Garfield
FAT CAT 3-PACK
VOLUME 7

BY
JIM DAVIS

BALLANTINE BOOKS • NEW YORK

2012 Ballantine Books Trade Paperback Edition

Published in the United States by Ballantine Books, an imprint of Random House, a division of Penguin Random House LLC, New York.

Originally published as three separate volumes, in both black and white and color, as *Garfield Hangs Out*, *Garfield Takes Up Space*, and *Garfield Says a Mouthful*. This compilation was originally published in black and white in 1996.

ISBN 978-0-345-52588-8

Printed in China

randomhousebooks.com

11

Garfield hangs out

BY JIM DAVIS

Ballantine Books • **New York**

PROFESSOR GARFIELD'S

NATURAL HISTORY OF DOGS

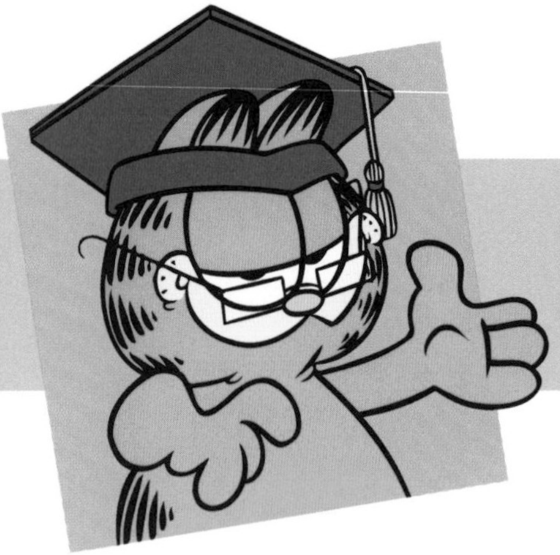

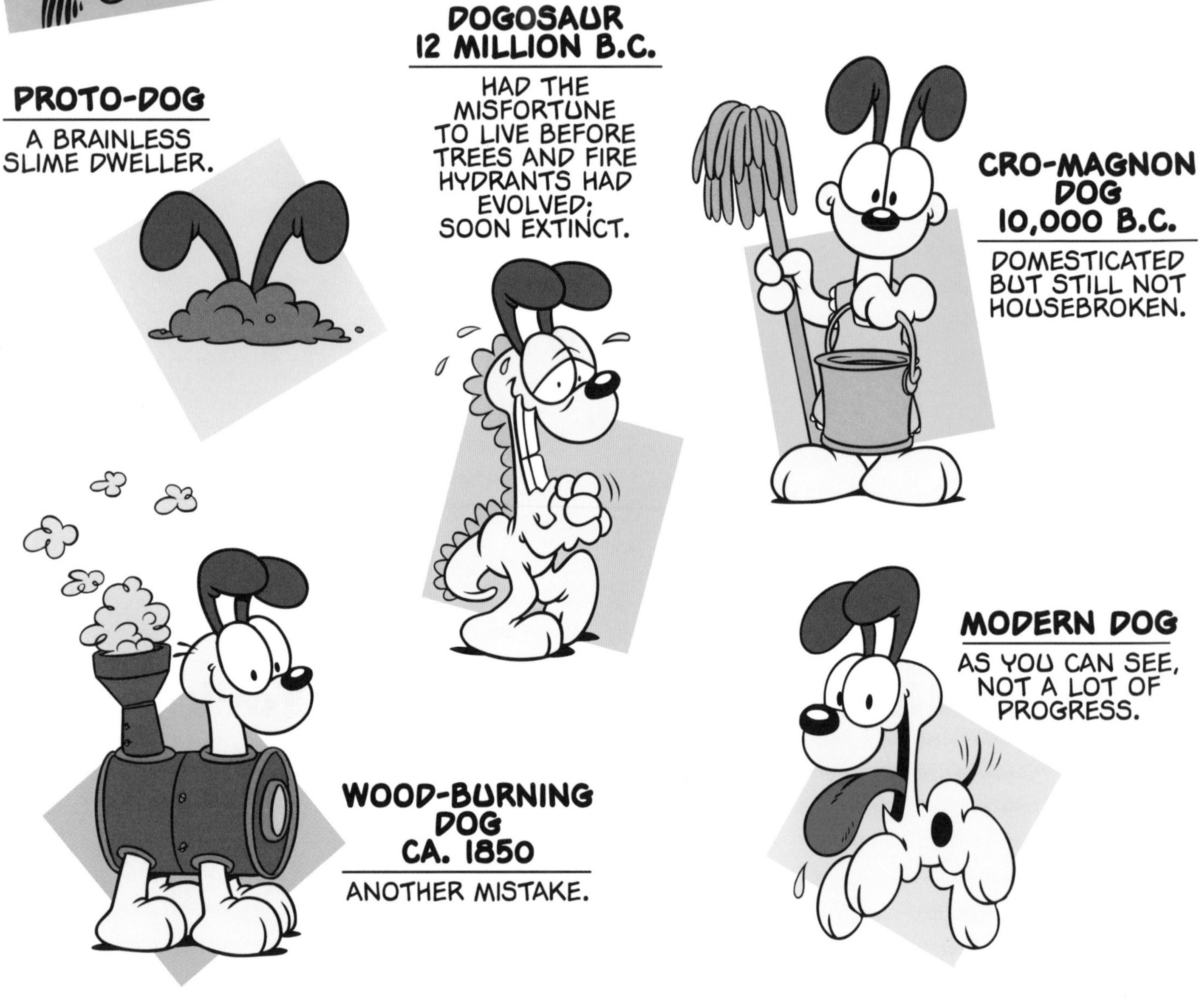
PROTO-DOG
A BRAINLESS SLIME DWELLER.
DOGOSAUR 12 MILLION B.C.
HAD THE MISFORTUNE TO LIVE BEFORE TREES AND FIRE HYDRANTS HAD EVOLVED; SOON EXTINCT.
CRO-MAGNON DOG 10,000 B.C.
DOMESTICATED BUT STILL NOT HOUSEBROKEN.
WOOD-BURNING DOG CA. 1850
ANOTHER MISTAKE.
MODERN DOG
AS YOU CAN SEE, NOT A LOT OF PROGRESS.

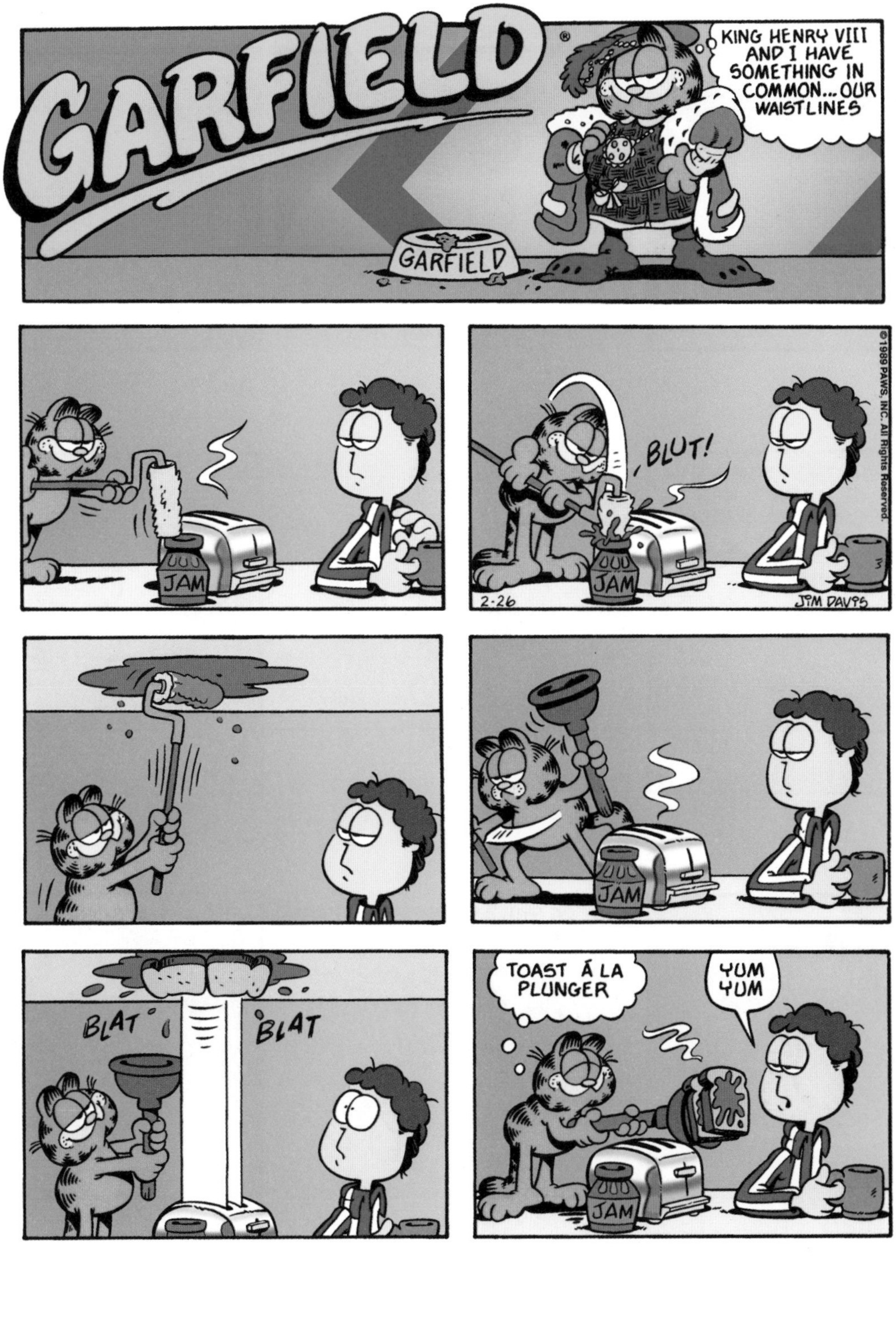
GARFIELD
KING HENRY VIII AND I HAVE SOMETHING IN COMMON... OUR WAISTLINES
GARFIELD
©1989 PAWS, INC. All Rights Reserved.
JAM
BLUT!
JAM
2·26
JIM DAVIS
JAM
BLAT
BLAT
TOAST Á LA PLUNGER
YUM YUM
JAM

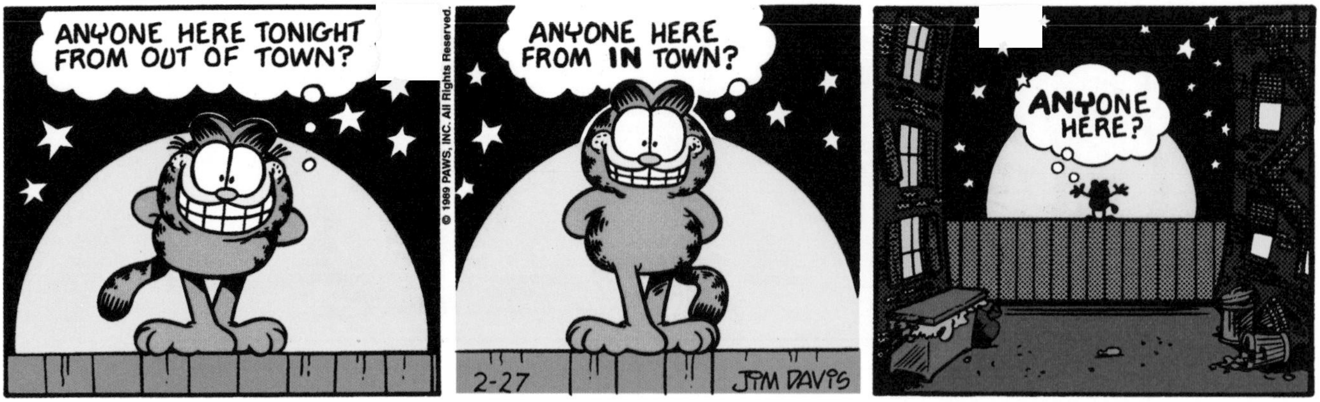
ANYONE HERE TONIGHT FROM OUT OF TOWN?
© 1989 PAWS, INC. All Rights Reserved.
ANYONE HERE FROM IN TOWN?
2-27
JIM DAVIS
ANYONE HERE?

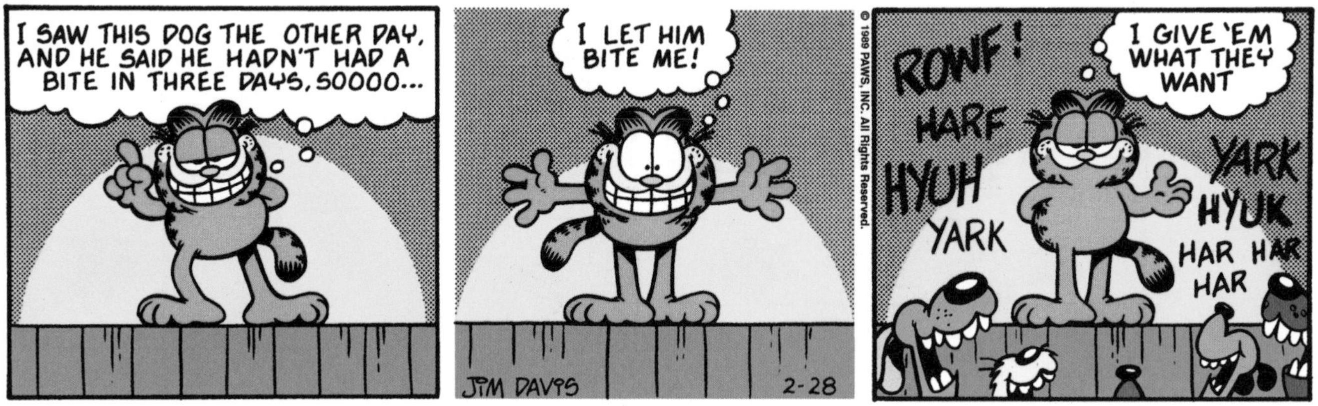
I SAW THIS DOG THE OTHER DAY, AND HE SAID HE HADN'T HAD A BITE IN THREE DAYS, SOOOO...
I LET HIM BITE ME!
JIM DAVIS
2-28
© 1989 PAWS, INC. All Rights Reserved.
ROWF!
HARF
HYUH
YARK
I GIVE 'EM WHAT THEY WANT
YARK
HYUK
HAR HAR HAR

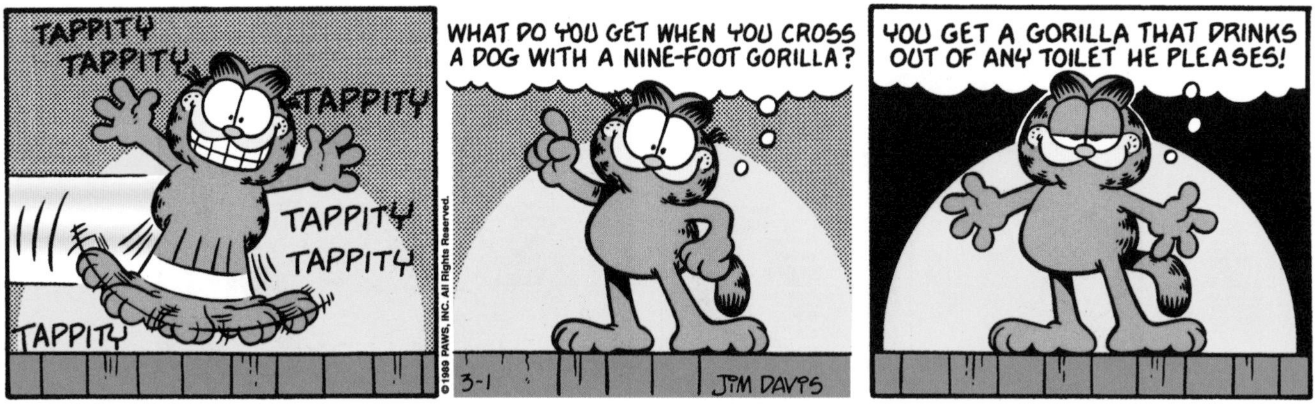
TAPPITY
TAPPITY
TAPPITY
TAPPITY
TAPPITY
TAPPITY
© 1989 PAWS, INC. All Rights Reserved.
WHAT DO YOU GET WHEN YOU CROSS A DOG WITH A NINE-FOOT GORILLA?
3-1
JIM DAVIS
YOU GET A GORILLA THAT DRINKS OUT OF ANY TOILET HE PLEASES!

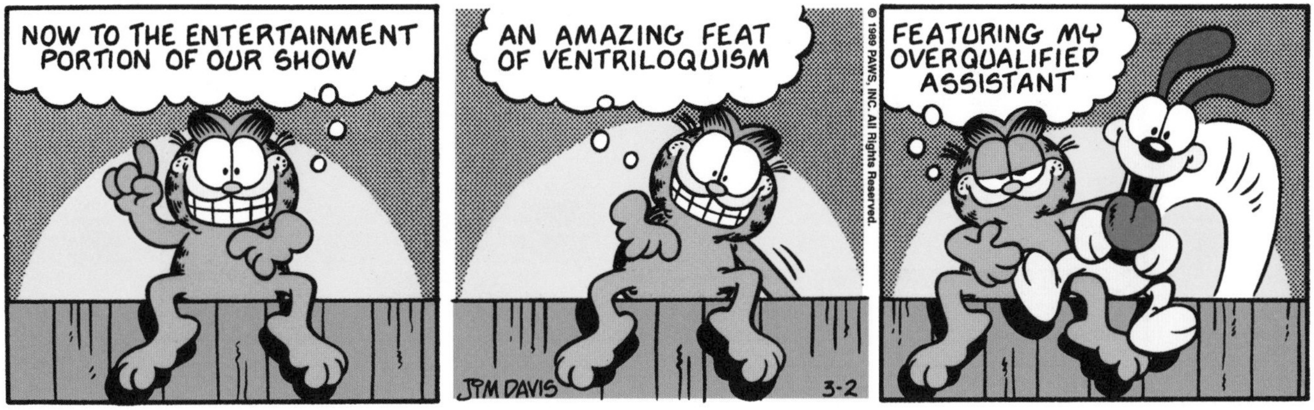
NOW TO THE ENTERTAINMENT PORTION OF OUR SHOW
AN AMAZING FEAT OF VENTRILOQUISM
JIM DAVIS
3-2
© 1989 PAWS, INC. All Rights Reserved.
FEATURING MY OVERQUALIFIED ASSISTANT

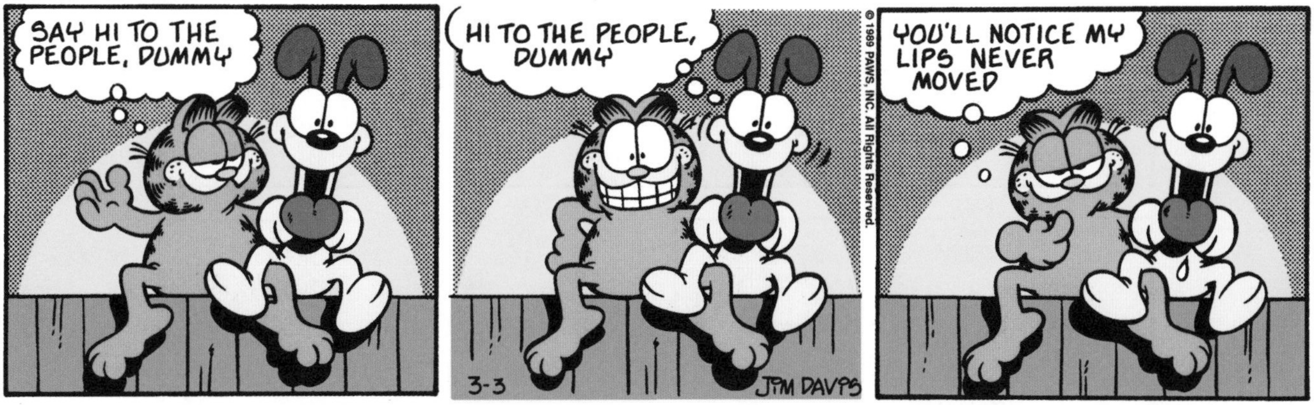
SAY HI TO THE PEOPLE, DUMMY
HI TO THE PEOPLE, DUMMY
3-3
JIM DAVIS
© 1989 PAWS, INC. All Rights Reserved.
YOU'LL NOTICE MY LIPS NEVER MOVED

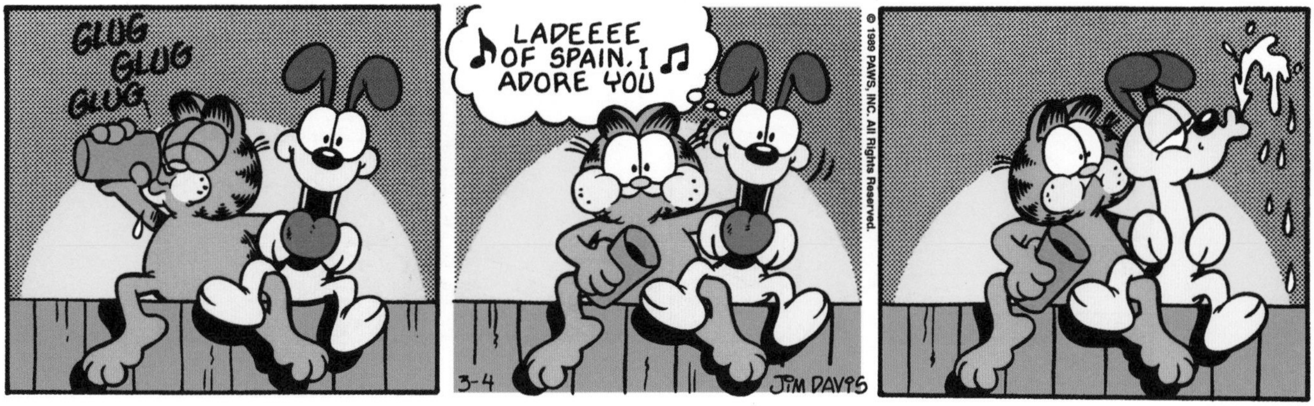
GLUG GLUG GLUG
♪ LADEEEE OF SPAIN, I ♫ ADORE YOU
3-4
JIM DAVIS
© 1989 PAWS, INC. All Rights Reserved.

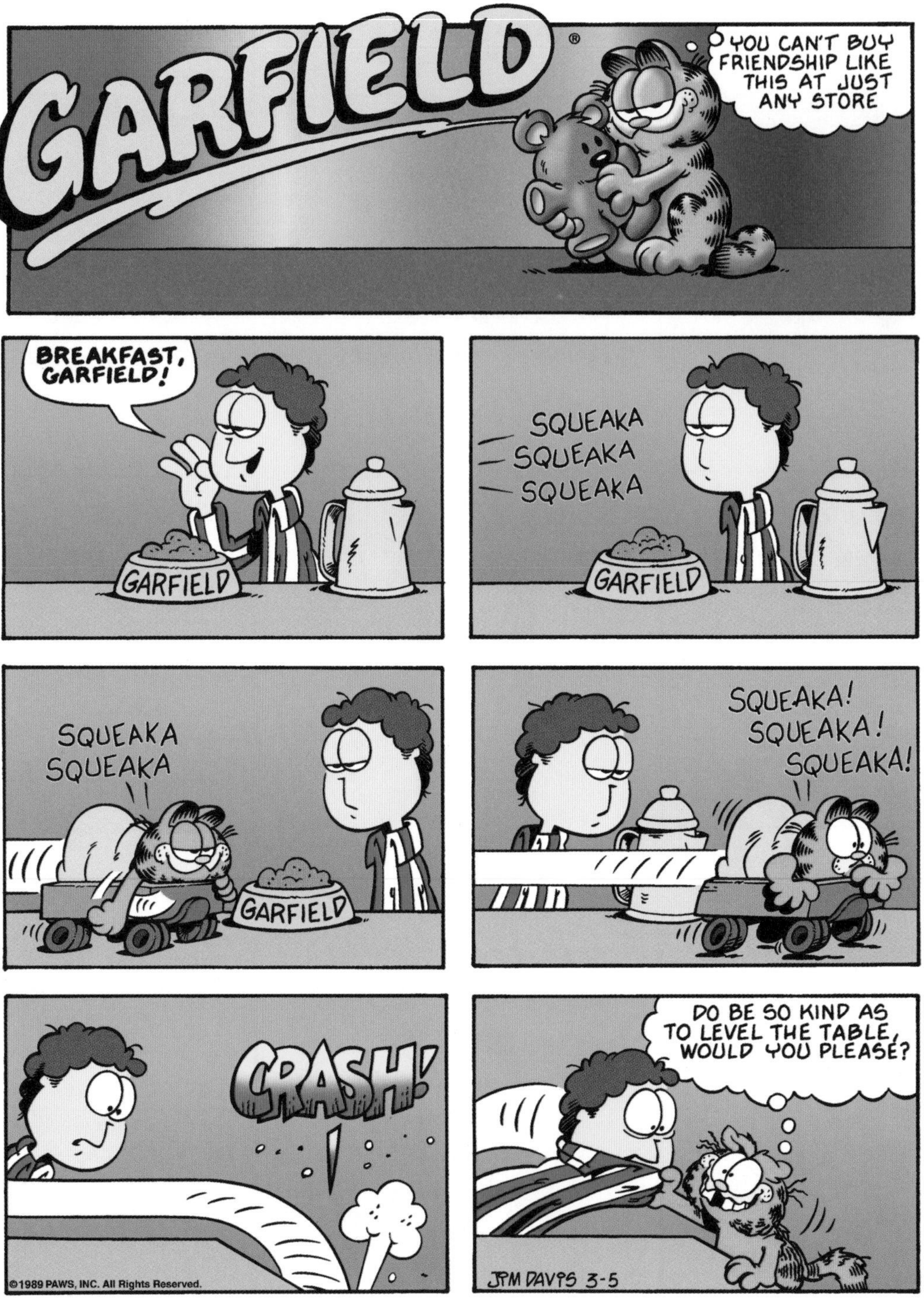
GARFIELD®
YOU CAN'T BUY FRIENDSHIP LIKE THIS AT JUST ANY STORE
BREAKFAST, GARFIELD!
GARFIELD
SQUEAKA SQUEAKA SQUEAKA
GARFIELD
SQUEAKA SQUEAKA
GARFIELD
SQUEAKA! SQUEAKA! SQUEAKA!
CRASH!
DO BE SO KIND AS TO LEVEL THE TABLE, WOULD YOU PLEASE?
JPM DAVIS 3-5
©1989 PAWS, INC. All Rights Reserved.

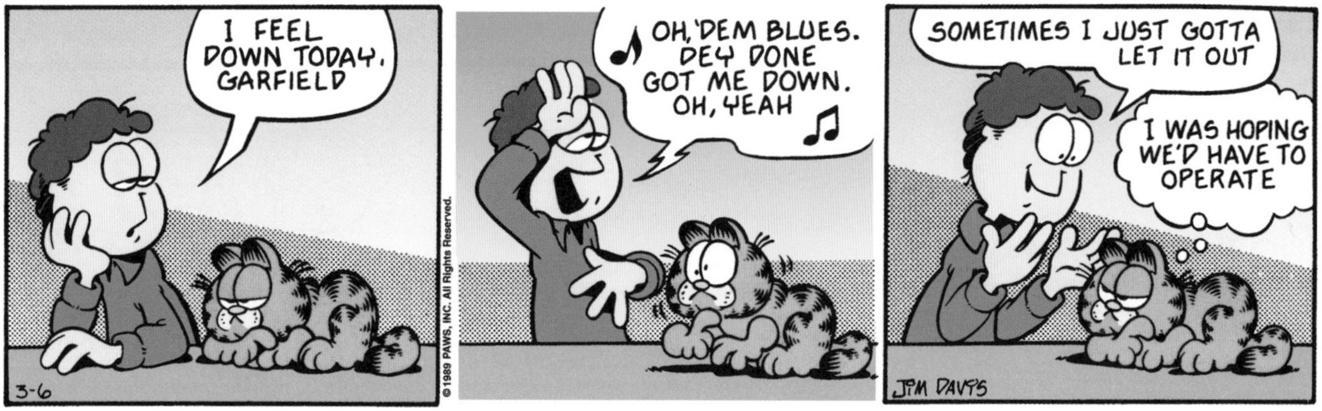
3-6
I FEEL DOWN TODAY, GARFIELD
OH, 'DEM BLUES. DEY DONE GOT ME DOWN. OH, YEAH
© 1989 PAWS, INC. All Rights Reserved.
SOMETIMES I JUST GOTTA LET IT OUT
I WAS HOPING WE'D HAVE TO OPERATE
JIM DAVIS

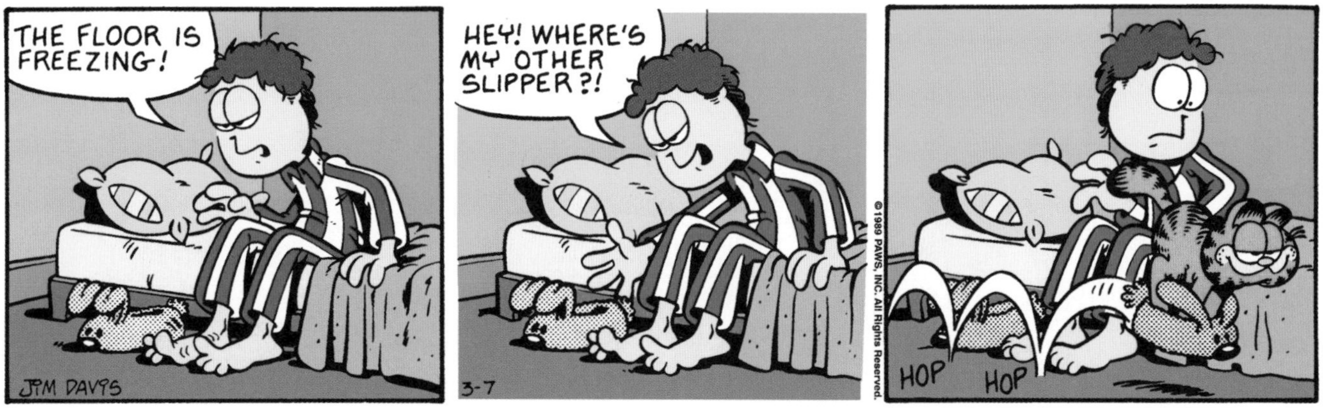
THE FLOOR IS FREEZING!
JIM DAVIS
HEY! WHERE'S MY OTHER SLIPPER?!
3-7
© 1989 PAWS, INC. All Rights Reserved.
HOP HOP

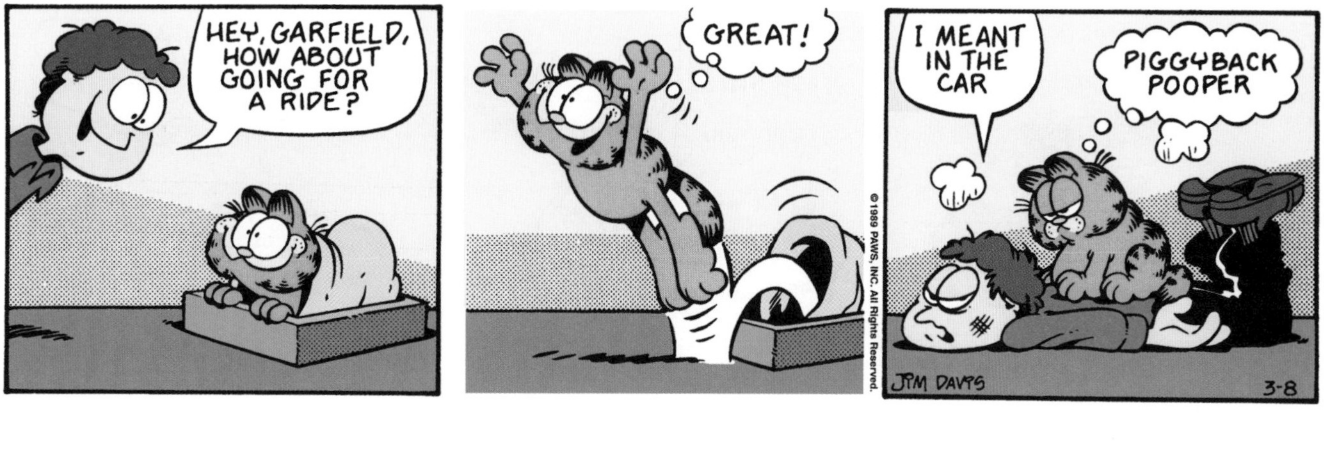
HEY, GARFIELD, HOW ABOUT GOING FOR A RIDE?
GREAT!
© 1989 PAWS, INC. All Rights Reserved.
I MEANT IN THE CAR
PIGGYBACK POOPER
JIM DAVIS
3-8

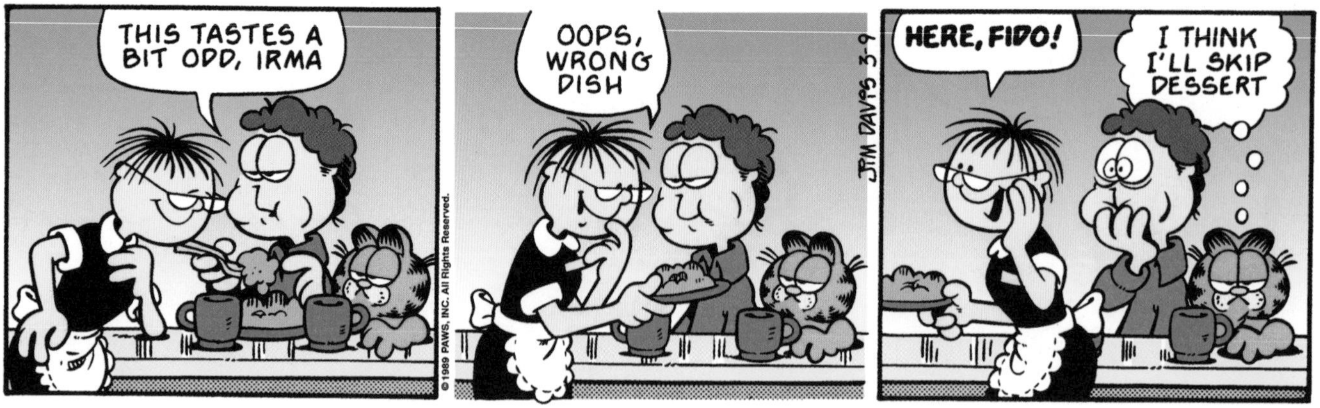
THIS TASTES A BIT ODD, IRMA
OOPS, WRONG DISH
JIM DAVIS 3-9
HERE, FIDO!
I THINK I'LL SKIP DESSERT
© 1989 PAWS, INC. All Rights Reserved.

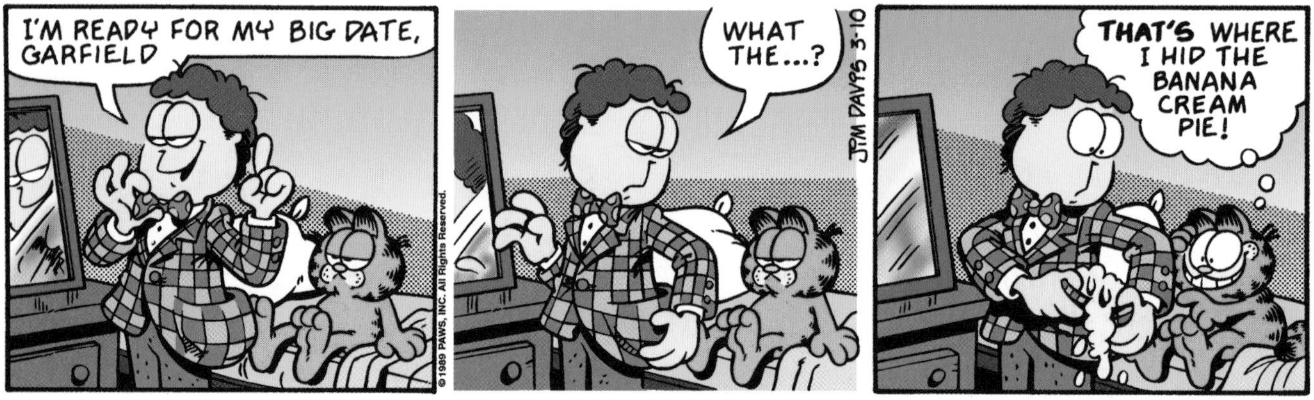
I'M READY FOR MY BIG DATE, GARFIELD
WHAT THE...?
JIM DAVIS 3-10
THAT'S WHERE I HID THE BANANA CREAM PIE!
© 1989 PAWS, INC. All Rights Reserved.

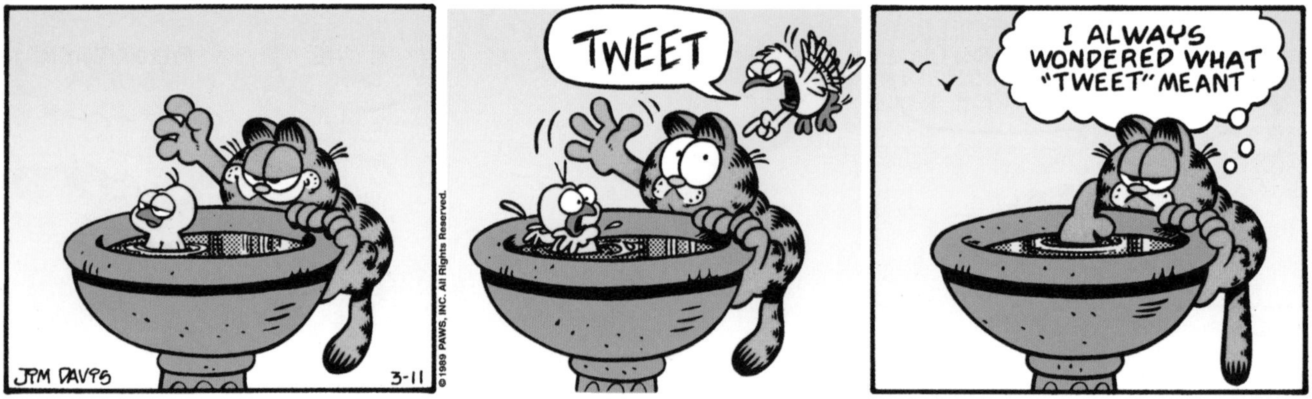
JIM DAVIS
3-11
TWEET
I ALWAYS WONDERED WHAT "TWEET" MEANT
© 1989 PAWS, INC. All Rights Reserved.

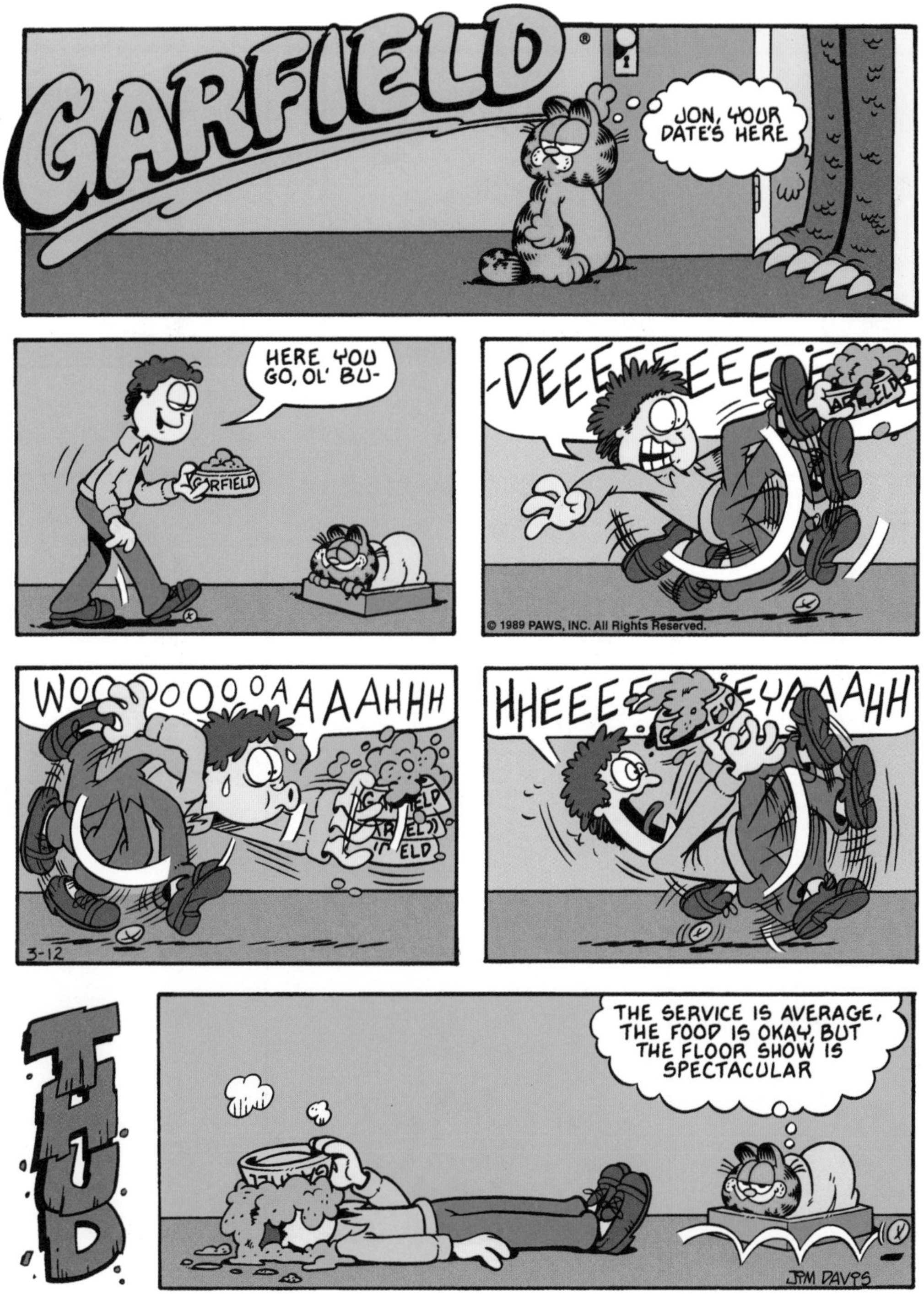
GARFIELD®
JON, YOUR DATE'S HERE
HERE YOU GO, OL' BU-
GARFIELD
-DEEEEEEEEEE
WOOOOOOOOAAAAHHH
HHEEEEEEEYAAAHH
THUD
THE SERVICE IS AVERAGE, THE FOOD IS OKAY, BUT THE FLOOR SHOW IS SPECTACULAR
3-12
JIM DAVIS

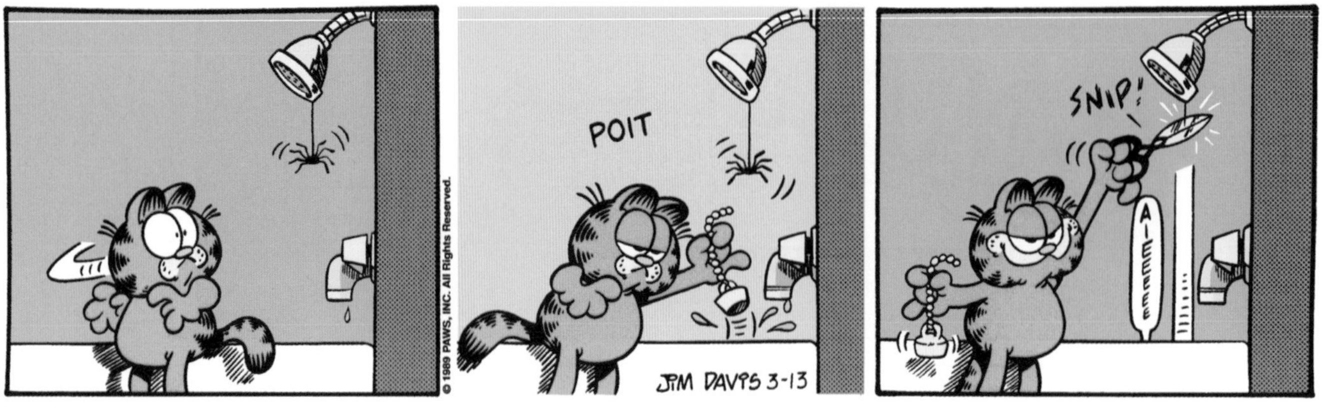
POIT
JIM DAVIS 3-13
© 1989 PAWS, INC. All Rights Reserved.
SNIP!
AIEEEEE

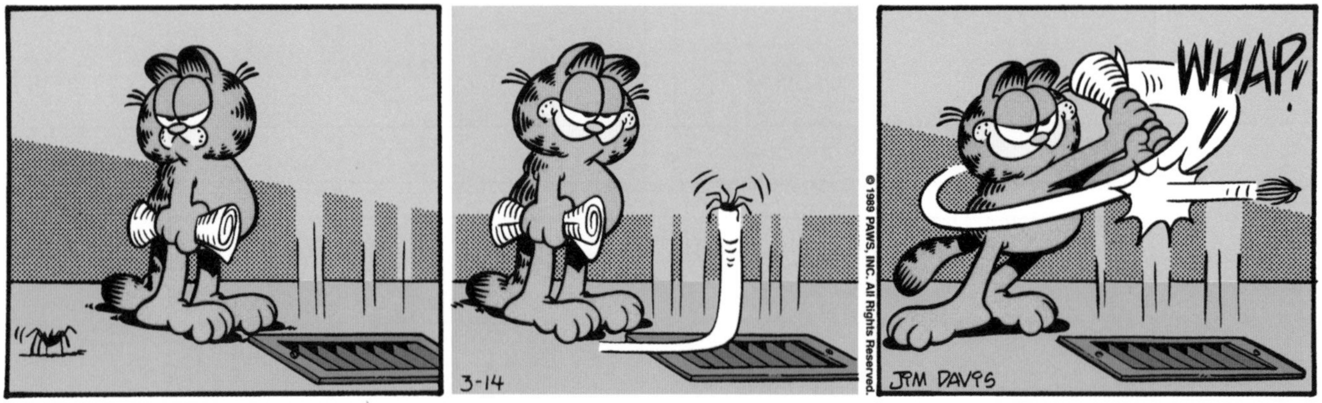
3-14
© 1989 PAWS, INC. All Rights Reserved.
WHAP!
JIM DAVIS

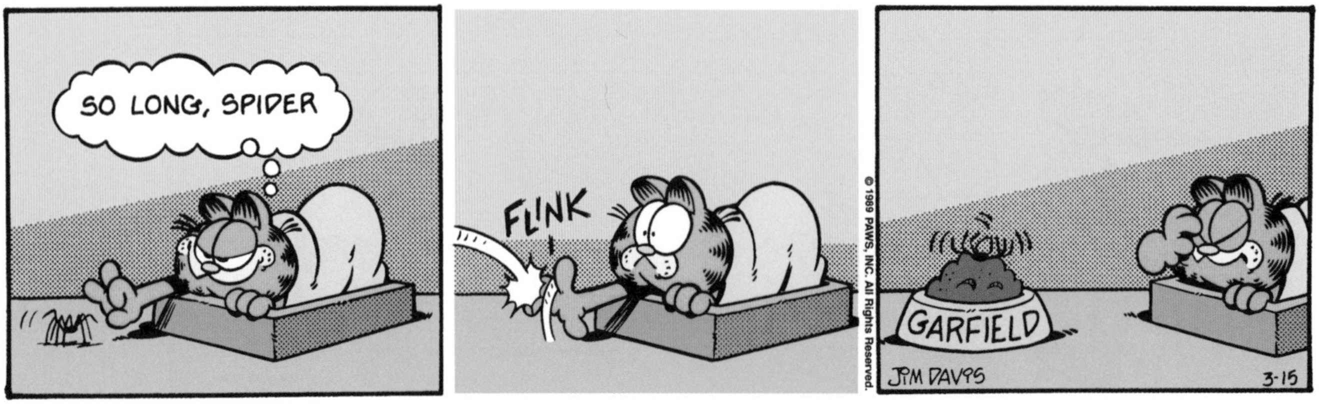
SO LONG, SPIDER
FLINK
© 1989 PAWS, INC. All Rights Reserved.
GARFIELD
JIM DAVIS
3-15

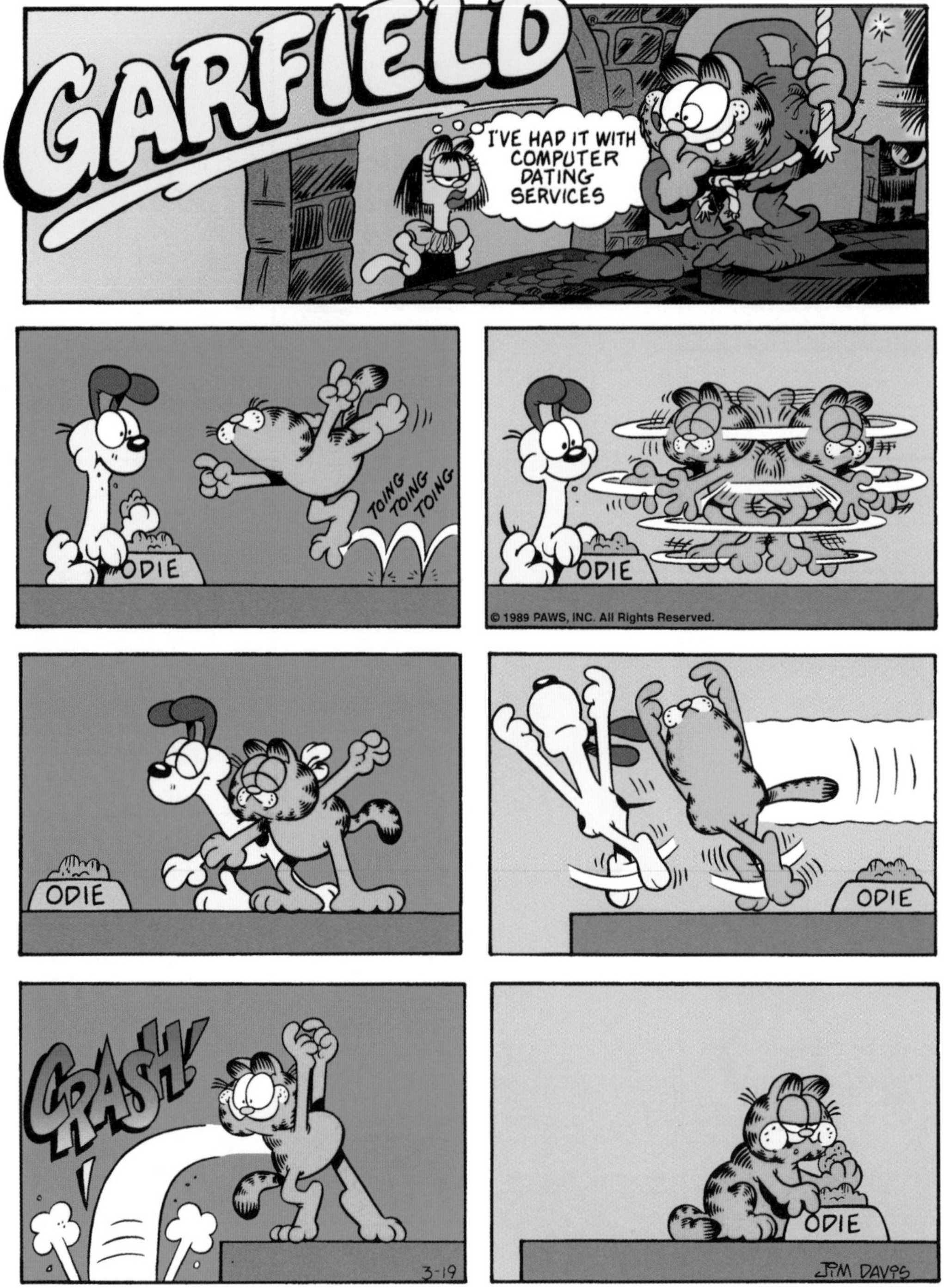
GARFIELD
I'VE HAD IT WITH COMPUTER DATING SERVICES
ODIE
TOING TOING TOING
ODIE
© 1989 PAWS, INC. All Rights Reserved.
ODIE
ODIE
CRASH!
3-19
ODIE
JIM DAVIS

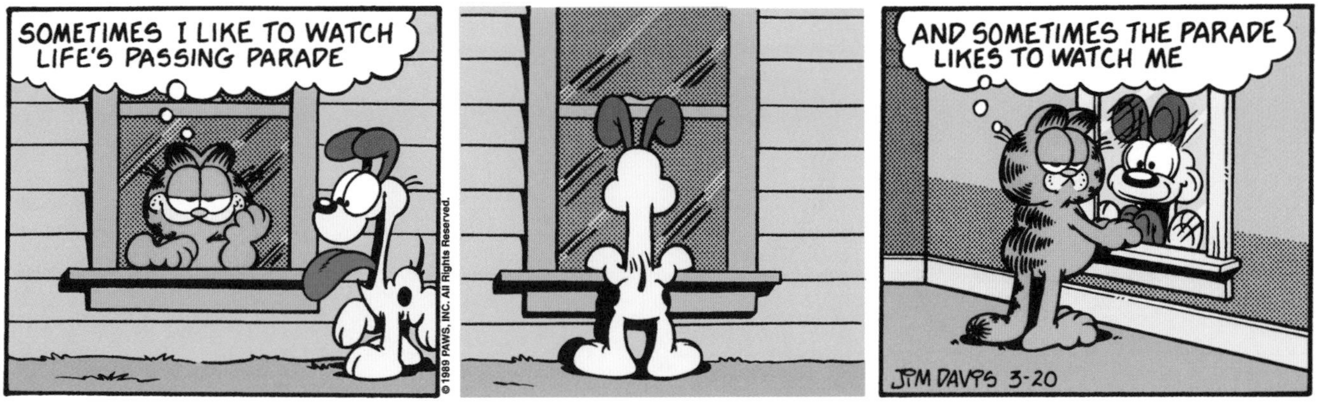
SOMETIMES I LIKE TO WATCH LIFE'S PASSING PARADE
© 1989 PAWS, INC. All Rights Reserved.
AND SOMETIMES THE PARADE LIKES TO WATCH ME
JIM DAVIS 3-20

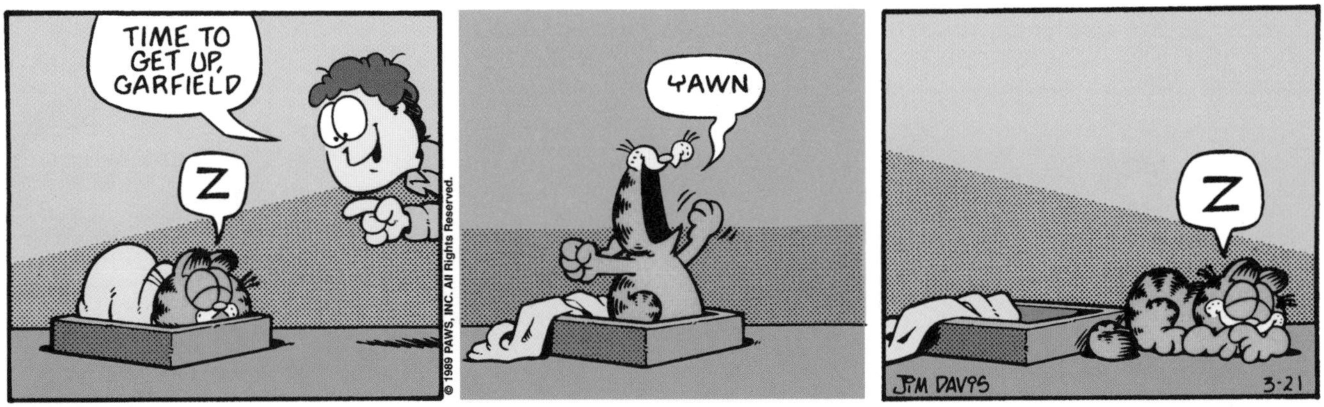
TIME TO GET UP, GARFIELD
Z
© 1989 PAWS, INC. All Rights Reserved.
YAWN
Z
JIM DAVIS 3-21

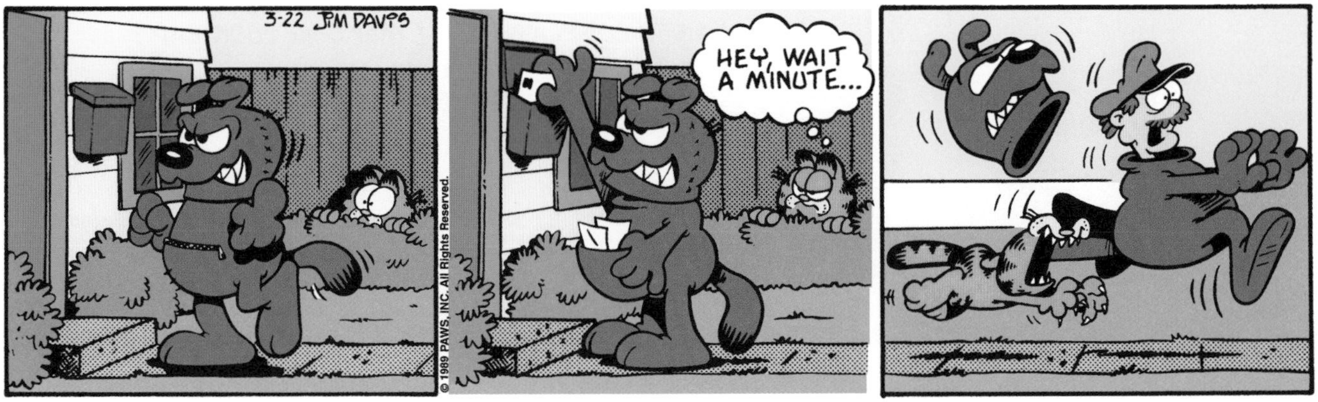
3-22 JIM DAVIS
© 1989 PAWS, INC. All Rights Reserved.
HEY, WAIT A MINUTE...

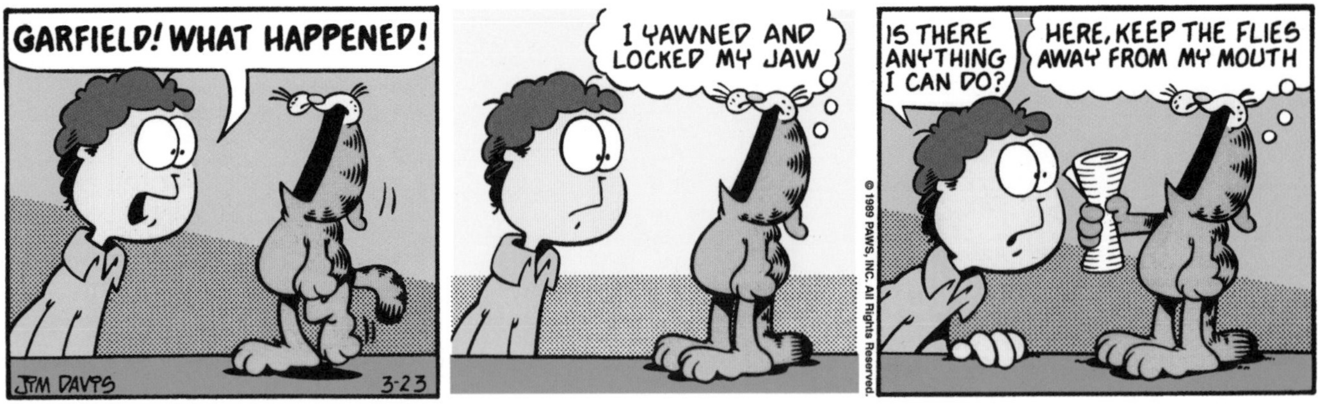
GARFIELD! WHAT HAPPENED!
JIM DAVIS 3-23
I YAWNED AND LOCKED MY JAW
© 1989 PAWS, INC. All Rights Reserved.
IS THERE ANYTHING I CAN DO?
HERE, KEEP THE FLIES AWAY FROM MY MOUTH

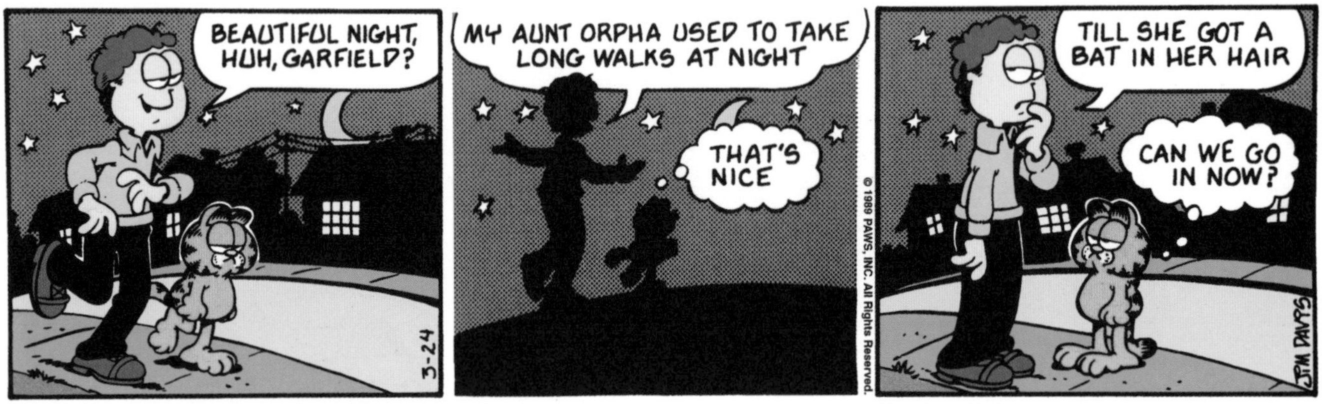
BEAUTIFUL NIGHT, HUH, GARFIELD?
3-24
MY AUNT ORPHA USED TO TAKE LONG WALKS AT NIGHT
THAT'S NICE
© 1989 PAWS, INC. All Rights Reserved.
TILL SHE GOT A BAT IN HER HAIR
CAN WE GO IN NOW?
JIM DAVIS

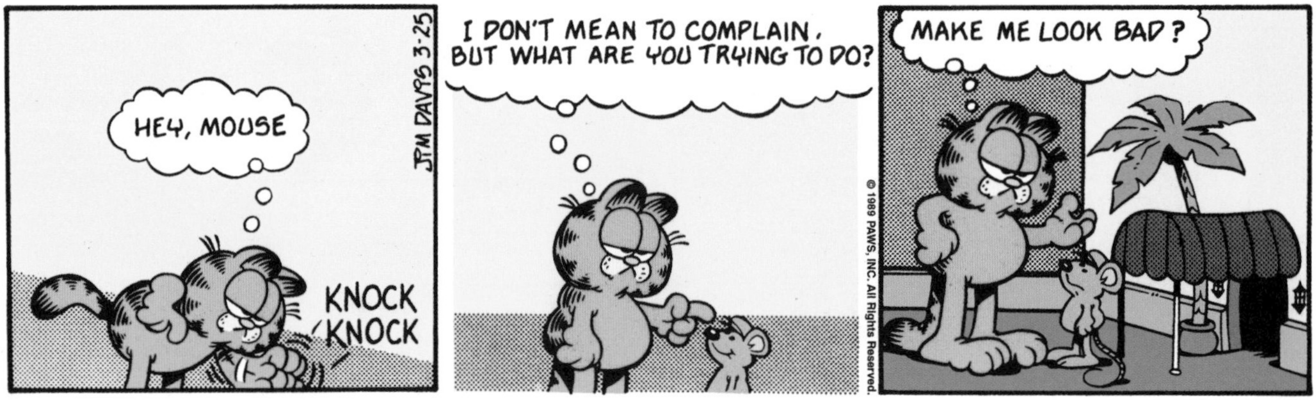
JIM DAVIS 3-25
HEY, MOUSE
KNOCK KNOCK
I DON'T MEAN TO COMPLAIN, BUT WHAT ARE YOU TRYING TO DO?
© 1989 PAWS, INC. All Rights Reserved.
MAKE ME LOOK BAD?

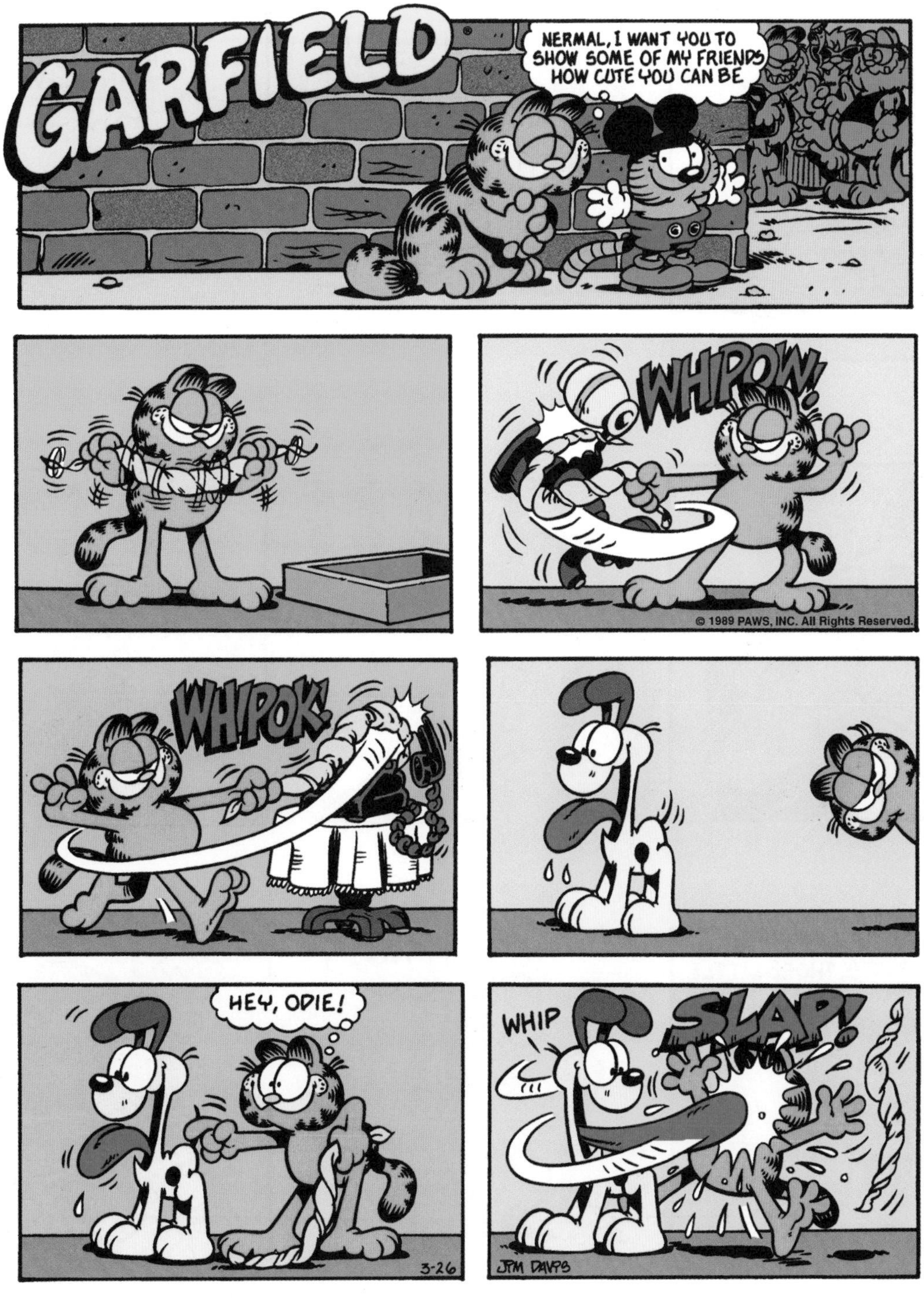
GARFIELD
NERMAL, I WANT YOU TO SHOW SOME OF MY FRIENDS HOW CUTE YOU CAN BE
WHIPOW!
WHIPOK!
HEY, ODIE!
WHIP
SLAP!
3-26
JPM DAVPS

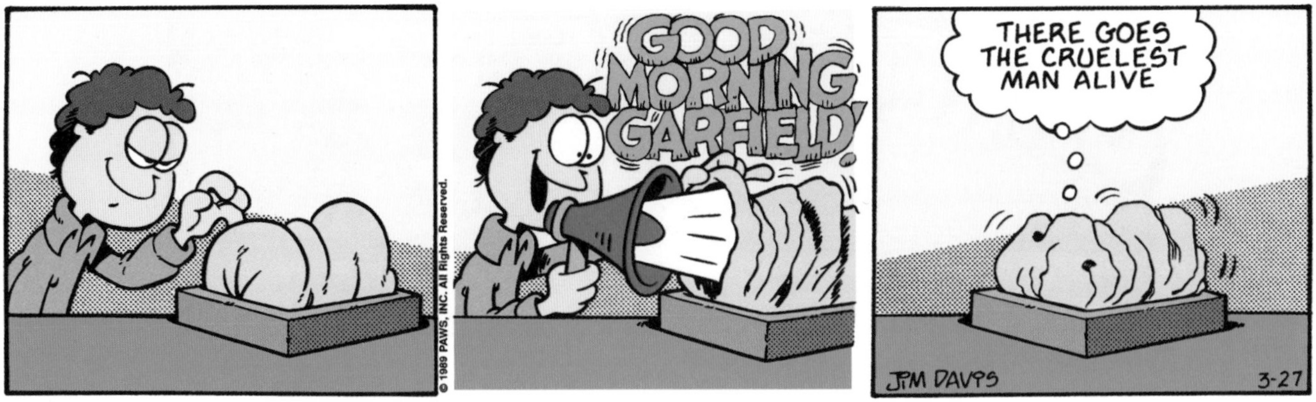
GOOD MORNING GARFIELD!
THERE GOES THE CRUELEST MAN ALIVE
JIM DAVIS
3-27
© 1989 PAWS, INC. All Rights Reserved.

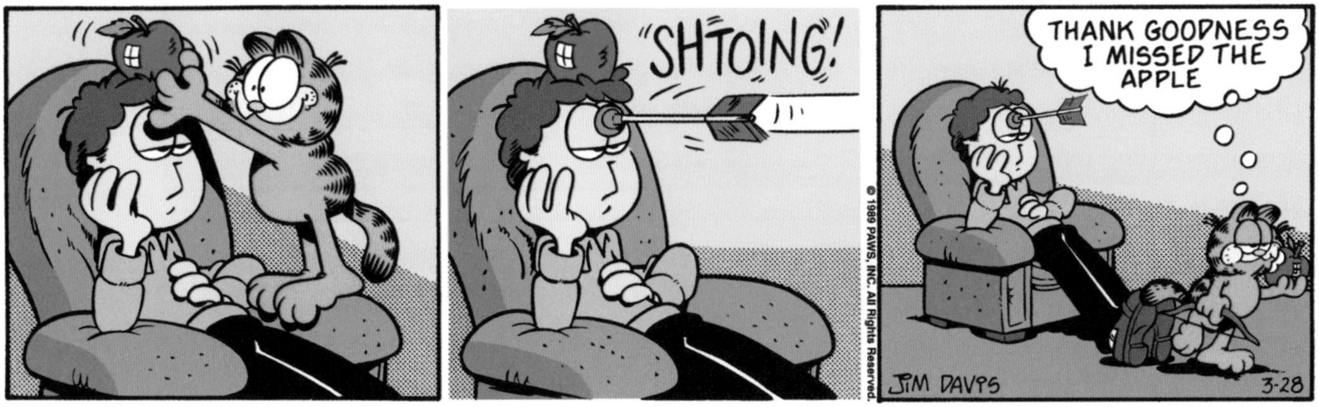
SHTOING!
THANK GOODNESS I MISSED THE APPLE
JIM DAVIS
3-28
© 1989 PAWS, INC. All Rights Reserved.

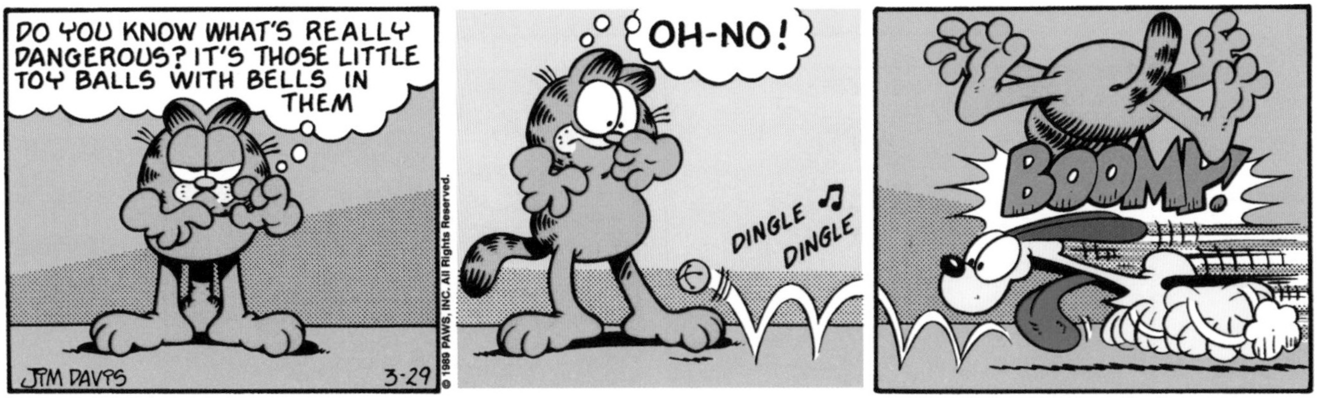
DO YOU KNOW WHAT'S REALLY DANGEROUS? IT'S THOSE LITTLE TOY BALLS WITH BELLS IN THEM
JIM DAVIS
3-29
© 1989 PAWS, INC. All Rights Reserved.
OH-NO!
DINGLE DINGLE
BOOM!

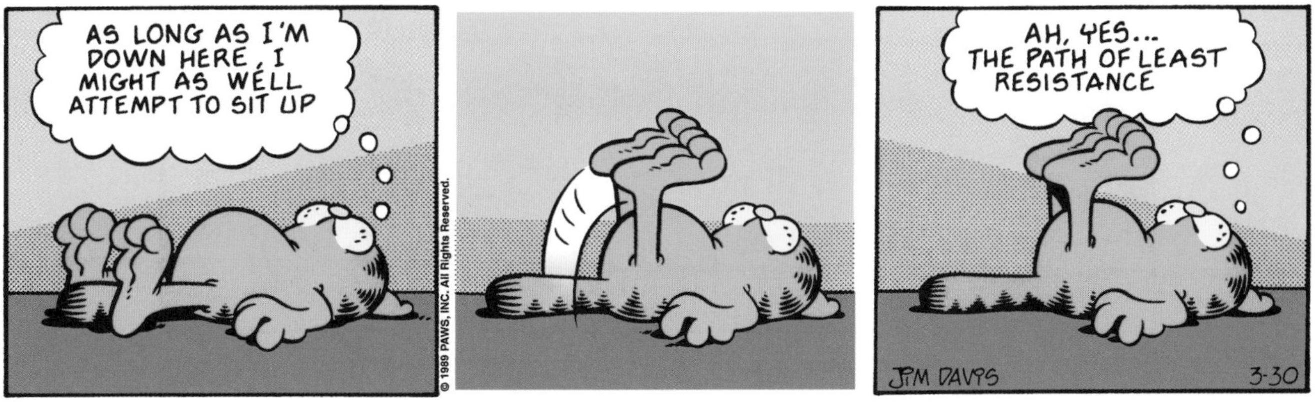
AS LONG AS I'M DOWN HERE, I MIGHT AS WELL ATTEMPT TO SIT UP
© 1989 PAWS, INC. All Rights Reserved.
AH, YES... THE PATH OF LEAST RESISTANCE
JIM DAVIS 3-30

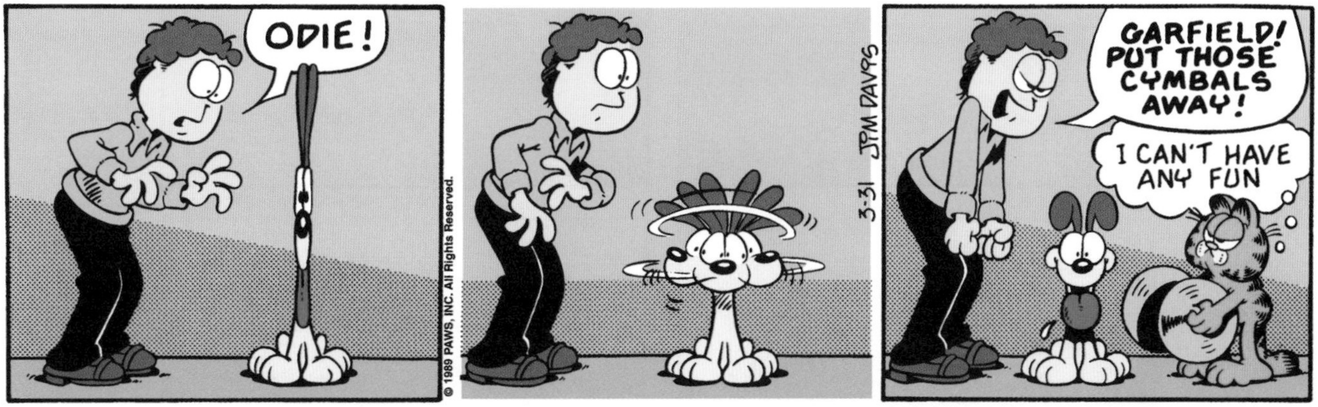
ODIE!
© 1989 PAWS, INC. All Rights Reserved.
JIM DAVIS 3-31
GARFIELD! PUT THOSE CYMBALS AWAY!
I CAN'T HAVE ANY FUN

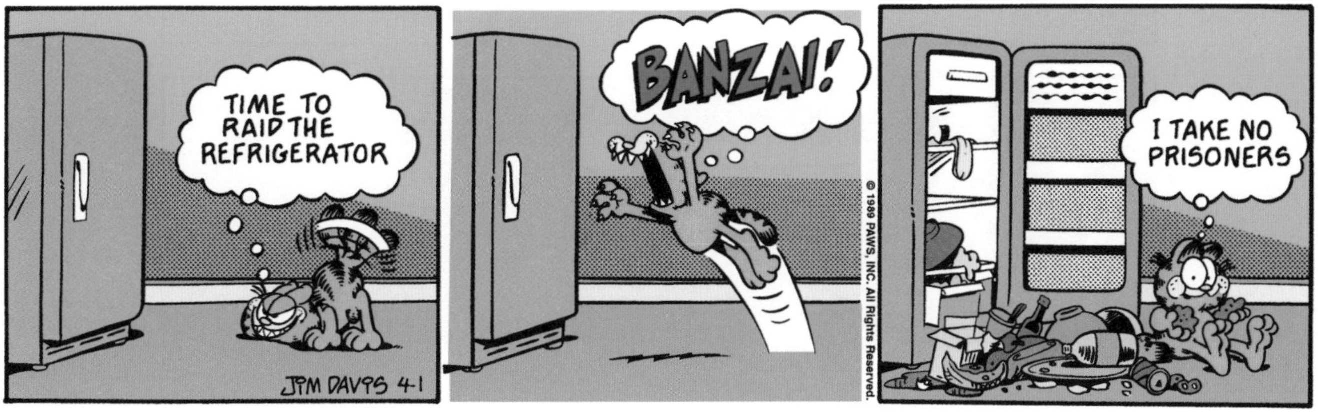
TIME TO RAID THE REFRIGERATOR
JIM DAVIS 4-1
BANZAI!
© 1989 PAWS, INC. All Rights Reserved.
I TAKE NO PRISONERS

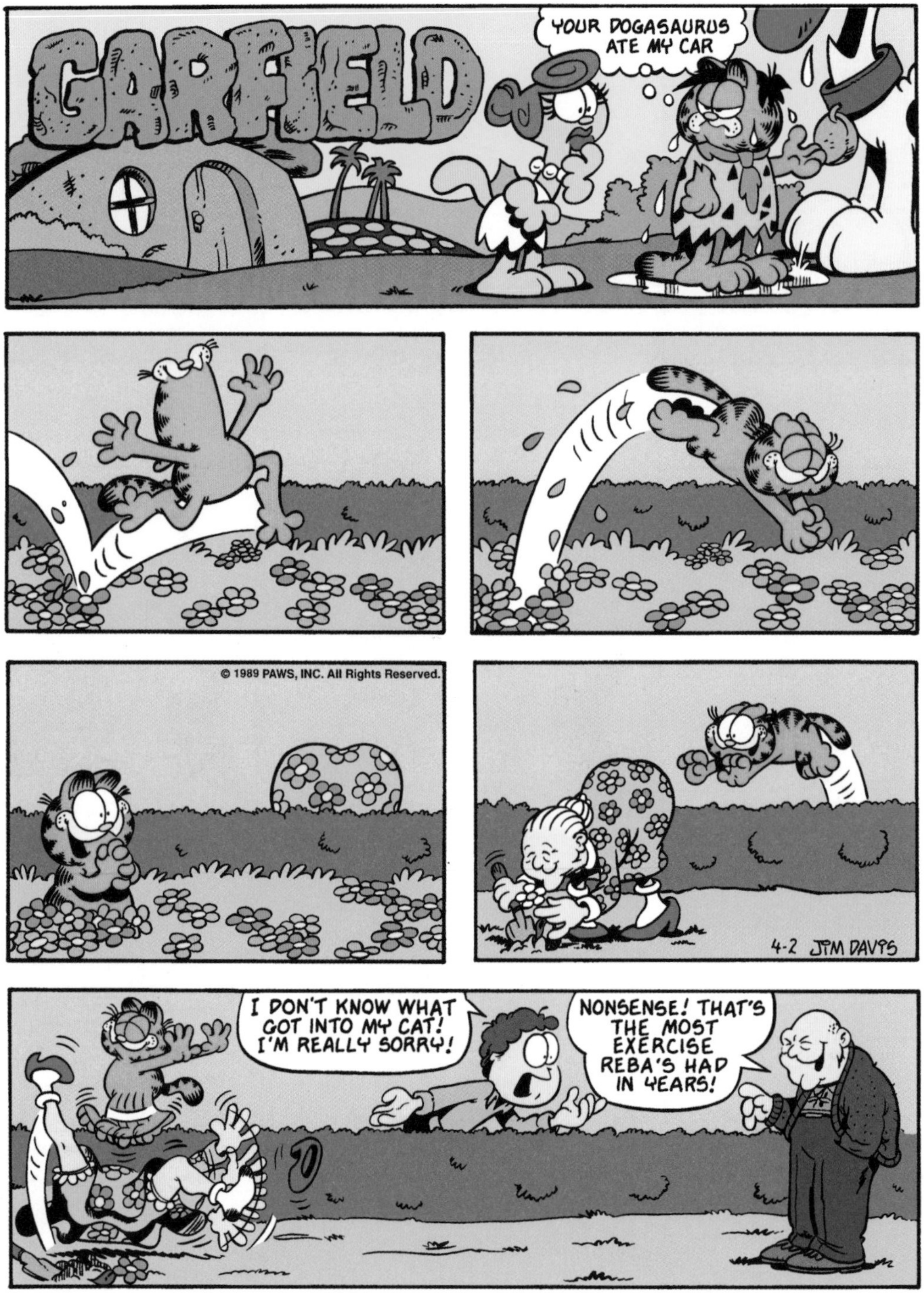
GARFIELD
YOUR DOGASAURUS ATE MY CAR
© 1989 PAWS, INC. All Rights Reserved.
4-2 JIM DAVIS
I DON'T KNOW WHAT GOT INTO MY CAT! I'M REALLY SORRY!
NONSENSE! THAT'S THE MOST EXERCISE REBA'S HAD IN YEARS!

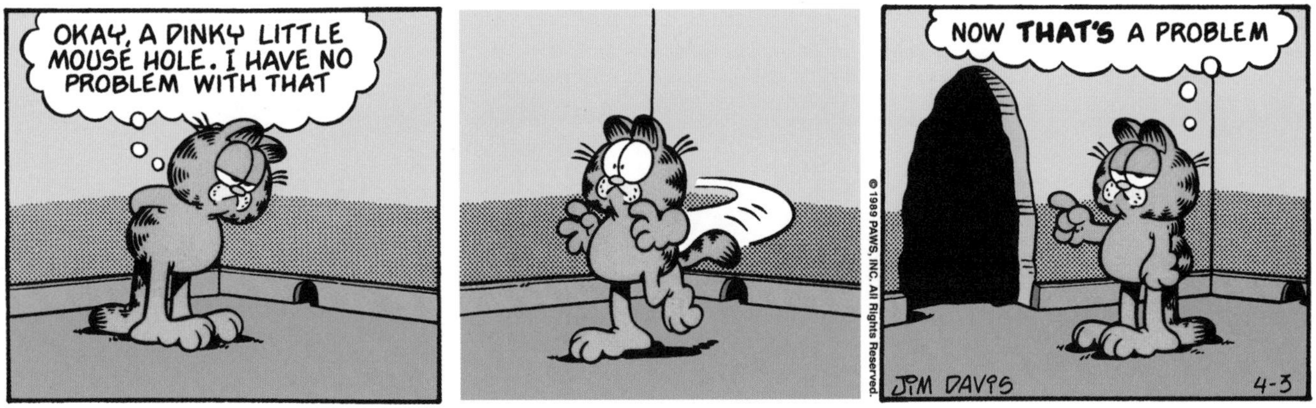
OKAY, A DINKY LITTLE MOUSE HOLE. I HAVE NO PROBLEM WITH THAT
NOW THAT'S A PROBLEM
© 1989 PAWS, INC. All Rights Reserved.
JIM DAVIS
4-3

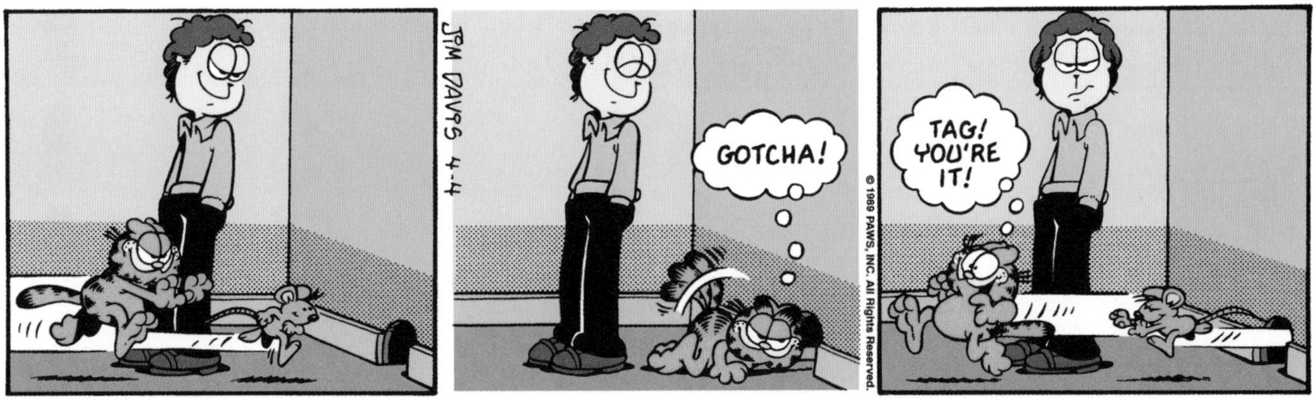
JIM DAVIS 4-4
GOTCHA!
© 1989 PAWS, INC. All Rights Reserved.
TAG! YOU'RE IT!

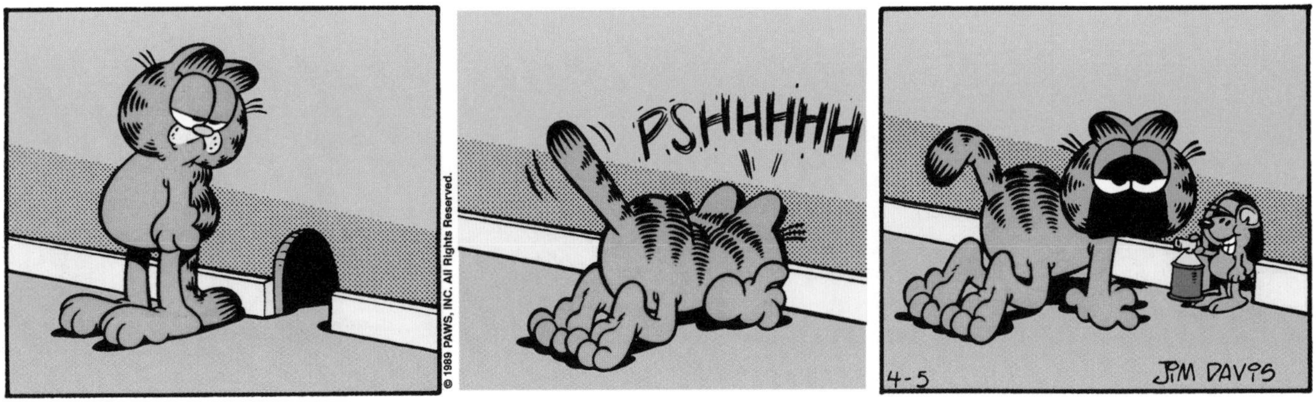
© 1989 PAWS, INC. All Rights Reserved.
PSHHHHH
4-5
JIM DAVIS

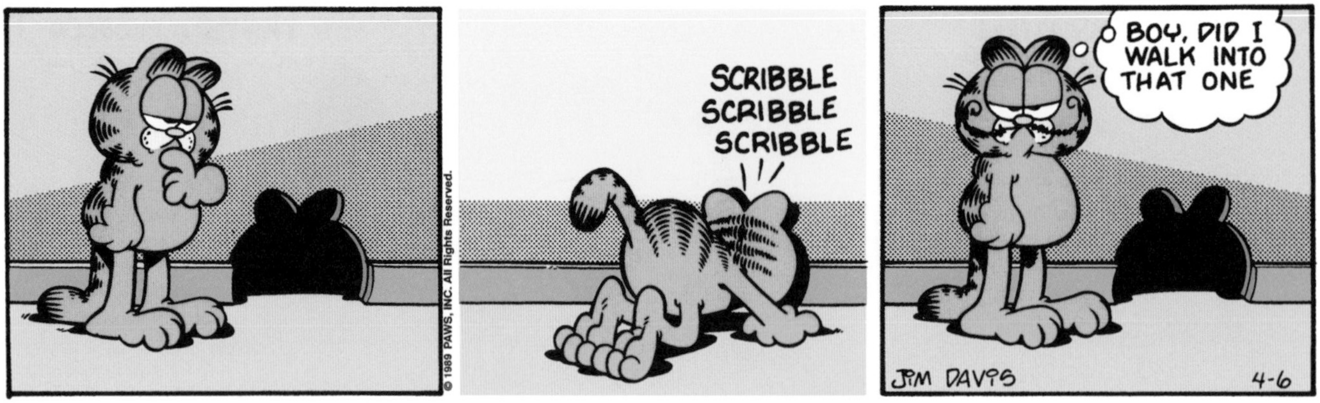
© 1989 PAWS, INC. All Rights Reserved.
SCRIBBLE
SCRIBBLE
SCRIBBLE
BOY, DID I WALK INTO THAT ONE
JIM DAVIS
4-6

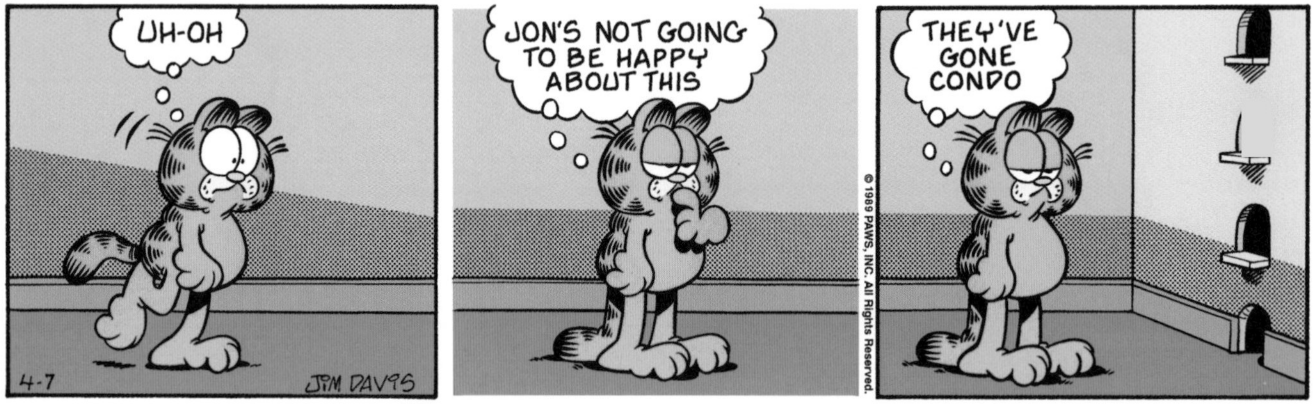
UH-OH
4-7
JIM DAVIS
JON'S NOT GOING TO BE HAPPY ABOUT THIS
© 1989 PAWS, INC. All Rights Reserved.
THEY'VE GONE CONDO

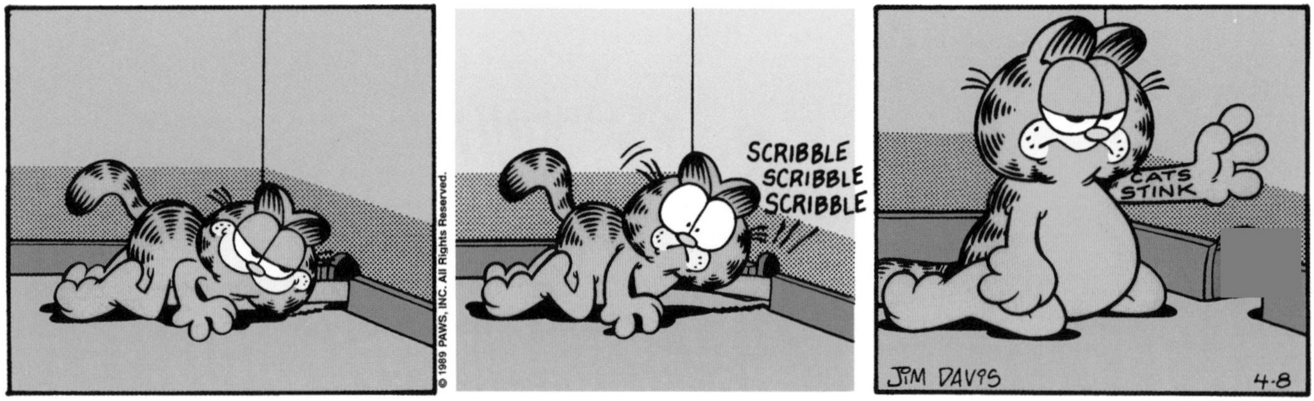
© 1989 PAWS, INC. All Rights Reserved.
SCRIBBLE
SCRIBBLE
SCRIBBLE
CATS STINK
JIM DAVIS
4-8

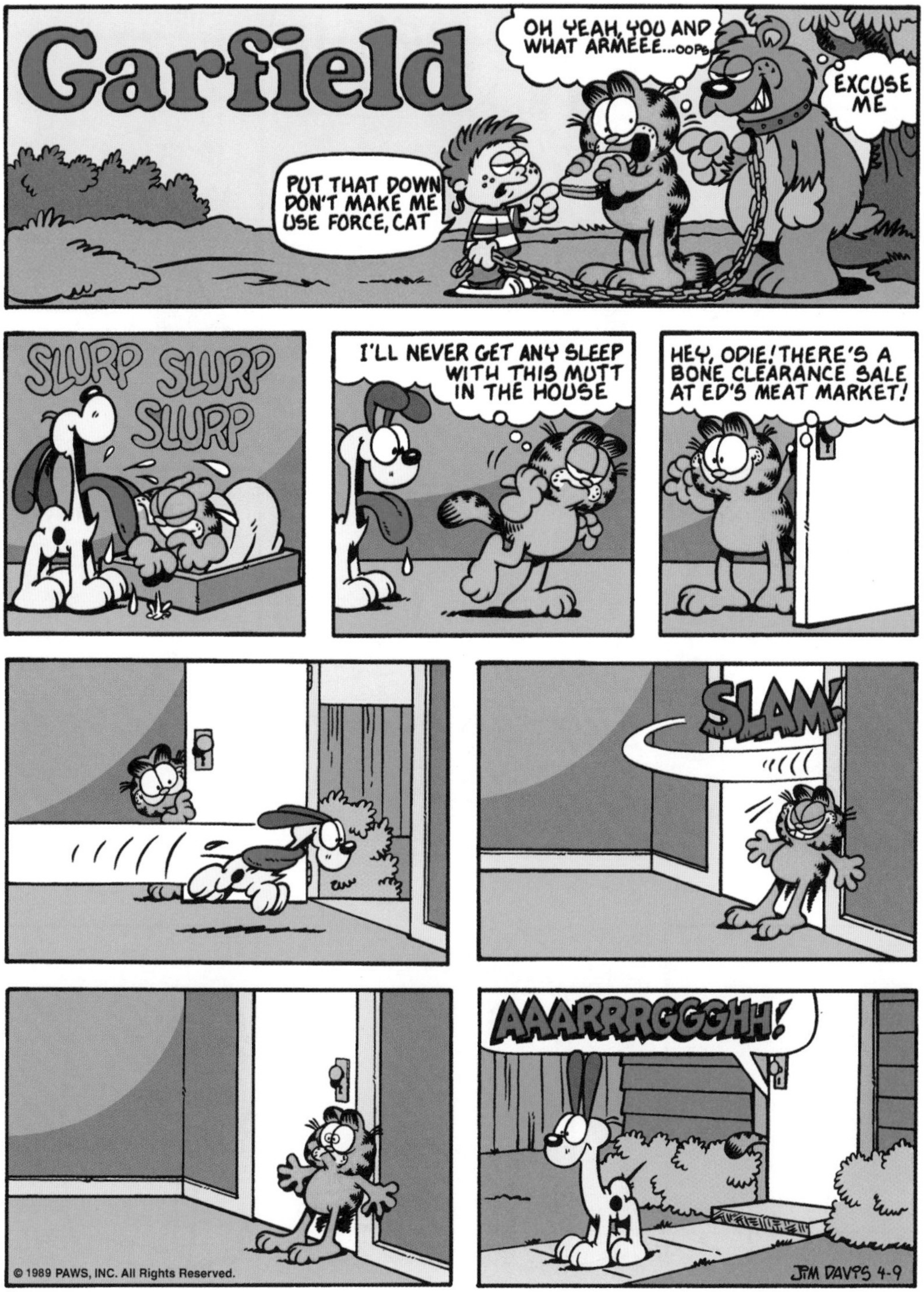
Garfield
OH YEAH, YOU AND WHAT ARMEEE...OOPS
EXCUSE ME
PUT THAT DOWN DON'T MAKE ME USE FORCE, CAT
SLURP SLURP SLURP
I'LL NEVER GET ANY SLEEP WITH THIS MUTT IN THE HOUSE
HEY, ODIE! THERE'S A BONE CLEARANCE SALE AT ED'S MEAT MARKET!
SLAM!
AAARRRGGGHH!
JIM DAVIS 4-9

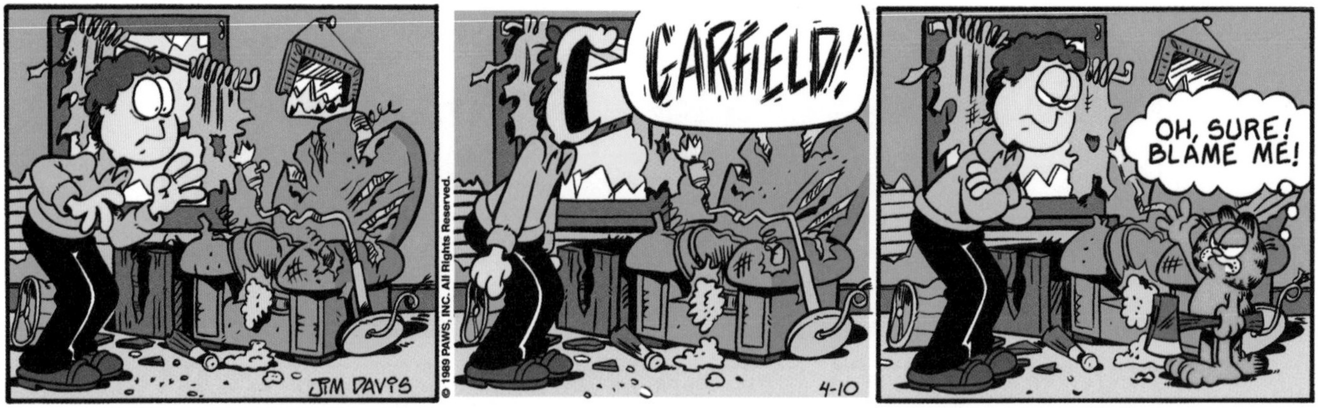
JIM DAVIS
© 1989 PAWS, INC. All Rights Reserved.
GARFIELD!
4-10
OH, SURE! BLAME ME!

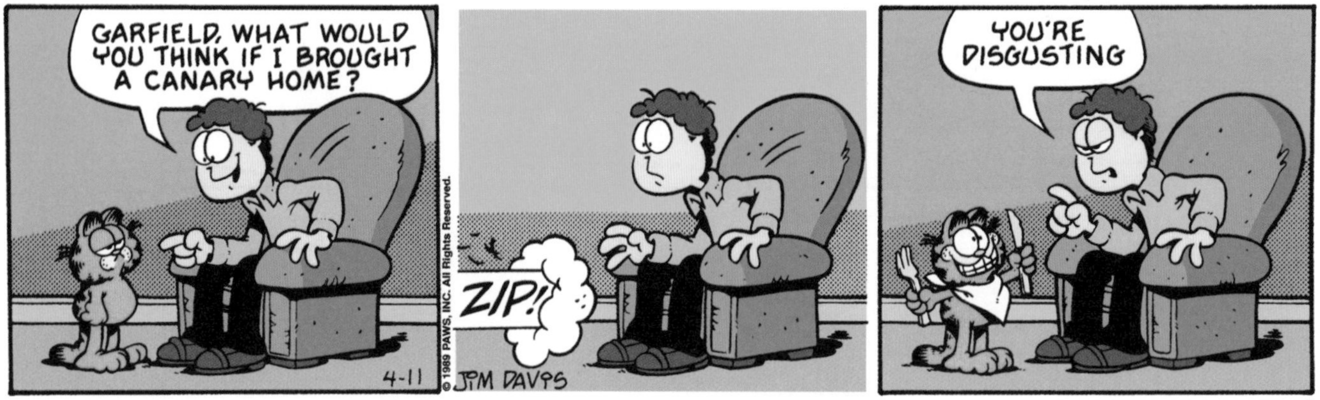
GARFIELD, WHAT WOULD YOU THINK IF I BROUGHT A CANARY HOME?
4-11
© 1989 PAWS, INC. All Rights Reserved.
ZIP!
JIM DAVIS
YOU'RE DISGUSTING

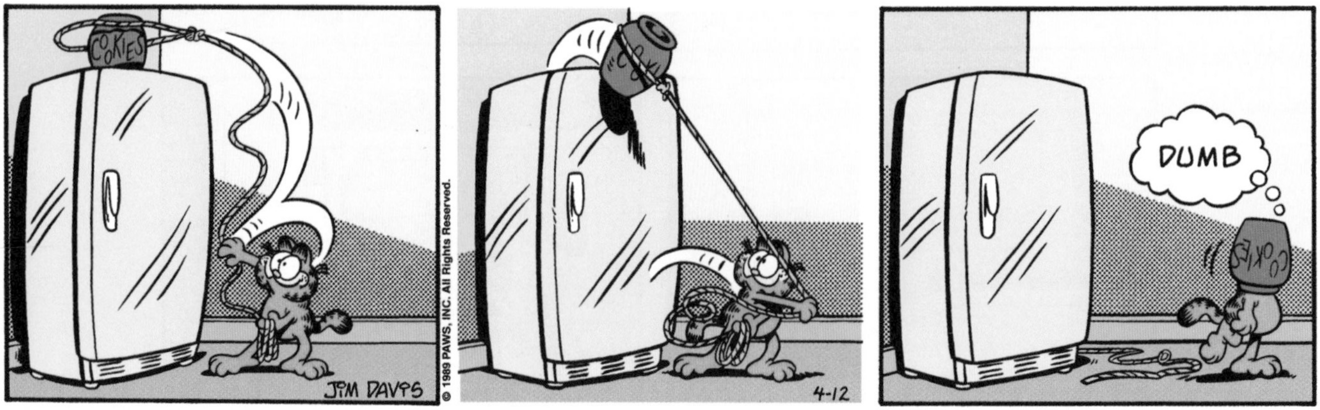
COOKIES
JIM DAVIS
© 1989 PAWS, INC. All Rights Reserved.
4-12
DUMB

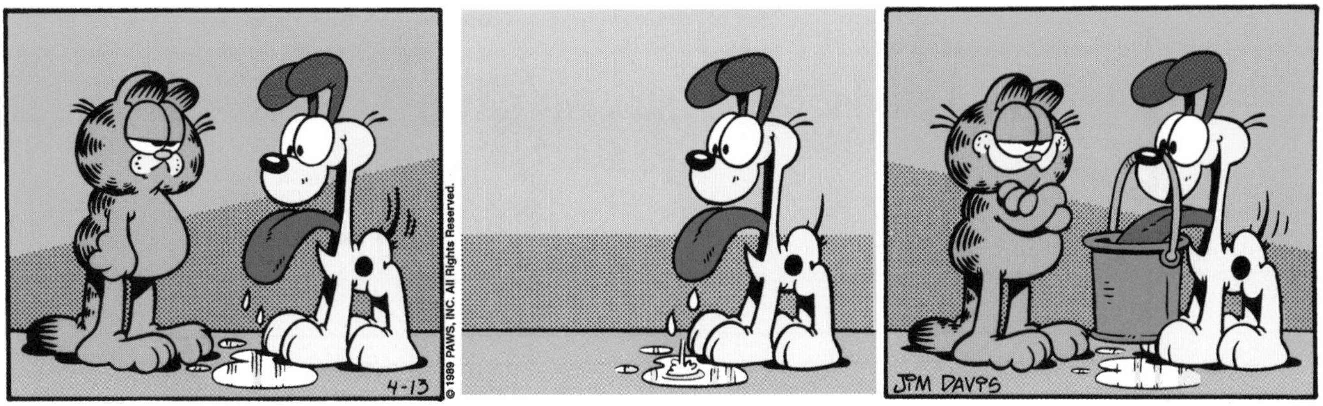
4-13
© 1989 PAWS, INC. All Rights Reserved.
JIM DAVIS

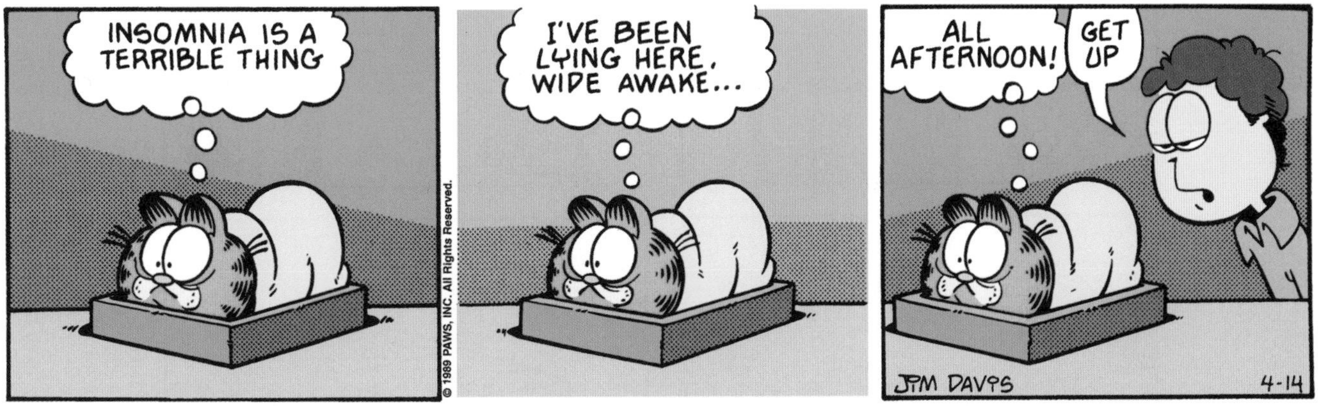
INSOMNIA IS A TERRIBLE THING
© 1989 PAWS, INC. All Rights Reserved.
I'VE BEEN LYING HERE, WIDE AWAKE...
ALL AFTERNOON!
GET UP
JIM DAVIS
4-14

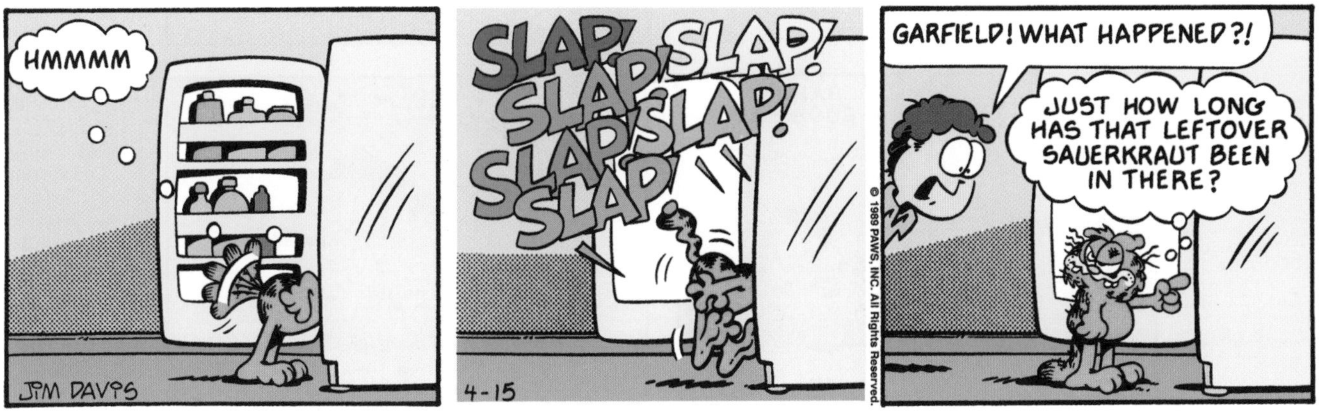
HMMMM
JIM DAVIS
SLAP! SLAP! SLAP! SLAP! SLAP! SLAP! SLAP!
4-15
© 1989 PAWS, INC. All Rights Reserved.
GARFIELD! WHAT HAPPENED?!
JUST HOW LONG HAS THAT LEFTOVER SAUERKRAUT BEEN IN THERE?

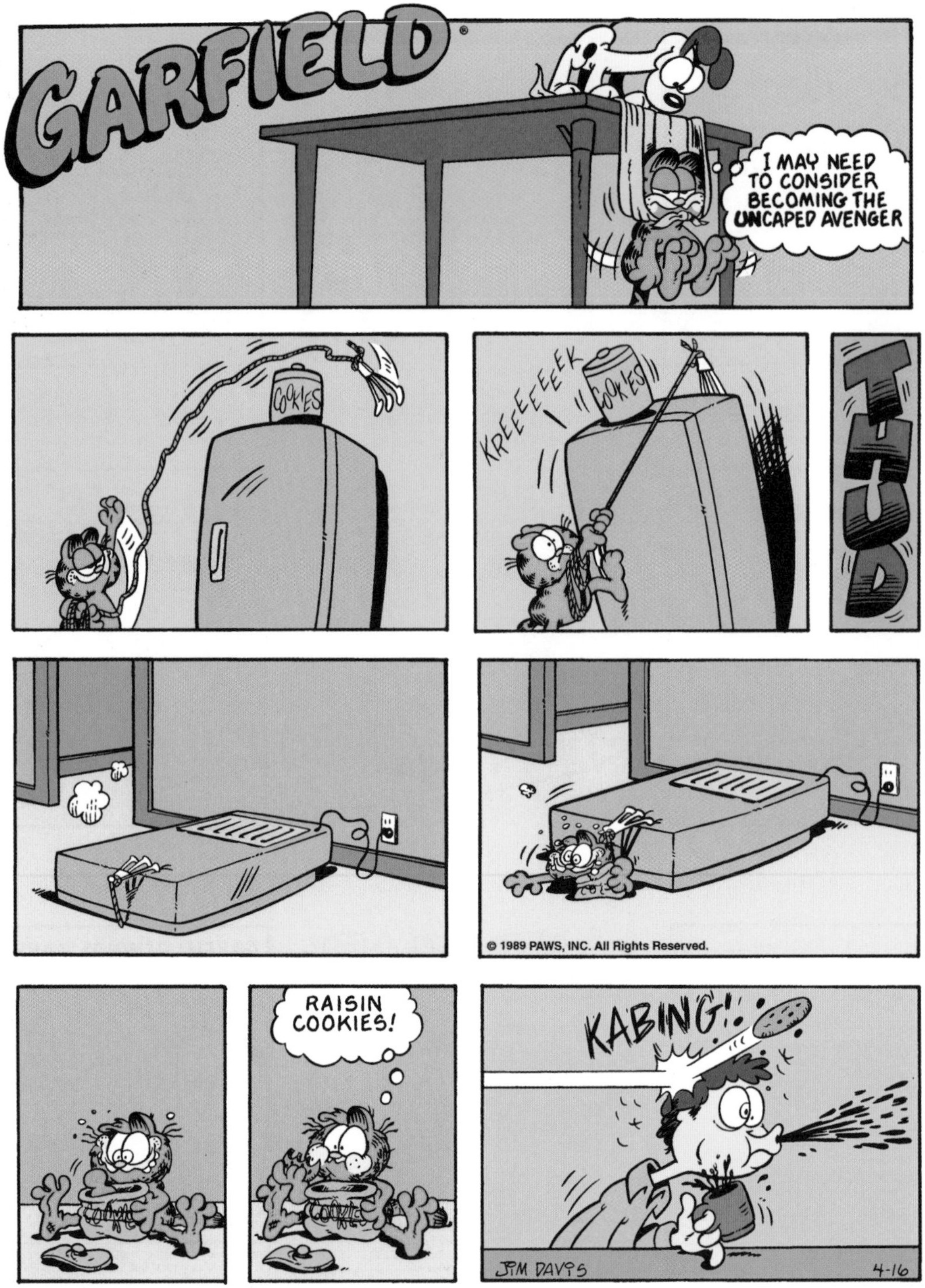
GARFIELD
I MAY NEED TO CONSIDER BECOMING THE UNCAPED AVENGER
COOKIES
KREEEEEEEK
COOKIES
THUD
© 1989 PAWS, INC. All Rights Reserved.
RAISIN COOKIES!
KABING!
JPM DAVIS
4-16

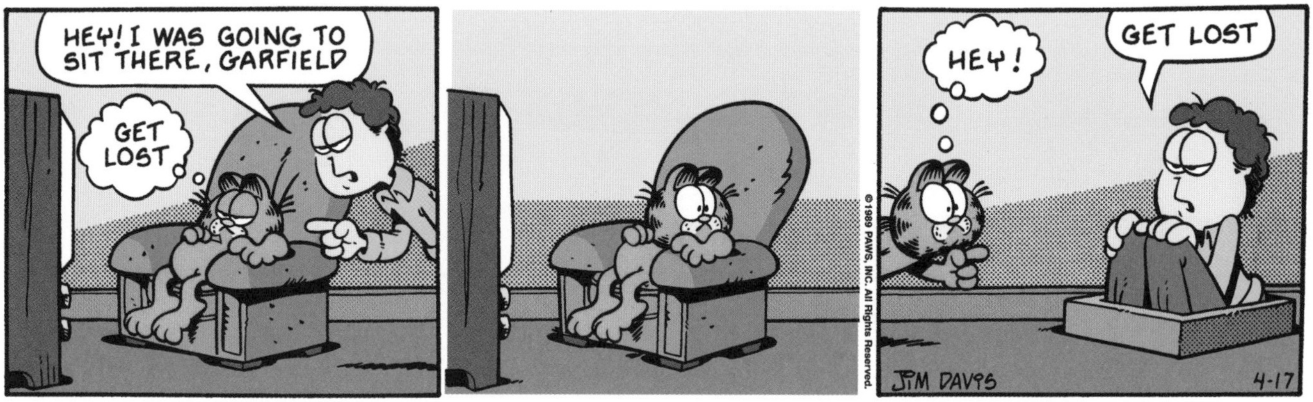
HEY! I WAS GOING TO SIT THERE, GARFIELD
GET LOST
© 1989 PAWS, INC. All Rights Reserved.
HEY!
GET LOST
JIM DAVIS
4-17

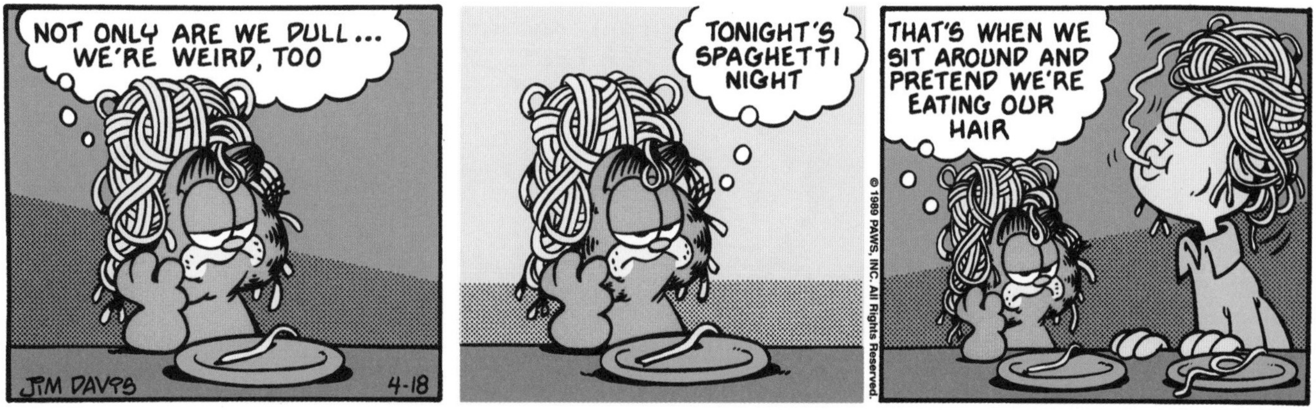
NOT ONLY ARE WE DULL... WE'RE WEIRD, TOO
JIM DAVIS
4-18
TONIGHT'S SPAGHETTI NIGHT
© 1989 PAWS, INC. All Rights Reserved.
THAT'S WHEN WE SIT AROUND AND PRETEND WE'RE EATING OUR HAIR

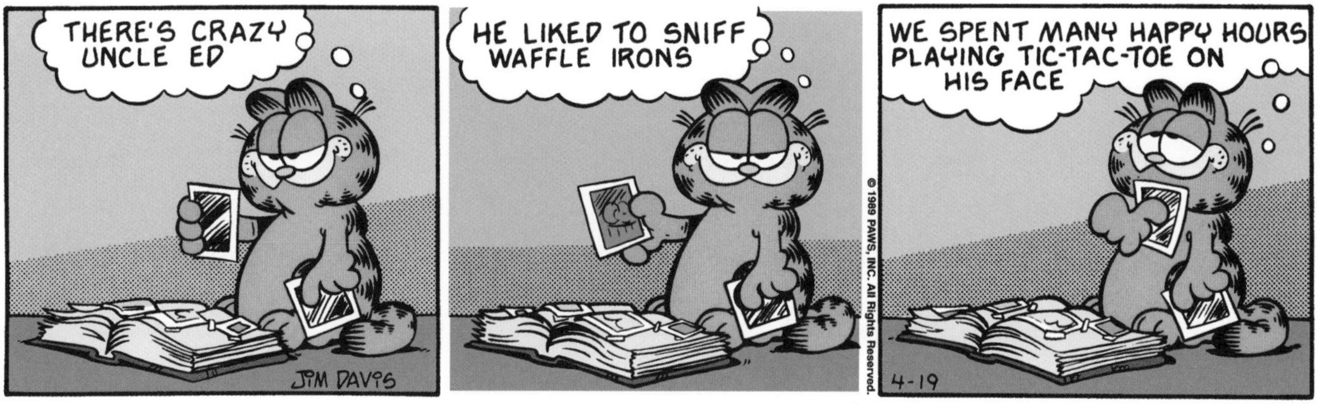
THERE'S CRAZY UNCLE ED
JIM DAVIS
HE LIKED TO SNIFF WAFFLE IRONS
© 1989 PAWS, INC. All Rights Reserved.
WE SPENT MANY HAPPY HOURS PLAYING TIC-TAC-TOE ON HIS FACE
4-19

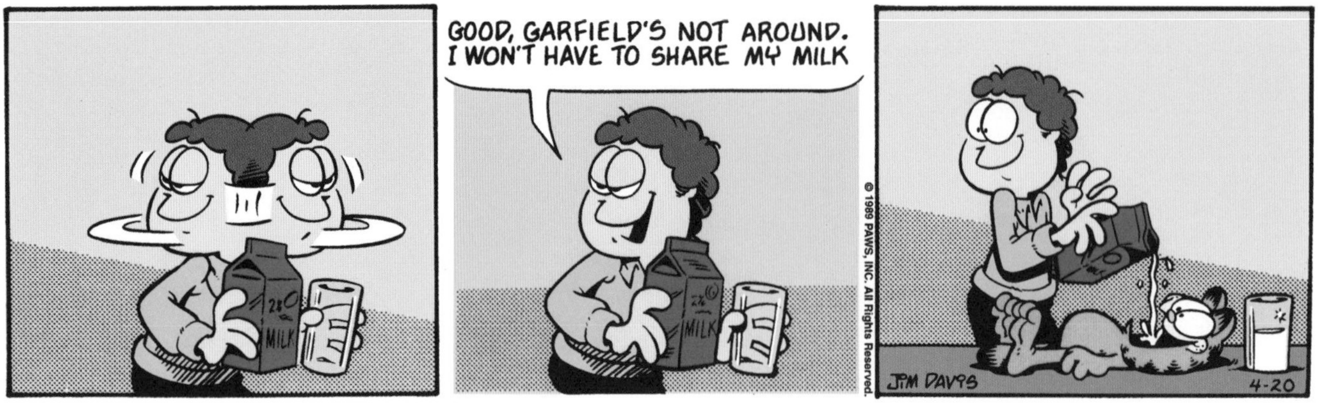
GOOD, GARFIELD'S NOT AROUND. I WON'T HAVE TO SHARE MY MILK
© 1989 PAWS, INC. All Rights Reserved.
JIM DAVIS
4-20

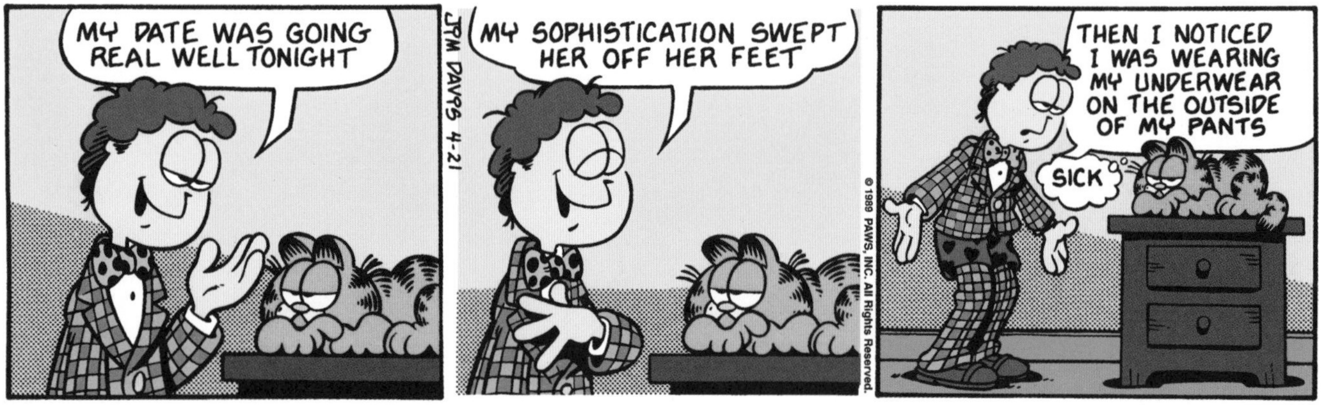
MY DATE WAS GOING REAL WELL TONIGHT
JIM DAVIS 4-21
MY SOPHISTICATION SWEPT HER OFF HER FEET
© 1989 PAWS, INC. All Rights Reserved.
THEN I NOTICED I WAS WEARING MY UNDERWEAR ON THE OUTSIDE OF MY PANTS
SICK

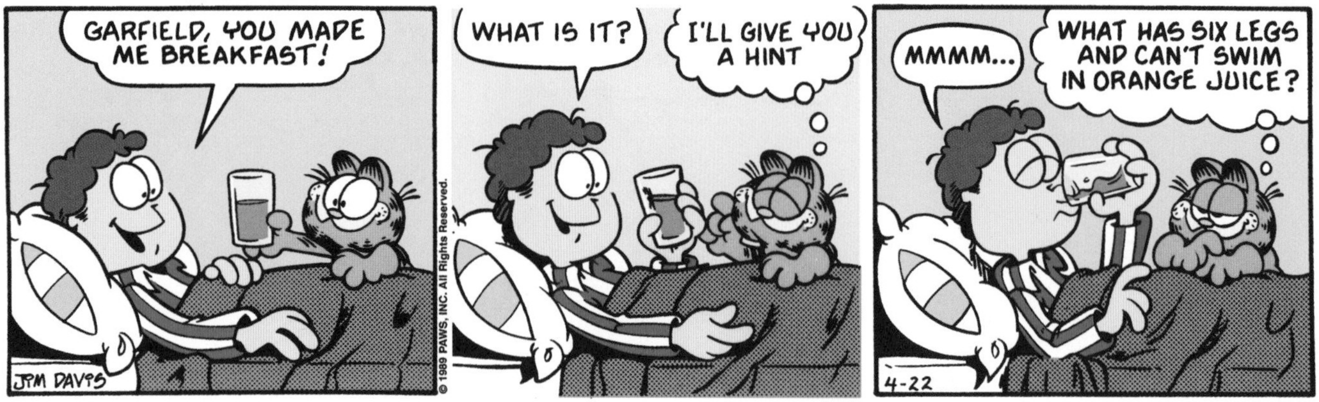
GARFIELD, YOU MADE ME BREAKFAST!
JIM DAVIS
© 1989 PAWS, INC. All Rights Reserved.
WHAT IS IT?
I'LL GIVE YOU A HINT
MMMM...
WHAT HAS SIX LEGS AND CAN'T SWIM IN ORANGE JUICE?
4-22

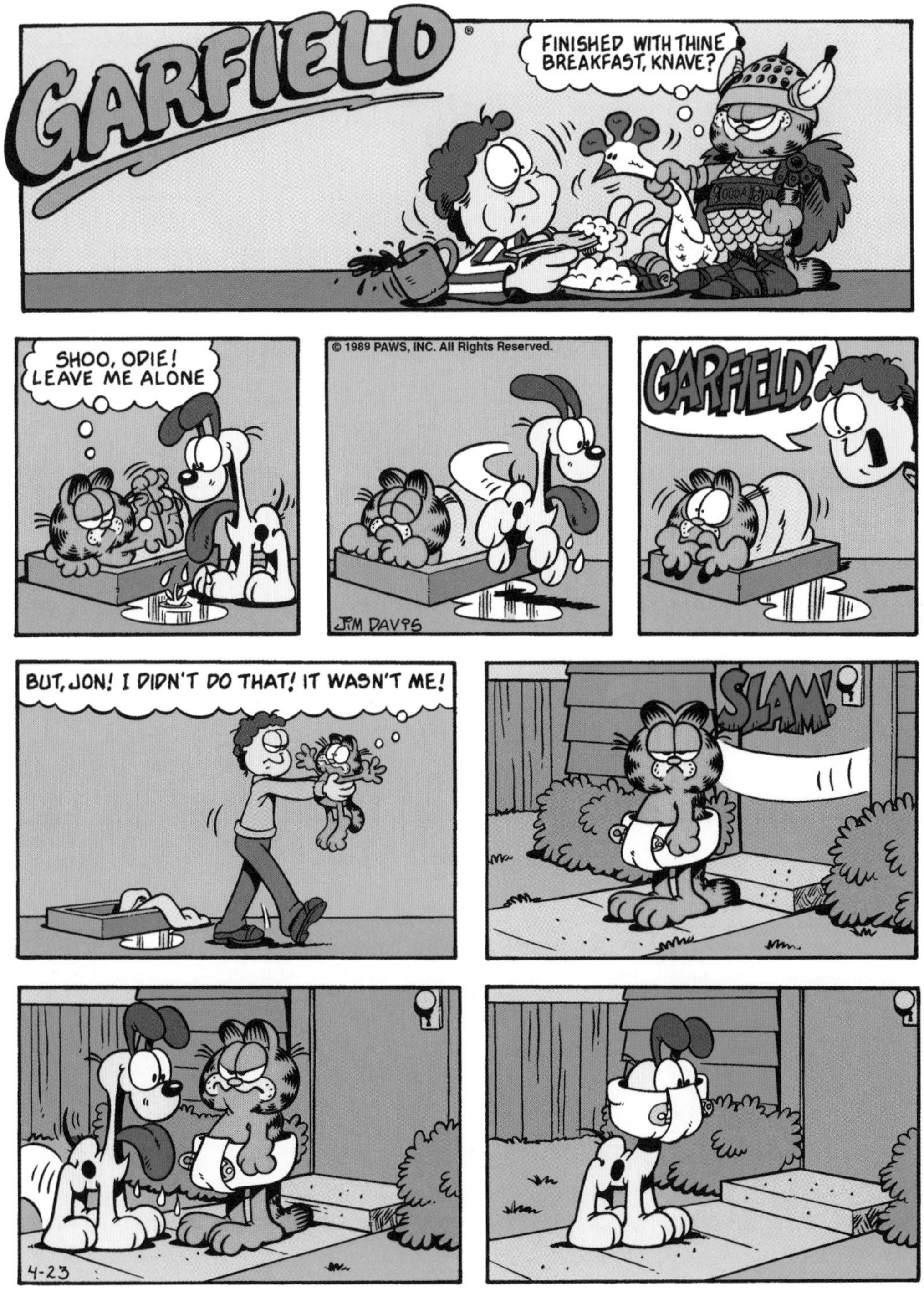
GARFIELD
FINISHED WITH THINE BREAKFAST, KNAVE?
SHOO, ODIE! LEAVE ME ALONE
© 1989 PAWS, INC. All Rights Reserved.
JIM DAVIS
GARFIELD!
BUT, JON! I DIDN'T DO THAT! IT WASN'T ME!
SLAM!
4-23

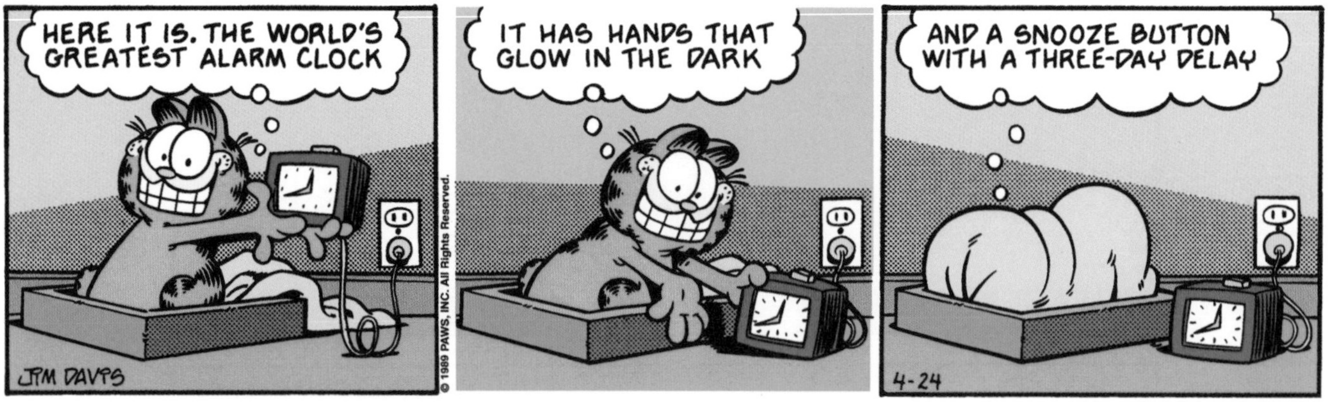
HERE IT IS. THE WORLD'S GREATEST ALARM CLOCK
JIM DAVIS
© 1989 PAWS, INC. All Rights Reserved.
IT HAS HANDS THAT GLOW IN THE DARK
AND A SNOOZE BUTTON WITH A THREE-DAY DELAY
4-24

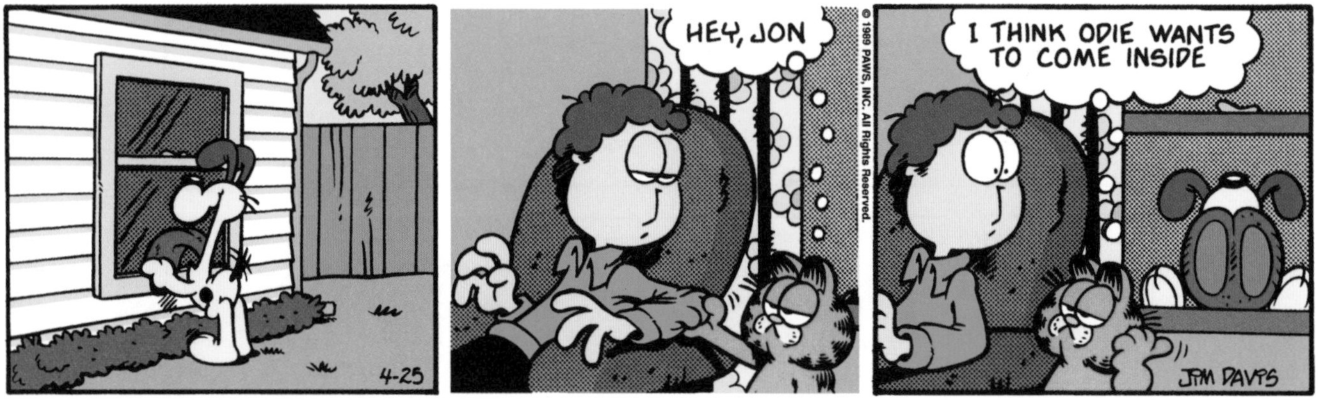
4-25
HEY, JON
© 1989 PAWS, INC. All Rights Reserved.
I THINK ODIE WANTS TO COME INSIDE
JIM DAVIS

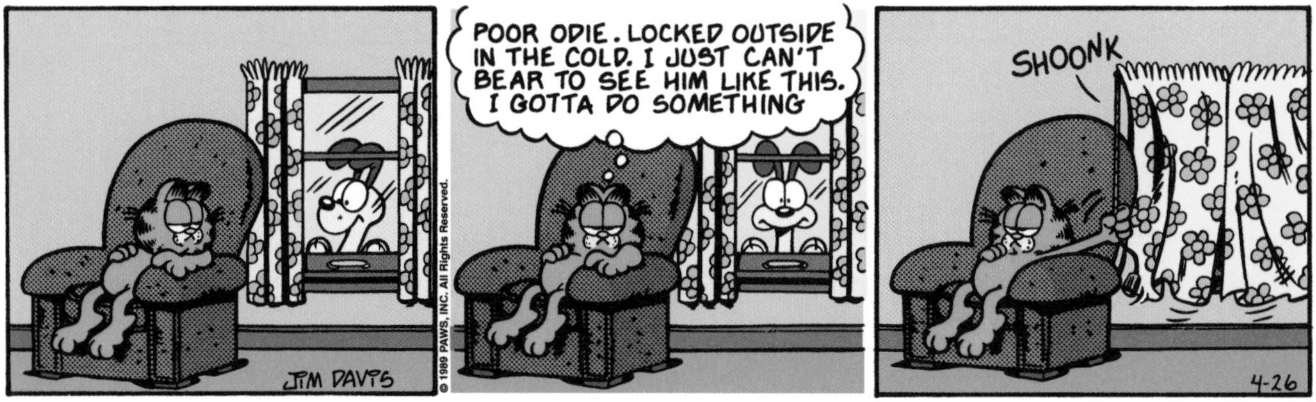
JIM DAVIS
© 1989 PAWS, INC. All Rights Reserved.
POOR ODIE. LOCKED OUTSIDE IN THE COLD. I JUST CAN'T BEAR TO SEE HIM LIKE THIS. I GOTTA DO SOMETHING
SHOONK
4-26

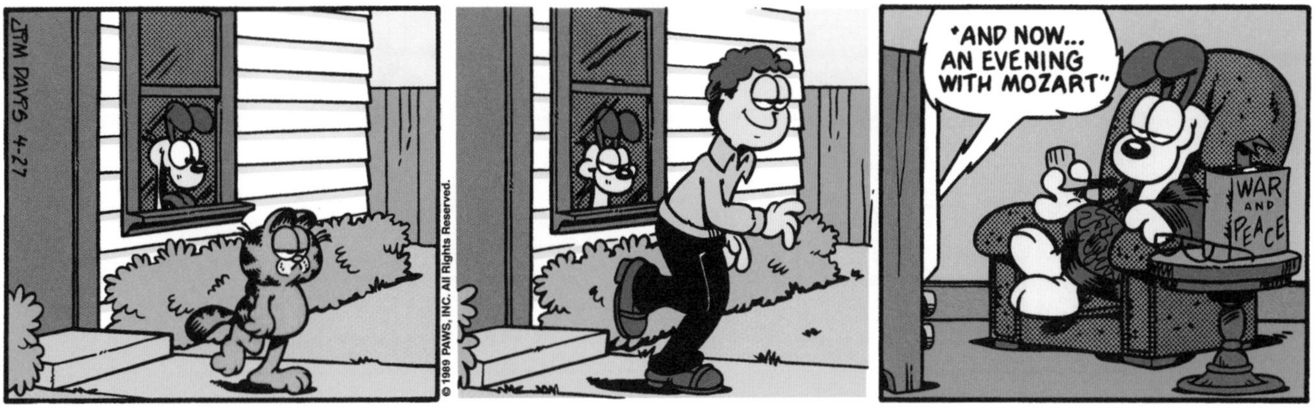
JIM DAVIS 4-27
© 1989 PAWS, INC. All Rights Reserved.
"AND NOW... AN EVENING WITH MOZART"
WAR AND PEACE

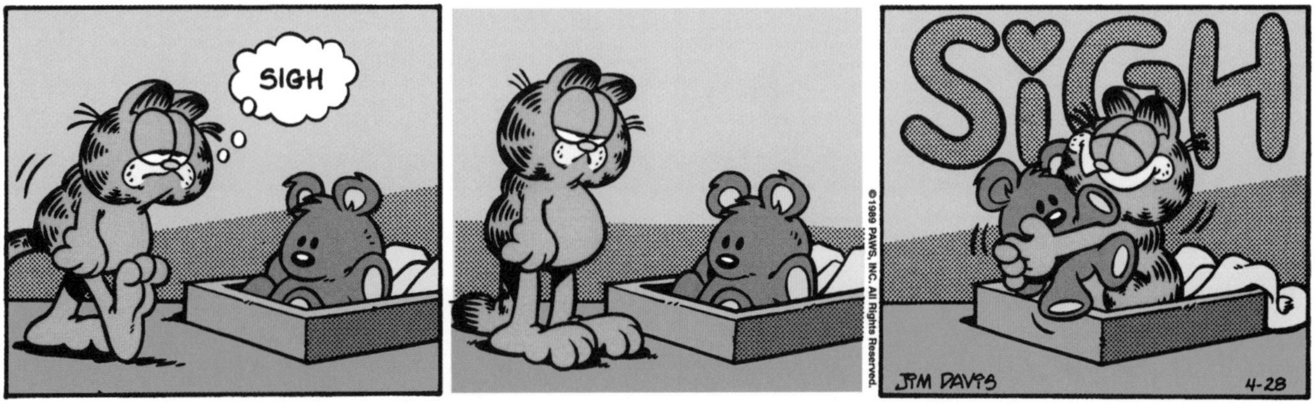
SIGH
© 1989 PAWS, INC. All Rights Reserved.
SIGH
JIM DAVIS
4-28

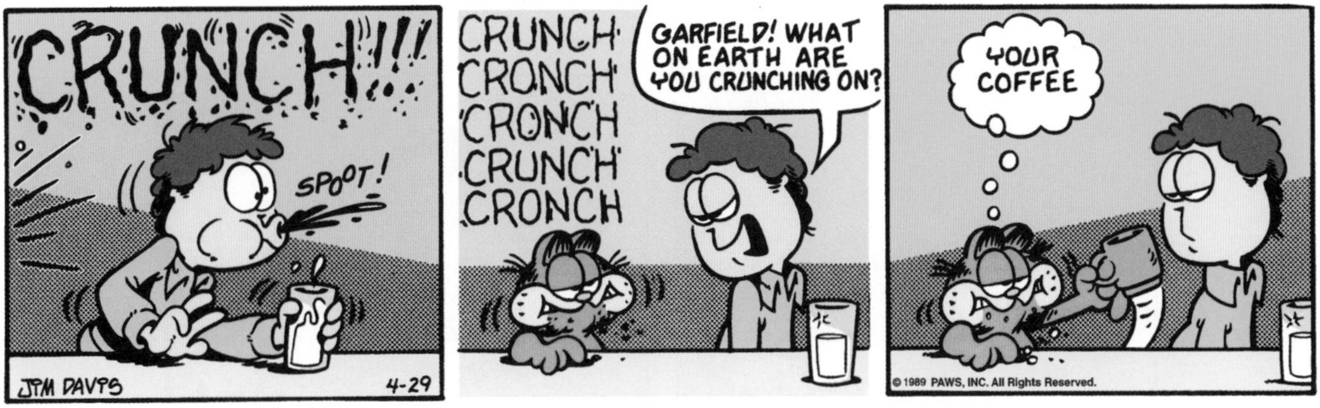
CRUNCH!!!
SPOOT!
JIM DAVIS
4-29
CRUNCH
CRONCH
CRONCH
CRUNCH
CRONCH
GARFIELD! WHAT ON EARTH ARE YOU CRUNCHING ON?
YOUR COFFEE
© 1989 PAWS, INC. All Rights Reserved.

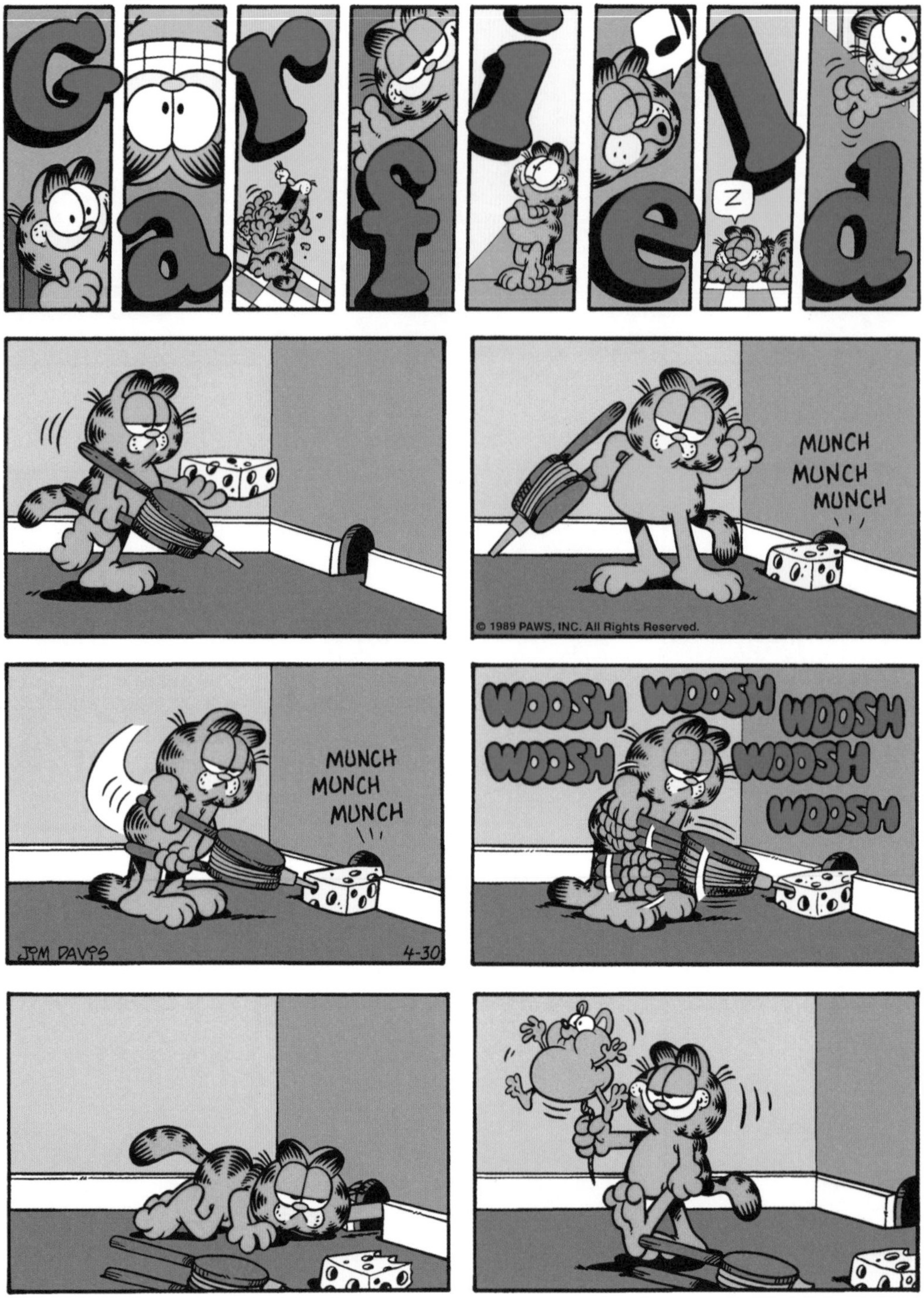
Garfield
Z
MUNCH
MUNCH
MUNCH
© 1989 PAWS, INC. All Rights Reserved.
MUNCH
MUNCH
MUNCH
JIM DAVIS
4-30
WOOSH WOOSH WOOSH
WOOSH WOOSH
WOOSH

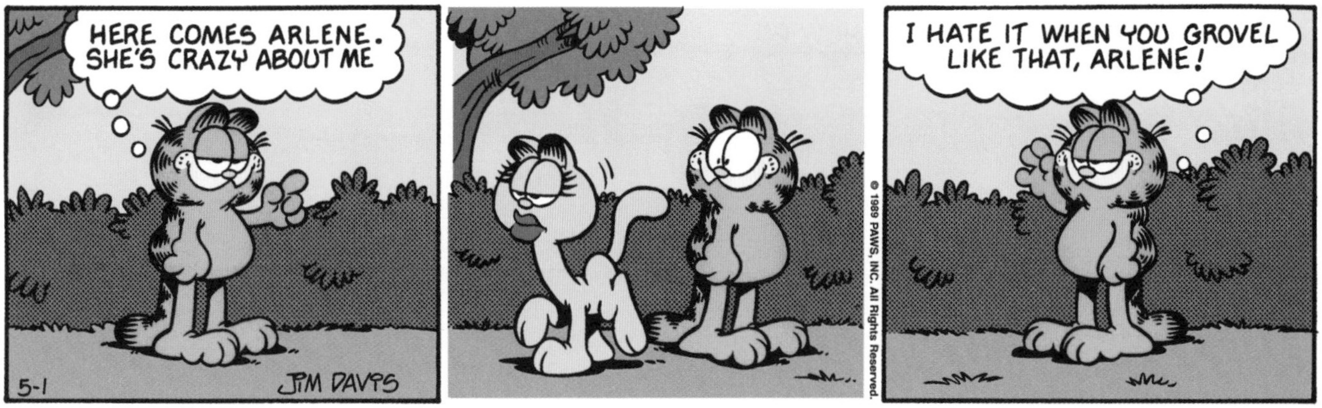
HERE COMES ARLENE. SHE'S CRAZY ABOUT ME
5-1
JIM DAVIS
© 1989 PAWS, INC. All Rights Reserved.
I HATE IT WHEN YOU GROVEL LIKE THAT, ARLENE!

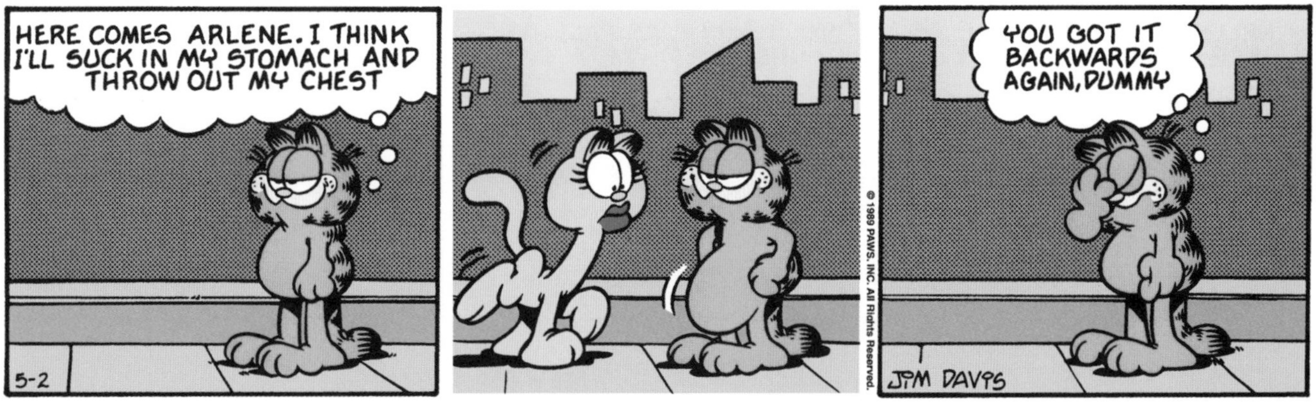
HERE COMES ARLENE. I THINK I'LL SUCK IN MY STOMACH AND THROW OUT MY CHEST
5-2
© 1989 PAWS, INC. All Rights Reserved.
YOU GOT IT BACKWARDS AGAIN, DUMMY
JIM DAVIS

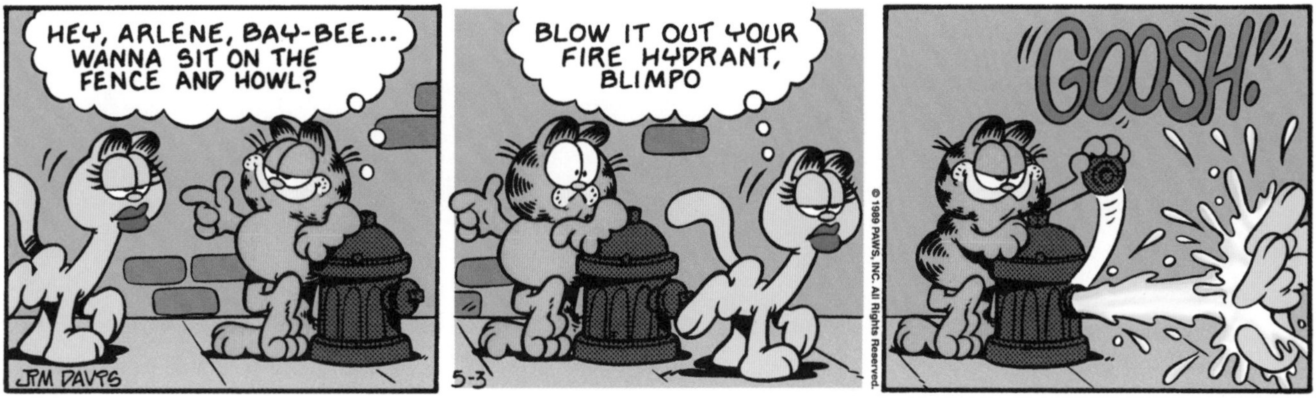
HEY, ARLENE, BAY-BEE... WANNA SIT ON THE FENCE AND HOWL?
JIM DAVIS
BLOW IT OUT YOUR FIRE HYDRANT, BLIMPO
5-3
© 1989 PAWS, INC. All Rights Reserved.
GOOSH!

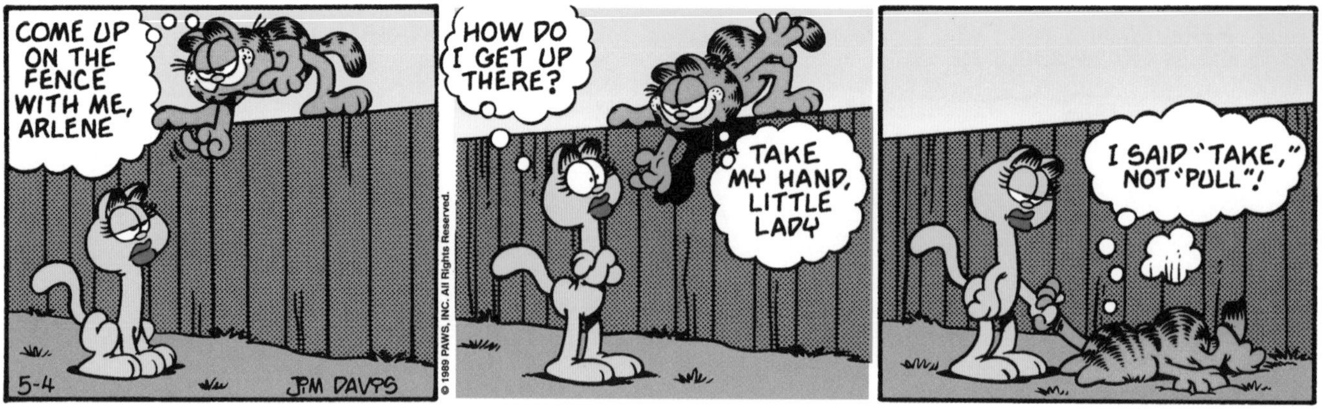
5-4
JIM DAVIS
COME UP ON THE FENCE WITH ME, ARLENE
© 1989 PAWS, INC. All Rights Reserved.
HOW DO I GET UP THERE?
TAKE MY HAND, LITTLE LADY
I SAID "TAKE," NOT "PULL"!

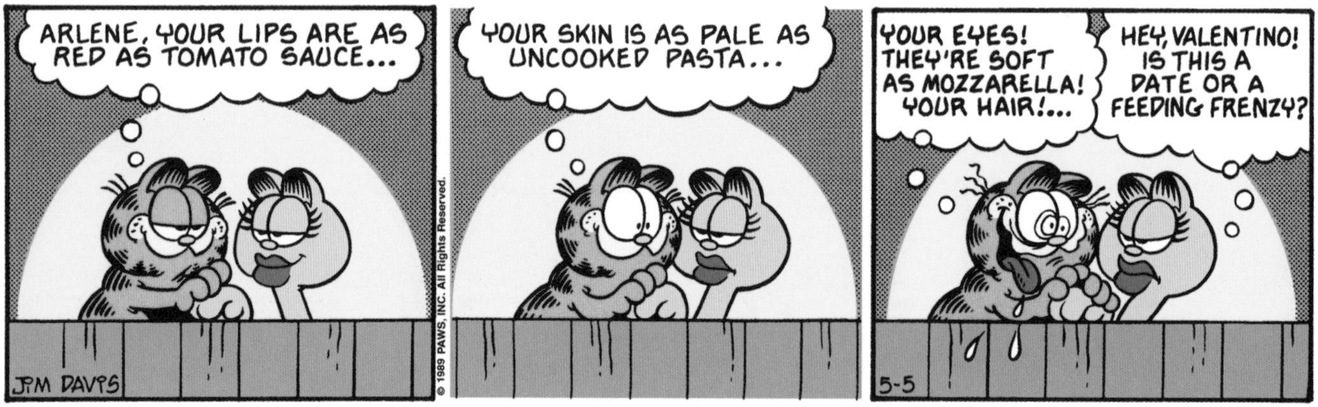
ARLENE, YOUR LIPS ARE AS RED AS TOMATO SAUCE...
JIM DAVIS
© 1989 PAWS, INC. All Rights Reserved.
YOUR SKIN IS AS PALE AS UNCOOKED PASTA...
YOUR EYES! THEY'RE SOFT AS MOZZARELLA! YOUR HAIR!...
HEY, VALENTINO! IS THIS A DATE OR A FEEDING FRENZY?
5-5

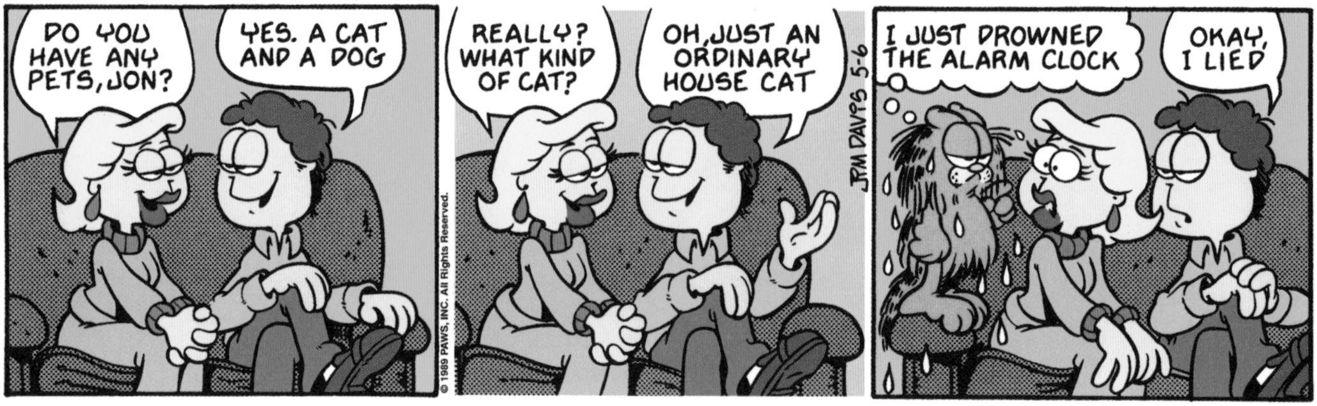
DO YOU HAVE ANY PETS, JON?
YES. A CAT AND A DOG
© 1989 PAWS, INC. All Rights Reserved.
REALLY? WHAT KIND OF CAT?
OH, JUST AN ORDINARY HOUSE CAT
JIM DAVIS 5-6
I JUST DROWNED THE ALARM CLOCK
OKAY, I LIED

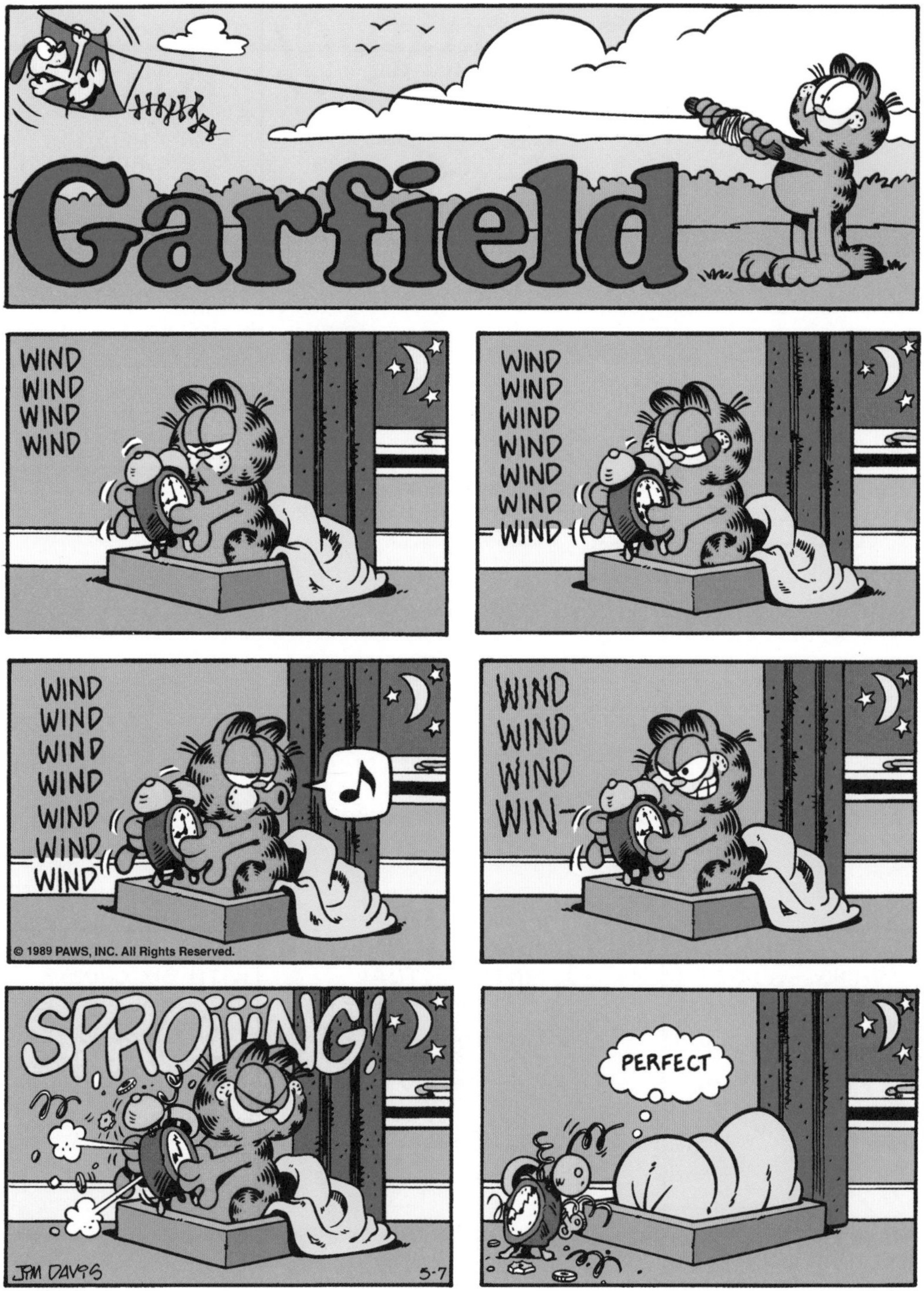
Garfield
WIND WIND WIND WIND
WIND WIND WIND WIND WIND WIND WIND
WIND WIND WIND WIND WIND WIND WIND
WIND WIND WIND WIN-
© 1989 PAWS, INC. All Rights Reserved.
SPROIIING!
JPM DAVIS 5-7
PERFECT

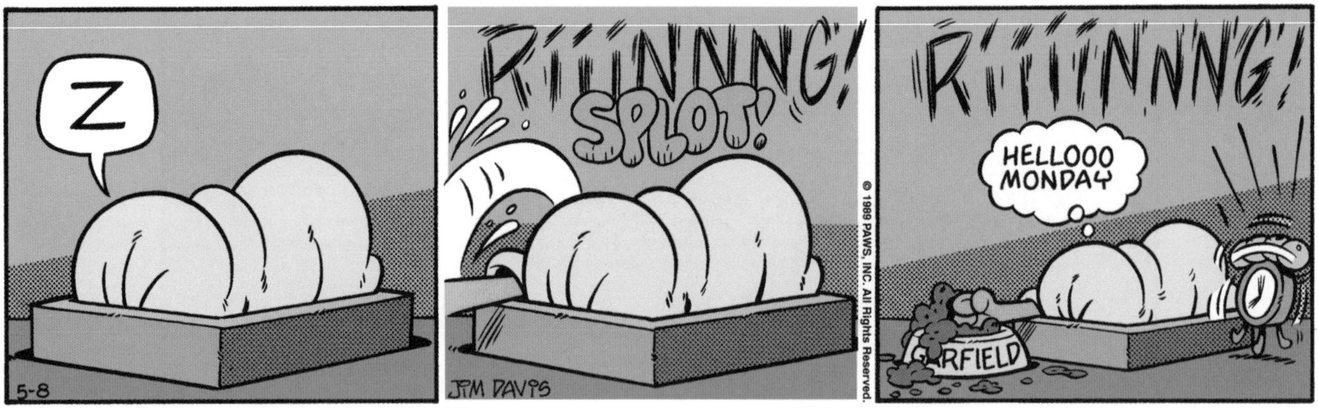
Z
RIIINNNG!
SPLOT!
© 1989 PAWS, INC. All Rights Reserved.
RIIIINNNG!
HELLOOO MONDAY
RFIELD
5-8
JIM DAVIS

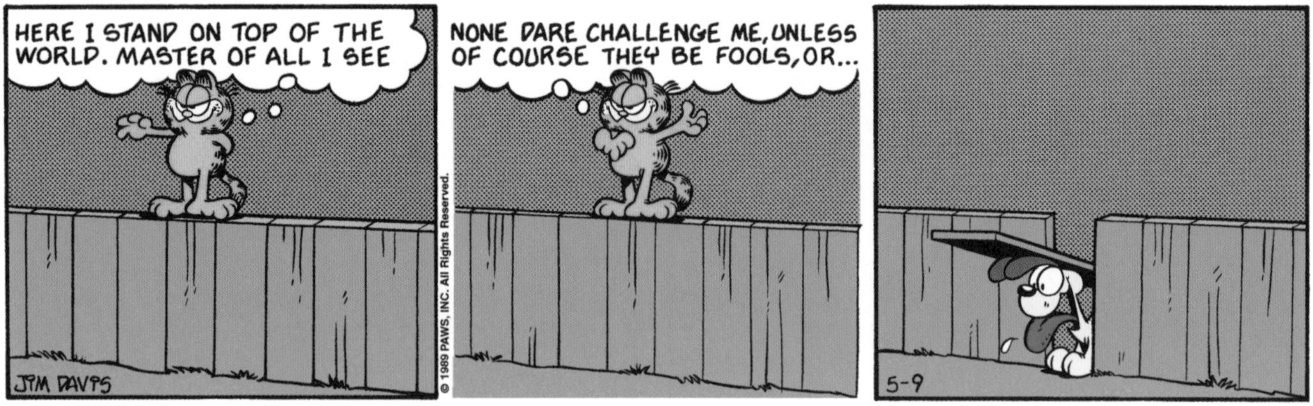
HERE I STAND ON TOP OF THE WORLD. MASTER OF ALL I SEE
© 1989 PAWS, INC. All Rights Reserved.
NONE DARE CHALLENGE ME, UNLESS OF COURSE THEY BE FOOLS, OR...
JIM DAVIS
5-9

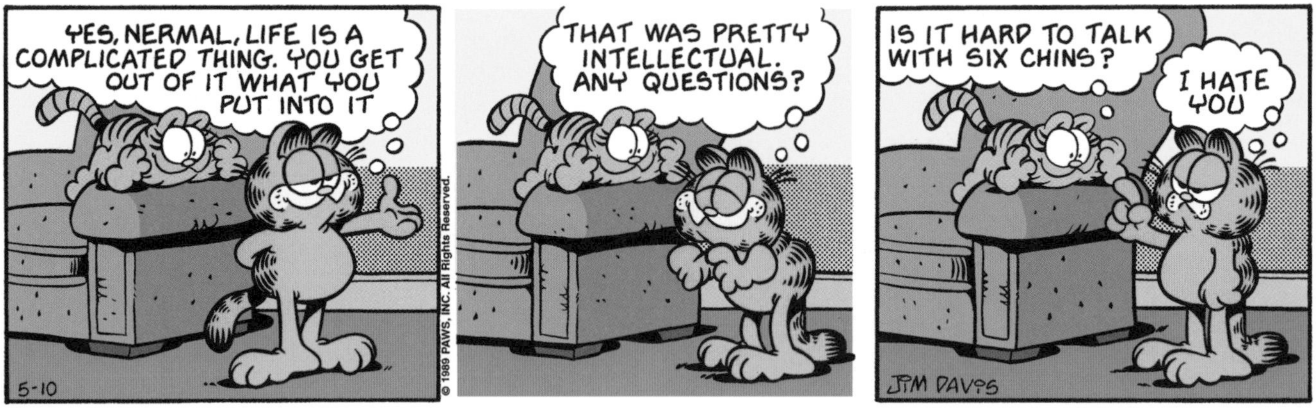
YES, NERMAL, LIFE IS A COMPLICATED THING. YOU GET OUT OF IT WHAT YOU PUT INTO IT
© 1989 PAWS, INC. All Rights Reserved.
THAT WAS PRETTY INTELLECTUAL. ANY QUESTIONS?
IS IT HARD TO TALK WITH SIX CHINS?
I HATE YOU
5-10
JIM DAVIS

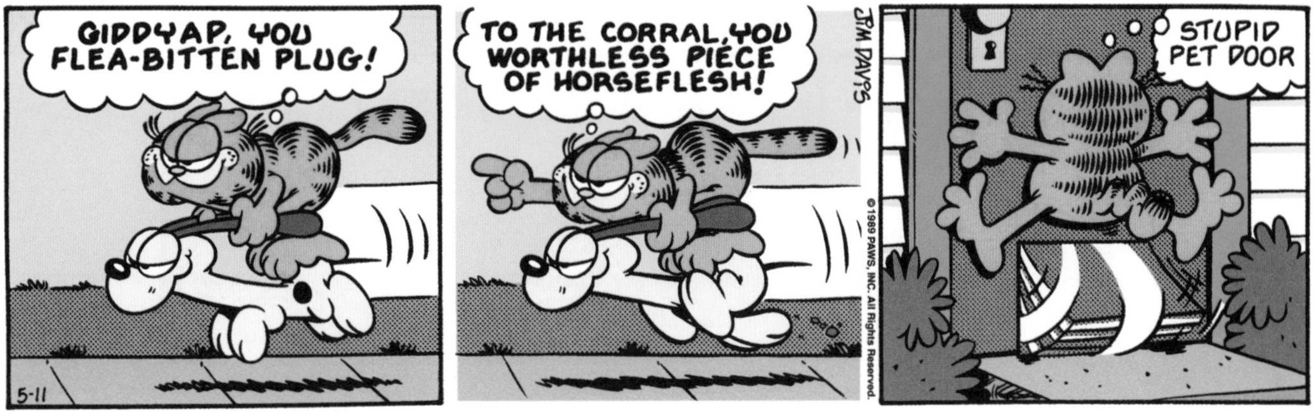
GIDDYAP, YOU FLEA-BITTEN PLUG!
TO THE CORRAL, YOU WORTHLESS PIECE OF HORSEFLESH!
STUPID PET DOOR
JIM DAVIS
© 1989 PAWS, INC. All Rights Reserved.
5-11

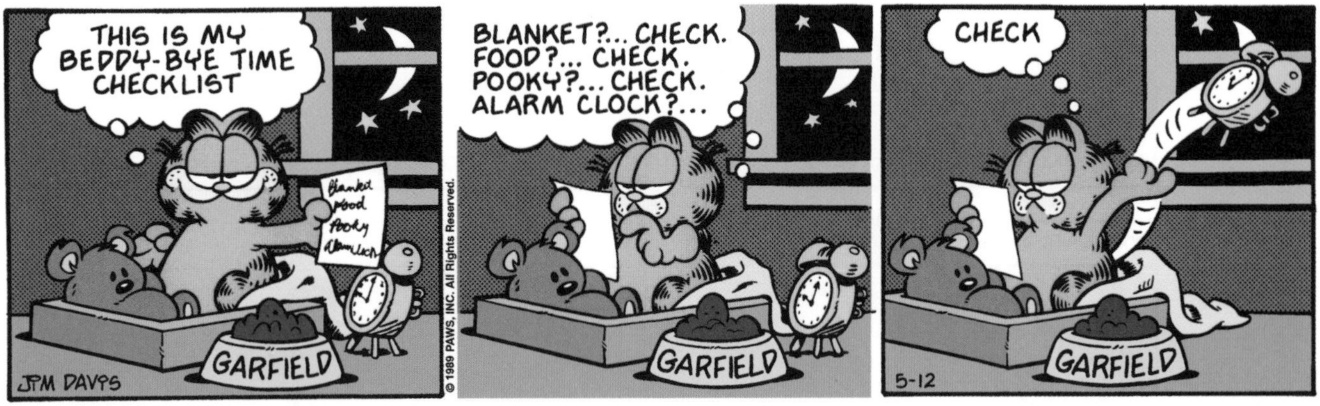
THIS IS MY BEDDY-BYE TIME CHECKLIST
GARFIELD
JIM DAVIS
© 1989 PAWS, INC. All Rights Reserved.
BLANKET?... CHECK. FOOD?... CHECK. POOKY?... CHECK. ALARM CLOCK?...
GARFIELD
CHECK
GARFIELD
5-12

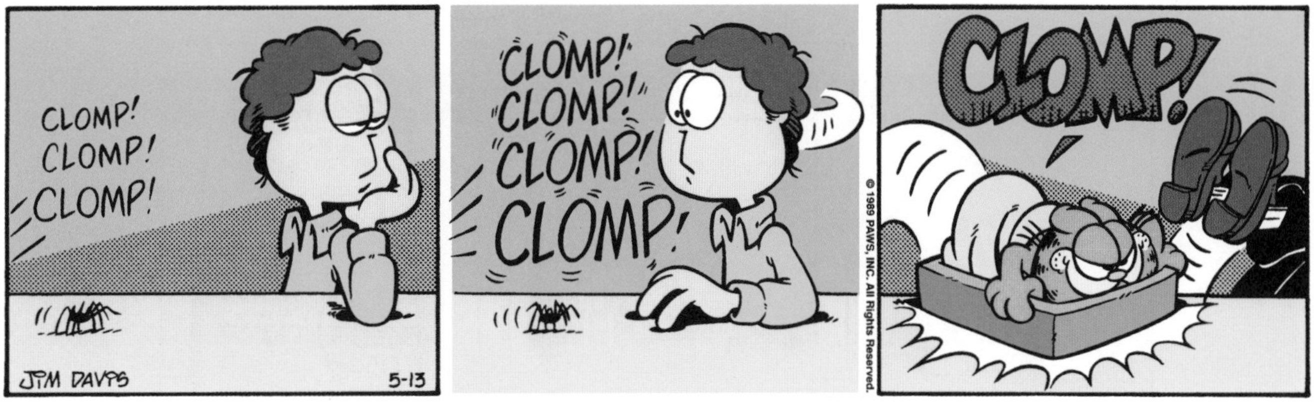
CLOMP! CLOMP! CLOMP!
JIM DAVIS
5-13
CLOMP! CLOMP! CLOMP! CLOMP!
© 1989 PAWS, INC. All Rights Reserved.
CLOMP!

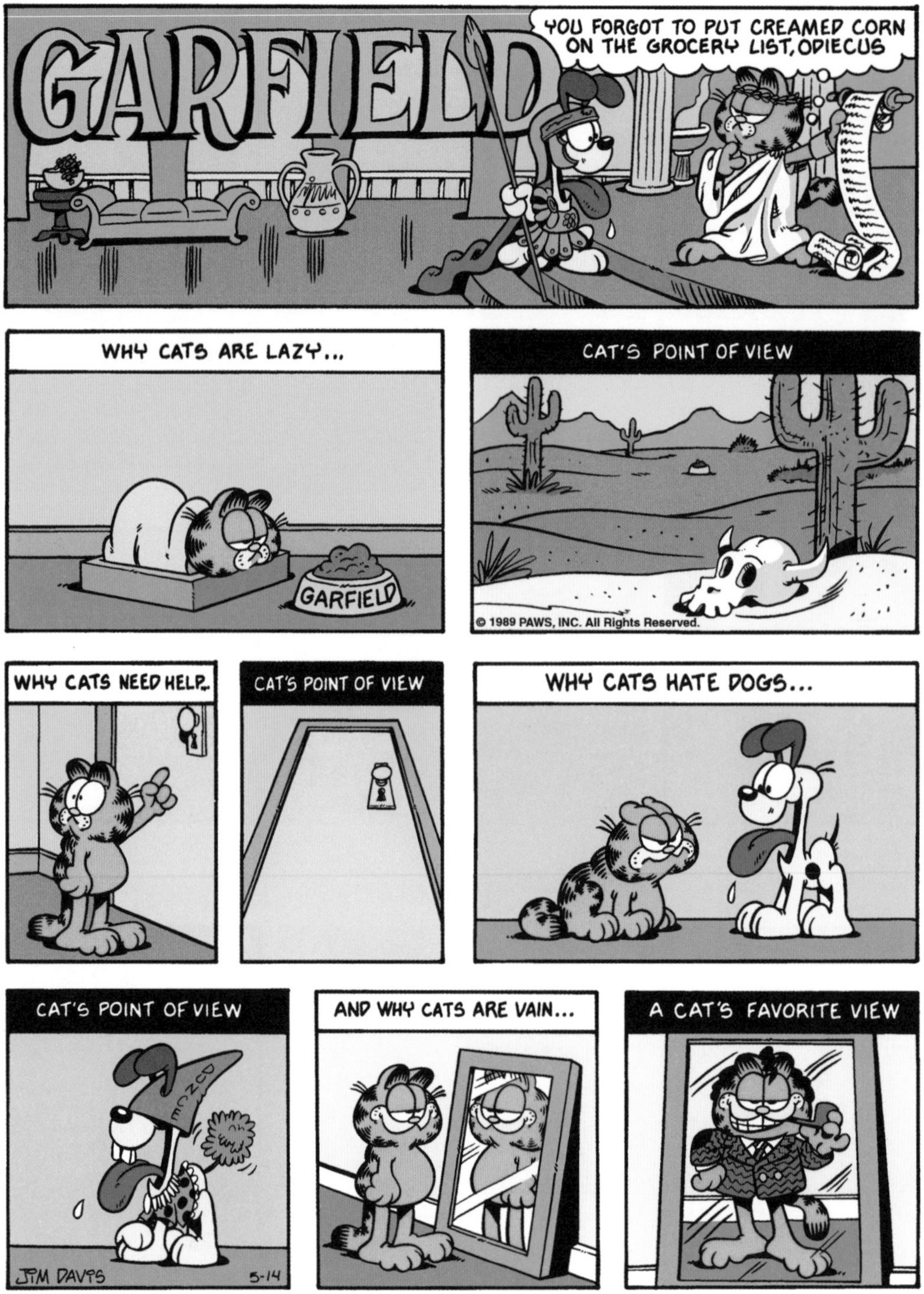
GARFIELD
YOU FORGOT TO PUT CREAMED CORN ON THE GROCERY LIST, ODIECUS
WHY CATS ARE LAZY...
GARFIELD
CAT'S POINT OF VIEW
© 1989 PAWS, INC. All Rights Reserved.
WHY CATS NEED HELP...
CAT'S POINT OF VIEW
WHY CATS HATE DOGS...
CAT'S POINT OF VIEW
JIM DAVIS
5-14
AND WHY CATS ARE VAIN...
A CAT'S FAVORITE VIEW

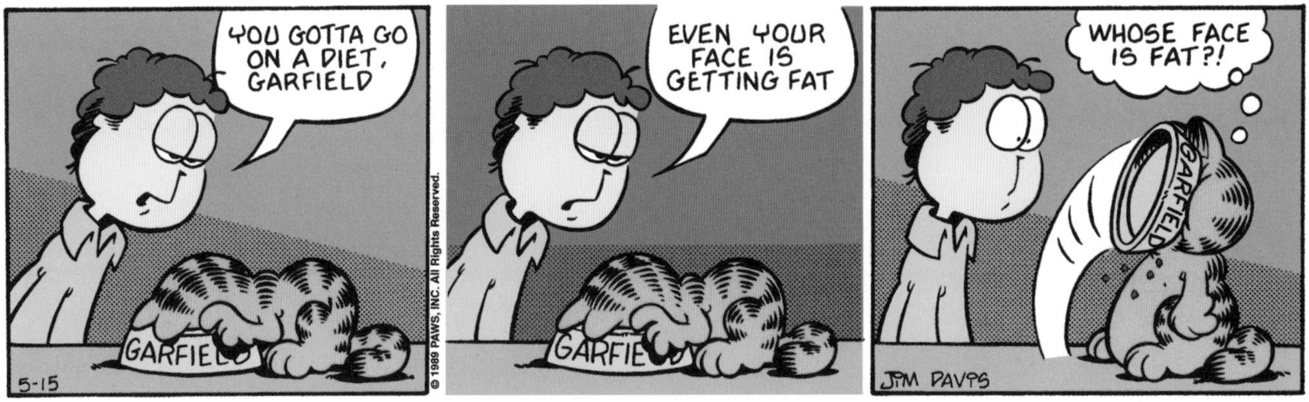
YOU GOTTA GO ON A DIET, GARFIELD
GARFIELD
5-15
© 1989 PAWS, INC. All Rights Reserved.
EVEN YOUR FACE IS GETTING FAT
WHOSE FACE IS FAT?!
GARFIELD
JIM DAVIS

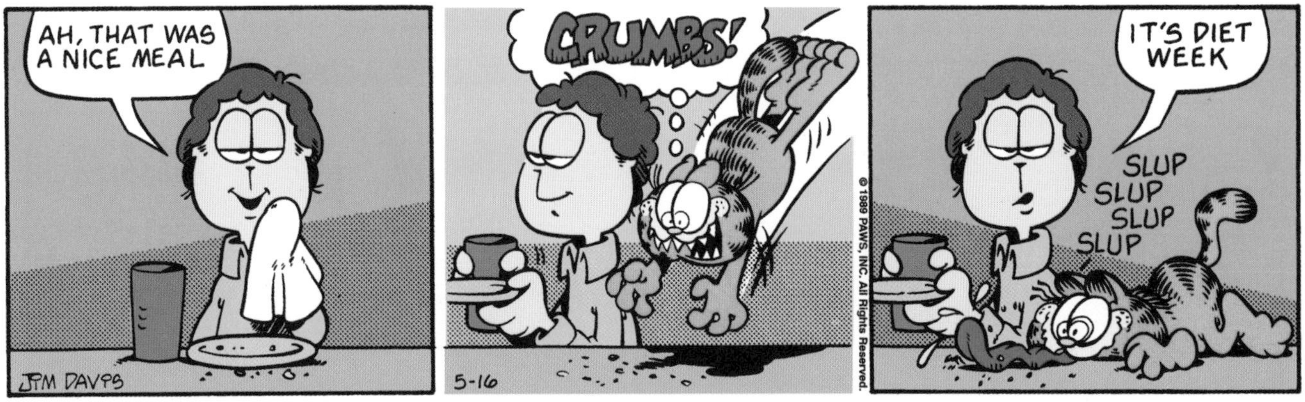
AH, THAT WAS A NICE MEAL
JIM DAVIS
CRUMBS!
5-16
© 1989 PAWS, INC. All Rights Reserved.
IT'S DIET WEEK
SLUP
SLUP
SLUP
SLUP

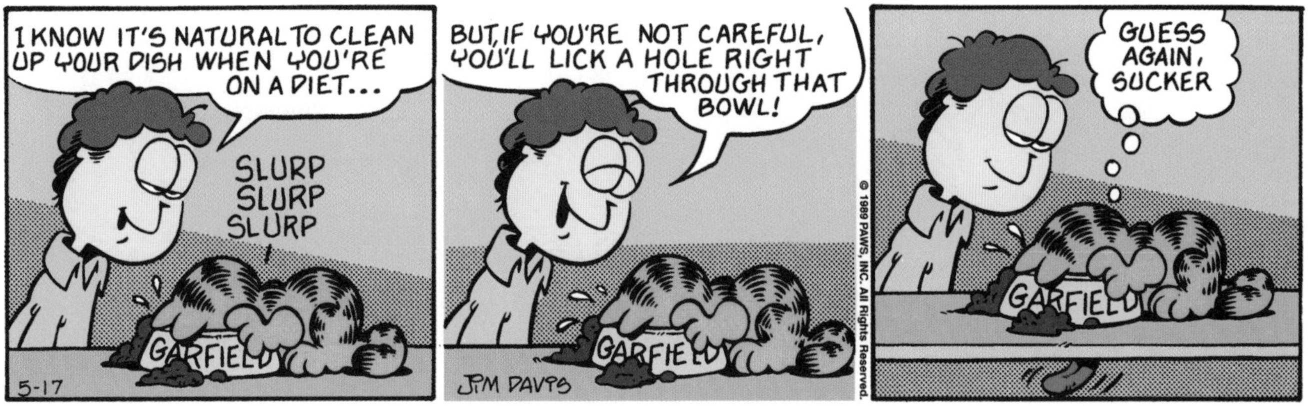
I KNOW IT'S NATURAL TO CLEAN UP YOUR DISH WHEN YOU'RE ON A DIET...
SLURP
SLURP
SLURP
GARFIELD
5-17
BUT, IF YOU'RE NOT CAREFUL, YOU'LL LICK A HOLE RIGHT THROUGH THAT BOWL!
GARFIELD
JIM DAVIS
© 1989 PAWS, INC. All Rights Reserved.
GUESS AGAIN, SUCKER
GARFIELD

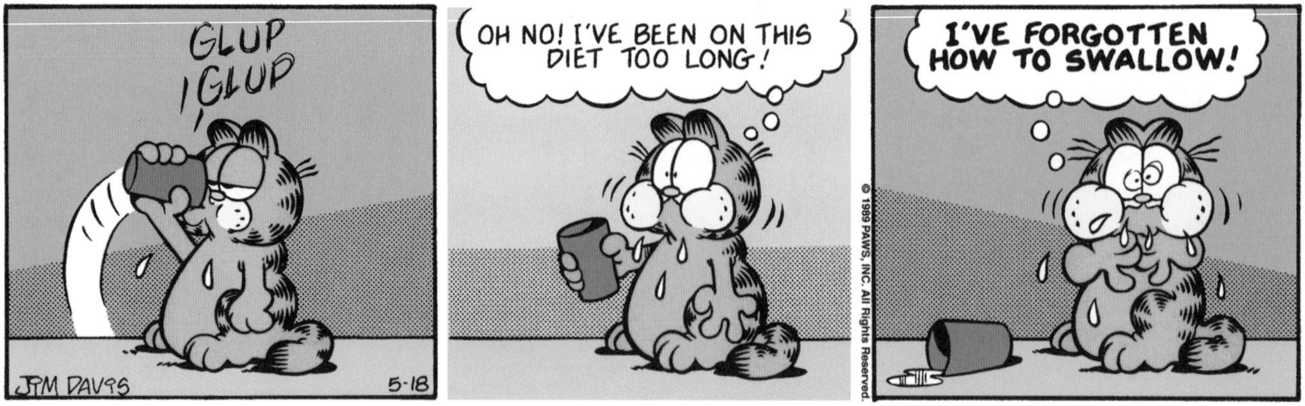
GLUP
GLUP
JIM DAVIS
5-18
OH NO! I'VE BEEN ON THIS DIET TOO LONG!
I'VE FORGOTTEN HOW TO SWALLOW!

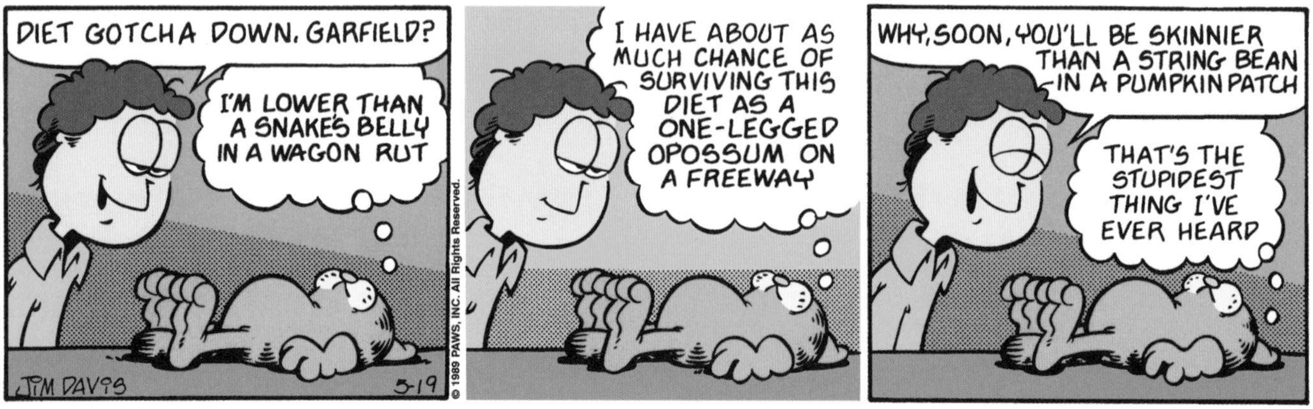
DIET GOTCHA DOWN, GARFIELD?
I'M LOWER THAN A SNAKE'S BELLY IN A WAGON RUT
JIM DAVIS
5-19
I HAVE ABOUT AS MUCH CHANCE OF SURVIVING THIS DIET AS A ONE-LEGGED OPOSSUM ON A FREEWAY
WHY, SOON, YOU'LL BE SKINNIER THAN A STRING BEAN IN A PUMPKIN PATCH
THAT'S THE STUPIDEST THING I'VE EVER HEARD

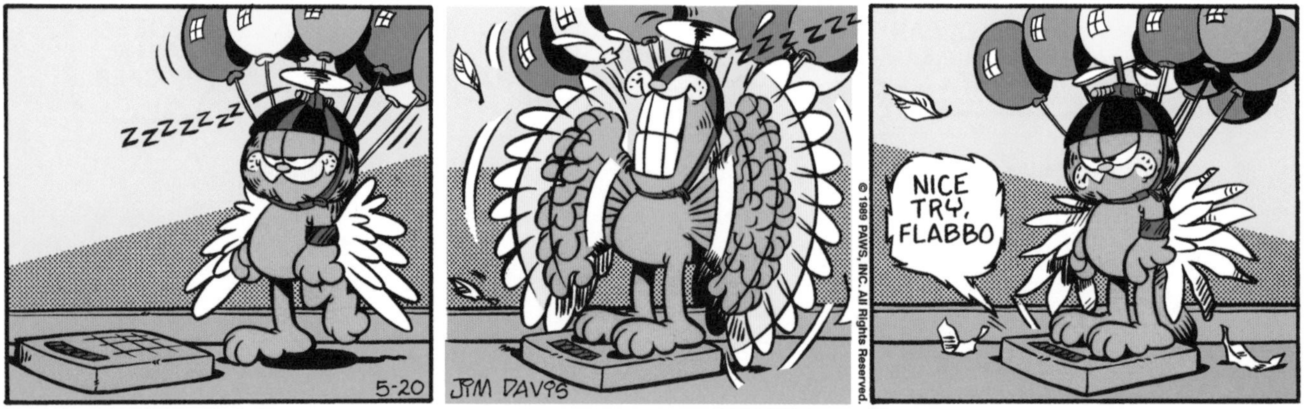
ZZZZZZZ
5-20
ZZZZZZ
JIM DAVIS
NICE TRY, FLABBO

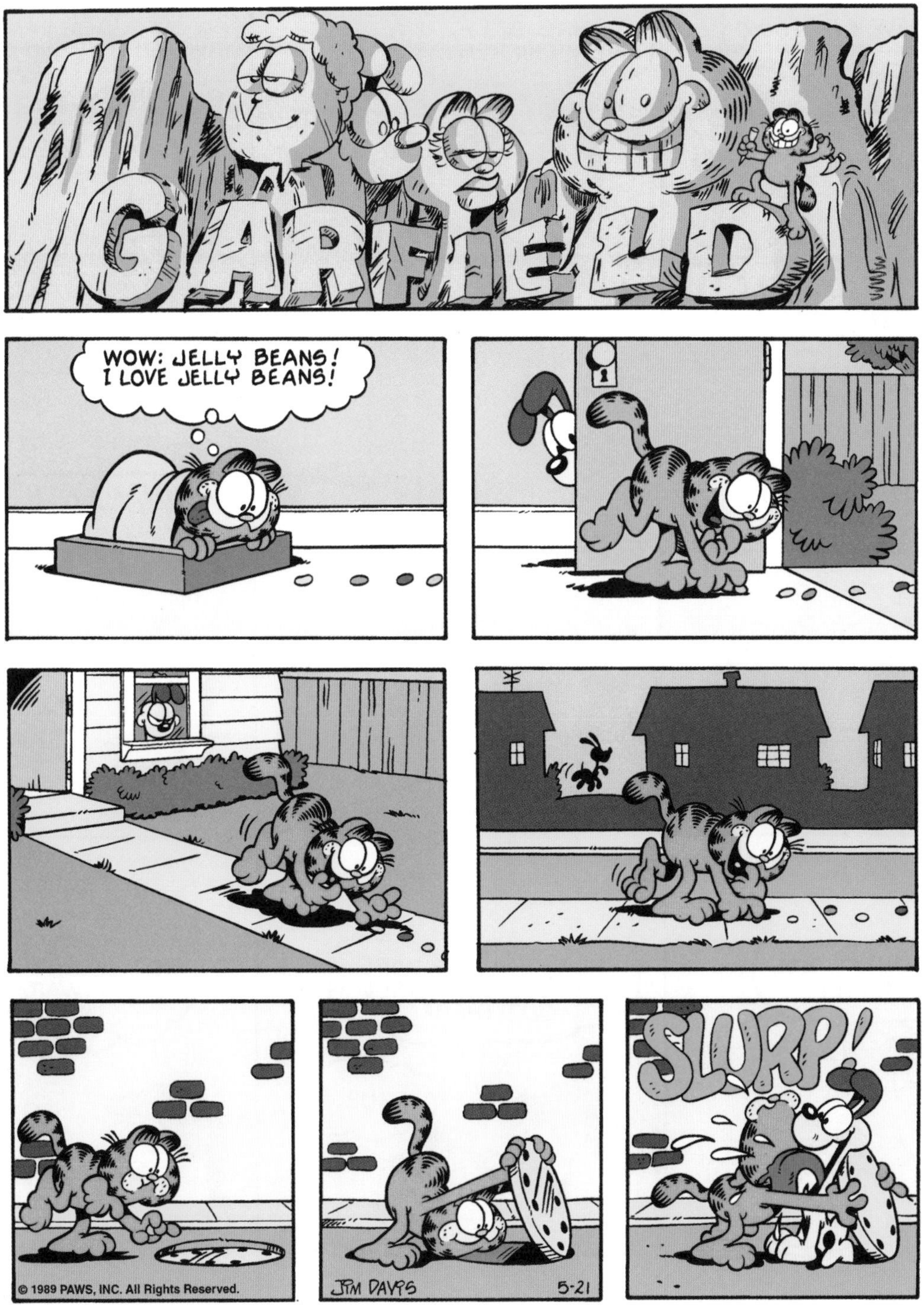
GARFIELD
WOW: JELLY BEANS! I LOVE JELLY BEANS!
SLURP!
JIM DAVIS
5-21

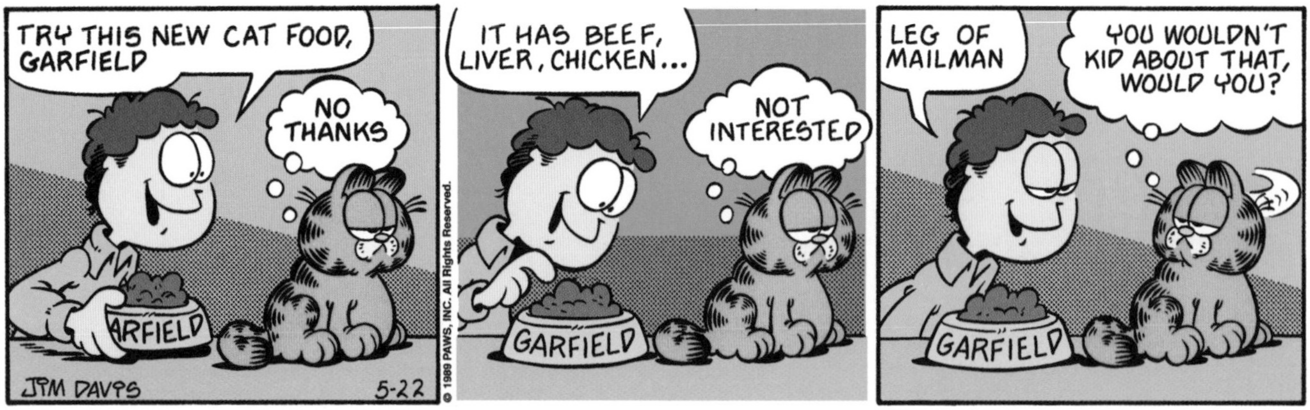
TRY THIS NEW CAT FOOD, GARFIELD
NO THANKS
ARFIELD
JIM DAVIS
5-22
© 1989 PAWS, INC. All Rights Reserved.
IT HAS BEEF, LIVER, CHICKEN...
NOT INTERESTED
GARFIELD
LEG OF MAILMAN
YOU WOULDN'T KID ABOUT THAT, WOULD YOU?
GARFIELD

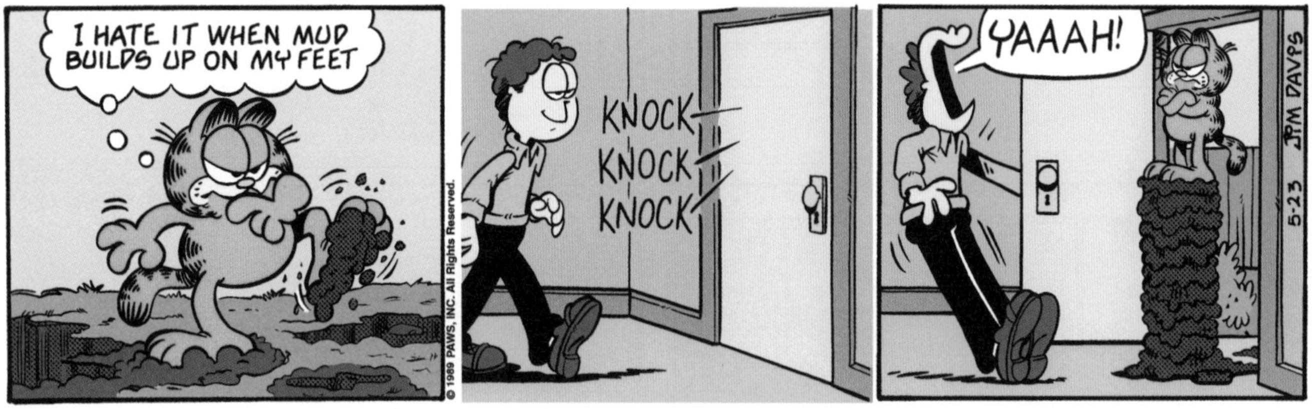
I HATE IT WHEN MUD BUILDS UP ON MY FEET
© 1989 PAWS, INC. All Rights Reserved.
KNOCK
KNOCK
KNOCK
YAAAH!
JIM DAVIS
5-23

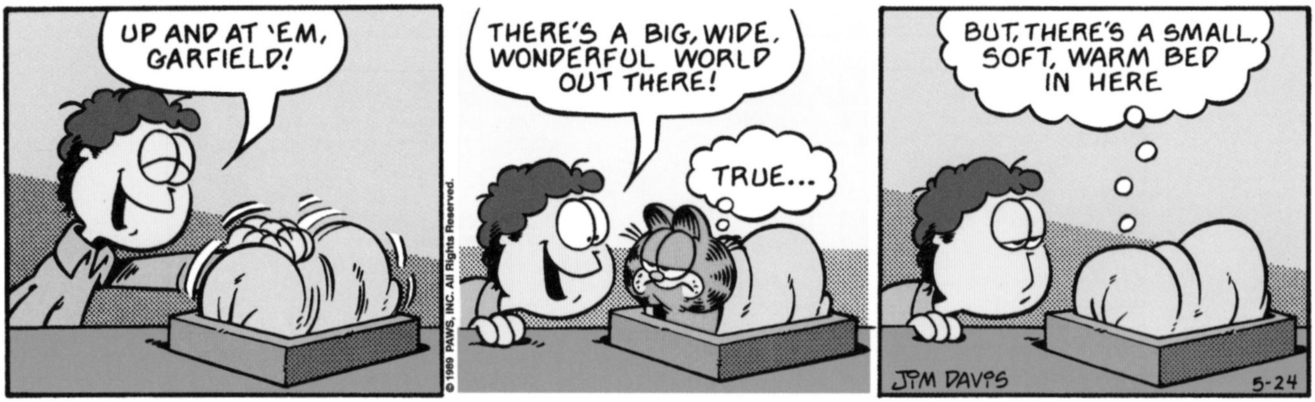
UP AND AT 'EM, GARFIELD!
© 1989 PAWS, INC. All Rights Reserved.
THERE'S A BIG, WIDE, WONDERFUL WORLD OUT THERE!
TRUE...
BUT, THERE'S A SMALL, SOFT, WARM BED IN HERE
JIM DAVIS
5-24

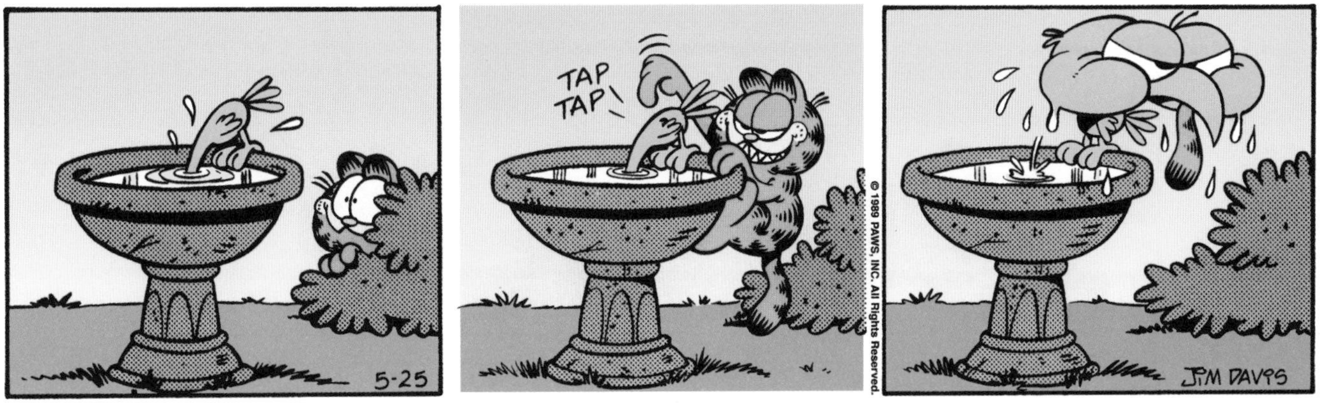
5-25
TAP TAP
© 1989 PAWS, INC. All Rights Reserved.
JIM DAVIS

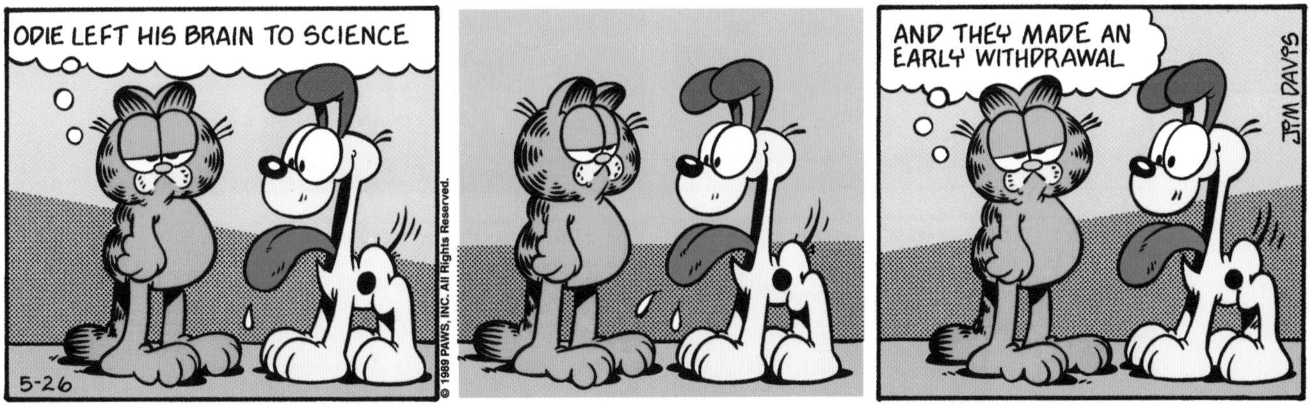
ODIE LEFT HIS BRAIN TO SCIENCE
5-26
© 1989 PAWS, INC. All Rights Reserved.
AND THEY MADE AN EARLY WITHDRAWAL
JIM DAVIS

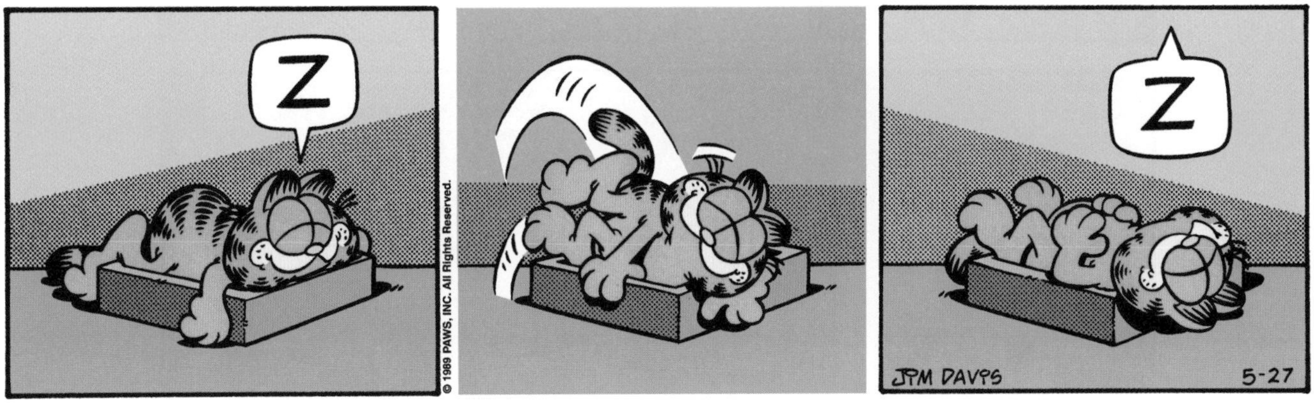
Z
© 1989 PAWS, INC. All Rights Reserved.
Z
JIM DAVIS
5-27

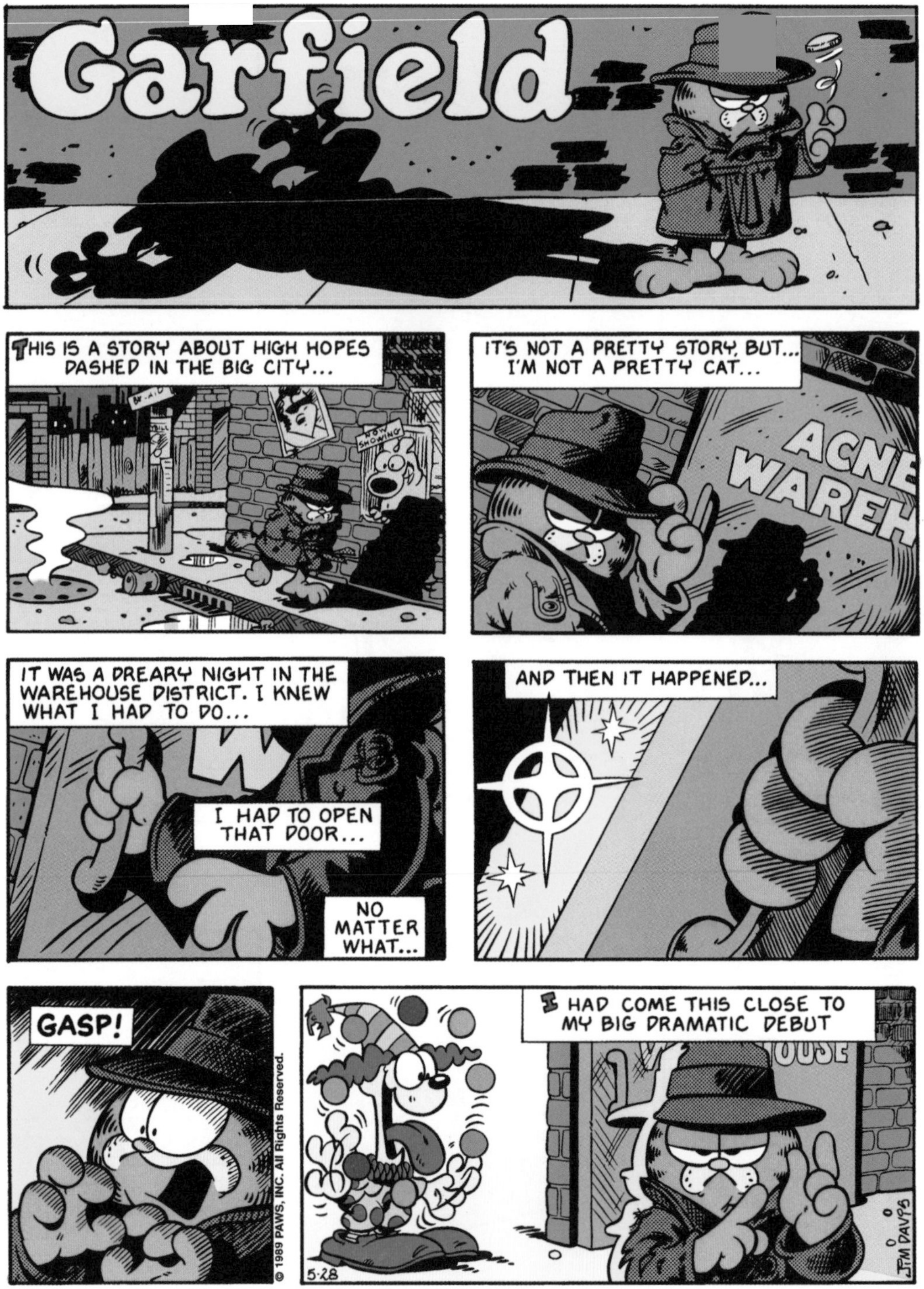
Garfield
THIS IS A STORY ABOUT HIGH HOPES DASHED IN THE BIG CITY...
NOW SHOWING
IT'S NOT A PRETTY STORY, BUT... I'M NOT A PRETTY CAT...
ACNE WAREH
IT WAS A DREARY NIGHT IN THE WAREHOUSE DISTRICT. I KNEW WHAT I HAD TO DO...
I HAD TO OPEN THAT DOOR...
NO MATTER WHAT...
AND THEN IT HAPPENED...
GASP!
© 1989 PAWS, INC. All Rights Reserved.
I HAD COME THIS CLOSE TO MY BIG DRAMATIC DEBUT
5-28
JIM DAVIS

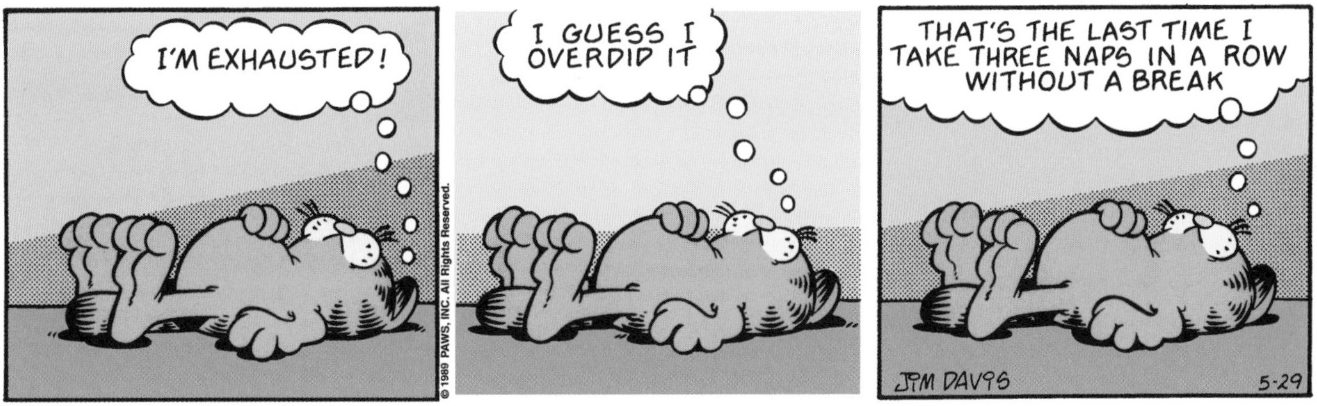
I'M EXHAUSTED!
I GUESS I OVERDID IT
THAT'S THE LAST TIME I TAKE THREE NAPS IN A ROW WITHOUT A BREAK
© 1989 PAWS, INC. All Rights Reserved.
JIM DAVIS 5-29

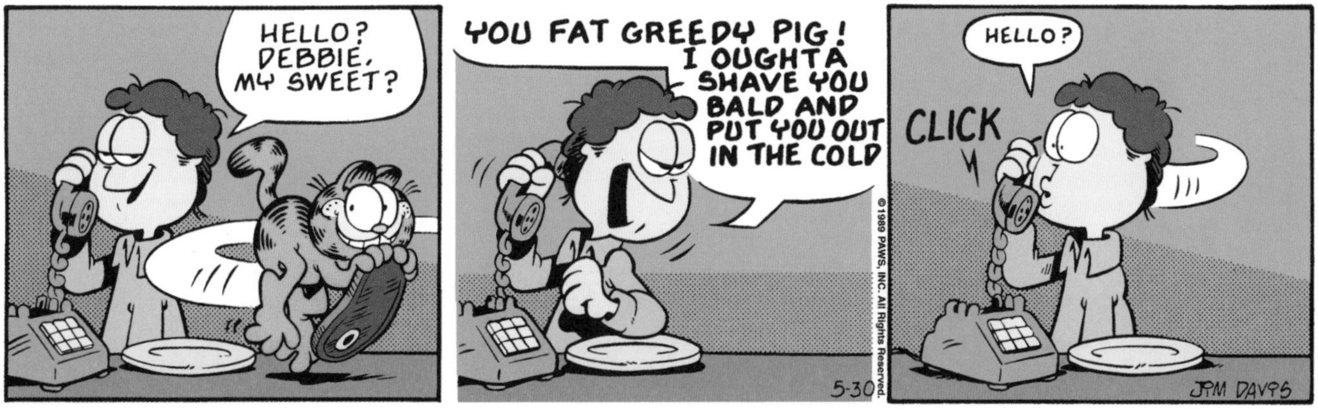
HELLO? DEBBIE, MY SWEET?
YOU FAT GREEDY PIG! I OUGHTA SHAVE YOU BALD AND PUT YOU OUT IN THE COLD
5-30
CLICK
HELLO?
© 1989 PAWS, INC. All Rights Reserved.
JIM DAVIS

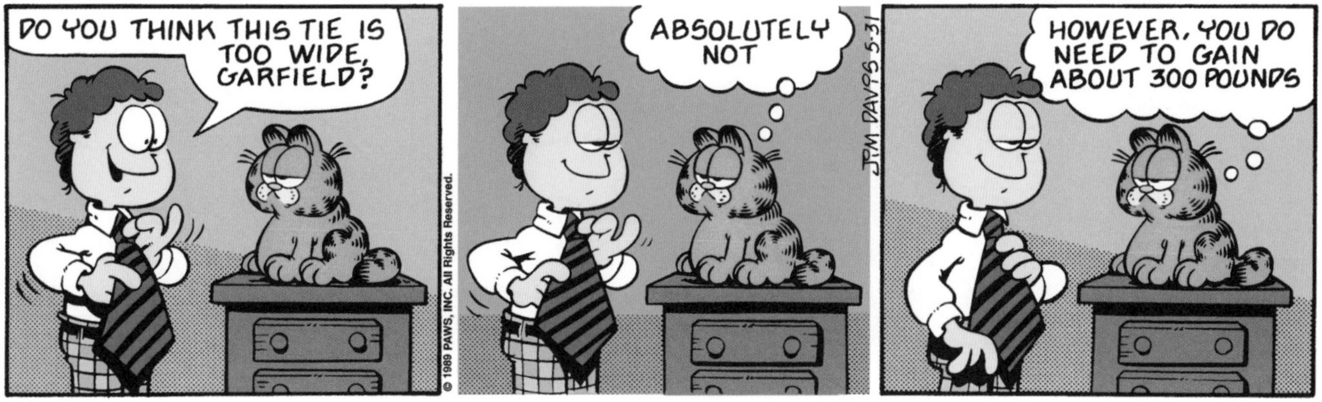
DO YOU THINK THIS TIE IS TOO WIDE, GARFIELD?
© 1989 PAWS, INC. All Rights Reserved.
ABSOLUTELY NOT
JIM DAVIS 5-31
HOWEVER, YOU DO NEED TO GAIN ABOUT 300 POUNDS

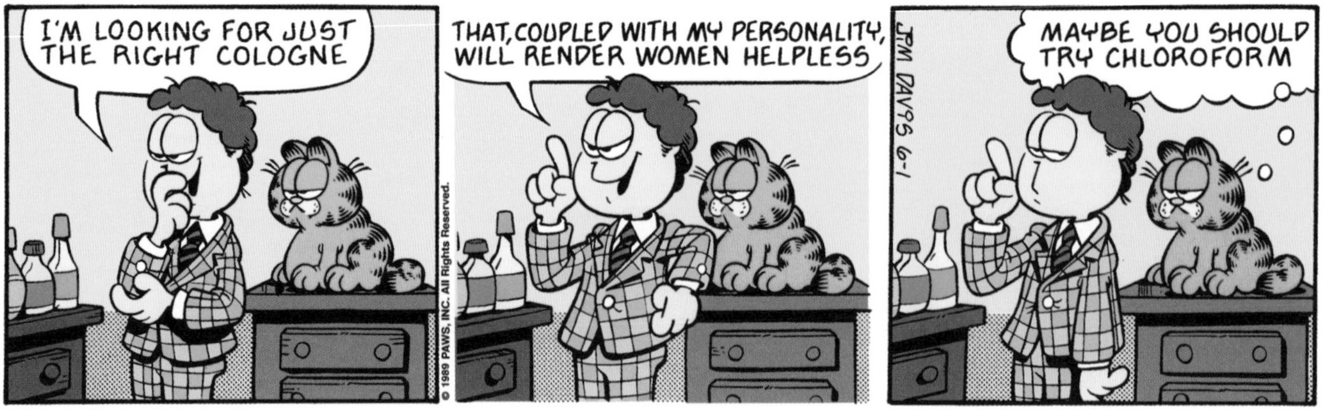
I'M LOOKING FOR JUST THE RIGHT COLOGNE
© 1989 PAWS, INC. All Rights Reserved.
THAT, COUPLED WITH MY PERSONALITY, WILL RENDER WOMEN HELPLESS
JIM DAVIS 6-1
MAYBE YOU SHOULD TRY CHLOROFORM

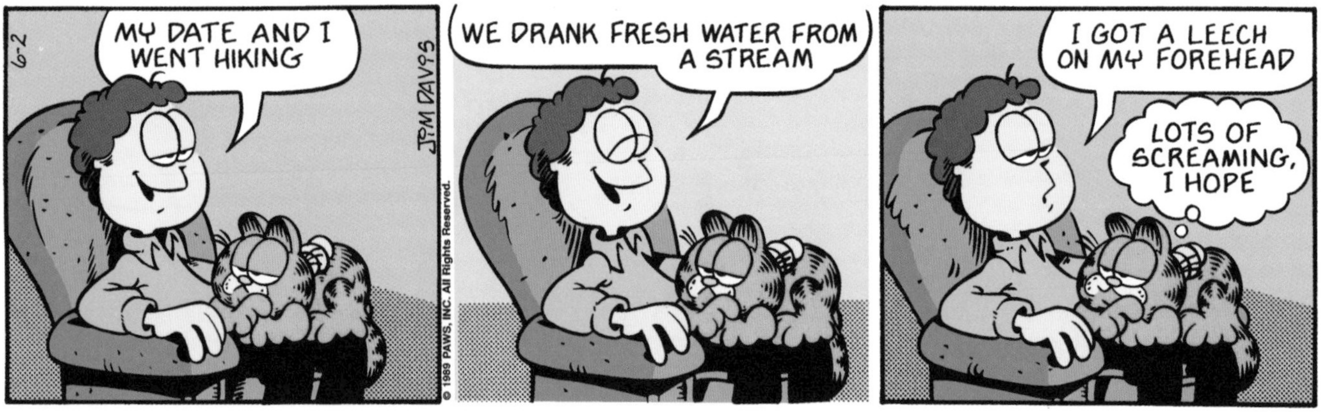
6-2
MY DATE AND I WENT HIKING
JIM DAVIS
© 1989 PAWS, INC. All Rights Reserved.
WE DRANK FRESH WATER FROM A STREAM
I GOT A LEECH ON MY FOREHEAD
LOTS OF SCREAMING, I HOPE

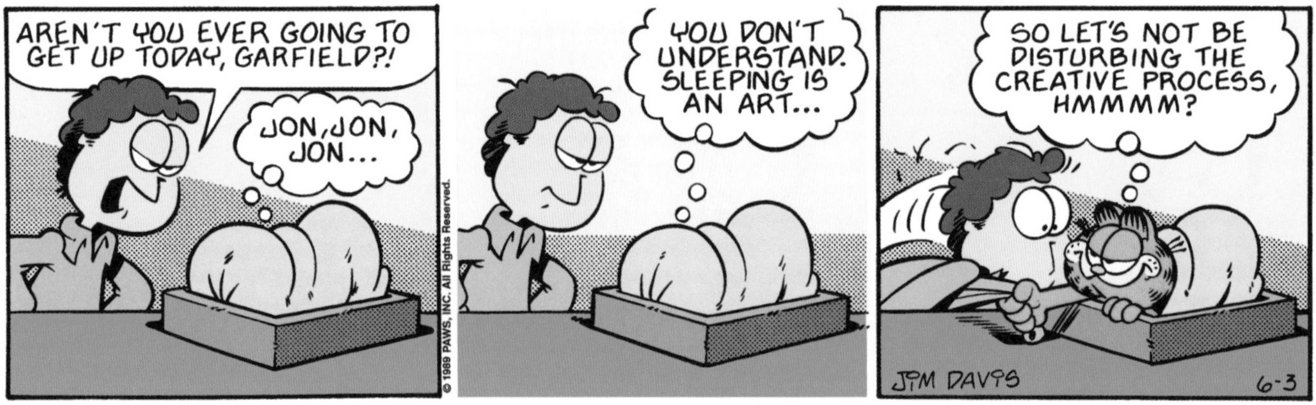
AREN'T YOU EVER GOING TO GET UP TODAY, GARFIELD?!
JON, JON, JON...
© 1989 PAWS, INC. All Rights Reserved.
YOU DON'T UNDERSTAND. SLEEPING IS AN ART...
SO LET'S NOT BE DISTURBING THE CREATIVE PROCESS, HMMMM?
JIM DAVIS
6-3

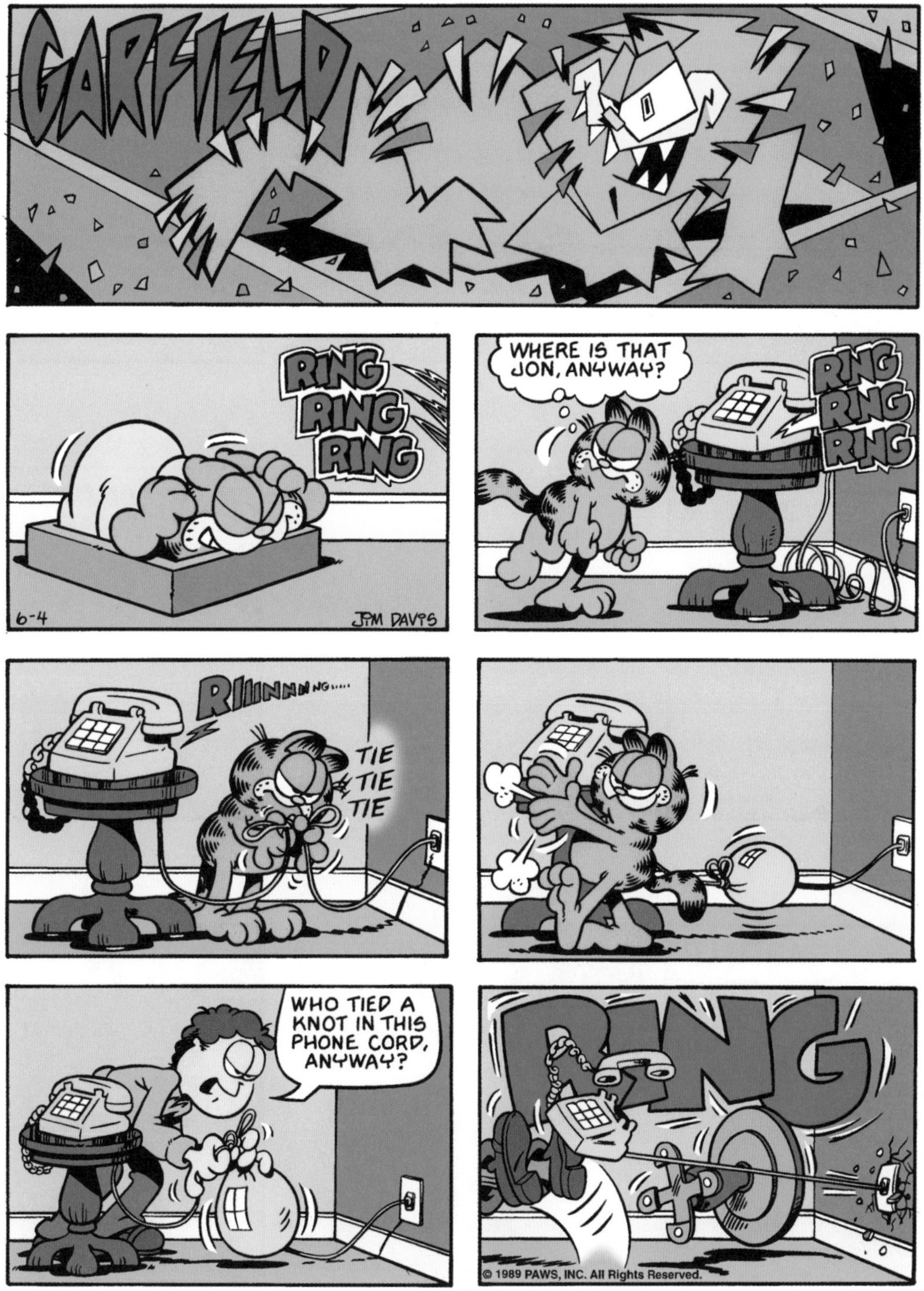
GARFIELD
RING RING RING
6-4
JIM DAVIS
WHERE IS THAT JON, ANYWAY?
RING RING RING
RIIINNNNNG.....
TIE TIE TIE
WHO TIED A KNOT IN THIS PHONE CORD, ANYWAY?
RING

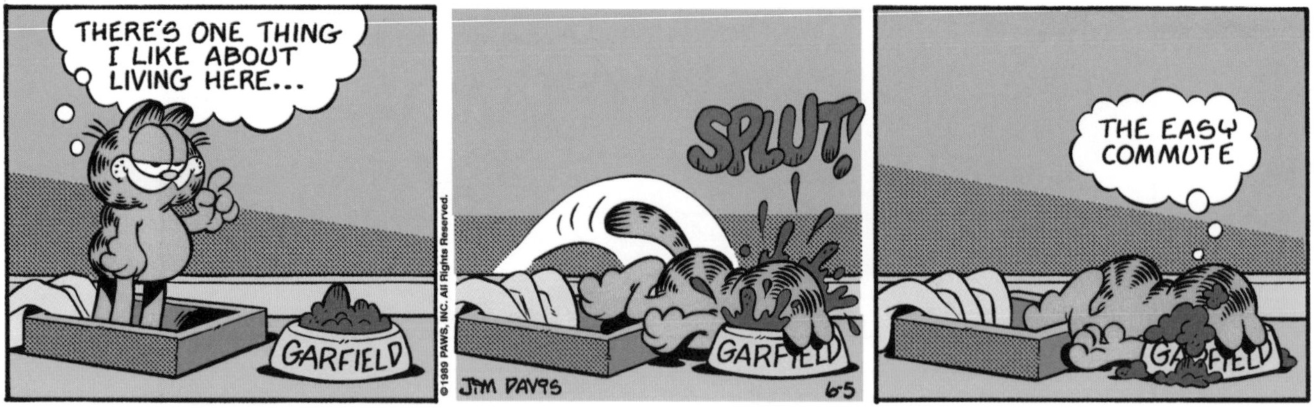
THERE'S ONE THING I LIKE ABOUT LIVING HERE...
GARFIELD
© 1989 PAWS, INC. All Rights Reserved.
SPLUT!
GARFIELD
JIM DAVIS
6-5
THE EASY COMMUTE

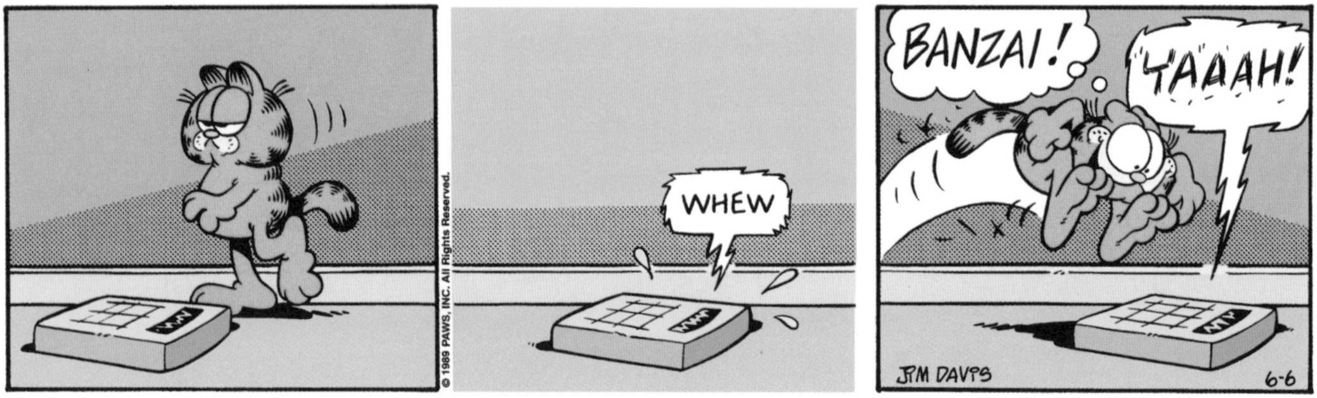
© 1989 PAWS, INC. All Rights Reserved.
WHEW
BANZAI!
YAAAH!
JIM DAVIS
6-6

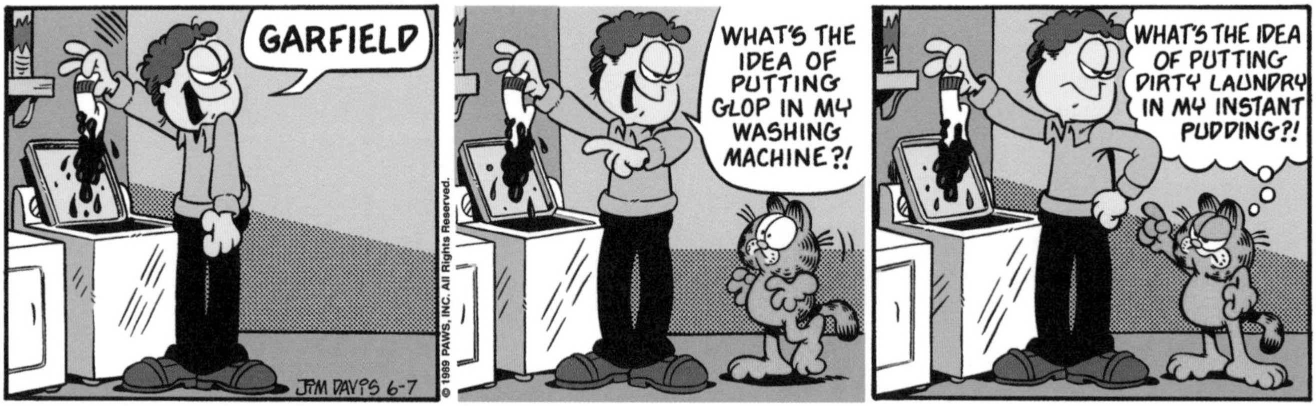
GARFIELD
JIM DAVIS 6-7
© 1989 PAWS, INC. All Rights Reserved.
WHAT'S THE IDEA OF PUTTING GLOP IN MY WASHING MACHINE?!
WHAT'S THE IDEA OF PUTTING DIRTY LAUNDRY IN MY INSTANT PUDDING?!

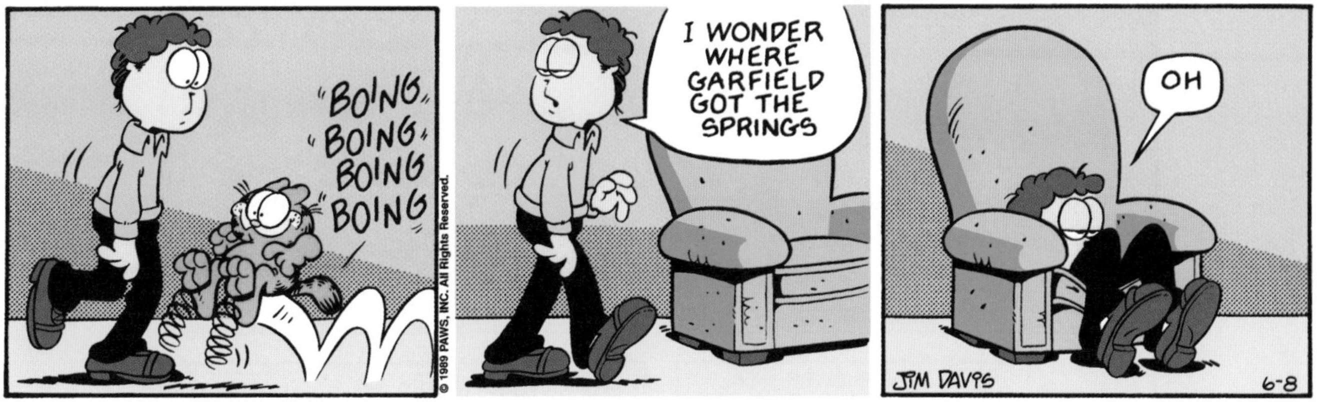
"BOING" "BOING" BOING "BOING
© 1989 PAWS, INC. All Rights Reserved.
I WONDER WHERE GARFIELD GOT THE SPRINGS
OH
JIM DAVIS 6-8

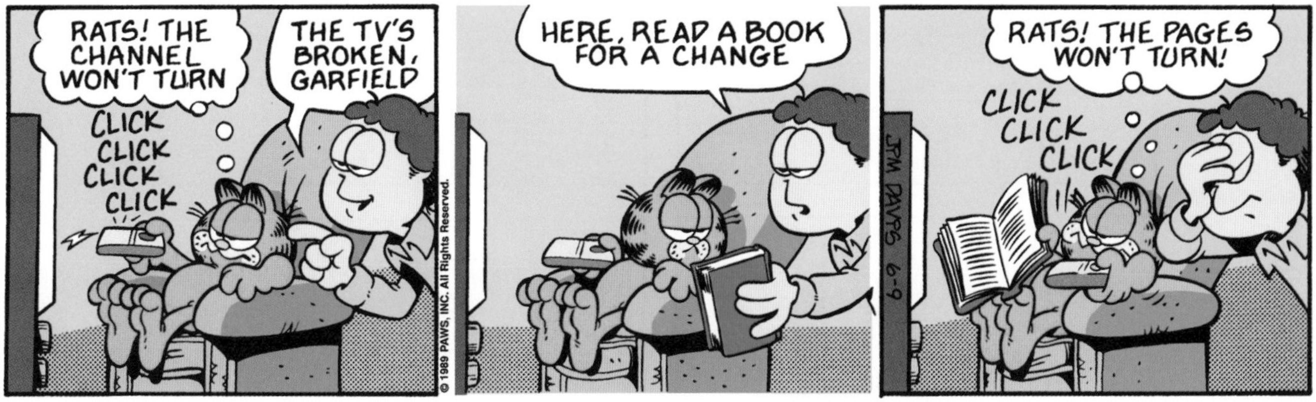
THE TV'S BROKEN, GARFIELD
RATS! THE CHANNEL WON'T TURN
CLICK CLICK CLICK CLICK
© 1989 PAWS, INC. All Rights Reserved.
HERE, READ A BOOK FOR A CHANGE
JIM DAVIS 6-9
RATS! THE PAGES WON'T TURN!
CLICK CLICK CLICK

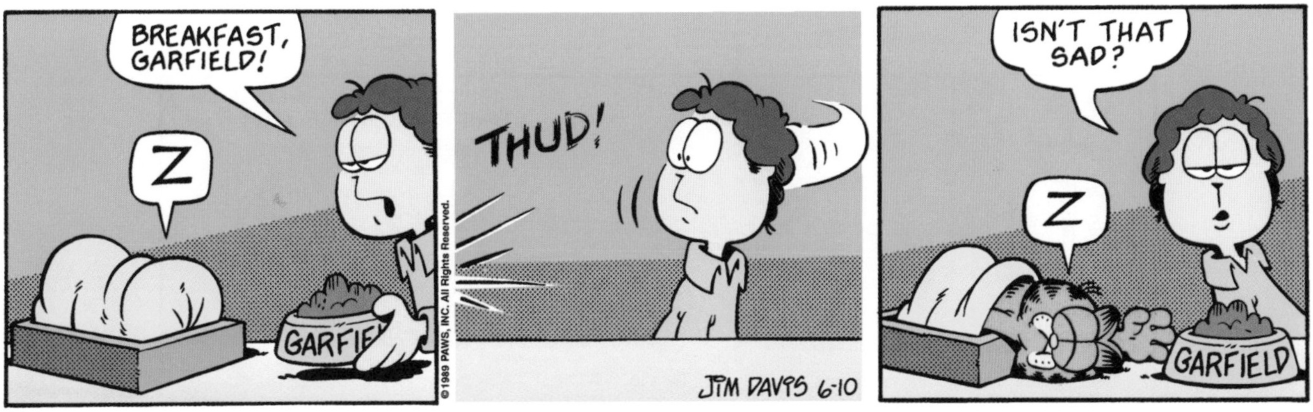
BREAKFAST, GARFIELD!
Z
GARFIE
© 1989 PAWS, INC. All Rights Reserved.
THUD!
JIM DAVIS 6-10
ISN'T THAT SAD?
Z
GARFIELD

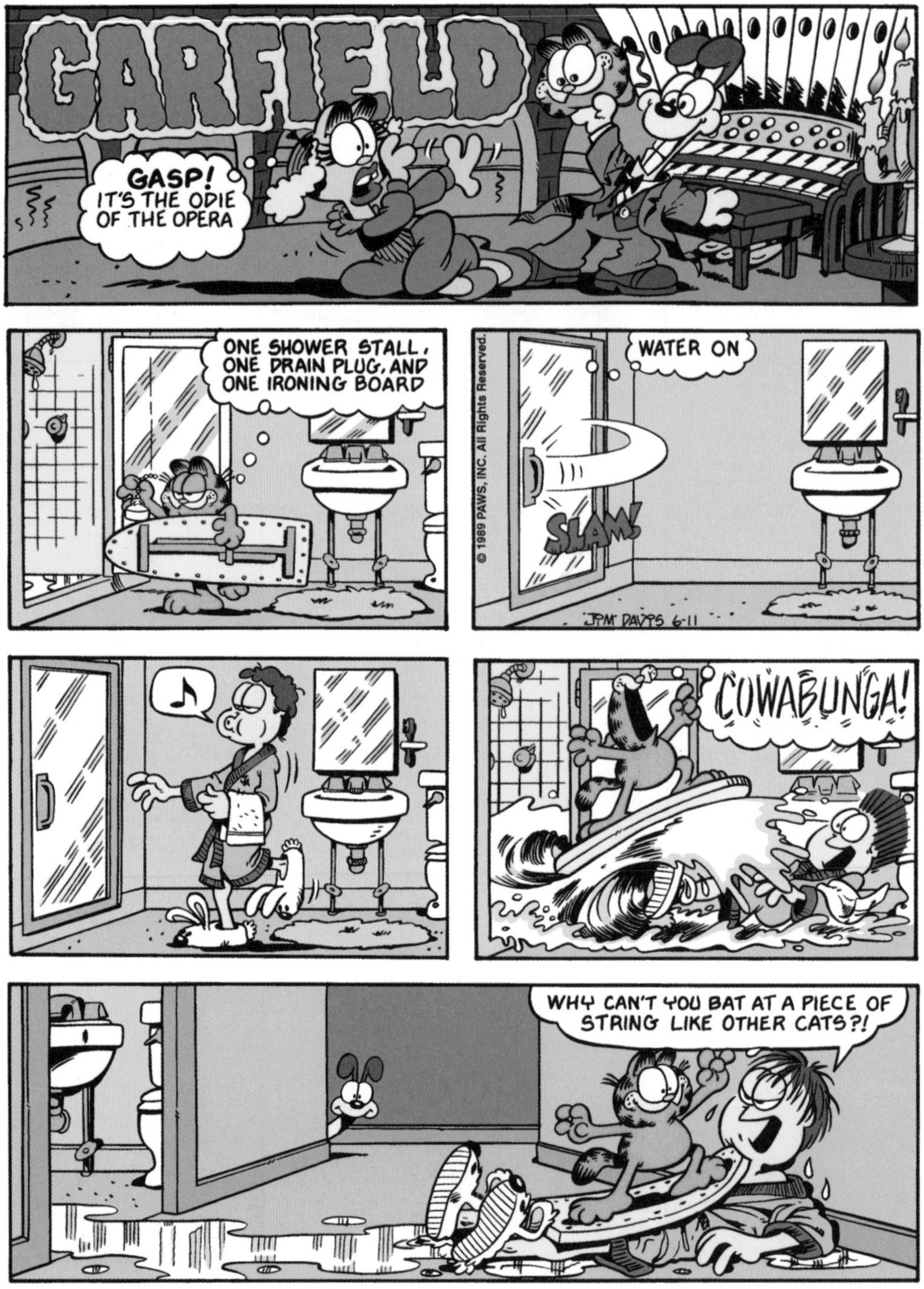
GARFIELD
GASP! IT'S THE ODIE OF THE OPERA
ONE SHOWER STALL, ONE DRAIN PLUG, AND ONE IRONING BOARD
© 1989 PAWS, INC. All Rights Reserved.
WATER ON
SLAM!
JPM DAVIS 6-11
♪
COWABUNGA!
WHY CAN'T YOU BAT AT A PIECE OF STRING LIKE OTHER CATS?!

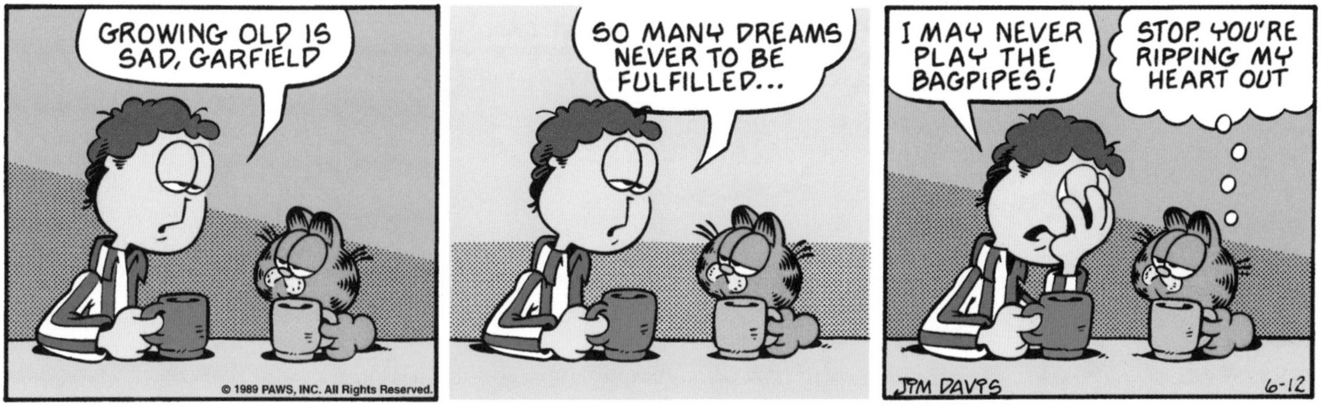
GROWING OLD IS SAD, GARFIELD
© 1989 PAWS, INC. All Rights Reserved.
SO MANY DREAMS NEVER TO BE FULFILLED...
I MAY NEVER PLAY THE BAGPIPES!
STOP. YOU'RE RIPPING MY HEART OUT
JIM DAVIS
6-12

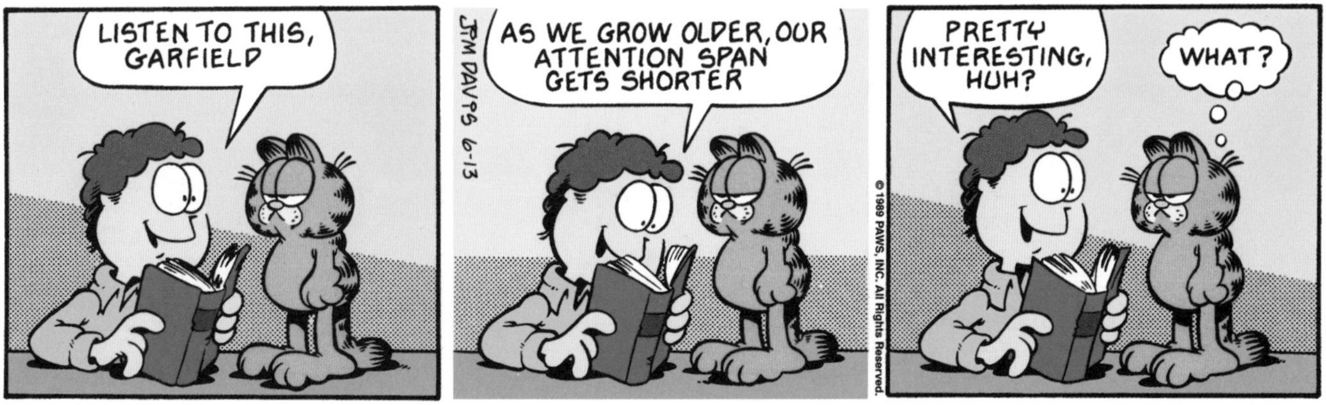
LISTEN TO THIS, GARFIELD
JIM DAVIS 6-13
AS WE GROW OLDER, OUR ATTENTION SPAN GETS SHORTER
© 1989 PAWS, INC. All Rights Reserved.
PRETTY INTERESTING, HUH?
WHAT?

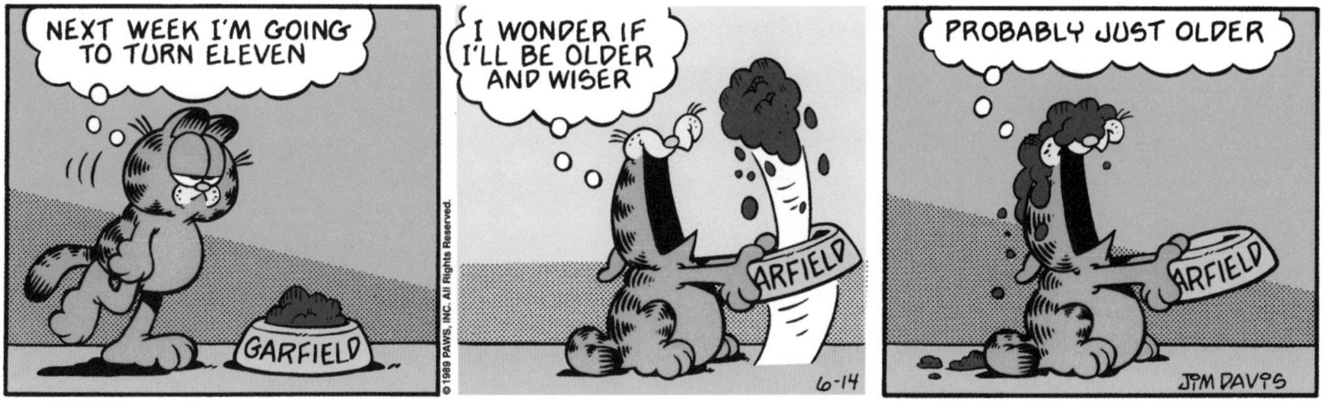
NEXT WEEK I'M GOING TO TURN ELEVEN
GARFIELD
© 1989 PAWS, INC. All Rights Reserved.
I WONDER IF I'LL BE OLDER AND WISER
ARFIELD
6-14
PROBABLY JUST OLDER
ARFIELD
JIM DAVIS

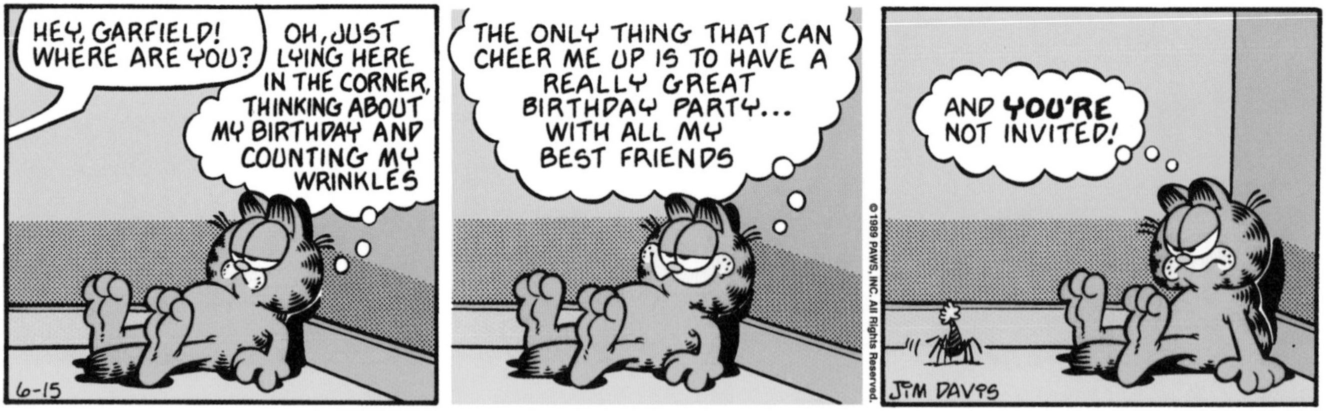
HEY, GARFIELD! WHERE ARE YOU?
OH, JUST LYING HERE IN THE CORNER, THINKING ABOUT MY BIRTHDAY AND COUNTING MY WRINKLES
6-15
THE ONLY THING THAT CAN CHEER ME UP IS TO HAVE A REALLY GREAT BIRTHDAY PARTY... WITH ALL MY BEST FRIENDS
© 1989 PAWS, INC. All Rights Reserved.
AND **YOU'RE** NOT INVITED!
JIM DAVIS

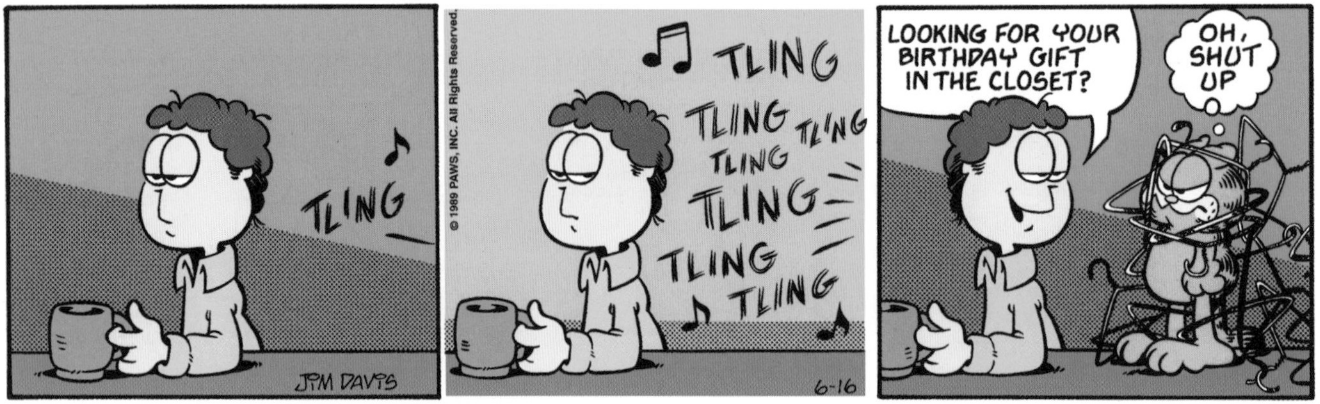
TLING
JIM DAVIS
© 1989 PAWS, INC. All Rights Reserved.
TLING
TLING TLING
TLING
TLING
TLING
TLING
6-16
LOOKING FOR YOUR BIRTHDAY GIFT IN THE CLOSET?
OH, SHUT UP

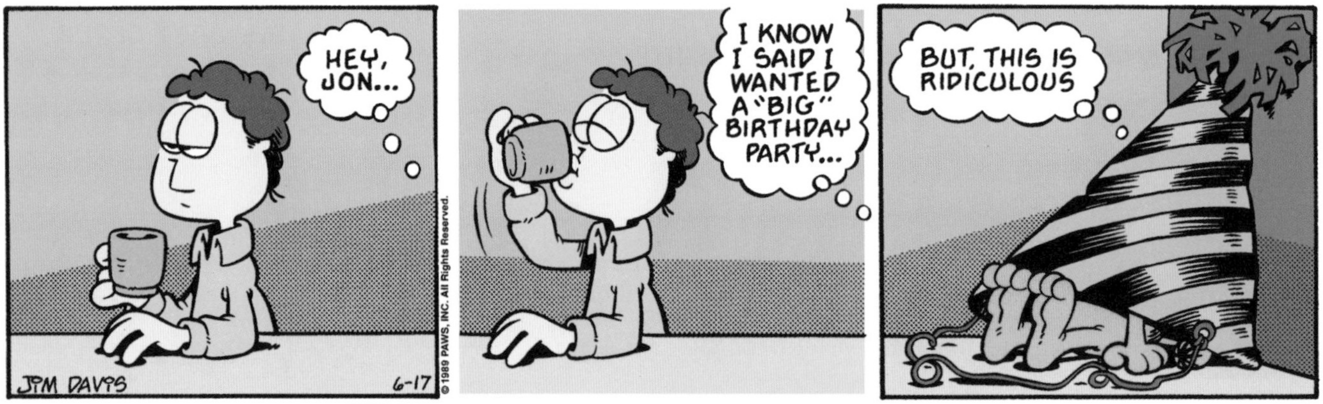
HEY, JON...
JIM DAVIS
6-17
© 1989 PAWS, INC. All Rights Reserved.
I KNOW I SAID I WANTED A "BIG" BIRTHDAY PARTY...
BUT, THIS IS RIDICULOUS

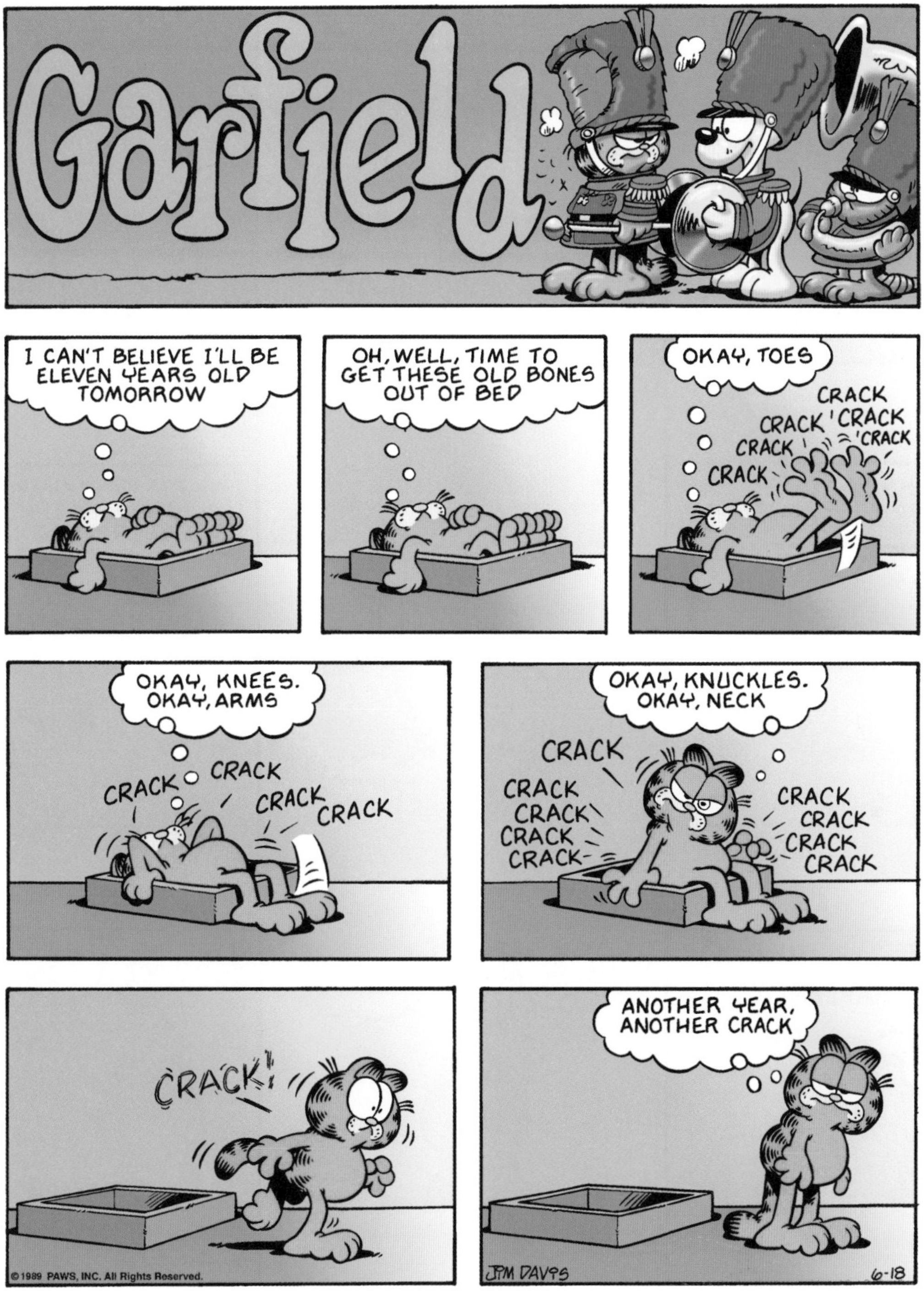

Garfield
I CAN'T BELIEVE I'LL BE ELEVEN YEARS OLD TOMORROW
OH, WELL, TIME TO GET THESE OLD BONES OUT OF BED
OKAY, TOES
CRACK CRACK CRACK CRACK CRACK CRACK
OKAY, KNEES. OKAY, ARMS
CRACK CRACK CRACK CRACK
OKAY, KNUCKLES. OKAY, NECK
CRACK CRACK CRACK CRACK CRACK CRACK CRACK CRACK CRACK
CRACK!
ANOTHER YEAR, ANOTHER CRACK
© 1989 PAWS, INC. All Rights Reserved.
JPM DAVPS
6-18

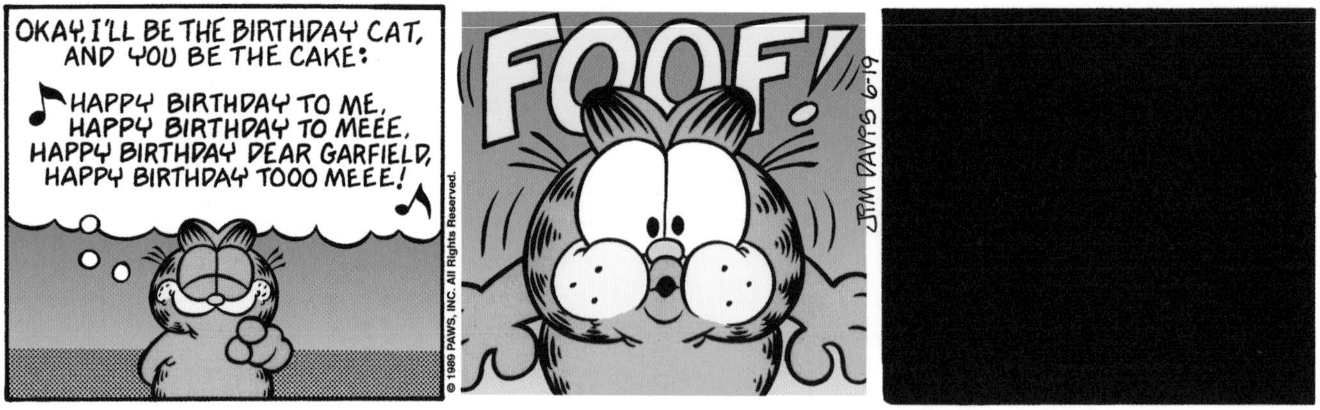
OKAY, I'LL BE THE BIRTHDAY CAT, AND YOU BE THE CAKE:
HAPPY BIRTHDAY TO ME, HAPPY BIRTHDAY TO MEEE, HAPPY BIRTHDAY DEAR GARFIELD, HAPPY BIRTHDAY TOOO MEEE!
© 1989 PAWS, INC. All Rights Reserved.
FOOF!
JIM DAVIS 6-19

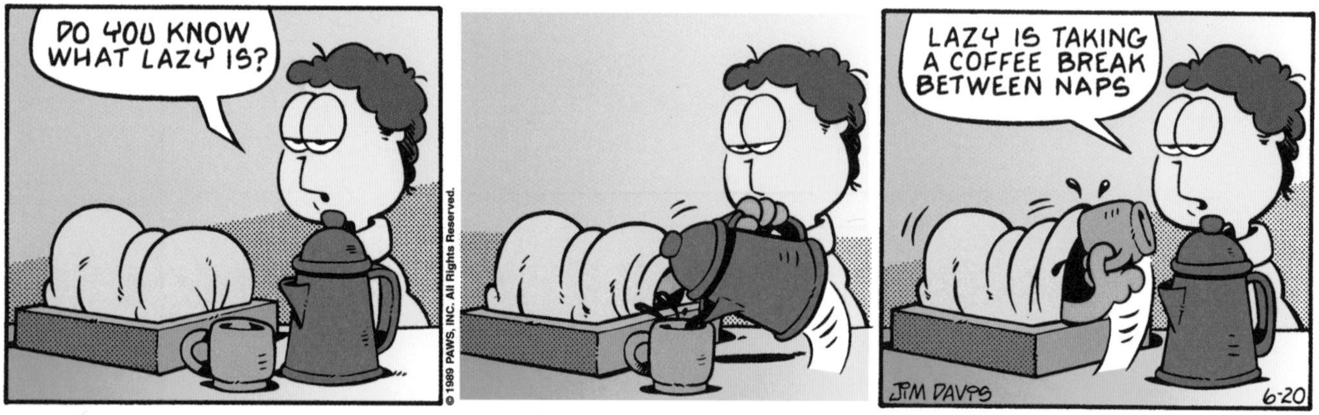
DO YOU KNOW WHAT LAZY IS?
© 1989 PAWS, INC. All Rights Reserved.
LAZY IS TAKING A COFFEE BREAK BETWEEN NAPS
JIM DAVIS
6-20

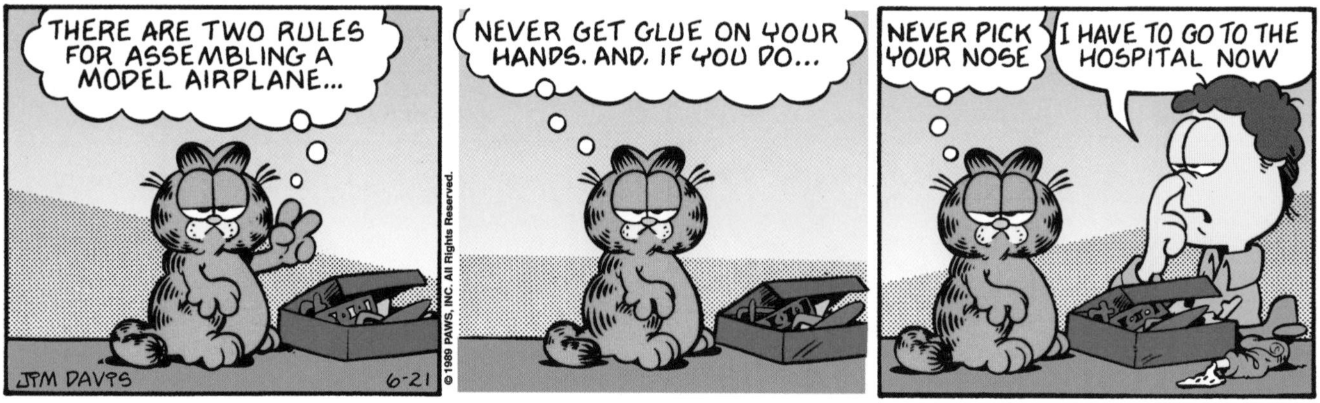
THERE ARE TWO RULES FOR ASSEMBLING A MODEL AIRPLANE...
JIM DAVIS
6-21
© 1989 PAWS, INC. All Rights Reserved.
NEVER GET GLUE ON YOUR HANDS. AND, IF YOU DO...
NEVER PICK YOUR NOSE
I HAVE TO GO TO THE HOSPITAL NOW

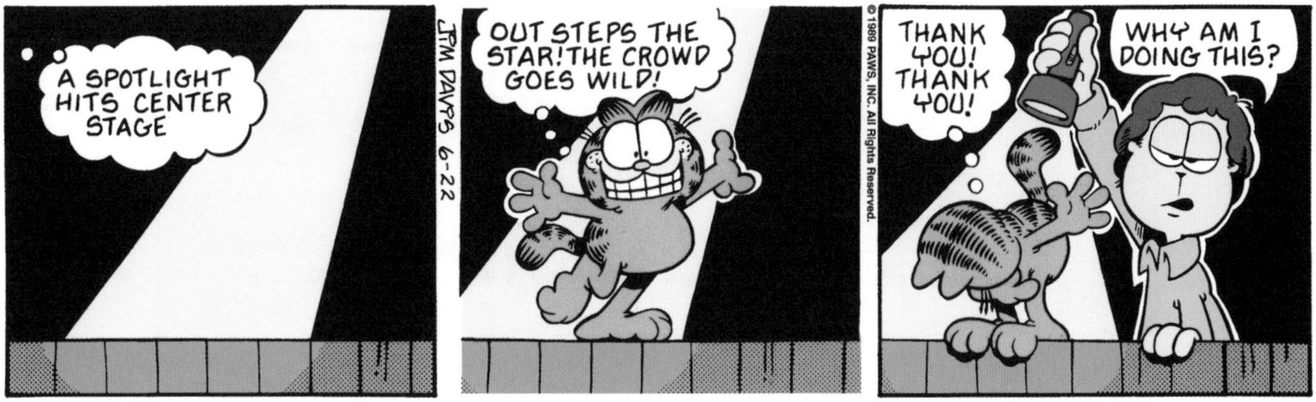
A SPOTLIGHT HITS CENTER STAGE
JIM DAVIS 6-22
OUT STEPS THE STAR! THE CROWD GOES WILD!
© 1989 PAWS, INC. All Rights Reserved.
THANK YOU! THANK YOU!
WHY AM I DOING THIS?

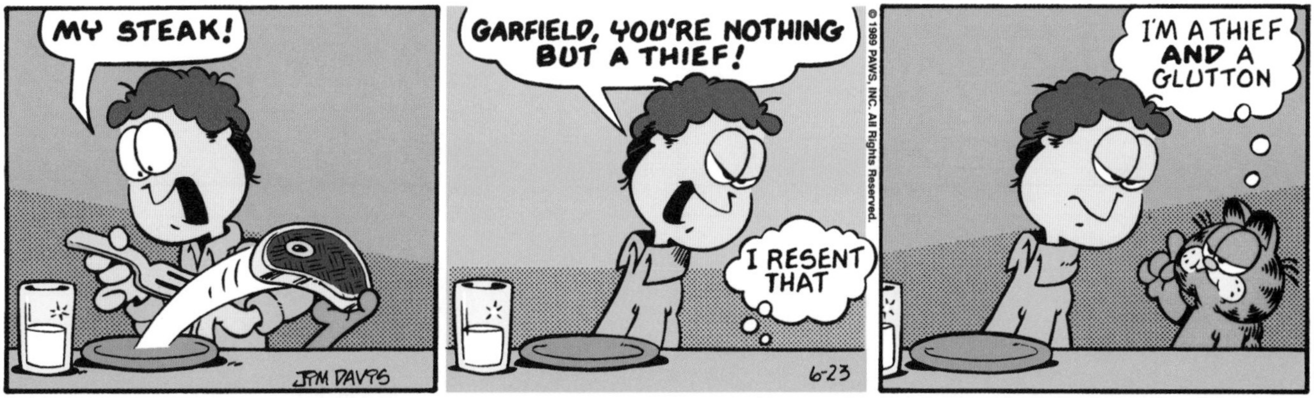
MY STEAK!
JIM DAVIS
GARFIELD, YOU'RE NOTHING BUT A THIEF!
I RESENT THAT
6-23
© 1989 PAWS, INC. All Rights Reserved.
I'M A THIEF **AND** A GLUTTON

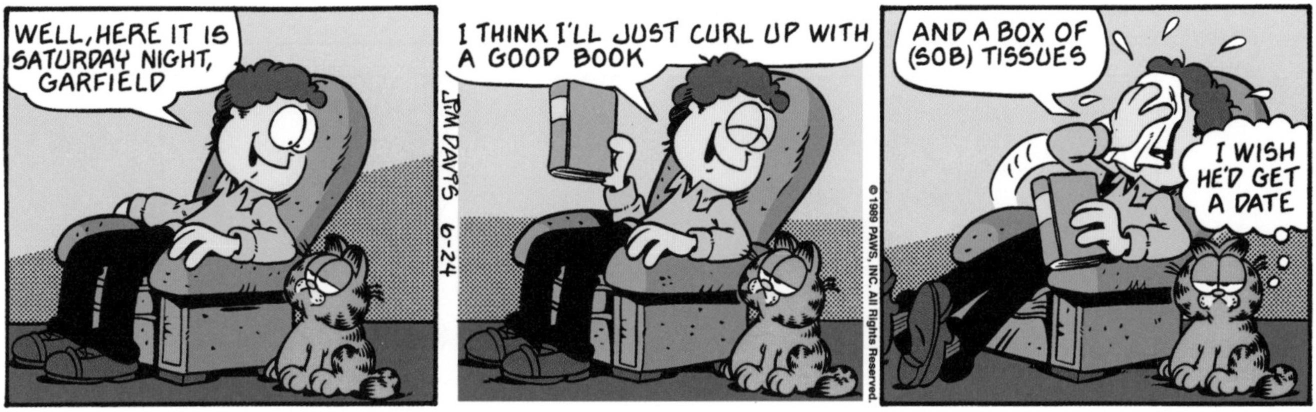
WELL, HERE IT IS SATURDAY NIGHT, GARFIELD
JIM DAVIS 6-24
I THINK I'LL JUST CURL UP WITH A GOOD BOOK
© 1989 PAWS, INC. All Rights Reserved.
AND A BOX OF (SOB) TISSUES
I WISH HE'D GET A DATE

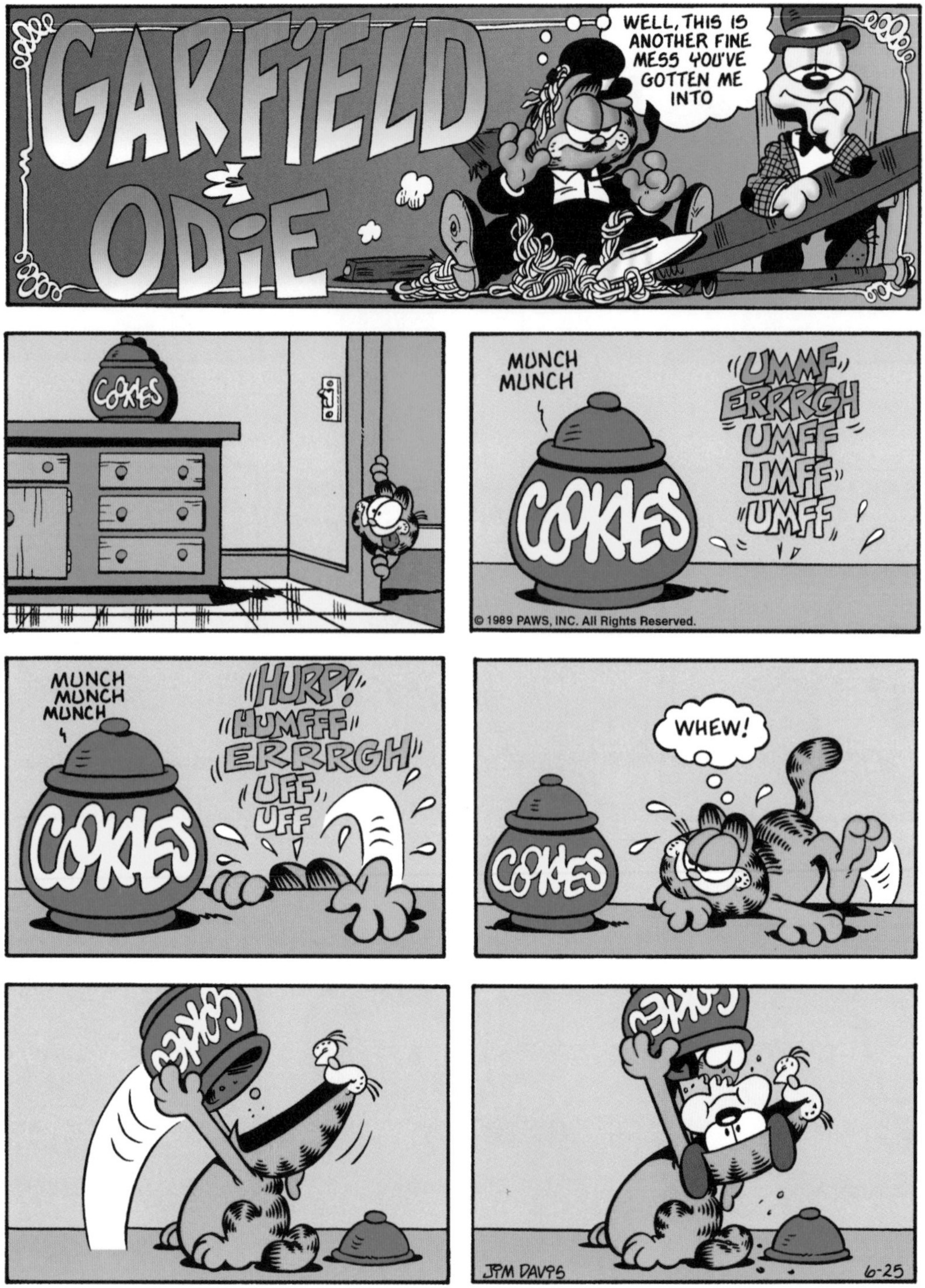
GARFIELD & ODIE
WELL, THIS IS ANOTHER FINE MESS YOU'VE GOTTEN ME INTO
COOKIES
MUNCH MUNCH
UMMF ERRRGH UMFF UMFF UMFF
© 1989 PAWS, INC. All Rights Reserved.
MUNCH MUNCH MUNCH
HURP! HUMFFF ERRRGH UFF UFF
WHEW!
JIM DAVIS
6-25

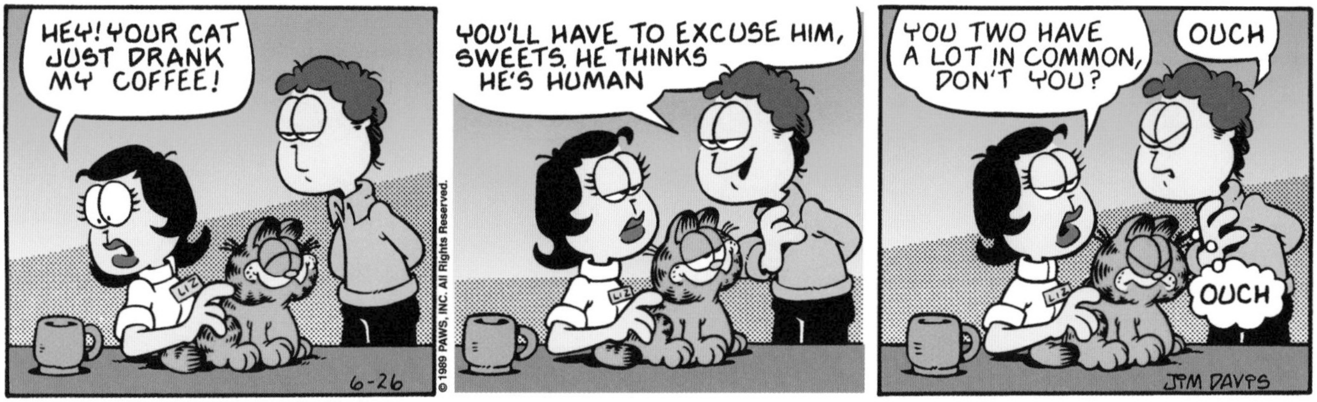
HEY! YOUR CAT JUST DRANK MY COFFEE!
6-26
© 1989 PAWS, INC. All Rights Reserved.
YOU'LL HAVE TO EXCUSE HIM, SWEETS. HE THINKS HE'S HUMAN
YOU TWO HAVE A LOT IN COMMON, DON'T YOU?
OUCH
OUCH
JIM DAVIS

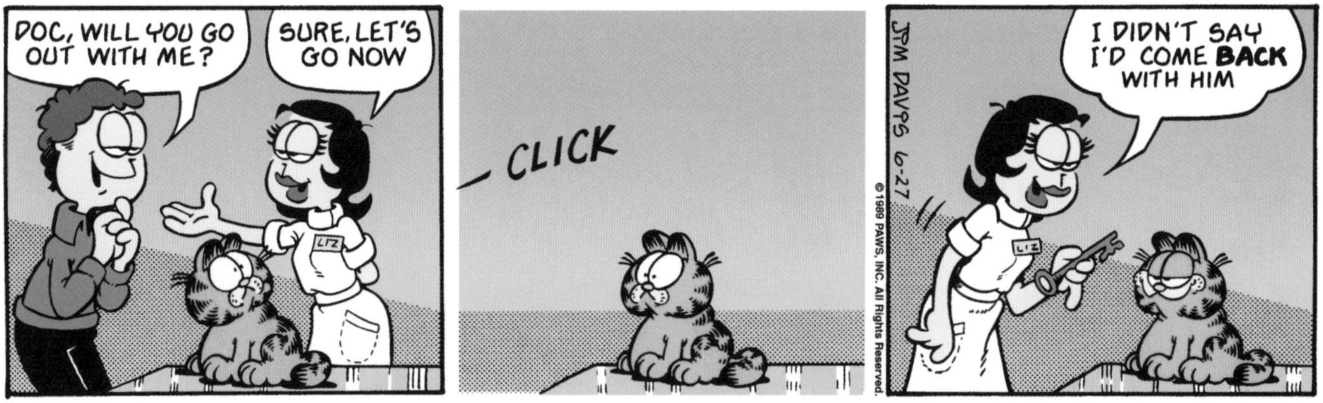
DOC, WILL YOU GO OUT WITH ME?
SURE, LET'S GO NOW
CLICK
JIM DAVIS 6-27
© 1989 PAWS, INC. All Rights Reserved.
I DIDN'T SAY I'D COME **BACK** WITH HIM
LIZ

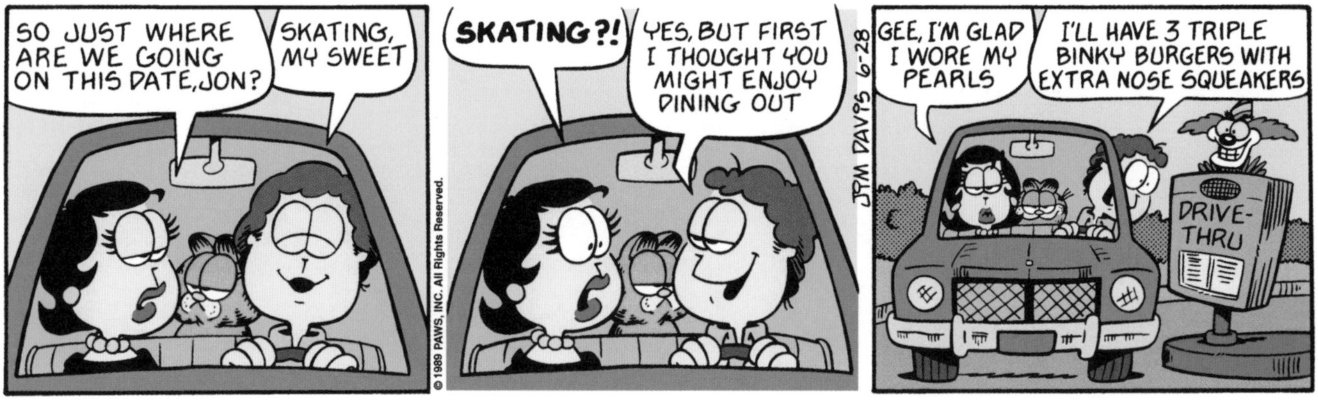
SO JUST WHERE ARE WE GOING ON THIS DATE, JON?
SKATING, MY SWEET
© 1989 PAWS, INC. All Rights Reserved.
SKATING?!
YES, BUT FIRST I THOUGHT YOU MIGHT ENJOY DINING OUT
JIM DAVIS 6-28
GEE, I'M GLAD I WORE MY PEARLS
I'LL HAVE 3 TRIPLE BINKY BURGERS WITH EXTRA NOSE SQUEAKERS
DRIVE-THRU

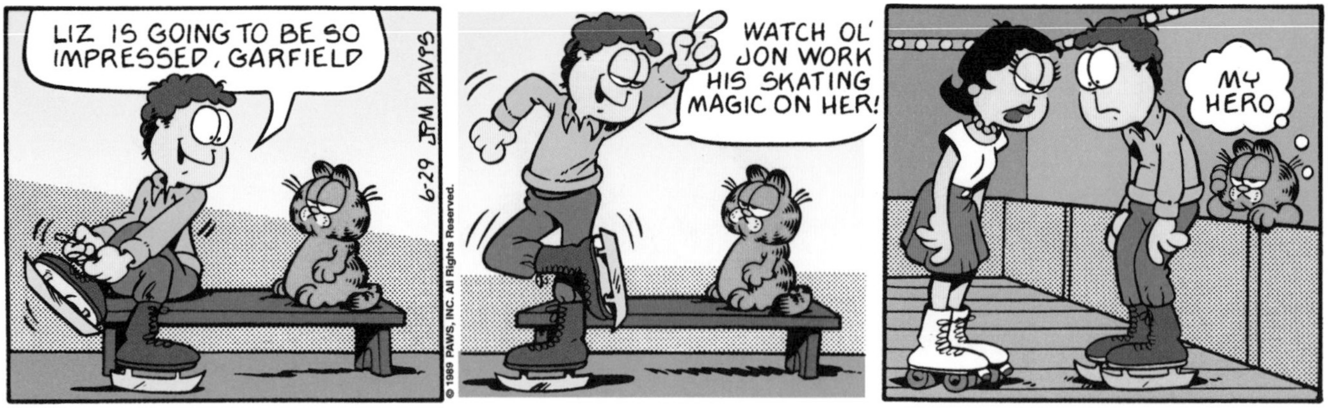
LIZ IS GOING TO BE SO IMPRESSED, GARFIELD
WATCH OL' JON WORK HIS SKATING MAGIC ON HER!
MY HERO
© 1989 PAWS, INC. All Rights Reserved.

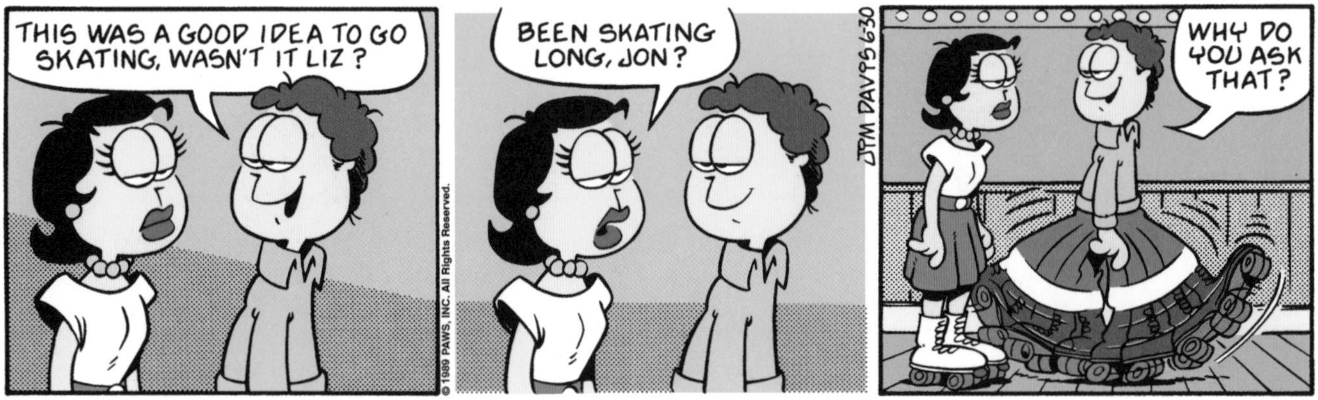
THIS WAS A GOOD IDEA TO GO SKATING, WASN'T IT LIZ?
BEEN SKATING LONG, JON?
WHY DO YOU ASK THAT?
© 1989 PAWS, INC. All Rights Reserved.

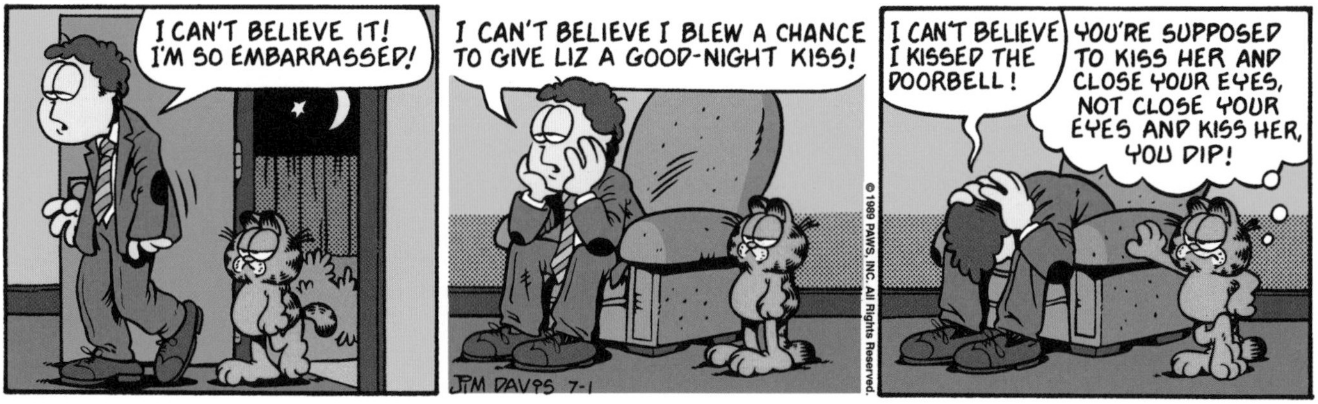
I CAN'T BELIEVE IT! I'M SO EMBARRASSED!
I CAN'T BELIEVE I BLEW A CHANCE TO GIVE LIZ A GOOD-NIGHT KISS!
I CAN'T BELIEVE I KISSED THE DOORBELL!
YOU'RE SUPPOSED TO KISS HER AND CLOSE YOUR EYES, NOT CLOSE YOUR EYES AND KISS HER, YOU DIP!
© 1989 PAWS, INC. All Rights Reserved.

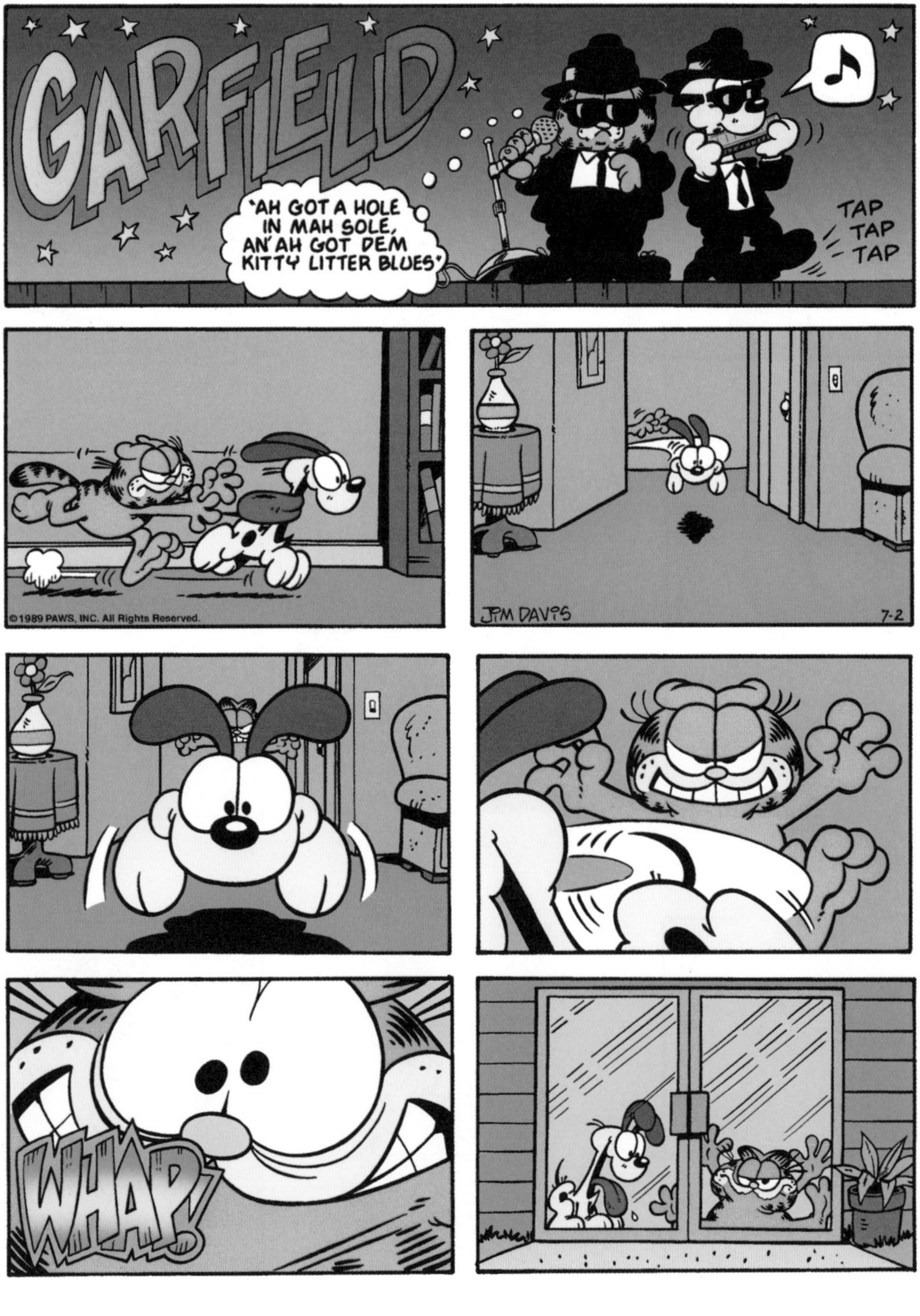
GARFIELD
"AH GOT A HOLE IN MAH SOLE, AN' AH GOT DEM KITTY LITTER BLUES"
TAP
TAP
TAP
©1989 PAWS, INC. All Rights Reserved.
JIM DAVIS
7-2
WHAP

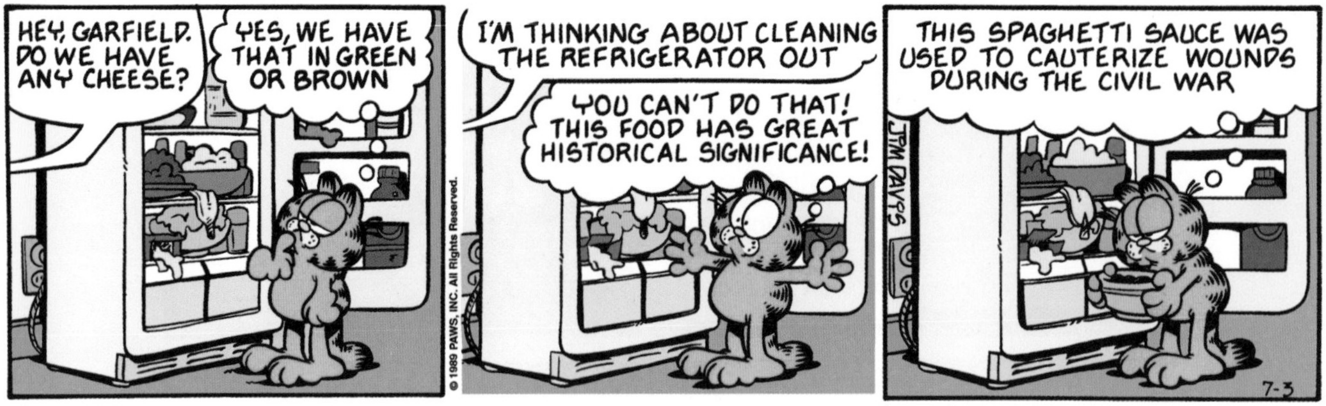
HEY, GARFIELD. DO WE HAVE ANY CHEESE?
YES, WE HAVE THAT IN GREEN OR BROWN
© 1989 PAWS, INC. All Rights Reserved.
I'M THINKING ABOUT CLEANING THE REFRIGERATOR OUT
YOU CAN'T DO THAT! THIS FOOD HAS GREAT HISTORICAL SIGNIFICANCE!
THIS SPAGHETTI SAUCE WAS USED TO CAUTERIZE WOUNDS DURING THE CIVIL WAR
JIM DAVIS
7-3

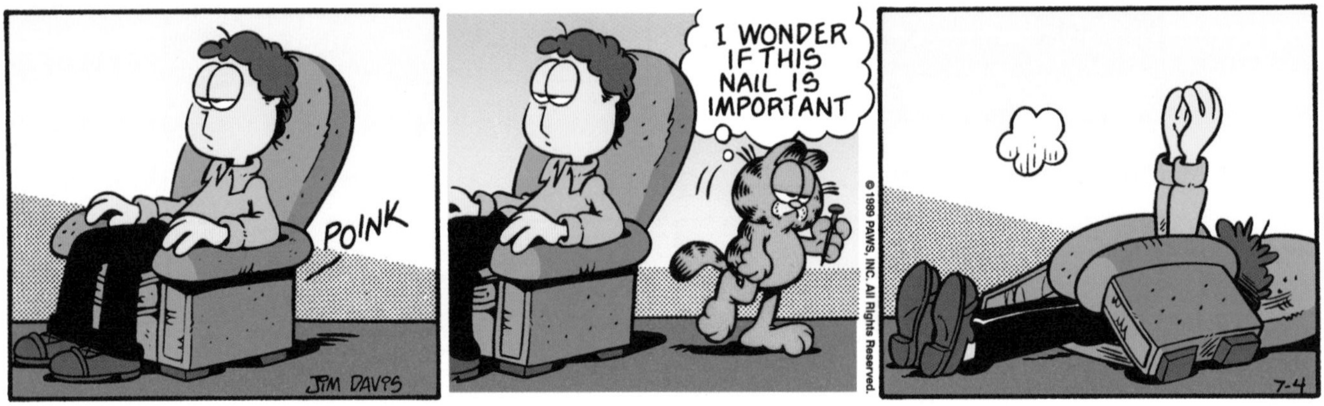
POINK
JIM DAVIS
I WONDER IF THIS NAIL IS IMPORTANT
© 1989 PAWS, INC. All Rights Reserved.
7-4

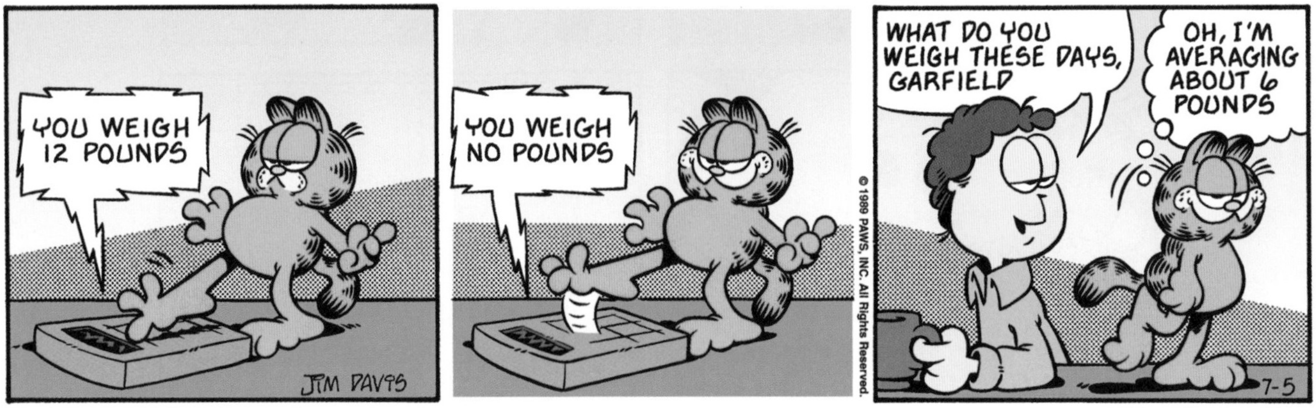
YOU WEIGH 12 POUNDS
JIM DAVIS
YOU WEIGH NO POUNDS
© 1989 PAWS, INC. All Rights Reserved.
WHAT DO YOU WEIGH THESE DAYS, GARFIELD
OH, I'M AVERAGING ABOUT 6 POUNDS
7-5

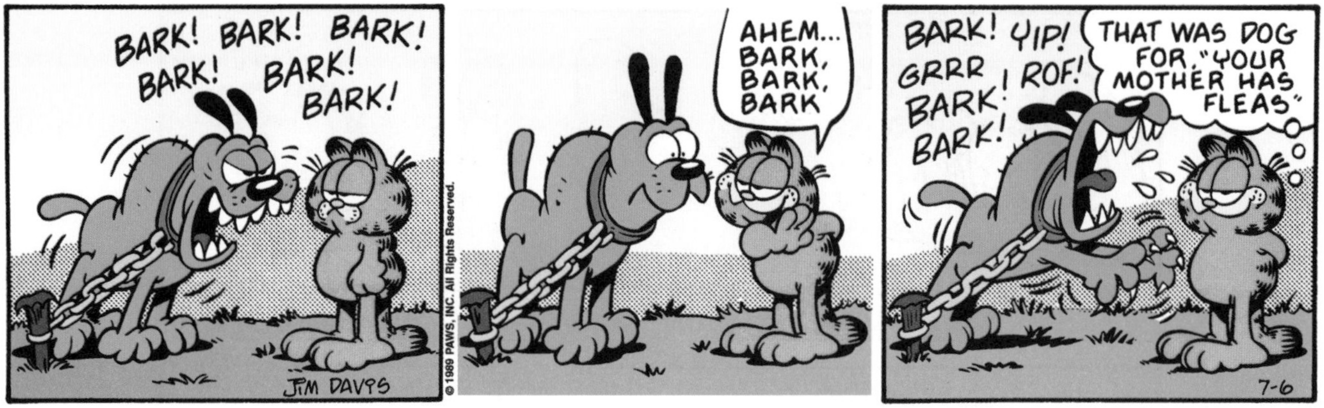
BARK! BARK! BARK!
BARK! BARK!
BARK!
JIM DAVIS
© 1989 PAWS, INC. All Rights Reserved.
AHEM... BARK, BARK, BARK
BARK! YIP!
GRRR ROF!
BARK!
BARK!
BARK!
THAT WAS DOG FOR, "YOUR MOTHER HAS FLEAS"
7-6

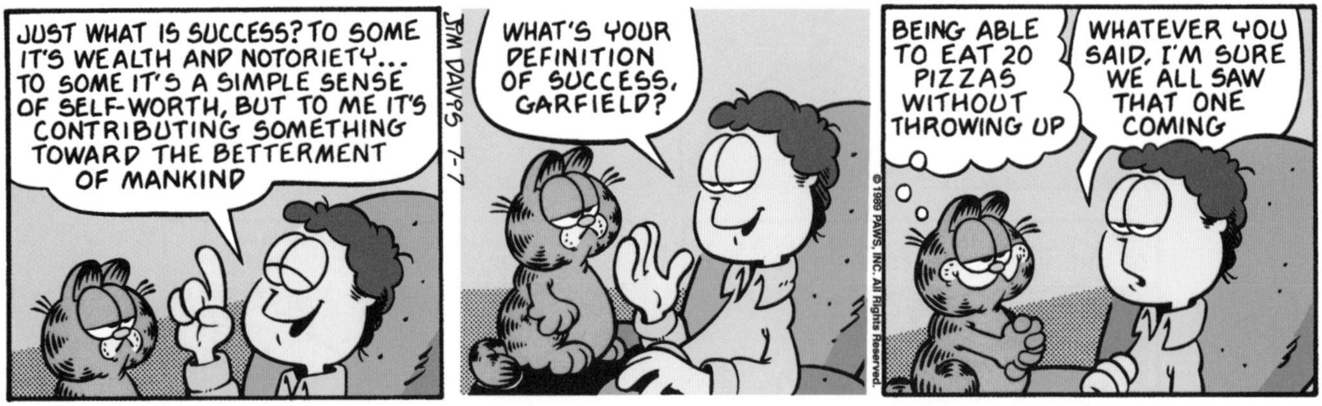
JUST WHAT IS SUCCESS? TO SOME IT'S WEALTH AND NOTORIETY... TO SOME IT'S A SIMPLE SENSE OF SELF-WORTH, BUT TO ME IT'S CONTRIBUTING SOMETHING TOWARD THE BETTERMENT OF MANKIND
JIM DAVIS 7-7
WHAT'S YOUR DEFINITION OF SUCCESS, GARFIELD?
© 1989 PAWS, INC. All Rights Reserved.
BEING ABLE TO EAT 20 PIZZAS WITHOUT THROWING UP
WHATEVER YOU SAID, I'M SURE WE ALL SAW THAT ONE COMING

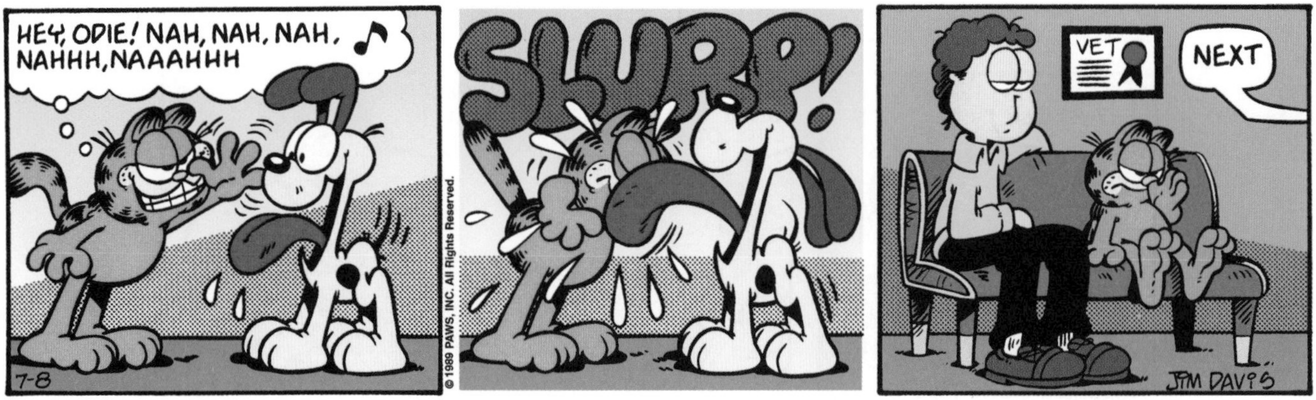
HEY, ODIE! NAH, NAH, NAH, NAHHH, NAAAHHH
7-8
© 1989 PAWS, INC. All Rights Reserved.
SLURP!
VET
NEXT
JIM DAVIS

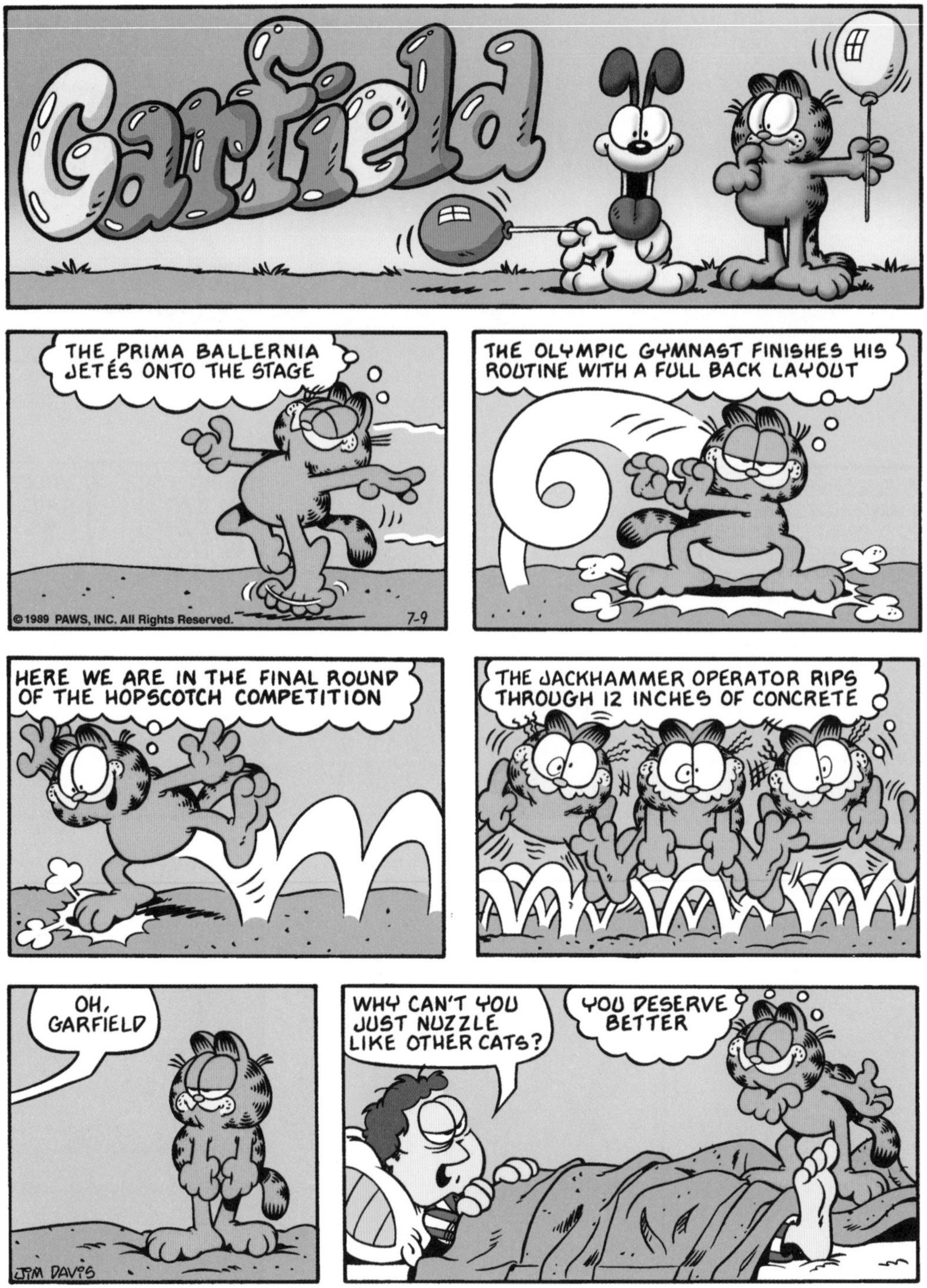
Garfield
THE PRIMA BALLERNIA JETÉS ONTO THE STAGE
©1989 PAWS, INC. All Rights Reserved.
7-9
THE OLYMPIC GYMNAST FINISHES HIS ROUTINE WITH A FULL BACK LAYOUT
HERE WE ARE IN THE FINAL ROUND OF THE HOPSCOTCH COMPETITION
THE JACKHAMMER OPERATOR RIPS THROUGH 12 INCHES OF CONCRETE
OH, GARFIELD
JIM DAVIS
WHY CAN'T YOU JUST NUZZLE LIKE OTHER CATS?
YOU DESERVE BETTER

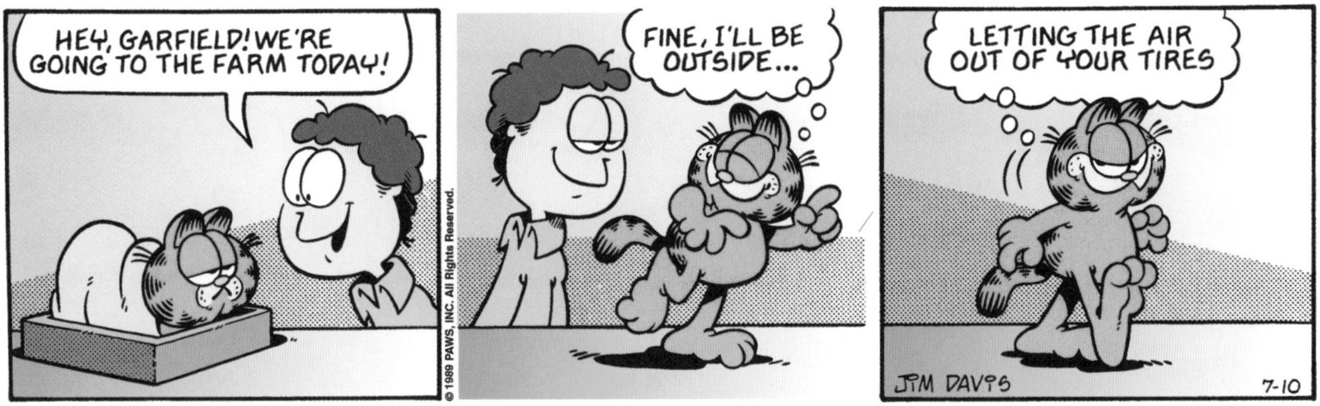
HEY, GARFIELD! WE'RE GOING TO THE FARM TODAY!
© 1989 PAWS, INC. All Rights Reserved.
FINE, I'LL BE OUTSIDE...
LETTING THE AIR OUT OF YOUR TIRES
JIM DAVIS
7-10

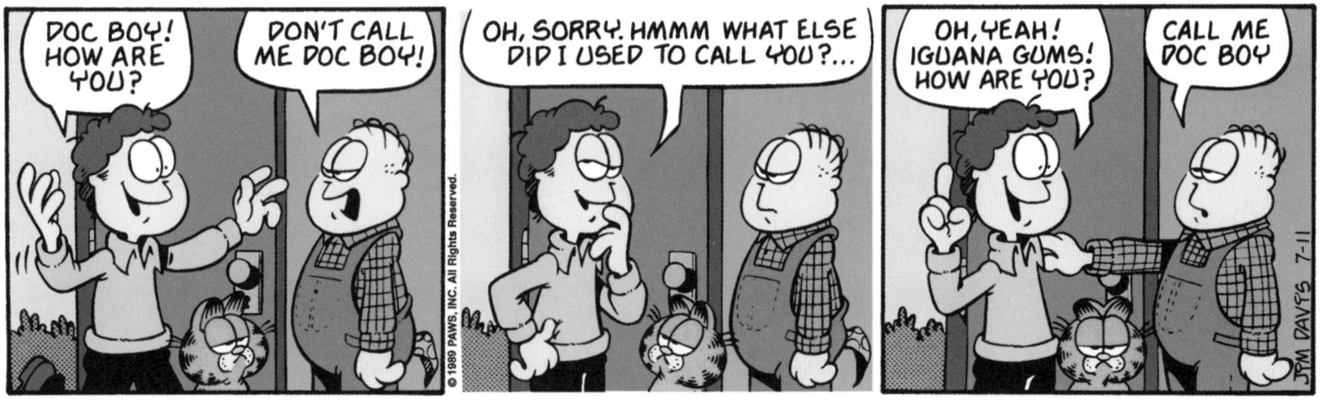
DOC BOY! HOW ARE YOU?
DON'T CALL ME DOC BOY!
© 1989 PAWS, INC. All Rights Reserved.
OH, SORRY. HMMM WHAT ELSE DID I USED TO CALL YOU?...
OH, YEAH! IGUANA GUMS! HOW ARE YOU?
CALL ME DOC BOY
JIM DAVIS 7-11

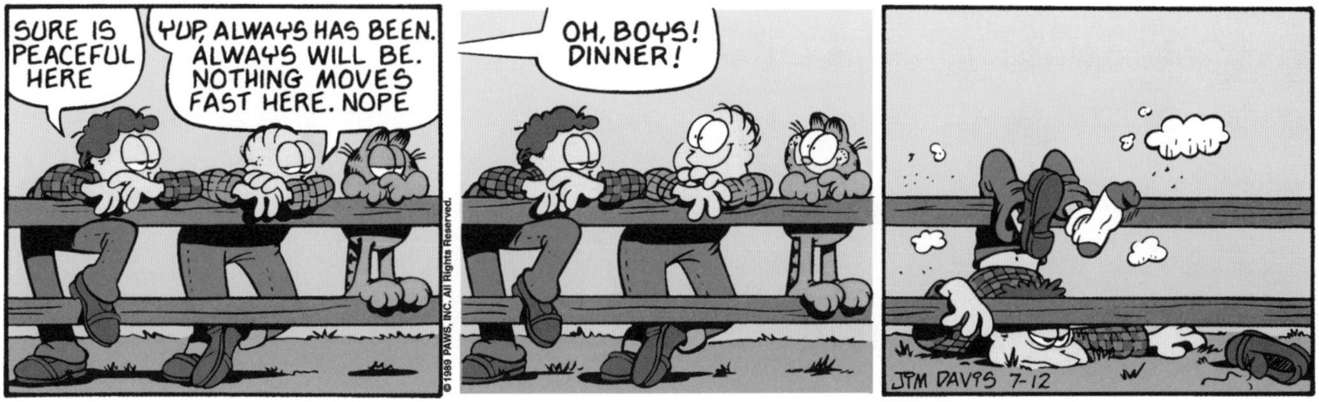
SURE IS PEACEFUL HERE
YUP, ALWAYS HAS BEEN. ALWAYS WILL BE. NOTHING MOVES FAST HERE. NOPE
© 1989 PAWS, INC. All Rights Reserved.
OH, BOYS! DINNER!
JIM DAVIS 7-12

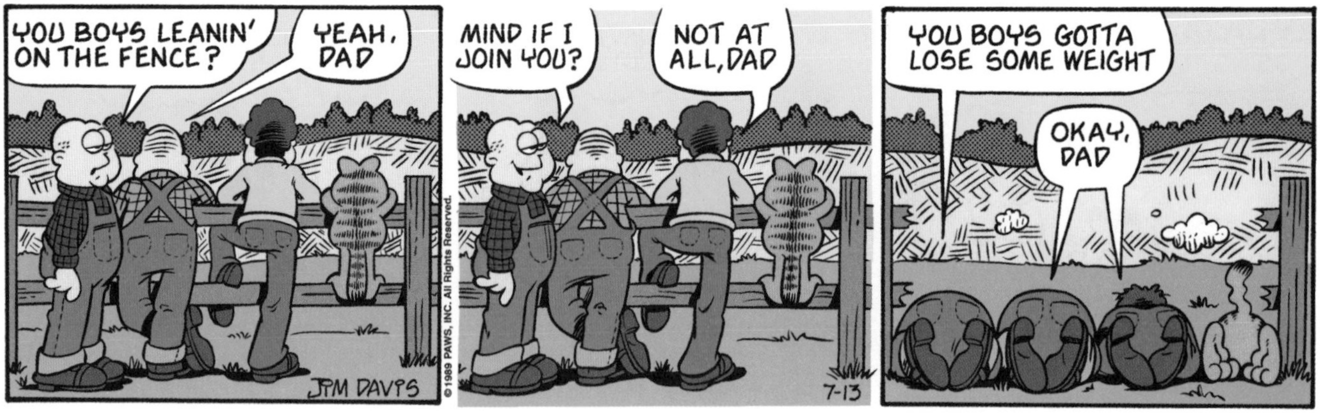
YOU BOYS LEANIN' ON THE FENCE?
YEAH, DAD
JIM DAVIS
© 1989 PAWS, INC. All Rights Reserved.
MIND IF I JOIN YOU?
NOT AT ALL, DAD
7-13
YOU BOYS GOTTA LOSE SOME WEIGHT
OKAY, DAD

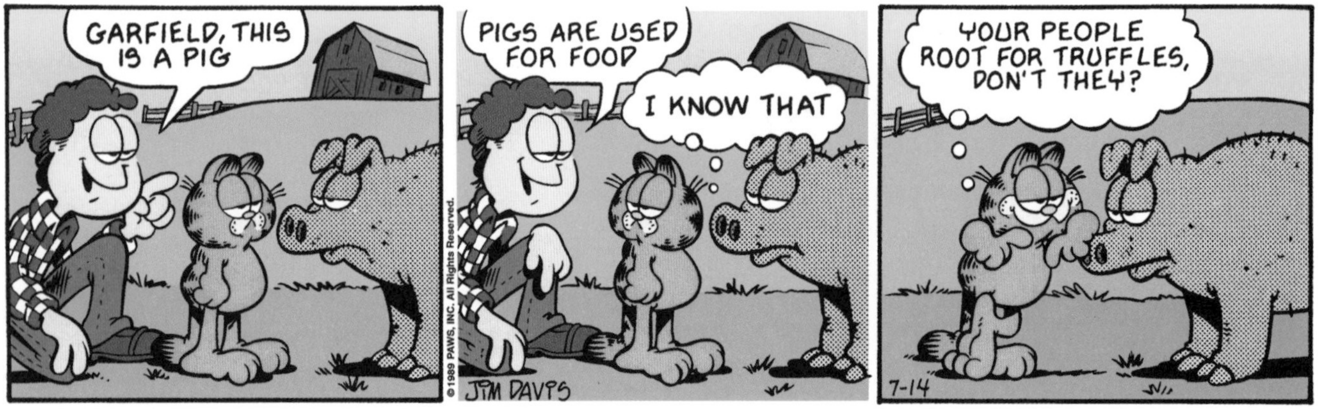
GARFIELD, THIS IS A PIG
© 1989 PAWS, INC. All Rights Reserved.
PIGS ARE USED FOR FOOD
I KNOW THAT
JIM DAVIS
YOUR PEOPLE ROOT FOR TRUFFLES, DON'T THEY?
7-14

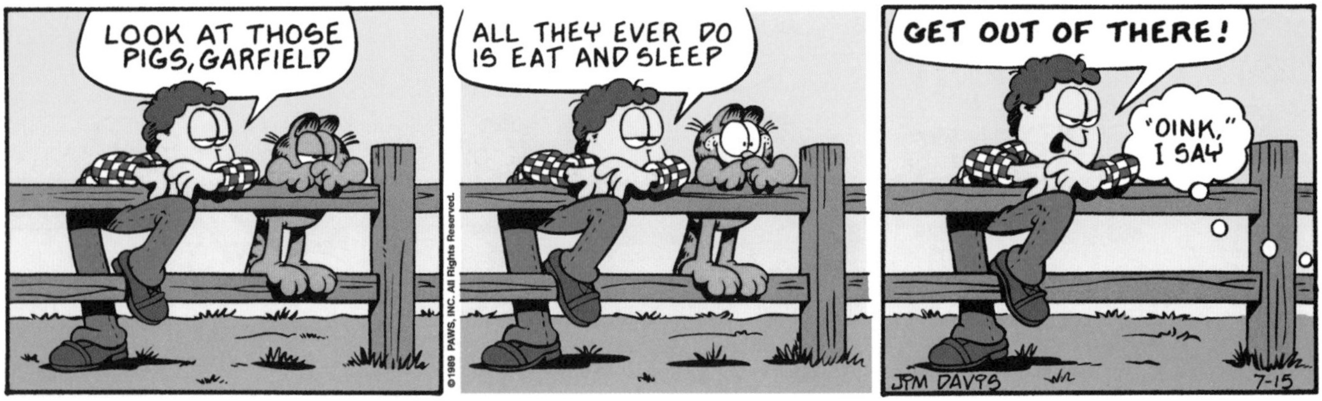
LOOK AT THOSE PIGS, GARFIELD
© 1989 PAWS, INC. All Rights Reserved.
ALL THEY EVER DO IS EAT AND SLEEP
GET OUT OF THERE!
"OINK," I SAY
JIM DAVIS
7-15

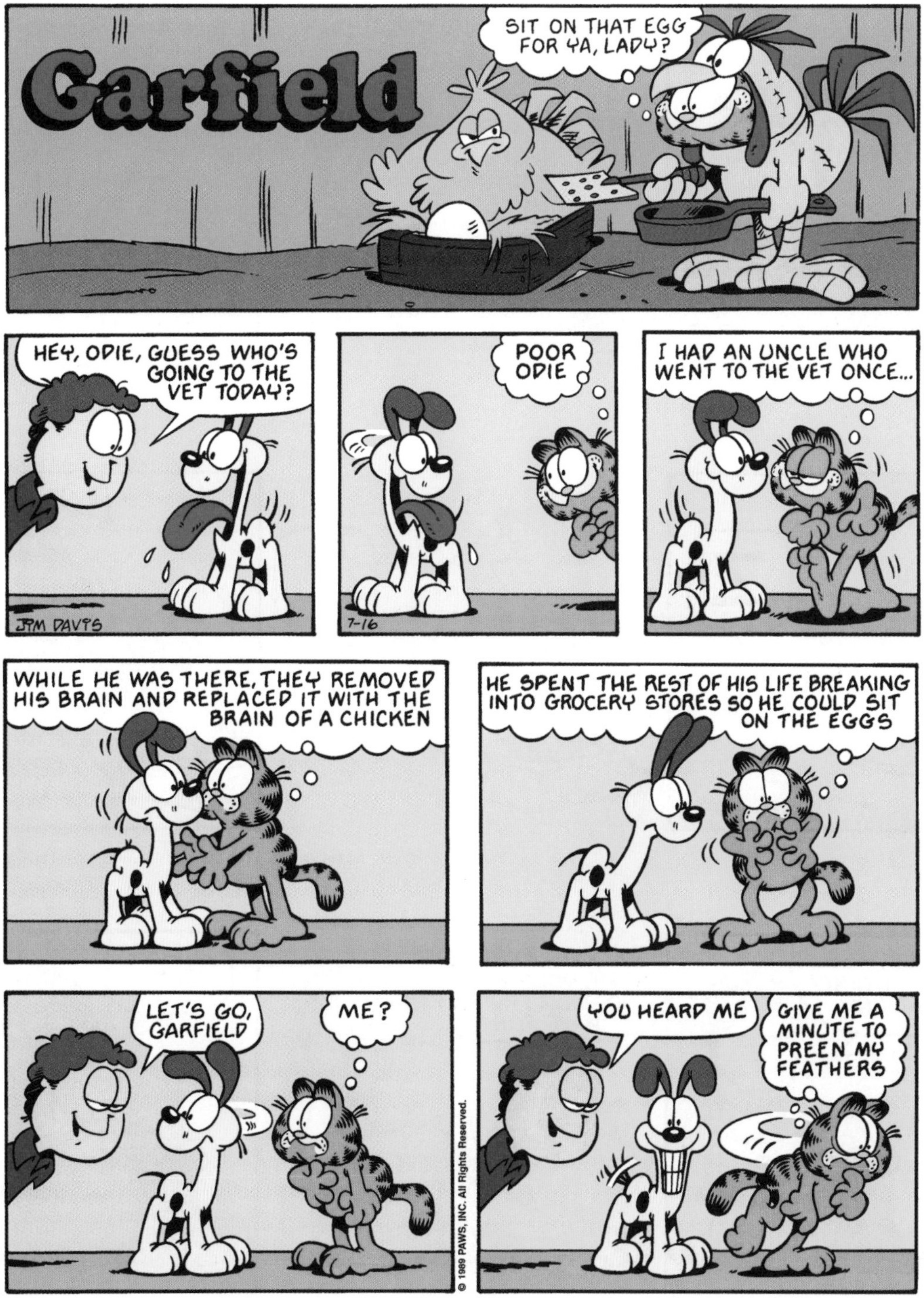
Garfield
SIT ON THAT EGG FOR YA, LADY?
HEY, ODIE, GUESS WHO'S GOING TO THE VET TODAY?
JIM DAVIS
POOR ODIE
7-16
I HAD AN UNCLE WHO WENT TO THE VET ONCE...
WHILE HE WAS THERE, THEY REMOVED HIS BRAIN AND REPLACED IT WITH THE BRAIN OF A CHICKEN
HE SPENT THE REST OF HIS LIFE BREAKING INTO GROCERY STORES SO HE COULD SIT ON THE EGGS
LET'S GO, GARFIELD
ME?
© 1989 PAWS, INC. All Rights Reserved.
YOU HEARD ME
GIVE ME A MINUTE TO PREEN MY FEATHERS

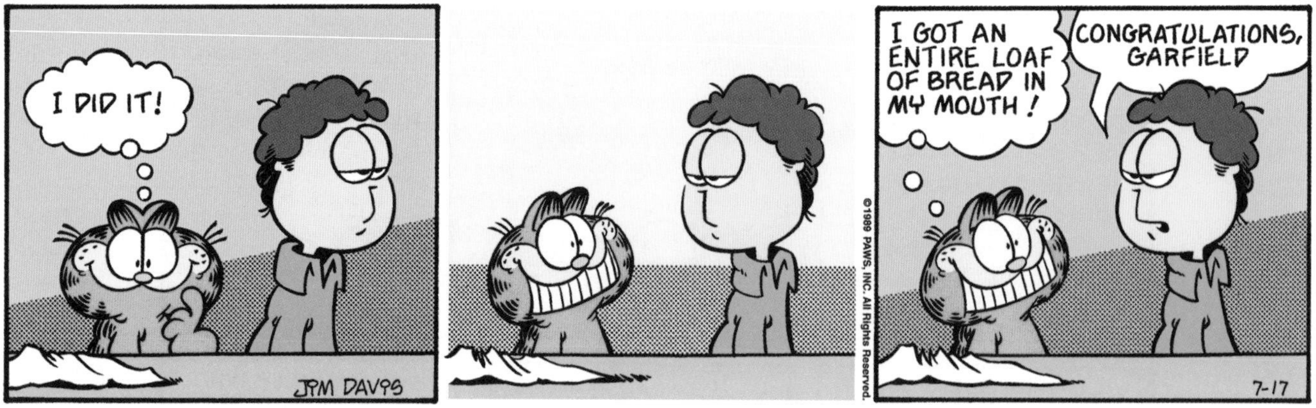
I DID IT!
JIM DAVIS
©1989 PAWS, INC. All Rights Reserved.
I GOT AN ENTIRE LOAF OF BREAD IN MY MOUTH!
CONGRATULATIONS, GARFIELD
7-17

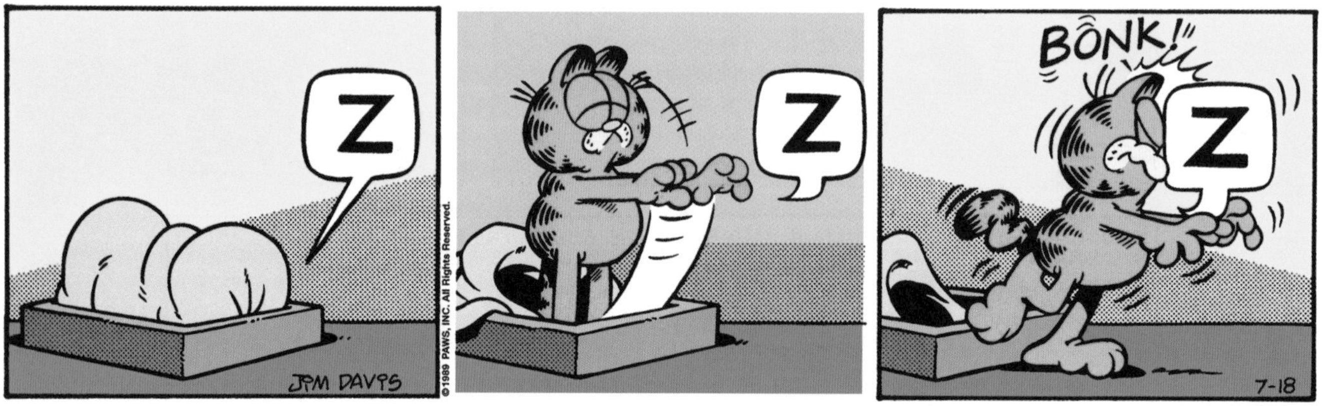
Z
JIM DAVIS
©1989 PAWS, INC. All Rights Reserved.
Z
BONK!
Z
7-18

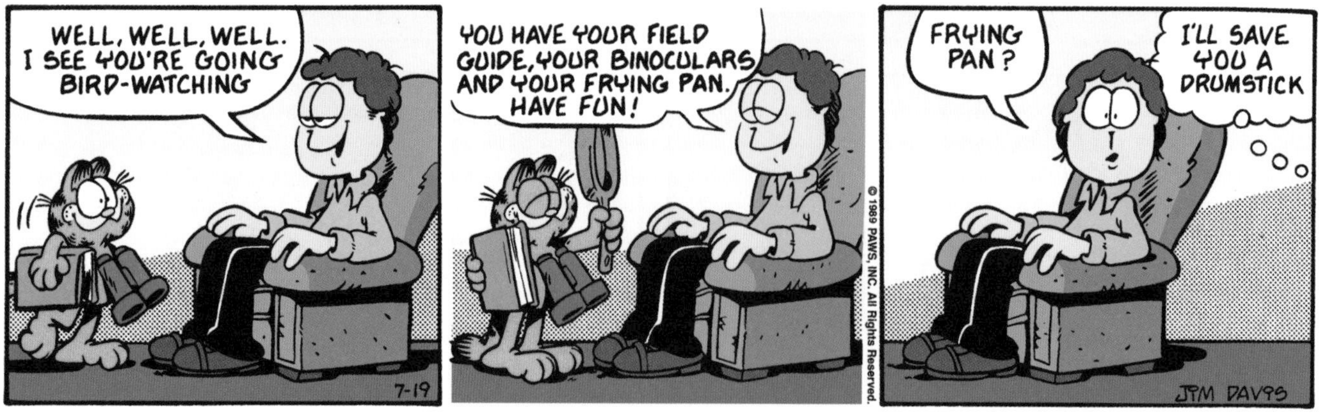
WELL, WELL, WELL. I SEE YOU'RE GOING BIRD-WATCHING
7-19
YOU HAVE YOUR FIELD GUIDE, YOUR BINOCULARS AND YOUR FRYING PAN. HAVE FUN!
©1989 PAWS, INC. All Rights Reserved.
FRYING PAN?
I'LL SAVE YOU A DRUMSTICK
JIM DAVIS

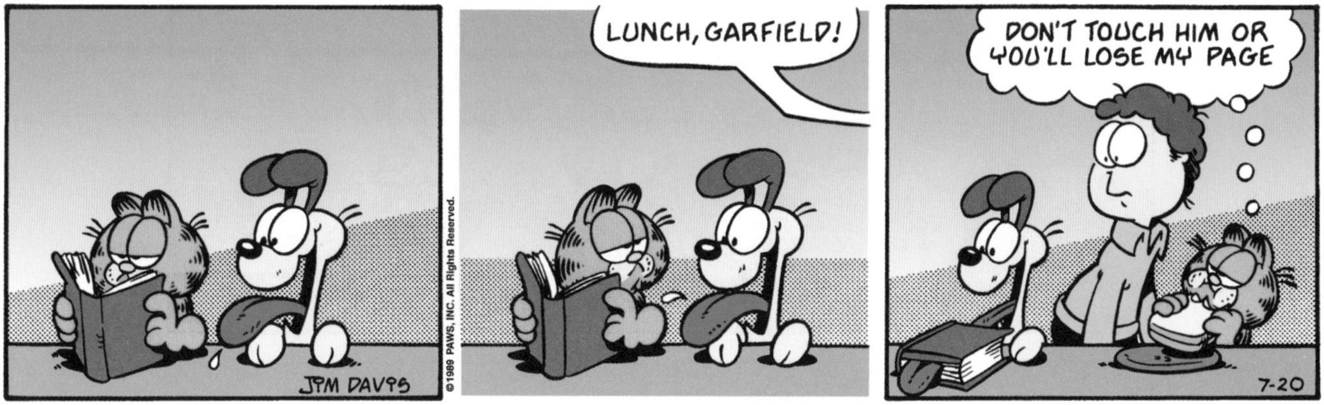
JIM DAVIS
©1989 PAWS, INC. All Rights Reserved.
LUNCH, GARFIELD!
DON'T TOUCH HIM OR YOU'LL LOSE MY PAGE
7-20

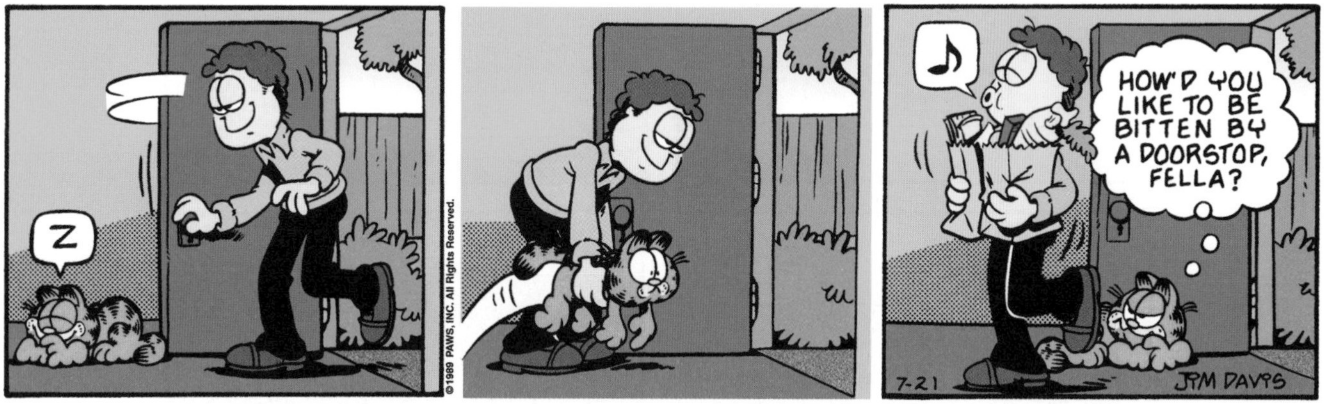
Z
©1989 PAWS, INC. All Rights Reserved.
♪
HOW'D YOU LIKE TO BE BITTEN BY A DOORSTOP, FELLA?
7-21
JIM DAVIS

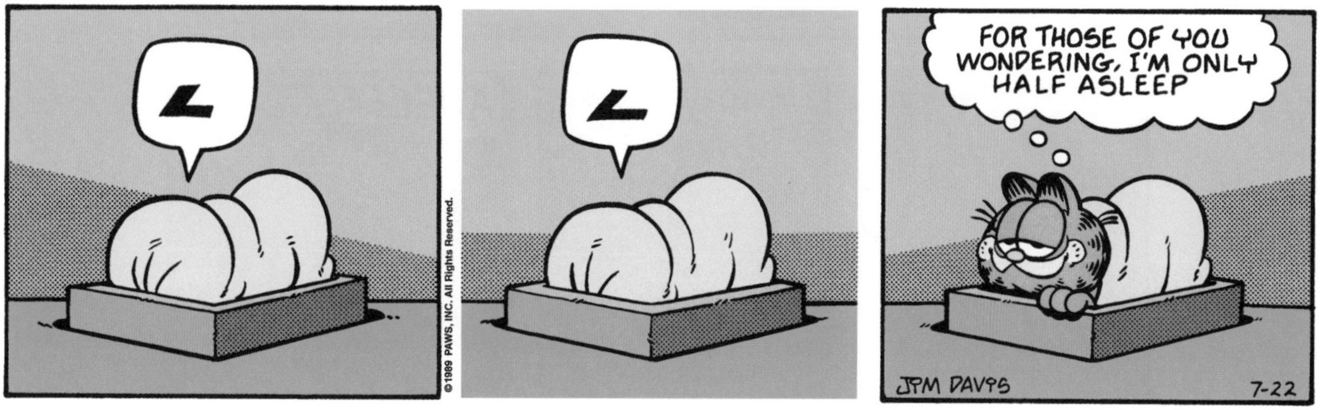
©1989 PAWS, INC. All Rights Reserved.
FOR THOSE OF YOU WONDERING, I'M ONLY HALF ASLEEP
JIM DAVIS
7-22

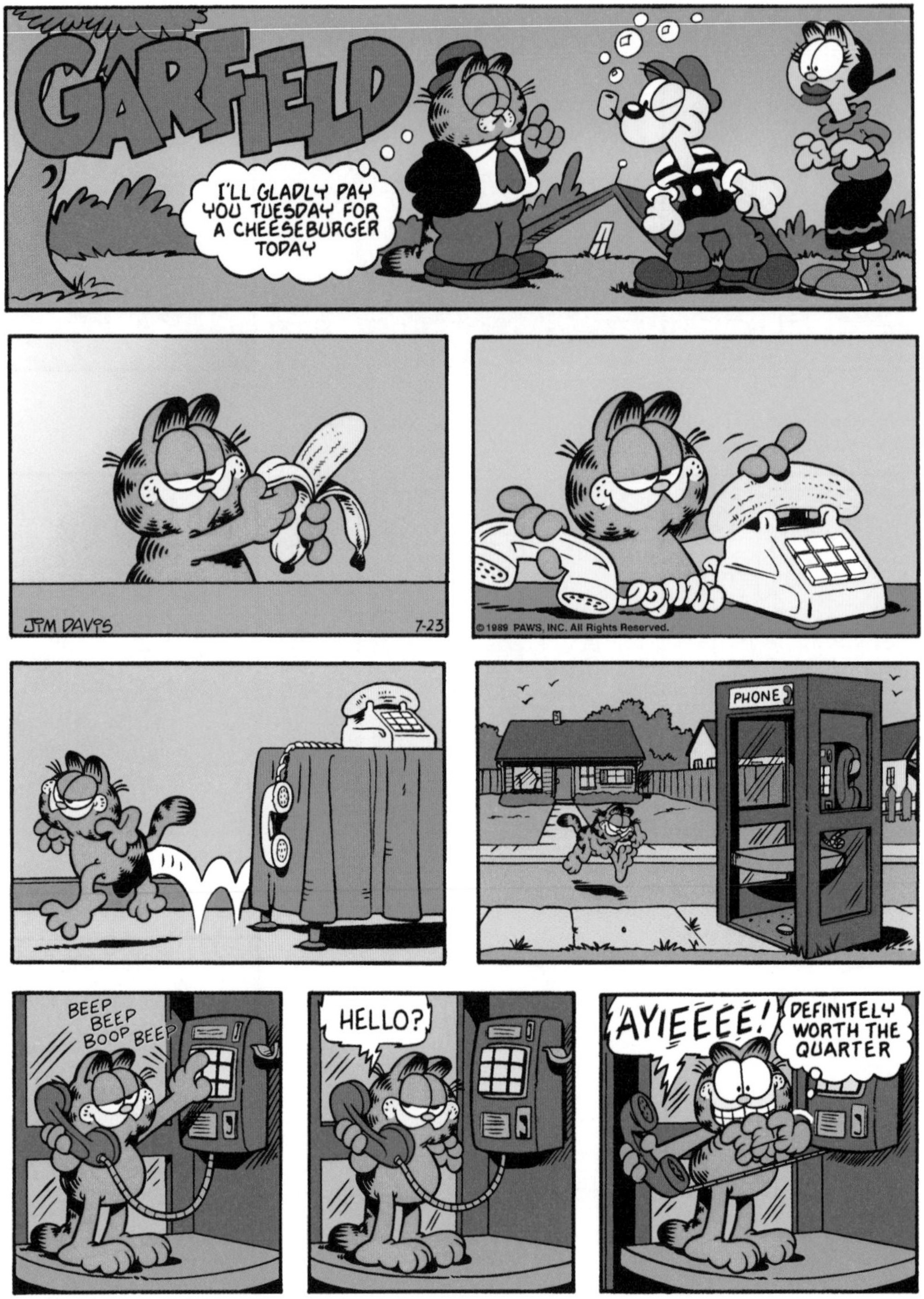
GARFIELD
I'LL GLADLY PAY YOU TUESDAY FOR A CHEESEBURGER TODAY
JIM DAVIS
7-23
© 1989 PAWS, INC. All Rights Reserved.
PHONE
BEEP BEEP BOOP BEEP
HELLO?
AYIEEEE!
DEFINITELY WORTH THE QUARTER

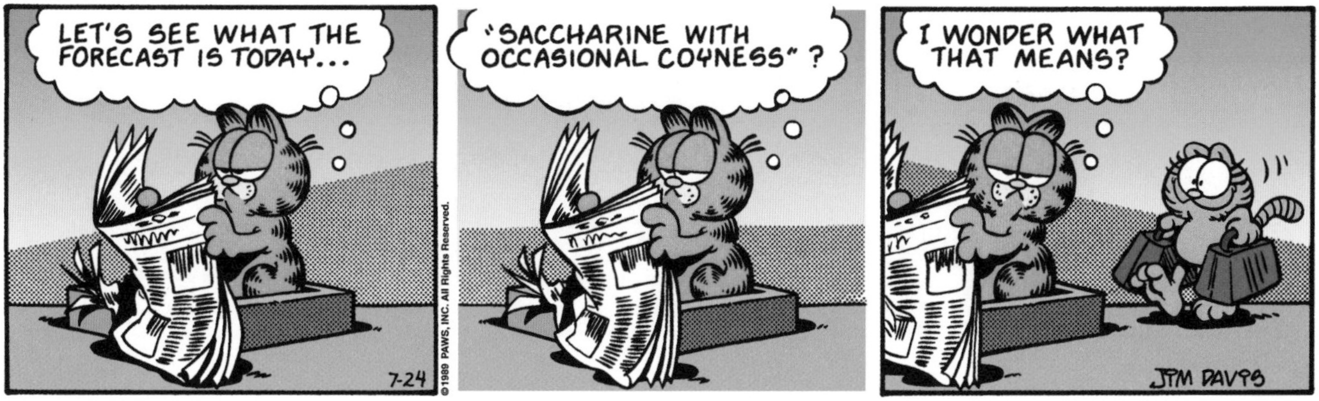
LET'S SEE WHAT THE FORECAST IS TODAY...
7-24
© 1989 PAWS, INC. All Rights Reserved.
"SACCHARINE WITH OCCASIONAL COYNESS"?
I WONDER WHAT THAT MEANS?
JIM DAVIS

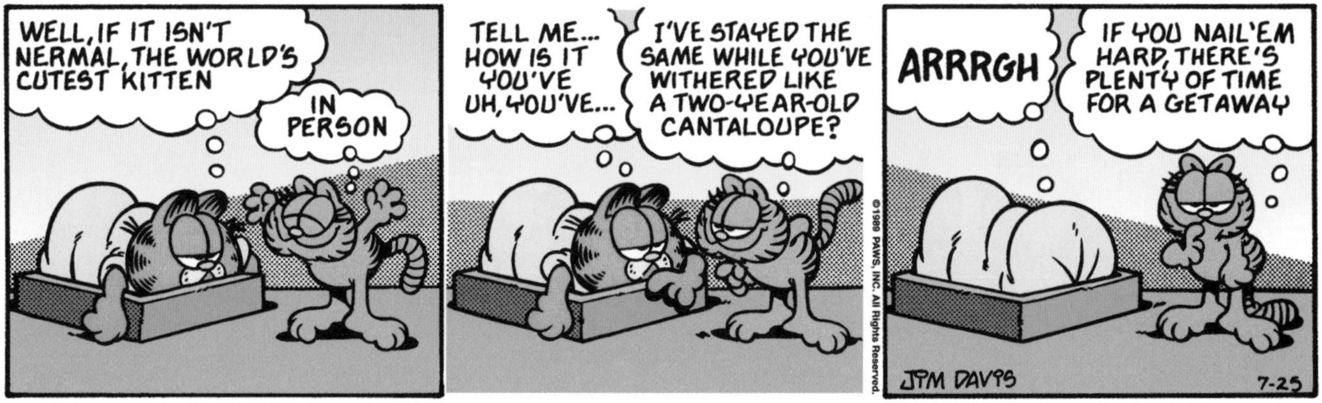
WELL, IF IT ISN'T NERMAL, THE WORLD'S CUTEST KITTEN
IN PERSON
TELL ME... HOW IS IT YOU'VE UH, YOU'VE...
I'VE STAYED THE SAME WHILE YOU'VE WITHERED LIKE A TWO-YEAR-OLD CANTALOUPE?
© 1989 PAWS, INC. All Rights Reserved.
ARRRGH
IF YOU NAIL'EM HARD, THERE'S PLENTY OF TIME FOR A GETAWAY
JIM DAVIS
7-25

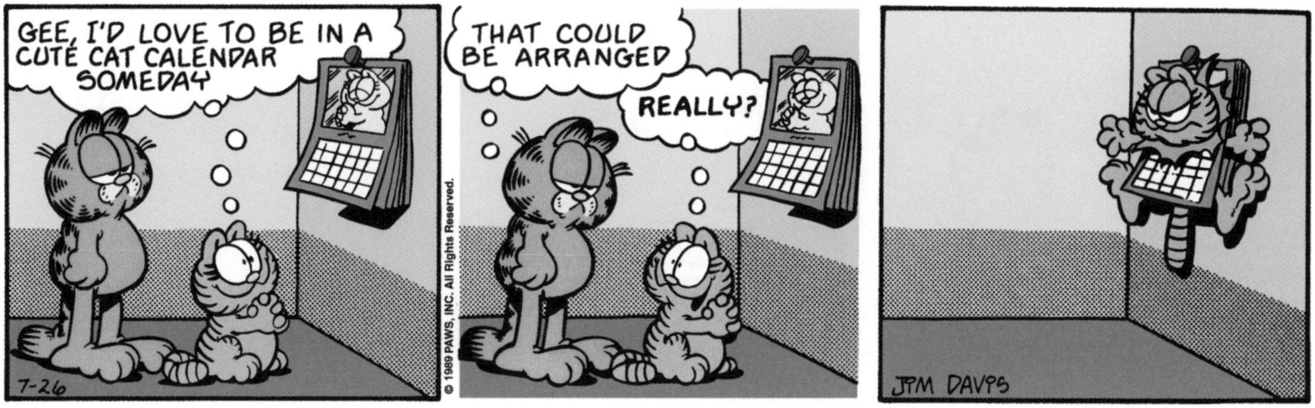
GEE, I'D LOVE TO BE IN A CUTE CAT CALENDAR SOMEDAY
7-26
© 1989 PAWS, INC. All Rights Reserved.
THAT COULD BE ARRANGED
REALLY?
JIM DAVIS

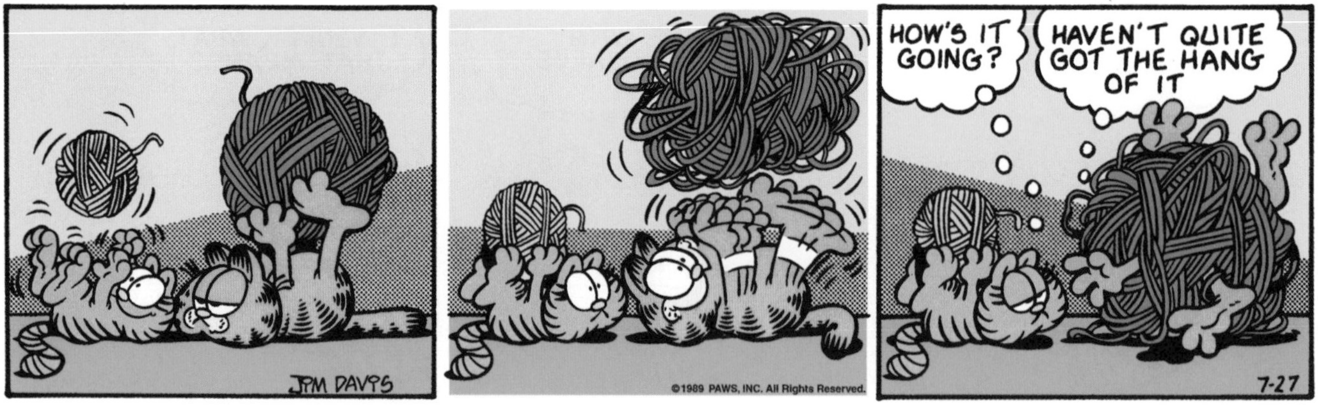
JIM DAVIS
©1989 PAWS, INC. All Rights Reserved.
HOW'S IT GOING?
HAVEN'T QUITE GOT THE HANG OF IT
7-27

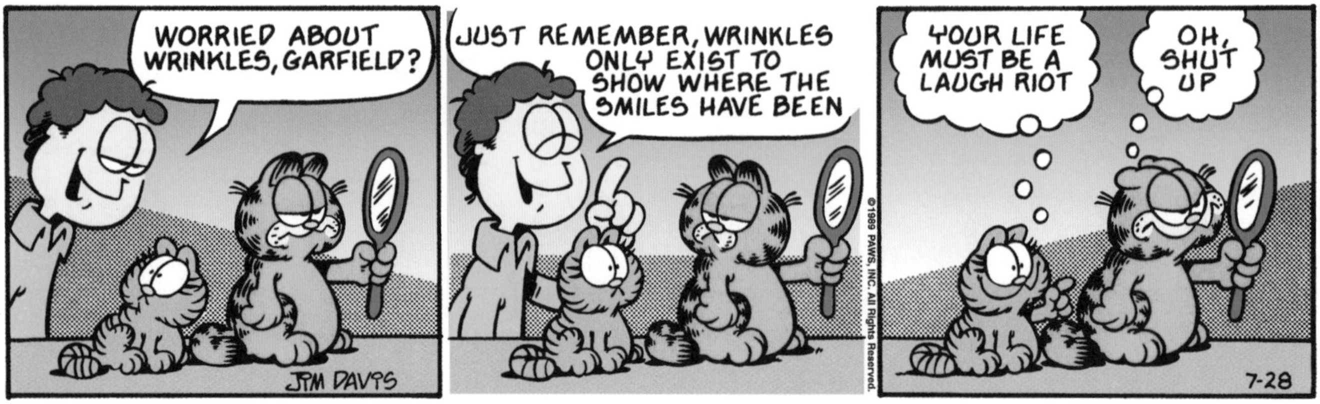
WORRIED ABOUT WRINKLES, GARFIELD?
JIM DAVIS
JUST REMEMBER, WRINKLES ONLY EXIST TO SHOW WHERE THE SMILES HAVE BEEN
©1989 PAWS, INC. All Rights Reserved.
YOUR LIFE MUST BE A LAUGH RIOT
OH, SHUT UP
7-28

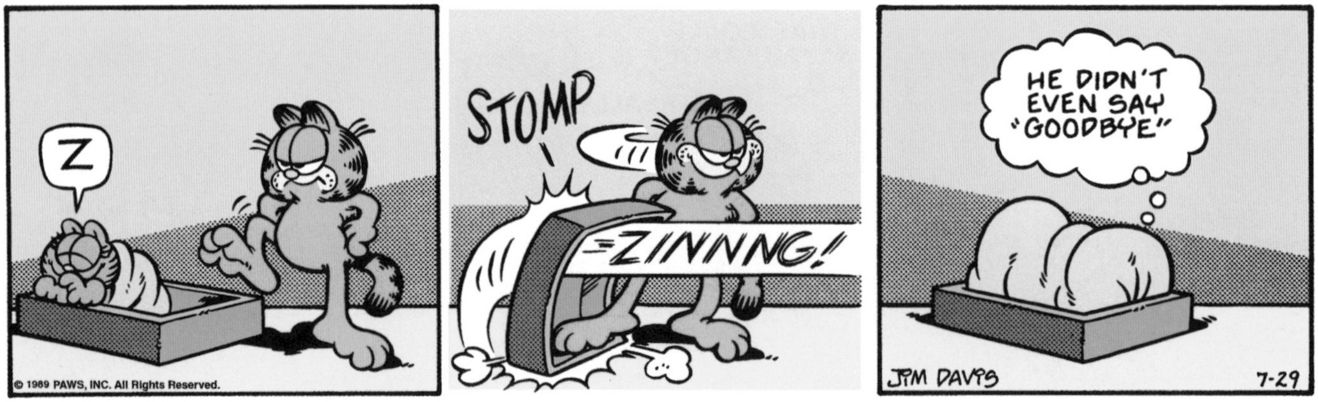
Z
© 1989 PAWS, INC. All Rights Reserved.
STOMP
ZINNNG!
HE DIDN'T EVEN SAY "GOODBYE"
JIM DAVIS
7-29

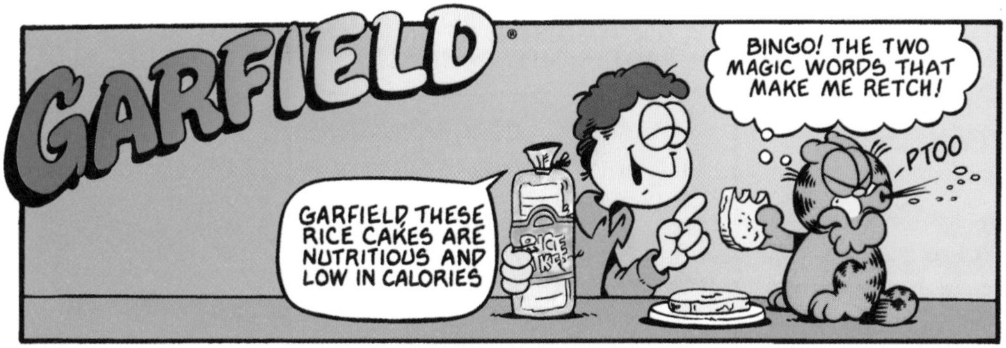
GARFIELD
GARFIELD THESE RICE CAKES ARE NUTRITIOUS AND LOW IN CALORIES
BINGO! THE TWO MAGIC WORDS THAT MAKE ME RETCH!
PTOO

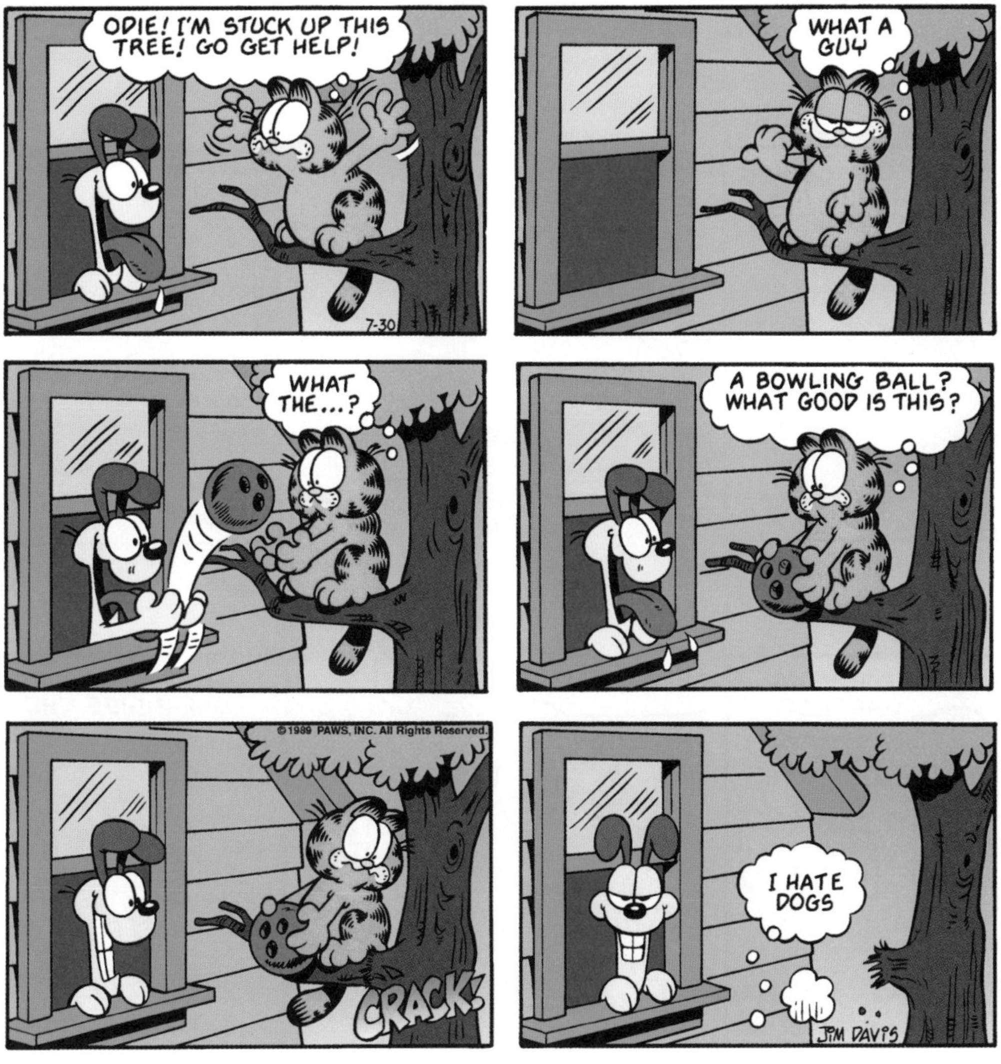
ODIE! I'M STUCK UP THIS TREE! GO GET HELP!
7-30
WHAT A GUY
WHAT THE...?
A BOWLING BALL? WHAT GOOD IS THIS?
©1989 PAWS, INC. All Rights Reserved.
CRACK!
I HATE DOGS
JIM DAVIS

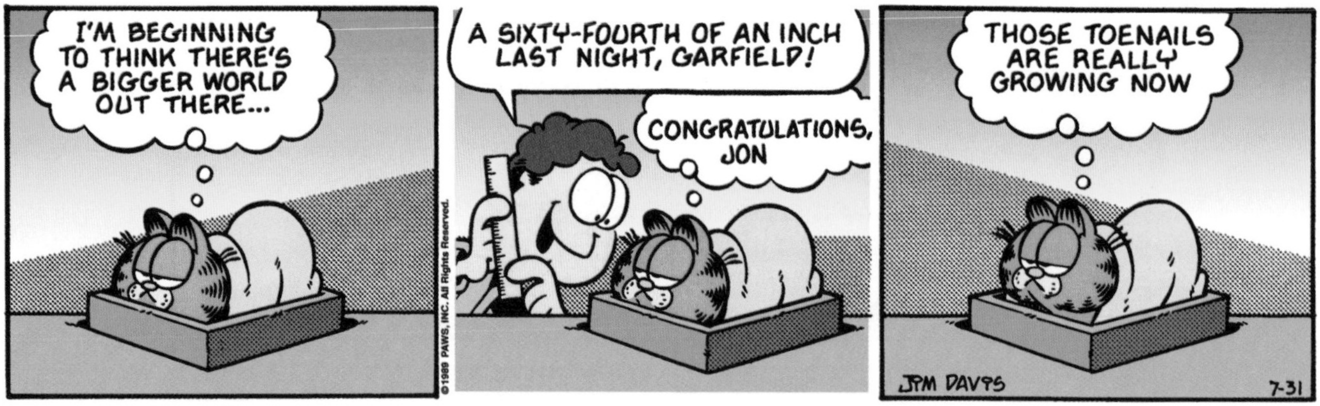
I'M BEGINNING TO THINK THERE'S A BIGGER WORLD OUT THERE...
A SIXTY-FOURTH OF AN INCH LAST NIGHT, GARFIELD!
CONGRATULATIONS, JON
THOSE TOENAILS ARE REALLY GROWING NOW
©1989 PAWS, INC. All Rights Reserved.
JIM DAVIS
7-31

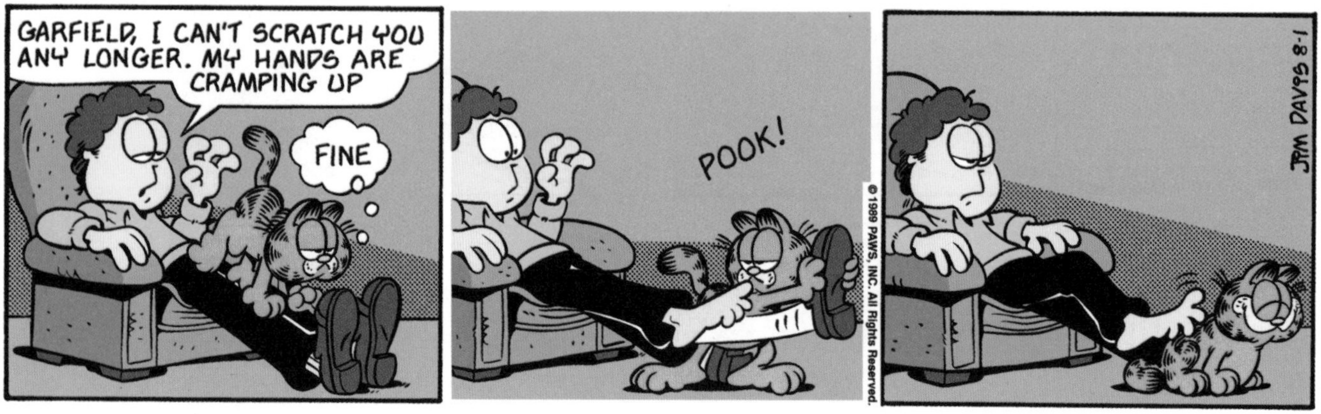
GARFIELD, I CAN'T SCRATCH YOU ANY LONGER. MY HANDS ARE CRAMPING UP
FINE
POOK!
© 1989 PAWS, INC. All Rights Reserved.
JIM DAVIS 8-1

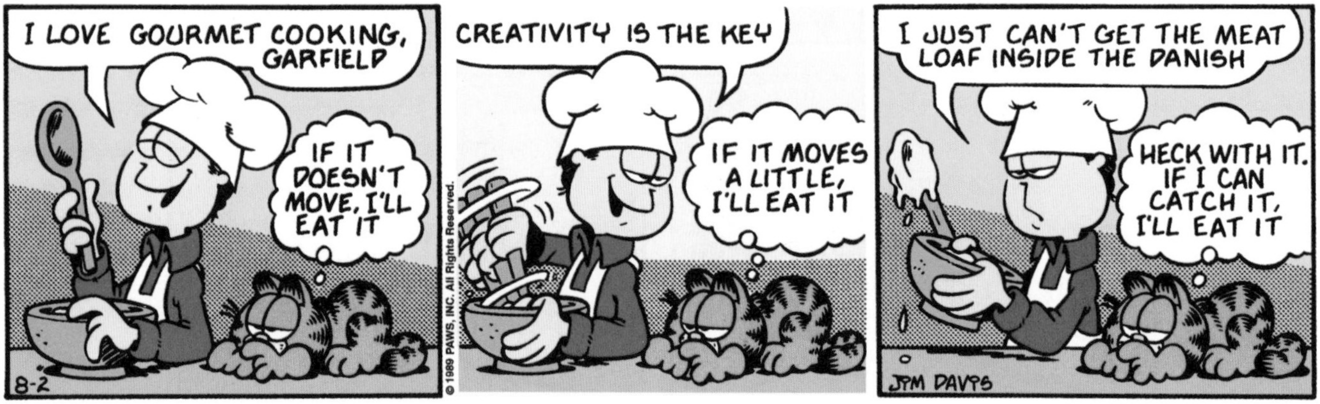
I LOVE GOURMET COOKING, GARFIELD
IF IT DOESN'T MOVE, I'LL EAT IT
8-2
CREATIVITY IS THE KEY
IF IT MOVES A LITTLE, I'LL EAT IT
© 1989 PAWS, INC. All Rights Reserved.
I JUST CAN'T GET THE MEAT LOAF INSIDE THE DANISH
HECK WITH IT. IF I CAN CATCH IT, I'LL EAT IT
JIM DAVIS

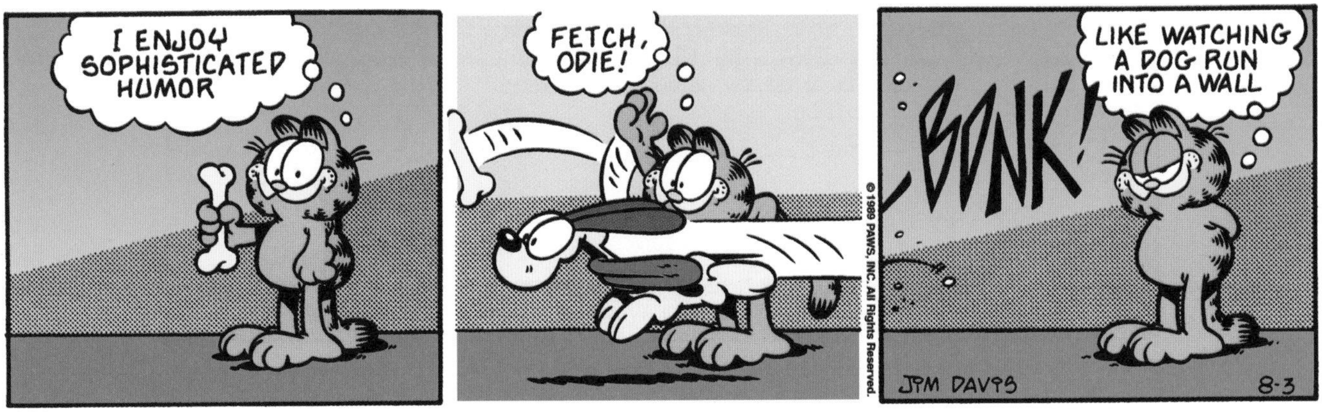
I ENJOY SOPHISTICATED HUMOR
FETCH, ODIE!
©1989 PAWS, INC. All Rights Reserved.
BONK!
LIKE WATCHING A DOG RUN INTO A WALL
JIM DAVIS
8-3

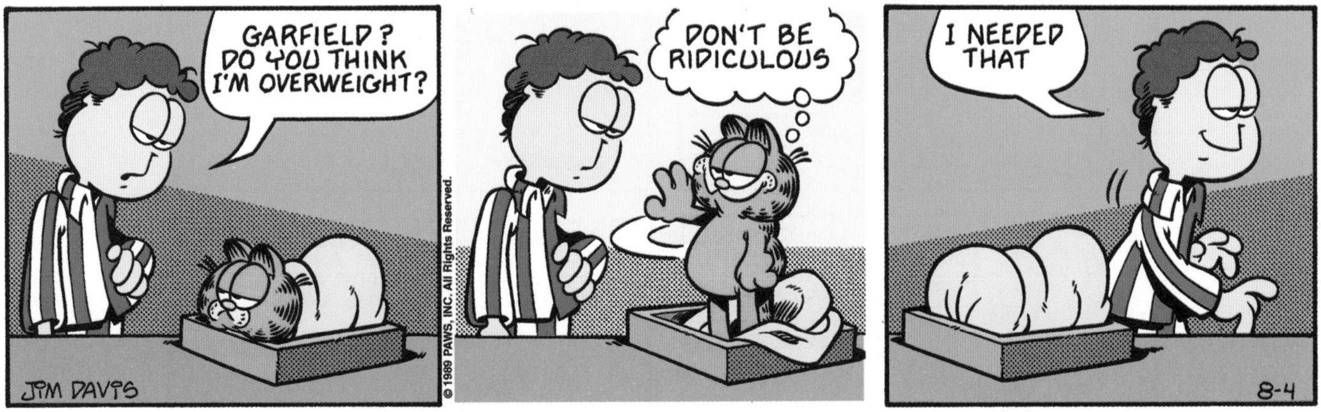
GARFIELD? DO YOU THINK I'M OVERWEIGHT?
JIM DAVIS
©1989 PAWS, INC. All Rights Reserved.
DON'T BE RIDICULOUS
I NEEDED THAT
8-4

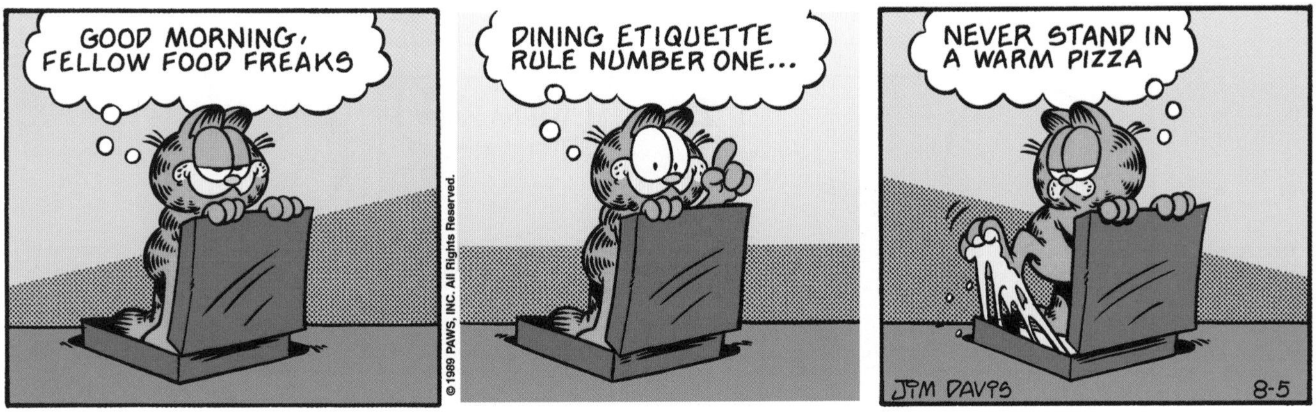
GOOD MORNING, FELLOW FOOD FREAKS
©1989 PAWS, INC. All Rights Reserved.
DINING ETIQUETTE RULE NUMBER ONE...
NEVER STAND IN A WARM PIZZA
JIM DAVIS
8-5

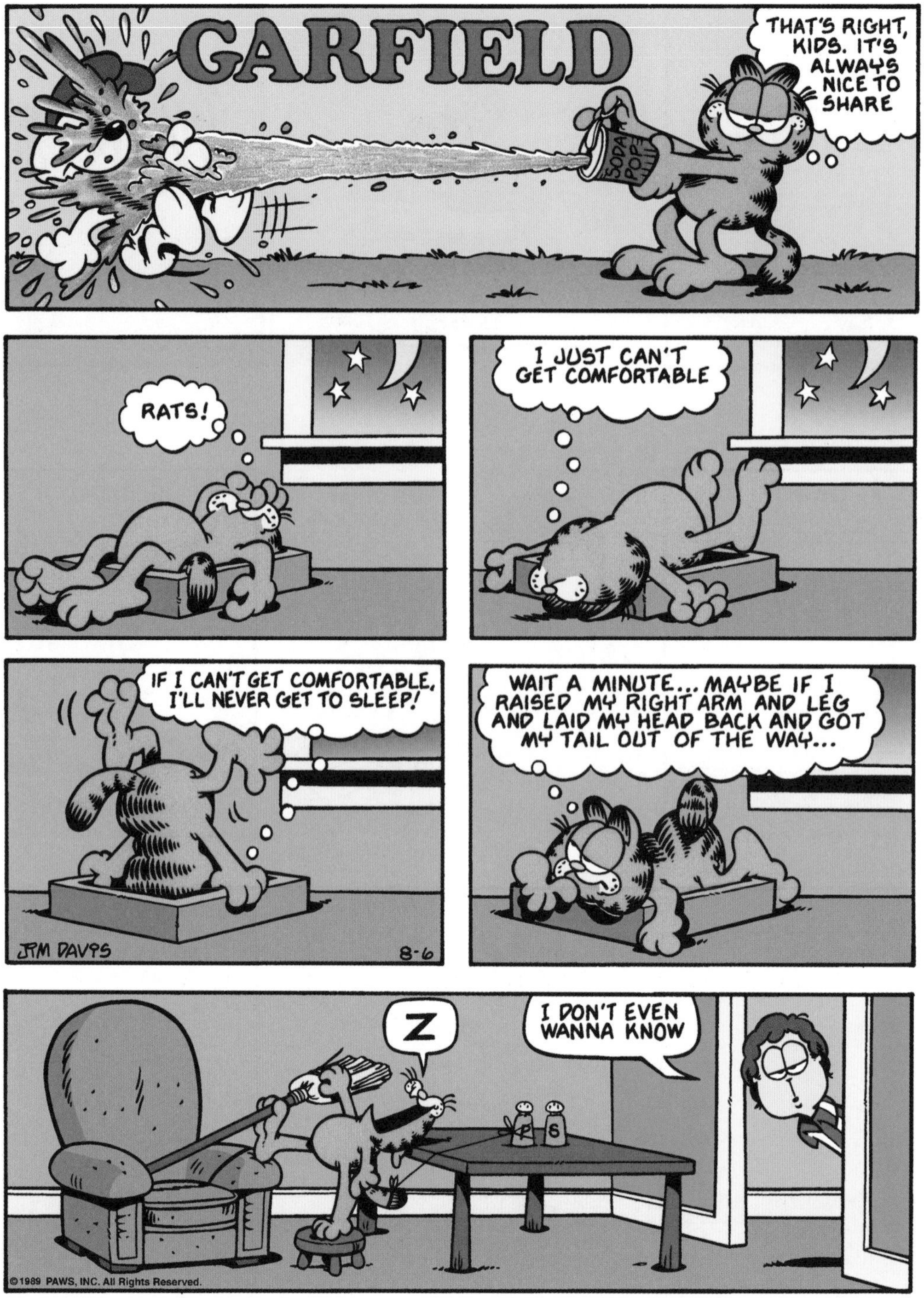
GARFIELD
THAT'S RIGHT, KIDS. IT'S ALWAYS NICE TO SHARE
SODA POP
RATS!
I JUST CAN'T GET COMFORTABLE
IF I CAN'T GET COMFORTABLE, I'LL NEVER GET TO SLEEP!
WAIT A MINUTE... MAYBE IF I RAISED MY RIGHT ARM AND LEG AND LAID MY HEAD BACK AND GOT MY TAIL OUT OF THE WAY...
JIM DAVIS 8-6
Z
I DON'T EVEN WANNA KNOW
P
S

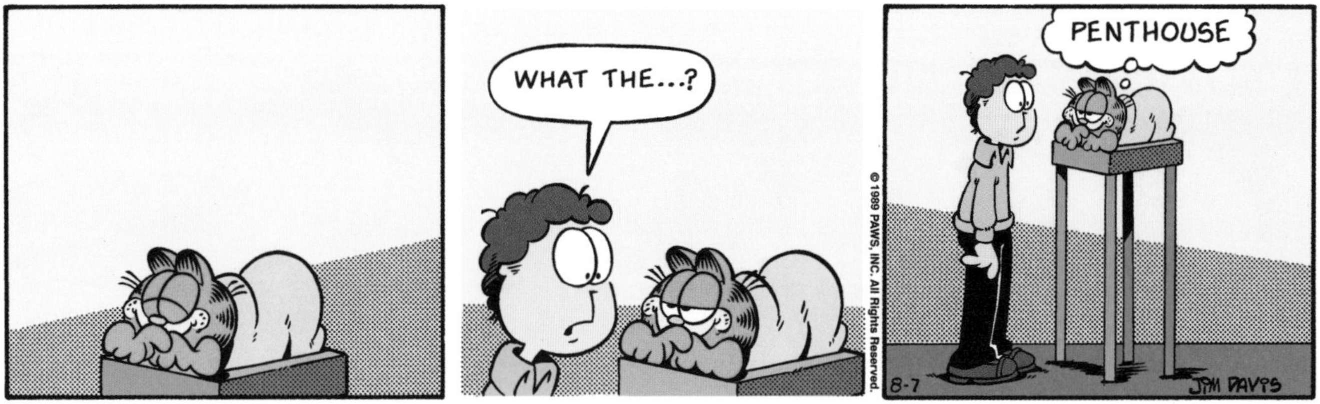
WHAT THE...?
PENTHOUSE
8-7
JIM DAVIS

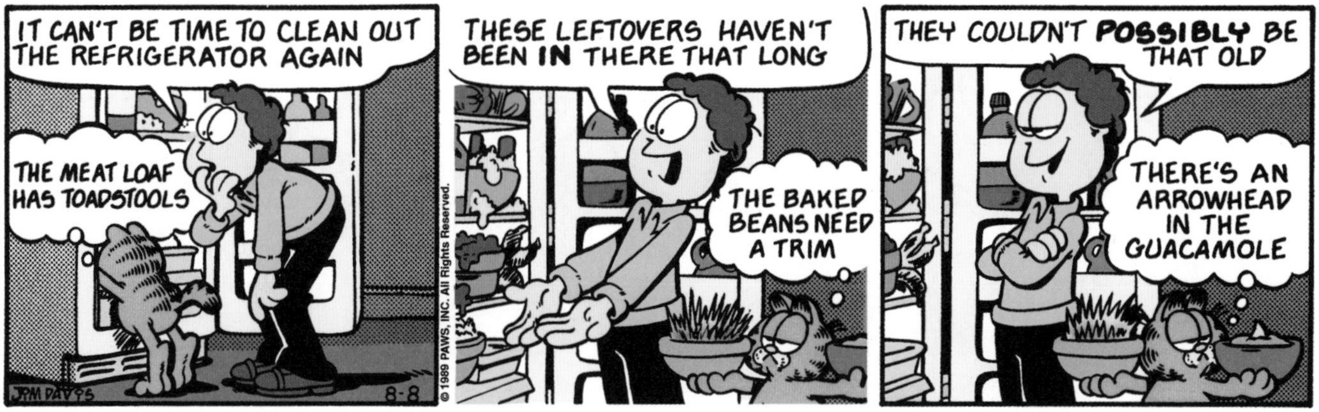
IT CAN'T BE TIME TO CLEAN OUT THE REFRIGERATOR AGAIN
THE MEAT LOAF HAS TOADSTOOLS
JIM DAVIS
8-8
THESE LEFTOVERS HAVEN'T BEEN **IN** THERE THAT LONG
THE BAKED BEANS NEED A TRIM
THEY COULDN'T **POSSIBLY** BE THAT OLD
THERE'S AN ARROWHEAD IN THE GUACAMOLE

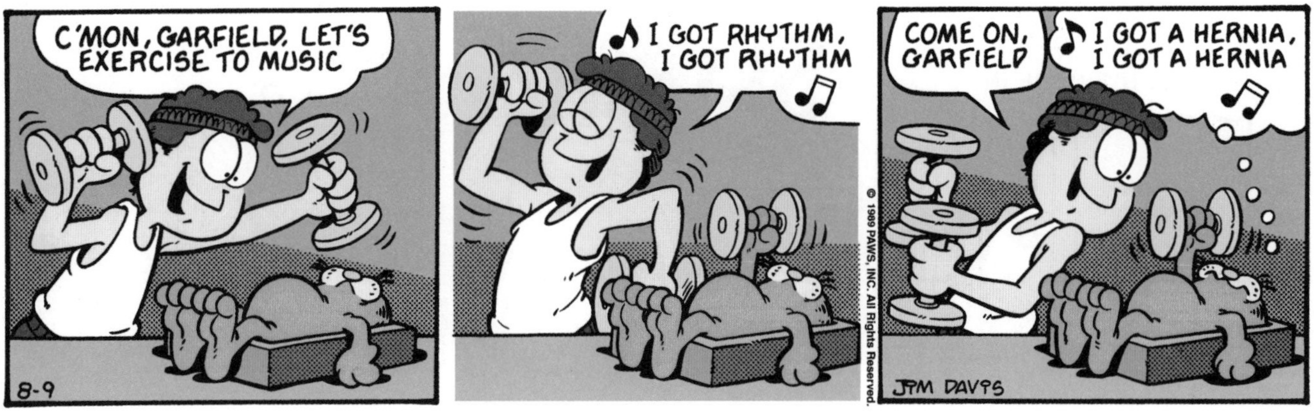
C'MON, GARFIELD, LET'S EXERCISE TO MUSIC
8-9
♪ I GOT RHYTHM, I GOT RHYTHM ♫
COME ON, GARFIELD
♪ I GOT A HERNIA, I GOT A HERNIA ♫
JIM DAVIS

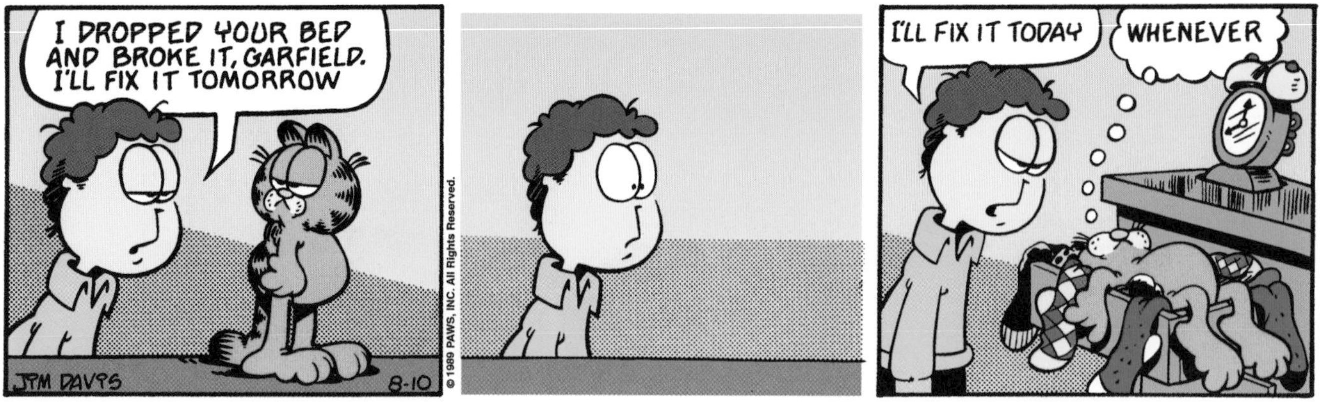
I DROPPED YOUR BED AND BROKE IT, GARFIELD. I'LL FIX IT TOMORROW
JIM DAVIS
8-10
©1989 PAWS, INC. All Rights Reserved.
I'LL FIX IT TODAY
WHENEVER

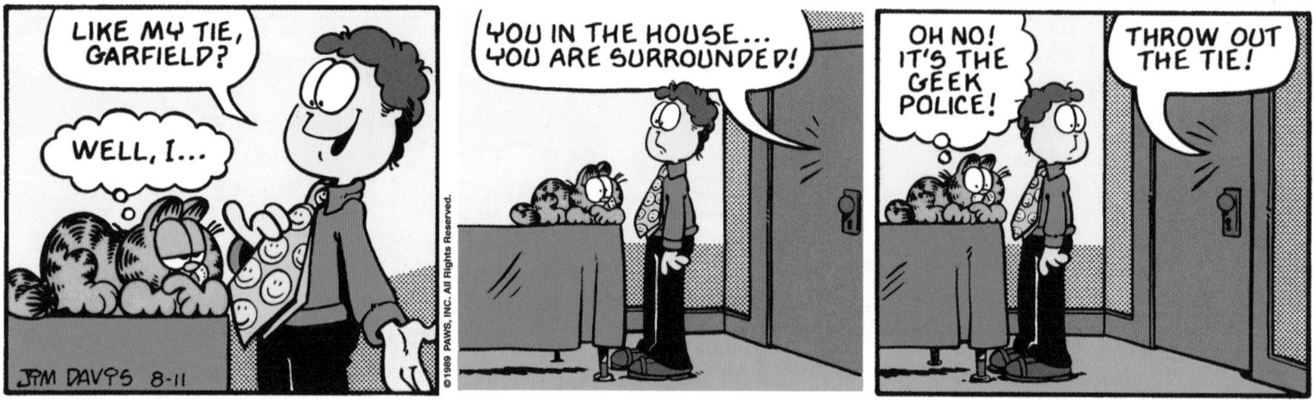
LIKE MY TIE, GARFIELD?
WELL, I...
JIM DAVIS 8-11
©1989 PAWS, INC. All Rights Reserved.
YOU IN THE HOUSE... YOU ARE SURROUNDED!
OH NO! IT'S THE GEEK POLICE!
THROW OUT THE TIE!

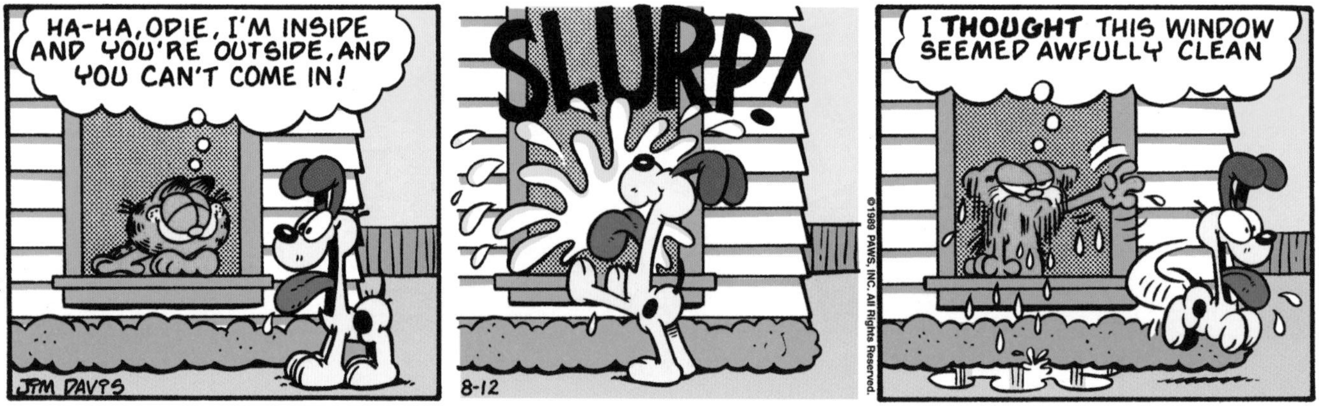
HA-HA, ODIE, I'M INSIDE AND YOU'RE OUTSIDE, AND YOU CAN'T COME IN!
JIM DAVIS
SLURP!
8-12
©1989 PAWS, INC. All Rights Reserved.
I THOUGHT THIS WINDOW SEEMED AWFULLY CLEAN

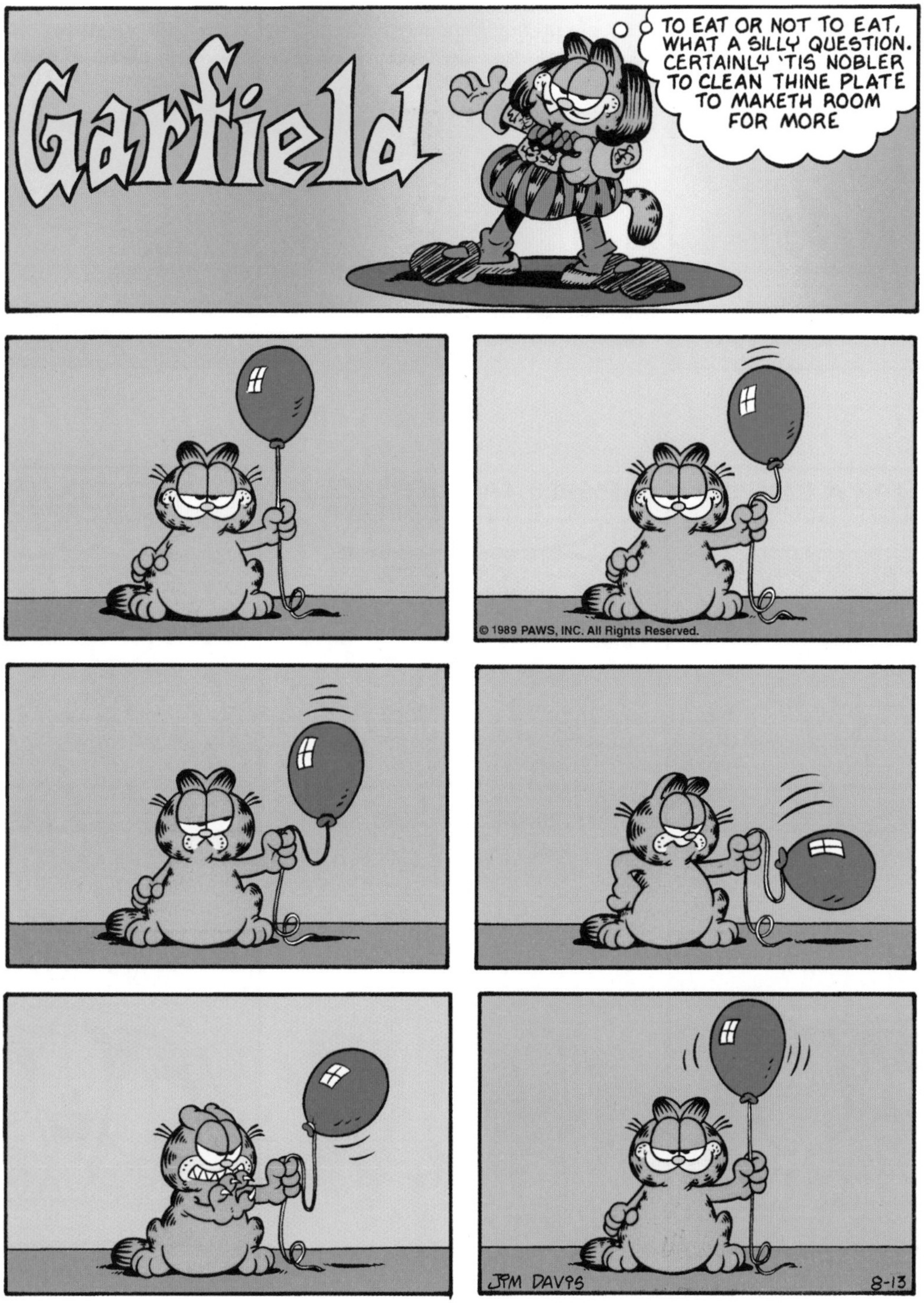
Garfield
TO EAT OR NOT TO EAT, WHAT A SILLY QUESTION. CERTAINLY 'TIS NOBLER TO CLEAN THINE PLATE TO MAKETH ROOM FOR MORE
© 1989 PAWS, INC. All Rights Reserved.
JIM DAVIS
8-13

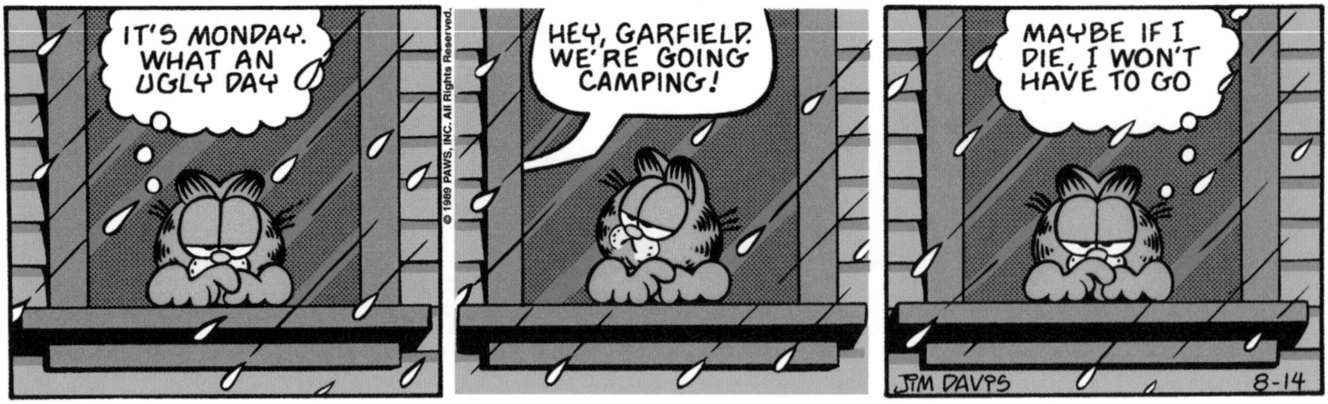
IT'S MONDAY. WHAT AN UGLY DAY
© 1989 PAWS, INC. All Rights Reserved.
HEY, GARFIELD. WE'RE GOING CAMPING!
MAYBE IF I DIE, I WON'T HAVE TO GO
JIM DAVIS 8-14

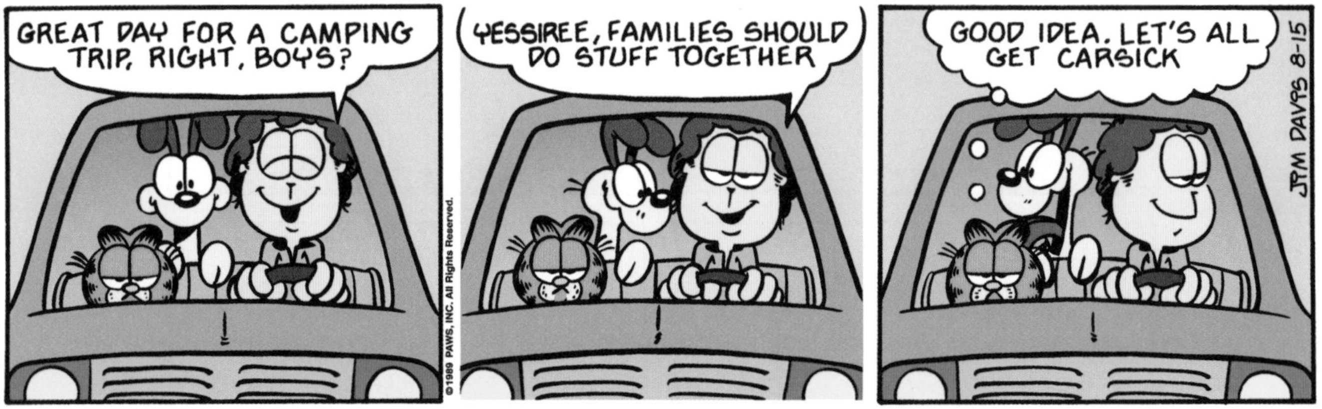
GREAT DAY FOR A CAMPING TRIP, RIGHT, BOYS?
© 1989 PAWS, INC. All Rights Reserved.
YESSIREE, FAMILIES SHOULD DO STUFF TOGETHER
GOOD IDEA. LET'S ALL GET CARSICK
JIM DAVIS 8-15

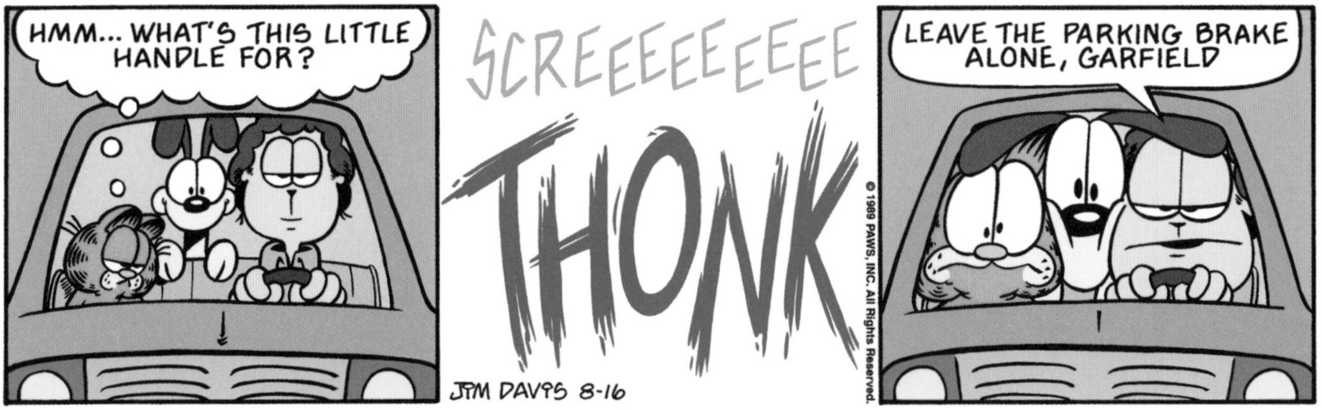
HMM... WHAT'S THIS LITTLE HANDLE FOR?
SCREEEEEEEEEE
THONK
JIM DAVIS 8-16
© 1989 PAWS, INC. All Rights Reserved.
LEAVE THE PARKING BRAKE ALONE, GARFIELD

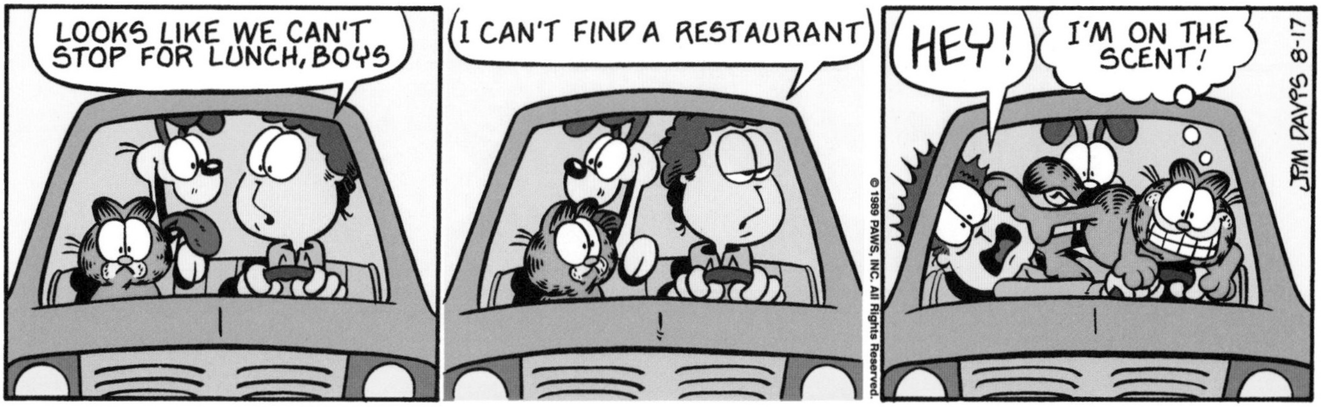
LOOKS LIKE WE CAN'T STOP FOR LUNCH, BOYS
I CAN'T FIND A RESTAURANT
HEY!
I'M ON THE SCENT!
© 1989 PAWS, INC. All Rights Reserved.

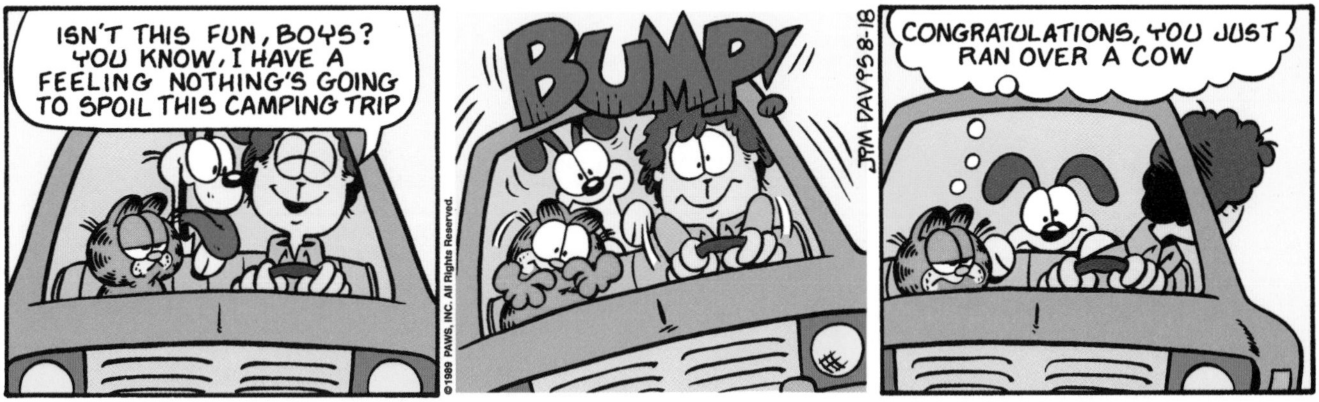
ISN'T THIS FUN, BOYS? YOU KNOW, I HAVE A FEELING NOTHING'S GOING TO SPOIL THIS CAMPING TRIP
BUMP!
CONGRATULATIONS, YOU JUST RAN OVER A COW
© 1989 PAWS, INC. All Rights Reserved.

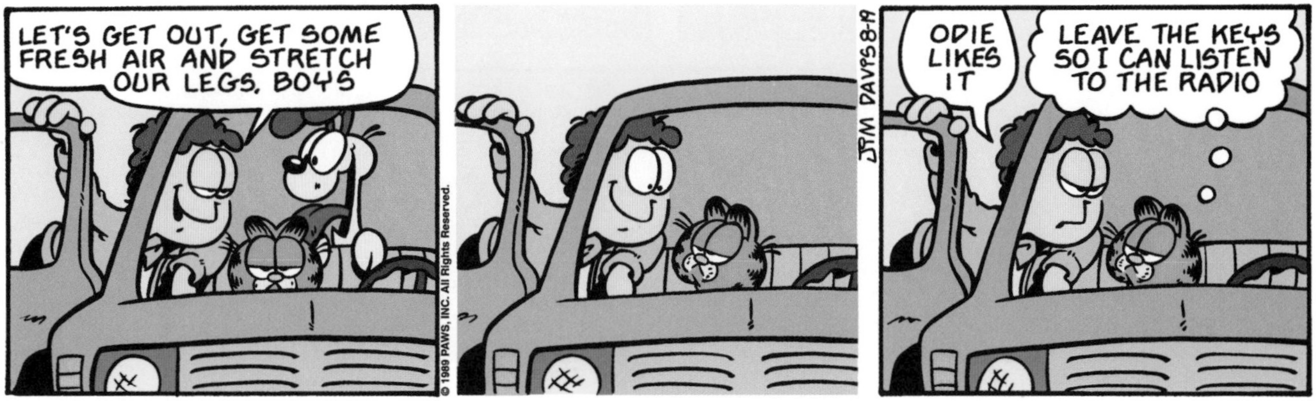
LET'S GET OUT, GET SOME FRESH AIR AND STRETCH OUR LEGS, BOYS
ODIE LIKES IT
LEAVE THE KEYS SO I CAN LISTEN TO THE RADIO
© 1989 PAWS, INC. All Rights Reserved.

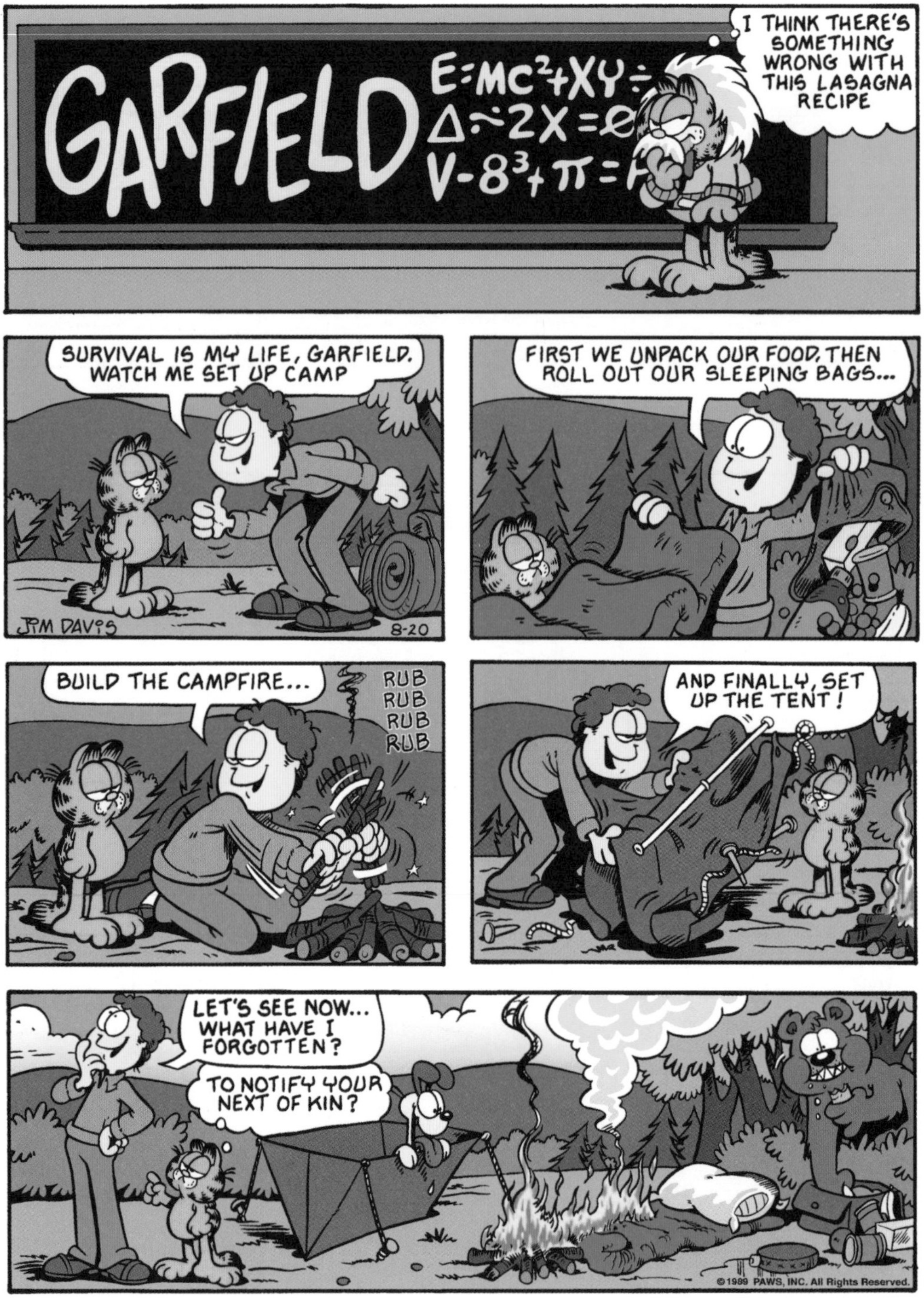
GARFIELD
E=MC²+XY÷
Δ≈2X=ℓ
V-8³+π=
I THINK THERE'S SOMETHING WRONG WITH THIS LASAGNA RECIPE
SURVIVAL IS MY LIFE, GARFIELD. WATCH ME SET UP CAMP
JIM DAVIS
8-20
FIRST WE UNPACK OUR FOOD, THEN ROLL OUT OUR SLEEPING BAGS...
BUILD THE CAMPFIRE...
RUB RUB RUB RUB
AND FINALLY, SET UP THE TENT!
LET'S SEE NOW... WHAT HAVE I FORGOTTEN?
TO NOTIFY YOUR NEXT OF KIN?
©1989 PAWS, INC. All Rights Reserved.

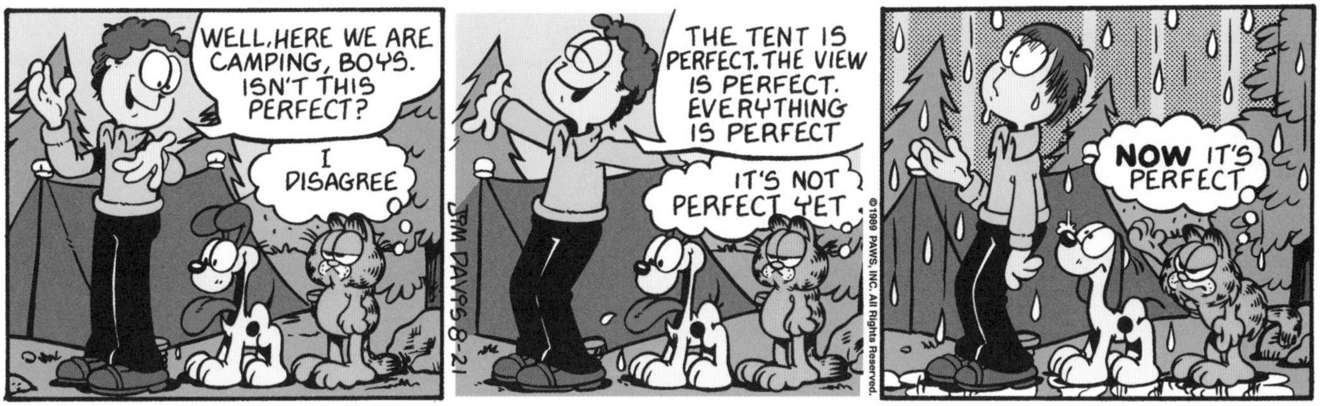
WELL, HERE WE ARE CAMPING, BOYS. ISN'T THIS PERFECT?
I DISAGREE
JIM DAVIS 8-21
THE TENT IS PERFECT. THE VIEW IS PERFECT. EVERYTHING IS PERFECT
IT'S NOT PERFECT YET
© 1989 PAWS, INC. All Rights Reserved.
NOW IT'S PERFECT

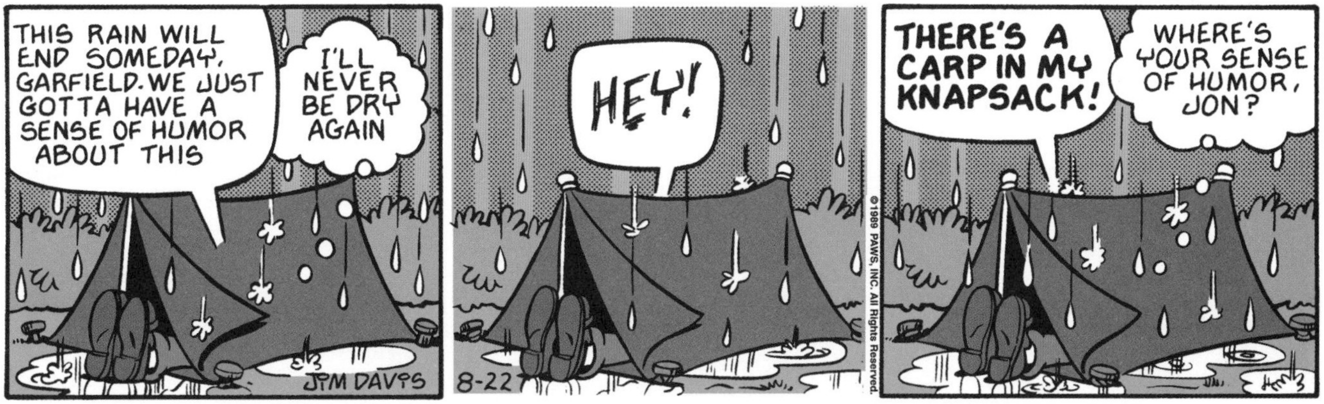
THIS RAIN WILL END SOMEDAY, GARFIELD. WE JUST GOTTA HAVE A SENSE OF HUMOR ABOUT THIS
I'LL NEVER BE DRY AGAIN
JIM DAVIS
HEY!
8-22
© 1989 PAWS, INC. All Rights Reserved.
THERE'S A CARP IN MY KNAPSACK!
WHERE'S YOUR SENSE OF HUMOR, JON?

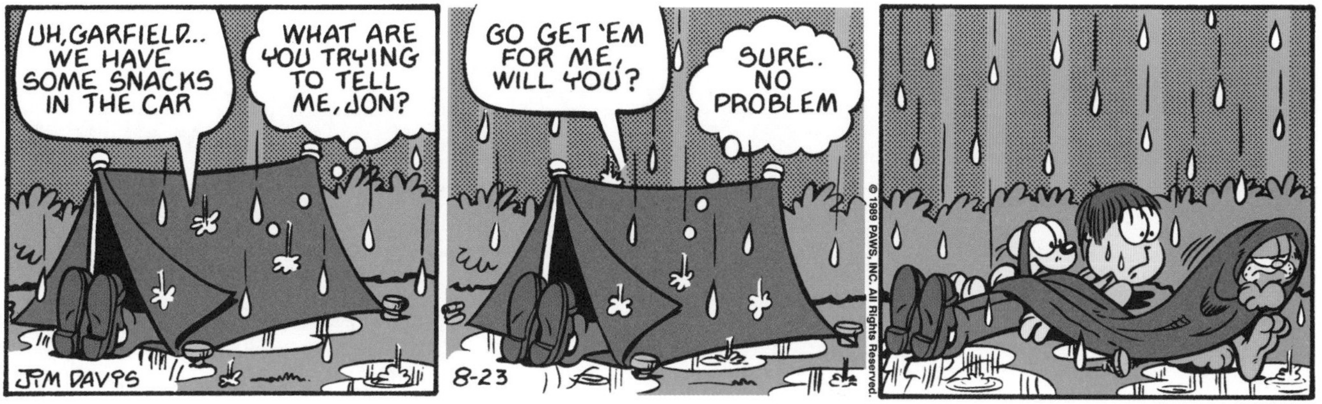
UH, GARFIELD... WE HAVE SOME SNACKS IN THE CAR
WHAT ARE YOU TRYING TO TELL ME, JON?
JIM DAVIS
GO GET 'EM FOR ME, WILL YOU?
SURE. NO PROBLEM
8-23
© 1989 PAWS, INC. All Rights Reserved.

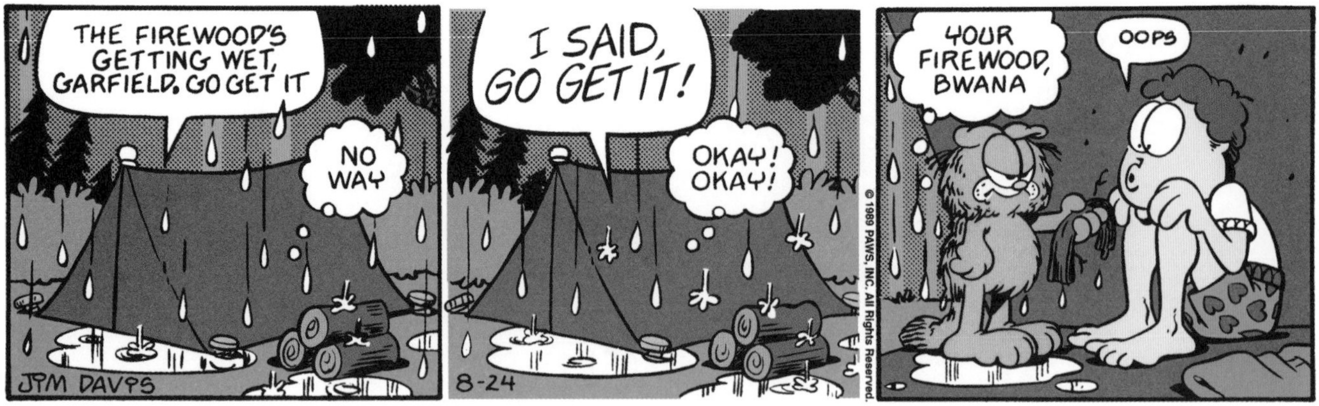
THE FIREWOOD'S GETTING WET, GARFIELD. GO GET IT
NO WAY
JIM DAVIS
I SAID, GO GET IT!
OKAY! OKAY!
8-24
© 1989 PAWS, INC. All Rights Reserved.
YOUR FIREWOOD, BWANA
OOPS

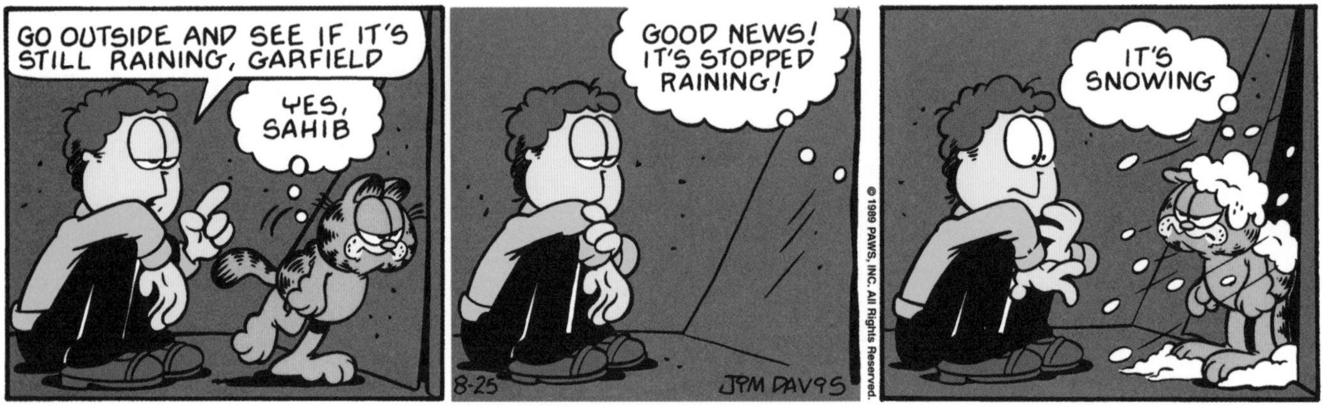
GO OUTSIDE AND SEE IF IT'S STILL RAINING, GARFIELD
YES, SAHIB
GOOD NEWS! IT'S STOPPED RAINING!
8-25
JIM DAVIS
© 1989 PAWS, INC. All Rights Reserved.
IT'S SNOWING

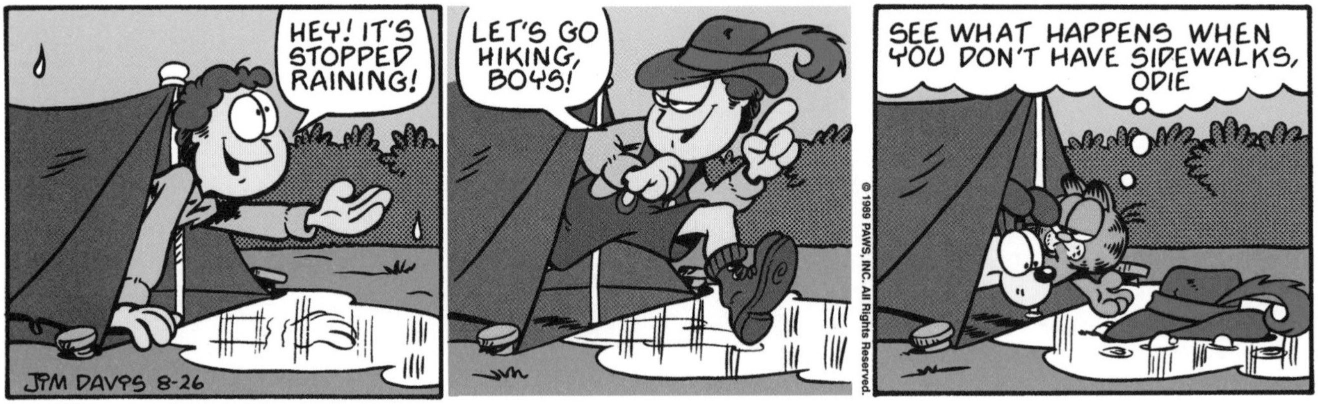
HEY! IT'S STOPPED RAINING!
JIM DAVIS 8-26
LET'S GO HIKING, BOYS!
© 1989 PAWS, INC. All Rights Reserved.
SEE WHAT HAPPENS WHEN YOU DON'T HAVE SIDEWALKS, ODIE

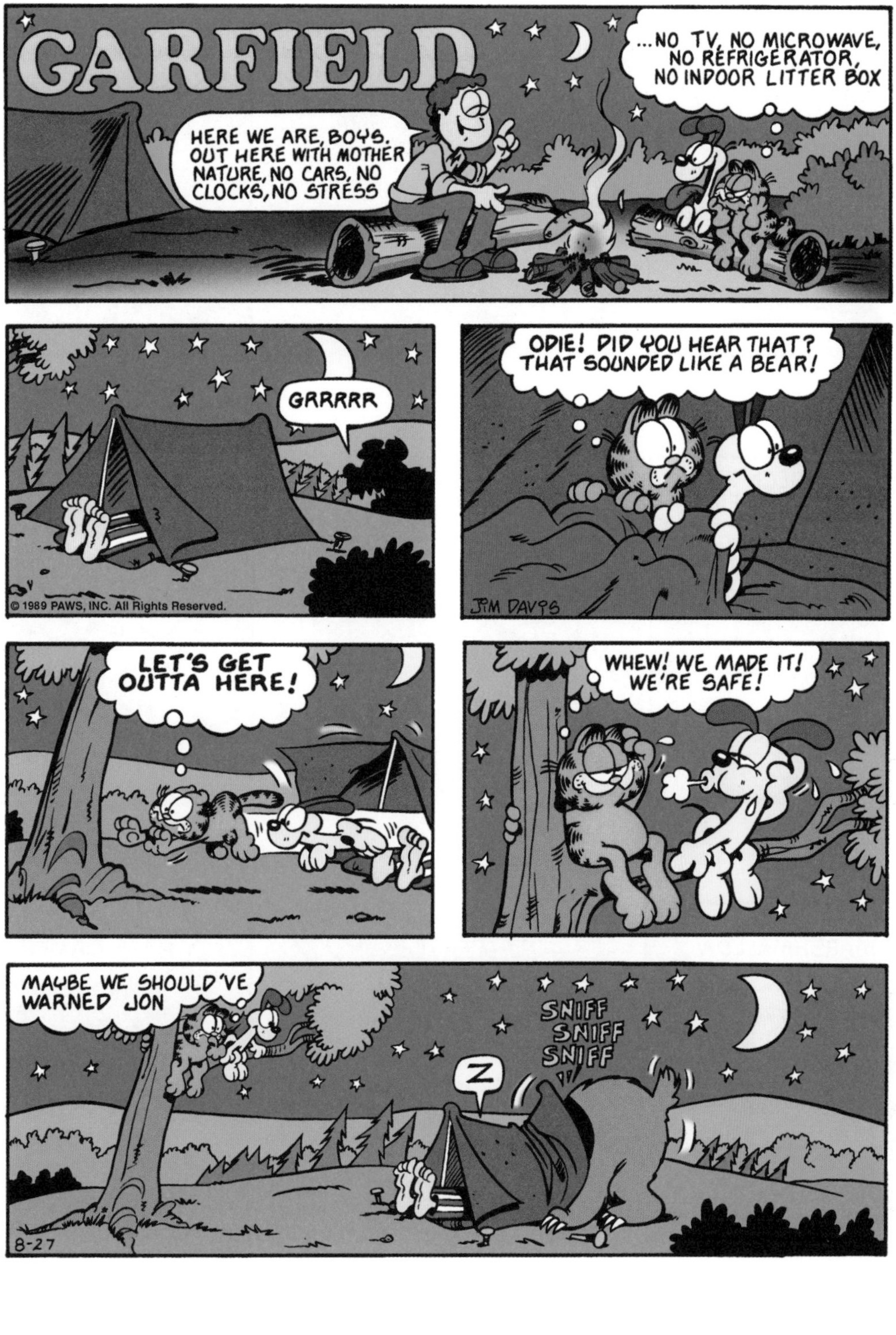
GARFIELD
HERE WE ARE, BOYS. OUT HERE WITH MOTHER NATURE, NO CARS, NO CLOCKS, NO STRESS
...NO TV, NO MICROWAVE, NO REFRIGERATOR, NO INDOOR LITTER BOX
GRRRRR
© 1989 PAWS, INC. All Rights Reserved.
ODIE! DID YOU HEAR THAT? THAT SOUNDED LIKE A BEAR!
JIM DAVIS
LET'S GET OUTTA HERE!
WHEW! WE MADE IT! WE'RE SAFE!
MAYBE WE SHOULD'VE WARNED JON
SNIFF SNIFF SNIFF
Z
8-27

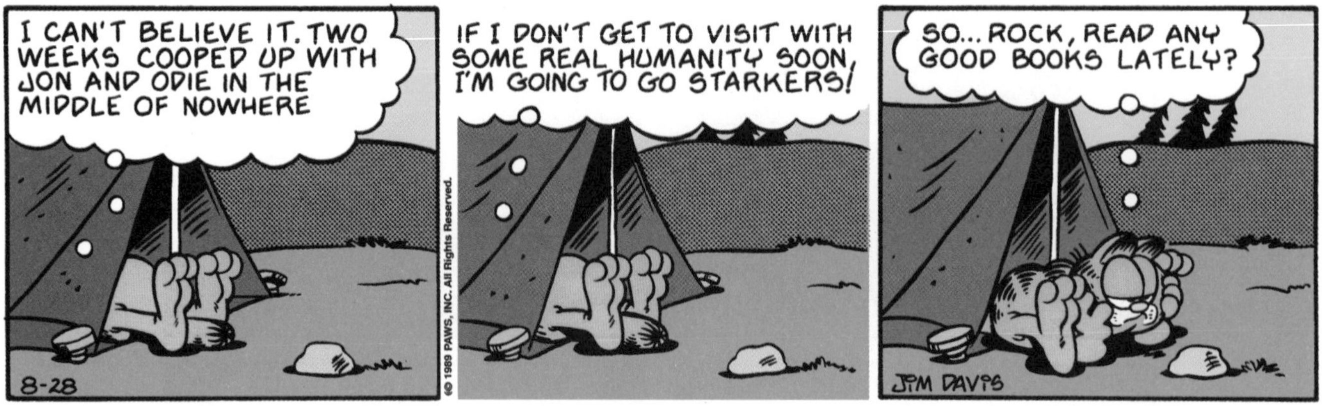
I CAN'T BELIEVE IT. TWO WEEKS COOPED UP WITH JON AND ODIE IN THE MIDDLE OF NOWHERE
IF I DON'T GET TO VISIT WITH SOME REAL HUMANITY SOON, I'M GOING TO GO STARKERS!
SO... ROCK, READ ANY GOOD BOOKS LATELY?
8-28
© 1989 PAWS, INC. All Rights Reserved.
JIM DAVIS

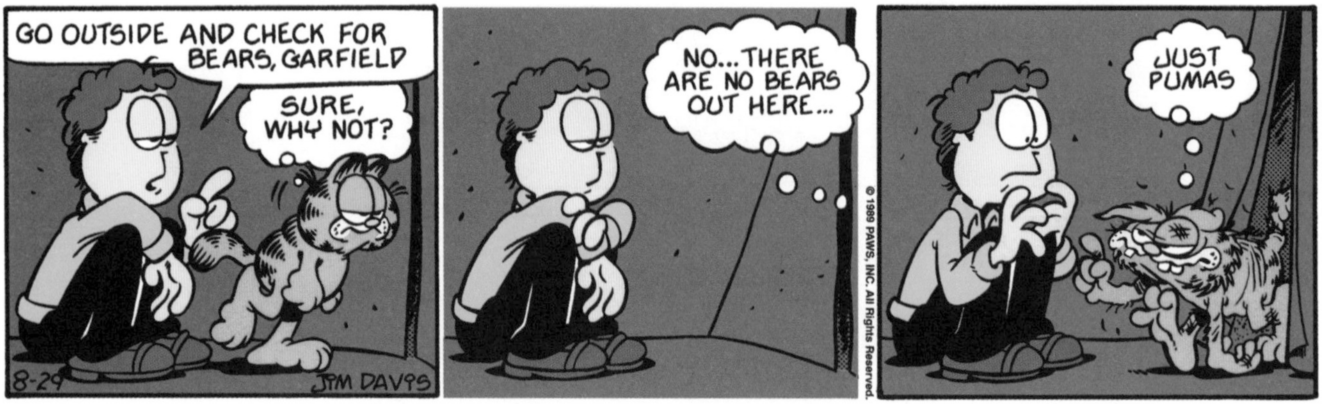
GO OUTSIDE AND CHECK FOR BEARS, GARFIELD
SURE, WHY NOT?
NO... THERE ARE NO BEARS OUT HERE...
JUST PUMAS
8-29
JIM DAVIS
© 1989 PAWS, INC. All Rights Reserved.

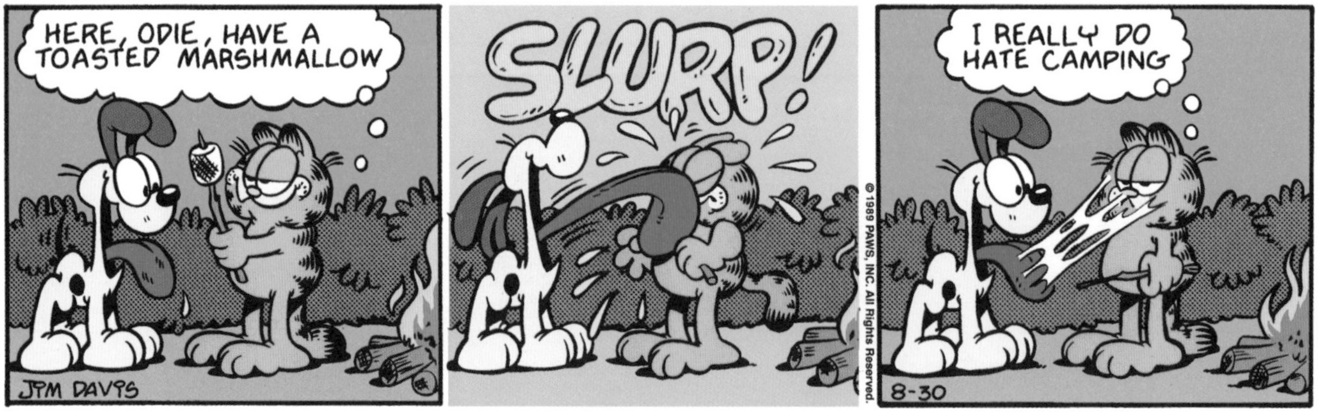
HERE, ODIE, HAVE A TOASTED MARSHMALLOW
SLURP!
I REALLY DO HATE CAMPING
JIM DAVIS
© 1989 PAWS, INC. All Rights Reserved.
8-30

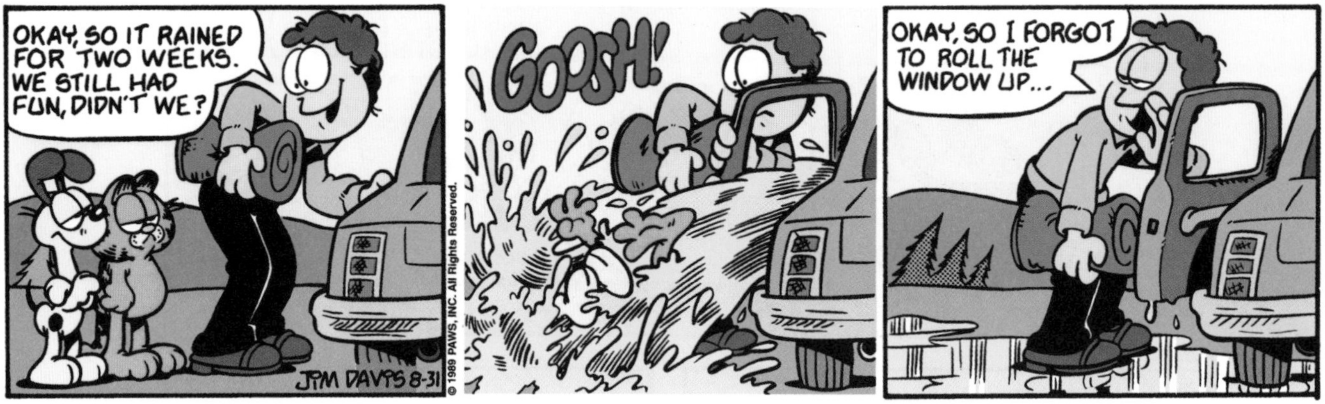
OKAY, SO IT RAINED FOR TWO WEEKS. WE STILL HAD FUN, DIDN'T WE?
JIM DAVIS 8-31
© 1989 PAWS, INC. All Rights Reserved.
GOOSH!
OKAY, SO I FORGOT TO ROLL THE WINDOW UP...

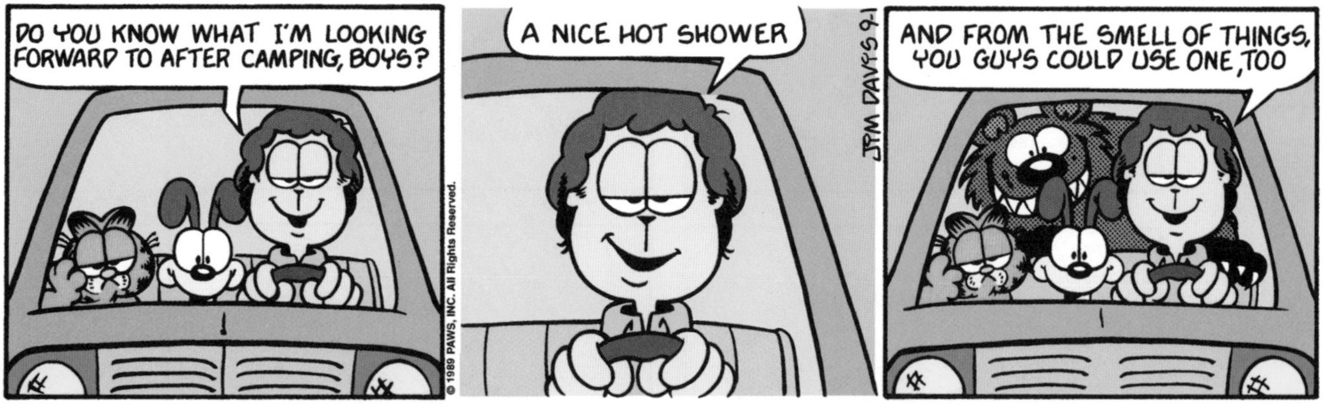
DO YOU KNOW WHAT I'M LOOKING FORWARD TO AFTER CAMPING, BOYS?
© 1989 PAWS, INC. All Rights Reserved.
A NICE HOT SHOWER
JIM DAVIS 9-1
AND FROM THE SMELL OF THINGS, YOU GUYS COULD USE ONE, TOO

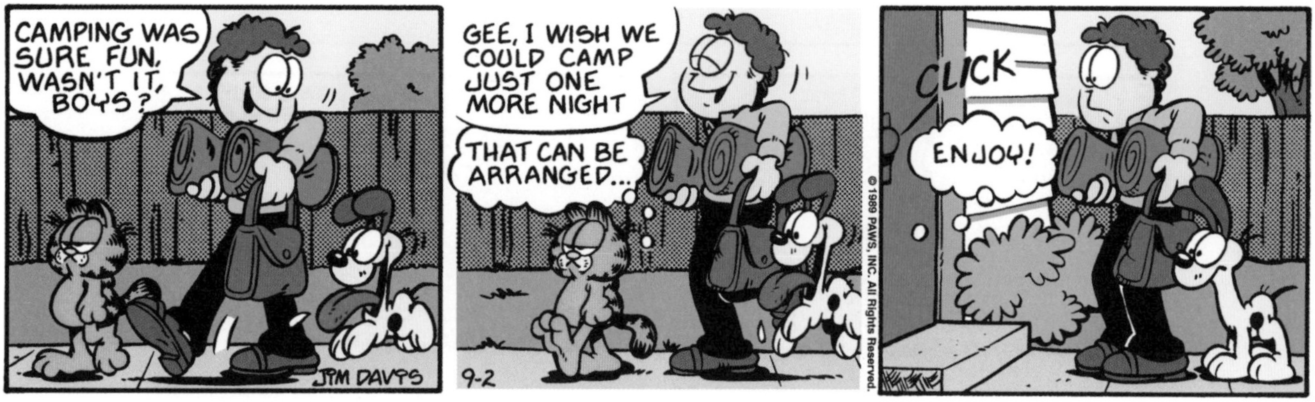
CAMPING WAS SURE FUN, WASN'T IT, BOYS?
JIM DAVIS
GEE, I WISH WE COULD CAMP JUST ONE MORE NIGHT
THAT CAN BE ARRANGED...
9-2
© 1989 PAWS, INC. All Rights Reserved.
CLICK
ENJOY!

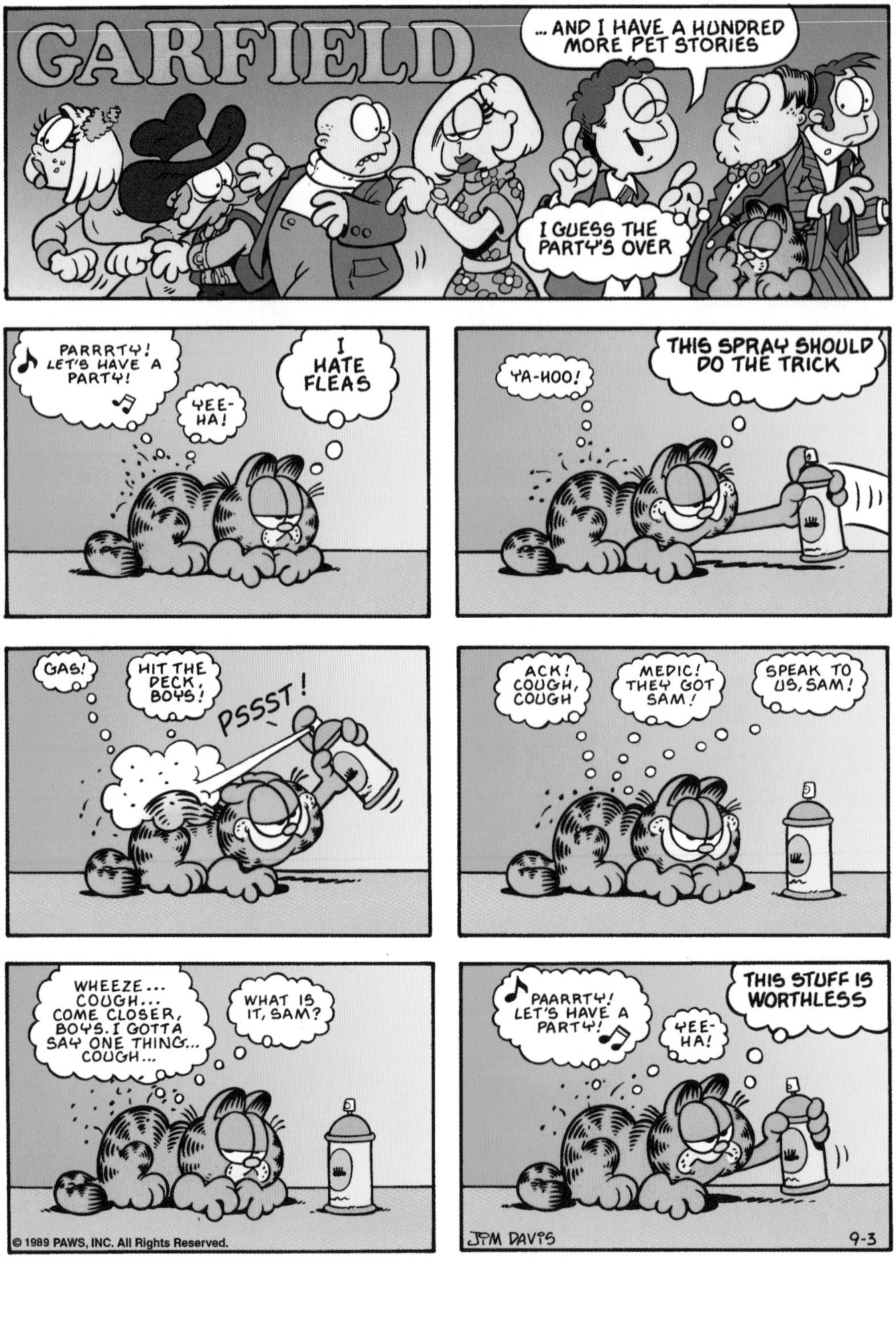
GARFIELD
... AND I HAVE A HUNDRED MORE PET STORIES
I GUESS THE PARTY'S OVER
PARRRTY! LET'S HAVE A PARTY!
YEE-HA!
I HATE FLEAS
YA-HOO!
THIS SPRAY SHOULD DO THE TRICK
GAS!
HIT THE DECK, BOYS!
PSSST!
ACK! COUGH, COUGH
MEDIC! THEY GOT SAM!
SPEAK TO US, SAM!
WHEEZE... COUGH... COME CLOSER, BOYS. I GOTTA SAY ONE THING... COUGH...
WHAT IS IT, SAM?
PAARRTY! LET'S HAVE A PARTY!
YEE-HA!
THIS STUFF IS WORTHLESS
© 1989 PAWS, INC. All Rights Reserved.
JIM DAVIS
9-3

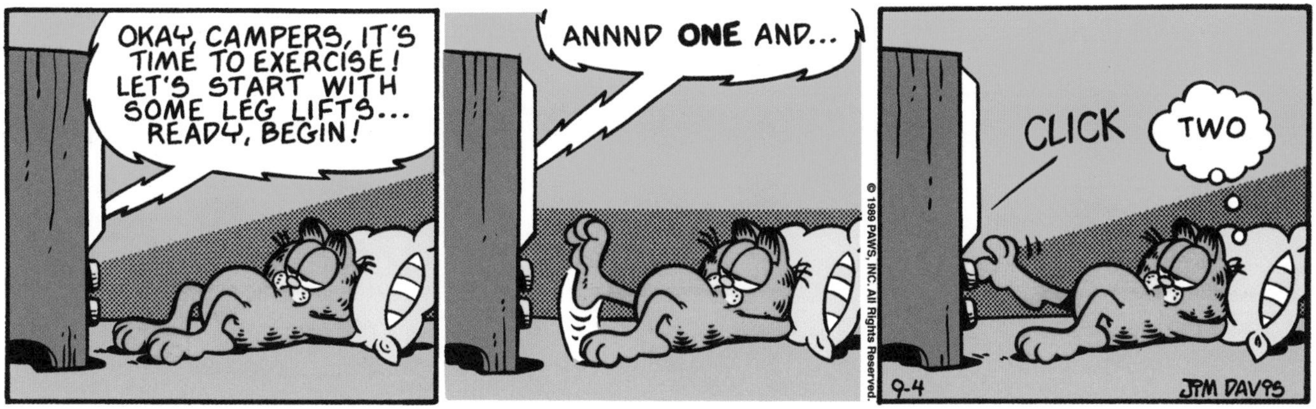
OKAY, CAMPERS, IT'S TIME TO EXERCISE! LET'S START WITH SOME LEG LIFTS... READY, BEGIN!
ANNND ONE AND...
CLICK
TWO
© 1989 PAWS, INC. All Rights Reserved.
9-4
JIM DAVIS

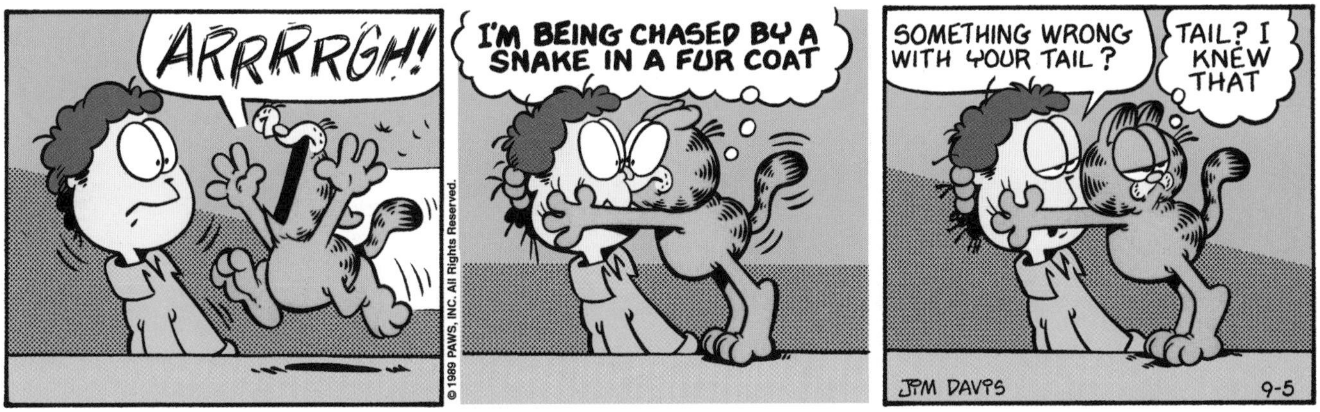
ARRRRGH!
I'M BEING CHASED BY A SNAKE IN A FUR COAT
SOMETHING WRONG WITH YOUR TAIL?
TAIL? I KNEW THAT
© 1989 PAWS, INC. All Rights Reserved.
JIM DAVIS
9-5

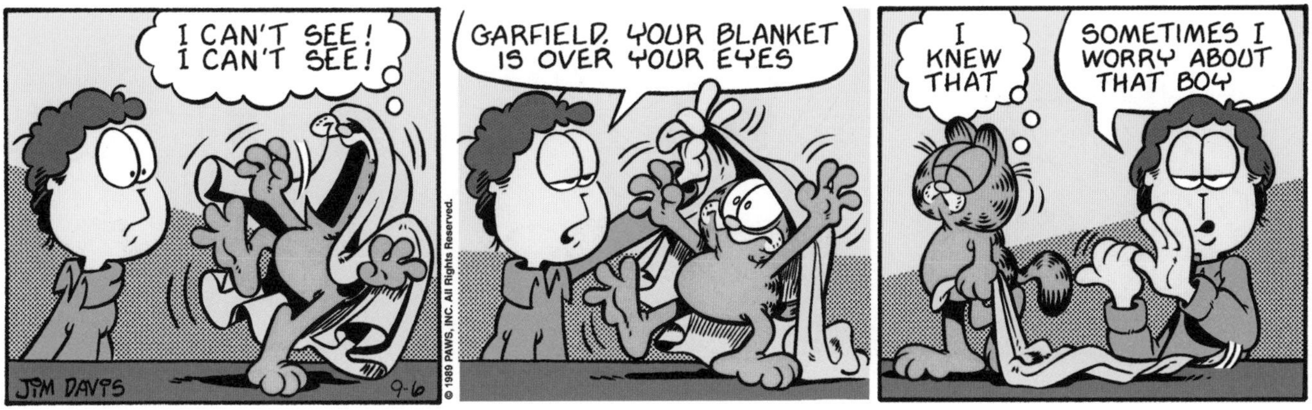
I CAN'T SEE! I CAN'T SEE!
GARFIELD, YOUR BLANKET IS OVER YOUR EYES
I KNEW THAT
SOMETIMES I WORRY ABOUT THAT BOY
© 1989 PAWS, INC. All Rights Reserved.
JIM DAVIS
9-6

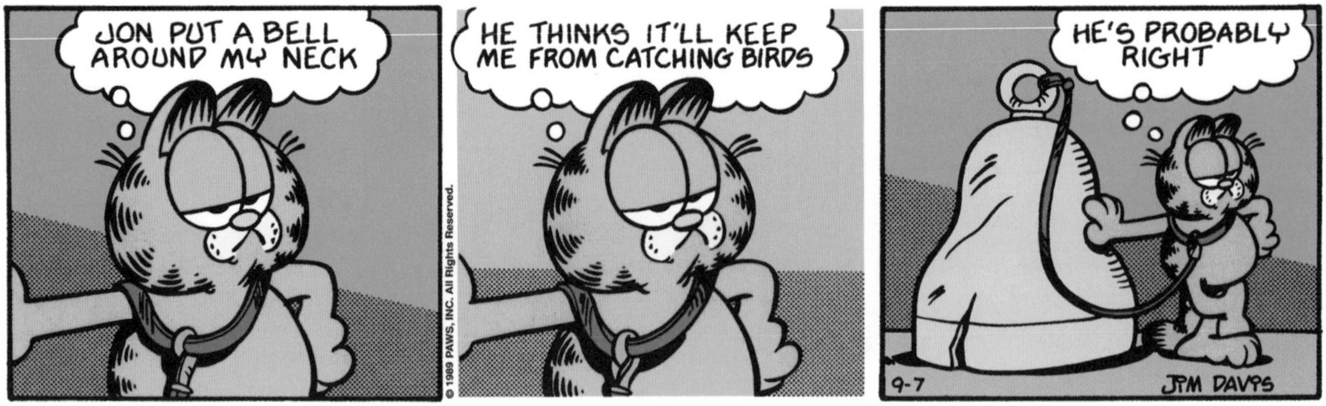
JON PUT A BELL AROUND MY NECK
HE THINKS IT'LL KEEP ME FROM CATCHING BIRDS
HE'S PROBABLY RIGHT
© 1989 PAWS, INC. All Rights Reserved.
9-7
JIM DAVIS

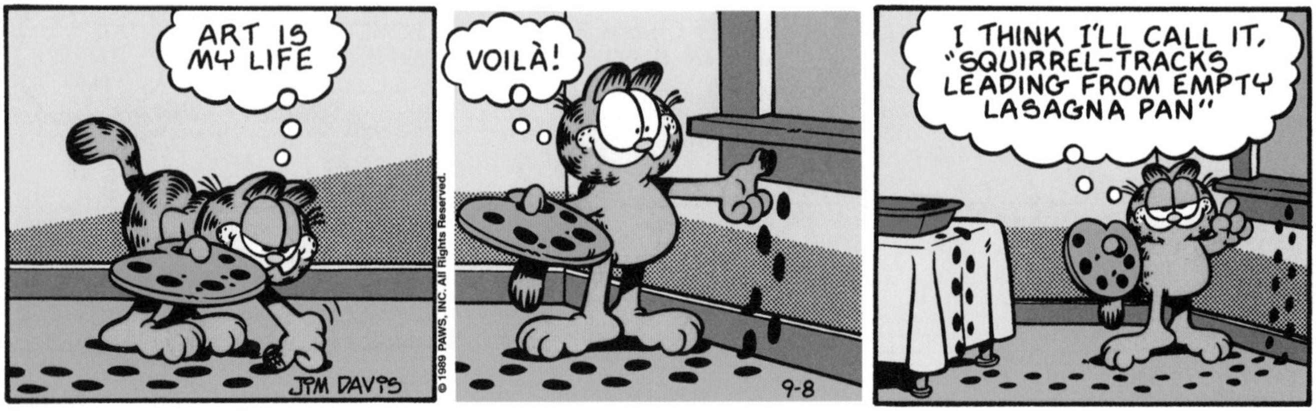
ART IS MY LIFE
JIM DAVIS
VOILÀ!
9-8
I THINK I'LL CALL IT, "SQUIRREL-TRACKS LEADING FROM EMPTY LASAGNA PAN"
© 1989 PAWS, INC. All Rights Reserved.

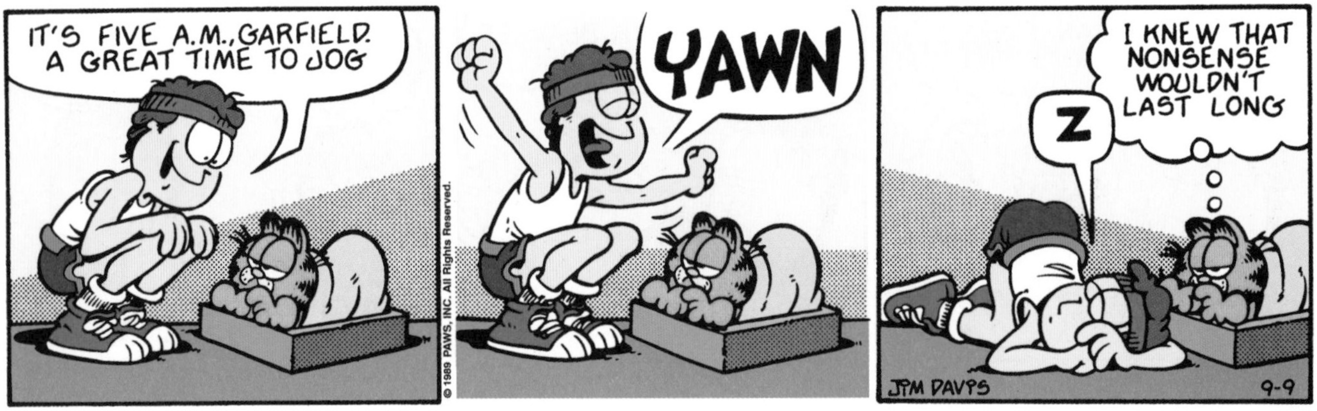
IT'S FIVE A.M., GARFIELD. A GREAT TIME TO JOG
YAWN
Z
I KNEW THAT NONSENSE WOULDN'T LAST LONG
© 1989 PAWS, INC. All Rights Reserved.
JIM DAVIS
9-9

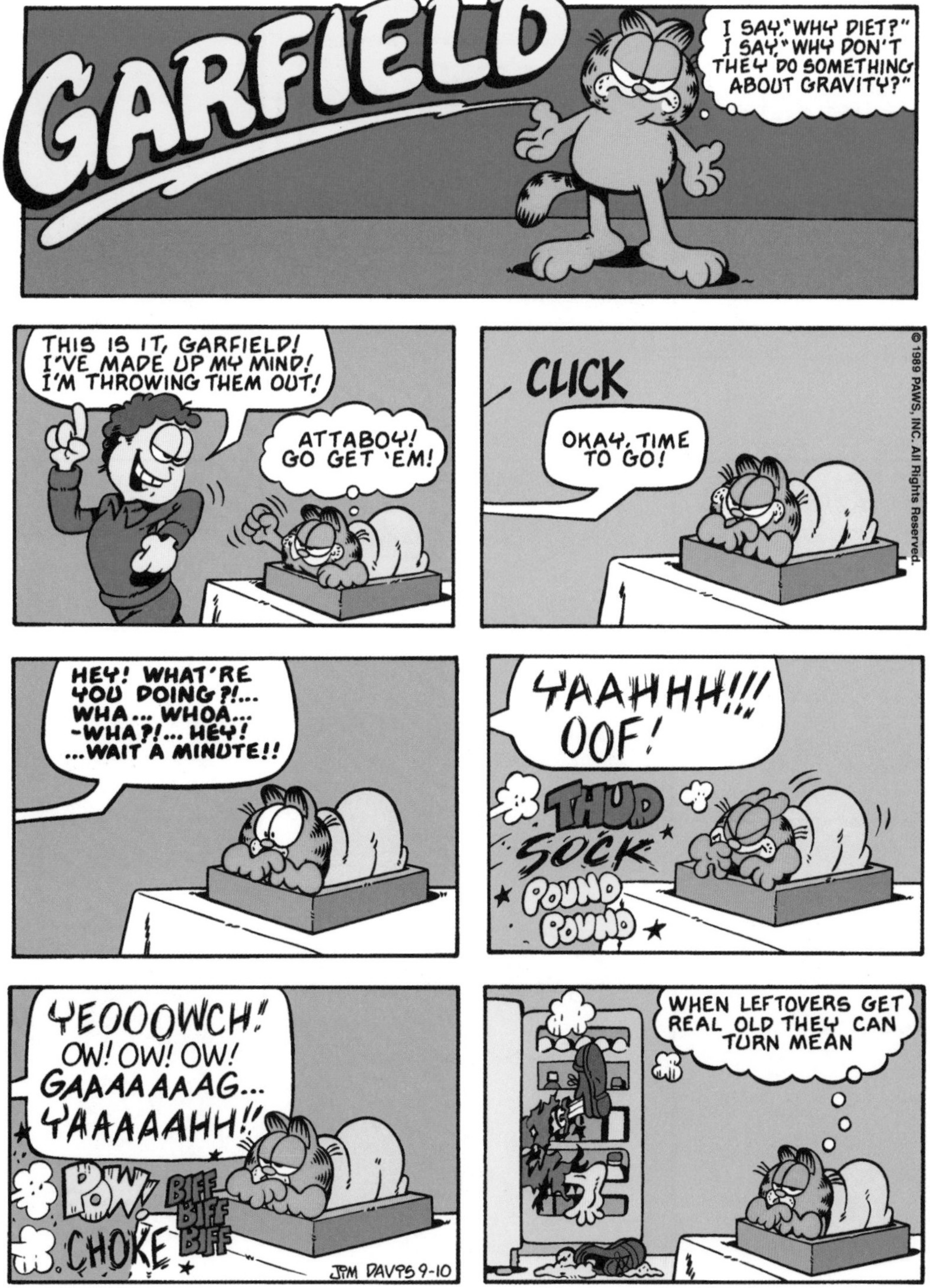
GARFIELD
I SAY, "WHY DIET?" I SAY, "WHY DON'T THEY DO SOMETHING ABOUT GRAVITY?"
THIS IS IT, GARFIELD! I'VE MADE UP MY MIND! I'M THROWING THEM OUT!
ATTABOY! GO GET 'EM!
CLICK
OKAY, TIME TO GO!
HEY! WHAT'RE YOU DOING?!... WHA... WHOA... -WHA?!... HEY! ...WAIT A MINUTE!!
YAAHHH!!! OOF!
THUD
SOCK
POUND
POUND
YEOOOWCH! OW! OW! OW! GAAAAAAAG... YAAAAAHH!!
POW!
BIFF
BIFF
BIFF
CHOKE
JIM DAVIS 9-10
WHEN LEFTOVERS GET REAL OLD THEY CAN TURN MEAN
© 1989 PAWS, INC. All Rights Reserved.

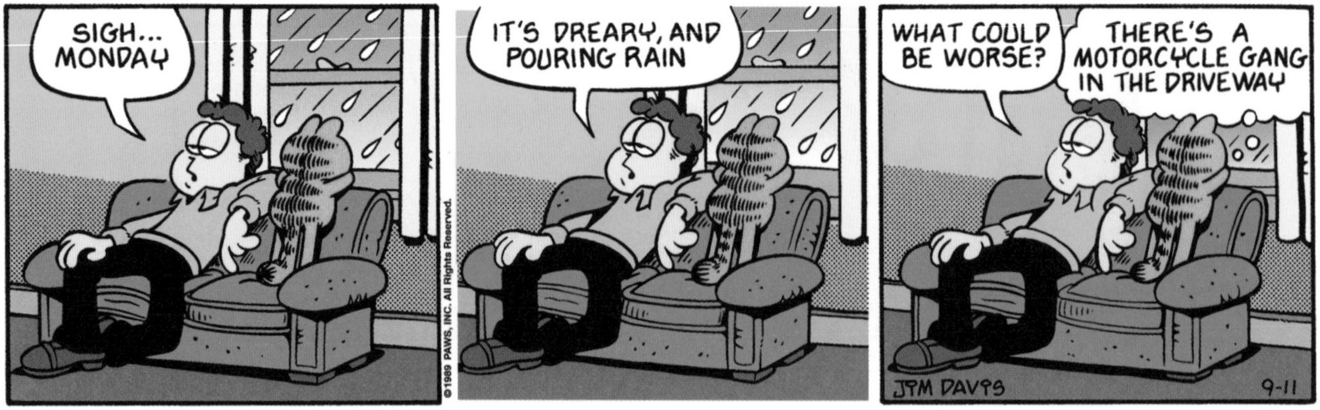
SIGH... MONDAY
©1989 PAWS, INC. All Rights Reserved.
IT'S DREARY, AND POURING RAIN
WHAT COULD BE WORSE?
THERE'S A MOTORCYCLE GANG IN THE DRIVEWAY
JIM DAVIS
9-11

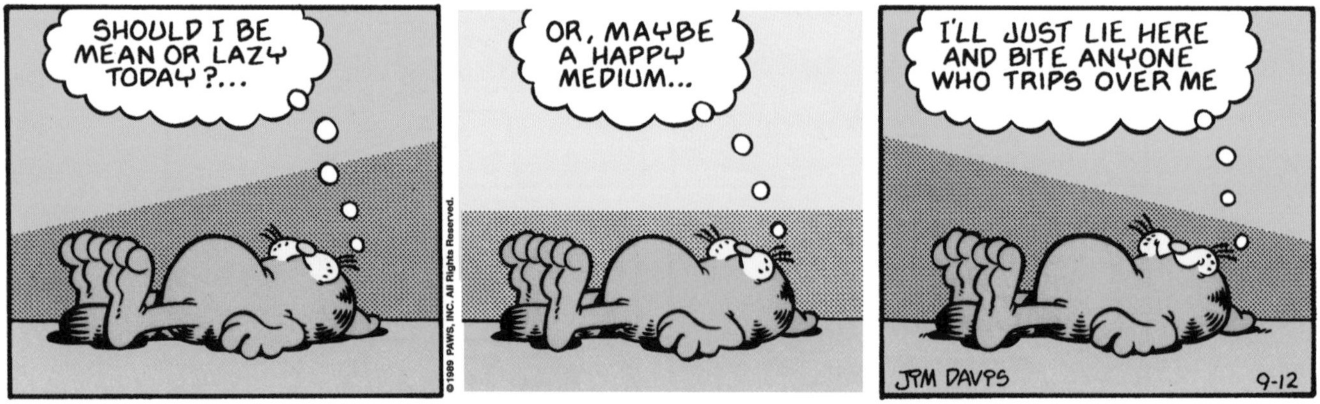
SHOULD I BE MEAN OR LAZY TODAY?...
©1989 PAWS, INC. All Rights Reserved.
OR, MAYBE A HAPPY MEDIUM...
I'LL JUST LIE HERE AND BITE ANYONE WHO TRIPS OVER ME
JIM DAVIS
9-12

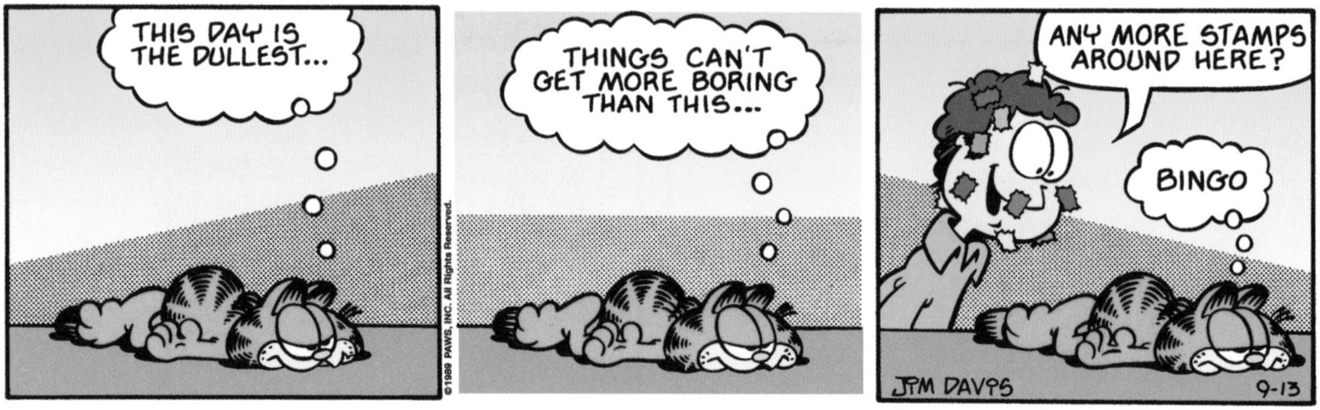
THIS DAY IS THE DULLEST...
©1989 PAWS, INC. All Rights Reserved.
THINGS CAN'T GET MORE BORING THAN THIS...
ANY MORE STAMPS AROUND HERE?
BINGO
JIM DAVIS
9-13

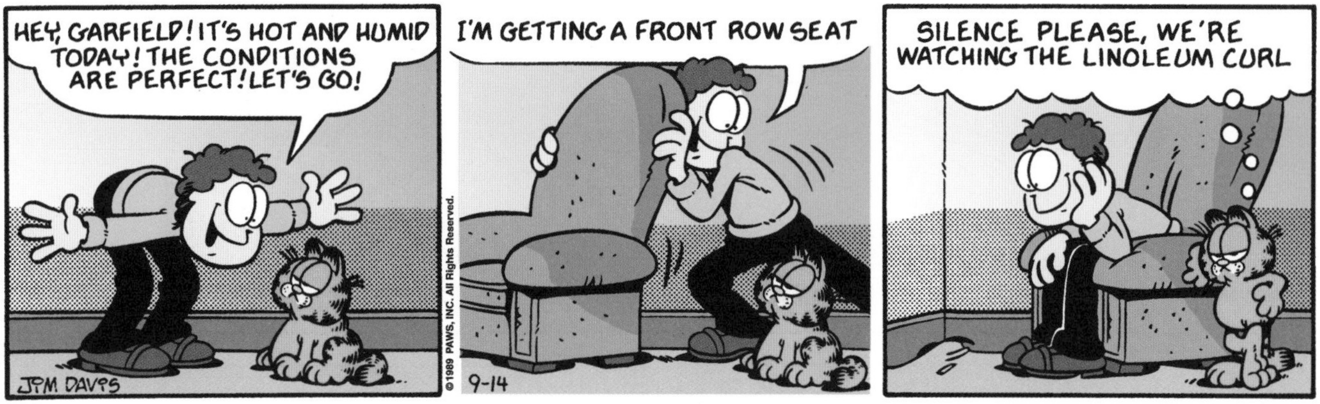
HEY, GARFIELD! IT'S HOT AND HUMID TODAY! THE CONDITIONS ARE PERFECT! LET'S GO!
JIM DAVIS
I'M GETTING A FRONT ROW SEAT
©1989 PAWS, INC. All Rights Reserved.
9-14
SILENCE PLEASE, WE'RE WATCHING THE LINOLEUM CURL

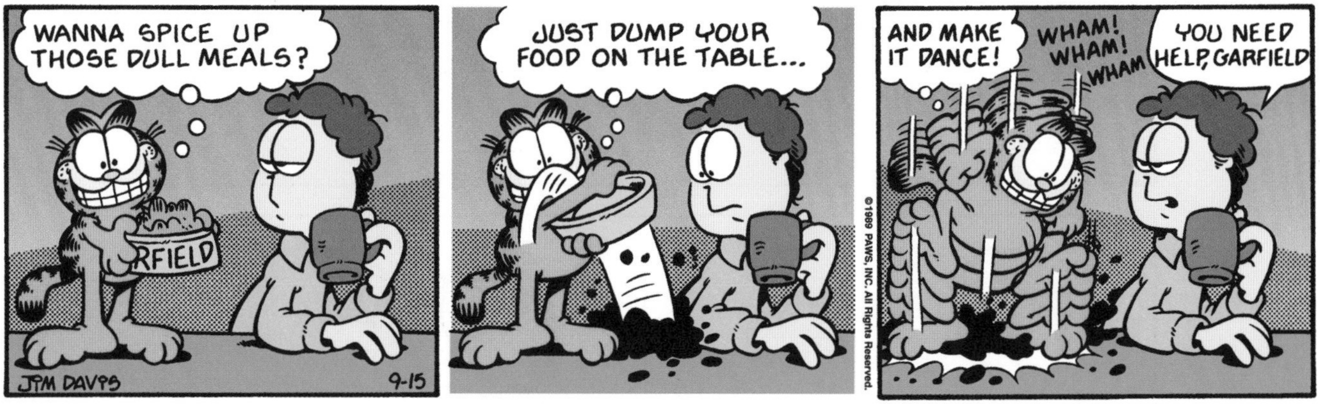
WANNA SPICE UP THOSE DULL MEALS?
RFIELD
JIM DAVIS
9-15
JUST DUMP YOUR FOOD ON THE TABLE...
©1989 PAWS, INC. All Rights Reserved.
AND MAKE IT DANCE!
WHAM! WHAM! WHAM
YOU NEED HELP, GARFIELD

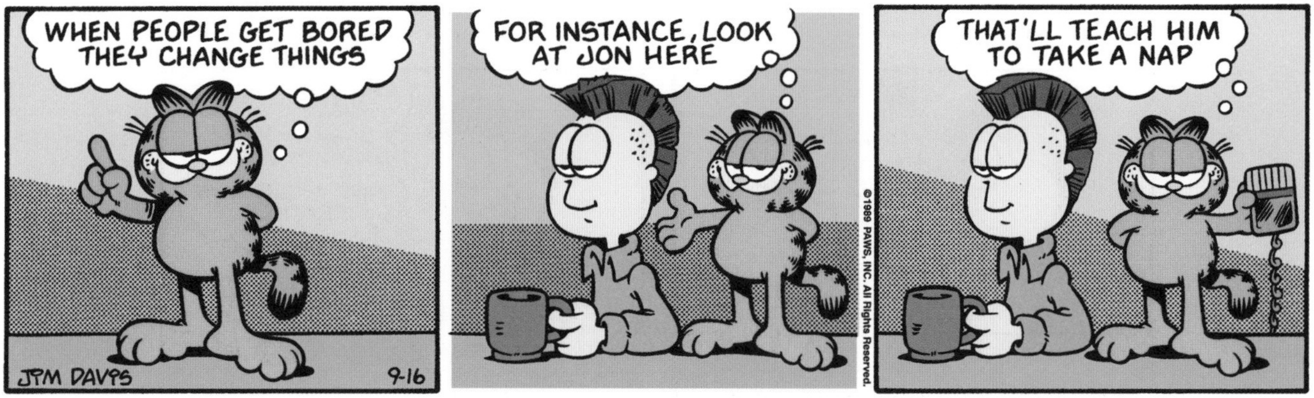
WHEN PEOPLE GET BORED THEY CHANGE THINGS
JIM DAVIS
9-16
FOR INSTANCE, LOOK AT JON HERE
©1989 PAWS, INC. All Rights Reserved.
THAT'LL TEACH HIM TO TAKE A NAP

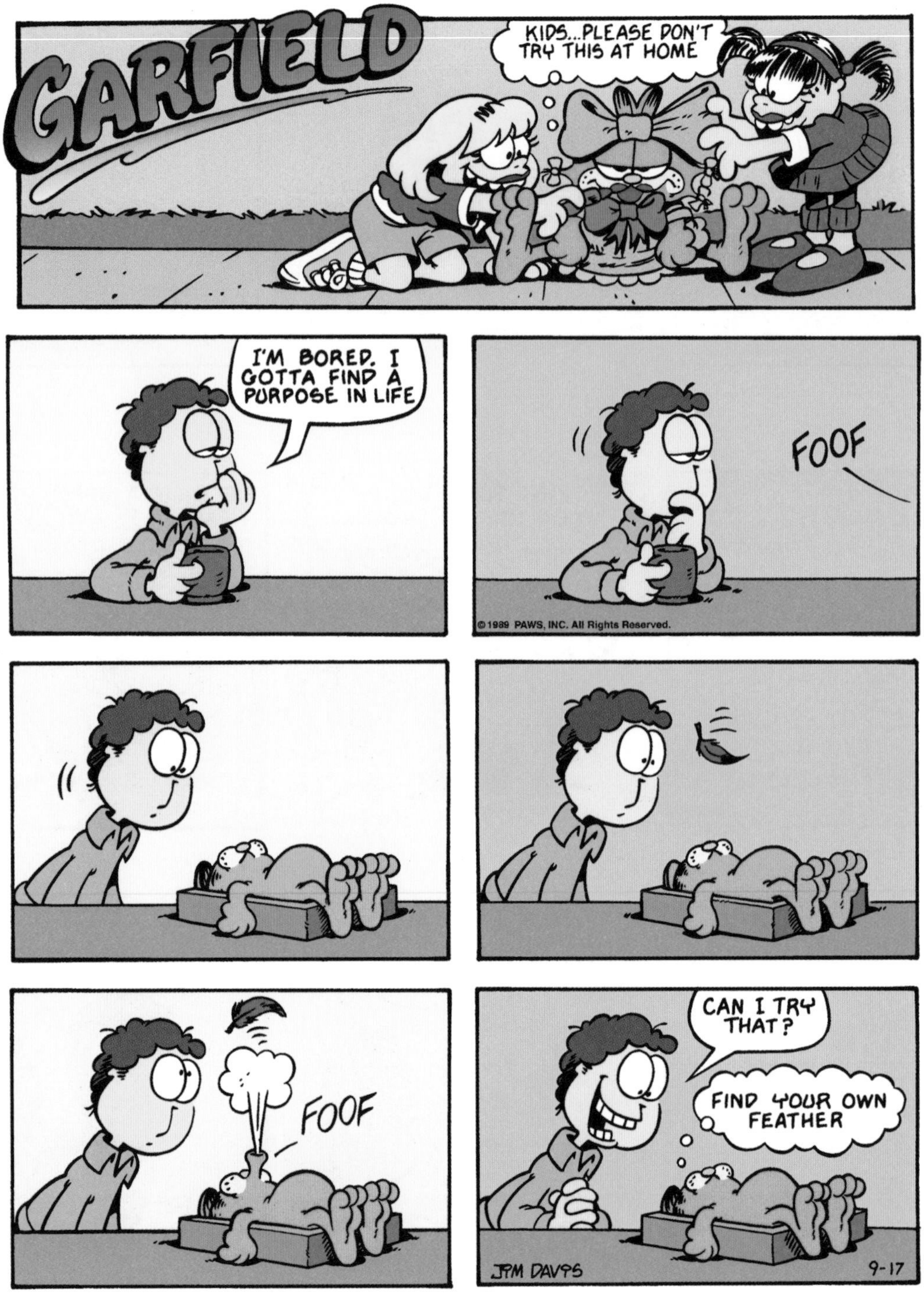
GARFIELD
KIDS...PLEASE DON'T TRY THIS AT HOME
I'M BORED. I GOTTA FIND A PURPOSE IN LIFE
FOOF
©1989 PAWS, INC. All Rights Reserved.
FOOF
CAN I TRY THAT?
FIND YOUR OWN FEATHER
JIM DAVIS
9-17

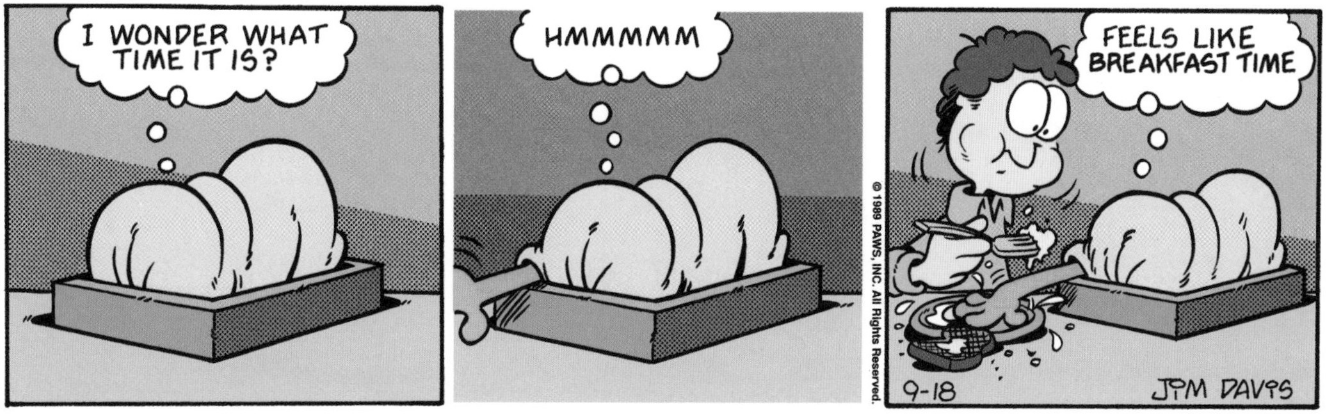
I WONDER WHAT TIME IT IS?
HMMMMM
FEELS LIKE BREAKFAST TIME
© 1989 PAWS, INC. All Rights Reserved.
9-18
JIM DAVIS

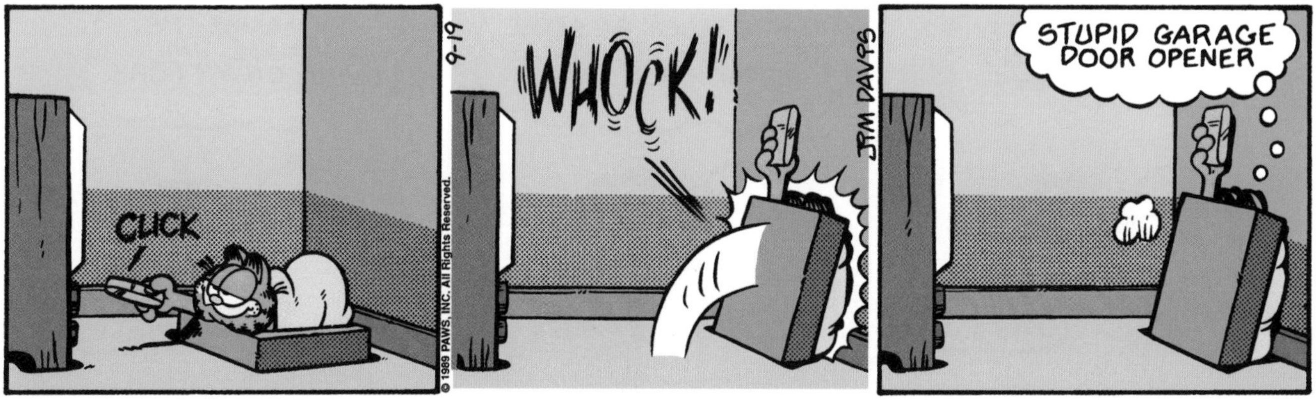
CLICK
© 1989 PAWS, INC. All Rights Reserved.
9-19
WHOCK!
JIM DAVIS
STUPID GARAGE DOOR OPENER

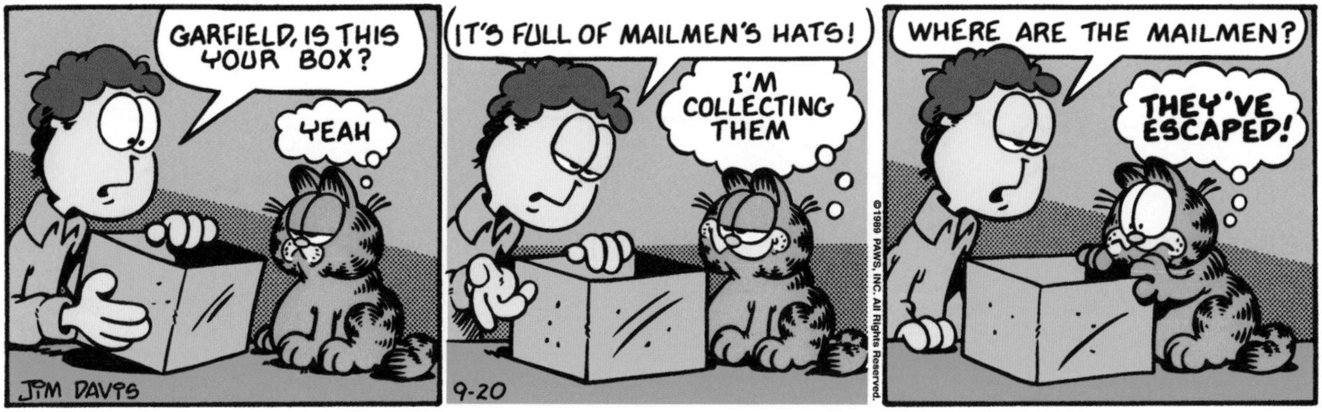
GARFIELD, IS THIS YOUR BOX?
YEAH
JIM DAVIS
IT'S FULL OF MAILMEN'S HATS!
I'M COLLECTING THEM
9-20
© 1989 PAWS, INC. All Rights Reserved.
WHERE ARE THE MAILMEN?
THEY'VE ESCAPED!

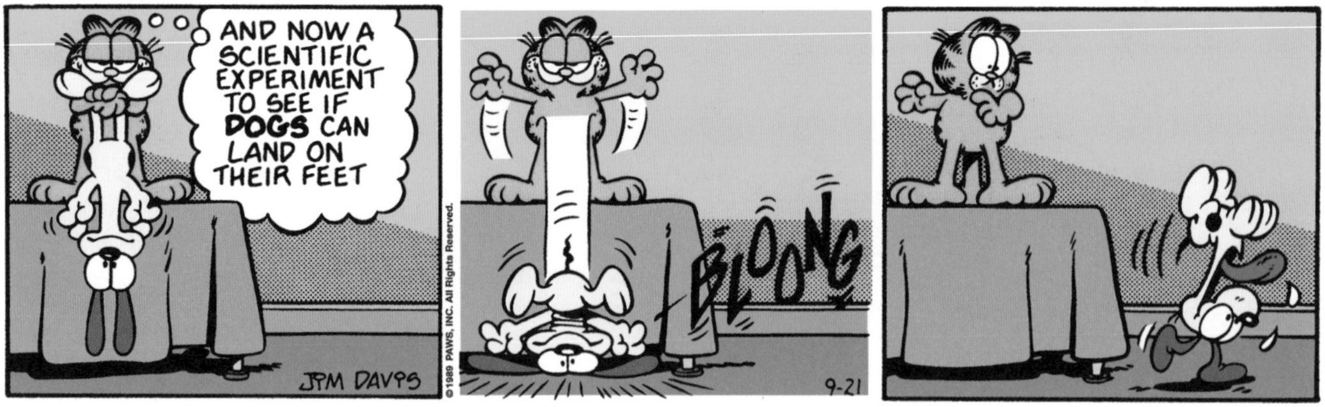
AND NOW A SCIENTIFIC EXPERIMENT TO SEE IF DOGS CAN LAND ON THEIR FEET
JIM DAVIS
©1989 PAWS, INC. All Rights Reserved.
BLOONG
9-21

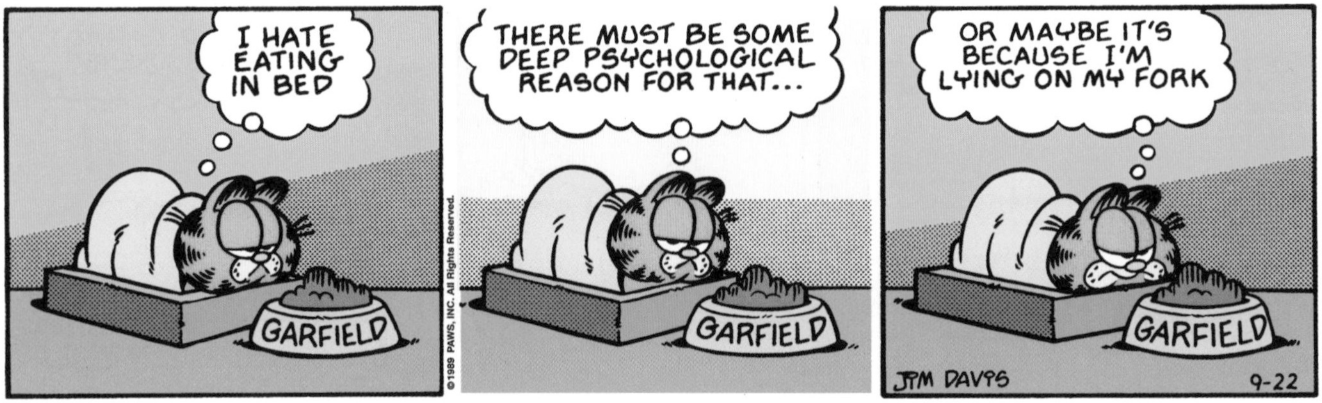
I HATE EATING IN BED
GARFIELD
©1989 PAWS, INC. All Rights Reserved.
THERE MUST BE SOME DEEP PSYCHOLOGICAL REASON FOR THAT...
GARFIELD
OR MAYBE IT'S BECAUSE I'M LYING ON MY FORK
GARFIELD
JIM DAVIS
9-22

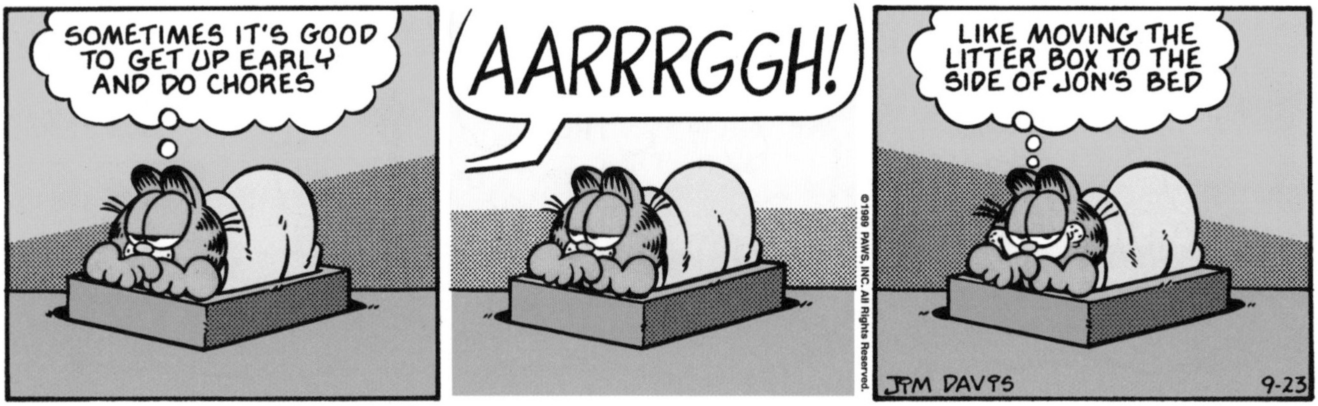
SOMETIMES IT'S GOOD TO GET UP EARLY AND DO CHORES
AARRRGGH!
©1989 PAWS, INC. All Rights Reserved.
LIKE MOVING THE LITTER BOX TO THE SIDE OF JON'S BED
JIM DAVIS
9-23

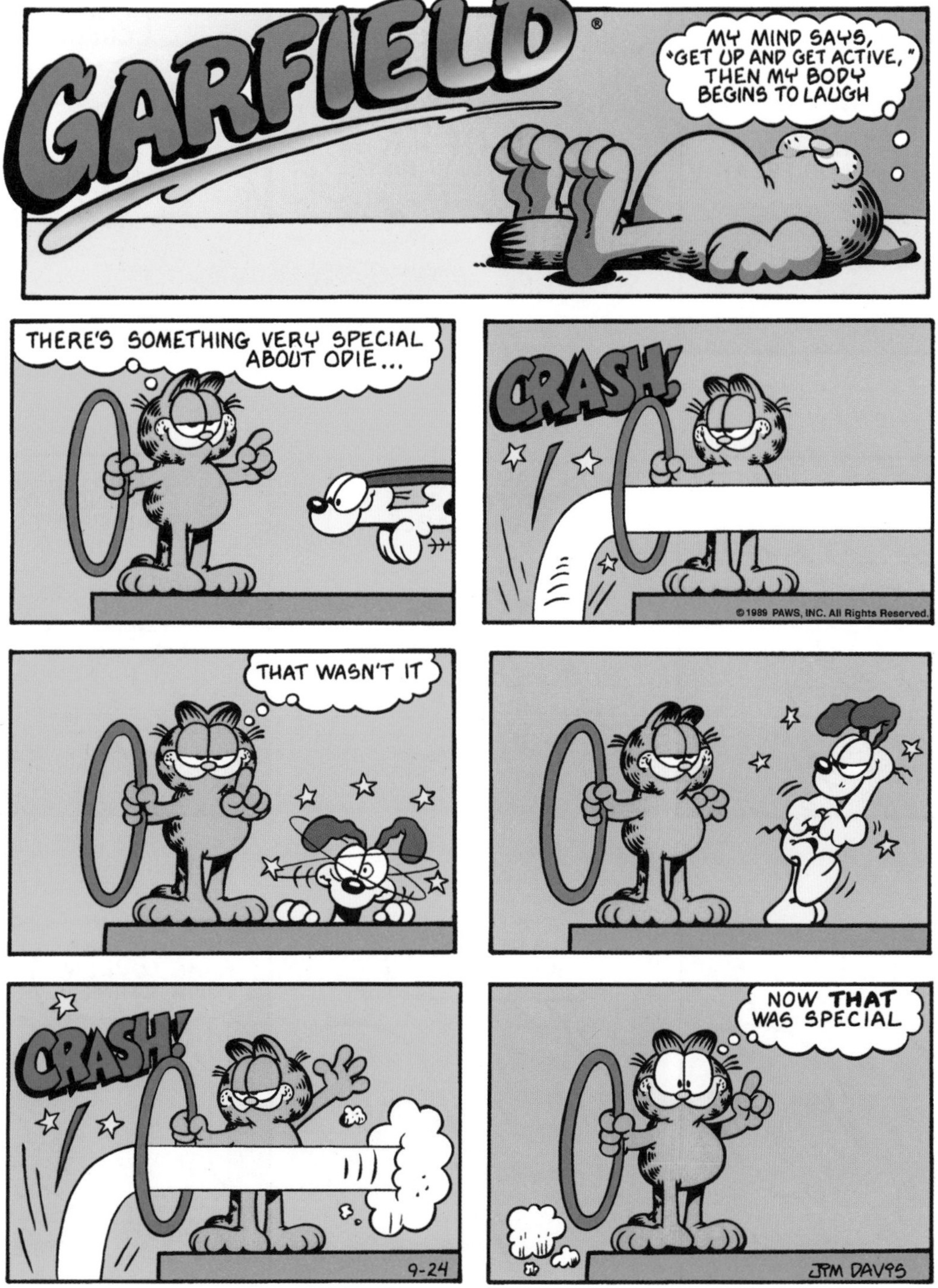
GARFIELD®
MY MIND SAYS, "GET UP AND GET ACTIVE," THEN MY BODY BEGINS TO LAUGH
THERE'S SOMETHING VERY SPECIAL ABOUT ODIE...
CRASH!
©1989 PAWS, INC. All Rights Reserved.
THAT WASN'T IT
CRASH!
9-24
NOW THAT WAS SPECIAL
JIM DAVIS

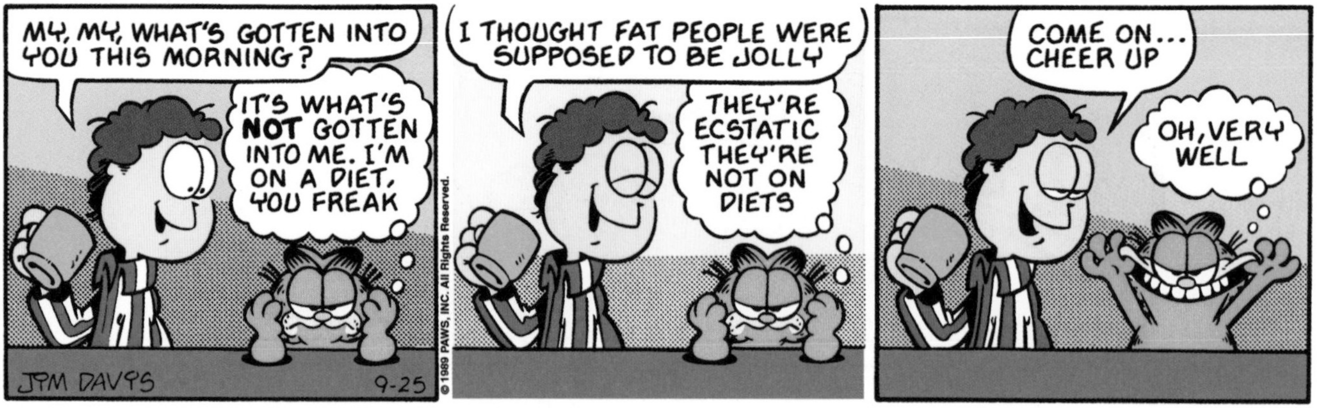
MY, MY, WHAT'S GOTTEN INTO YOU THIS MORNING?
IT'S WHAT'S **NOT** GOTTEN INTO ME. I'M ON A DIET, YOU FREAK
JIM DAVIS
9-25
© 1989 PAWS, INC. All Rights Reserved.
I THOUGHT FAT PEOPLE WERE SUPPOSED TO BE JOLLY
THEY'RE ECSTATIC THEY'RE NOT ON DIETS
COME ON... CHEER UP
OH, VERY WELL

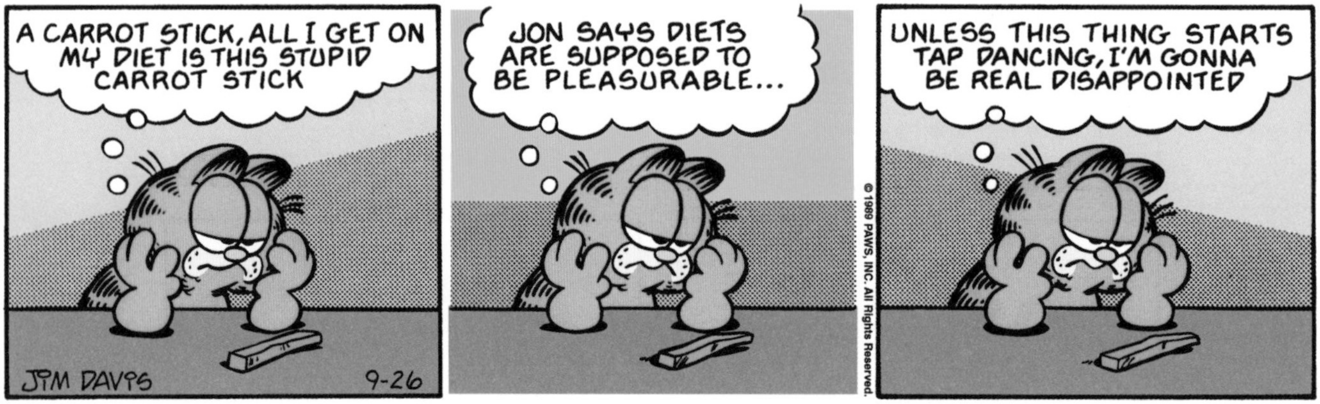
A CARROT STICK, ALL I GET ON MY DIET IS THIS STUPID CARROT STICK
JIM DAVIS
9-26
JON SAYS DIETS ARE SUPPOSED TO BE PLEASURABLE...
© 1989 PAWS, INC. All Rights Reserved.
UNLESS THIS THING STARTS TAP DANCING, I'M GONNA BE REAL DISAPPOINTED

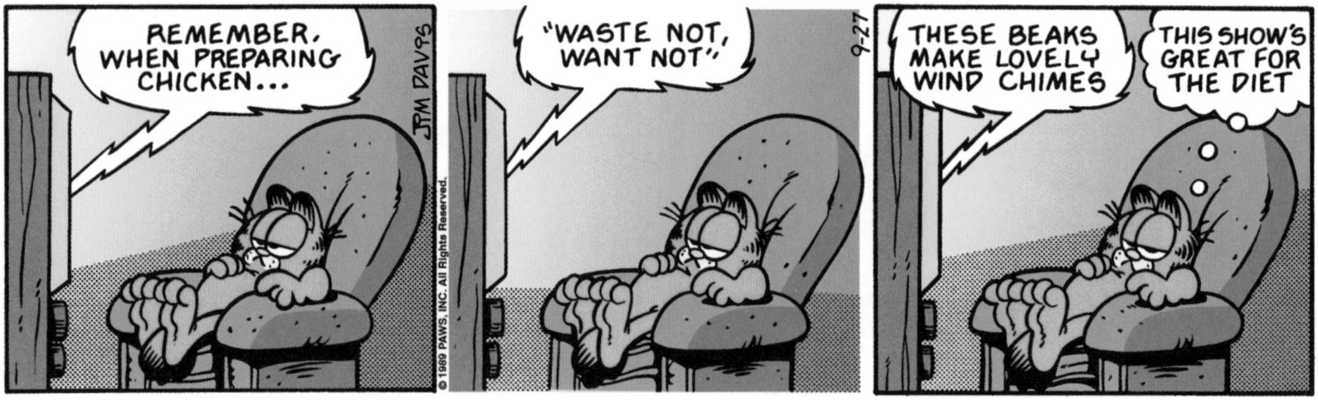
REMEMBER, WHEN PREPARING CHICKEN...
JIM DAVIS
© 1989 PAWS, INC. All Rights Reserved.
"WASTE NOT, WANT NOT"
9-27
THESE BEAKS MAKE LOVELY WIND CHIMES
THIS SHOW'S GREAT FOR THE DIET

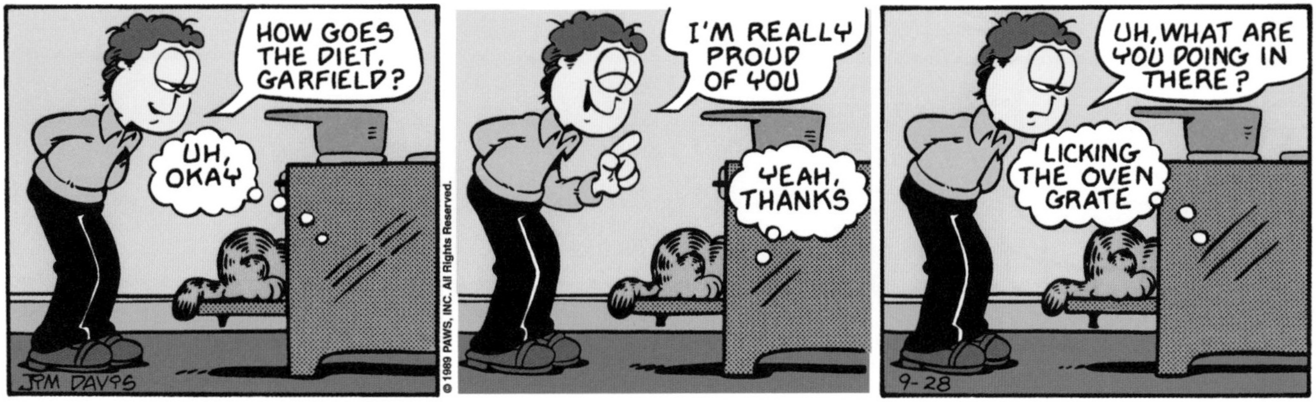
HOW GOES THE DIET, GARFIELD?
UH, OKAY
I'M REALLY PROUD OF YOU
YEAH, THANKS
UH, WHAT ARE YOU DOING IN THERE?
LICKING THE OVEN GRATE
JIM DAVIS
9-28
© 1989 PAWS, INC. All Rights Reserved.

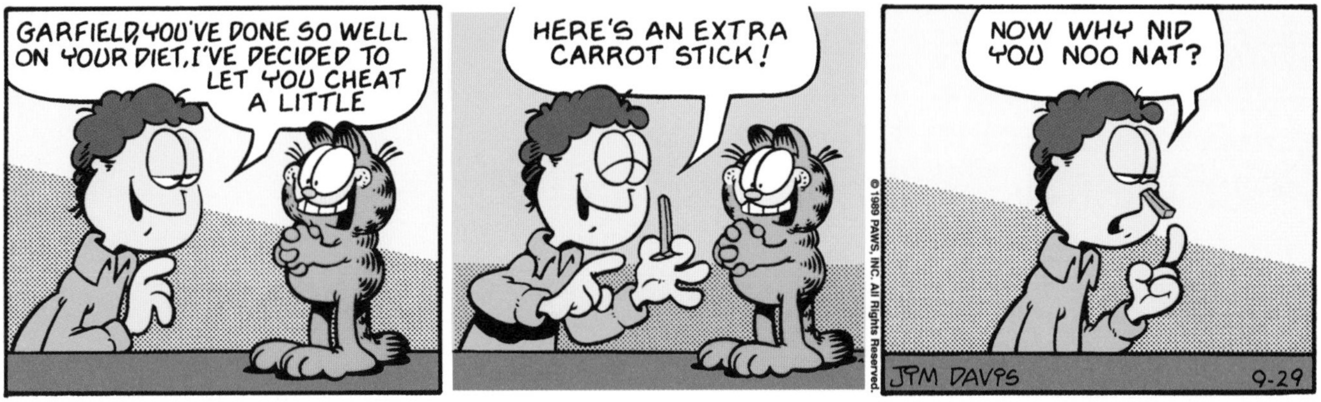
GARFIELD, YOU'VE DONE SO WELL ON YOUR DIET, I'VE DECIDED TO LET YOU CHEAT A LITTLE
HERE'S AN EXTRA CARROT STICK!
NOW WHY NID YOU NOO NAT?
JIM DAVIS
9-29
© 1989 PAWS, INC. All Rights Reserved.

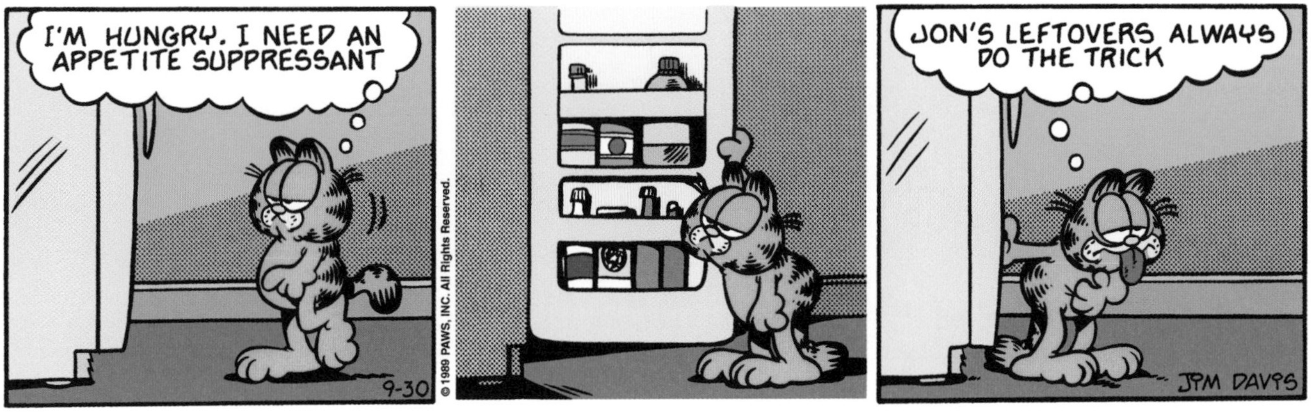
I'M HUNGRY. I NEED AN APPETITE SUPPRESSANT
JON'S LEFTOVERS ALWAYS DO THE TRICK
9-30
JIM DAVIS
© 1989 PAWS, INC. All Rights Reserved.

Ask a cat.

Q: Why does a cat always land on its feet?
A: Because it beats landing on its face.

Q: Can cats see in the dark?
A: Yes. They see a whole lot of dark.

Q: Is there more than one way to skin a cat?
A: I have given your name to the authorities.

Q: Why do cats eat plants?
A: To get rid of that mouse aftertaste.

Q: How often should I take my cat to the vet?
A: As often as you would like to have your lips ripped off.

Q: Should I have my cat fixed?
A: Why? Is it broken?

Q: Why do cats spend so much time napping?
A: To rest up for bedtime.

Q: How much food should my cat eat?
A: How much have you got?

Garfield takes up space

BY JIM DAVIS

Ballantine Books • New York

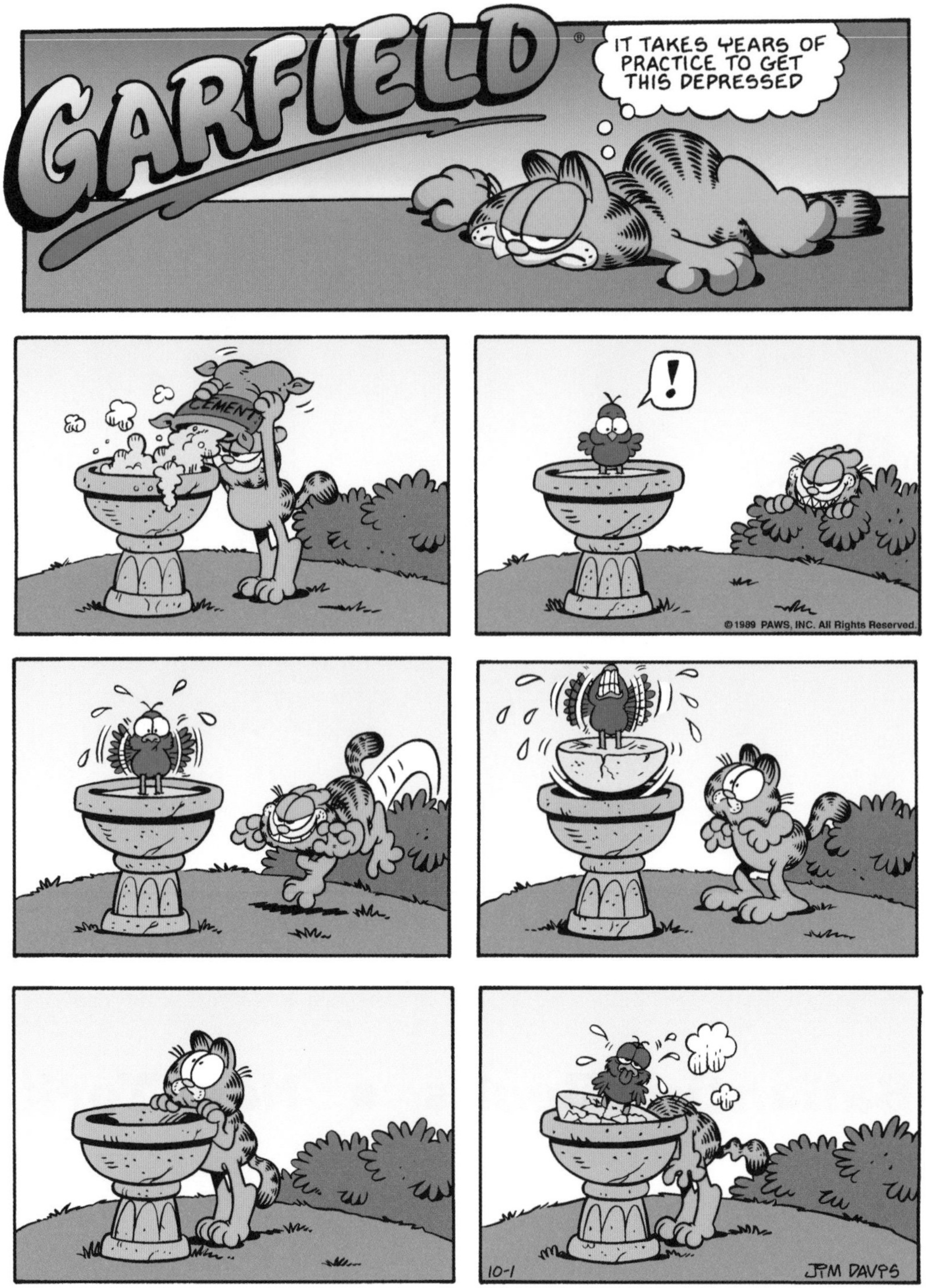
GARFIELD®
IT TAKES YEARS OF PRACTICE TO GET THIS DEPRESSED
CEMENT
!
© 1989 PAWS, INC. All Rights Reserved.
10-1
JIM DAVIS

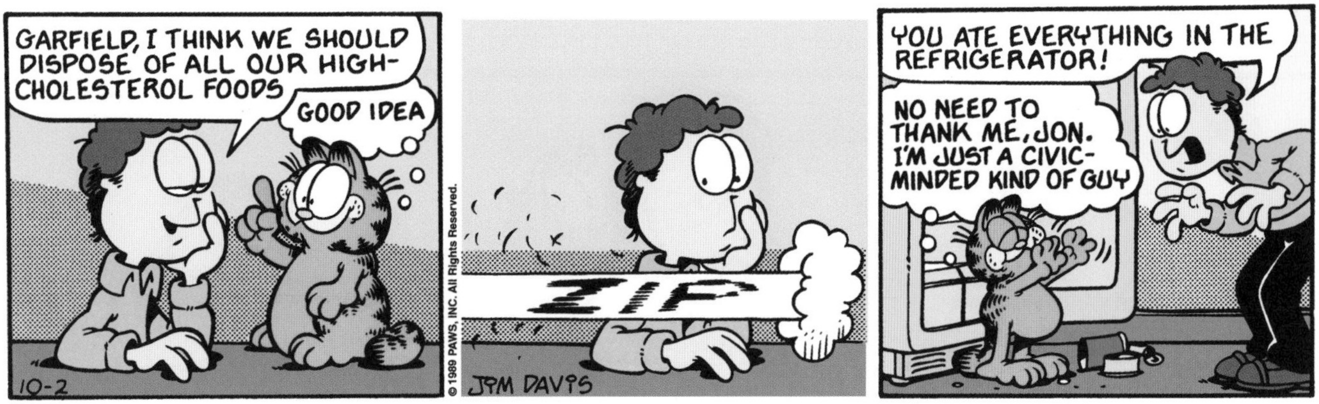
GARFIELD, I THINK WE SHOULD DISPOSE OF ALL OUR HIGH-CHOLESTEROL FOODS
GOOD IDEA
ZIP
YOU ATE EVERYTHING IN THE REFRIGERATOR!
NO NEED TO THANK ME, JON. I'M JUST A CIVIC-MINDED KIND OF GUY
© 1989 PAWS, INC. All Rights Reserved.

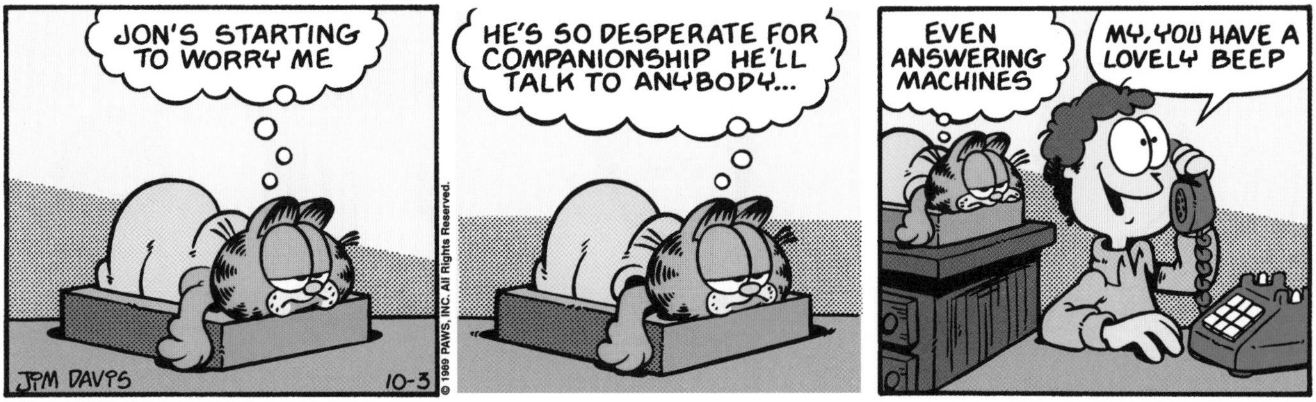
JON'S STARTING TO WORRY ME
HE'S SO DESPERATE FOR COMPANIONSHIP HE'LL TALK TO ANYBODY...
EVEN ANSWERING MACHINES
MY, YOU HAVE A LOVELY BEEP
© 1989 PAWS, INC. All Rights Reserved.

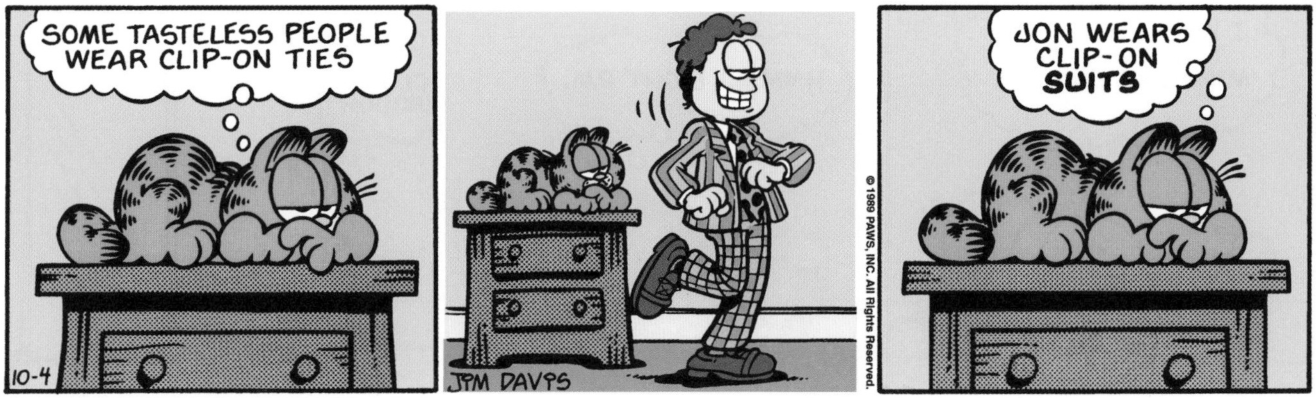
SOME TASTELESS PEOPLE WEAR CLIP-ON TIES
JON WEARS CLIP-ON **SUITS**
© 1989 PAWS, INC. All Rights Reserved.

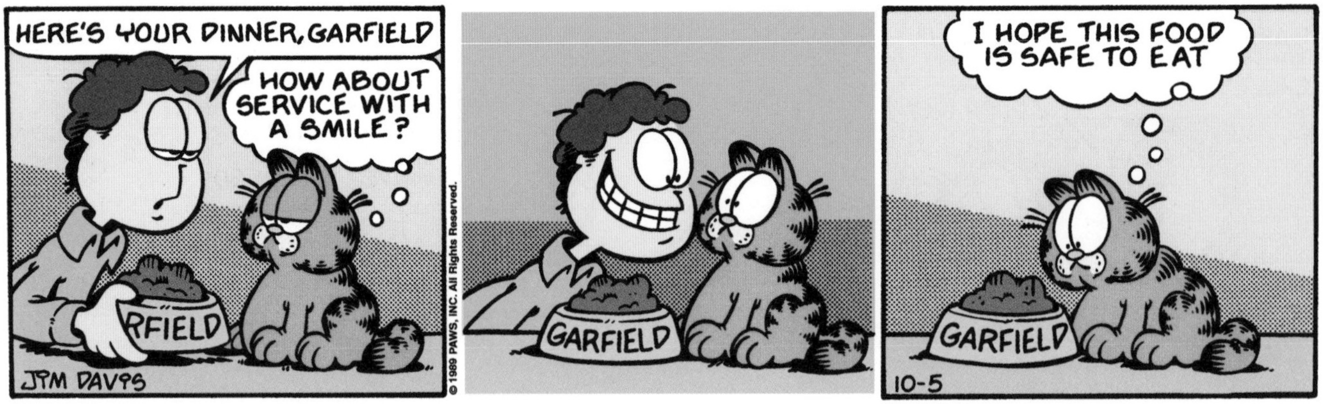
HERE'S YOUR DINNER, GARFIELD
HOW ABOUT SERVICE WITH A SMILE?
RFIELD
JIM DAVIS
© 1989 PAWS, INC. All Rights Reserved.
GARFIELD
I HOPE THIS FOOD IS SAFE TO EAT
GARFIELD
10-5

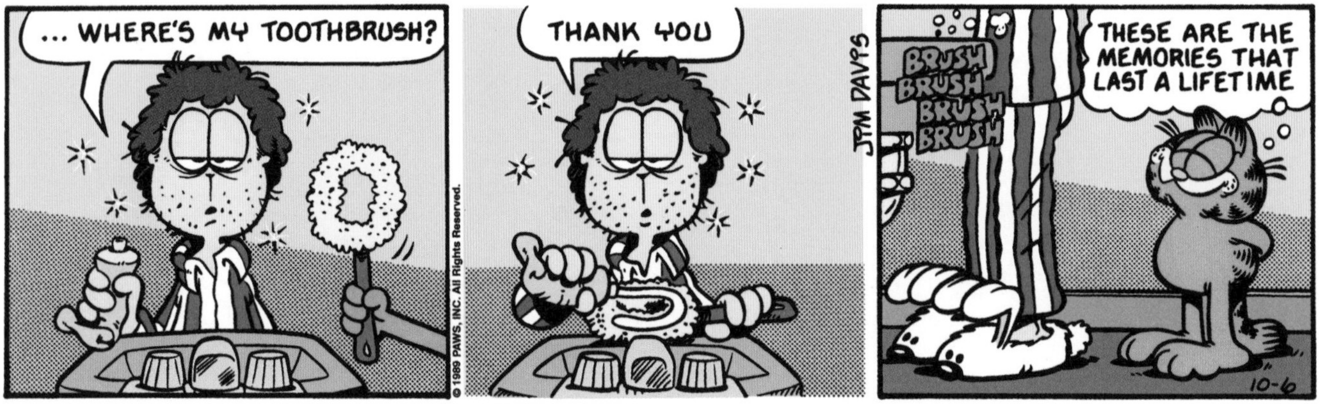
... WHERE'S MY TOOTHBRUSH?
© 1989 PAWS, INC. All Rights Reserved.
THANK YOU
JIM DAVIS
BRUSH BRUSH BRUSH BRUSH
THESE ARE THE MEMORIES THAT LAST A LIFETIME
10-6

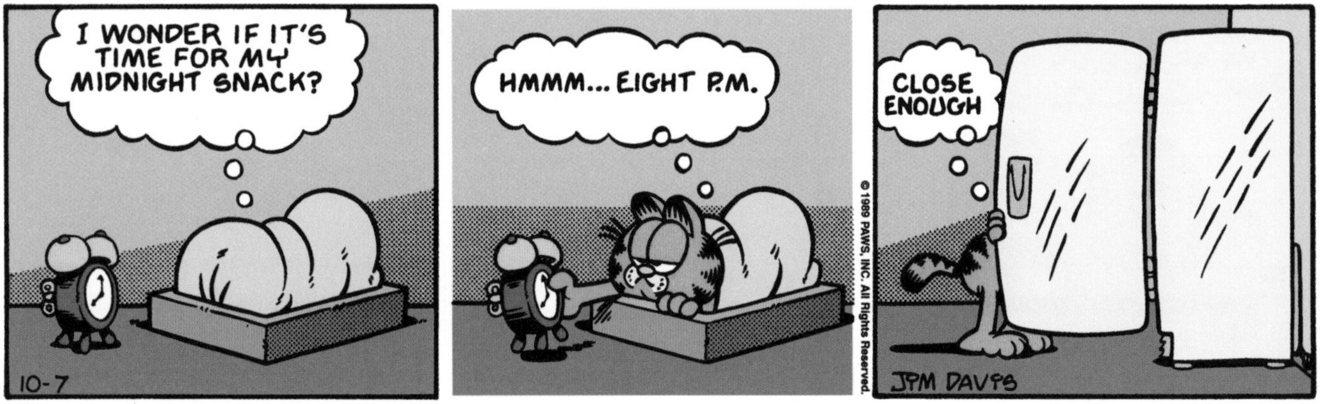
I WONDER IF IT'S TIME FOR MY MIDNIGHT SNACK?
10-7
HMMM... EIGHT P.M.
© 1989 PAWS, INC. All Rights Reserved.
CLOSE ENOUGH
JIM DAVIS

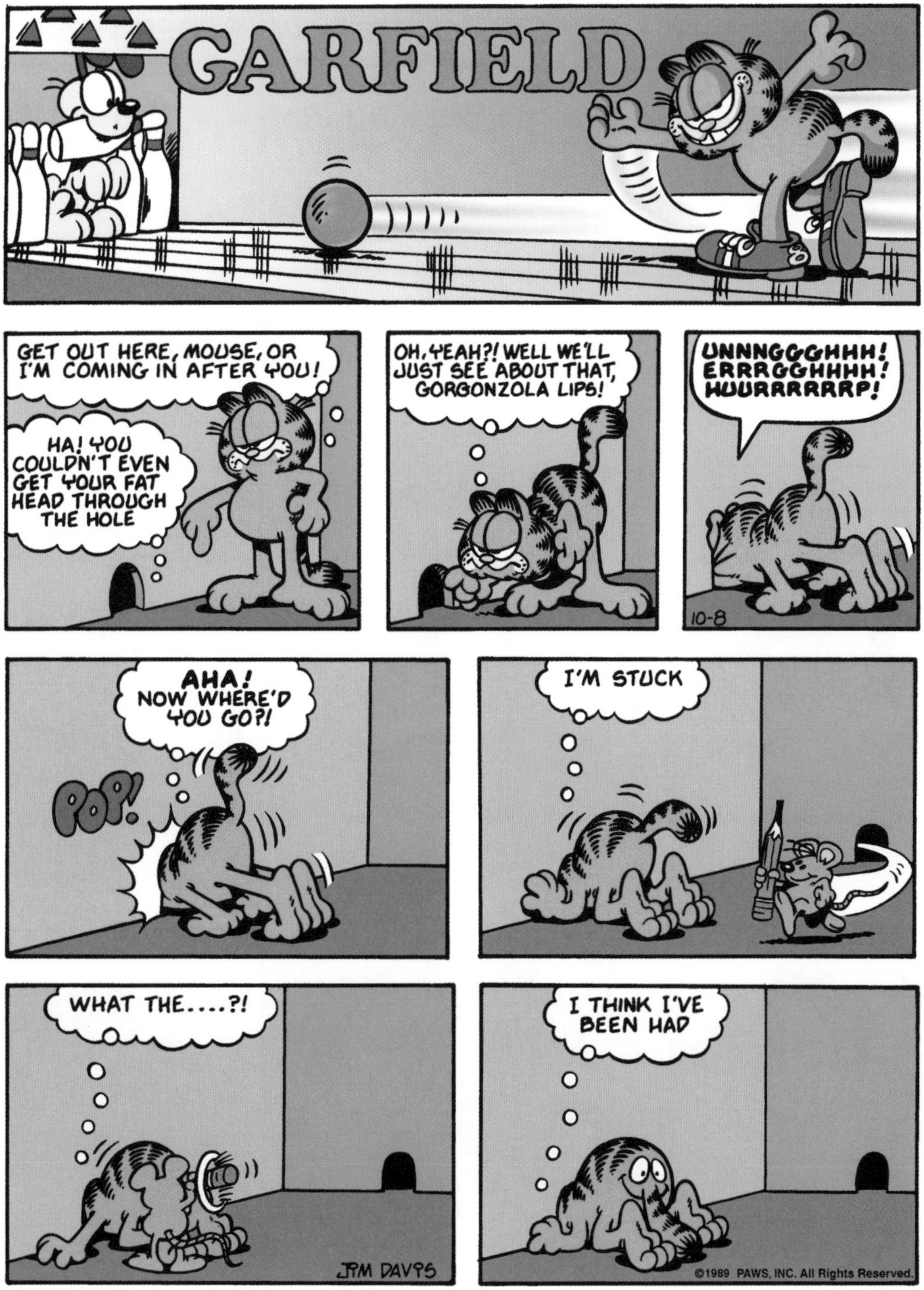
GARFIELD
GET OUT HERE, MOUSE, OR I'M COMING IN AFTER YOU!
HA! YOU COULDN'T EVEN GET YOUR FAT HEAD THROUGH THE HOLE
OH, YEAH?! WELL WE'LL JUST SEE ABOUT THAT, GORGONZOLA LIPS!
UNNNGGGHHH! ERRRGGHHHH! HUURRRRRRP!
10-8
AHA! NOW WHERE'D YOU GO?!
POP!
I'M STUCK
WHAT THE....?!
JIM DAVIS
I THINK I'VE BEEN HAD
©1989 PAWS, INC. All Rights Reserved.

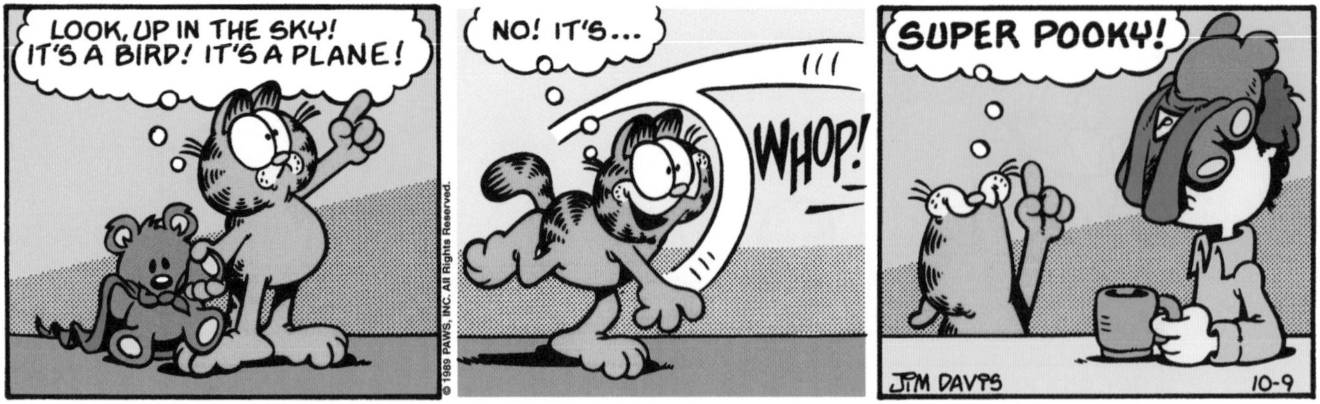
LOOK, UP IN THE SKY! IT'S A BIRD! IT'S A PLANE!
© 1989 PAWS, INC. All Rights Reserved.
NO! IT'S...
WHOP!
SUPER POOKY!
JIM DAVIS
10-9

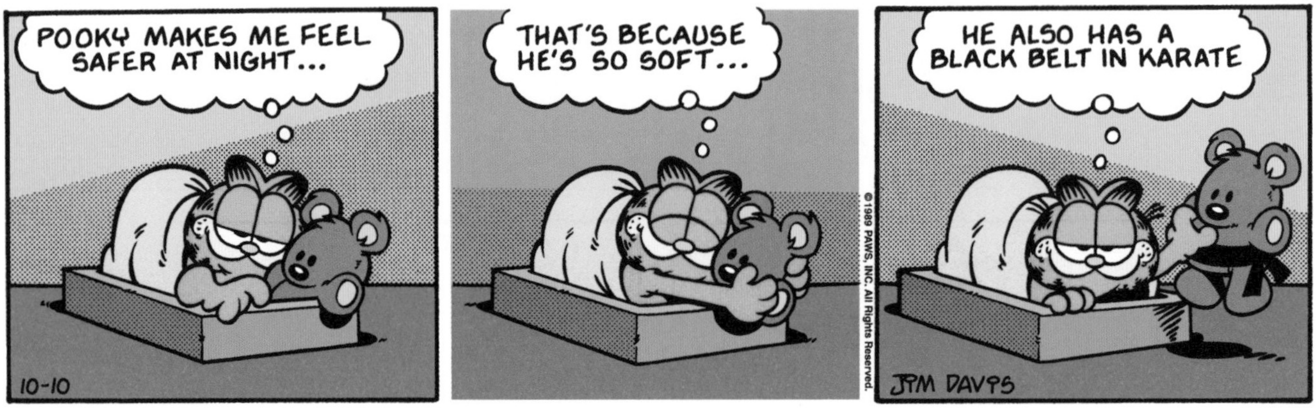
POOKY MAKES ME FEEL SAFER AT NIGHT...
10-10
THAT'S BECAUSE HE'S SO SOFT...
© 1989 PAWS, INC. All Rights Reserved.
HE ALSO HAS A BLACK BELT IN KARATE
JIM DAVIS

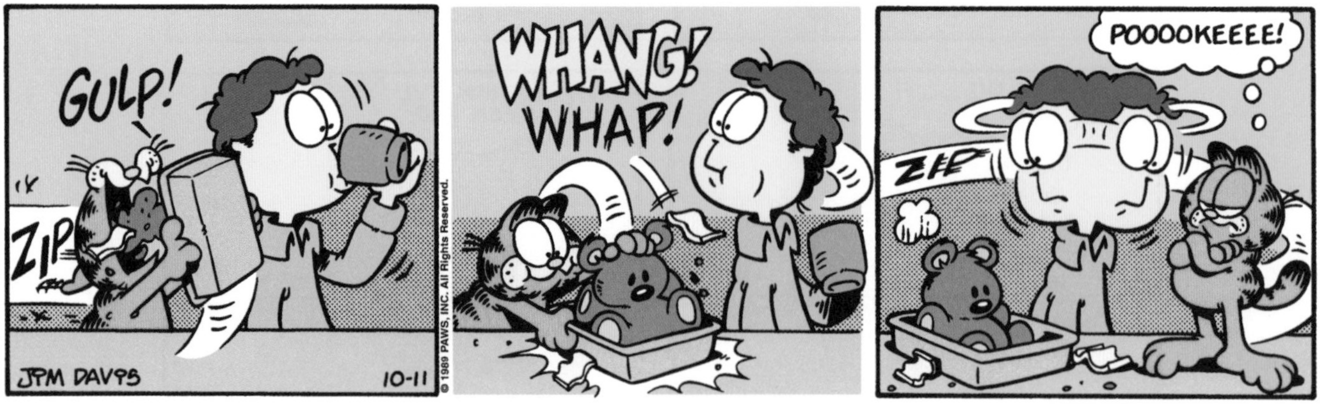
GULP!
ZIP
JIM DAVIS
10-11
© 1989 PAWS, INC. All Rights Reserved.
WHANG!
WHAP!
POOOOKEEEE!
ZIP

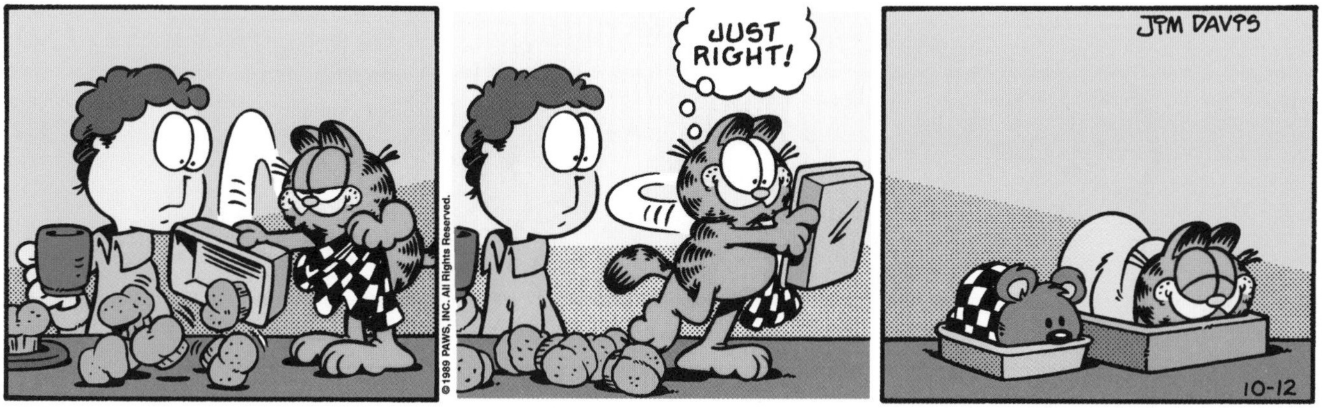
JUST RIGHT!
© 1989 PAWS, INC. All Rights Reserved.
JIM DAVIS
10-12

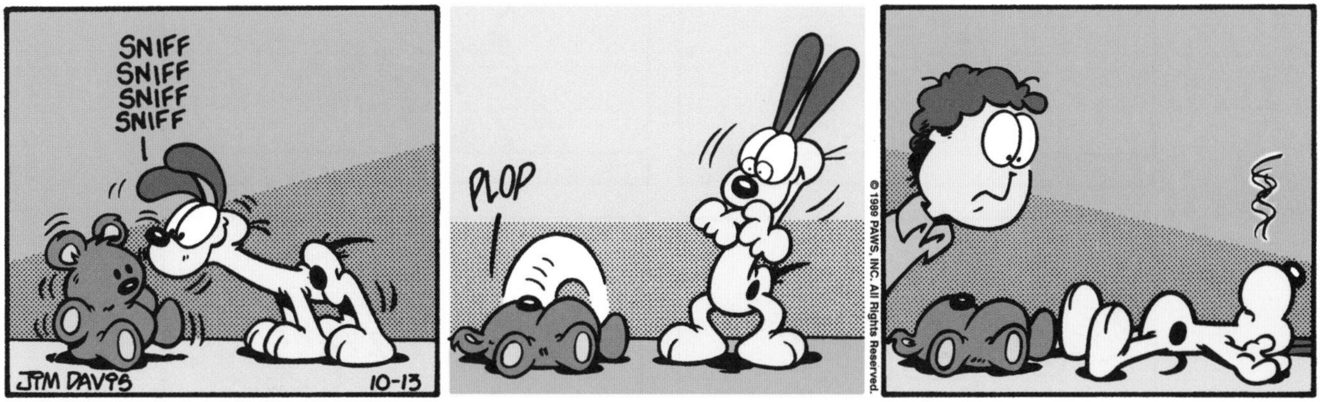
SNIFF SNIFF SNIFF SNIFF
JIM DAVIS
10-13
PLOP
© 1989 PAWS, INC. All Rights Reserved.

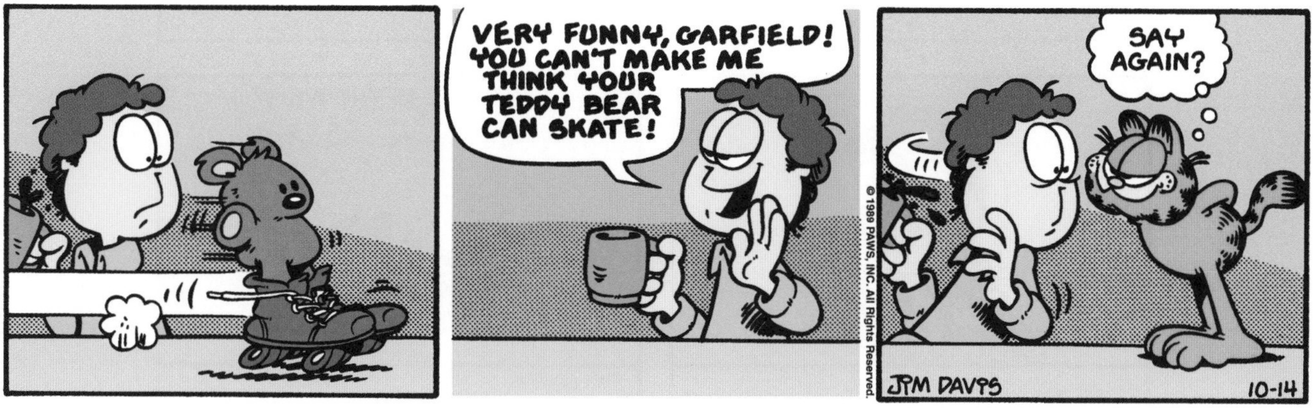
VERY FUNNY, GARFIELD! YOU CAN'T MAKE ME THINK YOUR TEDDY BEAR CAN SKATE!
© 1989 PAWS, INC. All Rights Reserved.
SAY AGAIN?
JIM DAVIS
10-14

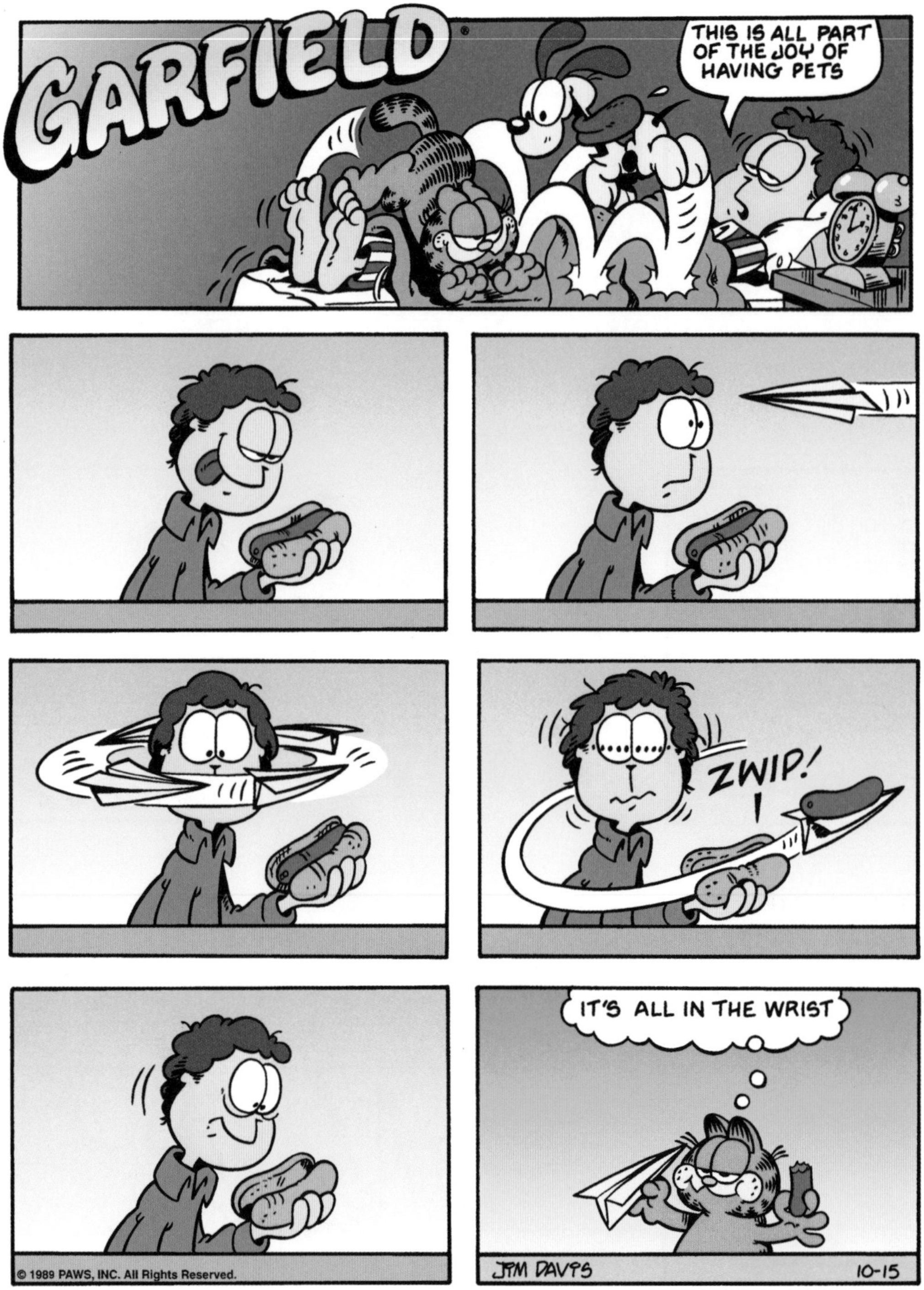
GARFIELD
THIS IS ALL PART OF THE JOY OF HAVING PETS
ZWIP!
IT'S ALL IN THE WRIST
JIM DAVIS
10-15

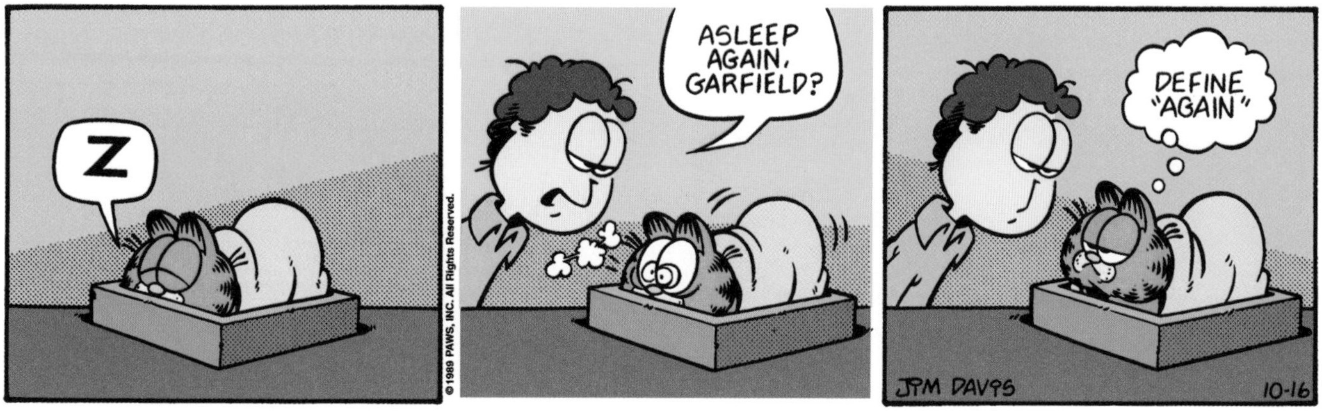
Z
ASLEEP AGAIN, GARFIELD?
DEFINE "AGAIN"
© 1989 PAWS, INC. All Rights Reserved.
JIM DAVIS
10-16

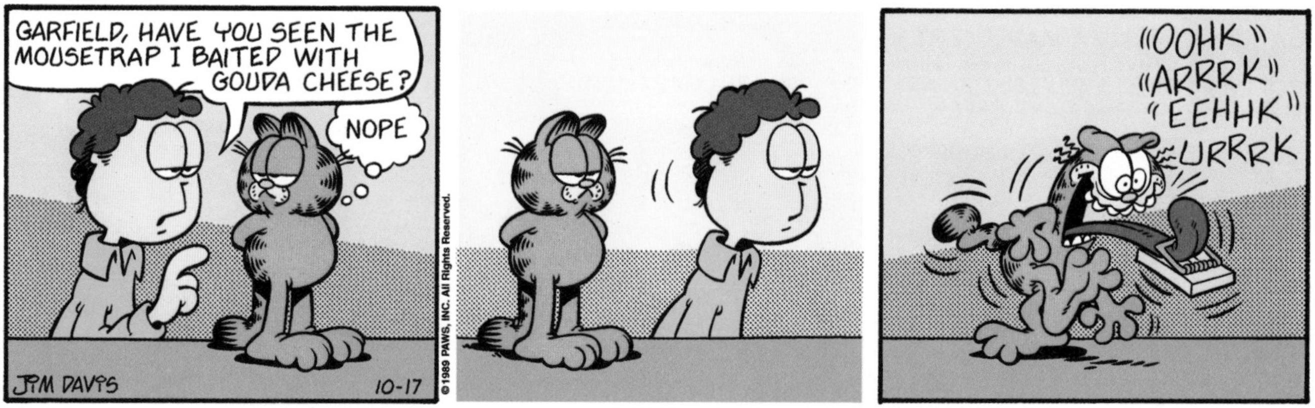
GARFIELD, HAVE YOU SEEN THE MOUSETRAP I BAITED WITH GOUDA CHEESE?
NOPE
«OOHK»
«ARRRK»
"EEHHK"
URRRK
© 1989 PAWS, INC. All Rights Reserved.
JIM DAVIS
10-17

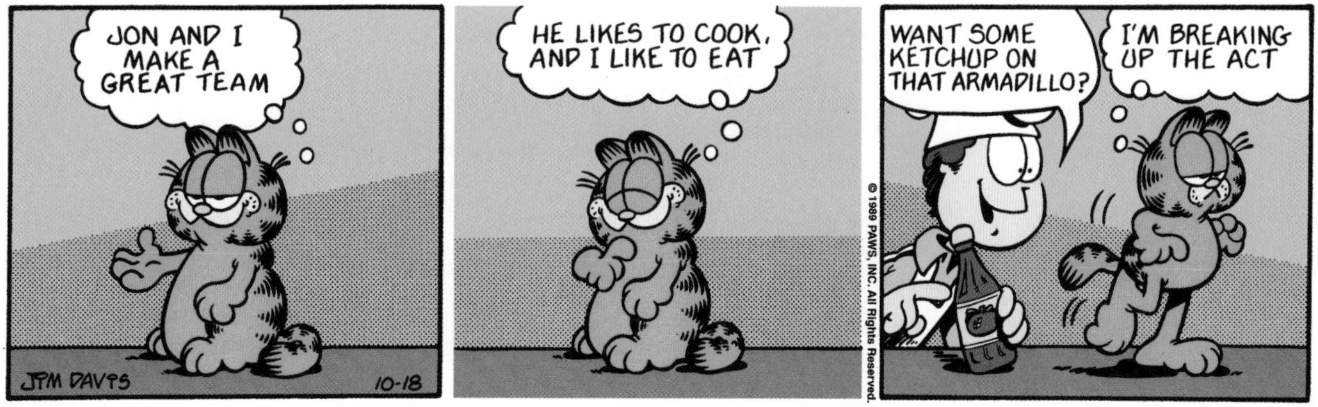
JON AND I MAKE A GREAT TEAM
HE LIKES TO COOK, AND I LIKE TO EAT
WANT SOME KETCHUP ON THAT ARMADILLO?
I'M BREAKING UP THE ACT
© 1989 PAWS, INC. All Rights Reserved.
JIM DAVIS
10-18

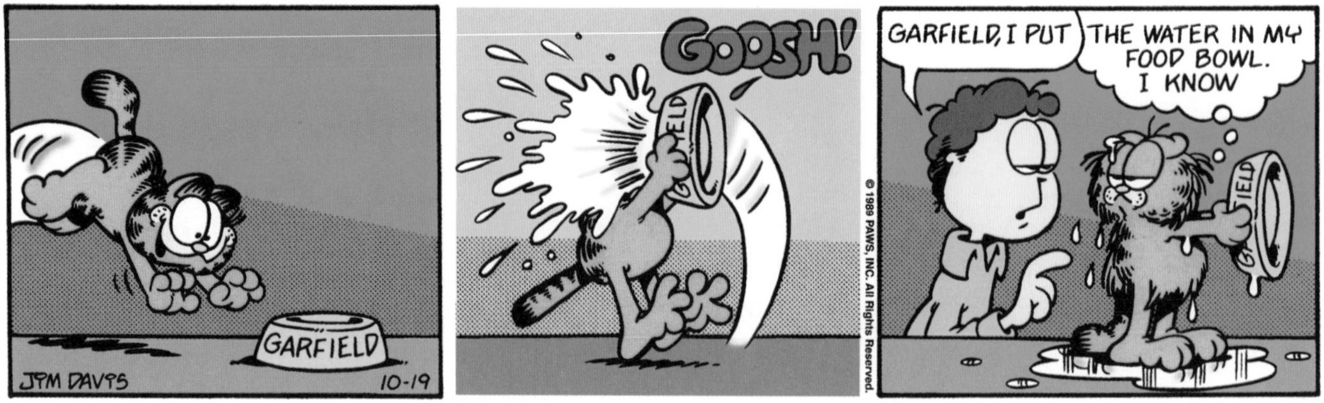
JIM DAVIS
10-19
GOOSH!
© 1989 PAWS, INC. All Rights Reserved.
GARFIELD, I PUT
THE WATER IN MY FOOD BOWL. I KNOW

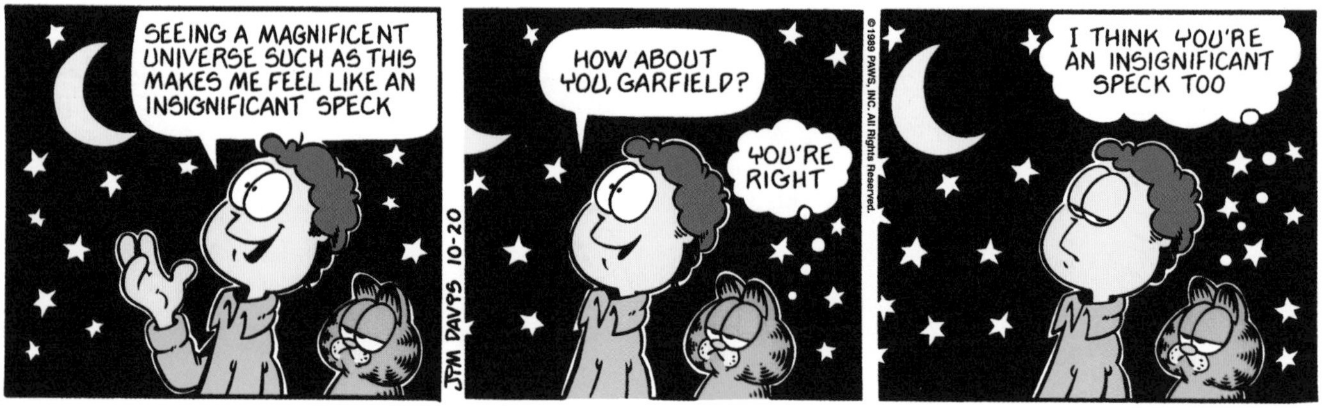
SEEING A MAGNIFICENT UNIVERSE SUCH AS THIS MAKES ME FEEL LIKE AN INSIGNIFICANT SPECK
JIM DAVIS 10-20
HOW ABOUT YOU, GARFIELD?
YOU'RE RIGHT
© 1989 PAWS, INC. All Rights Reserved.
I THINK YOU'RE AN INSIGNIFICANT SPECK TOO

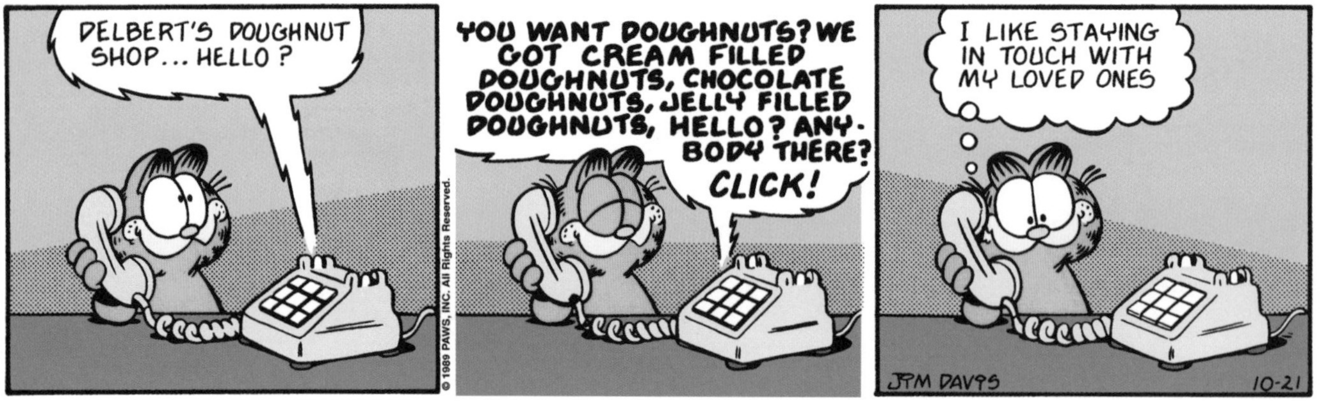
DELBERT'S DOUGHNUT SHOP... HELLO?
© 1989 PAWS, INC. All Rights Reserved.
YOU WANT DOUGHNUTS? WE GOT CREAM FILLED DOUGHNUTS, CHOCOLATE DOUGHNUTS, JELLY FILLED DOUGHNUTS, HELLO? ANY-BODY THERE?
CLICK!
I LIKE STAYING IN TOUCH WITH MY LOVED ONES
JIM DAVIS
10-21

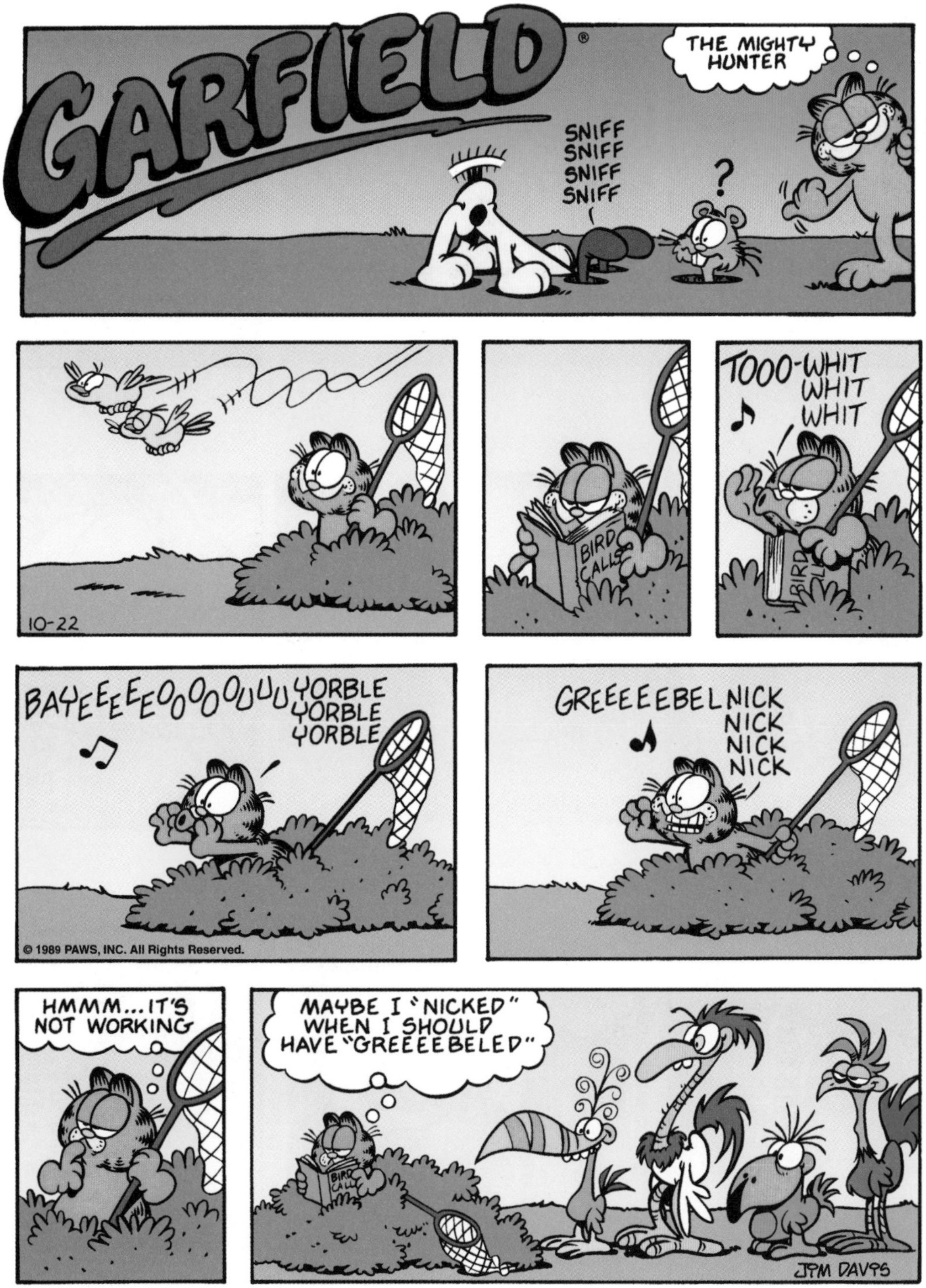
GARFIELD
THE MIGHTY HUNTER
SNIFF SNIFF SNIFF SNIFF
?
10-22
BIRD CALLS
TOOO-WHIT WHIT WHIT
BAYEEEEEOOOOOUUUYORBLE YORBLE YORBLE
GREEEEEBELNICK NICK NICK NICK
© 1989 PAWS, INC. All Rights Reserved.
HMMM... IT'S NOT WORKING
MAYBE I "NICKED" WHEN I SHOULD HAVE "GREEEEBELED"
BIRD CALLS
JIM DAVIS

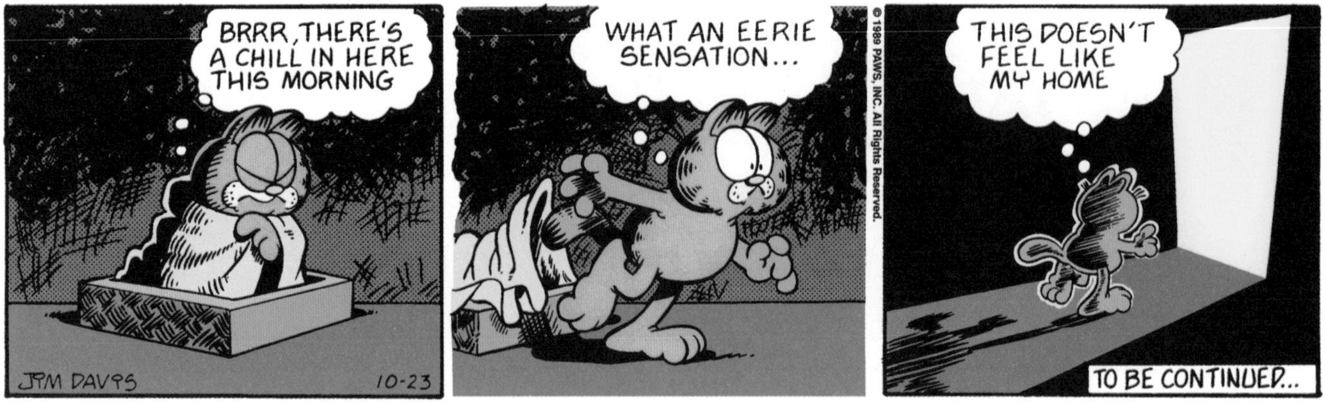
BRRR, THERE'S A CHILL IN HERE THIS MORNING
JIM DAVIS
10-23
WHAT AN EERIE SENSATION...
© 1989 PAWS, INC. All Rights Reserved.
THIS DOESN'T FEEL LIKE MY HOME
TO BE CONTINUED...

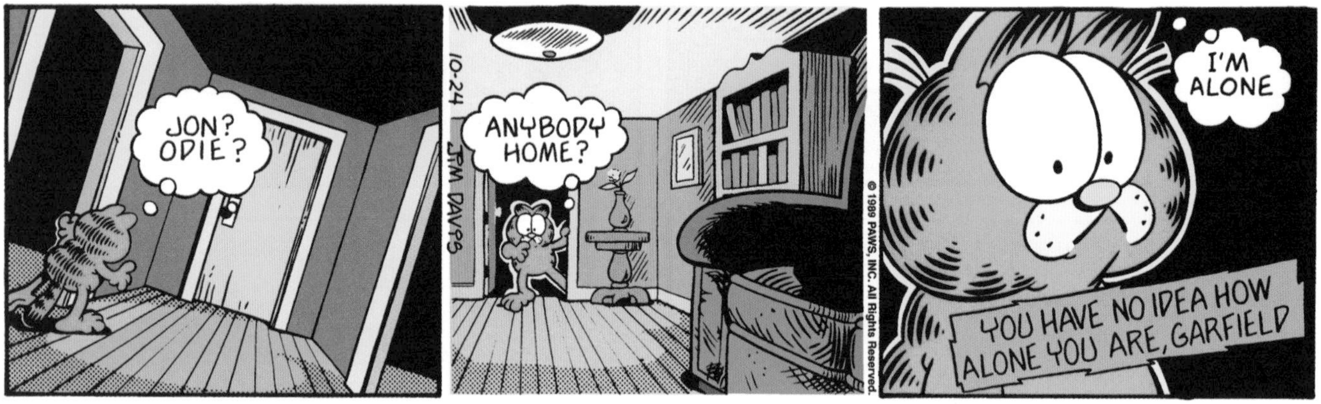
JON? ODIE?
10-24
JIM DAVIS
ANYBODY HOME?
© 1989 PAWS, INC. All Rights Reserved.
I'M ALONE
YOU HAVE NO IDEA HOW ALONE YOU ARE, GARFIELD

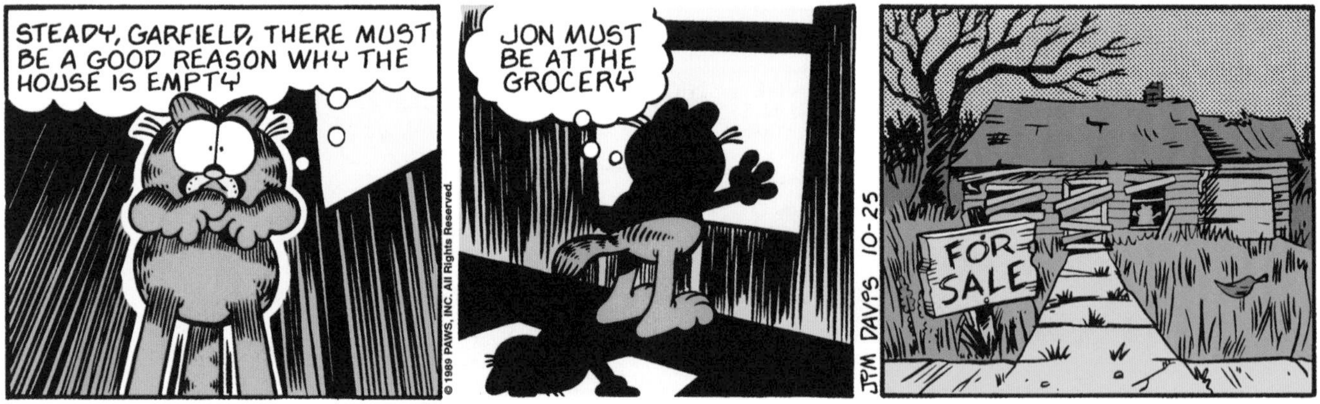
STEADY, GARFIELD, THERE MUST BE A GOOD REASON WHY THE HOUSE IS EMPTY
© 1989 PAWS, INC. All Rights Reserved.
JON MUST BE AT THE GROCERY
JIM DAVIS 10-25
FOR SALE

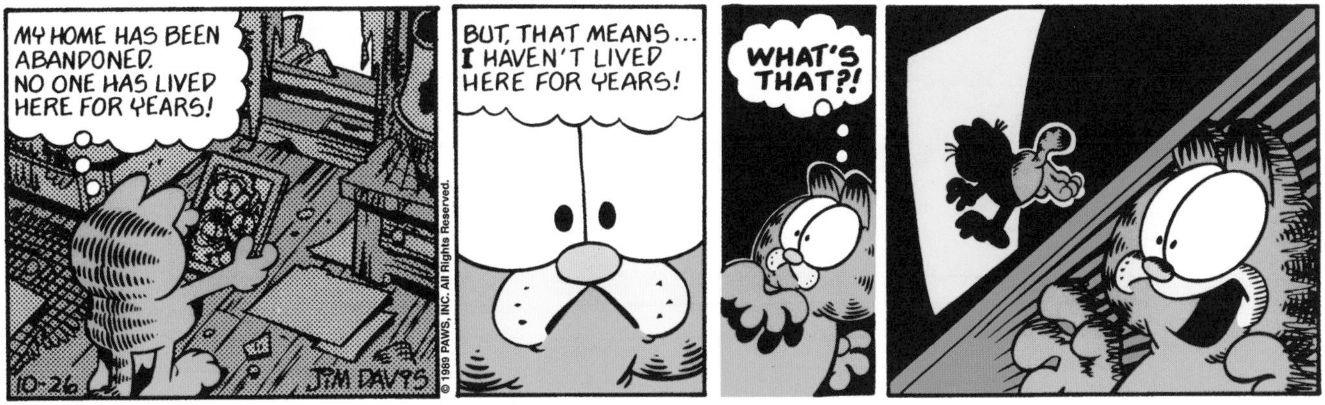
MY HOME HAS BEEN ABANDONED. NO ONE HAS LIVED HERE FOR YEARS!
10-26
JIM DAVIS
© 1989 PAWS, INC. All Rights Reserved.
BUT, THAT MEANS... I HAVEN'T LIVED HERE FOR YEARS!
WHAT'S THAT?!

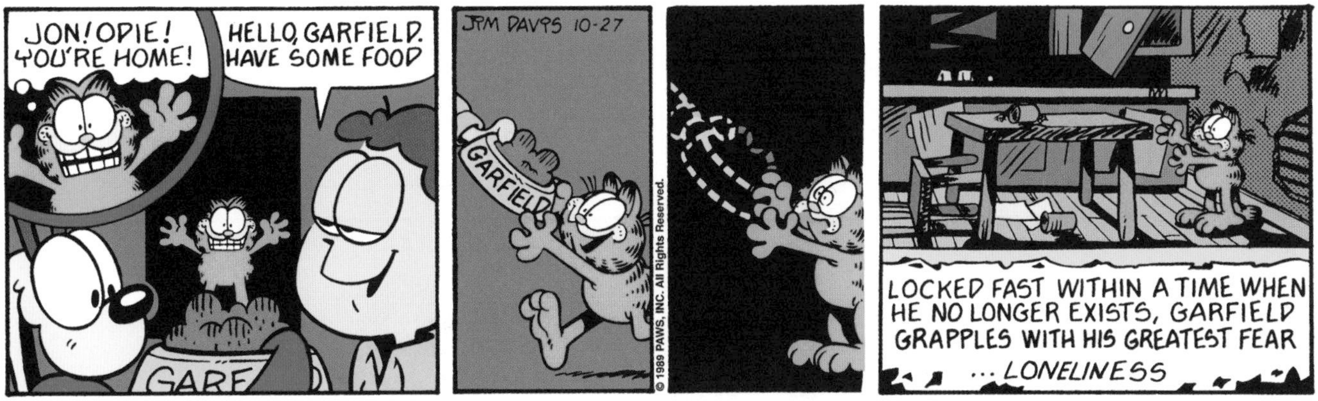
JON! ODIE! YOU'RE HOME!
HELLO, GARFIELD. HAVE SOME FOOD
GARF
JIM DAVIS 10-27
GARFIELD
© 1989 PAWS, INC. All Rights Reserved.
LOCKED FAST WITHIN A TIME WHEN HE NO LONGER EXISTS, GARFIELD GRAPPLES WITH HIS GREATEST FEAR
... LONELINESS

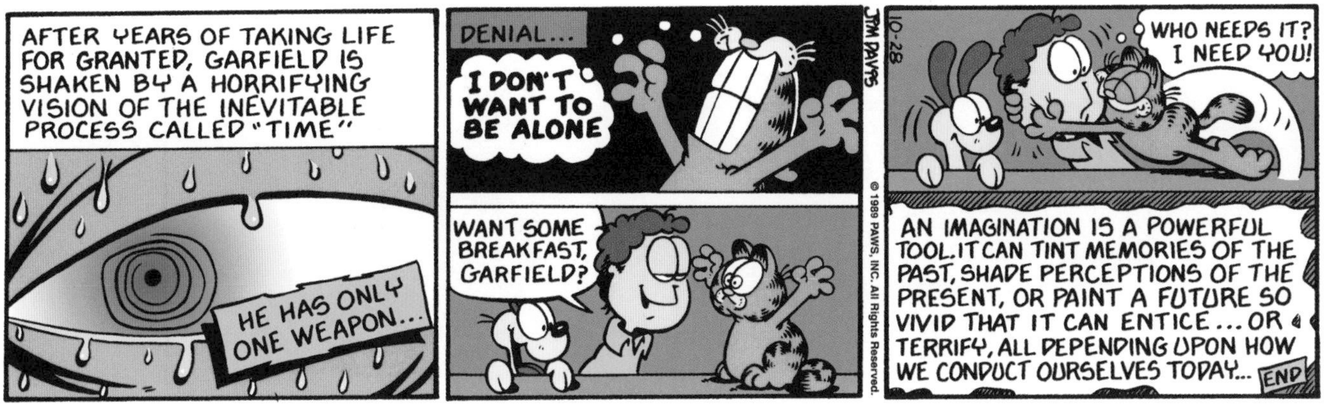
AFTER YEARS OF TAKING LIFE FOR GRANTED, GARFIELD IS SHAKEN BY A HORRIFYING VISION OF THE INEVITABLE PROCESS CALLED "TIME"
HE HAS ONLY ONE WEAPON...
DENIAL...
I DON'T WANT TO BE ALONE
WANT SOME BREAKFAST, GARFIELD?
JIM DAVIS 10-28
© 1989 PAWS, INC. All Rights Reserved.
WHO NEEDS IT? I NEED YOU!
AN IMAGINATION IS A POWERFUL TOOL. IT CAN TINT MEMORIES OF THE PAST, SHADE PERCEPTIONS OF THE PRESENT, OR PAINT A FUTURE SO VIVID THAT IT CAN ENTICE... OR TERRIFY, ALL DEPENDING UPON HOW WE CONDUCT OURSELVES TODAY...
END

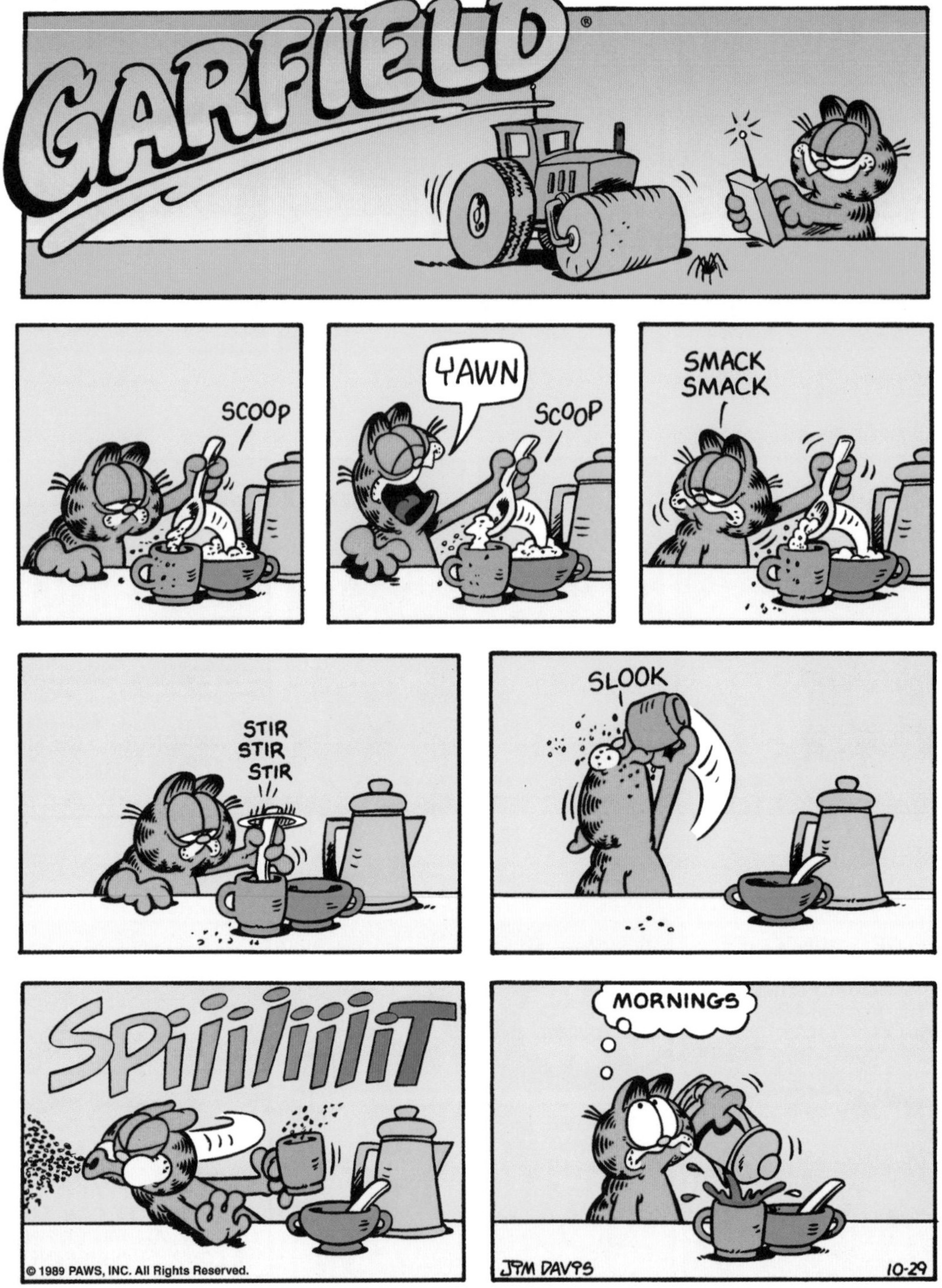
GARFIELD
SCOOP
YAWN
SCOOP
SMACK SMACK
STIR STIR STIR
SLOOK
SPIIIIIIIT
MORNINGS
© 1989 PAWS, INC. All Rights Reserved.
JIM DAVIS
10-29

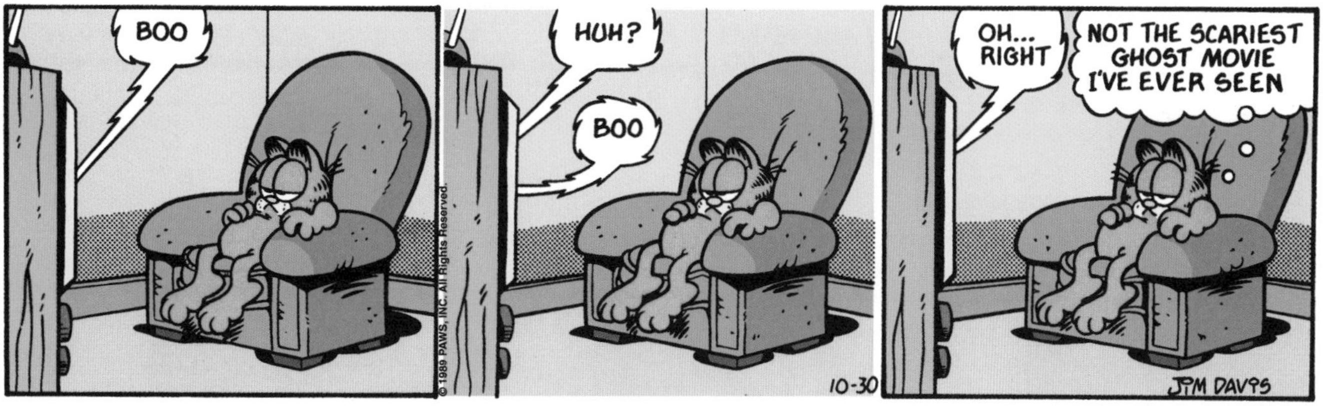
BOO
HUH?
BOO
OH... RIGHT
NOT THE SCARIEST GHOST MOVIE I'VE EVER SEEN
© 1989 PAWS, INC. All Rights Reserved.
10-30
JIM DAVIS

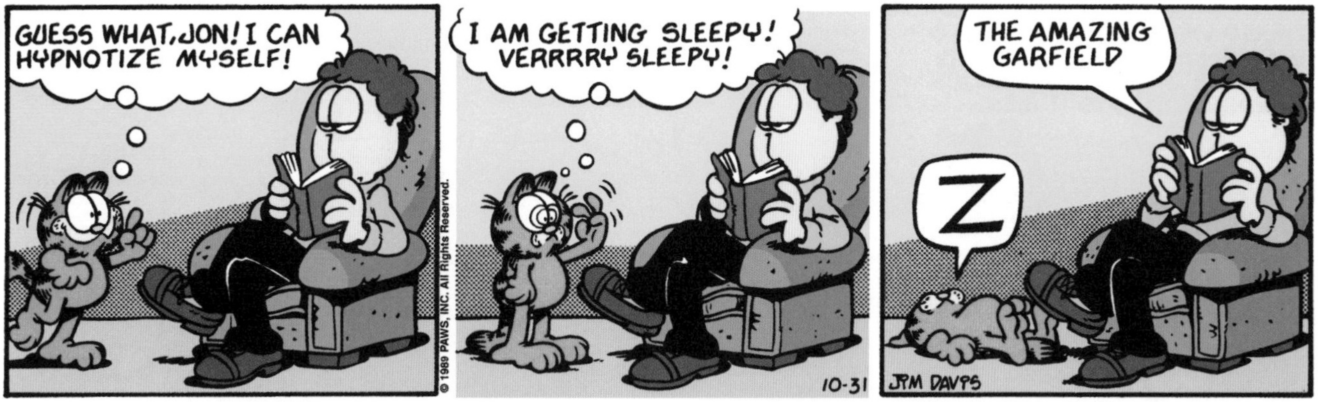
GUESS WHAT, JON! I CAN HYPNOTIZE MYSELF!
I AM GETTING SLEEPY! VERRRRY SLEEPY!
THE AMAZING GARFIELD
Z
© 1989 PAWS, INC. All Rights Reserved.
10-31
JIM DAVIS

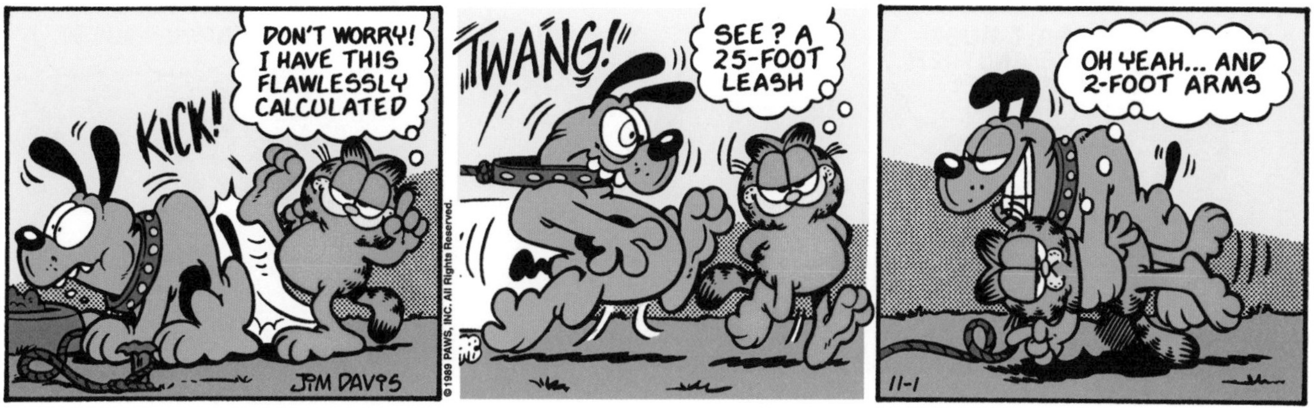
KICK!
DON'T WORRY! I HAVE THIS FLAWLESSLY CALCULATED
TWANG!
SEE? A 25-FOOT LEASH
OH YEAH... AND 2-FOOT ARMS
© 1989 PAWS, INC. All Rights Reserved.
JIM DAVIS
11-1

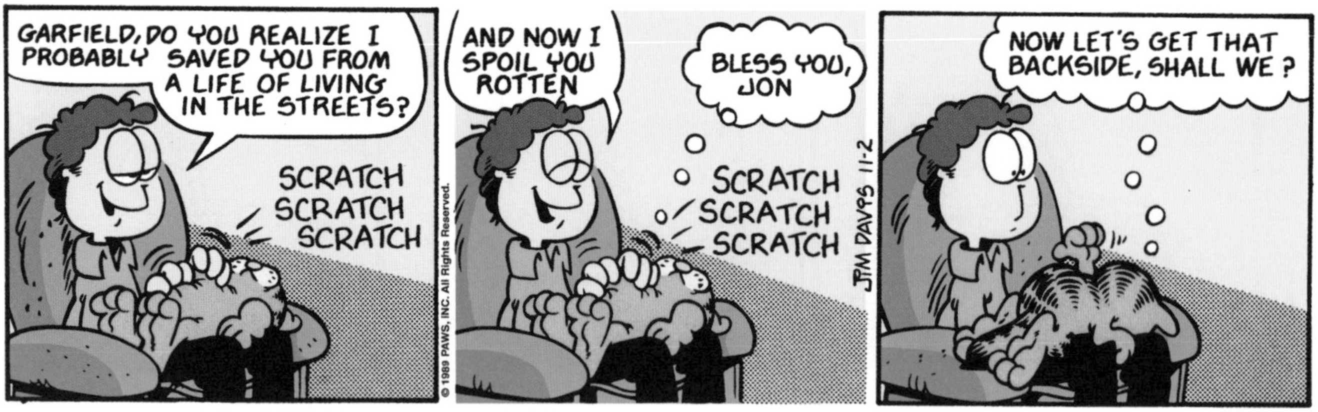
GARFIELD, DO YOU REALIZE I PROBABLY SAVED YOU FROM A LIFE OF LIVING IN THE STREETS?
SCRATCH SCRATCH SCRATCH
© 1989 PAWS, INC. All Rights Reserved.
AND NOW I SPOIL YOU ROTTEN
BLESS YOU, JON
SCRATCH SCRATCH SCRATCH
JIM DAVIS 11-2
NOW LET'S GET THAT BACKSIDE, SHALL WE?

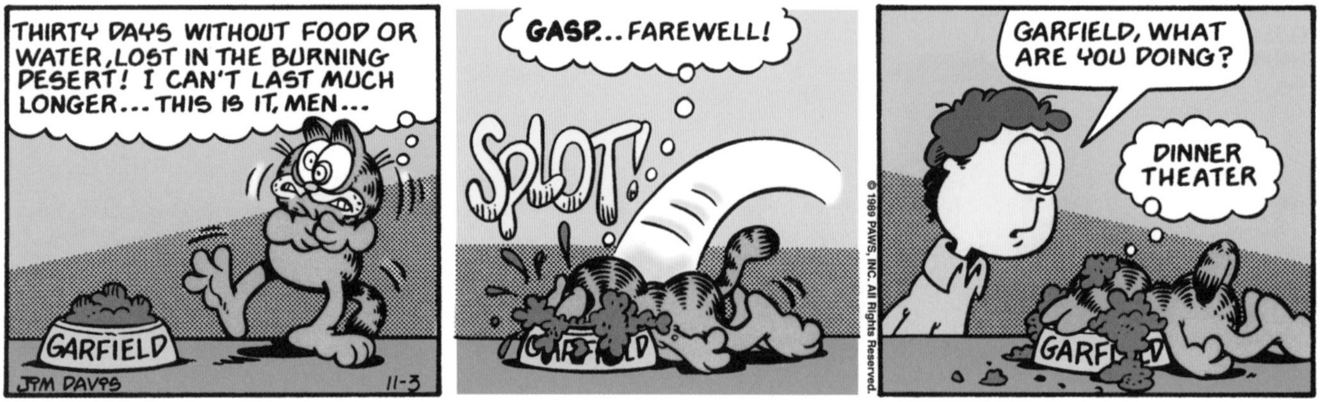
THIRTY DAYS WITHOUT FOOD OR WATER, LOST IN THE BURNING DESERT! I CAN'T LAST MUCH LONGER... THIS IS IT, MEN...
GARFIELD
JIM DAVIS 11-3
GASP... FAREWELL!
SPLOT!
© 1989 PAWS, INC. All Rights Reserved.
GARFIELD, WHAT ARE YOU DOING?
DINNER THEATER

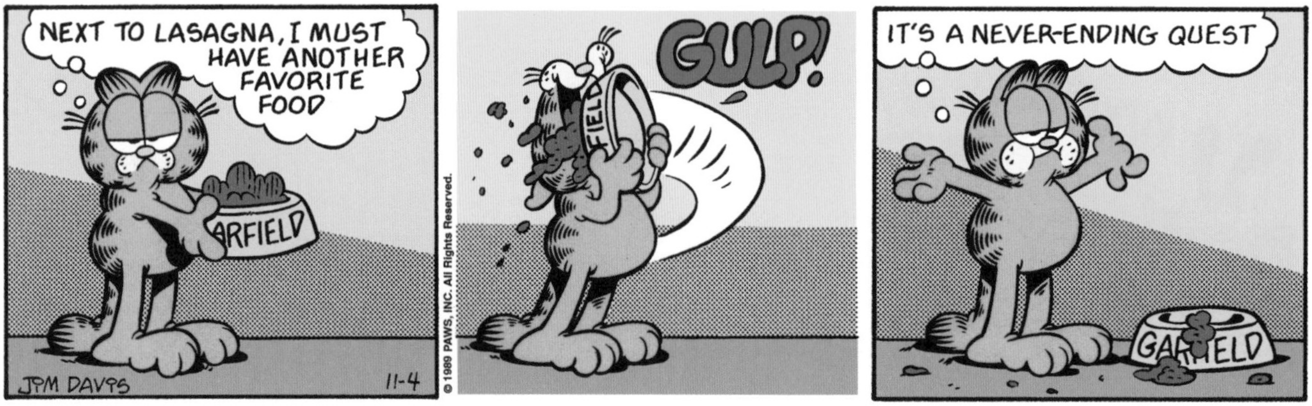
NEXT TO LASAGNA, I MUST HAVE ANOTHER FAVORITE FOOD
ARFIELD
JIM DAVIS 11-4
© 1989 PAWS, INC. All Rights Reserved.
GULP!
IT'S A NEVER-ENDING QUEST

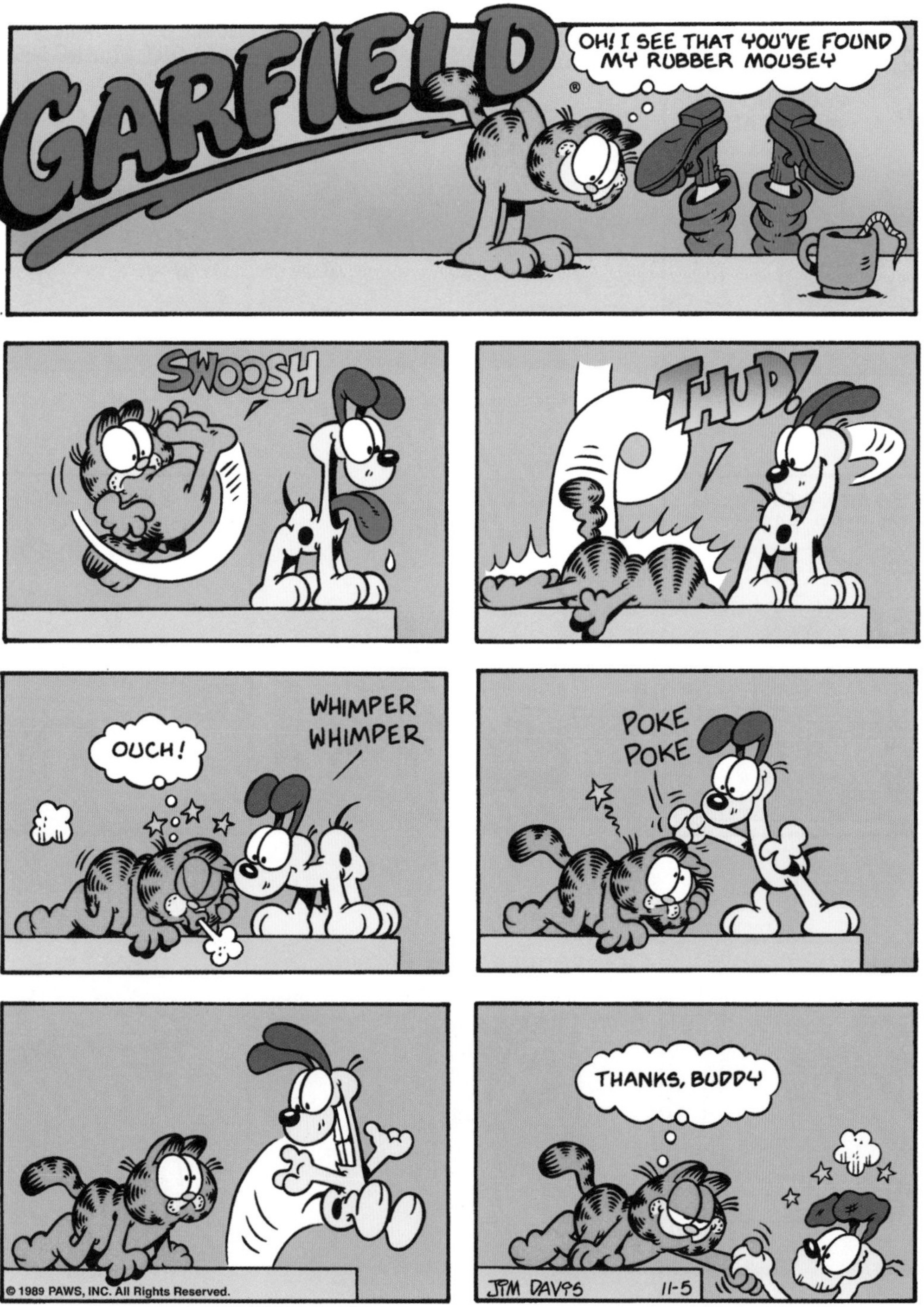
GARFIELD®
OH! I SEE THAT YOU'VE FOUND MY RUBBER MOUSEY
SWOOSH
THUD!
OUCH!
WHIMPER WHIMPER
POKE POKE
THANKS, BUDDY
© 1989 PAWS, INC. All Rights Reserved.
JIM DAVIS
11-5

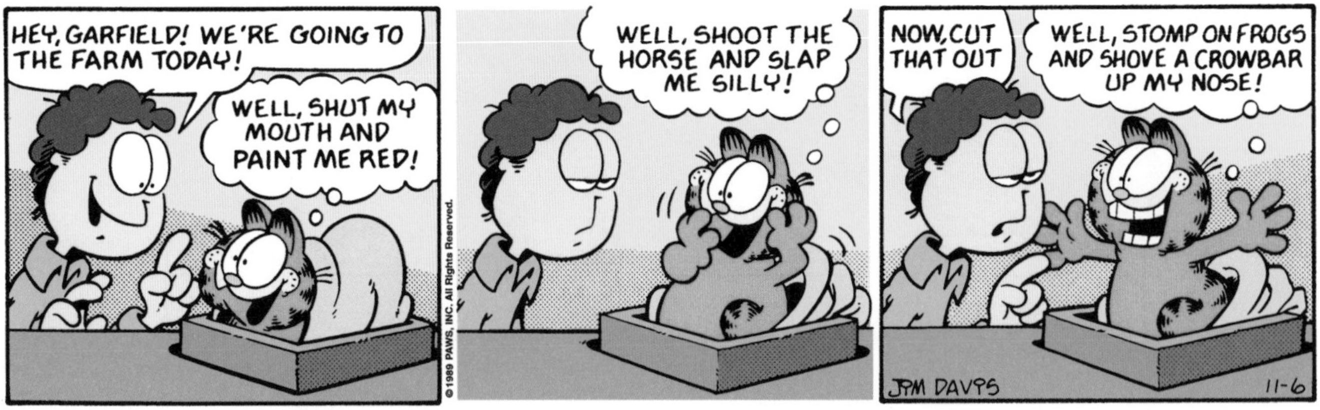
HEY, GARFIELD! WE'RE GOING TO THE FARM TODAY!
WELL, SHUT MY MOUTH AND PAINT ME RED!
© 1989 PAWS, INC. All Rights Reserved.
WELL, SHOOT THE HORSE AND SLAP ME SILLY!
NOW, CUT THAT OUT
WELL, STOMP ON FROGS AND SHOVE A CROWBAR UP MY NOSE!
JIM DAVIS
11-6

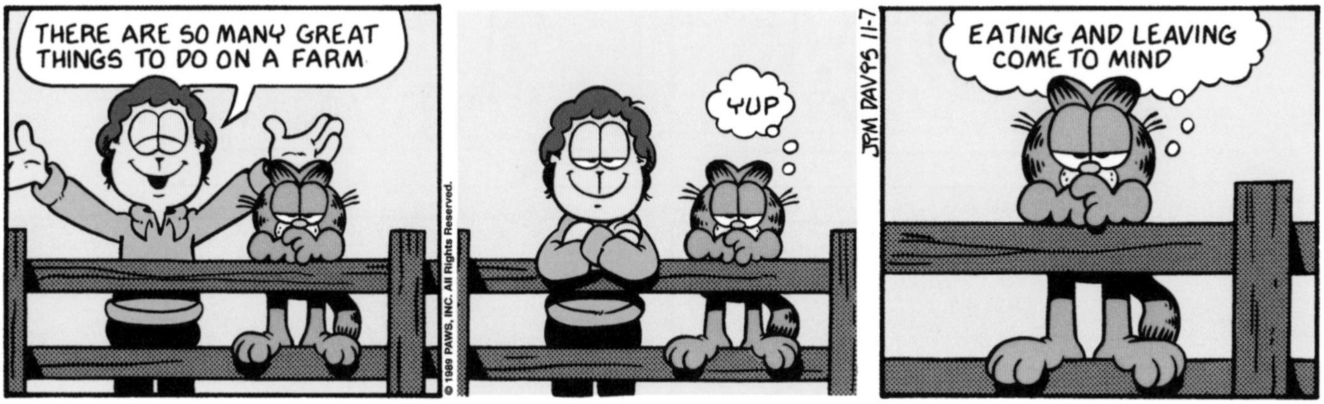
THERE ARE SO MANY GREAT THINGS TO DO ON A FARM
© 1989 PAWS, INC. All Rights Reserved.
YUP
JIM DAVIS 11-7
EATING AND LEAVING COME TO MIND

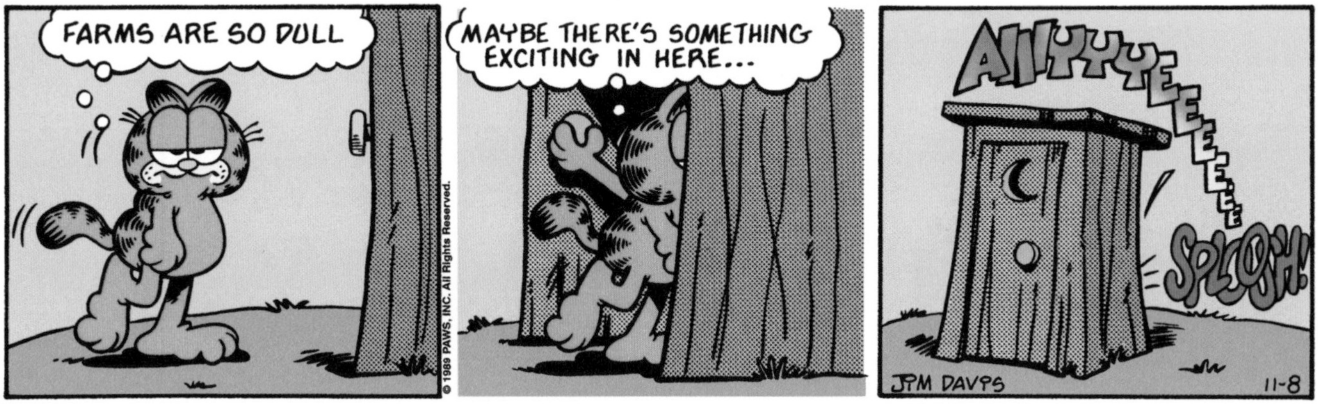
FARMS ARE SO DULL
© 1989 PAWS, INC. All Rights Reserved.
MAYBE THERE'S SOMETHING EXCITING IN HERE...
AIIYYYEEEEEEE
SPLOOSH!
JIM DAVIS
11-8

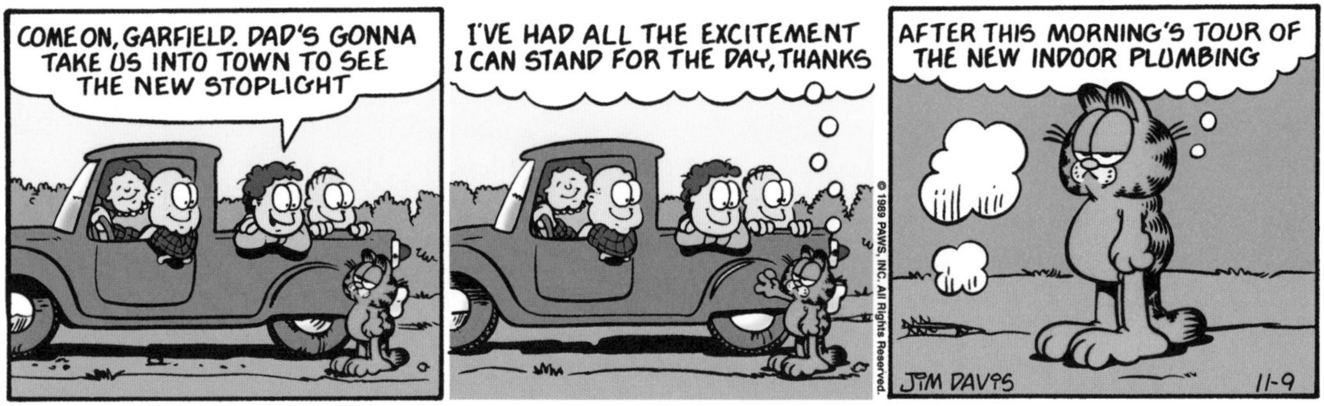
COME ON, GARFIELD. DAD'S GONNA TAKE US INTO TOWN TO SEE THE NEW STOPLIGHT
I'VE HAD ALL THE EXCITEMENT I CAN STAND FOR THE DAY, THANKS
AFTER THIS MORNING'S TOUR OF THE NEW INDOOR PLUMBING
© 1989 PAWS, INC. All Rights Reserved.
JIM DAVIS
11-9

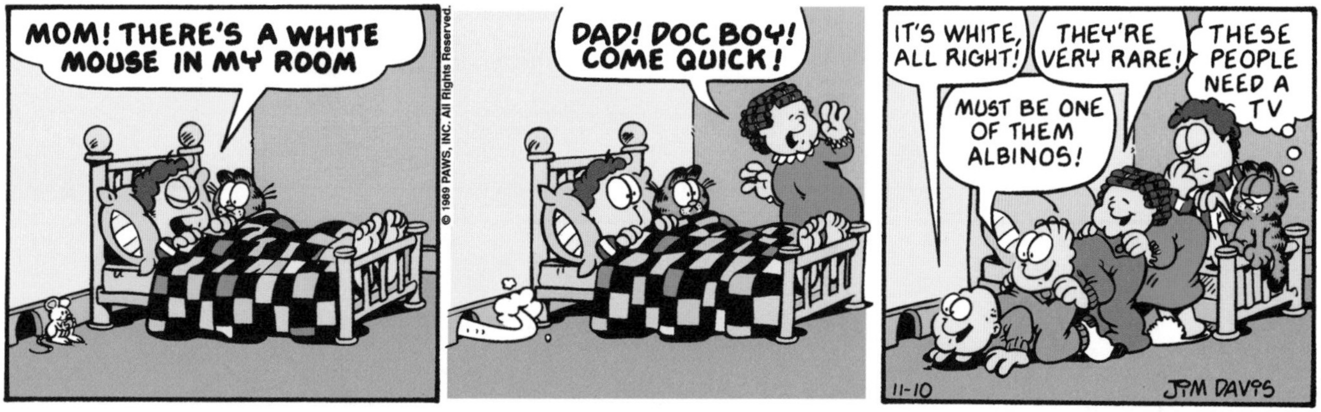
MOM! THERE'S A WHITE MOUSE IN MY ROOM
© 1989 PAWS, INC. All Rights Reserved.
DAD! DOC BOY! COME QUICK!
IT'S WHITE, ALL RIGHT!
THEY'RE VERY RARE!
MUST BE ONE OF THEM ALBINOS!
THESE PEOPLE NEED A
TV
11-10
JIM DAVIS

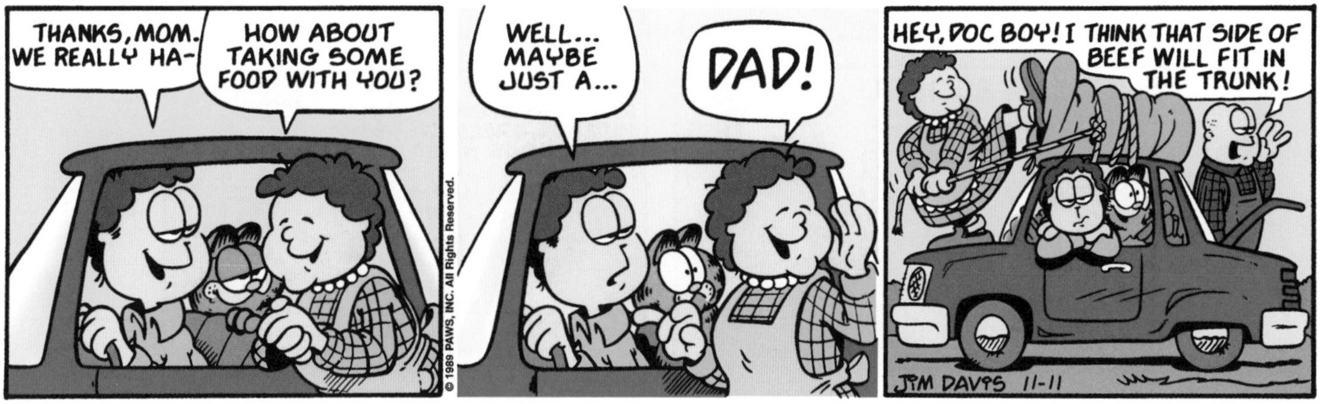
THANKS, MOM. WE REALLY HA-
HOW ABOUT TAKING SOME FOOD WITH YOU?
© 1989 PAWS, INC. All Rights Reserved.
WELL... MAYBE JUST A...
DAD!
HEY, DOC BOY! I THINK THAT SIDE OF BEEF WILL FIT IN THE TRUNK!
JIM DAVIS 11-11

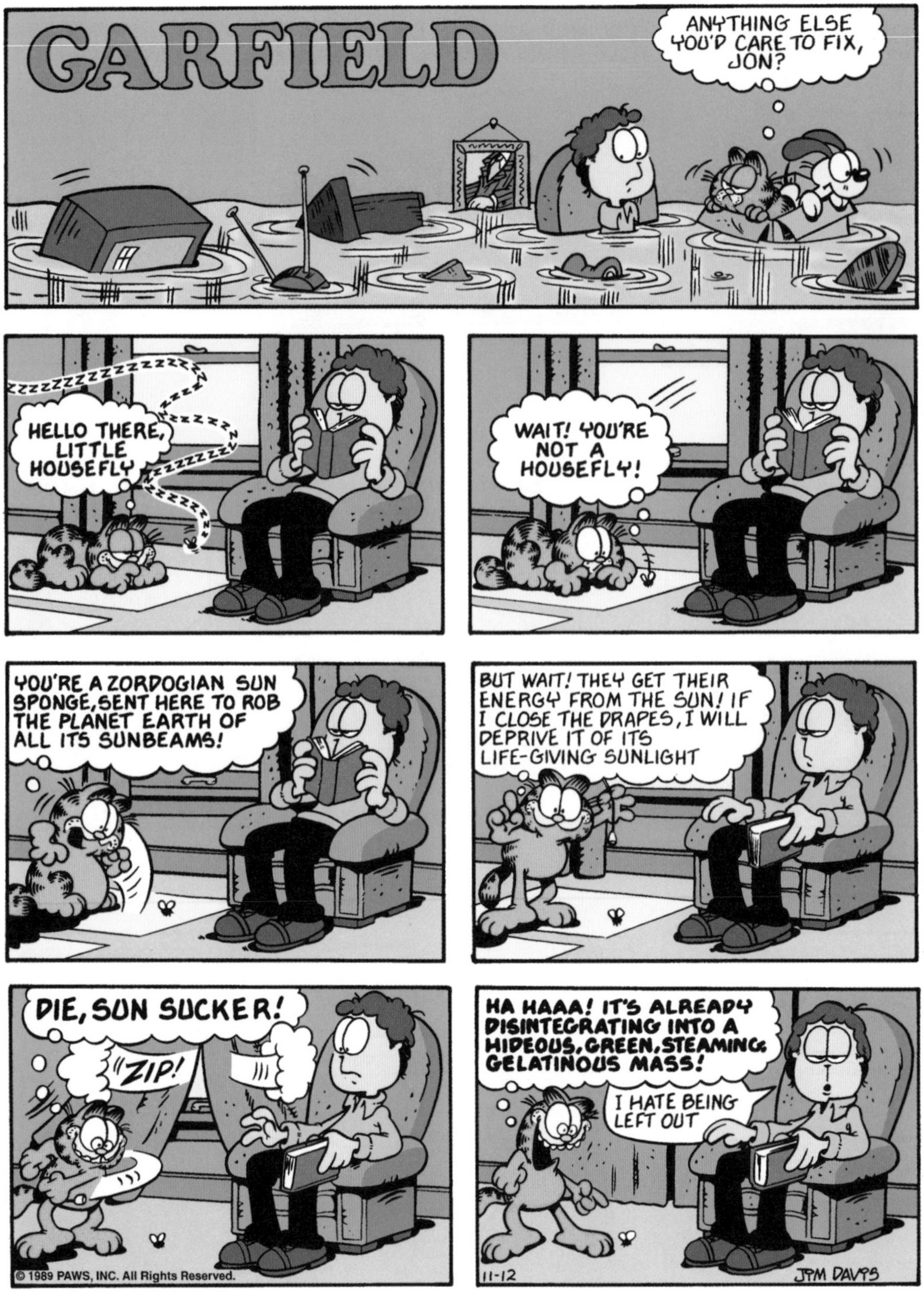
GARFIELD
ANYTHING ELSE YOU'D CARE TO FIX, JON?
HELLO THERE, LITTLE HOUSEFLY
WAIT! YOU'RE NOT A HOUSEFLY!
YOU'RE A ZORDOGIAN SUN SPONGE, SENT HERE TO ROB THE PLANET EARTH OF ALL ITS SUNBEAMS!
BUT WAIT! THEY GET THEIR ENERGY FROM THE SUN! IF I CLOSE THE DRAPES, I WILL DEPRIVE IT OF ITS LIFE-GIVING SUNLIGHT
DIE, SUN SUCKER!
ZIP!
HA HAAA! IT'S ALREADY DISINTEGRATING INTO A HIDEOUS, GREEN, STEAMING, GELATINOUS MASS!
I HATE BEING LEFT OUT
11-12
JIM DAVIS

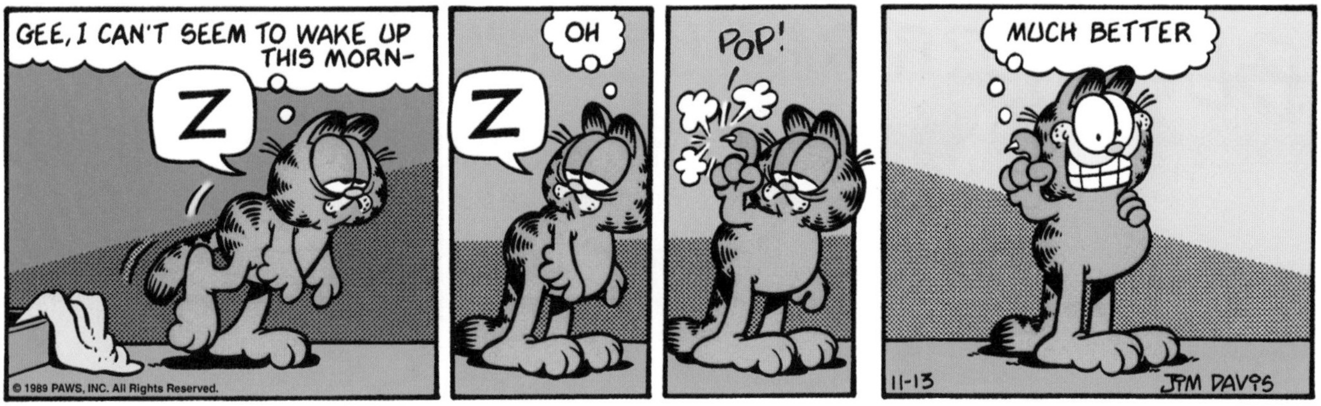
GEE, I CAN'T SEEM TO WAKE UP THIS MORN-
Z
© 1989 PAWS, INC. All Rights Reserved.
OH
Z
POP!
MUCH BETTER
11-13
JIM DAVIS

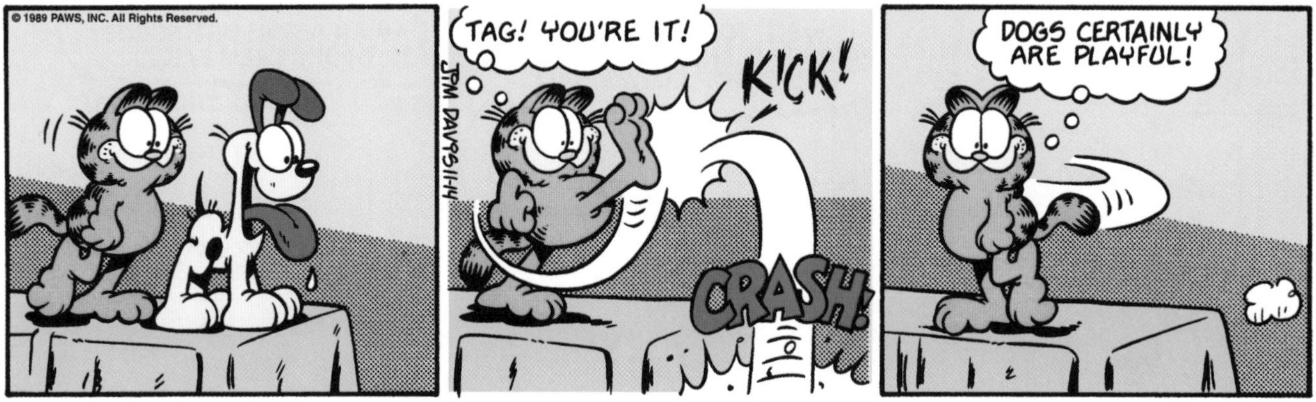
© 1989 PAWS, INC. All Rights Reserved.
TAG! YOU'RE IT!
JIM DAVIS 11-14
KICK!
CRASH!
DOGS CERTAINLY ARE PLAYFUL!

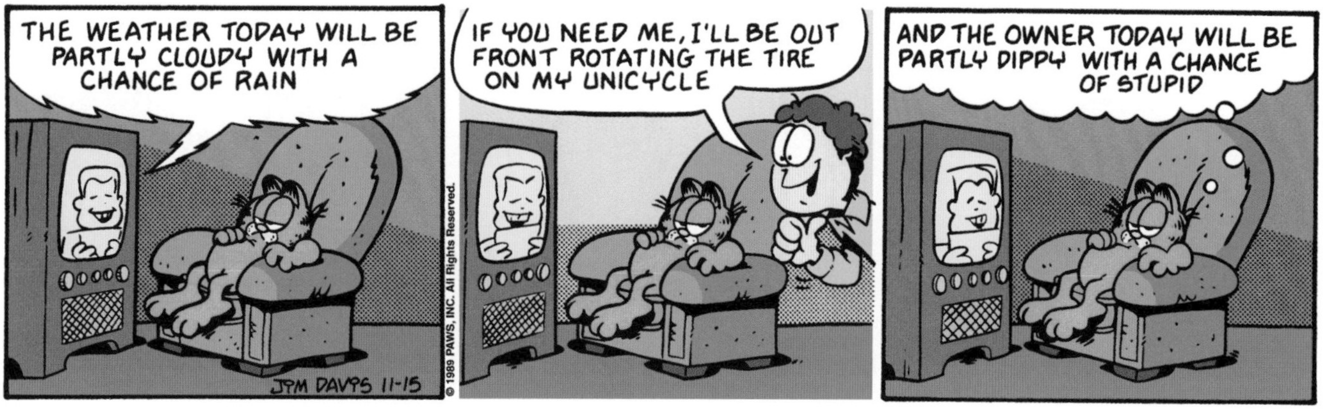
THE WEATHER TODAY WILL BE PARTLY CLOUDY WITH A CHANCE OF RAIN
JIM DAVIS 11-15
© 1989 PAWS, INC. All Rights Reserved.
IF YOU NEED ME, I'LL BE OUT FRONT ROTATING THE TIRE ON MY UNICYCLE
AND THE OWNER TODAY WILL BE PARTLY DIPPY WITH A CHANCE OF STUPID

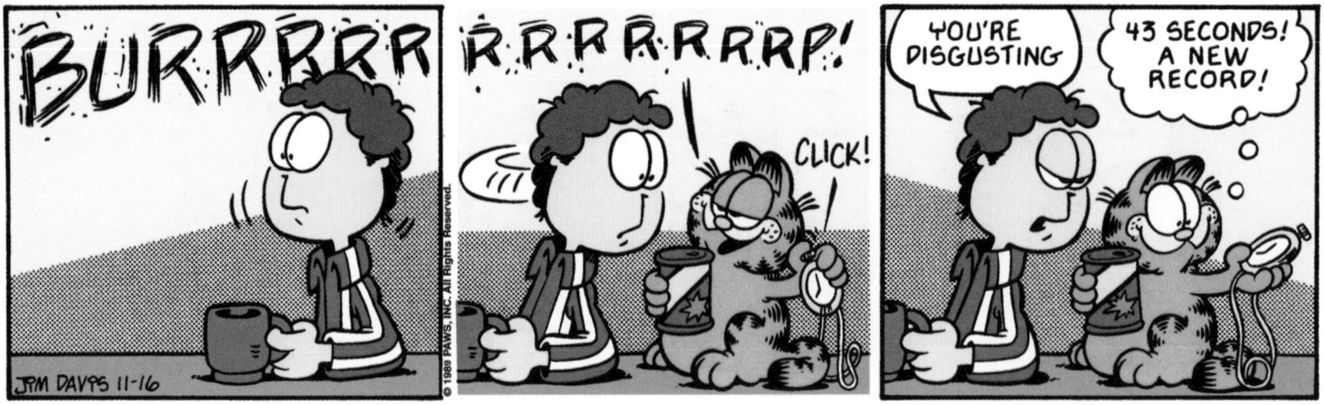
BURRRRRR
RRRRRRRP!
CLICK!
YOU'RE DISGUSTING
43 SECONDS! A NEW RECORD!
JIM DAVIS 11-16
© 1989 PAWS, INC. All Rights Reserved.

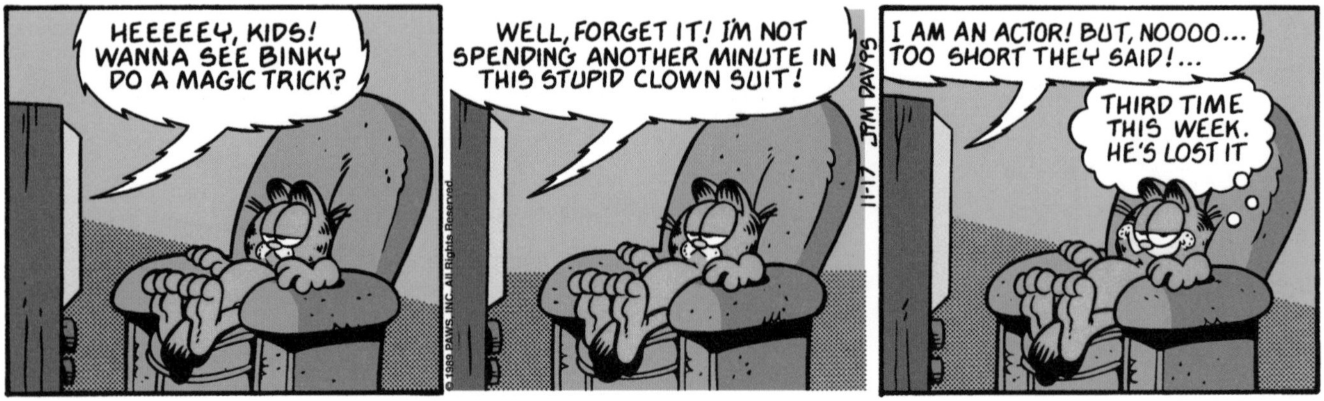
HEEEEEY, KIDS! WANNA SEE BINKY DO A MAGIC TRICK?
WELL, FORGET IT! I'M NOT SPENDING ANOTHER MINUTE IN THIS STUPID CLOWN SUIT!
I AM AN ACTOR! BUT, NOOOO... TOO SHORT THEY SAID!...
THIRD TIME THIS WEEK. HE'S LOST IT
JIM DAVIS 11-17
© 1989 PAWS, INC. All Rights Reserved.

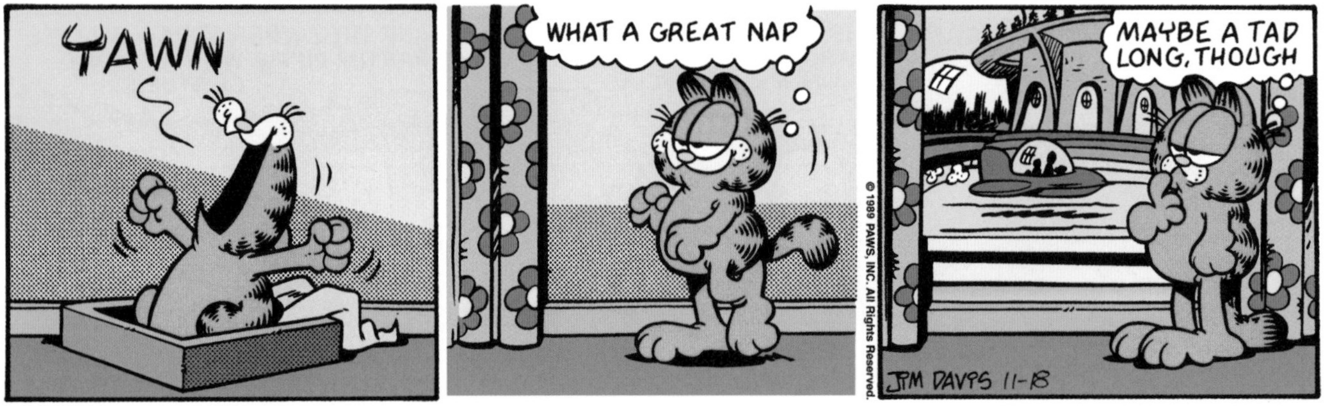
YAWN
WHAT A GREAT NAP
MAYBE A TAD LONG, THOUGH
JIM DAVIS 11-18
© 1989 PAWS, INC. All Rights Reserved.

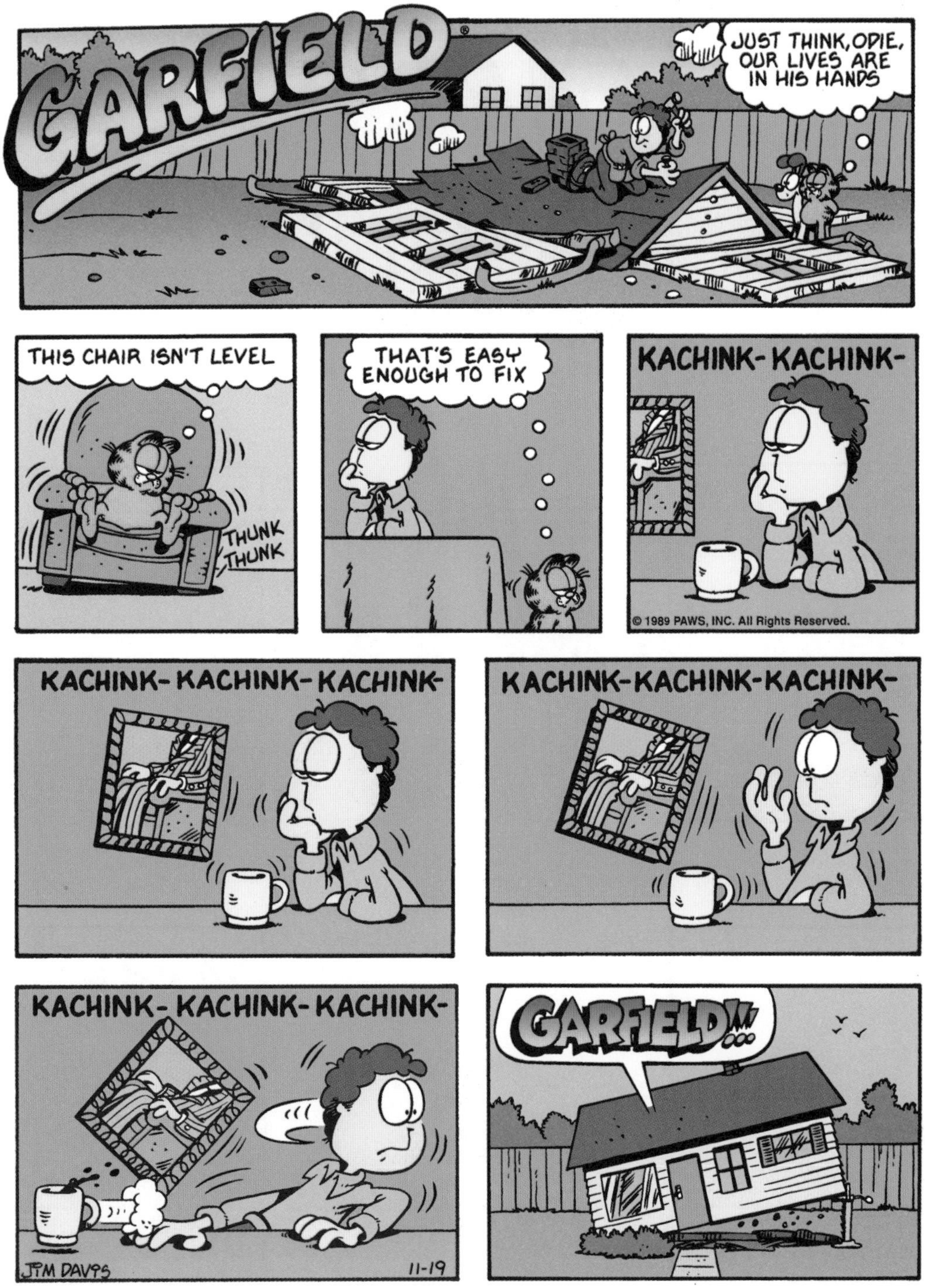
GARFIELD®
JUST THINK, ODIE, OUR LIVES ARE IN HIS HANDS
THIS CHAIR ISN'T LEVEL
THUNK THUNK
THAT'S EASY ENOUGH TO FIX
KACHINK- KACHINK-
© 1989 PAWS, INC. All Rights Reserved.
KACHINK- KACHINK- KACHINK-
KACHINK- KACHINK- KACHINK-
KACHINK- KACHINK- KACHINK-
JIM DAVIS
11-19
GARFIELD!!

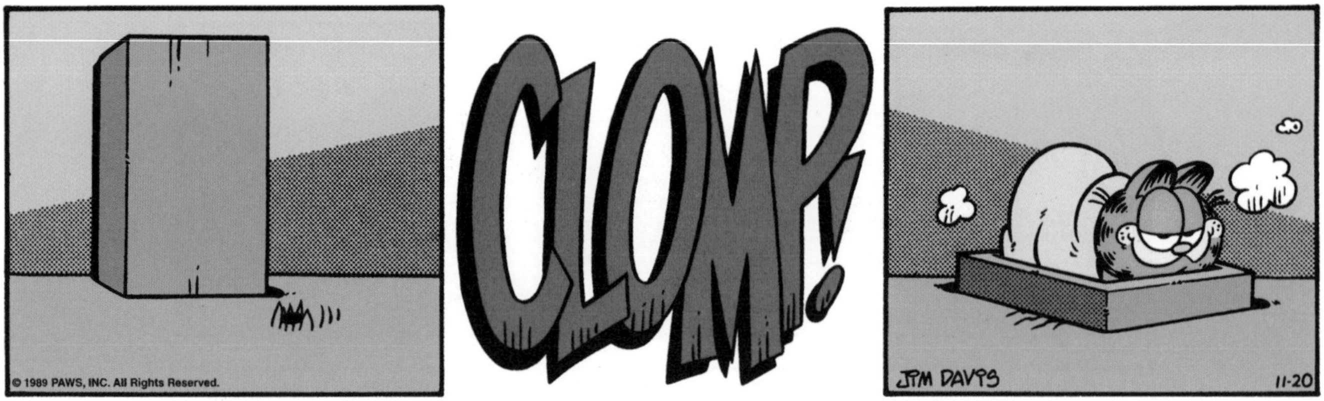
© 1989 PAWS, INC. All Rights Reserved.
CLOMP!
JIM DAVIS
11-20

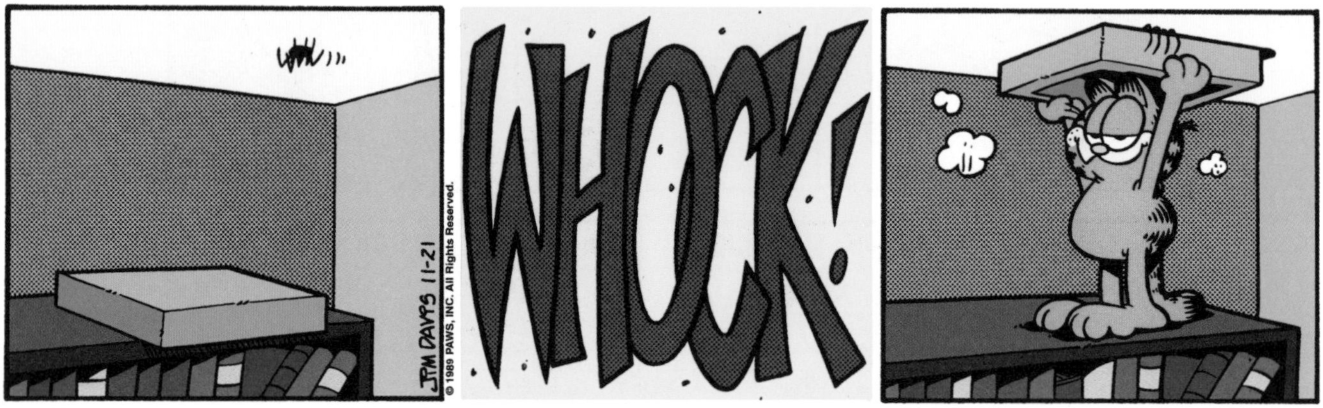
JIM DAVIS 11-21
© 1989 PAWS, INC. All Rights Reserved.
WHOCK!

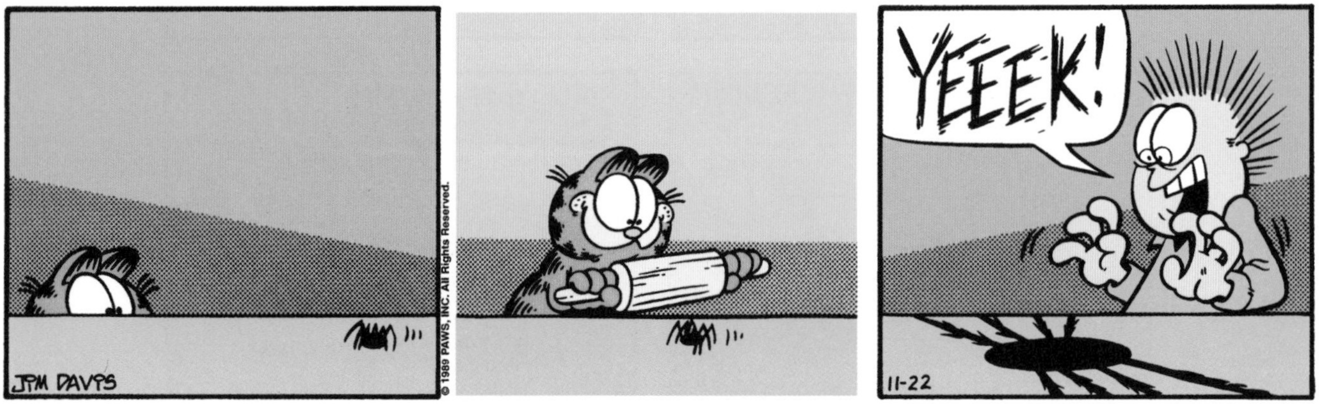
JIM DAVIS
© 1989 PAWS, INC. All Rights Reserved.
YEEEK!
11-22

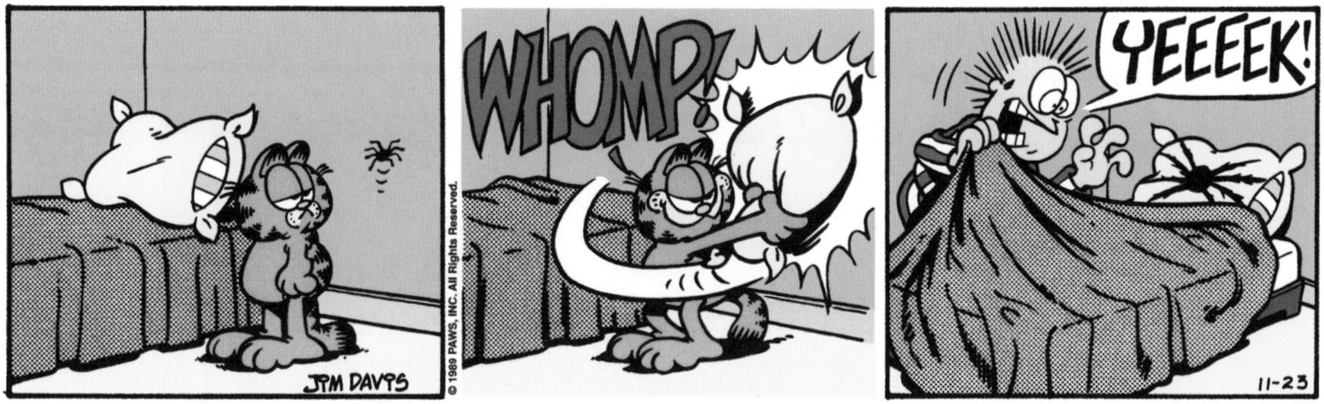
JIM DAVIS
© 1989 PAWS, INC. All Rights Reserved.
WHOMP!
YEEEEK!
11-23

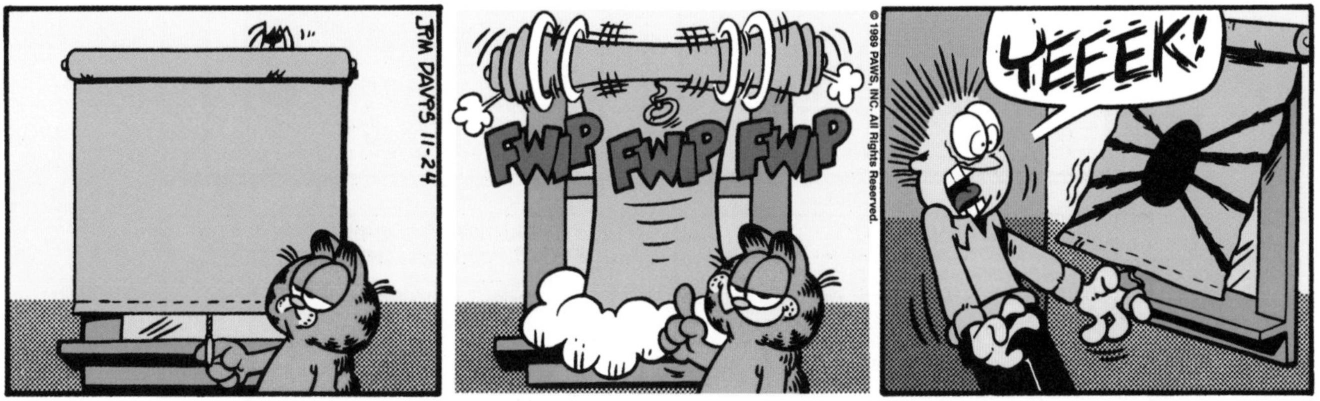
JIM DAVIS 11-24
FWIP FWIP FWIP
© 1989 PAWS, INC. All Rights Reserved.
YEEEK!

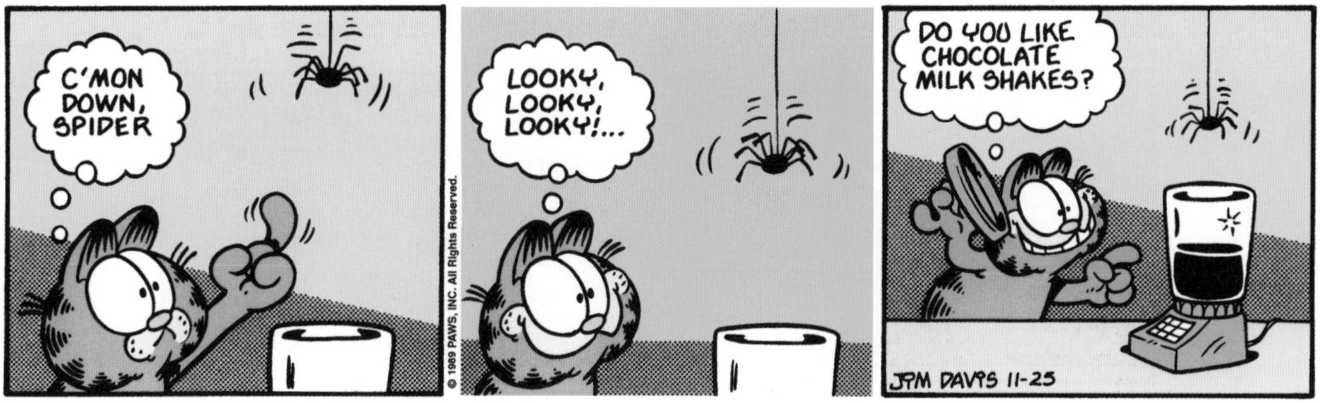
C'MON DOWN, SPIDER
© 1989 PAWS, INC. All Rights Reserved.
LOOKY, LOOKY, LOOKY!...
DO YOU LIKE CHOCOLATE MILK SHAKES?
JIM DAVIS 11-25

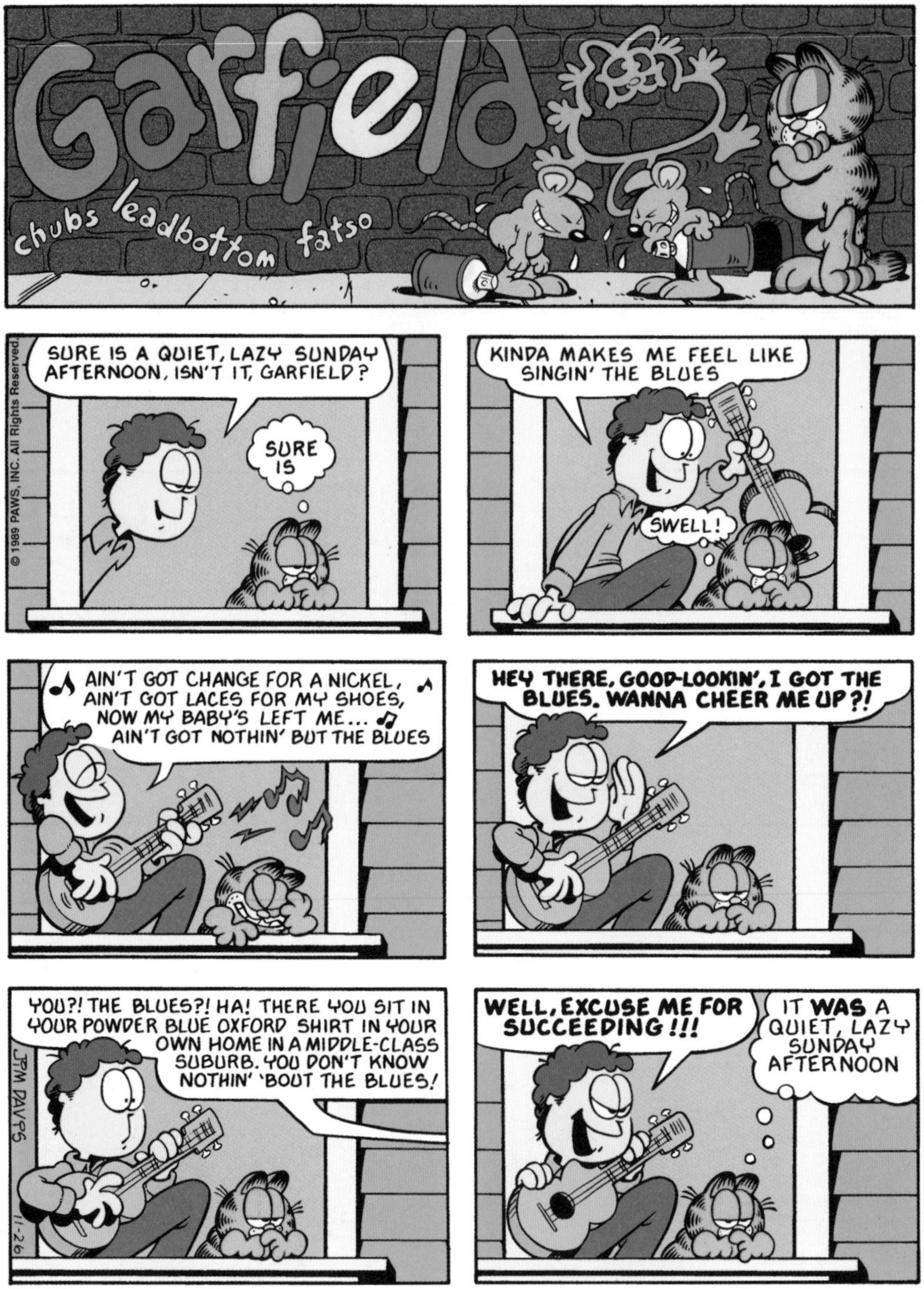
Garfield
chubs leadbottom fatso
SURE IS A QUIET, LAZY SUNDAY AFTERNOON, ISN'T IT, GARFIELD?
SURE IS
KINDA MAKES ME FEEL LIKE SINGIN' THE BLUES
SWELL!
AIN'T GOT CHANGE FOR A NICKEL, AIN'T GOT LACES FOR MY SHOES, NOW MY BABY'S LEFT ME... AIN'T GOT NOTHIN' BUT THE BLUES
HEY THERE, GOOD-LOOKIN', I GOT THE BLUES. WANNA CHEER ME UP?!
YOU?! THE BLUES?! HA! THERE YOU SIT IN YOUR POWDER BLUE OXFORD SHIRT IN YOUR OWN HOME IN A MIDDLE-CLASS SUBURB. YOU DON'T KNOW NOTHIN' 'BOUT THE BLUES!
JIM DAVIS
11-26
WELL, EXCUSE ME FOR SUCCEEDING!!!
IT WAS A QUIET, LAZY SUNDAY AFTERNOON

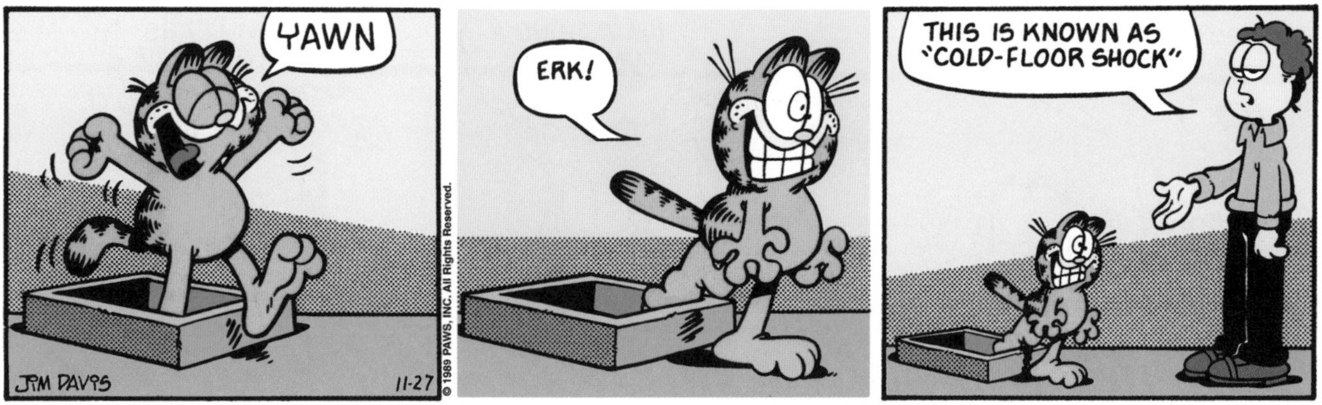
YAWN
JIM DAVIS 11-27
© 1989 PAWS, INC. All Rights Reserved.
ERK!
THIS IS KNOWN AS "COLD-FLOOR SHOCK"

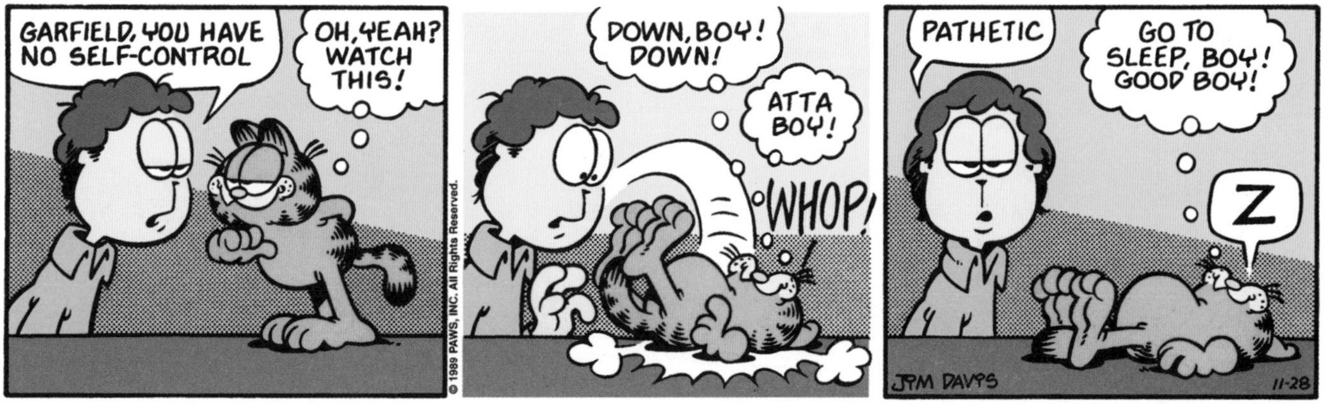
GARFIELD, YOU HAVE NO SELF-CONTROL
OH, YEAH? WATCH THIS!
© 1989 PAWS, INC. All Rights Reserved.
DOWN, BOY! DOWN!
ATTA BOY!
WHOP!
PATHETIC
GO TO SLEEP, BOY! GOOD BOY!
Z
JIM DAVIS 11-28

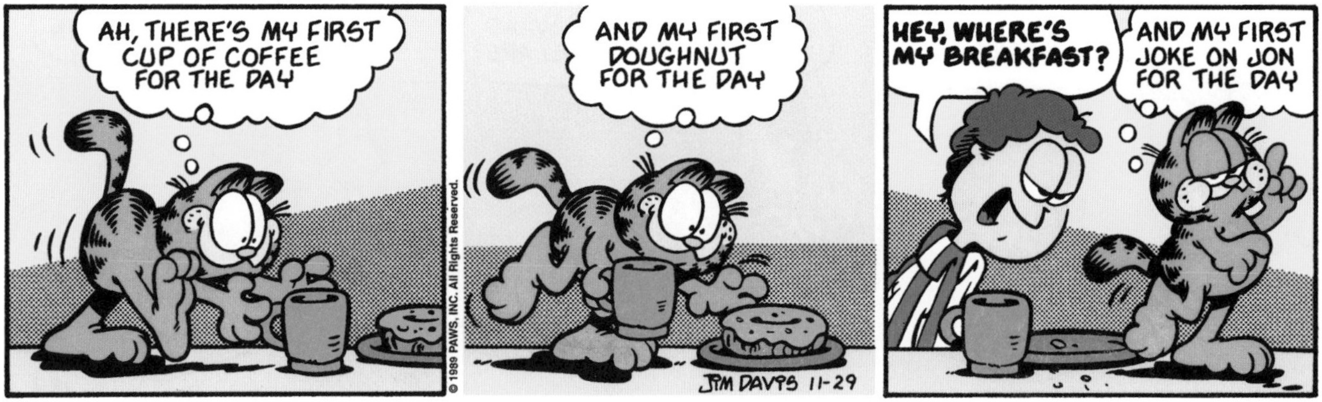
AH, THERE'S MY FIRST CUP OF COFFEE FOR THE DAY
© 1989 PAWS, INC. All Rights Reserved.
AND MY FIRST DOUGHNUT FOR THE DAY
JIM DAVIS 11-29
HEY, WHERE'S MY BREAKFAST?
AND MY FIRST JOKE ON JON FOR THE DAY

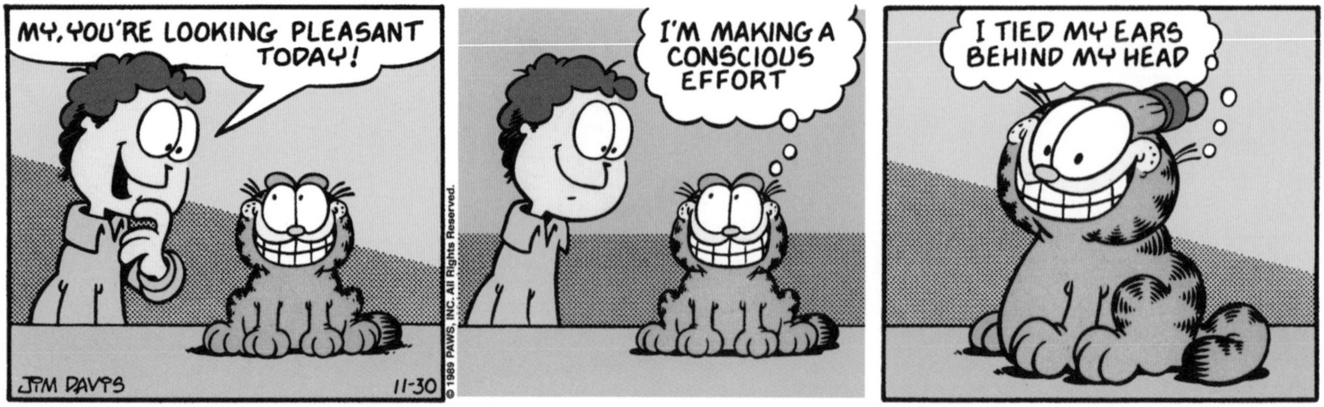
MY, YOU'RE LOOKING PLEASANT TODAY!
JIM DAVIS
11-30
© 1989 PAWS, INC. All Rights Reserved.
I'M MAKING A CONSCIOUS EFFORT
I TIED MY EARS BEHIND MY HEAD

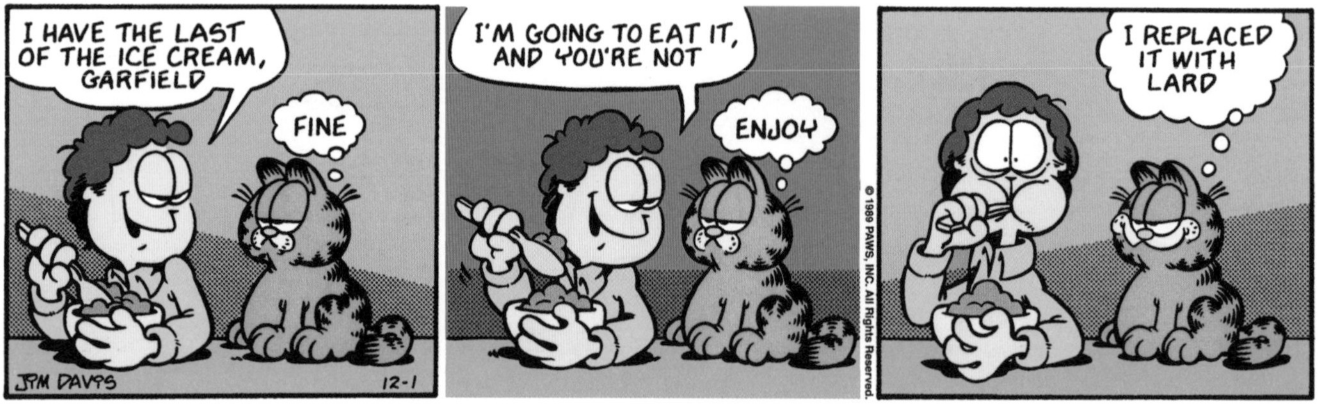
I HAVE THE LAST OF THE ICE CREAM, GARFIELD
FINE
JIM DAVIS
12-1
I'M GOING TO EAT IT, AND YOU'RE NOT
ENJOY
© 1989 PAWS, INC. All Rights Reserved.
I REPLACED IT WITH LARD

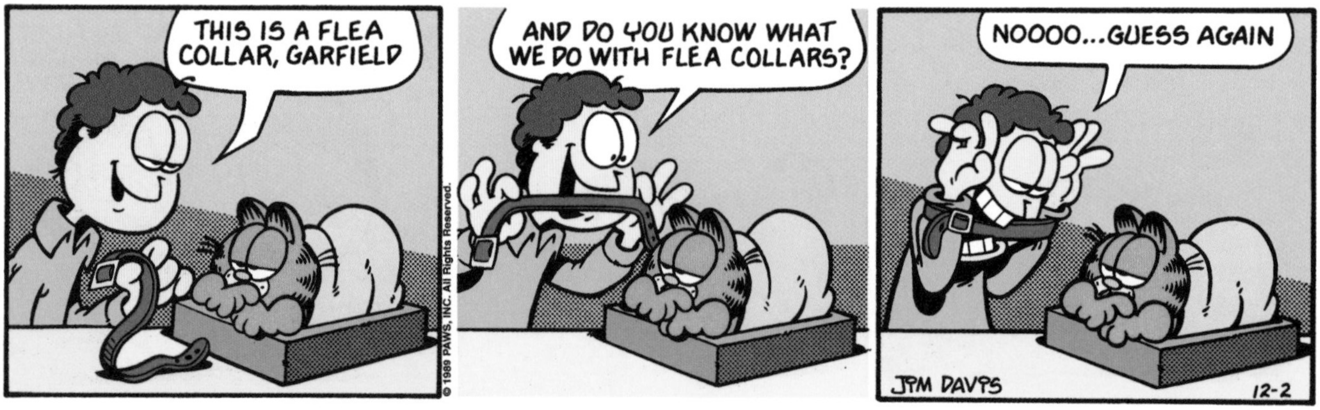
THIS IS A FLEA COLLAR, GARFIELD
© 1989 PAWS, INC. All Rights Reserved.
AND DO YOU KNOW WHAT WE DO WITH FLEA COLLARS?
NOOOO...GUESS AGAIN
JIM DAVIS
12-2

GARFIELD
I COULD HAVE SWORN I LEFT MY SECRET FORMULA HERE SOMEWHERE
JIM DAVIS
12-3
© 1989 PAWS, INC. All Rights Reserved.
CLICK
HEEEY, KIDS!

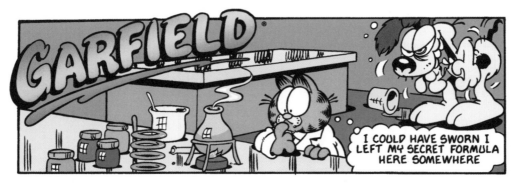

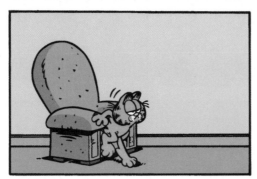

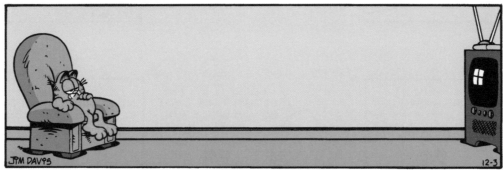

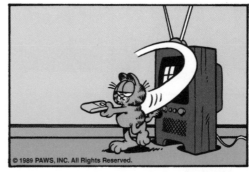

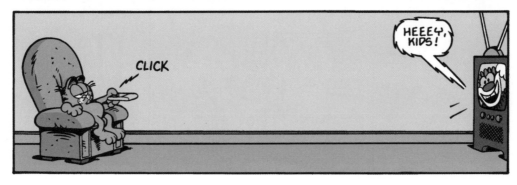

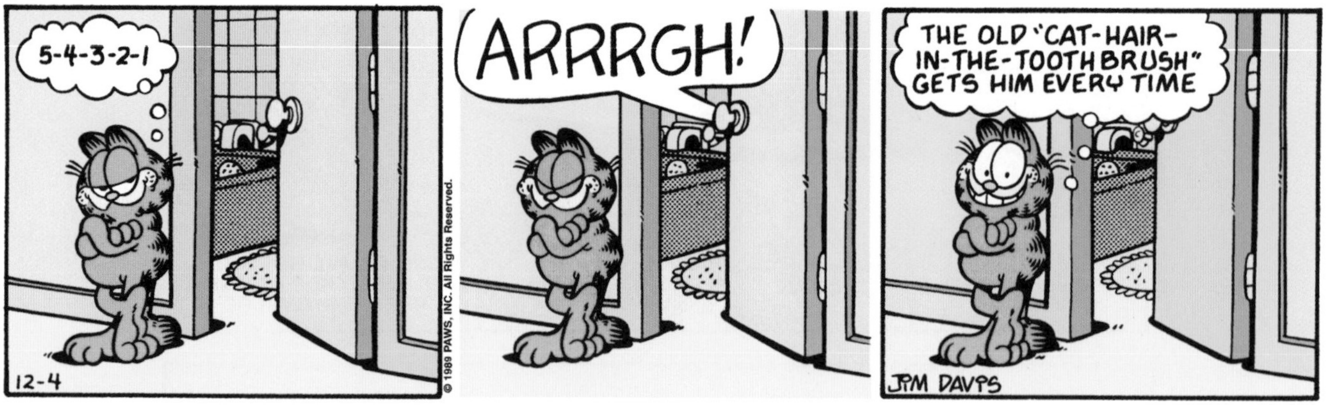
5-4-3-2-1
12-4
© 1989 PAWS, INC. All Rights Reserved.
ARRRGH!
THE OLD "CAT-HAIR-IN-THE-TOOTHBRUSH" GETS HIM EVERY TIME
JIM DAVIS

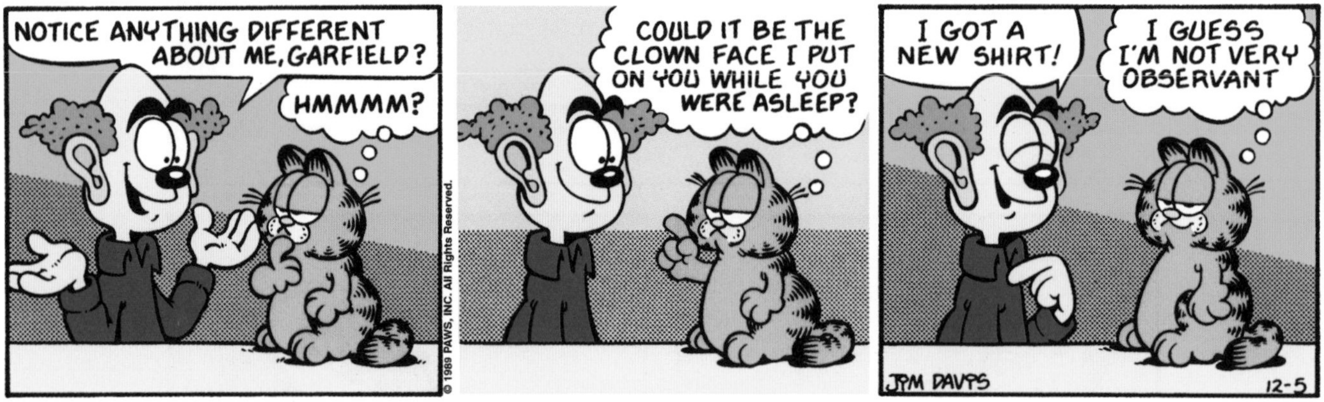
NOTICE ANYTHING DIFFERENT ABOUT ME, GARFIELD?
HMMMM?
© 1989 PAWS, INC. All Rights Reserved.
COULD IT BE THE CLOWN FACE I PUT ON YOU WHILE YOU WERE ASLEEP?
I GOT A NEW SHIRT!
I GUESS I'M NOT VERY OBSERVANT
JIM DAVIS
12-5

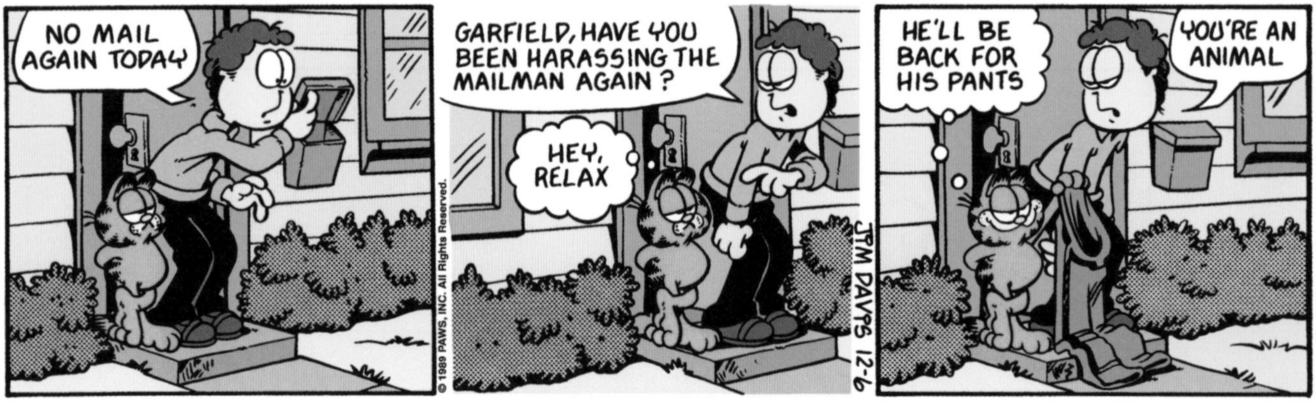
NO MAIL AGAIN TODAY
© 1989 PAWS, INC. All Rights Reserved.
GARFIELD, HAVE YOU BEEN HARASSING THE MAILMAN AGAIN?
HEY, RELAX
JIM DAVIS 12-6
HE'LL BE BACK FOR HIS PANTS
YOU'RE AN ANIMAL

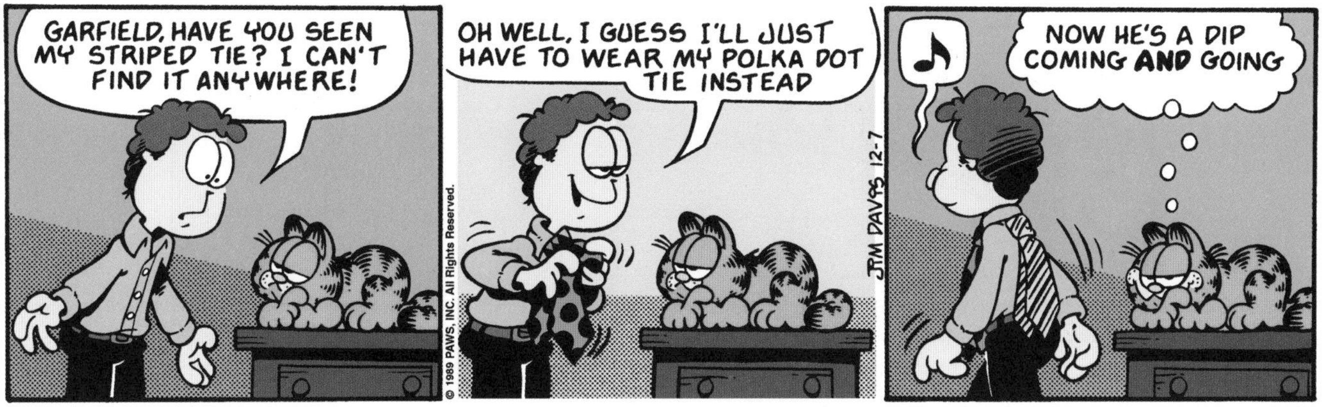
GARFIELD, HAVE YOU SEEN MY STRIPED TIE? I CAN'T FIND IT ANYWHERE!
OH WELL, I GUESS I'LL JUST HAVE TO WEAR MY POLKA DOT TIE INSTEAD
NOW HE'S A DIP COMING **AND** GOING
© 1989 PAWS, INC. All Rights Reserved.
JIM DAVIS 12-7

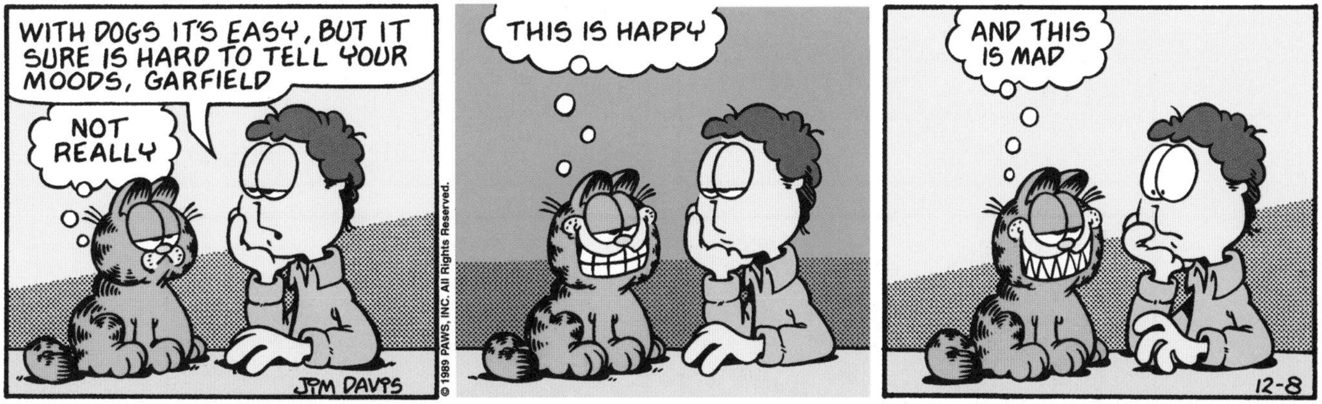
WITH DOGS IT'S EASY, BUT IT SURE IS HARD TO TELL YOUR MOODS, GARFIELD
NOT REALLY
JIM DAVIS
© 1989 PAWS, INC. All Rights Reserved.
THIS IS HAPPY
AND THIS IS MAD
12-8

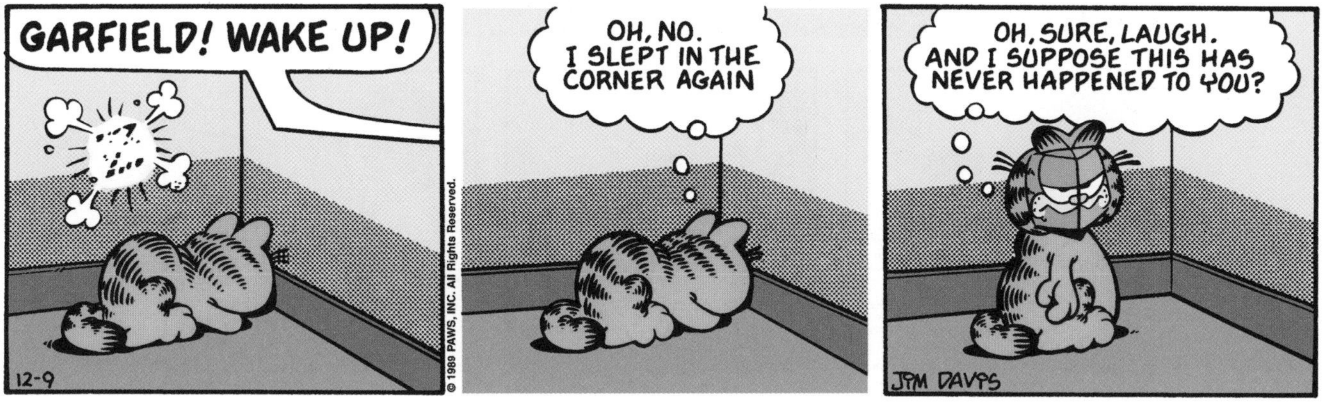
GARFIELD! WAKE UP!
12-9
© 1989 PAWS, INC. All Rights Reserved.
OH, NO. I SLEPT IN THE CORNER AGAIN
OH, SURE, LAUGH. AND I SUPPOSE THIS HAS NEVER HAPPENED TO YOU?
JIM DAVIS

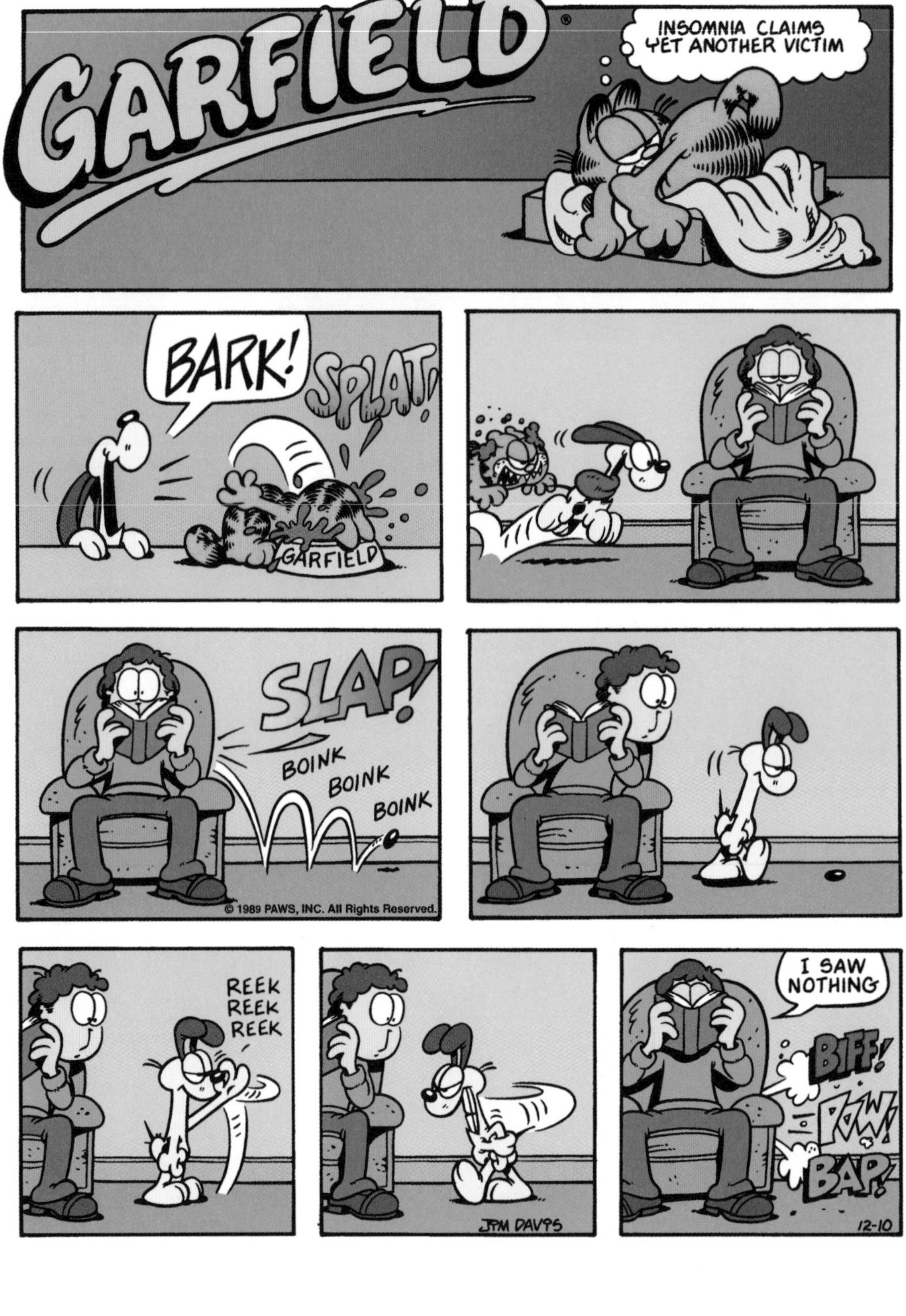
GARFIELD®
INSOMNIA CLAIMS YET ANOTHER VICTIM
BARK!
SPLAT!
GARFIELD
SLAP!
BOINK
BOINK
BOINK
© 1989 PAWS, INC. All Rights Reserved.
REEK
REEK
REEK
JPM DAVPS
I SAW NOTHING
BIFF!
POW!
BAP!
12-10

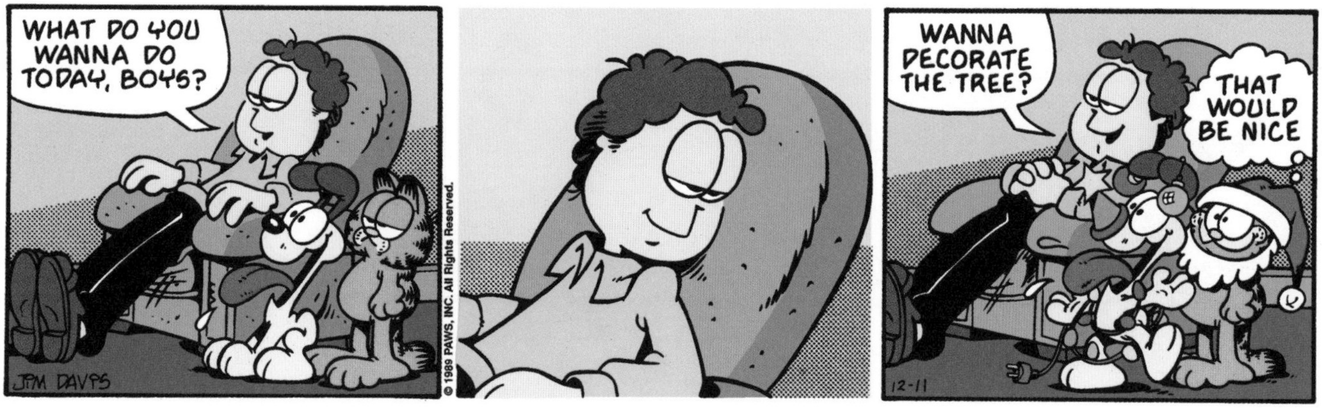
WHAT DO YOU WANNA DO TODAY, BOYS?
JIM DAVIS
© 1989 PAWS, INC. All Rights Reserved.
WANNA DECORATE THE TREE?
THAT WOULD BE NICE
12-11

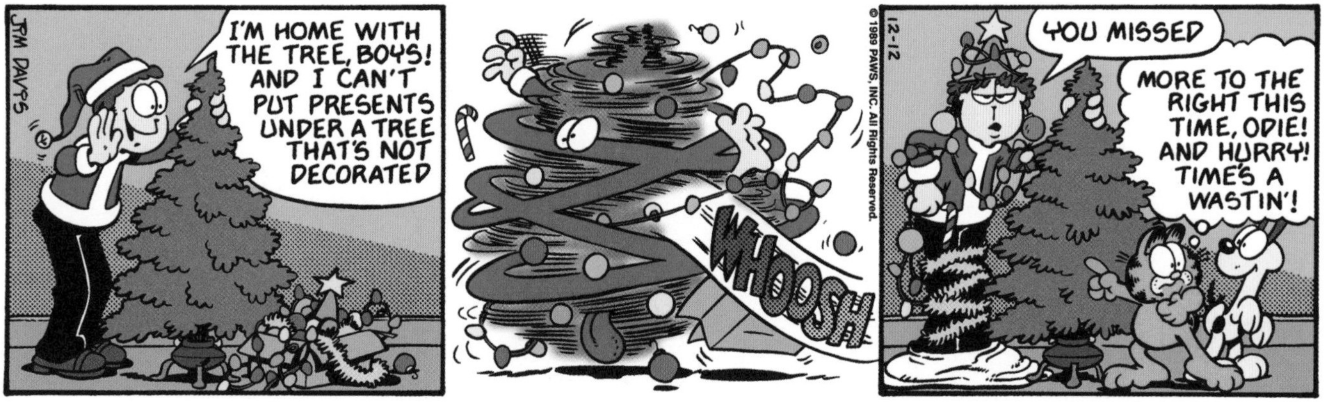
JIM DAVIS
I'M HOME WITH THE TREE, BOYS! AND I CAN'T PUT PRESENTS UNDER A TREE THAT'S NOT DECORATED
WHOOSH
© 1989 PAWS, INC. All Rights Reserved.
12-12
YOU MISSED
MORE TO THE RIGHT THIS TIME, ODIE! AND HURRY! TIME'S A WASTIN'!

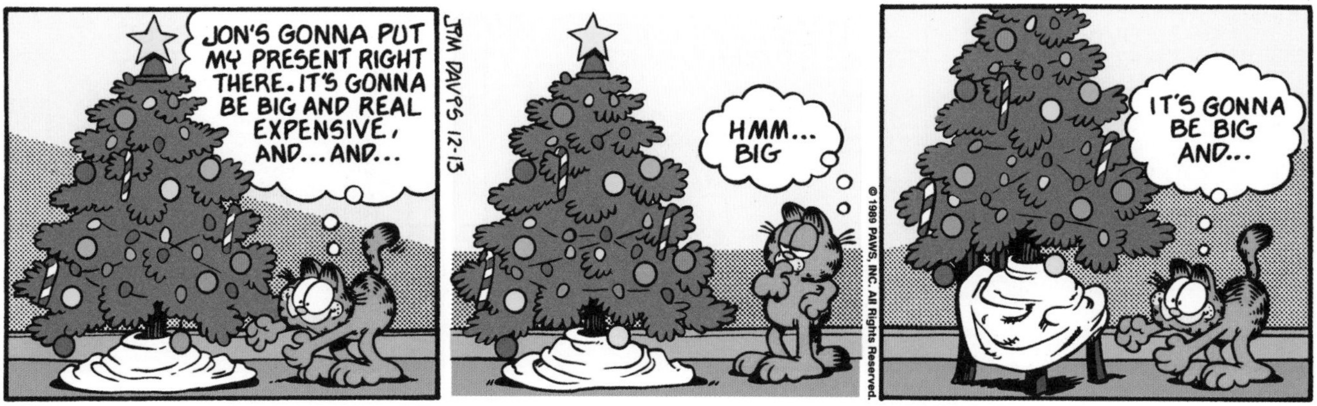
JON'S GONNA PUT MY PRESENT RIGHT THERE. IT'S GONNA BE BIG AND REAL EXPENSIVE, AND... AND...
JIM DAVIS 12-13
HMM... BIG
© 1989 PAWS, INC. All Rights Reserved.
IT'S GONNA BE BIG AND...

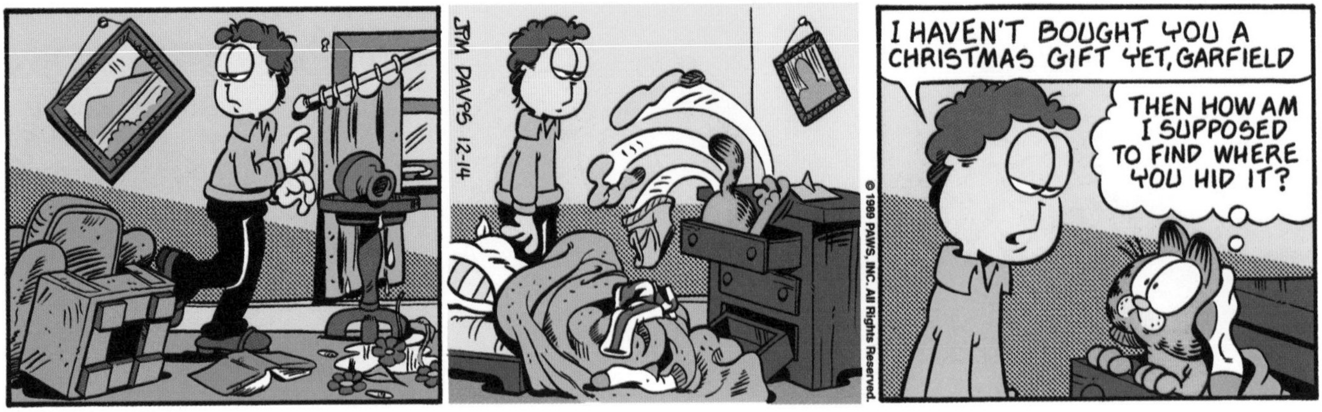
JIM DAVIS 12-14
I HAVEN'T BOUGHT YOU A CHRISTMAS GIFT YET, GARFIELD
THEN HOW AM I SUPPOSED TO FIND WHERE YOU HID IT?
© 1989 PAWS, INC. All Rights Reserved.

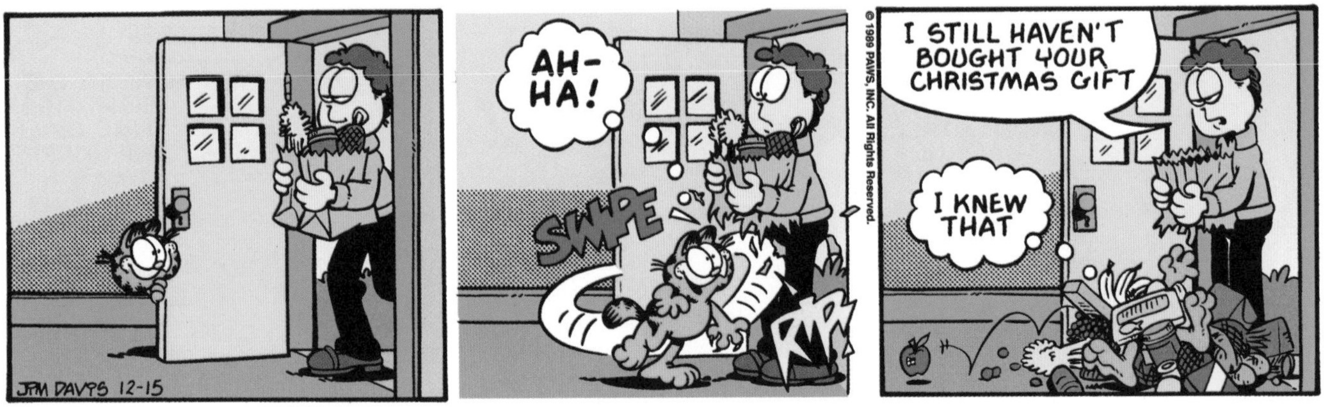
JIM DAVIS 12-15
AH-HA!
SWIPE
RIP
© 1989 PAWS, INC. All Rights Reserved.
I STILL HAVEN'T BOUGHT YOUR CHRISTMAS GIFT
I KNEW THAT

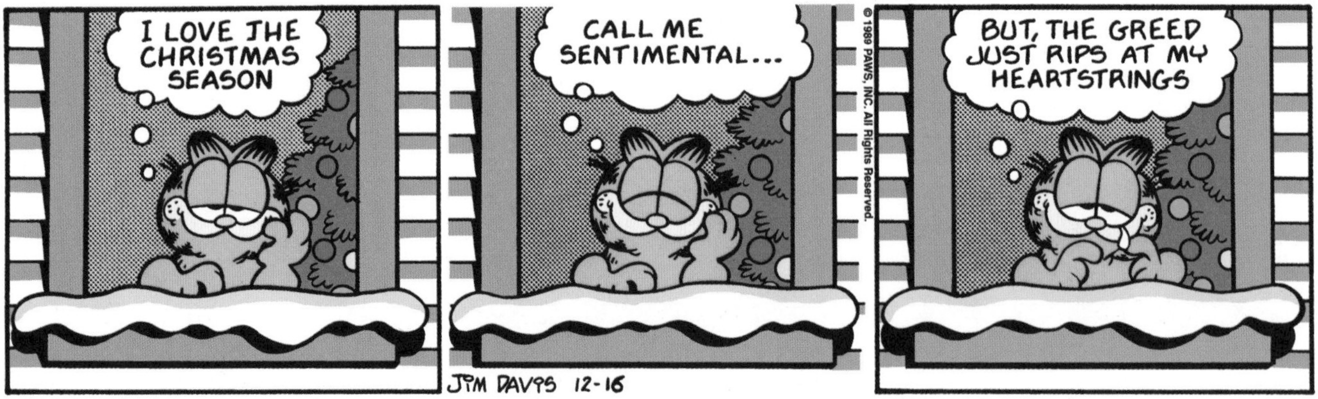
I LOVE THE CHRISTMAS SEASON
CALL ME SENTIMENTAL...
JIM DAVIS 12-16
© 1989 PAWS, INC. All Rights Reserved.
BUT, THE GREED JUST RIPS AT MY HEARTSTRINGS

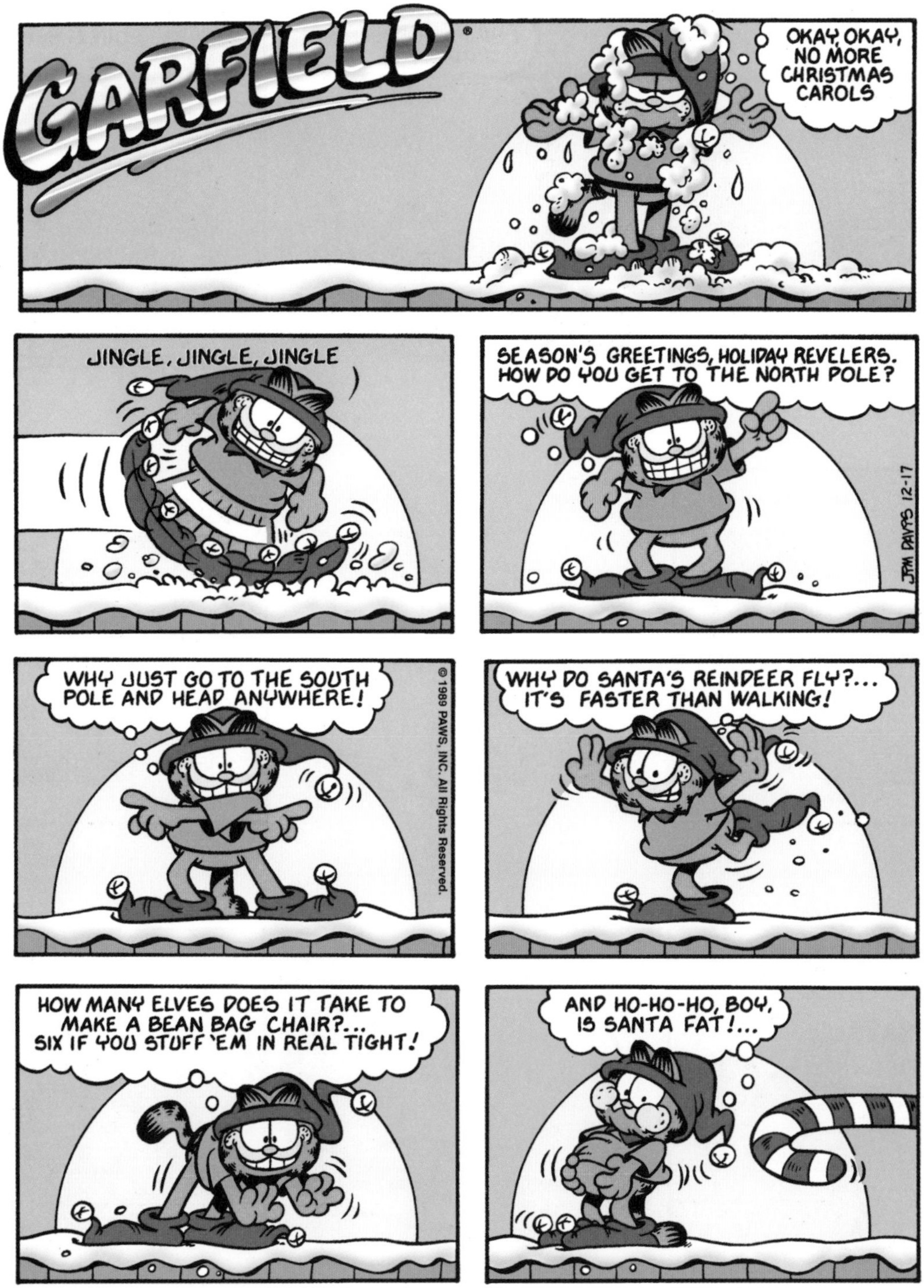
GARFIELD
OKAY, OKAY, NO MORE CHRISTMAS CAROLS
JINGLE, JINGLE, JINGLE
SEASON'S GREETINGS, HOLIDAY REVELERS. HOW DO YOU GET TO THE NORTH POLE?
JIM DAVIS 12-17
WHY JUST GO TO THE SOUTH POLE AND HEAD ANYWHERE!
© 1989 PAWS, INC. All Rights Reserved.
WHY DO SANTA'S REINDEER FLY?... IT'S FASTER THAN WALKING!
HOW MANY ELVES DOES IT TAKE TO MAKE A BEAN BAG CHAIR?... SIX IF YOU STUFF 'EM IN REAL TIGHT!
AND HO-HO-HO, BOY, IS SANTA FAT!...

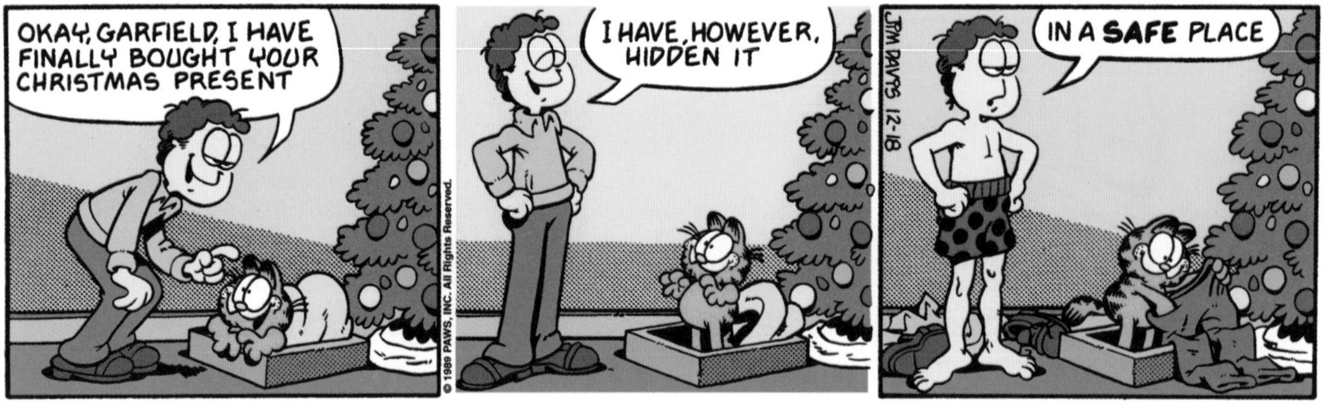
OKAY, GARFIELD, I HAVE FINALLY BOUGHT YOUR CHRISTMAS PRESENT
I HAVE, HOWEVER, HIDDEN IT
IN A **SAFE** PLACE
JIM DAVIS 12-18

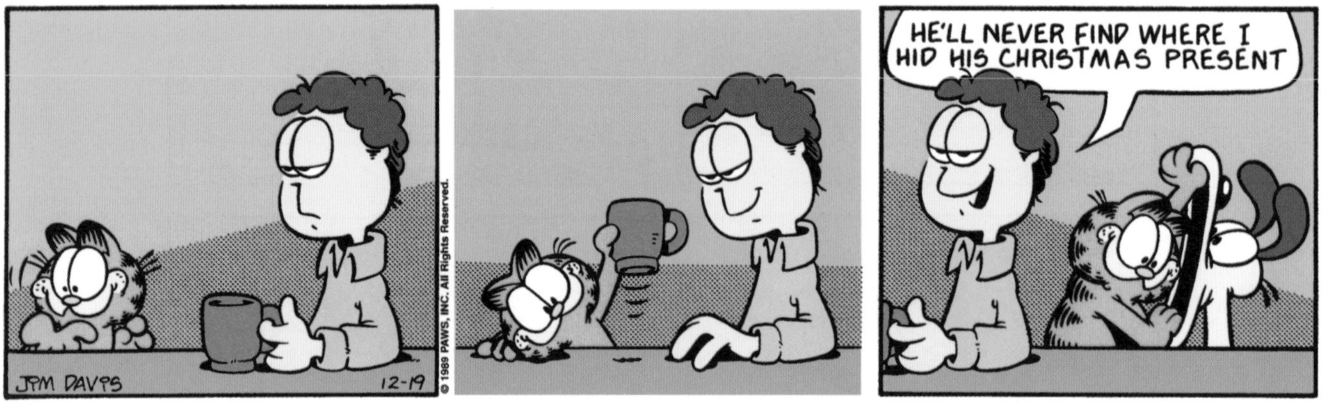
JIM DAVIS
12-19
HE'LL NEVER FIND WHERE I HID HIS CHRISTMAS PRESENT

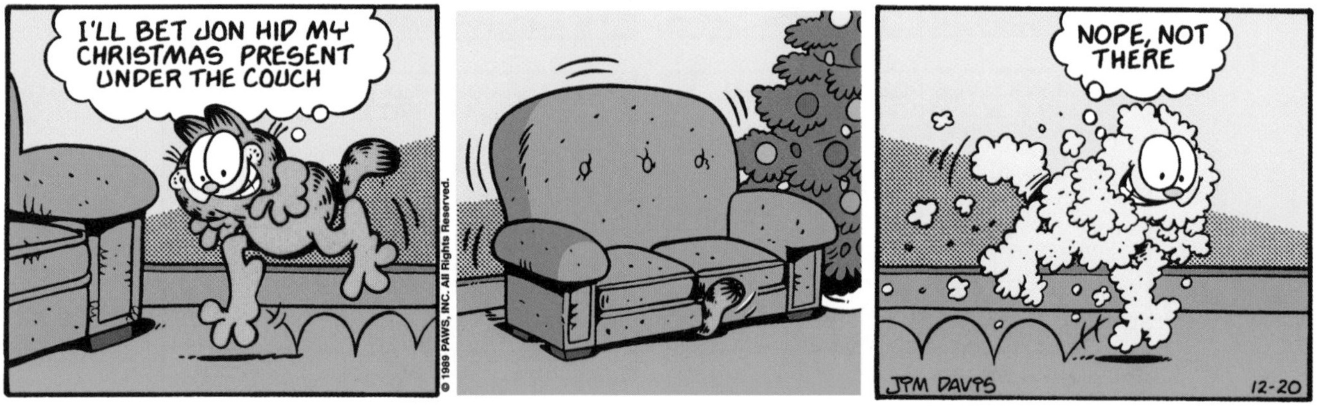
I'LL BET JON HID MY CHRISTMAS PRESENT UNDER THE COUCH
NOPE, NOT THERE
JIM DAVIS
12-20

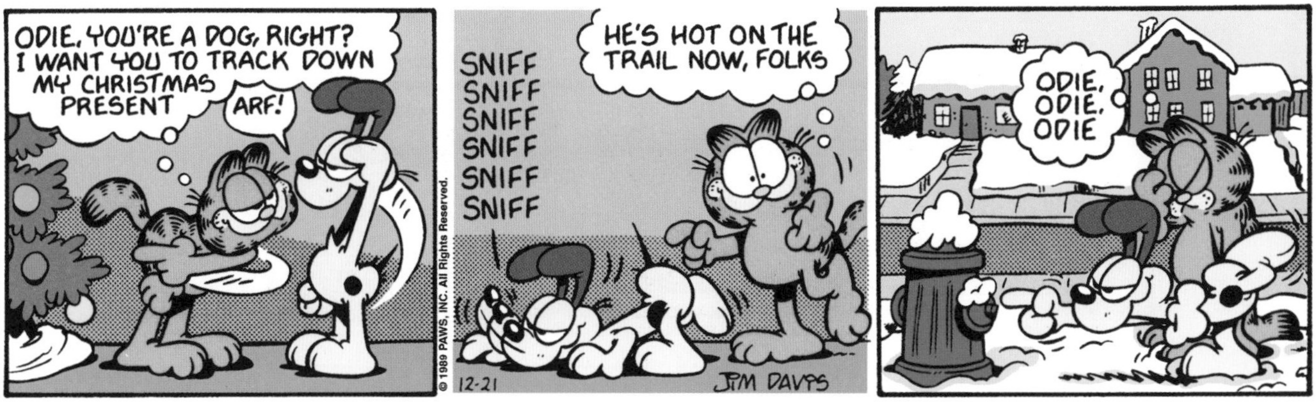
ODIE, YOU'RE A DOG, RIGHT? I WANT YOU TO TRACK DOWN MY CHRISTMAS PRESENT
ARF!
SNIFF SNIFF SNIFF SNIFF SNIFF SNIFF
HE'S HOT ON THE TRAIL NOW, FOLKS
© 1989 PAWS, INC. All Rights Reserved.
12-21
JIM DAVIS
ODIE, ODIE, ODIE

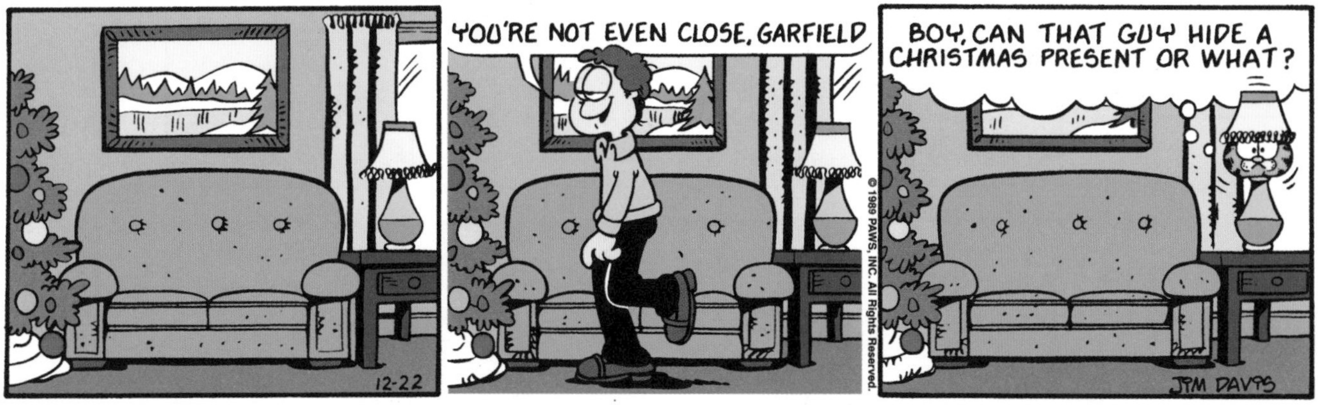
12-22
YOU'RE NOT EVEN CLOSE, GARFIELD
© 1989 PAWS, INC. All Rights Reserved.
BOY, CAN THAT GUY HIDE A CHRISTMAS PRESENT OR WHAT?
JIM DAVIS

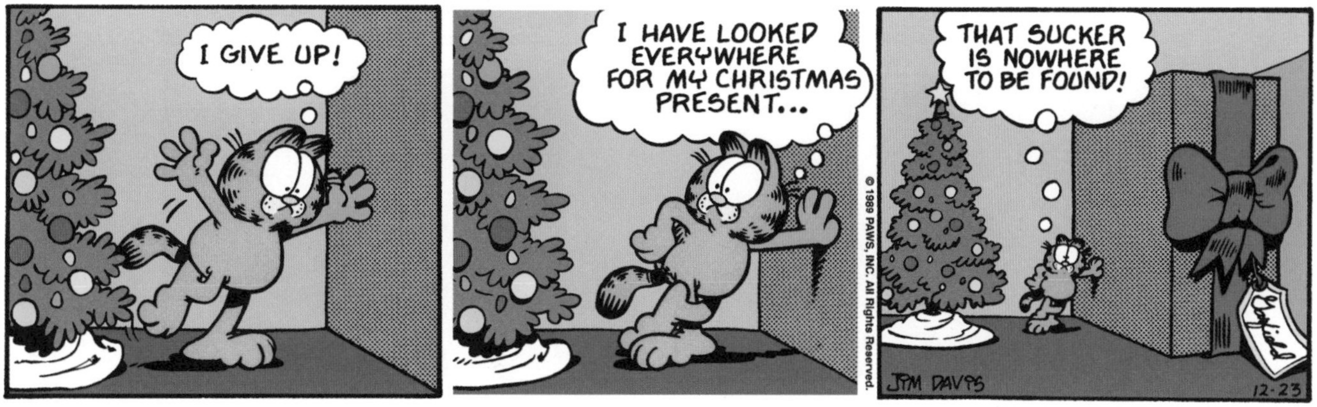
I GIVE UP!
I HAVE LOOKED EVERYWHERE FOR MY CHRISTMAS PRESENT...
© 1989 PAWS, INC. All Rights Reserved.
THAT SUCKER IS NOWHERE TO BE FOUND!
JIM DAVIS
12-23

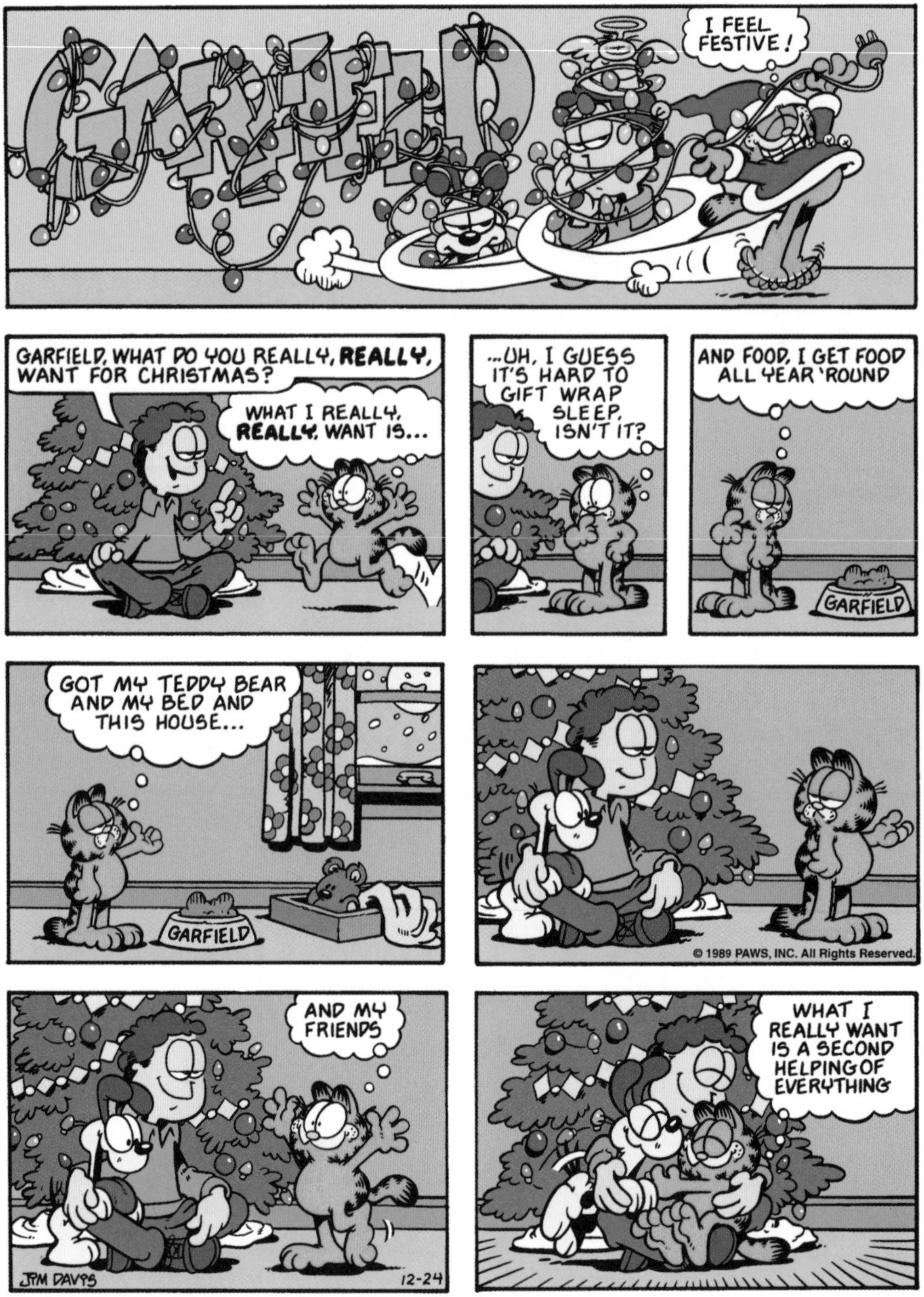
GARFIELD
I FEEL FESTIVE!
GARFIELD, WHAT DO YOU REALLY, **REALLY**, WANT FOR CHRISTMAS?
WHAT I REALLY, **REALLY**, WANT IS...
...UH, I GUESS IT'S HARD TO GIFT WRAP SLEEP, ISN'T IT?
AND FOOD, I GET FOOD ALL YEAR 'ROUND
GARFIELD
GOT MY TEDDY BEAR AND MY BED AND THIS HOUSE...
GARFIELD
© 1989 PAWS, INC. All Rights Reserved.
AND MY FRIENDS
JIM DAVIS
12-24
WHAT I REALLY WANT IS A SECOND HELPING OF EVERYTHING

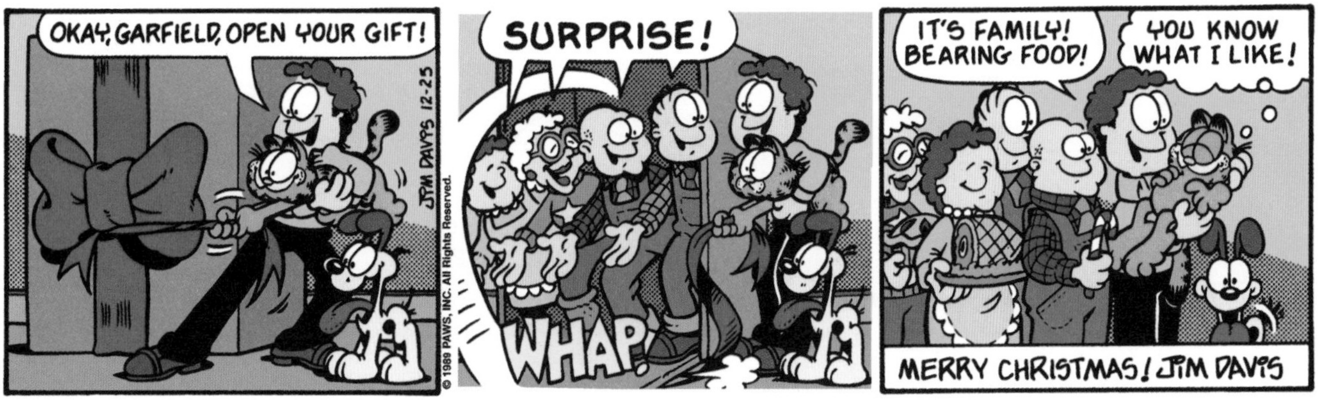
OKAY, GARFIELD, OPEN YOUR GIFT!
JIM DAVIS 12-25
© 1989 PAWS, INC. All Rights Reserved.
SURPRISE!
WHAP!
IT'S FAMILY! BEARING FOOD!
YOU KNOW WHAT I LIKE!
MERRY CHRISTMAS! JIM DAVIS

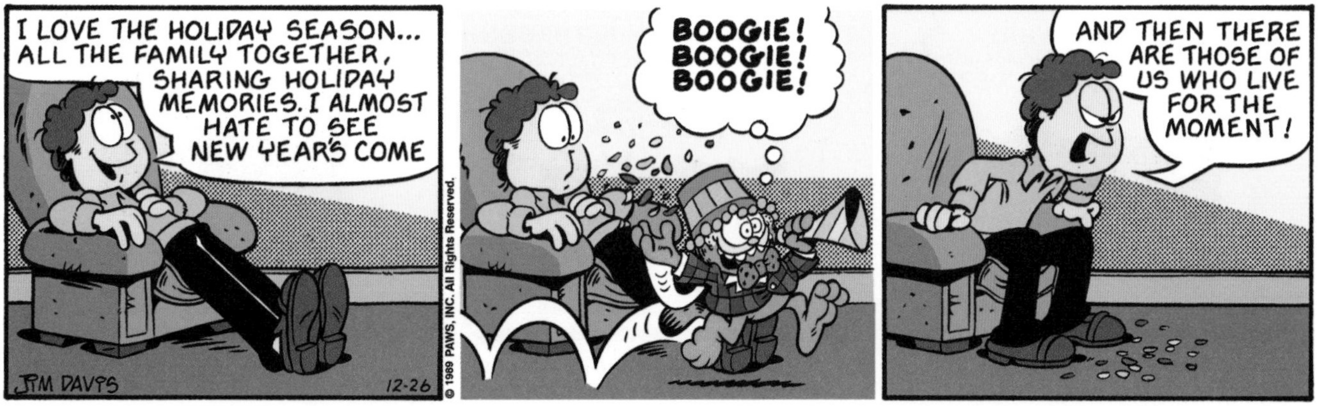
I LOVE THE HOLIDAY SEASON... ALL THE FAMILY TOGETHER, SHARING HOLIDAY MEMORIES. I ALMOST HATE TO SEE NEW YEAR'S COME
JIM DAVIS
12-26
© 1989 PAWS, INC. All Rights Reserved.
BOOGIE! BOOGIE! BOOGIE!
AND THEN THERE ARE THOSE OF US WHO LIVE FOR THE MOMENT!

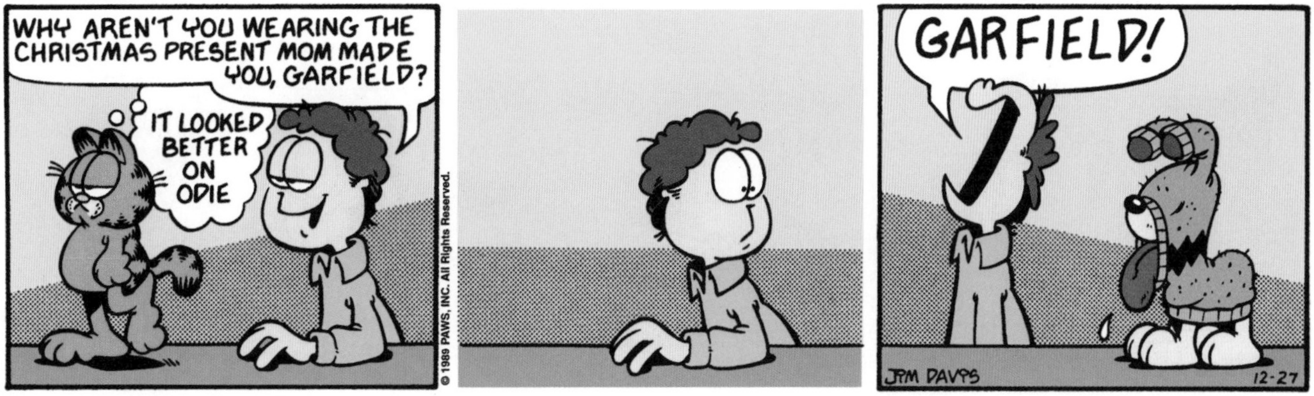
WHY AREN'T YOU WEARING THE CHRISTMAS PRESENT MOM MADE YOU, GARFIELD?
IT LOOKED BETTER ON ODIE
© 1989 PAWS, INC. All Rights Reserved.
GARFIELD!
JIM DAVIS
12-27

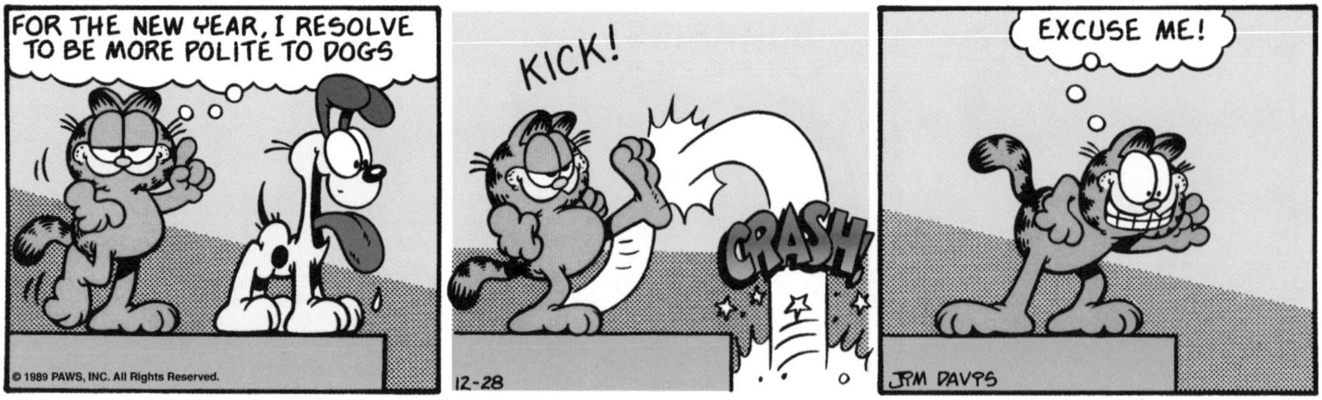
FOR THE NEW YEAR, I RESOLVE TO BE MORE POLITE TO DOGS
© 1989 PAWS, INC. All Rights Reserved.
KICK!
CRASH!
12-28
EXCUSE ME!
JIM DAVIS

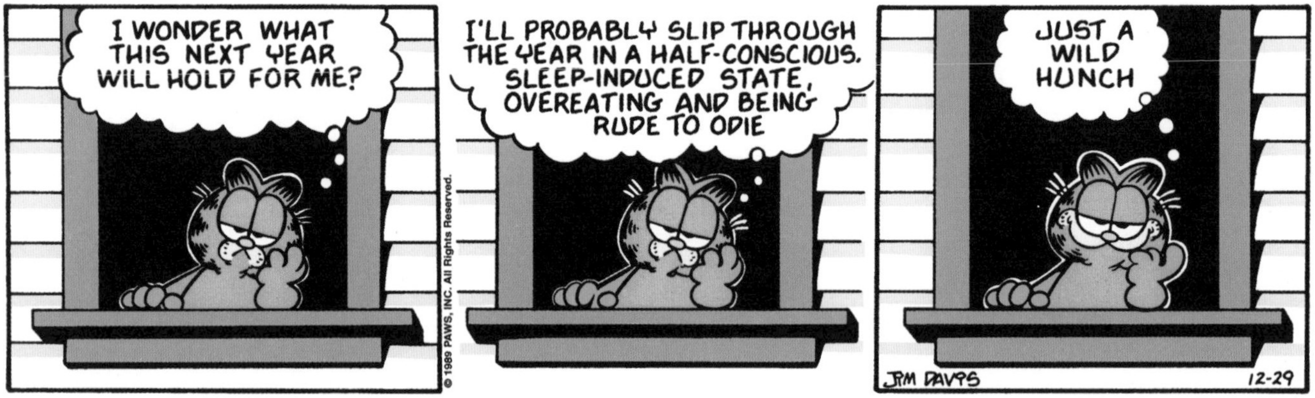
I WONDER WHAT THIS NEXT YEAR WILL HOLD FOR ME?
© 1989 PAWS, INC. All Rights Reserved.
I'LL PROBABLY SLIP THROUGH THE YEAR IN A HALF-CONSCIOUS, SLEEP-INDUCED STATE, OVEREATING AND BEING RUDE TO ODIE
JUST A WILD HUNCH
JIM DAVIS
12-29

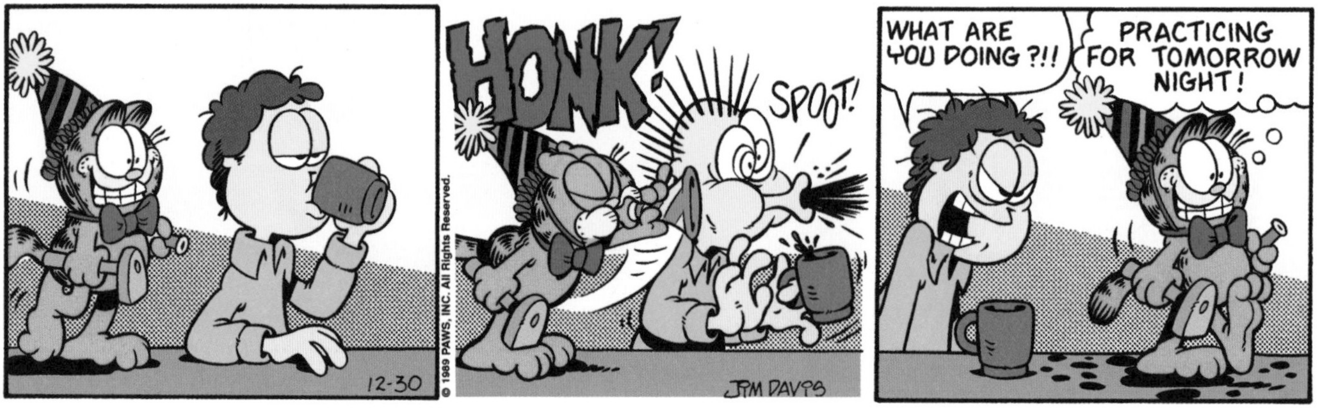
12-30
© 1989 PAWS, INC. All Rights Reserved.
HONK!
SPOOT!
JIM DAVIS
WHAT ARE YOU DOING ?!!
PRACTICING FOR TOMORROW NIGHT!

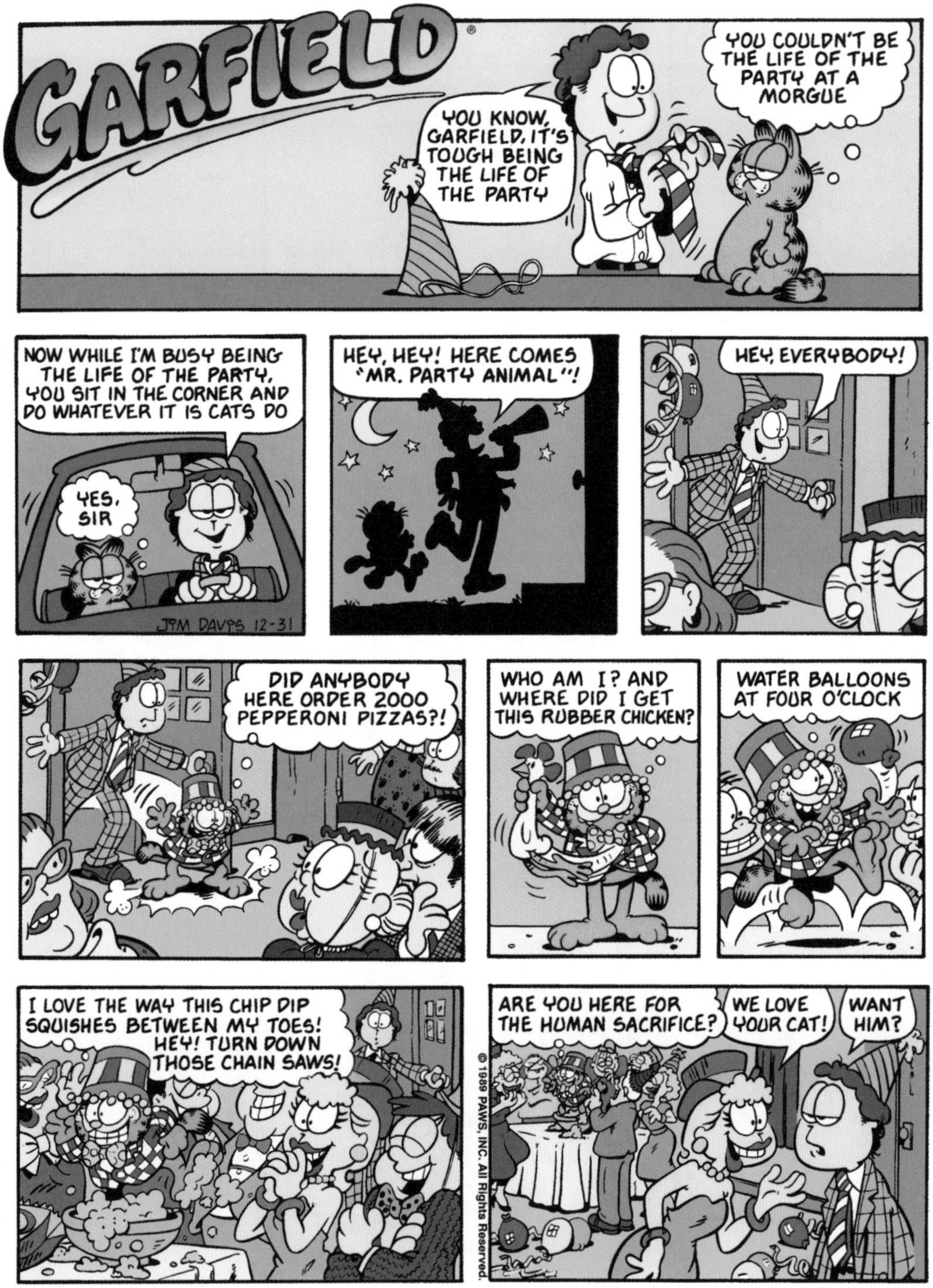
GARFIELD
YOU KNOW, GARFIELD, IT'S TOUGH BEING THE LIFE OF THE PARTY
YOU COULDN'T BE THE LIFE OF THE PARTY AT A MORGUE
NOW WHILE I'M BUSY BEING THE LIFE OF THE PARTY, YOU SIT IN THE CORNER AND DO WHATEVER IT IS CATS DO
YES, SIR
JIM DAVIS 12-31
HEY, HEY! HERE COMES "MR. PARTY ANIMAL"!
HEY, EVERYBODY!
DID ANYBODY HERE ORDER 2000 PEPPERONI PIZZAS?!
WHO AM I? AND WHERE DID I GET THIS RUBBER CHICKEN?
WATER BALLOONS AT FOUR O'CLOCK
I LOVE THE WAY THIS CHIP DIP SQUISHES BETWEEN MY TOES!
HEY! TURN DOWN THOSE CHAIN SAWS!
ARE YOU HERE FOR THE HUMAN SACRIFICE?
WE LOVE YOUR CAT!
WANT HIM?

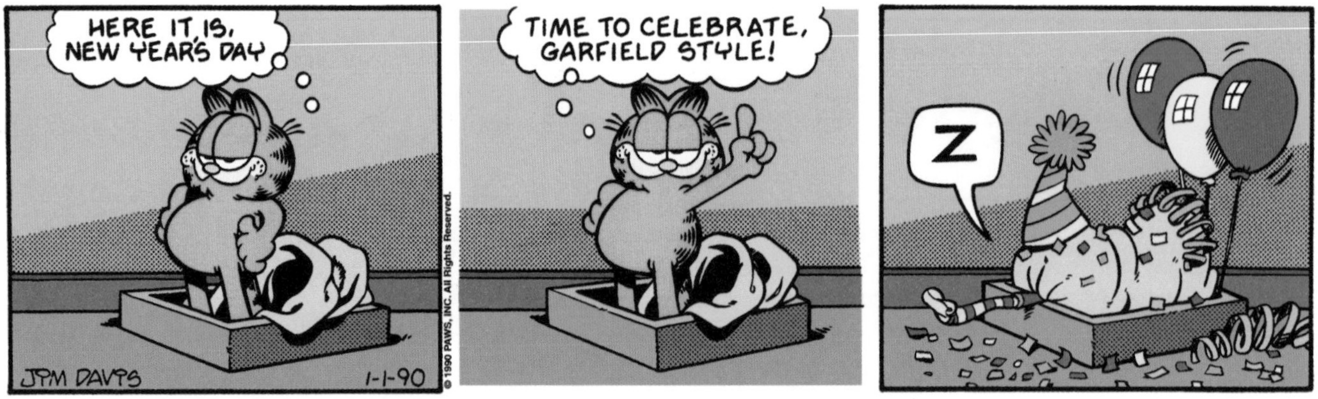
HERE IT IS, NEW YEAR'S DAY
JPM DAVPS 1-1-90
© 1990 PAWS, INC. All Rights Reserved.
TIME TO CELEBRATE, GARFIELD STYLE!
Z

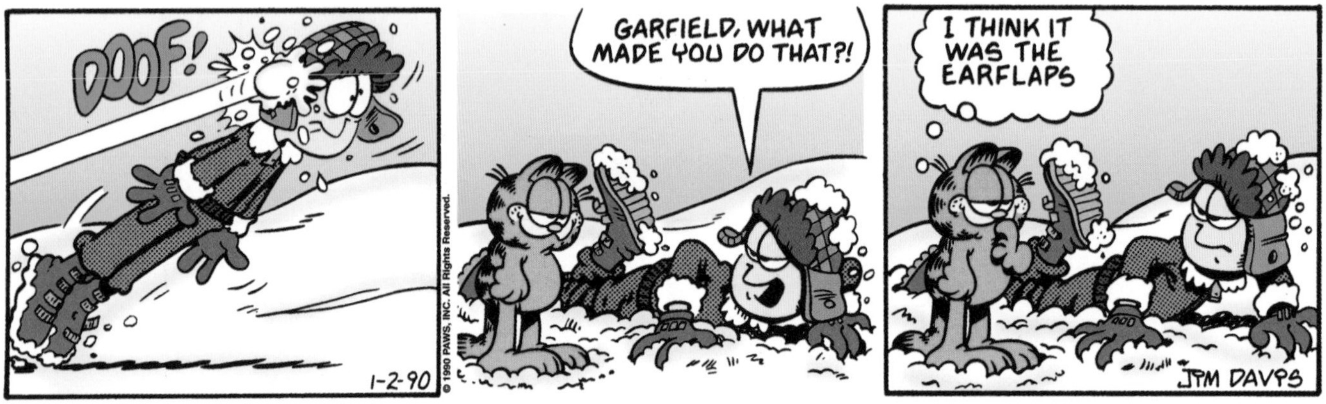
DOOF!
1-2-90
© 1990 PAWS, INC. All Rights Reserved.
GARFIELD, WHAT MADE YOU DO THAT?!
I THINK IT WAS THE EARFLAPS
JPM DAVPS

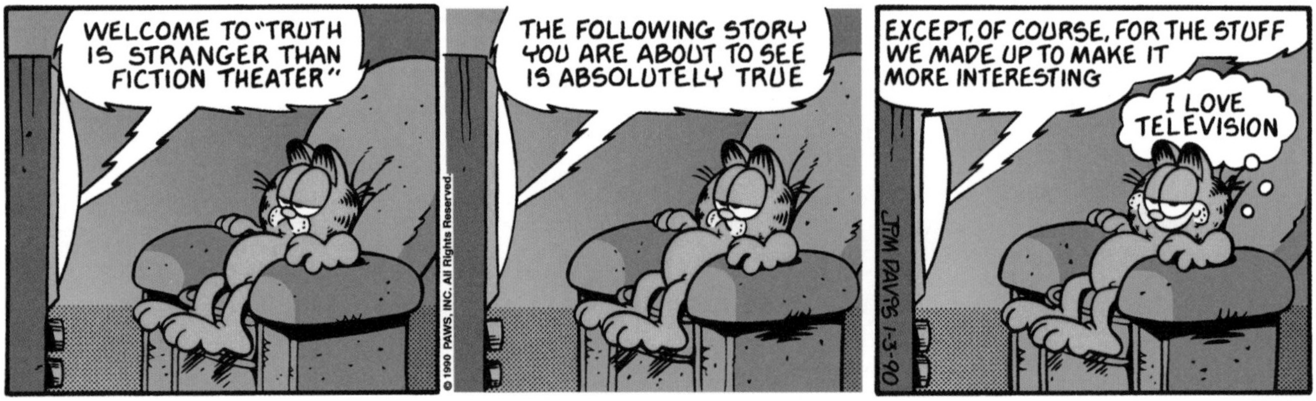
WELCOME TO "TRUTH IS STRANGER THAN FICTION THEATER"
© 1990 PAWS, INC. All Rights Reserved.
THE FOLLOWING STORY YOU ARE ABOUT TO SEE IS ABSOLUTELY TRUE
EXCEPT, OF COURSE, FOR THE STUFF WE MADE UP TO MAKE IT MORE INTERESTING
I LOVE TELEVISION
JPM DAVPS 1-3-90

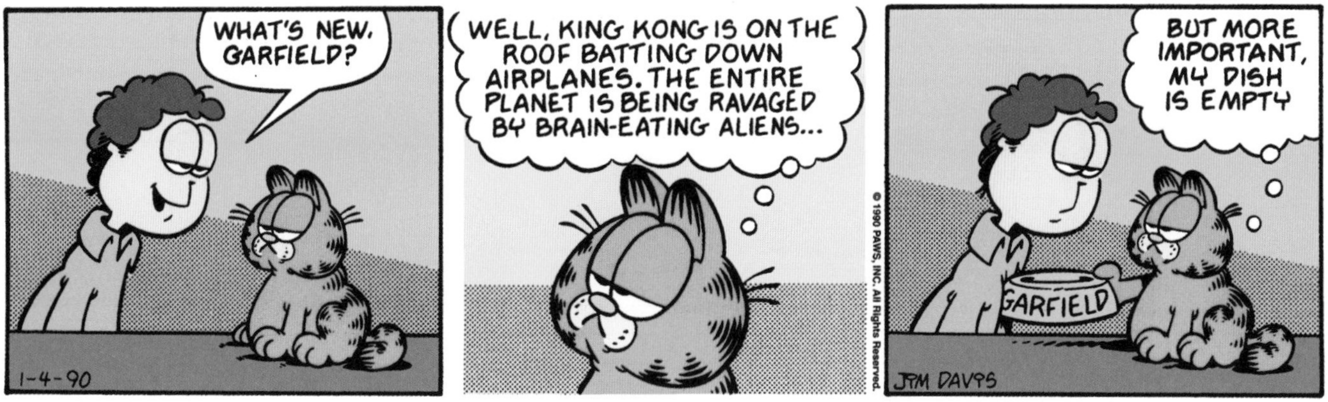
WHAT'S NEW, GARFIELD?
1-4-90
WELL, KING KONG IS ON THE ROOF BATTING DOWN AIRPLANES. THE ENTIRE PLANET IS BEING RAVAGED BY BRAIN-EATING ALIENS...
© 1990 PAWS, INC. All Rights Reserved.
BUT MORE IMPORTANT, MY DISH IS EMPTY
GARFIELD
JIM DAVIS

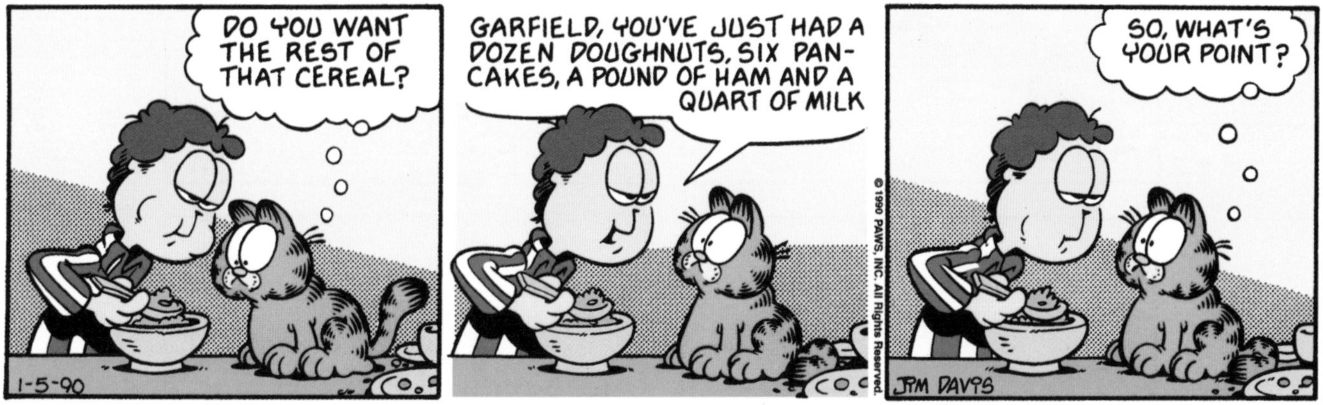
DO YOU WANT THE REST OF THAT CEREAL?
1-5-90
GARFIELD, YOU'VE JUST HAD A DOZEN DOUGHNUTS, SIX PANCAKES, A POUND OF HAM AND A QUART OF MILK
© 1990 PAWS, INC. All Rights Reserved.
SO, WHAT'S YOUR POINT?
JIM DAVIS

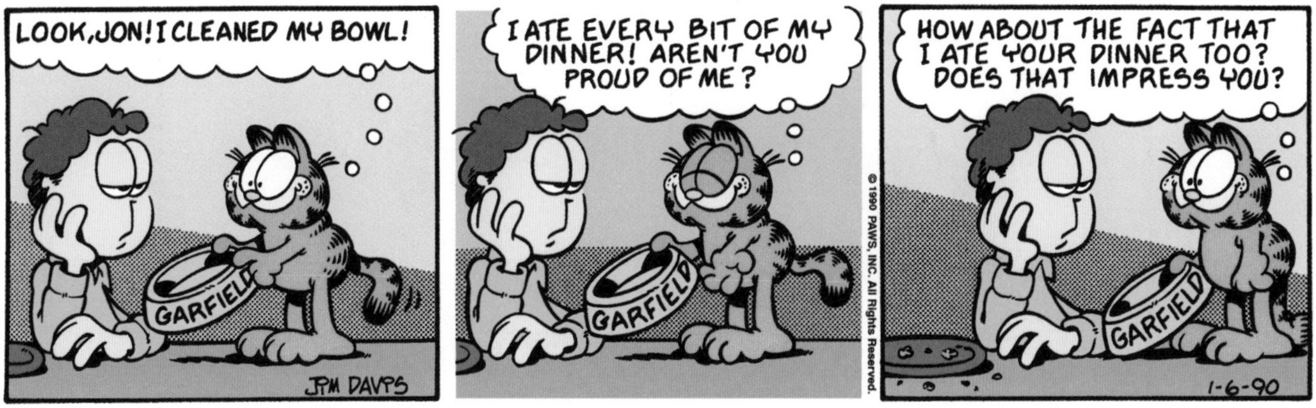
LOOK, JON! I CLEANED MY BOWL!
GARFIELD
JIM DAVIS
I ATE EVERY BIT OF MY DINNER! AREN'T YOU PROUD OF ME?
GARFIELD
© 1990 PAWS, INC. All Rights Reserved.
HOW ABOUT THE FACT THAT I ATE YOUR DINNER TOO? DOES THAT IMPRESS YOU?
GARFIELD
1-6-90

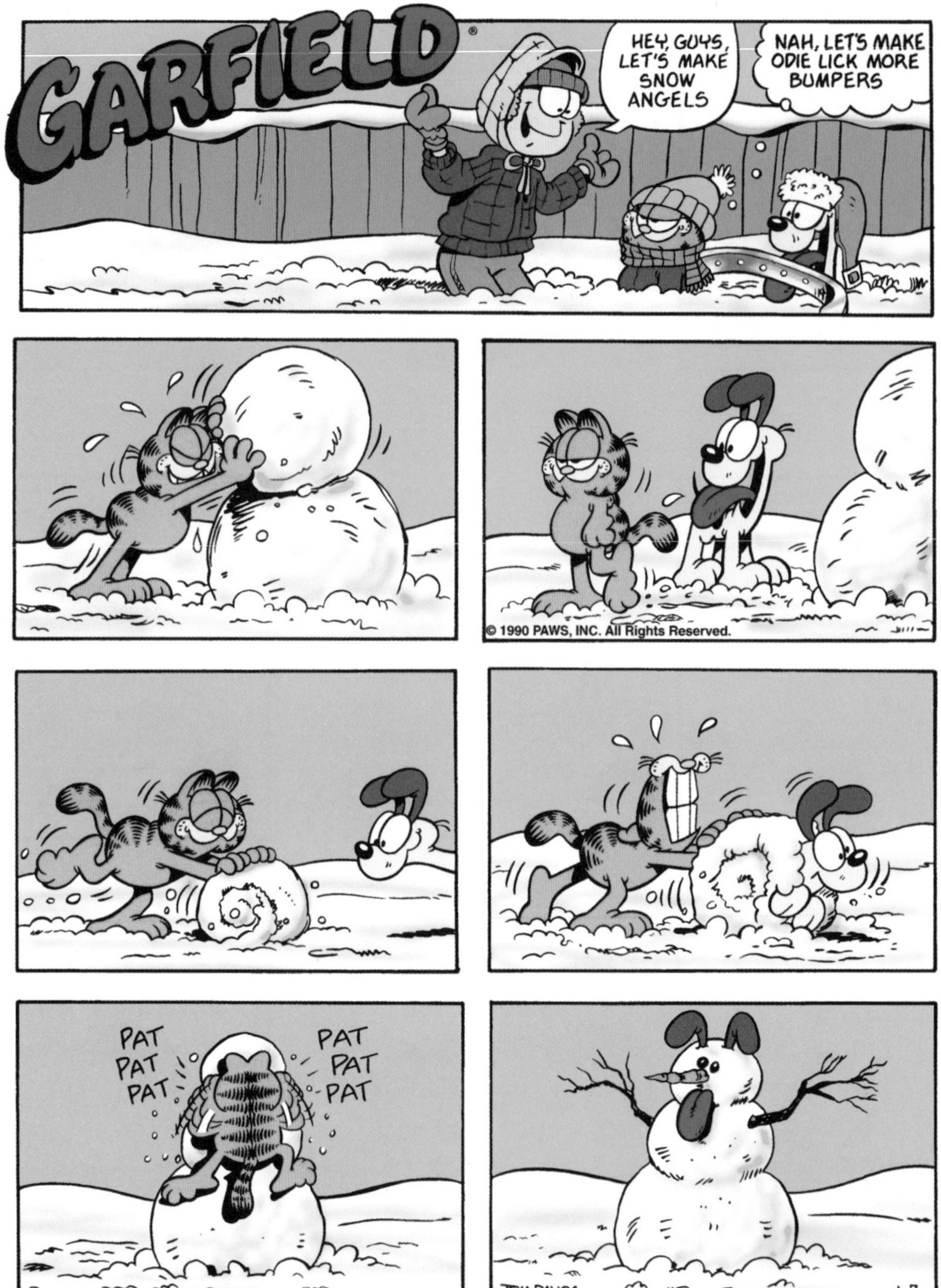
GARFIELD
HEY, GUYS, LET'S MAKE SNOW ANGELS
NAH, LET'S MAKE ODIE LICK MORE BUMPERS
© 1990 PAWS, INC. All Rights Reserved.
PAT PAT PAT
PAT PAT PAT
JIM DAVIS
1-7

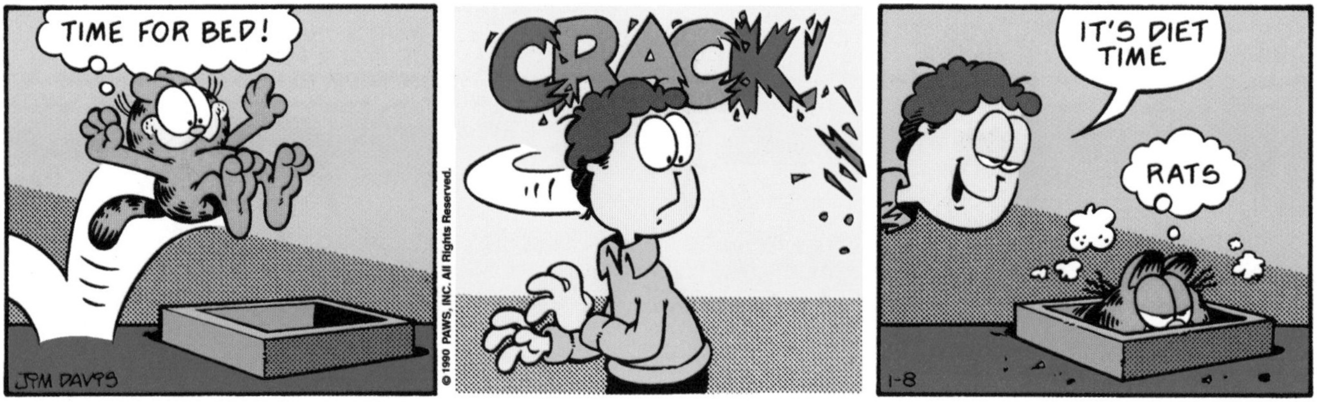
TIME FOR BED!
CRACK!
© 1990 PAWS, INC. All Rights Reserved.
IT'S DIET TIME
RATS
JIM DAVIS
1-8

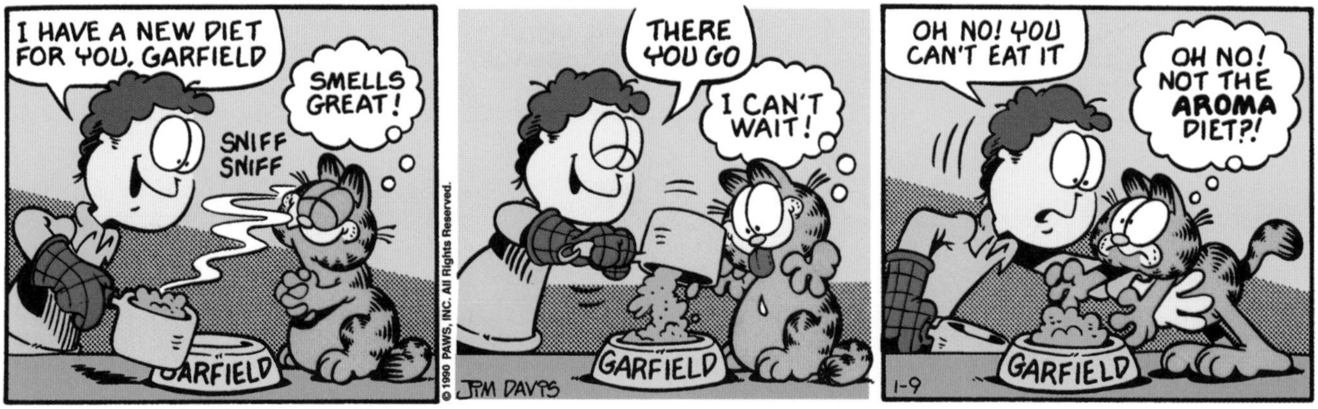
I HAVE A NEW DIET FOR YOU, GARFIELD
SMELLS GREAT!
SNIFF SNIFF
GARFIELD
© 1990 PAWS, INC. All Rights Reserved.
THERE YOU GO
I CAN'T WAIT!
GARFIELD
JIM DAVIS
OH NO! YOU CAN'T EAT IT
OH NO! NOT THE **AROMA** DIET?!
GARFIELD
1-9

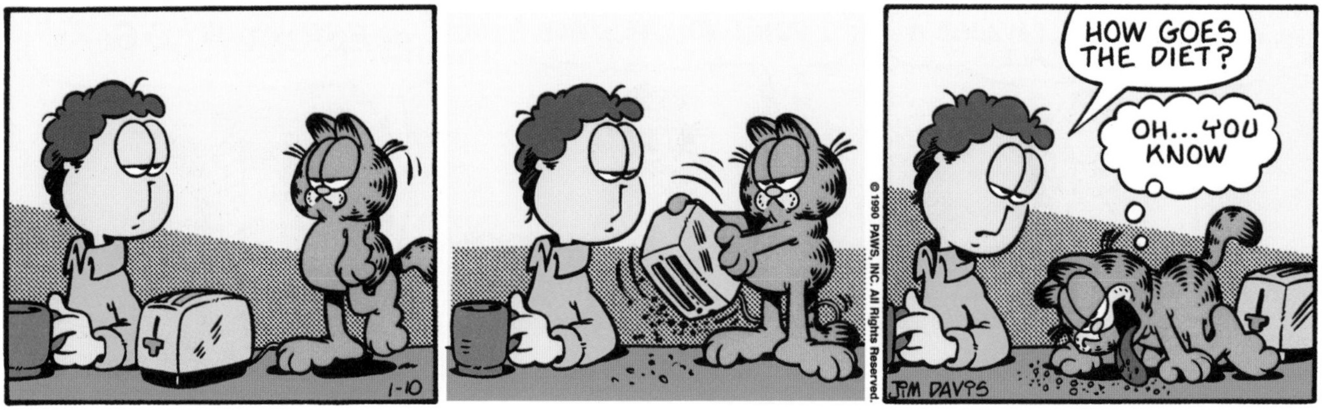
1-10
© 1990 PAWS, INC. All Rights Reserved.
HOW GOES THE DIET?
OH...YOU KNOW
JIM DAVIS

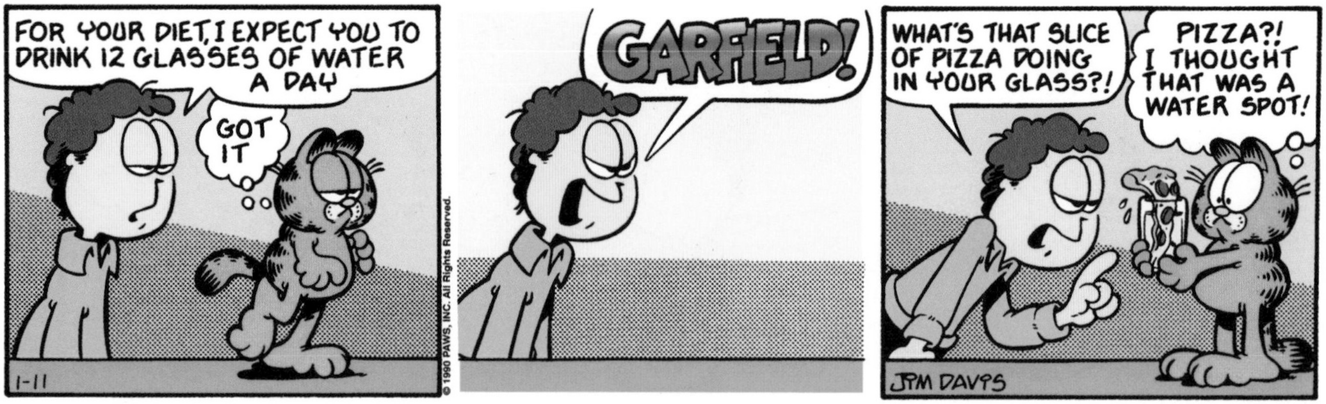
FOR YOUR DIET, I EXPECT YOU TO DRINK 12 GLASSES OF WATER A DAY
GOT IT
1-11
© 1990 PAWS, INC. All Rights Reserved.
GARFIELD!
WHAT'S THAT SLICE OF PIZZA DOING IN YOUR GLASS?!
PIZZA?! I THOUGHT THAT WAS A WATER SPOT!
JIM DAVIS

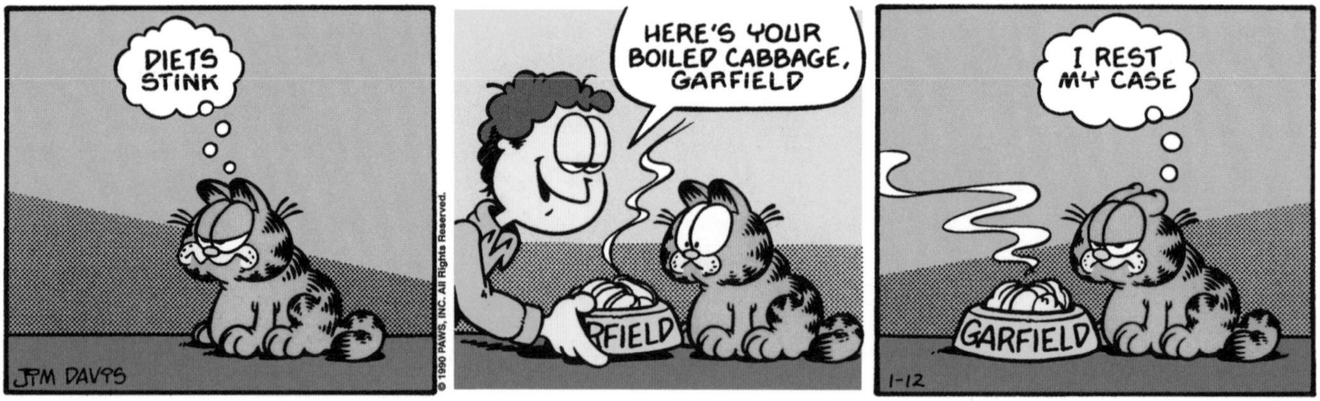
DIETS STINK
JIM DAVIS
© 1990 PAWS, INC. All Rights Reserved.
HERE'S YOUR BOILED CABBAGE, GARFIELD
RFIELD
I REST MY CASE
GARFIELD
1-12

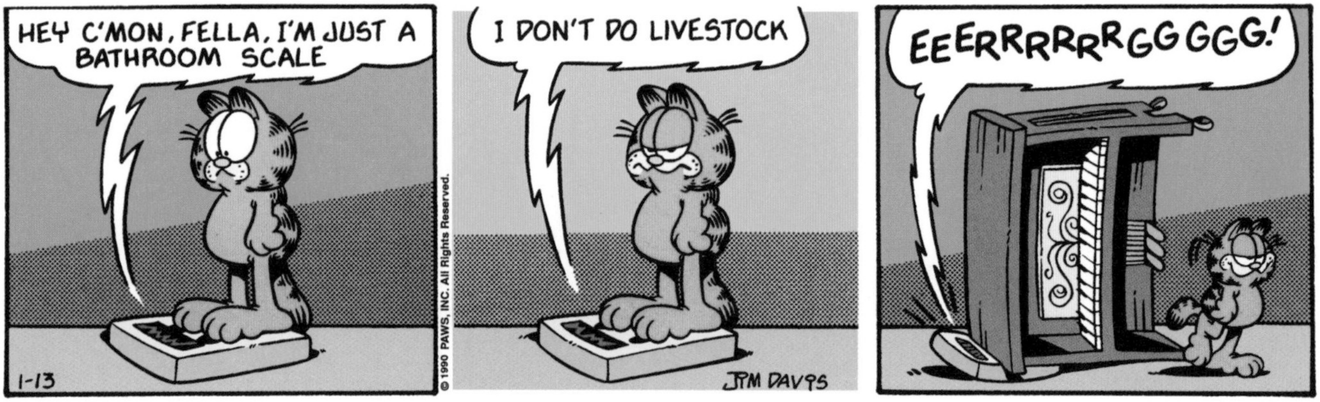
HEY C'MON, FELLA, I'M JUST A BATHROOM SCALE
1-13
© 1990 PAWS, INC. All Rights Reserved.
I DON'T DO LIVESTOCK
JIM DAVIS
EEERRRRRRGGGGG!

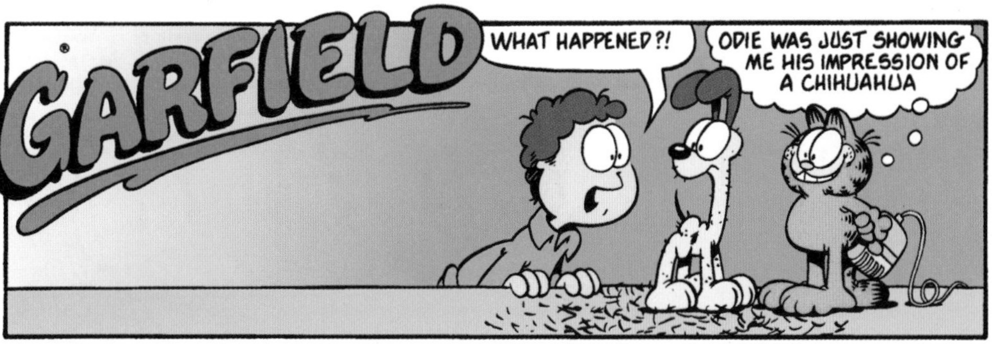
GARFIELD
WHAT HAPPENED?!
ODIE WAS JUST SHOWING ME HIS IMPRESSION OF A CHIHUAHUA

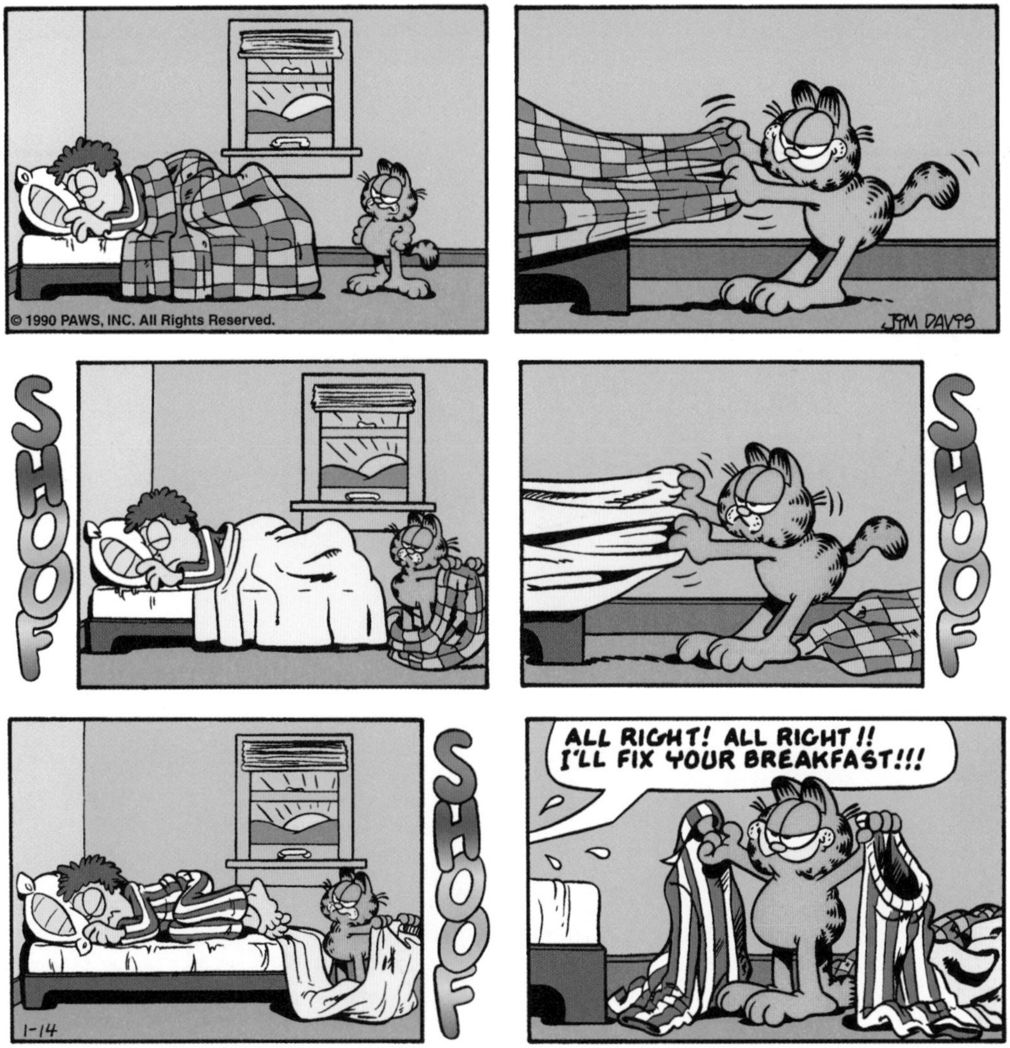
© 1990 PAWS, INC. All Rights Reserved.
JIM DAVIS
SHOOF
SHOOF
1-14
SHOOF
ALL RIGHT! ALL RIGHT!! I'LL FIX YOUR BREAKFAST!!!

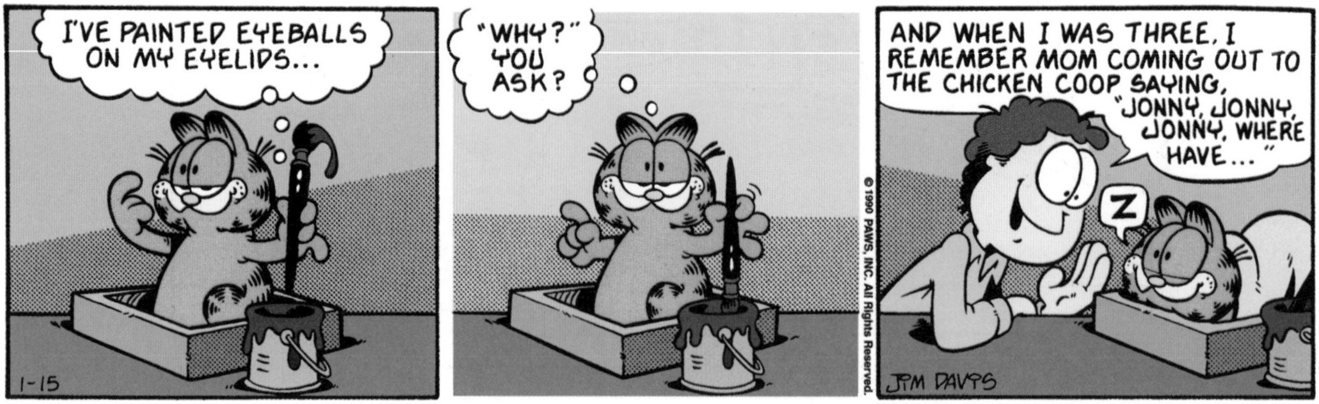
I'VE PAINTED EYEBALLS ON MY EYELIDS...
"WHY?" YOU ASK?
AND WHEN I WAS THREE, I REMEMBER MOM COMING OUT TO THE CHICKEN COOP SAYING, "JONNY, JONNY, JONNY, WHERE HAVE..."
Z
1-15
© 1990 PAWS, INC. All Rights Reserved.
JIM DAVIS

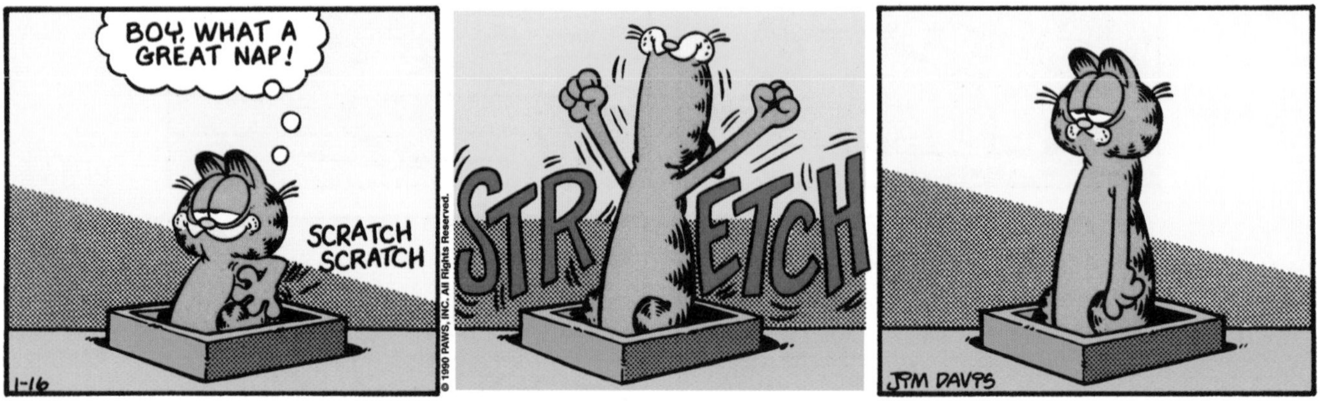
BOY, WHAT A GREAT NAP!
SCRATCH SCRATCH
STRETCH
1-16
© 1990 PAWS, INC. All Rights Reserved.
JIM DAVIS

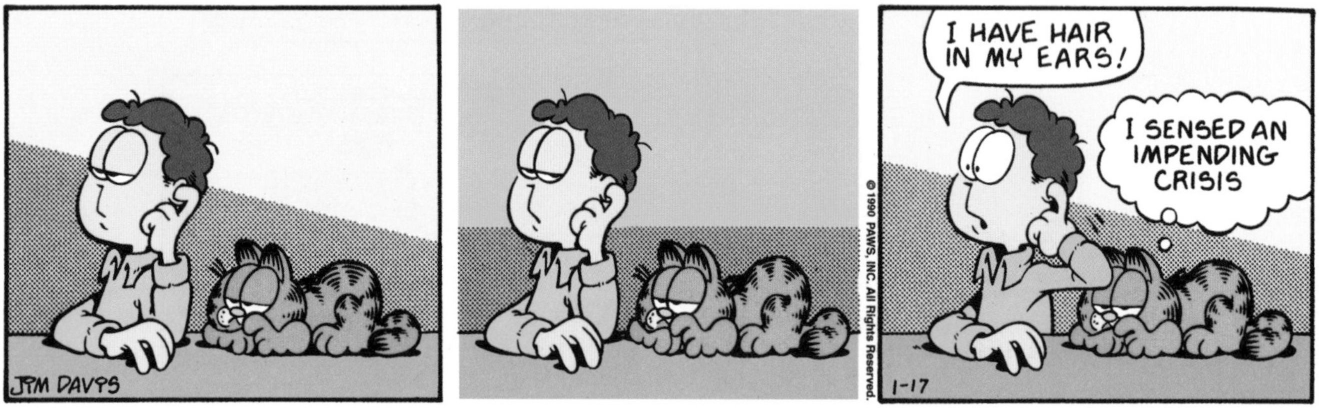
I HAVE HAIR IN MY EARS!
I SENSED AN IMPENDING CRISIS
JIM DAVIS
© 1990 PAWS, INC. All Rights Reserved.
1-17

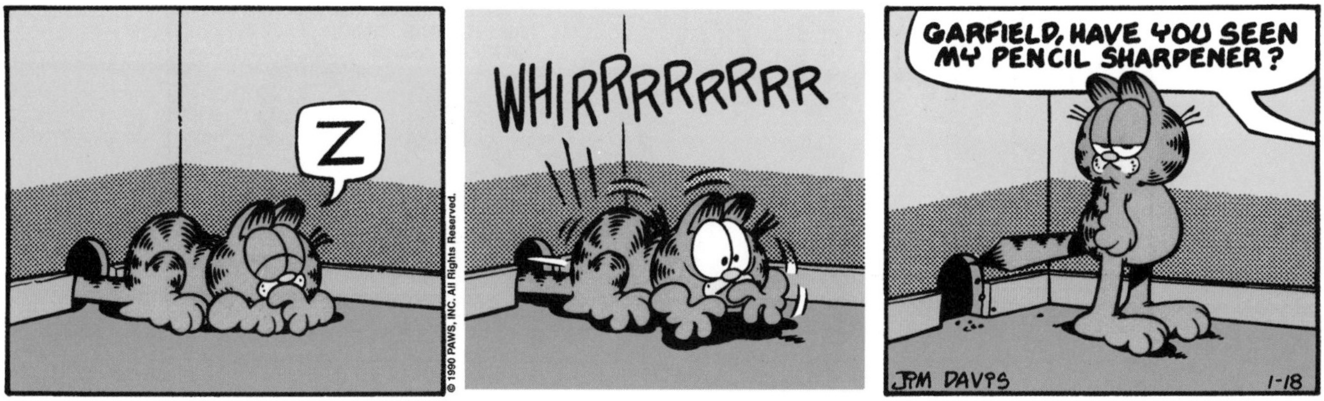
Z
© 1990 PAWS, INC. All Rights Reserved.
WHIRRRRRRRR
GARFIELD, HAVE YOU SEEN MY PENCIL SHARPENER?
1-18

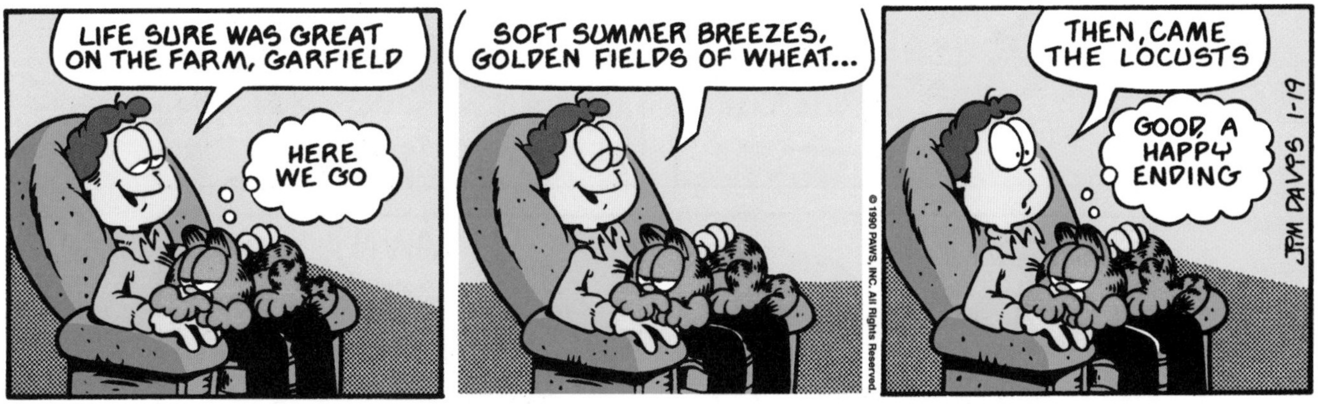
LIFE SURE WAS GREAT ON THE FARM, GARFIELD
HERE WE GO
SOFT SUMMER BREEZES, GOLDEN FIELDS OF WHEAT...
© 1990 PAWS, INC. All Rights Reserved.
THEN, CAME THE LOCUSTS
GOOD, A HAPPY ENDING
1-19

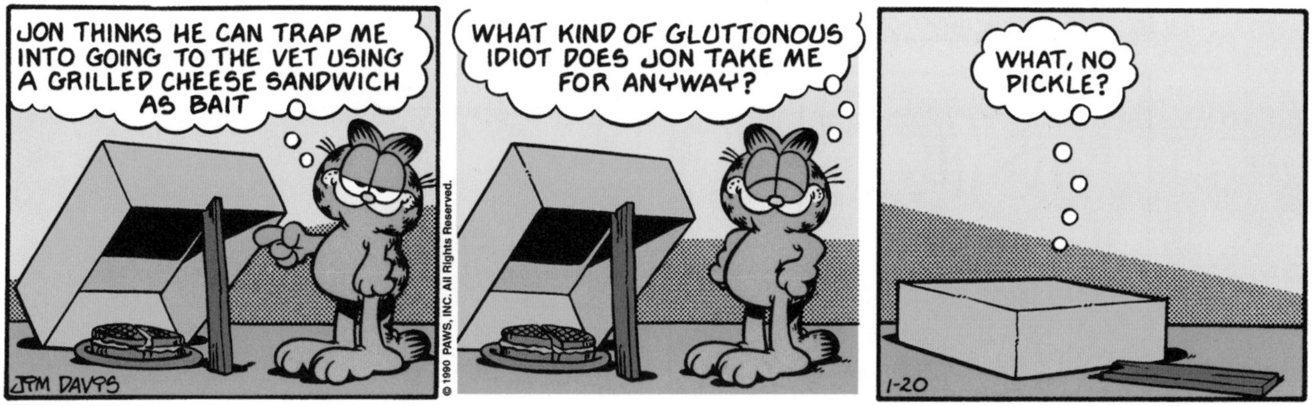
JON THINKS HE CAN TRAP ME INTO GOING TO THE VET USING A GRILLED CHEESE SANDWICH AS BAIT
© 1990 PAWS, INC. All Rights Reserved.
WHAT KIND OF GLUTTONOUS IDIOT DOES JON TAKE ME FOR ANYWAY?
WHAT, NO PICKLE?
1-20

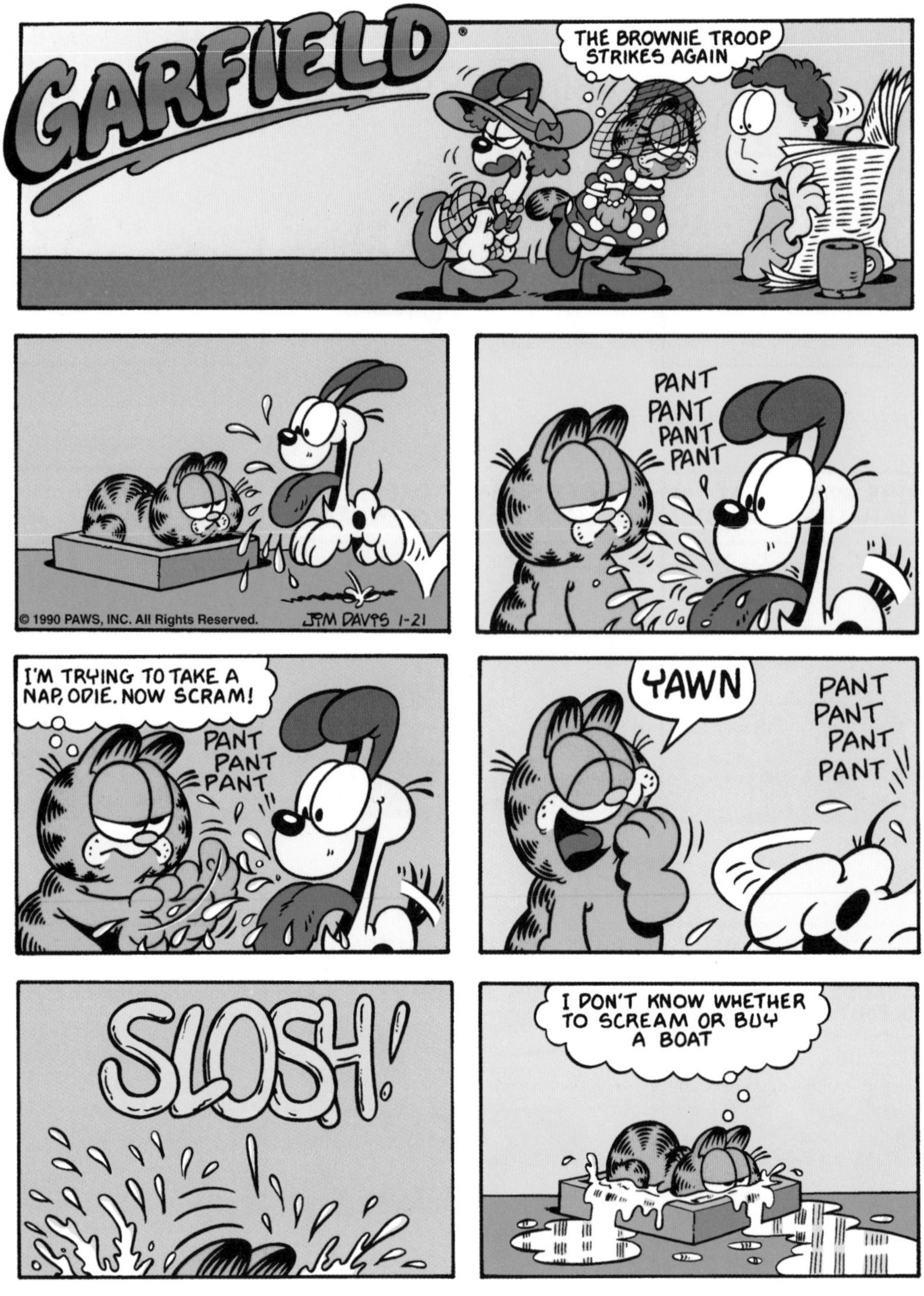
GARFIELD
THE BROWNIE TROOP STRIKES AGAIN
© 1990 PAWS, INC. All Rights Reserved.
JIM DAVIS 1-21
PANT PANT PANT PANT
I'M TRYING TO TAKE A NAP, ODIE. NOW SCRAM!
PANT PANT PANT
YAWN
PANT PANT PANT PANT
SLOSH!
I DON'T KNOW WHETHER TO SCREAM OR BUY A BOAT

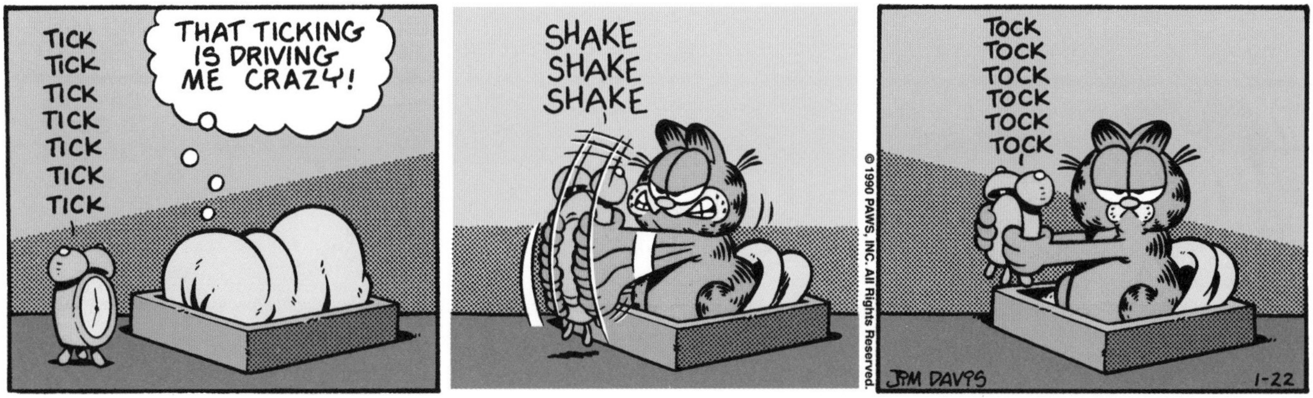
TICK TICK TICK TICK TICK TICK TICK
THAT TICKING IS DRIVING ME CRAZY!
SHAKE SHAKE SHAKE
© 1990 PAWS, INC. All Rights Reserved.
TOCK TOCK TOCK TOCK TOCK TOCK
JIM DAVIS
1-22

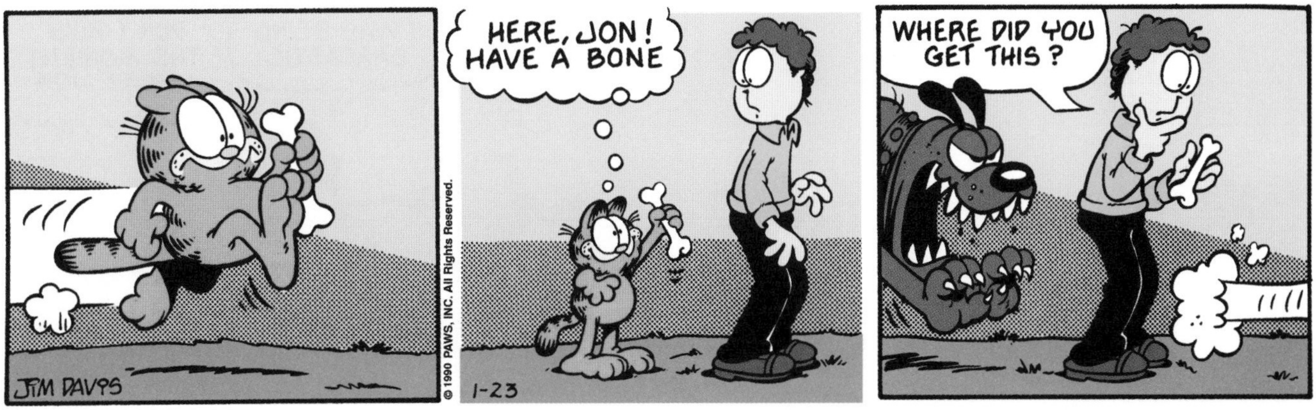
JIM DAVIS
© 1990 PAWS, INC. All Rights Reserved.
HERE, JON! HAVE A BONE
1-23
WHERE DID YOU GET THIS?

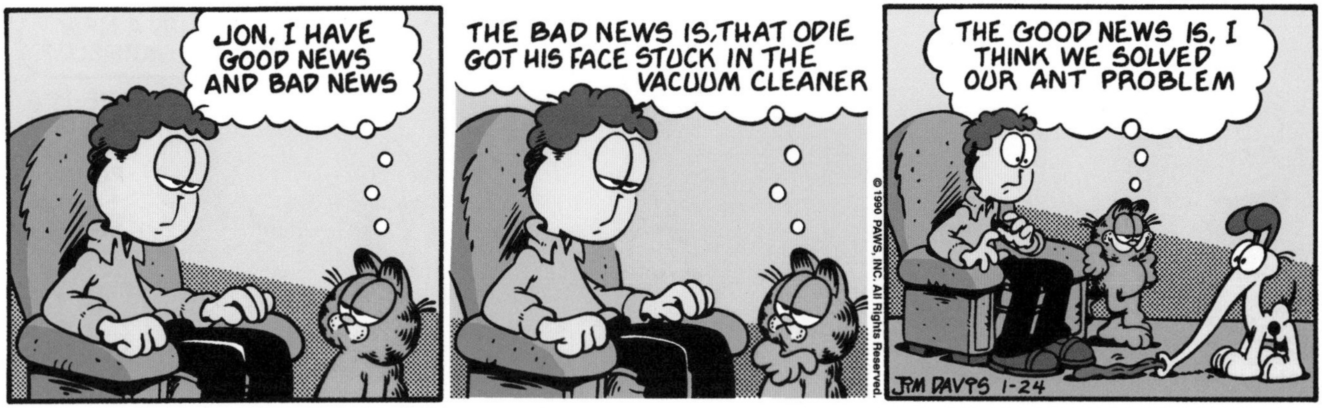
JON, I HAVE GOOD NEWS AND BAD NEWS
THE BAD NEWS IS, THAT ODIE GOT HIS FACE STUCK IN THE VACUUM CLEANER
© 1990 PAWS, INC. All Rights Reserved.
THE GOOD NEWS IS, I THINK WE SOLVED OUR ANT PROBLEM
JIM DAVIS 1-24

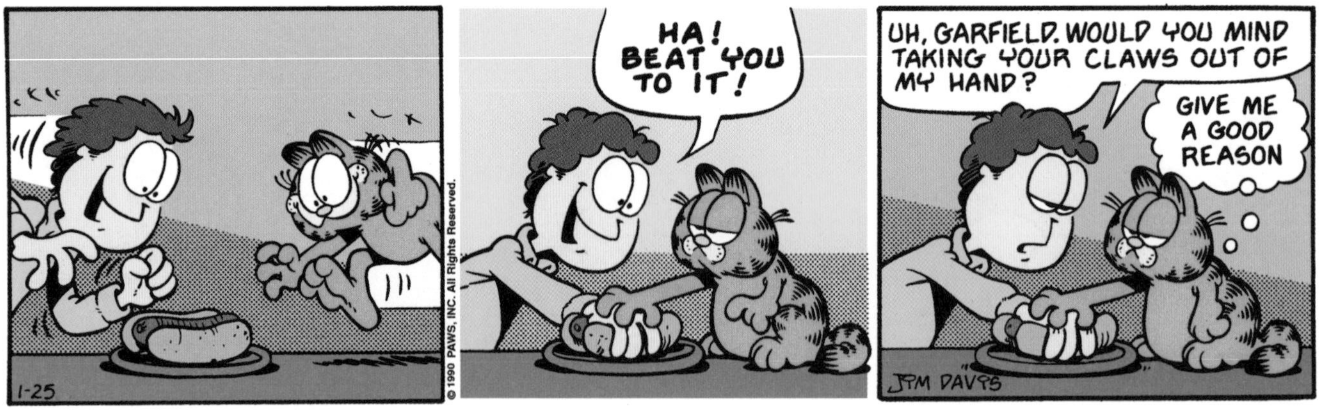
1-25
© 1990 PAWS, INC. All Rights Reserved.
HA! BEAT YOU TO IT!
UH, GARFIELD. WOULD YOU MIND TAKING YOUR CLAWS OUT OF MY HAND?
GIVE ME A GOOD REASON
JIM DAVIS

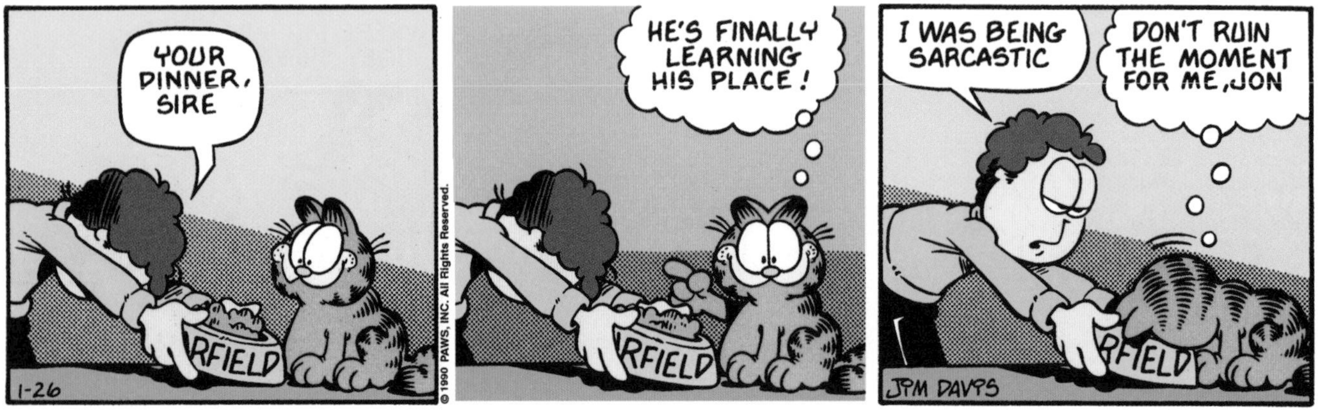
YOUR DINNER, SIRE
RFIELD
1-26
© 1990 PAWS, INC. All Rights Reserved.
HE'S FINALLY LEARNING HIS PLACE!
I WAS BEING SARCASTIC
DON'T RUIN THE MOMENT FOR ME, JON
JIM DAVIS

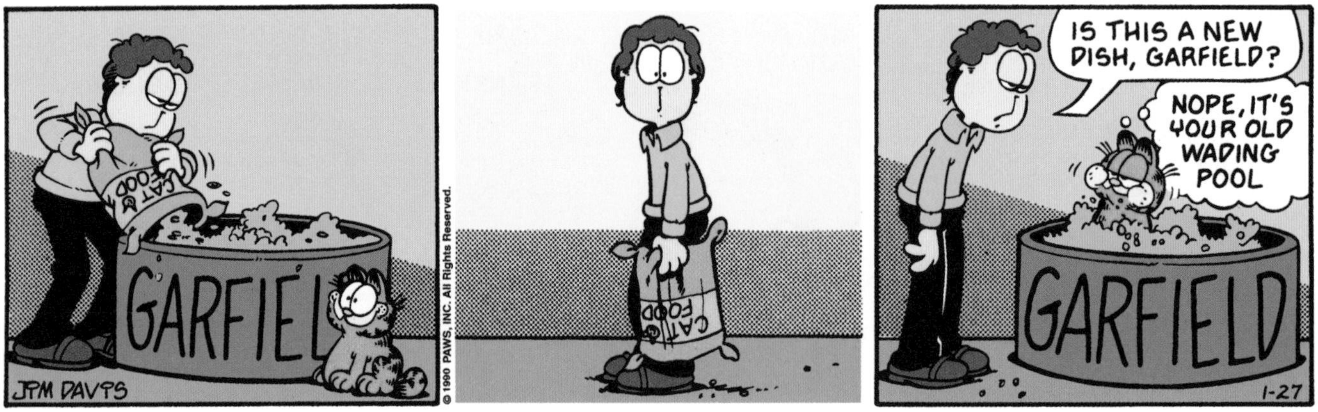
CAT FOOD
GARFIEL
JIM DAVIS
© 1990 PAWS, INC. All Rights Reserved.
IS THIS A NEW DISH, GARFIELD?
NOPE, IT'S YOUR OLD WADING POOL
GARFIELD
1-27

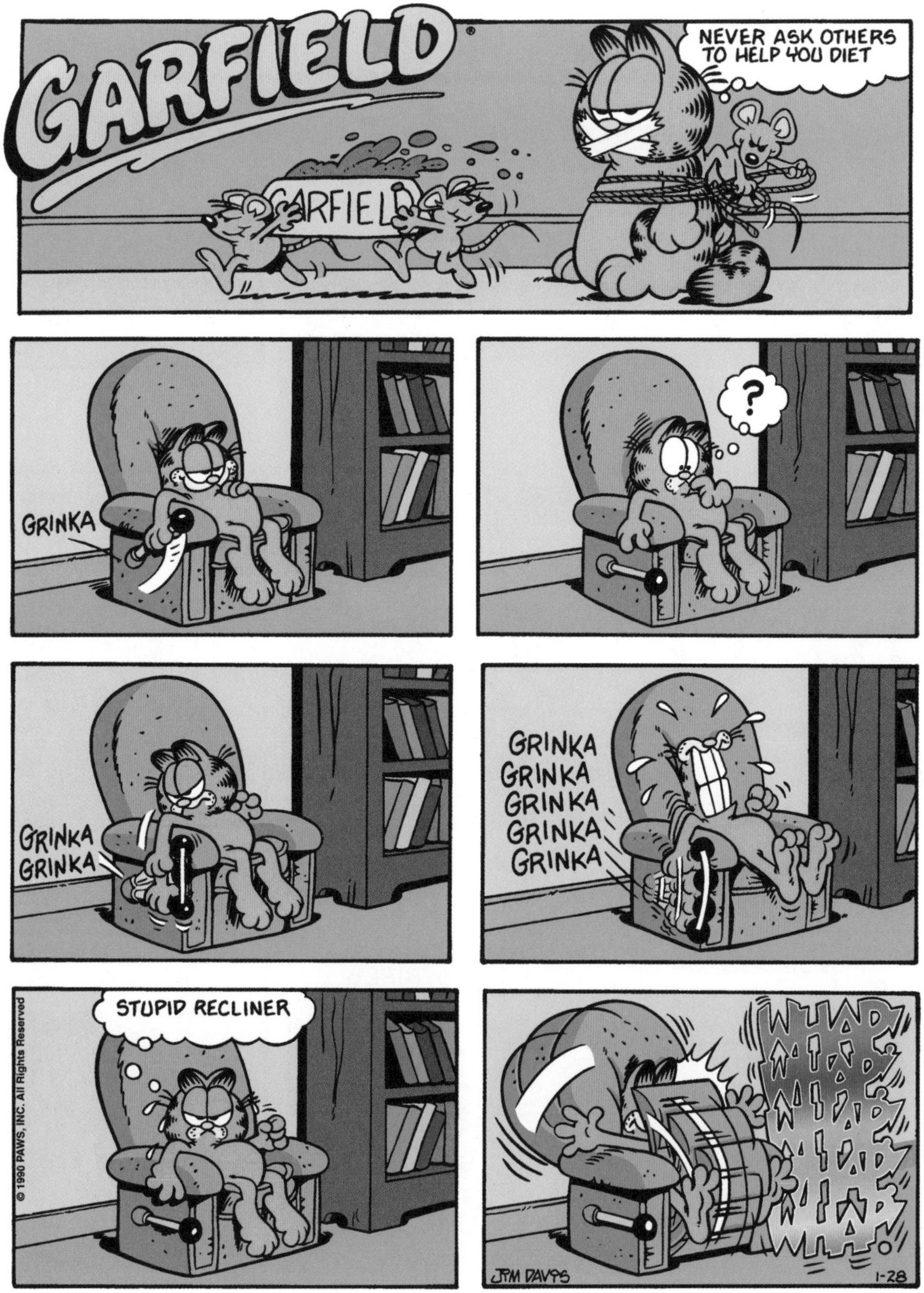
GARFIELD
GARFIELD
NEVER ASK OTHERS TO HELP YOU DIET
GRINKA
?
GRINKA GRINKA
GRINKA GRINKA GRINKA GRINKA GRINKA
STUPID RECLINER
© 1990 PAWS, INC. All Rights Reserved
WHAP! WHAP! WHAP! WHAP! WHAP! WHAP!
JIM DAVIS
1-28

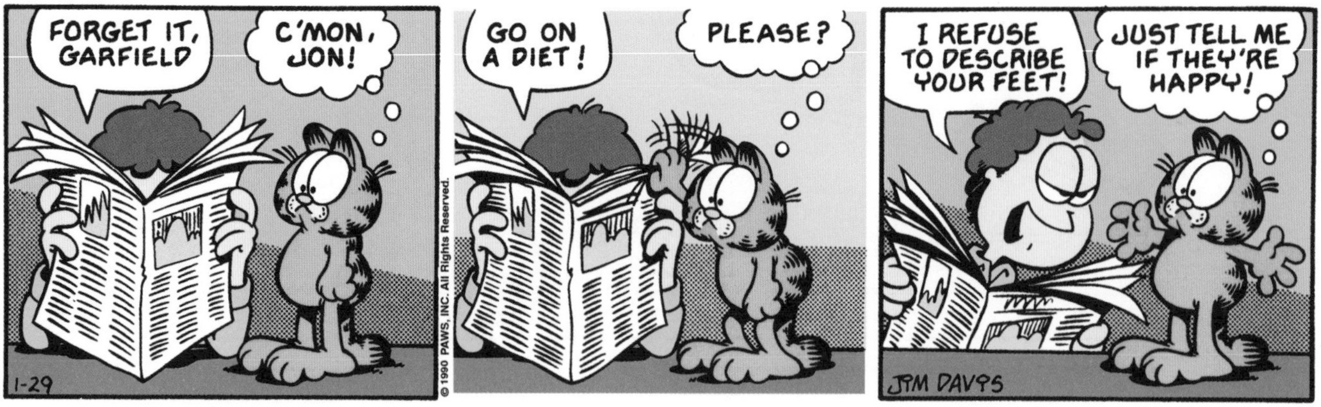
FORGET IT, GARFIELD
C'MON, JON!
1-29
© 1990 PAWS, INC. All Rights Reserved.
GO ON A DIET!
PLEASE?
I REFUSE TO DESCRIBE YOUR FEET!
JUST TELL ME IF THEY'RE HAPPY!
JIM DAVIS

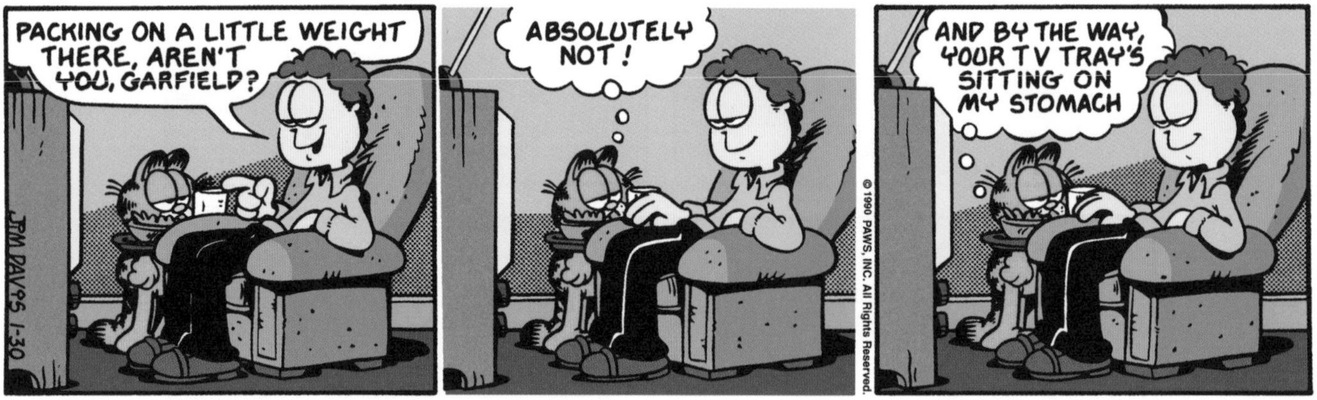
PACKING ON A LITTLE WEIGHT THERE, AREN'T YOU, GARFIELD?
JIM DAVIS 1-30
ABSOLUTELY NOT!
© 1990 PAWS, INC. All Rights Reserved.
AND BY THE WAY, YOUR TV TRAY'S SITTING ON MY STOMACH

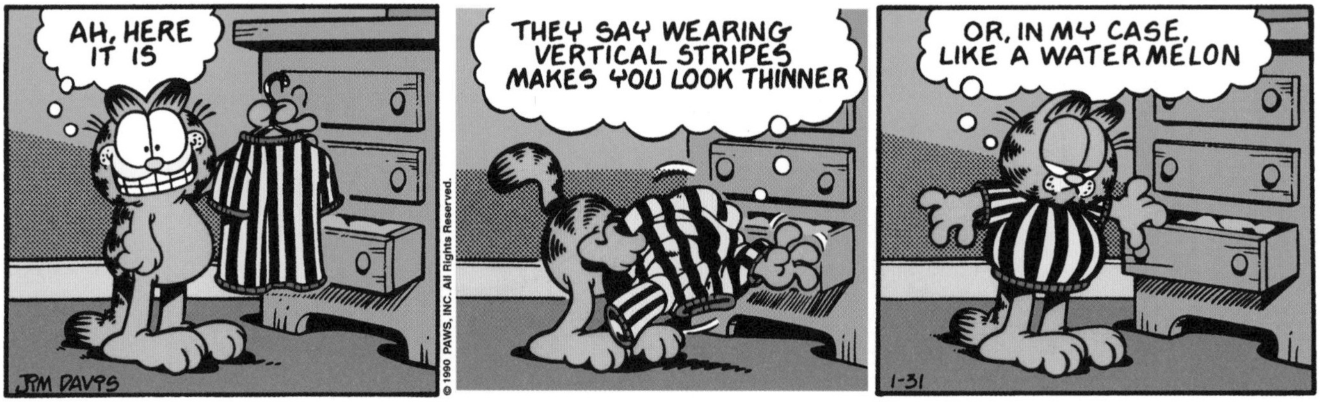
AH, HERE IT IS
JIM DAVIS
© 1990 PAWS, INC. All Rights Reserved.
THEY SAY WEARING VERTICAL STRIPES MAKES YOU LOOK THINNER
OR, IN MY CASE, LIKE A WATERMELON
1-31

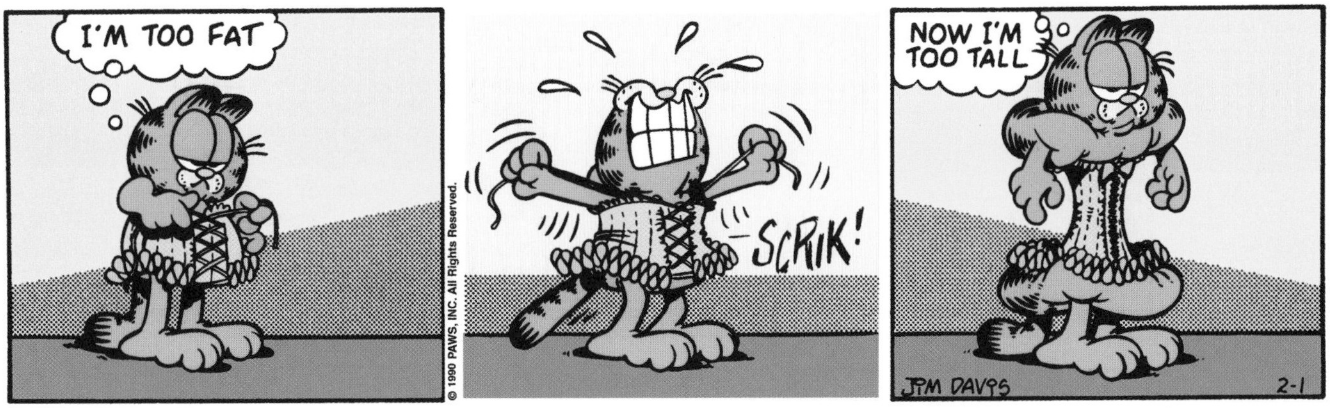
I'M TOO FAT
© 1990 PAWS, INC. All Rights Reserved.
SCRIK!
NOW I'M TOO TALL
JIM DAVIS
2-1

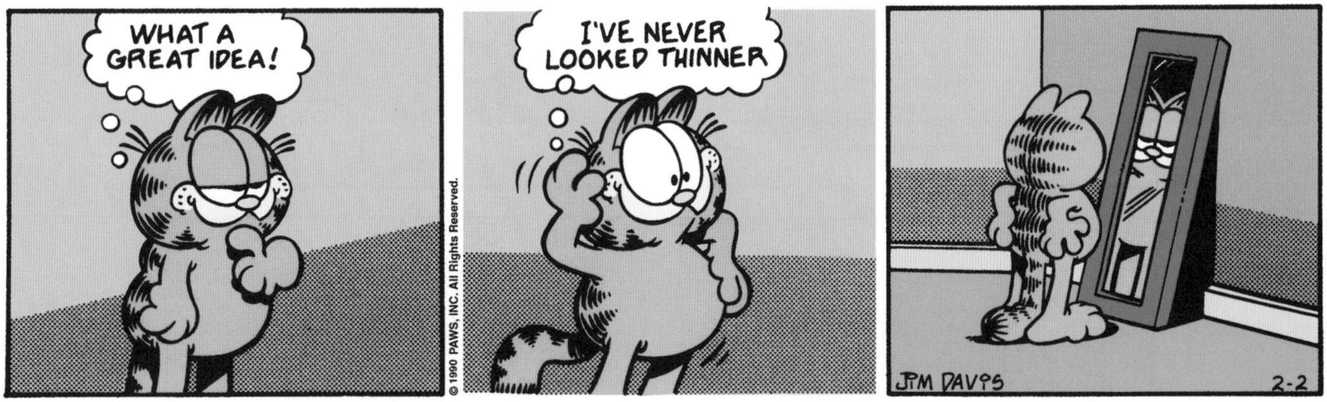
WHAT A GREAT IDEA!
© 1990 PAWS, INC. All Rights Reserved.
I'VE NEVER LOOKED THINNER
JIM DAVIS
2-2

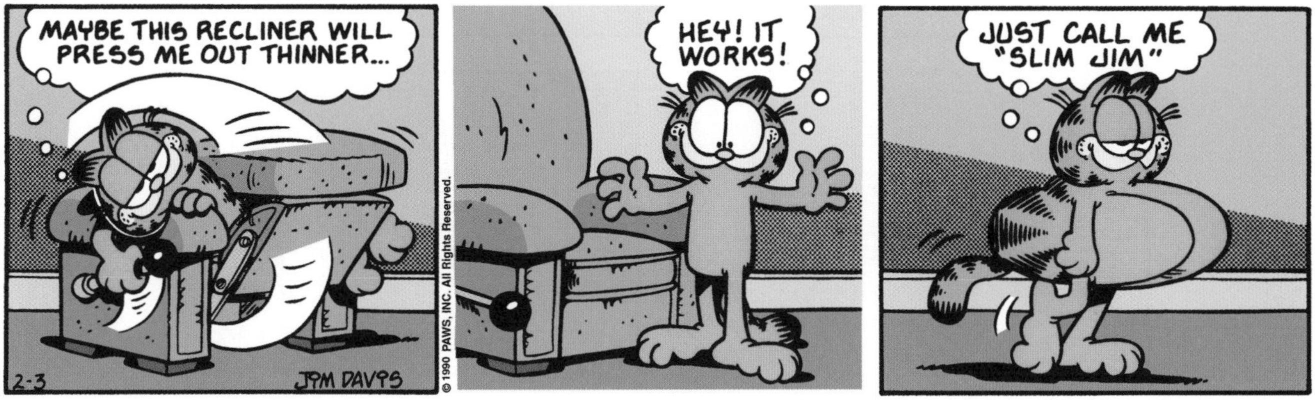
MAYBE THIS RECLINER WILL PRESS ME OUT THINNER...
2-3
JIM DAVIS
© 1990 PAWS, INC. All Rights Reserved.
HEY! IT WORKS!
JUST CALL ME "SLIM JIM"

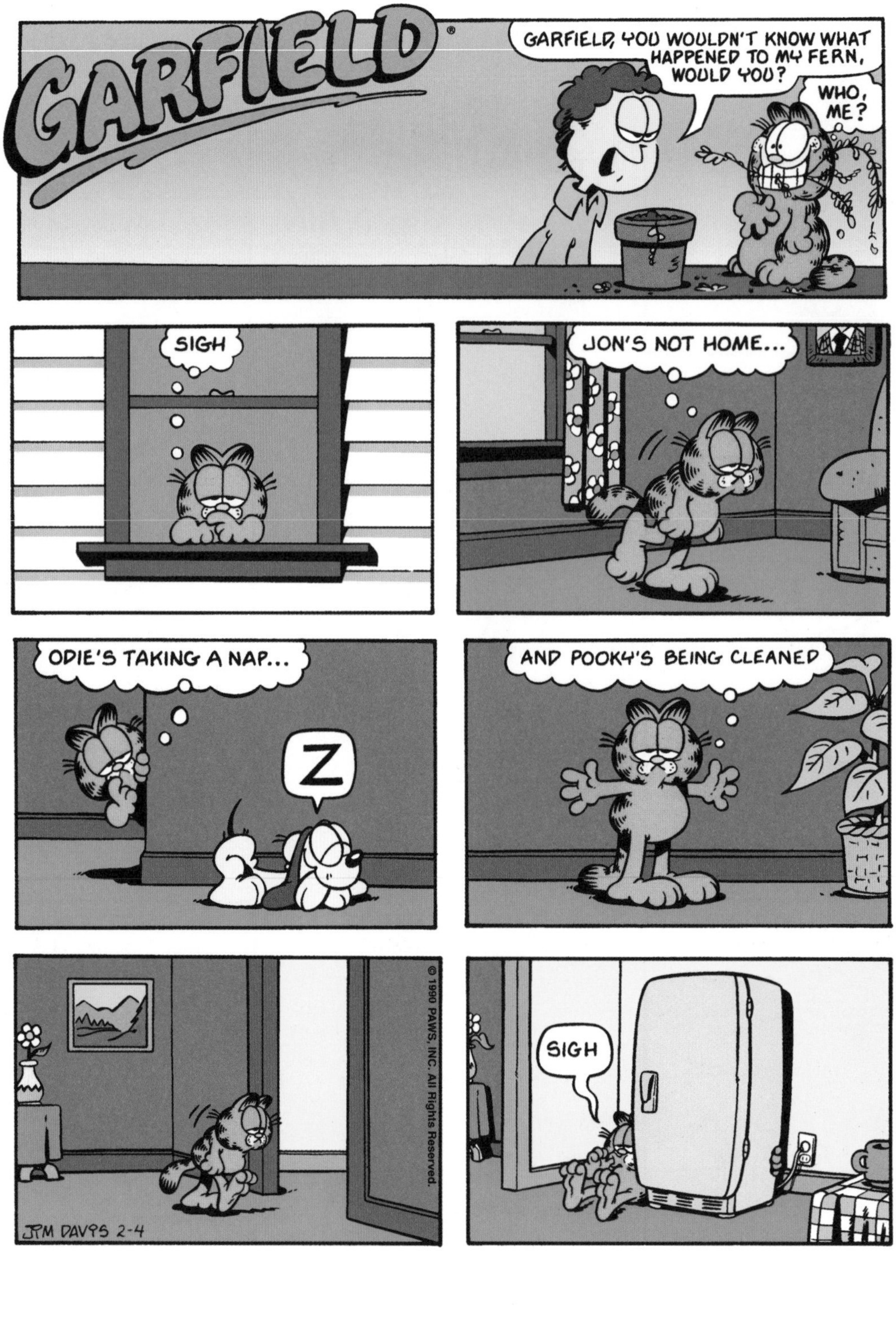
GARFIELD®
GARFIELD, YOU WOULDN'T KNOW WHAT HAPPENED TO MY FERN, WOULD YOU?
WHO, ME?
SIGH
JON'S NOT HOME...
ODIE'S TAKING A NAP...
Z
AND POOKY'S BEING CLEANED
© 1990 PAWS, INC. All Rights Reserved.
JIM DAVIS 2-4
SIGH

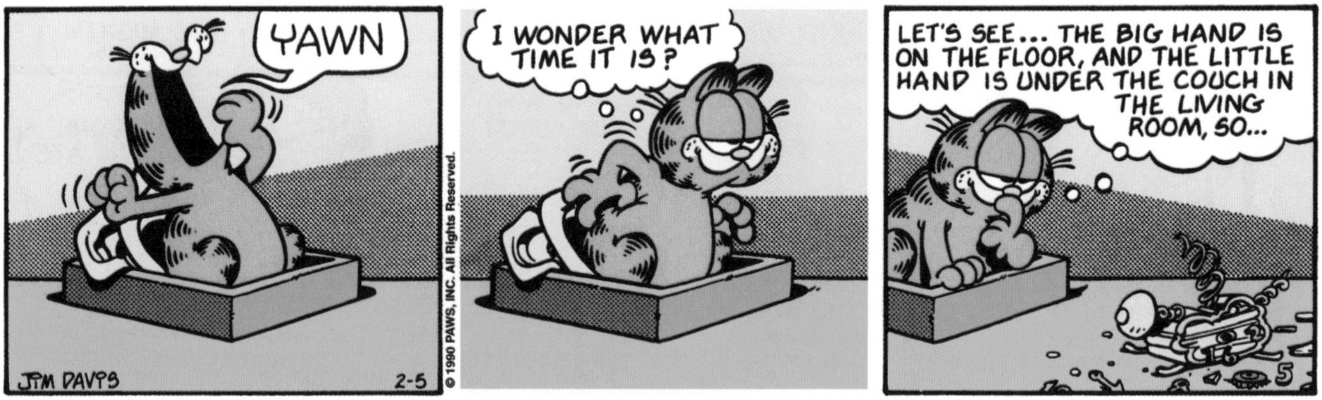
YAWN
JIM DAVIS 2-5
© 1990 PAWS, INC. All Rights Reserved.
I WONDER WHAT TIME IT IS?
LET'S SEE... THE BIG HAND IS ON THE FLOOR, AND THE LITTLE HAND IS UNDER THE COUCH IN THE LIVING ROOM, SO...
5

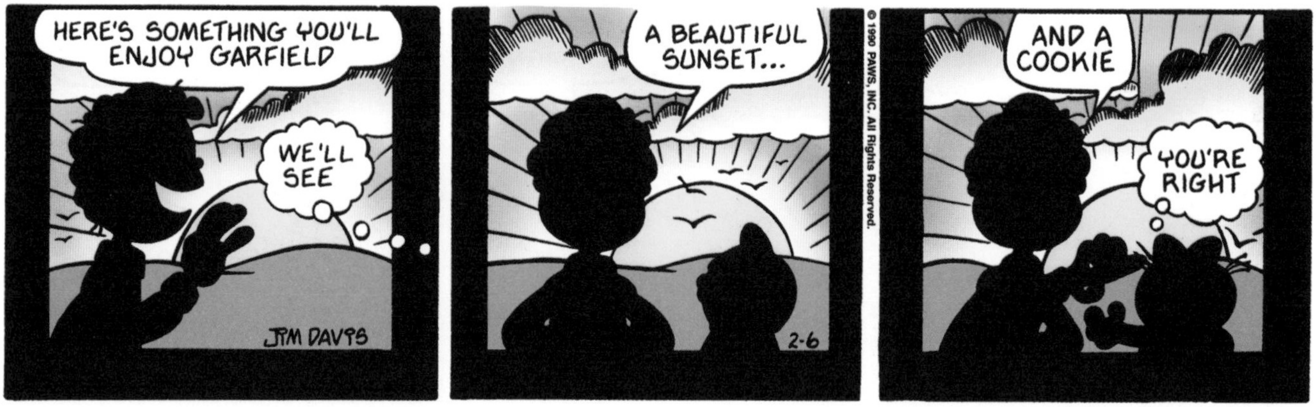
HERE'S SOMETHING YOU'LL ENJOY GARFIELD
WE'LL SEE
JIM DAVIS
A BEAUTIFUL SUNSET...
2-6
© 1990 PAWS, INC. All Rights Reserved.
AND A COOKIE
YOU'RE RIGHT

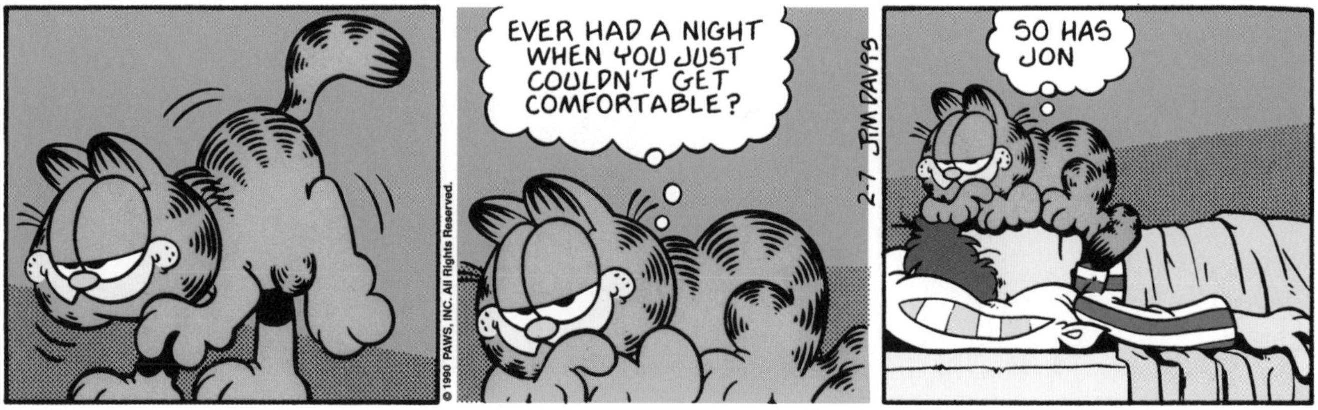
© 1990 PAWS, INC. All Rights Reserved.
EVER HAD A NIGHT WHEN YOU JUST COULDN'T GET COMFORTABLE?
2-7 JIM DAVIS
SO HAS JON

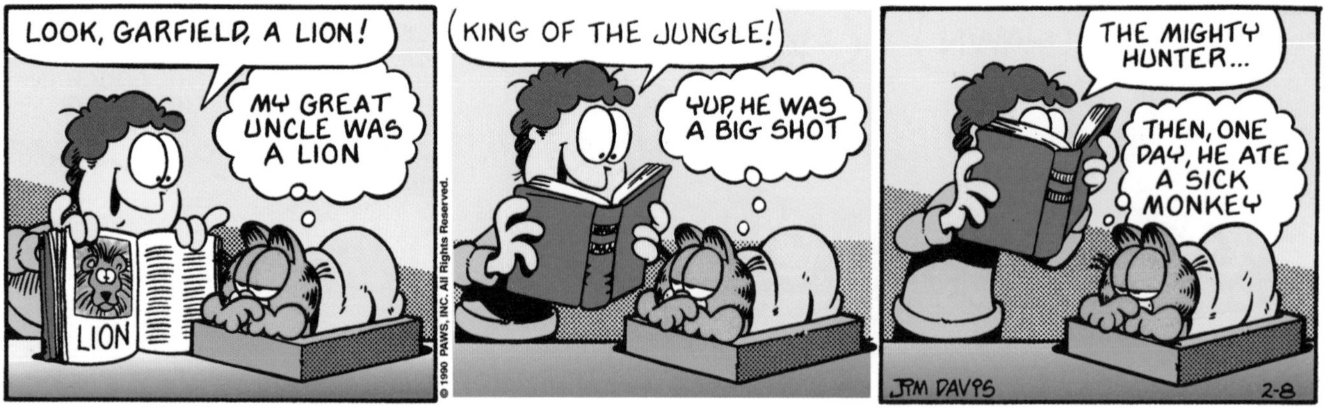
LOOK, GARFIELD, A LION!
MY GREAT UNCLE WAS A LION
LION
© 1990 PAWS, INC. All Rights Reserved.
KING OF THE JUNGLE!
YUP, HE WAS A BIG SHOT
THE MIGHTY HUNTER...
THEN, ONE DAY, HE ATE A SICK MONKEY
JIM DAVIS
2-8

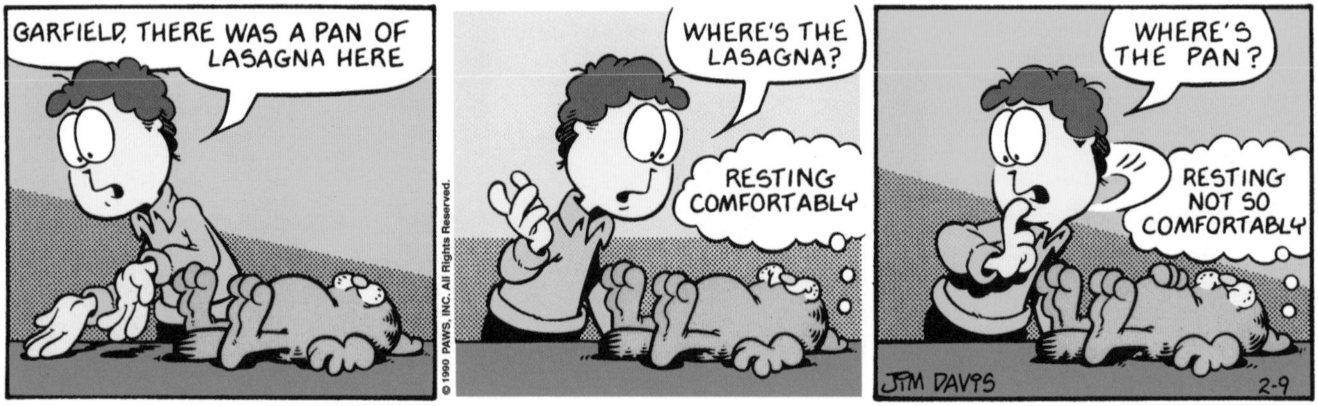
GARFIELD, THERE WAS A PAN OF LASAGNA HERE
© 1990 PAWS, INC. All Rights Reserved.
WHERE'S THE LASAGNA?
RESTING COMFORTABLY
WHERE'S THE PAN?
RESTING NOT SO COMFORTABLY
JIM DAVIS
2-9

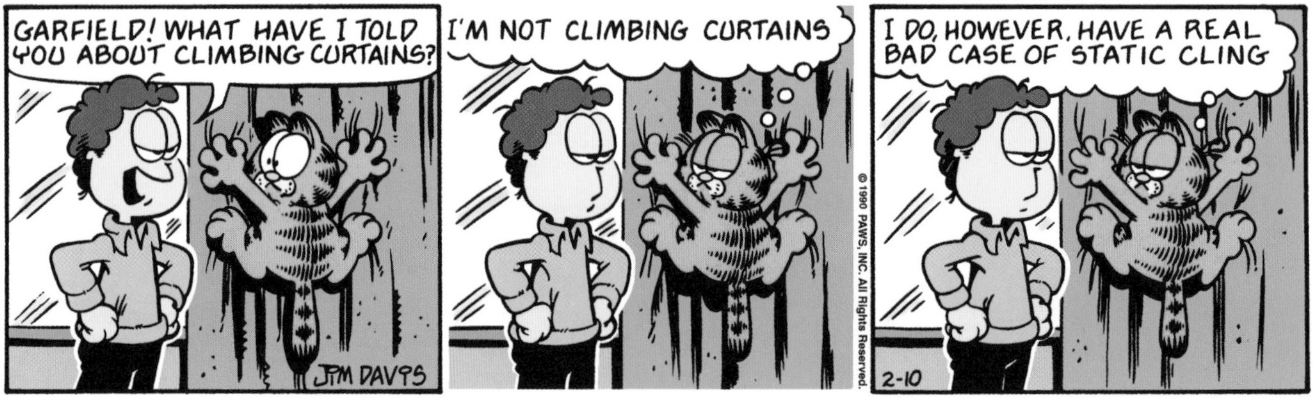
GARFIELD! WHAT HAVE I TOLD YOU ABOUT CLIMBING CURTAINS?
JIM DAVIS
I'M NOT CLIMBING CURTAINS
© 1990 PAWS, INC. All Rights Reserved.
I DO, HOWEVER, HAVE A REAL BAD CASE OF STATIC CLING
2-10

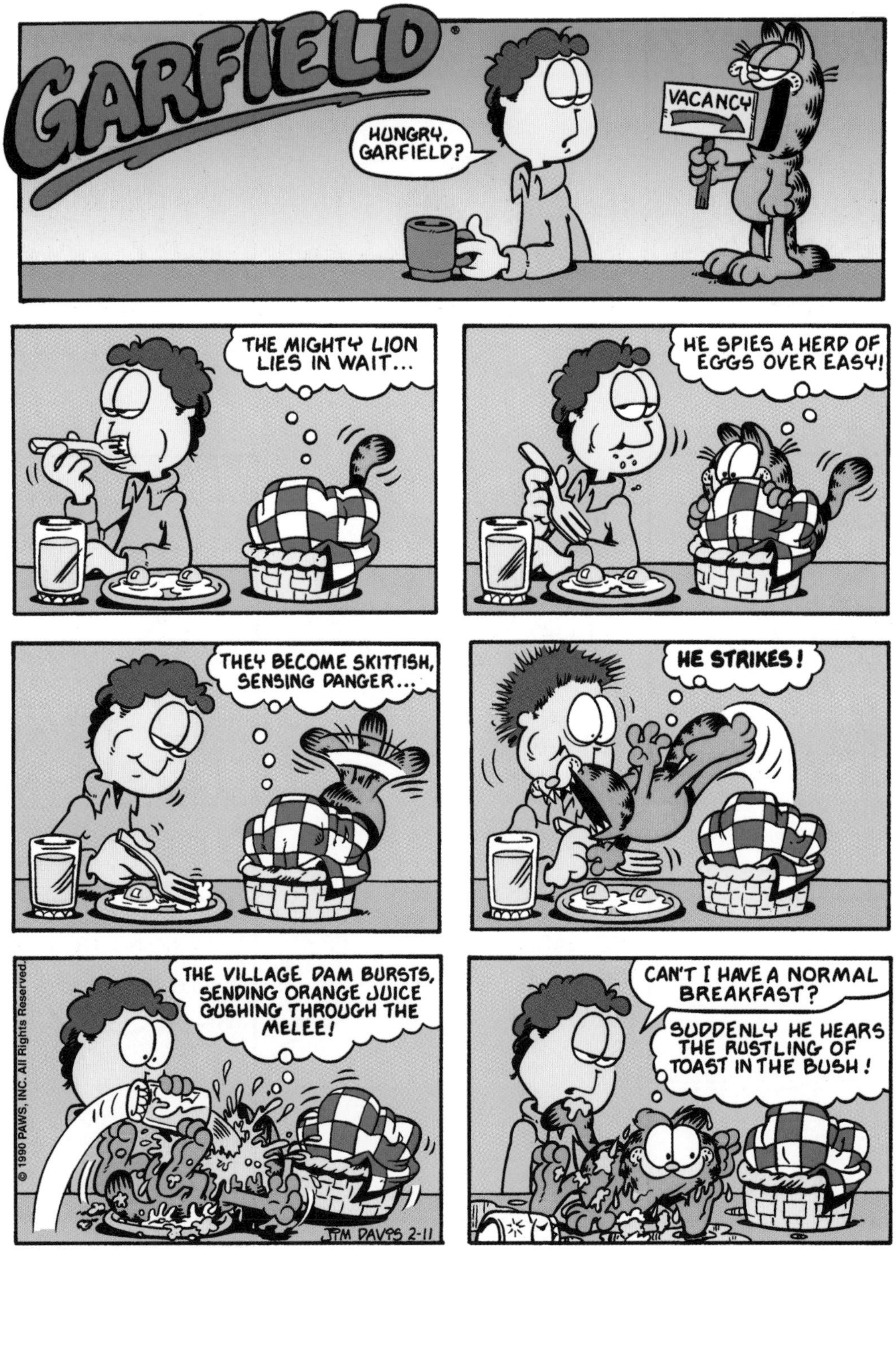
GARFIELD®
HUNGRY, GARFIELD?
VACANCY
THE MIGHTY LION LIES IN WAIT...
HE SPIES A HERD OF EGGS OVER EASY!
THEY BECOME SKITTISH, SENSING DANGER...
HE STRIKES!
THE VILLAGE DAM BURSTS, SENDING ORANGE JUICE GUSHING THROUGH THE MELEE!
© 1990 PAWS, INC. All Rights Reserved.
JIM DAVIS 2-11
CAN'T I HAVE A NORMAL BREAKFAST?
SUDDENLY HE HEARS THE RUSTLING OF TOAST IN THE BUSH!

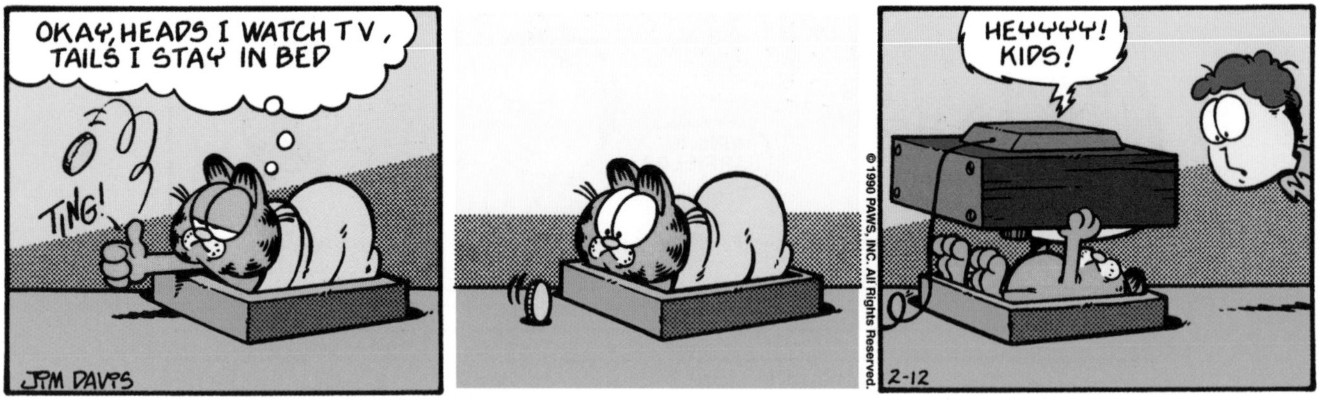
OKAY, HEADS I WATCH TV, TAILS I STAY IN BED
TING!
JPM DAVPS
© 1990 PAWS, INC. All Rights Reserved.
HEYYYY! KIDS!
2-12

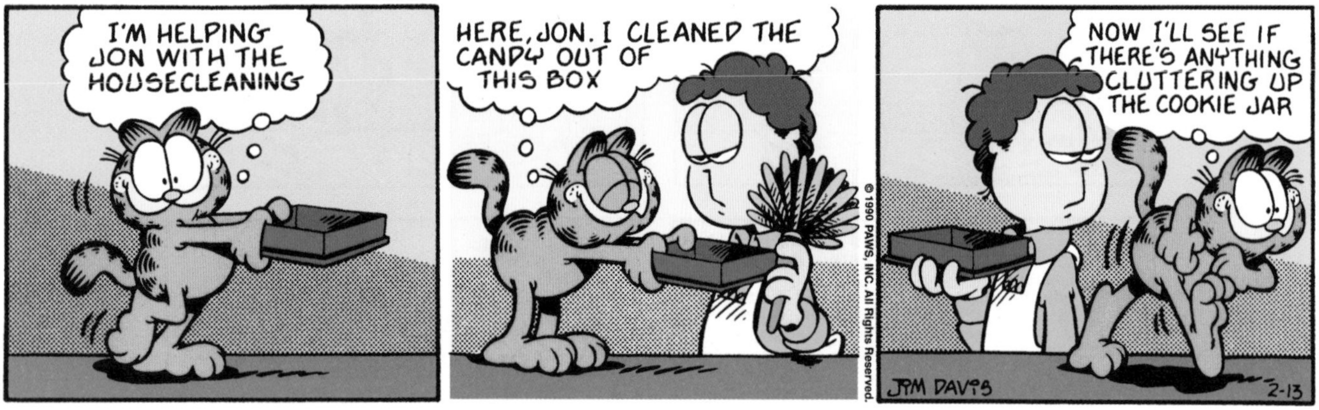
I'M HELPING JON WITH THE HOUSECLEANING
HERE, JON. I CLEANED THE CANDY OUT OF THIS BOX
© 1990 PAWS, INC. All Rights Reserved.
NOW I'LL SEE IF THERE'S ANYTHING CLUTTERING UP THE COOKIE JAR
JPM DAVPS
2-13

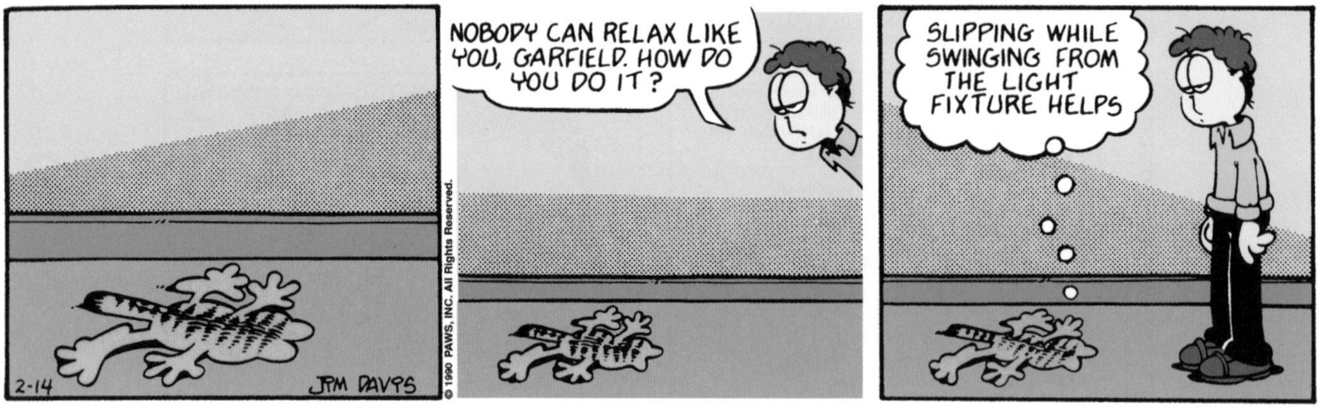
2-14
JPM DAVPS
© 1990 PAWS, INC. All Rights Reserved.
NOBODY CAN RELAX LIKE YOU, GARFIELD. HOW DO YOU DO IT?
SLIPPING WHILE SWINGING FROM THE LIGHT FIXTURE HELPS

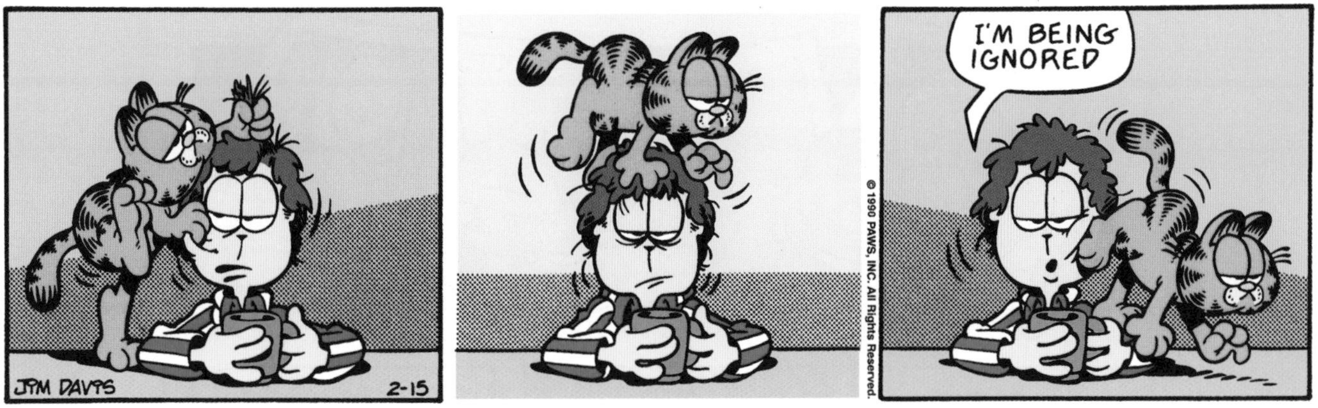
JIM DAVIS
2-15
I'M BEING IGNORED

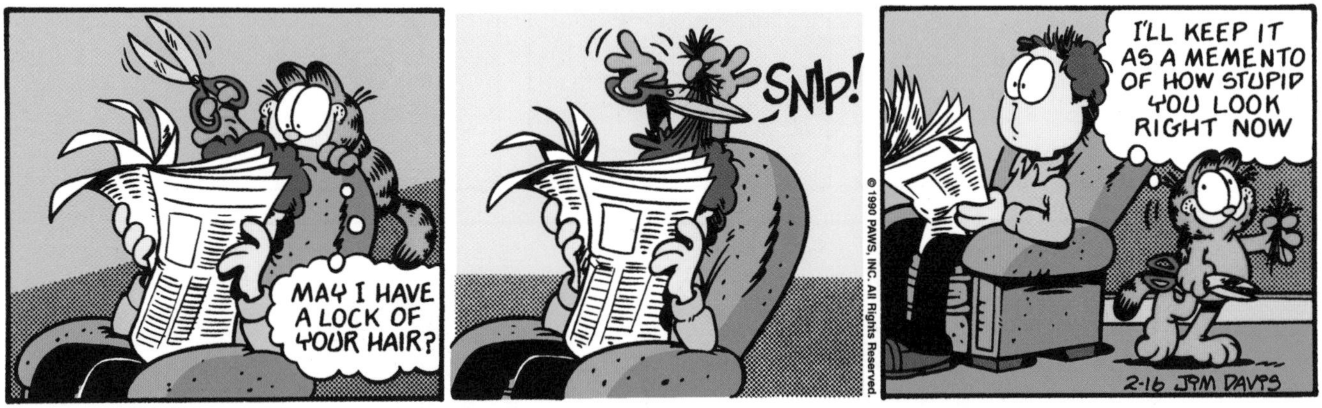
MAY I HAVE A LOCK OF YOUR HAIR?
SNIP!
I'LL KEEP IT AS A MEMENTO OF HOW STUPID YOU LOOK RIGHT NOW
2-16 JIM DAVIS

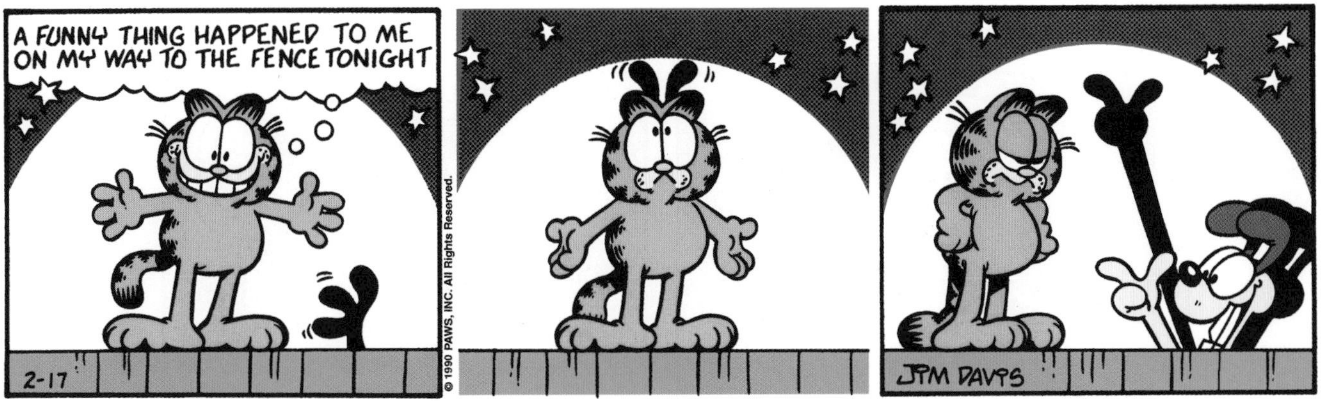
A FUNNY THING HAPPENED TO ME ON MY WAY TO THE FENCE TONIGHT
2-17
JIM DAVIS

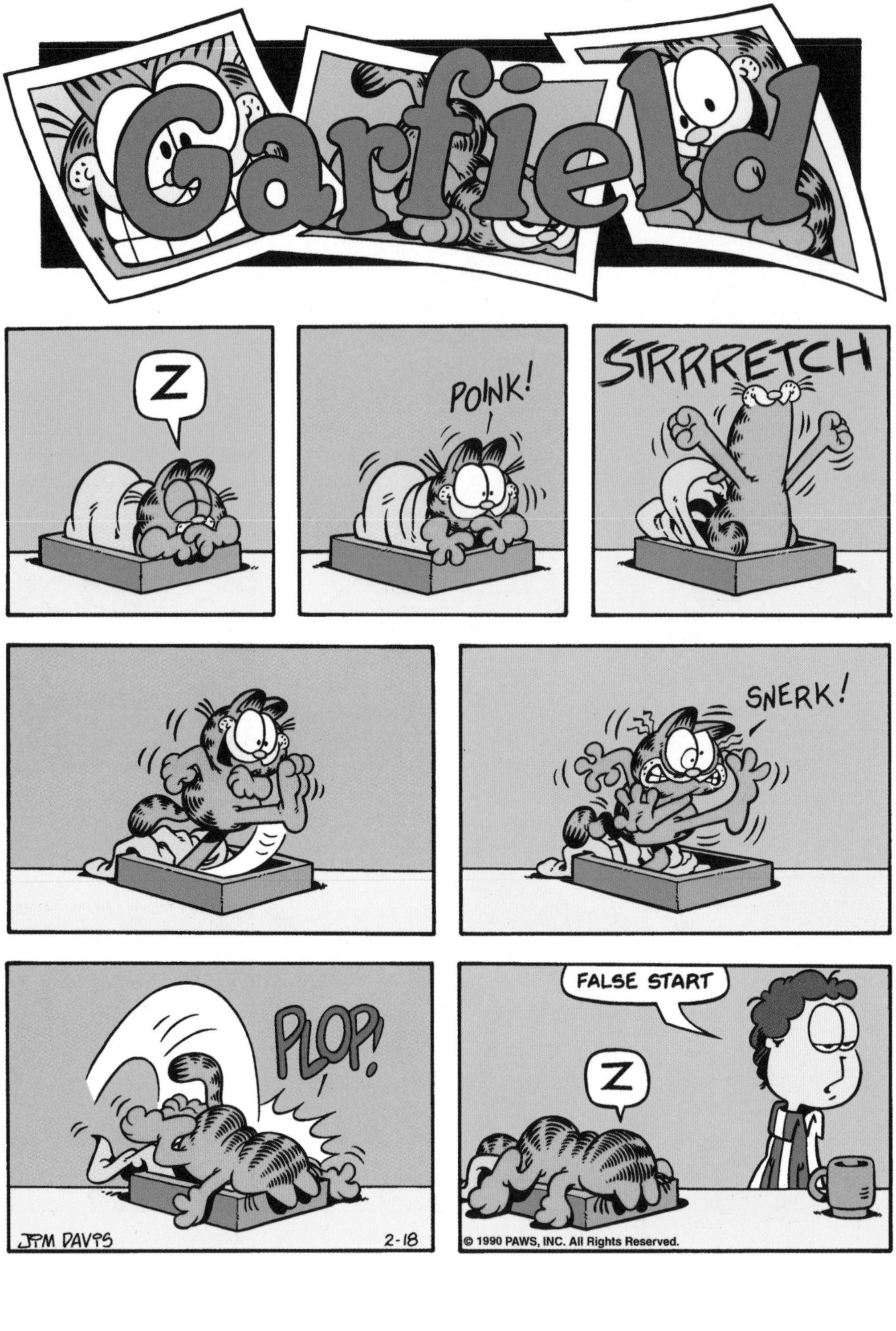
Garfield
Z
POINK!
STRRRETCH
SNERK!
PLOP!
JIM DAVIS
2-18
FALSE START
Z
© 1990 PAWS, INC. All Rights Reserved.

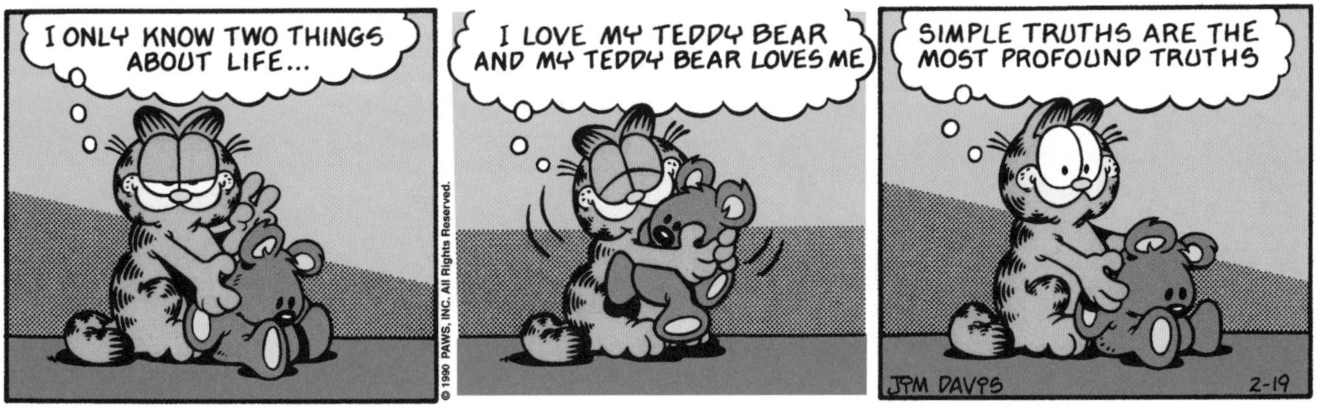
I ONLY KNOW TWO THINGS ABOUT LIFE...
© 1990 PAWS, INC. All Rights Reserved.
I LOVE MY TEDDY BEAR AND MY TEDDY BEAR LOVES ME
SIMPLE TRUTHS ARE THE MOST PROFOUND TRUTHS
JIM DAVIS
2-19

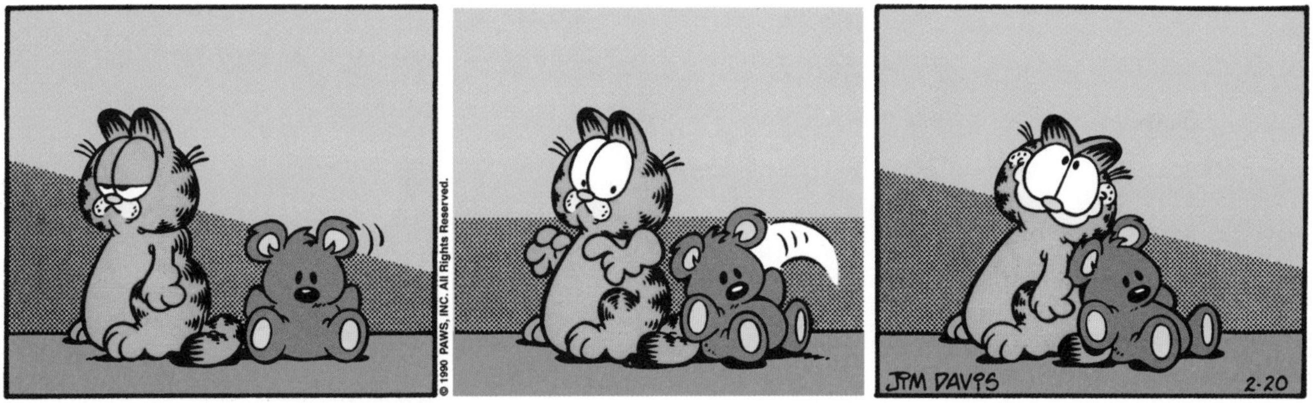
© 1990 PAWS, INC. All Rights Reserved.
JIM DAVIS
2-20

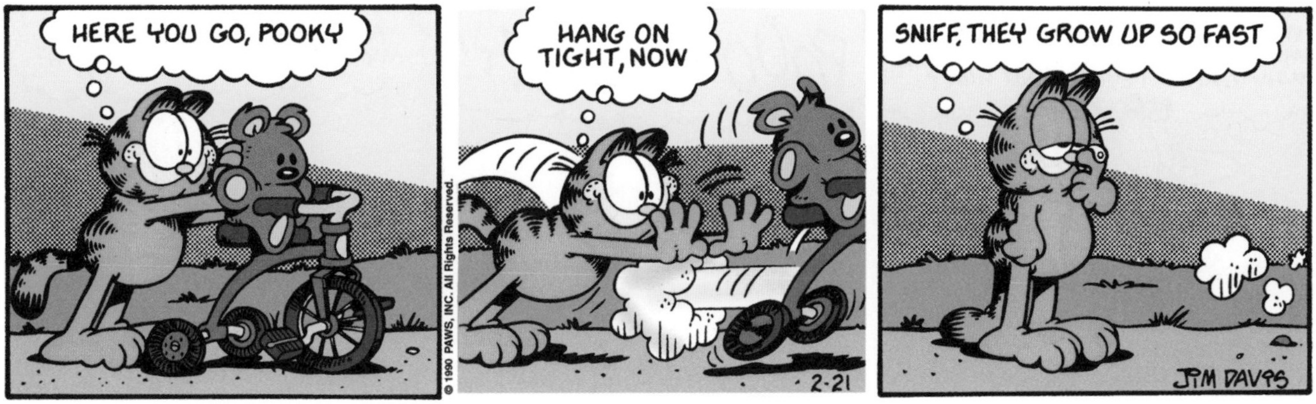
HERE YOU GO, POOKY
© 1990 PAWS, INC. All Rights Reserved.
HANG ON TIGHT, NOW
2-21
SNIFF, THEY GROW UP SO FAST
JIM DAVIS

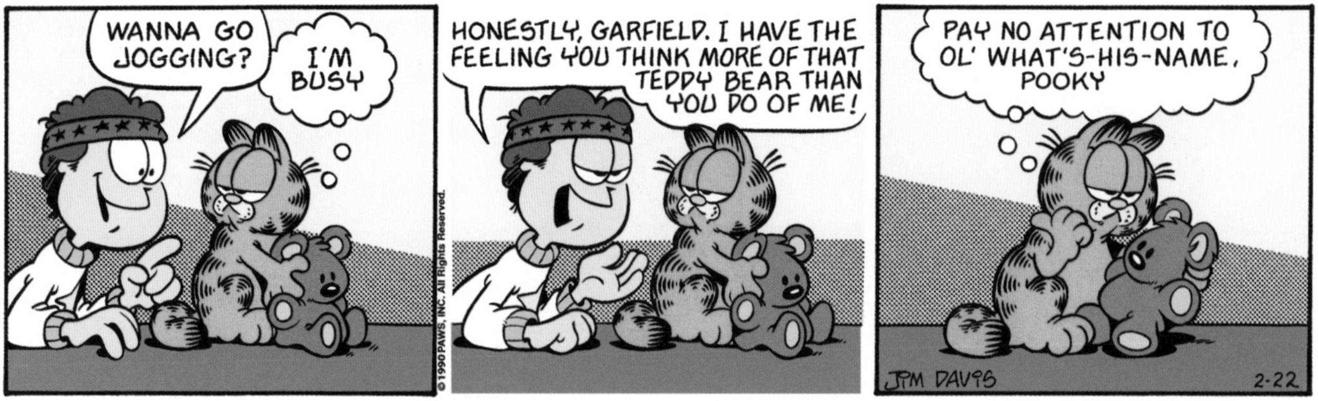
WANNA GO JOGGING?
I'M BUSY
© 1990 PAWS, INC. All Rights Reserved.
HONESTLY, GARFIELD. I HAVE THE FEELING YOU THINK MORE OF THAT TEDDY BEAR THAN YOU DO OF ME!
PAY NO ATTENTION TO OL' WHAT'S-HIS-NAME, POOKY
JIM DAVIS
2-22

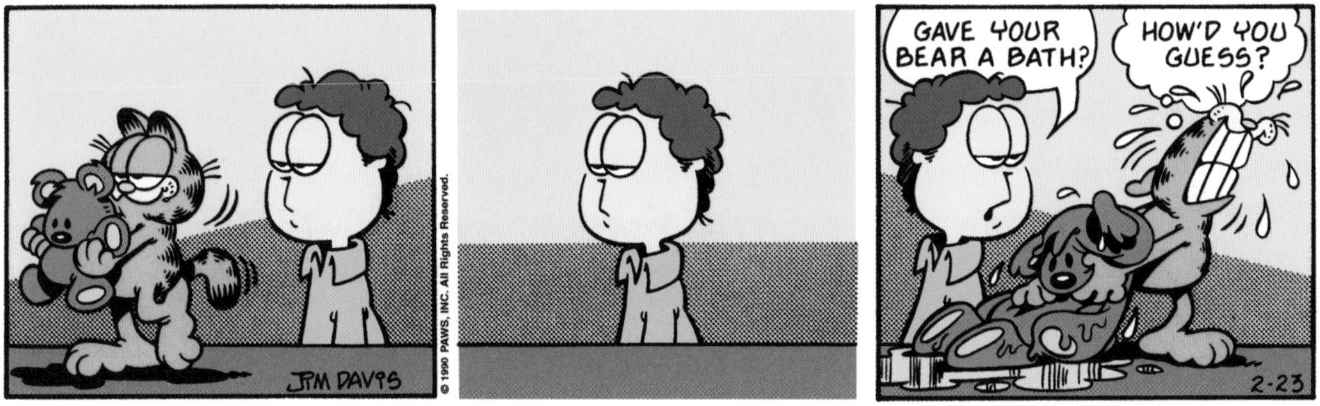
JIM DAVIS
© 1990 PAWS, INC. All Rights Reserved.
GAVE YOUR BEAR A BATH?
HOW'D YOU GUESS?
2-23

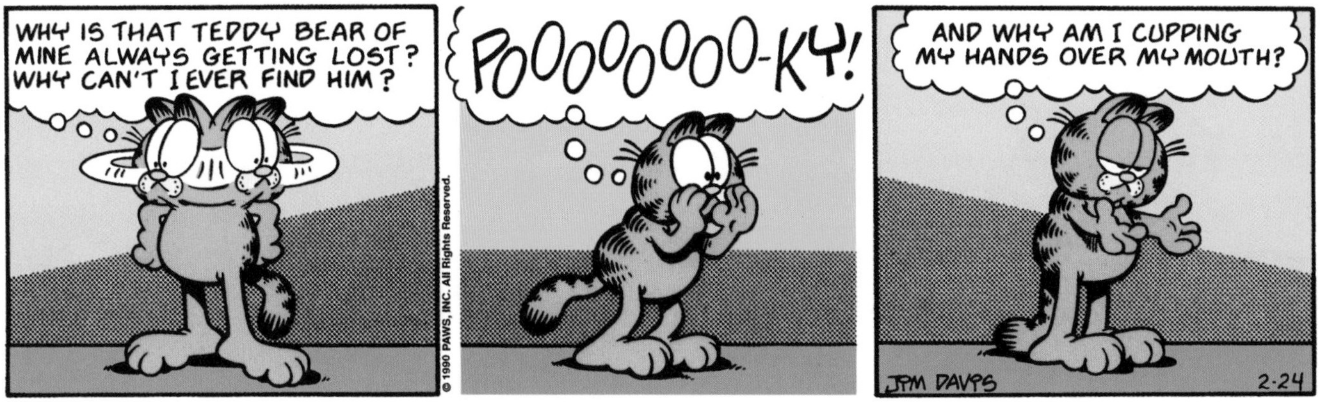
WHY IS THAT TEDDY BEAR OF MINE ALWAYS GETTING LOST? WHY CAN'T I EVER FIND HIM?
© 1990 PAWS, INC. All Rights Reserved.
POOOOOOOO-KY!
AND WHY AM I CUPPING MY HANDS OVER MY MOUTH?
JIM DAVIS
2-24

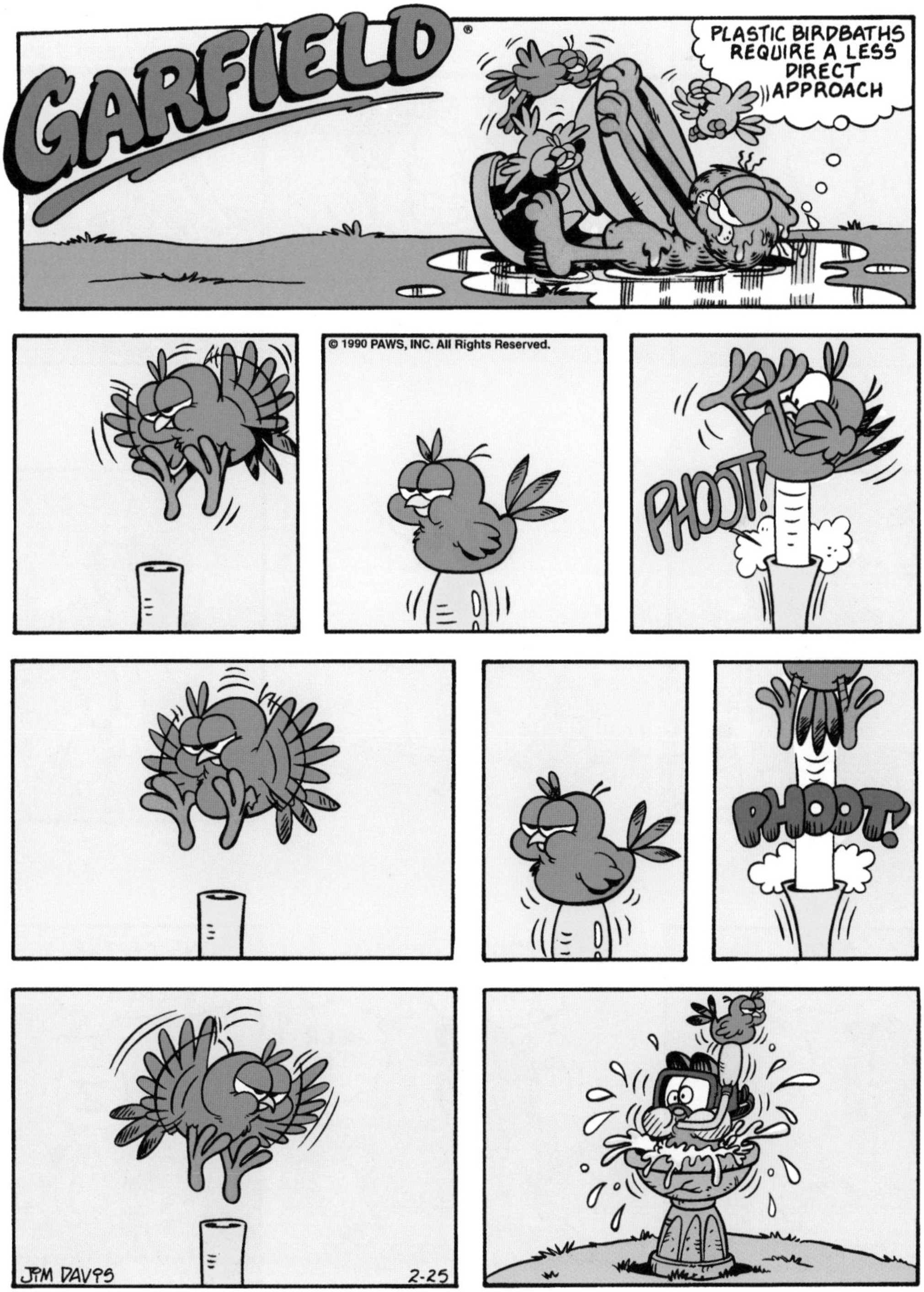
GARFIELD®
PLASTIC BIRDBATHS REQUIRE A LESS DIRECT APPROACH
© 1990 PAWS, INC. All Rights Reserved.
PHOOT!
PHOOT!
JIM DAVIS
2-25

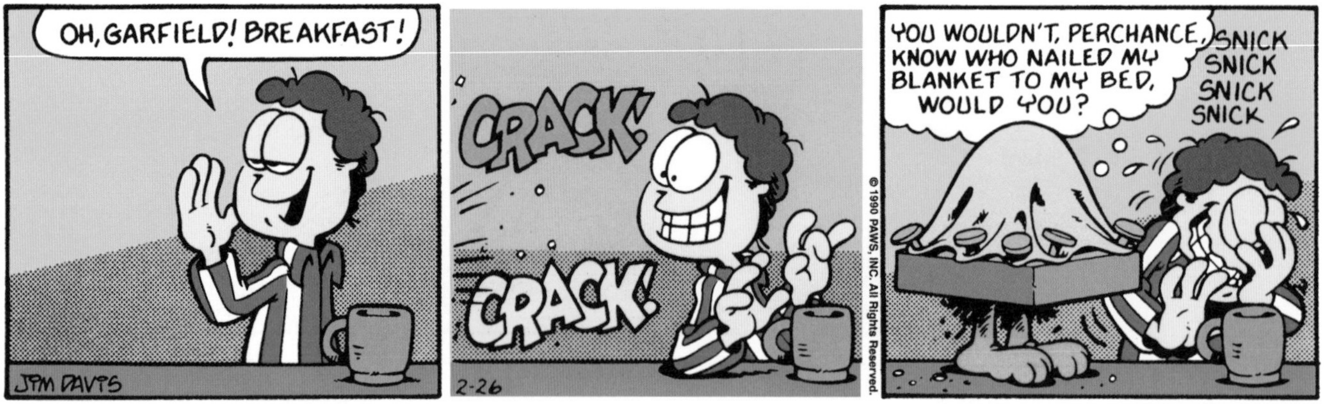
OH, GARFIELD! BREAKFAST!
CRACK!
CRACK!
YOU WOULDN'T, PERCHANCE, KNOW WHO NAILED MY BLANKET TO MY BED, WOULD YOU?
SNICK SNICK SNICK SNICK
JPM DAVPS
2-26
© 1990 PAWS, INC. All Rights Reserved.

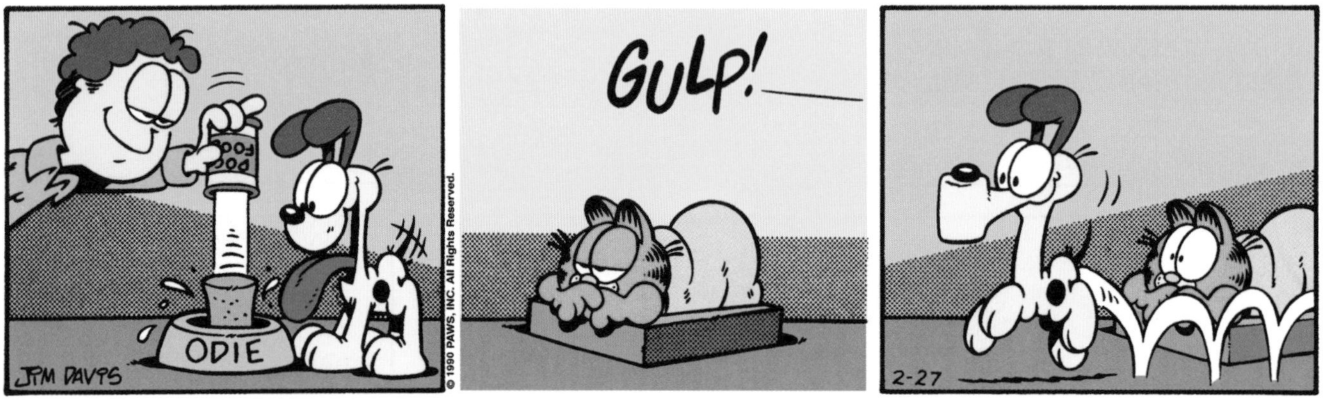
DOG FOOD
ODIE
GULP!
JPM DAVPS
2-27
© 1990 PAWS, INC. All Rights Reserved.

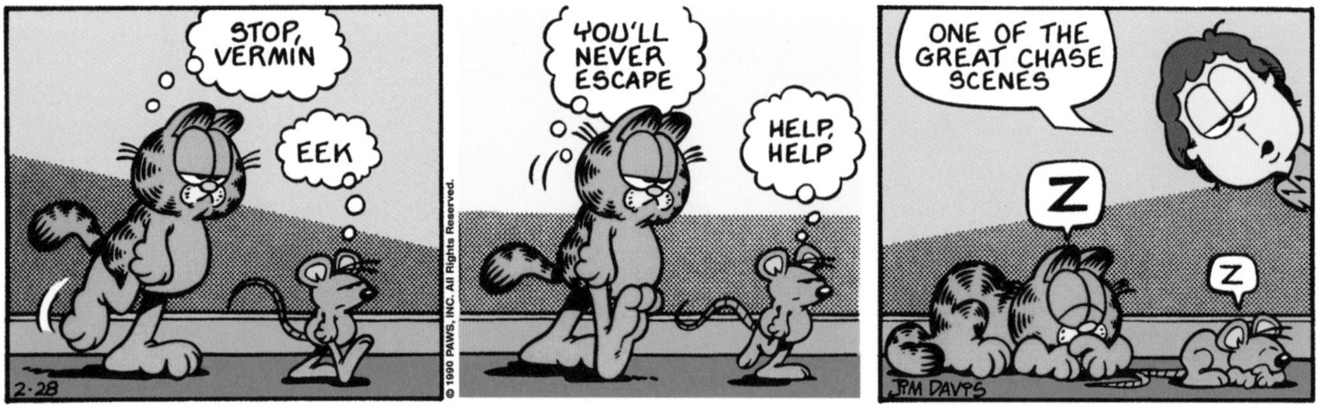
STOP, VERMIN
EEK
YOU'LL NEVER ESCAPE
HELP, HELP
ONE OF THE GREAT CHASE SCENES
Z
Z
2-28
JPM DAVPS
© 1990 PAWS, INC. All Rights Reserved.

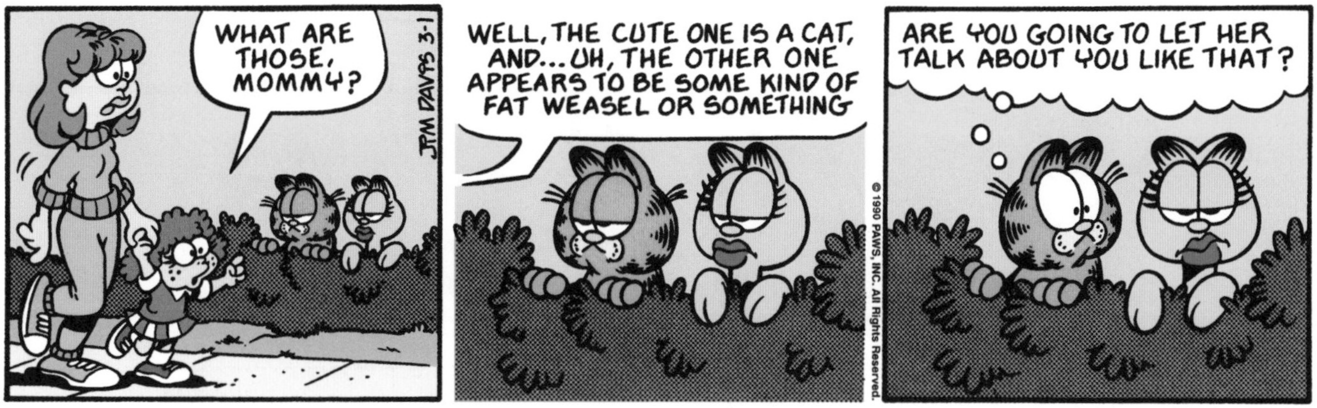
WHAT ARE THOSE, MOMMY?
JIM DAVIS 3-1
WELL, THE CUTE ONE IS A CAT, AND... UH, THE OTHER ONE APPEARS TO BE SOME KIND OF FAT WEASEL OR SOMETHING
© 1990 PAWS, INC. All Rights Reserved.
ARE YOU GOING TO LET HER TALK ABOUT YOU LIKE THAT?

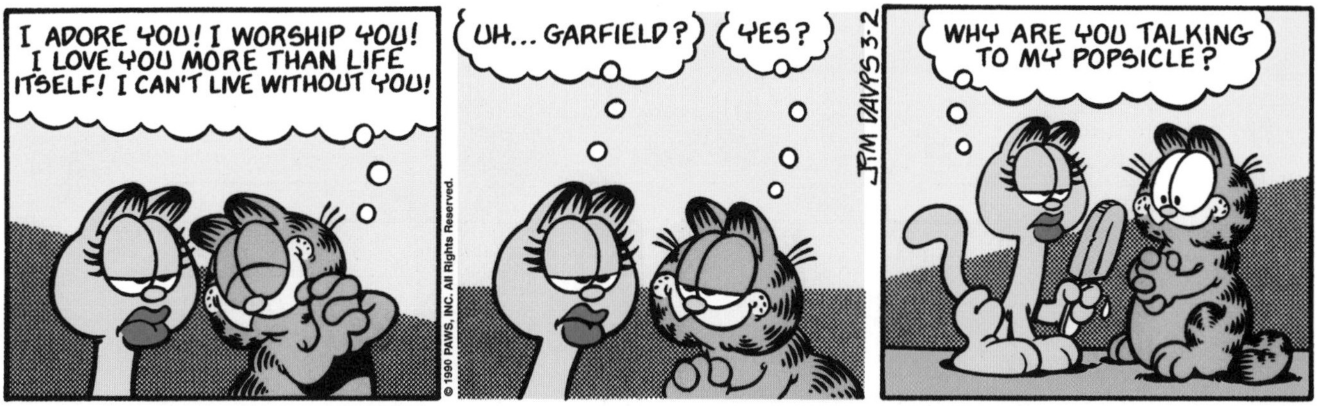
I ADORE YOU! I WORSHIP YOU! I LOVE YOU MORE THAN LIFE ITSELF! I CAN'T LIVE WITHOUT YOU!
© 1990 PAWS, INC. All Rights Reserved.
UH... GARFIELD?
YES?
JIM DAVIS 3-2
WHY ARE YOU TALKING TO MY POPSICLE?

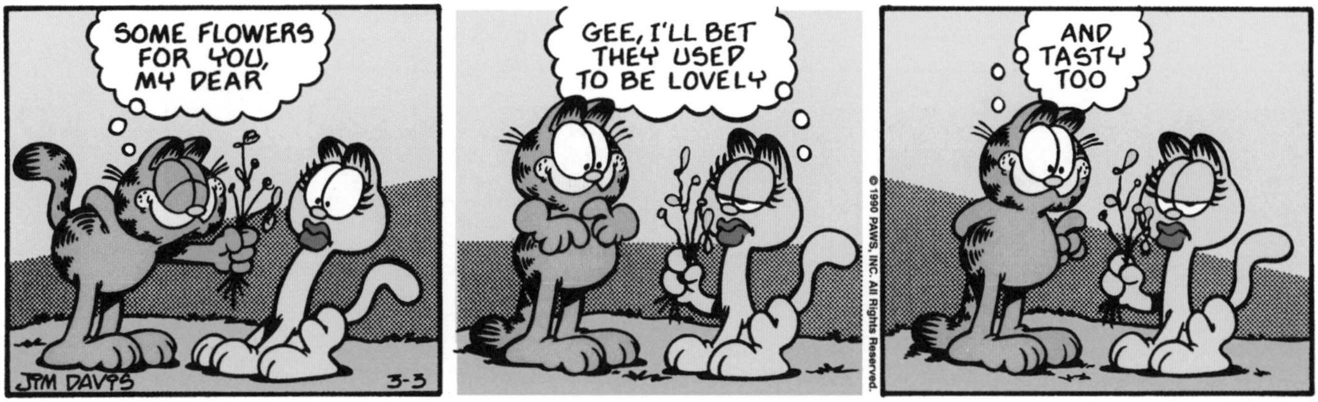
SOME FLOWERS FOR YOU, MY DEAR
JIM DAVIS 3-3
GEE, I'LL BET THEY USED TO BE LOVELY
© 1990 PAWS, INC. All Rights Reserved.
AND TASTY TOO

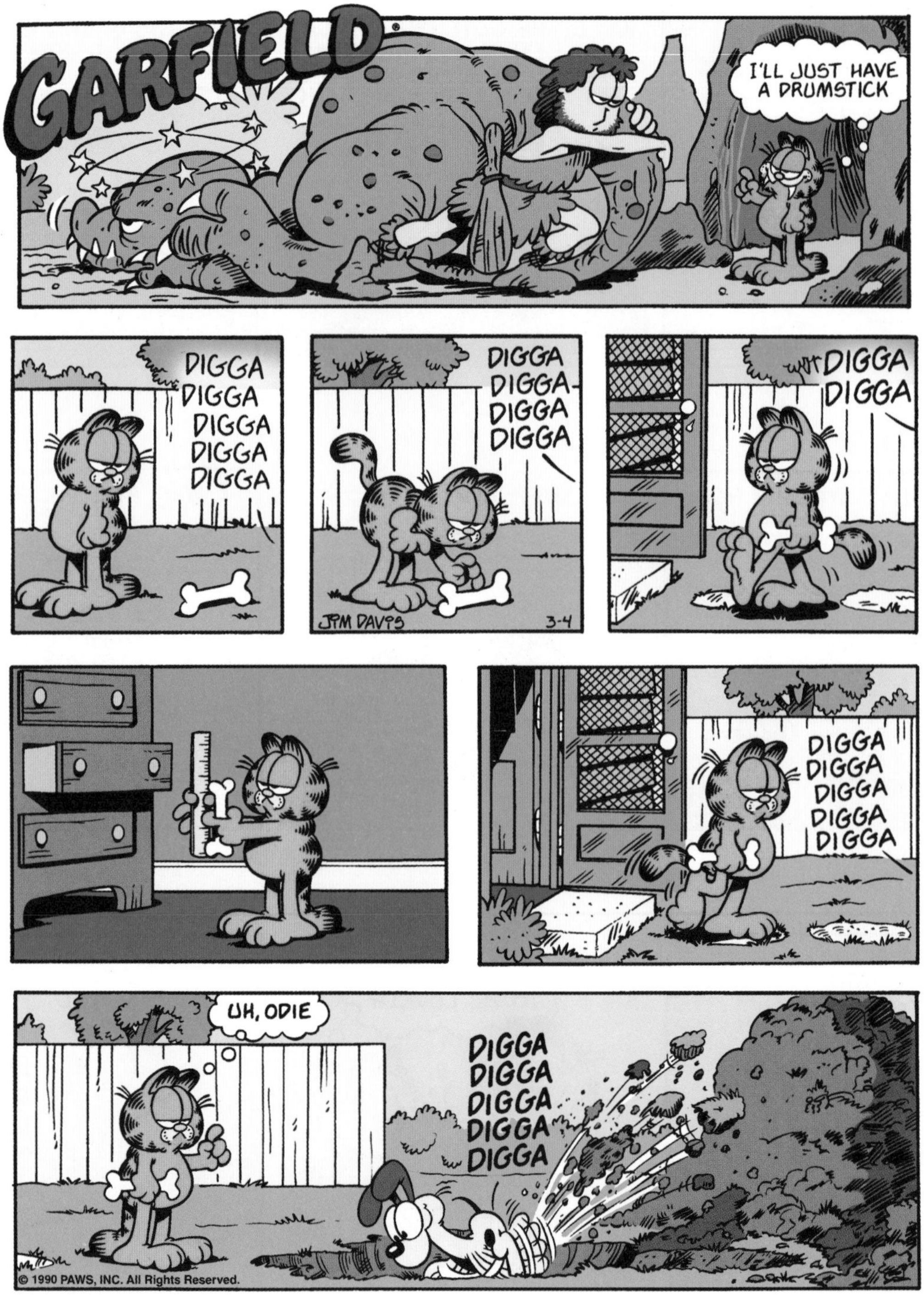
GARFIELD
I'LL JUST HAVE A DRUMSTICK
DIGGA DIGGA DIGGA DIGGA DIGGA
DIGGA DIGGA DIGGA DIGGA
JIM DAVIS 3-4
DIGGA DIGGA
DIGGA DIGGA DIGGA DIGGA DIGGA
UH, ODIE
DIGGA DIGGA DIGGA DIGGA DIGGA
© 1990 PAWS, INC. All Rights Reserved.

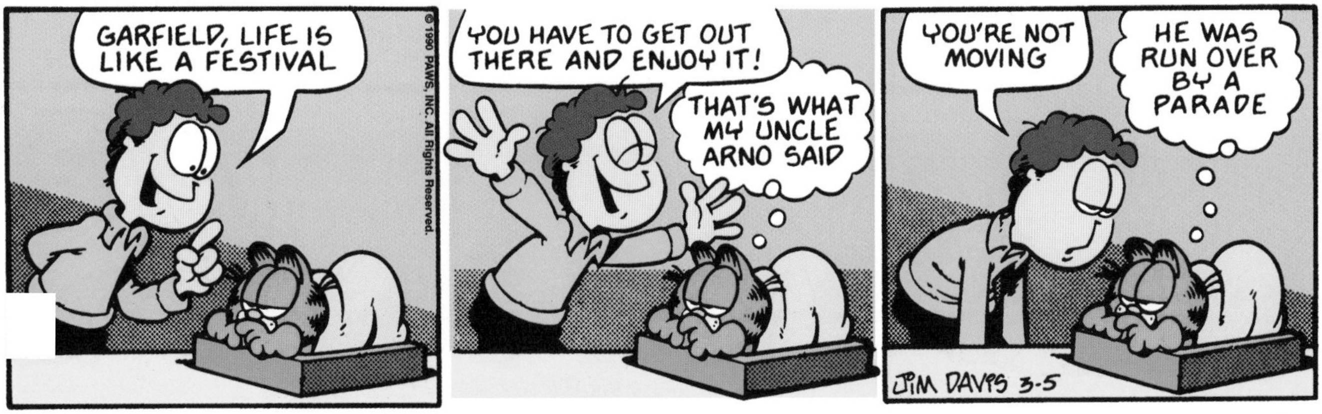
GARFIELD, LIFE IS LIKE A FESTIVAL
© 1990 PAWS, INC. All Rights Reserved.
YOU HAVE TO GET OUT THERE AND ENJOY IT!
THAT'S WHAT MY UNCLE ARNO SAID
YOU'RE NOT MOVING
HE WAS RUN OVER BY A PARADE
JIM DAVIS 3-5

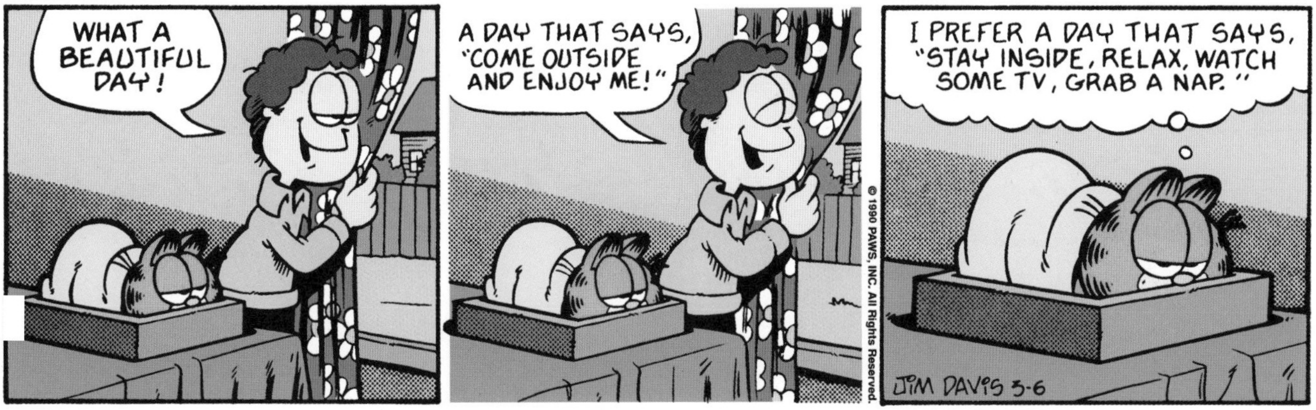
WHAT A BEAUTIFUL DAY!
A DAY THAT SAYS, "COME OUTSIDE AND ENJOY ME!"
© 1990 PAWS, INC. All Rights Reserved.
I PREFER A DAY THAT SAYS, "STAY INSIDE, RELAX, WATCH SOME TV, GRAB A NAP."
JIM DAVIS 3-6

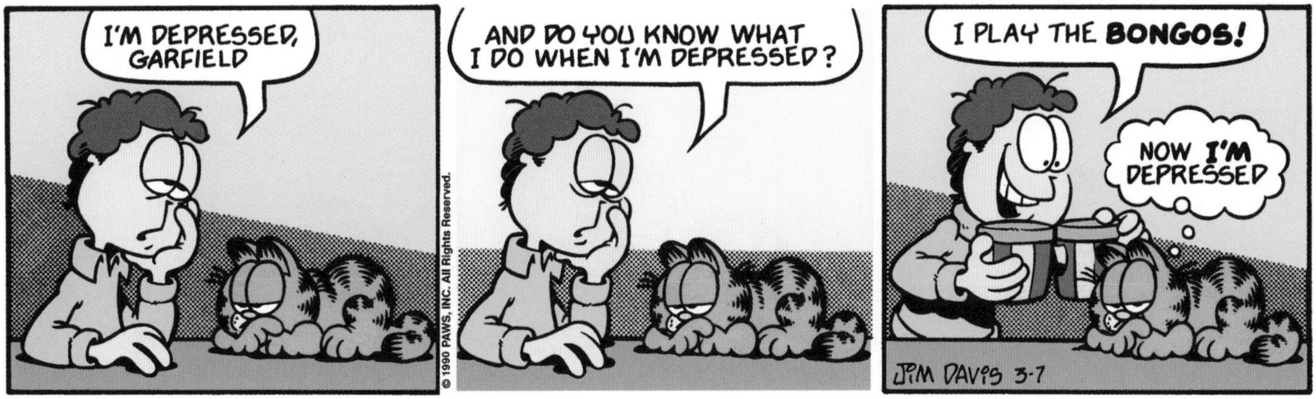
I'M DEPRESSED, GARFIELD
© 1990 PAWS, INC. All Rights Reserved.
AND DO YOU KNOW WHAT I DO WHEN I'M DEPRESSED?
I PLAY THE **BONGOS!**
NOW **I'M** DEPRESSED
JIM DAVIS 3-7

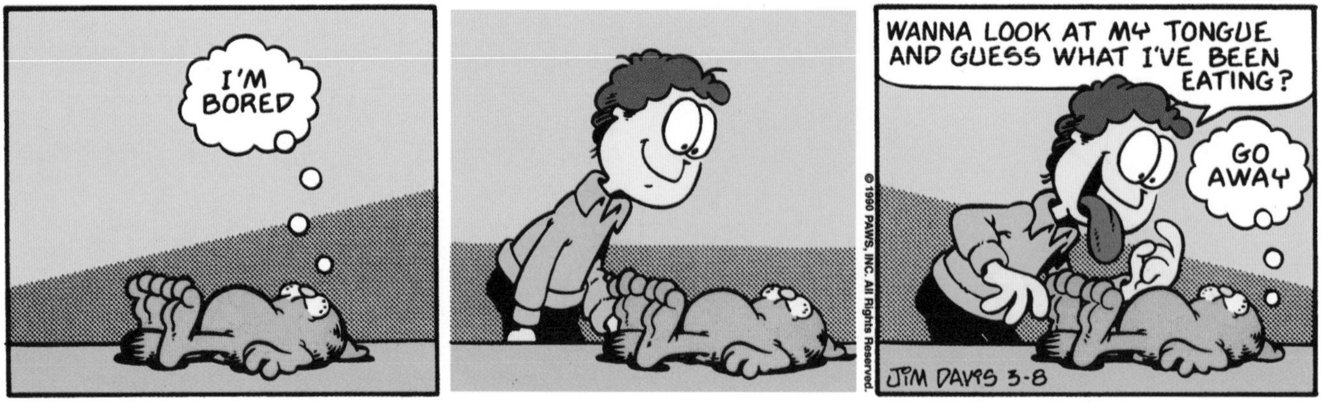
I'M BORED
WANNA LOOK AT MY TONGUE AND GUESS WHAT I'VE BEEN EATING?
GO AWAY
© 1990 PAWS, INC. All Rights Reserved.
JIM DAVIS 3-8

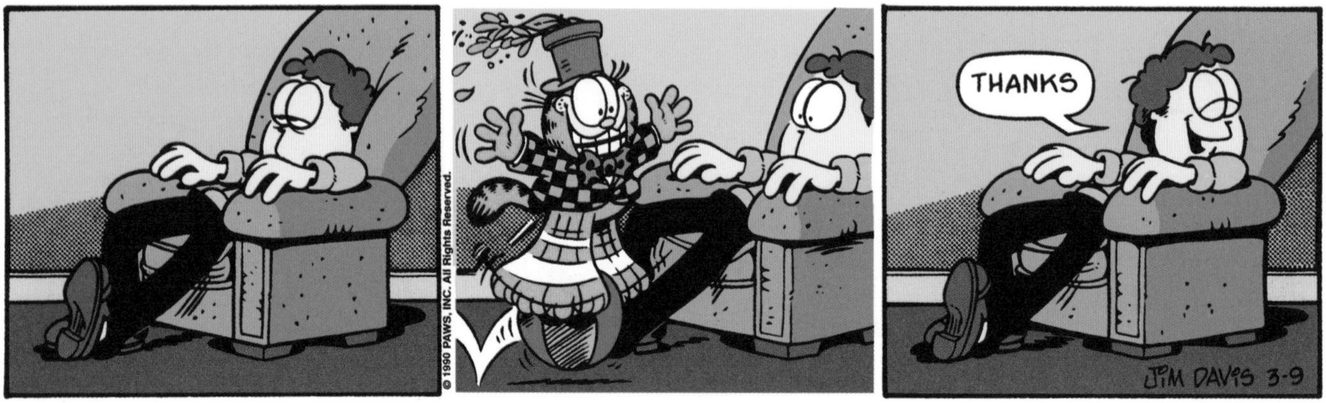
© 1990 PAWS, INC. All Rights Reserved.
THANKS
JIM DAVIS 3-9

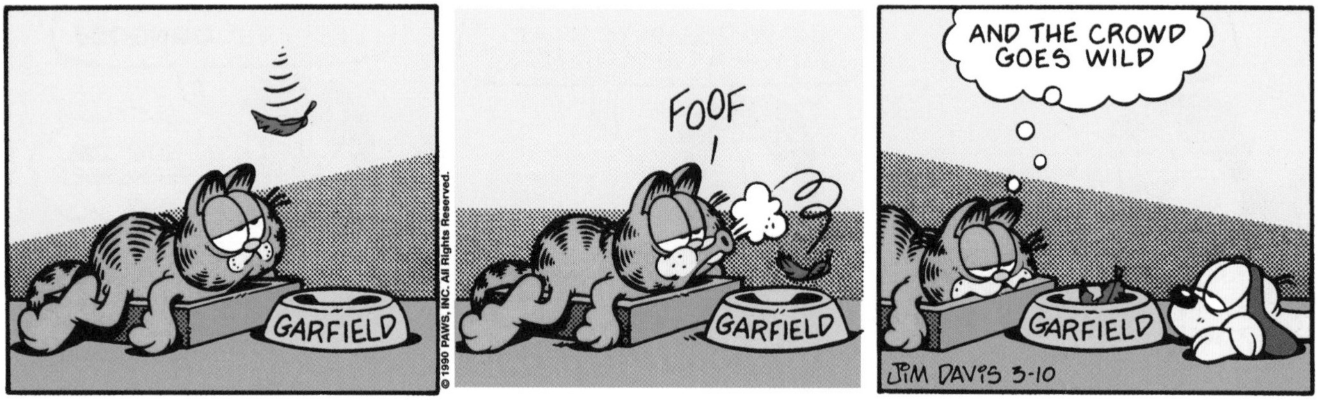
GARFIELD
© 1990 PAWS, INC. All Rights Reserved.
FOOF
GARFIELD
AND THE CROWD GOES WILD
GARFIELD
JIM DAVIS 3-10

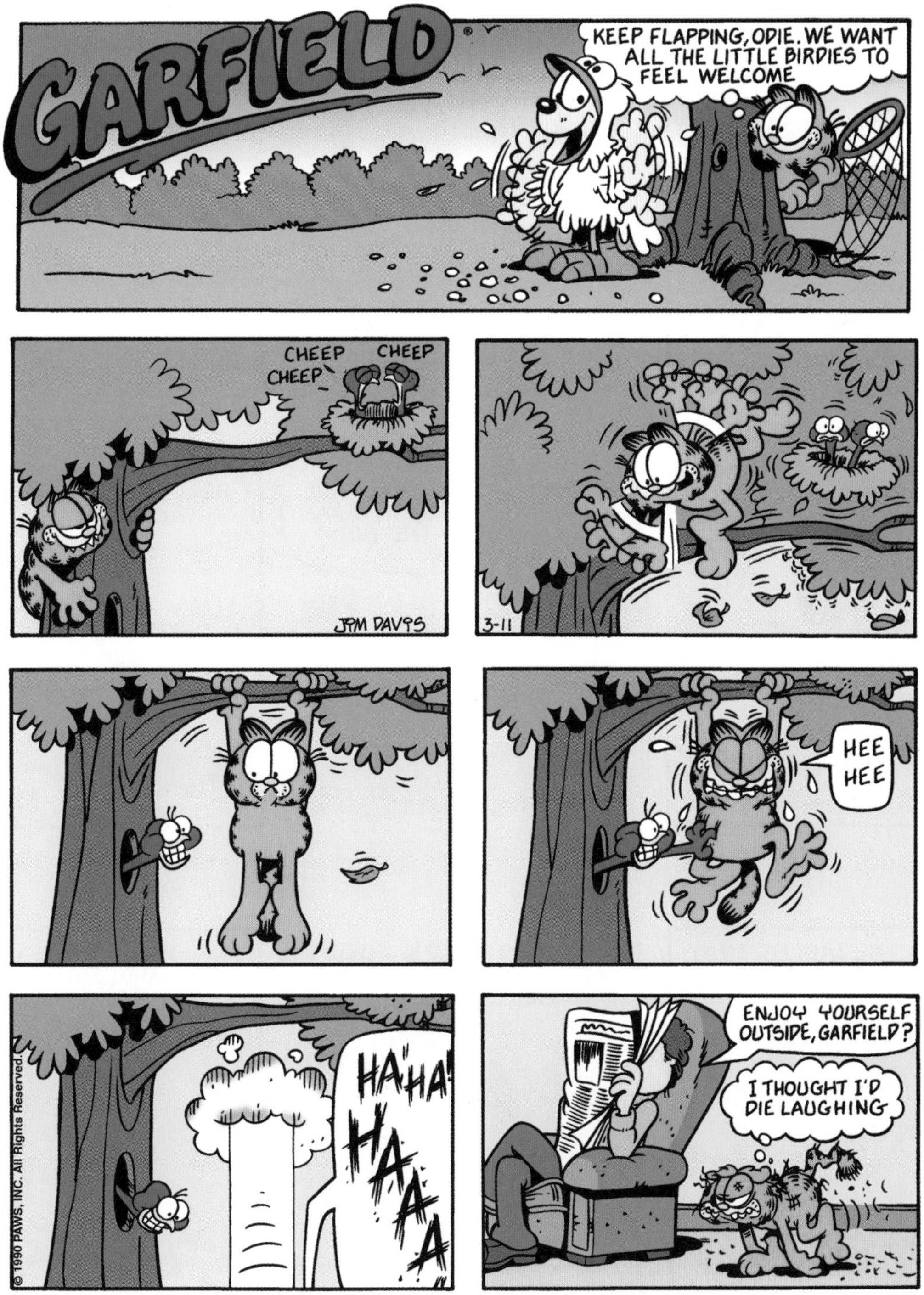
GARFIELD
KEEP FLAPPING, ODIE. WE WANT ALL THE LITTLE BIRDIES TO FEEL WELCOME
CHEEP CHEEP CHEEP
JIM DAVIS
3-11
HEE HEE
HA HA! HA HAAA
© 1990 PAWS, INC. All Rights Reserved.
ENJOY YOURSELF OUTSIDE, GARFIELD?
I THOUGHT I'D DIE LAUGHING

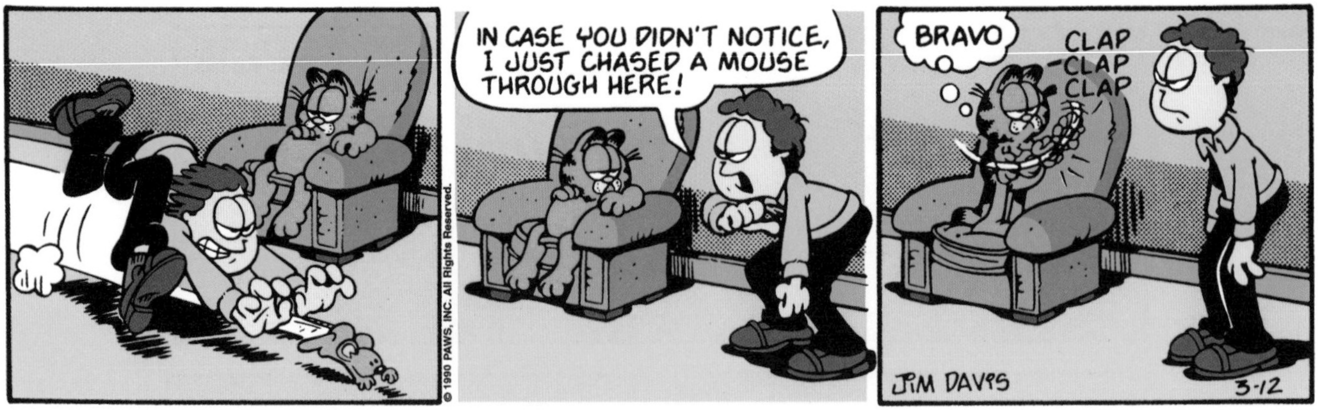
© 1990 PAWS, INC. All Rights Reserved.
IN CASE YOU DIDN'T NOTICE, I JUST CHASED A MOUSE THROUGH HERE!
BRAVO
CLAP CLAP CLAP
JIM DAVIS
3-12

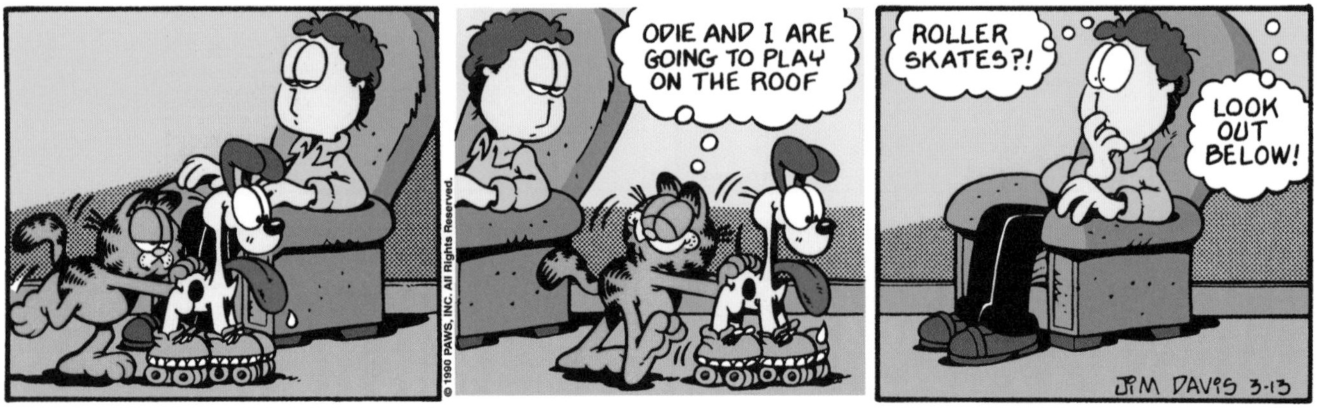
© 1990 PAWS, INC. All Rights Reserved.
ODIE AND I ARE GOING TO PLAY ON THE ROOF
ROLLER SKATES?!
LOOK OUT BELOW!
JIM DAVIS 3-13

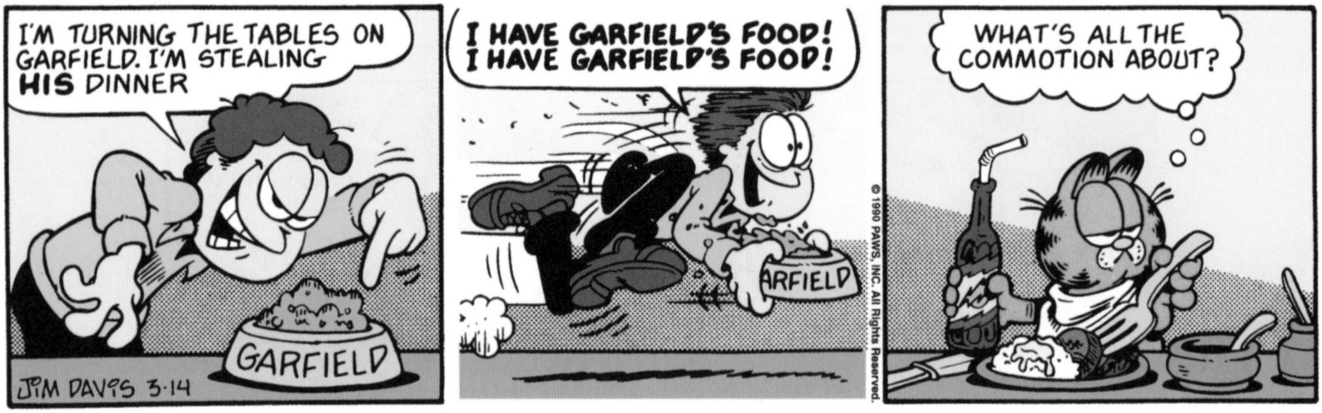
I'M TURNING THE TABLES ON GARFIELD. I'M STEALING **HIS** DINNER
GARFIELD
JIM DAVIS 3-14
I HAVE GARFIELD'S FOOD! I HAVE GARFIELD'S FOOD!
ARFIELD
© 1990 PAWS, INC. All Rights Reserved.
WHAT'S ALL THE COMMOTION ABOUT?

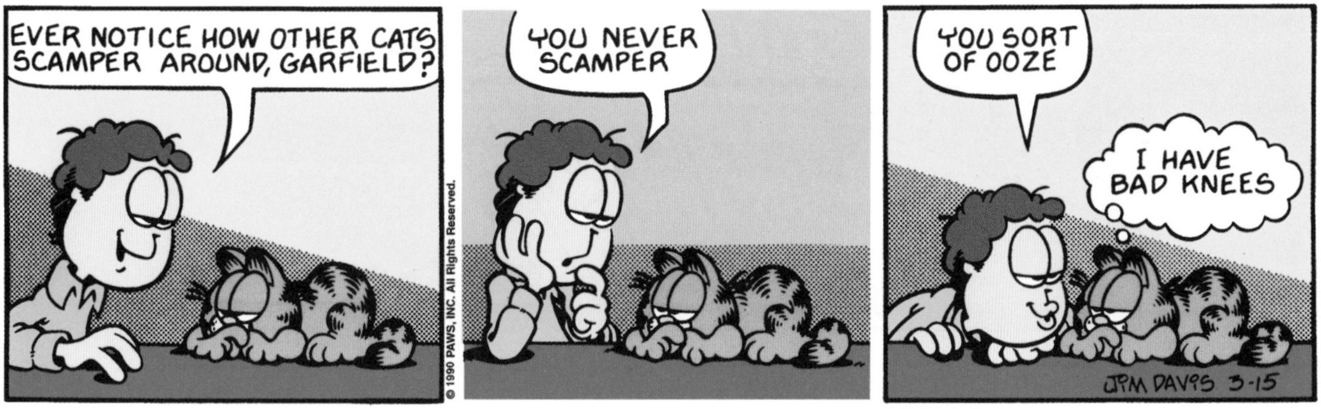
EVER NOTICE HOW OTHER CATS SCAMPER AROUND, GARFIELD?
YOU NEVER SCAMPER
YOU SORT OF OOZE
I HAVE BAD KNEES
© 1990 PAWS, INC. All Rights Reserved.
JIM DAVIS 3-15

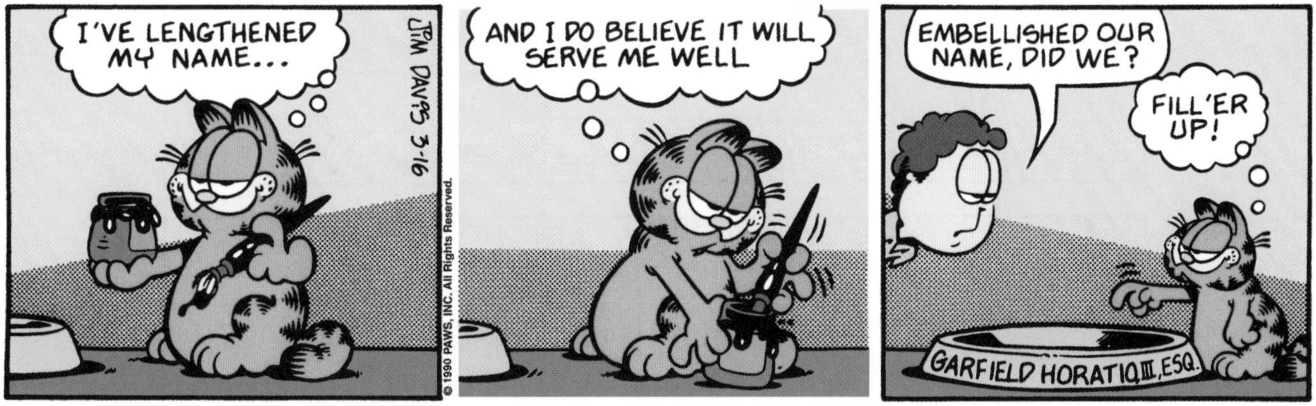
I'VE LENGTHENED MY NAME...
JIM DAVIS 3-16
AND I DO BELIEVE IT WILL SERVE ME WELL
EMBELLISHED OUR NAME, DID WE?
FILL'ER UP!
GARFIELD HORATIO III, ESQ.
© 1990 PAWS, INC. All Rights Reserved.

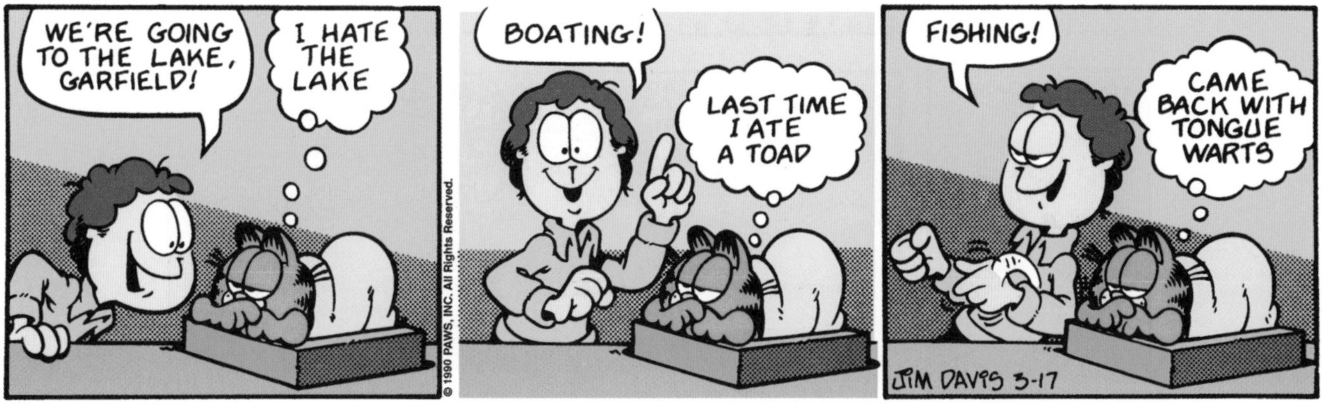
WE'RE GOING TO THE LAKE, GARFIELD!
I HATE THE LAKE
BOATING!
LAST TIME I ATE A TOAD
FISHING!
CAME BACK WITH TONGUE WARTS
© 1990 PAWS, INC. All Rights Reserved.
JIM DAVIS 3-17

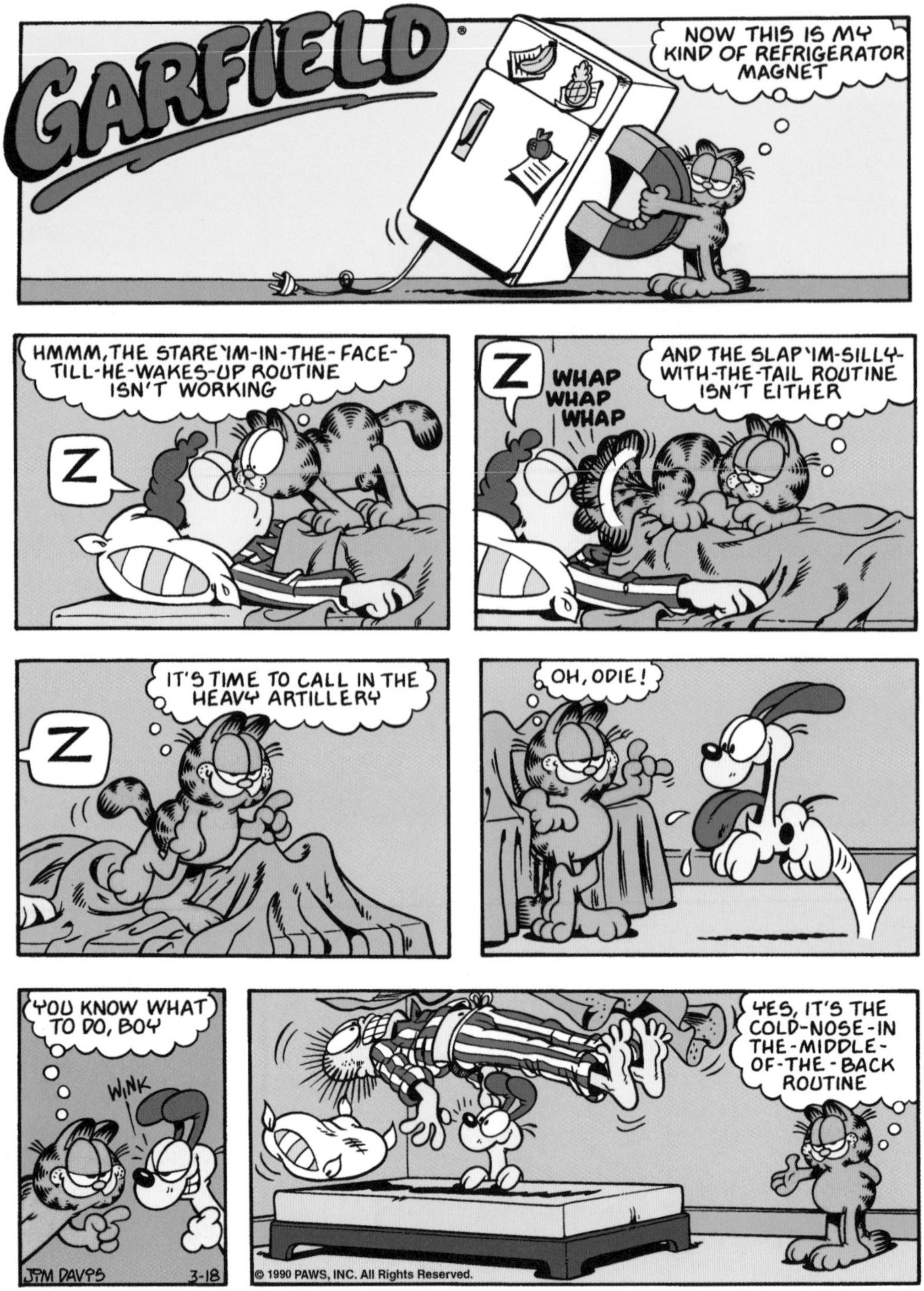
GARFIELD
NOW THIS IS MY KIND OF REFRIGERATOR MAGNET
HMMM, THE STARE 'IM-IN-THE-FACE-TILL-HE-WAKES-UP ROUTINE ISN'T WORKING
Z
Z
WHAP WHAP WHAP
AND THE SLAP 'IM-SILLY-WITH-THE-TAIL ROUTINE ISN'T EITHER
IT'S TIME TO CALL IN THE HEAVY ARTILLERY
Z
OH, ODIE!
YOU KNOW WHAT TO DO, BOY
WINK
YES, IT'S THE COLD-NOSE-IN THE-MIDDLE-OF-THE-BACK ROUTINE
JIM DAVIS 3-18
© 1990 PAWS, INC. All Rights Reserved.

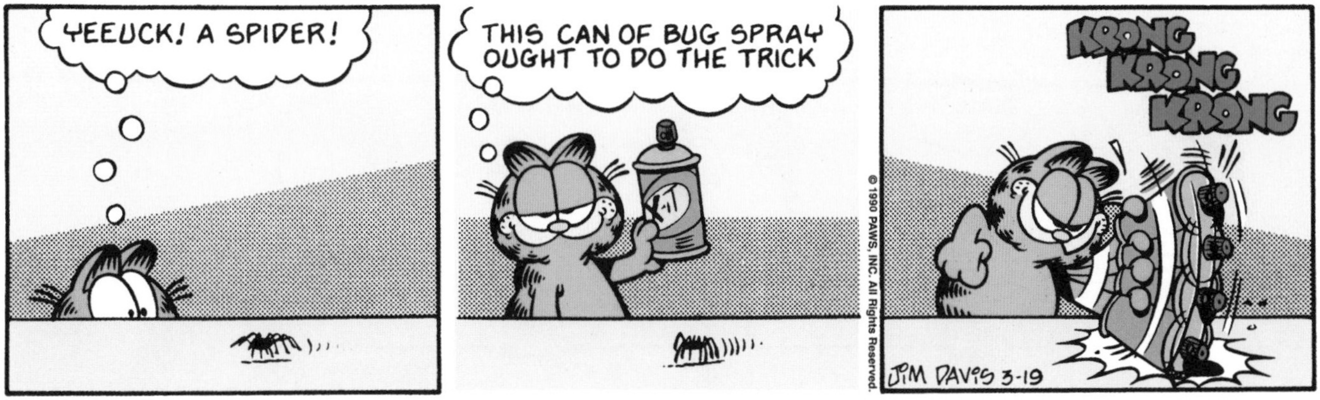
YEEUCK! A SPIDER!
THIS CAN OF BUG SPRAY OUGHT TO DO THE TRICK
KRONG KRONG KRONG
© 1990 PAWS, INC. All Rights Reserved.
JIM DAVIS 3-19

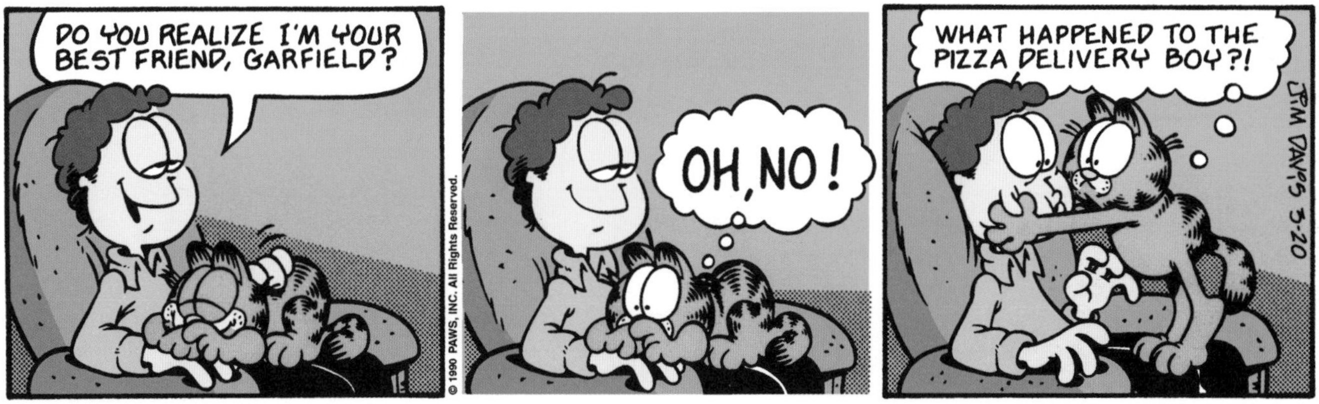
DO YOU REALIZE I'M YOUR BEST FRIEND, GARFIELD?
© 1990 PAWS, INC. All Rights Reserved.
OH, NO!
WHAT HAPPENED TO THE PIZZA DELIVERY BOY?!
JIM DAVIS 3-20

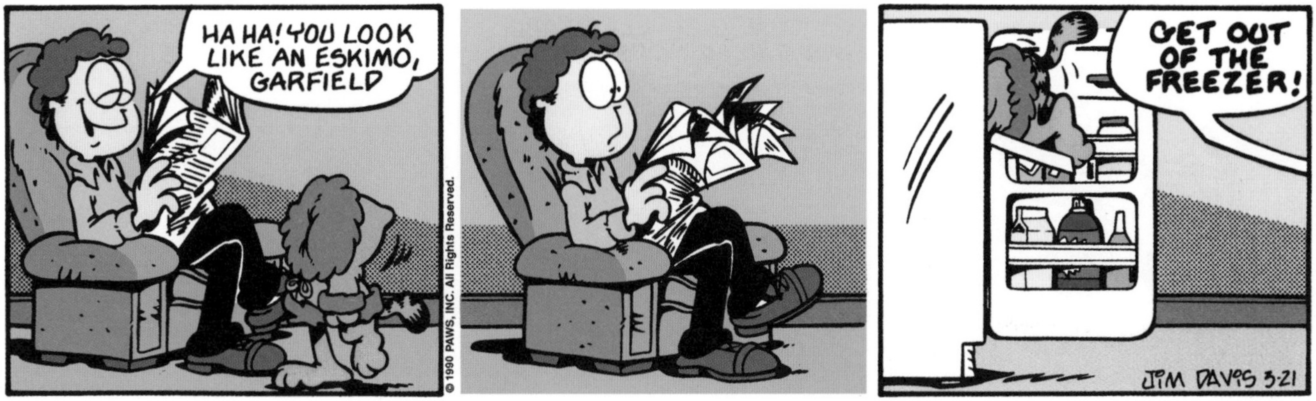
HA HA! YOU LOOK LIKE AN ESKIMO, GARFIELD
© 1990 PAWS, INC. All Rights Reserved.
GET OUT OF THE FREEZER!
JIM DAVIS 3-21

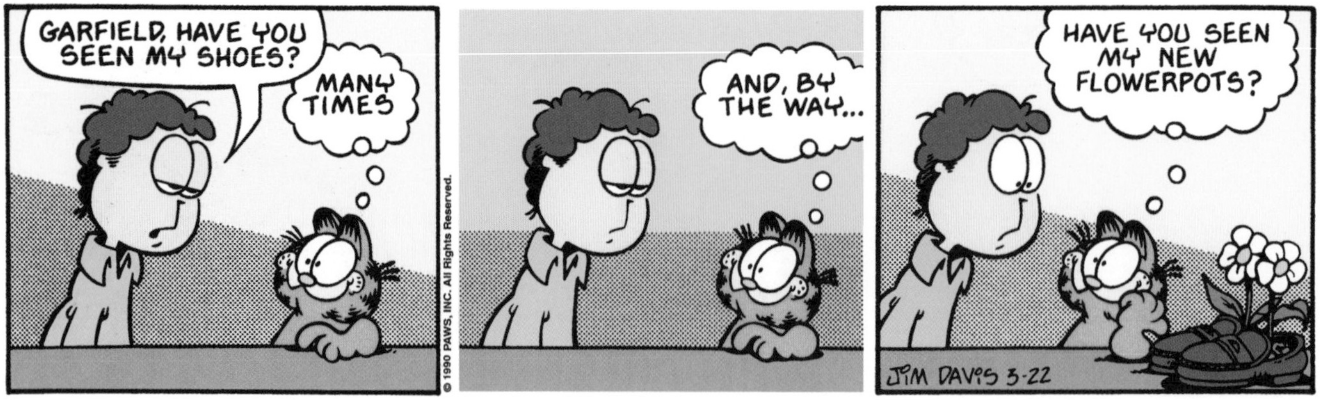
GARFIELD, HAVE YOU SEEN MY SHOES?
MANY TIMES
© 1990 PAWS, INC. All Rights Reserved.
AND, BY THE WAY...
HAVE YOU SEEN MY NEW FLOWERPOTS?
JIM DAVIS 3-22

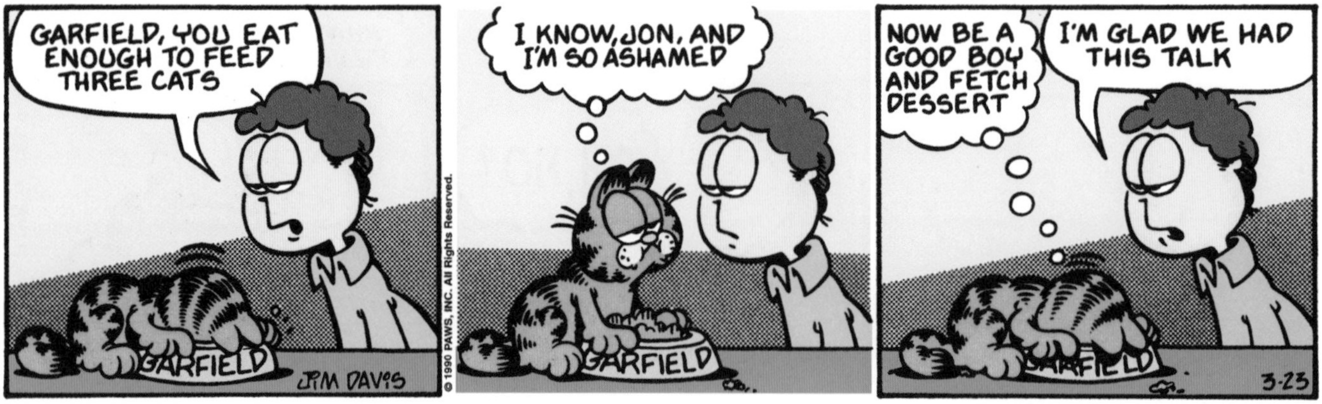
GARFIELD, YOU EAT ENOUGH TO FEED THREE CATS
GARFIELD
JIM DAVIS
© 1990 PAWS, INC. All Rights Reserved.
I KNOW, JON, AND I'M SO ASHAMED
GARFIELD
NOW BE A GOOD BOY AND FETCH DESSERT
I'M GLAD WE HAD THIS TALK
GARFIELD
3-23

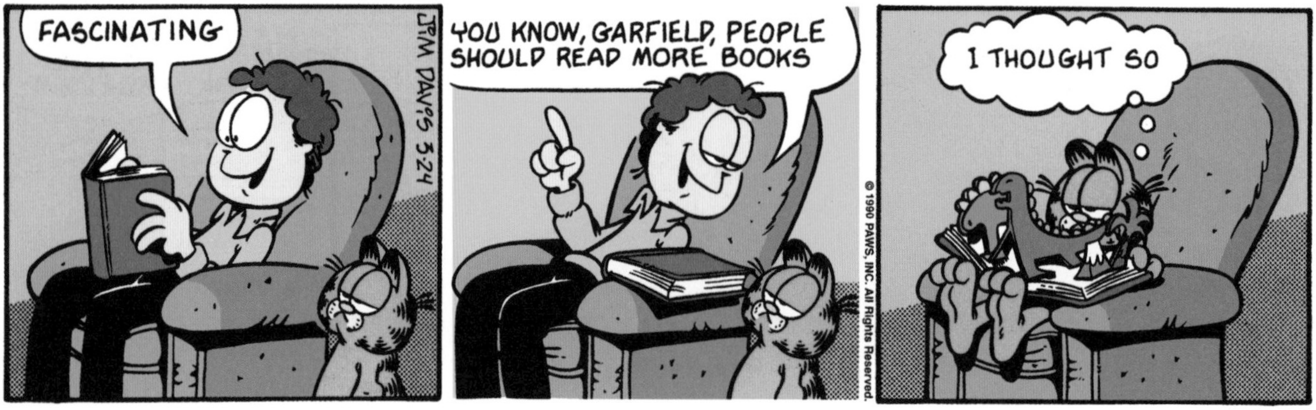
FASCINATING
JIM DAVIS 3-24
YOU KNOW, GARFIELD, PEOPLE SHOULD READ MORE BOOKS
© 1990 PAWS, INC. All Rights Reserved.
I THOUGHT SO

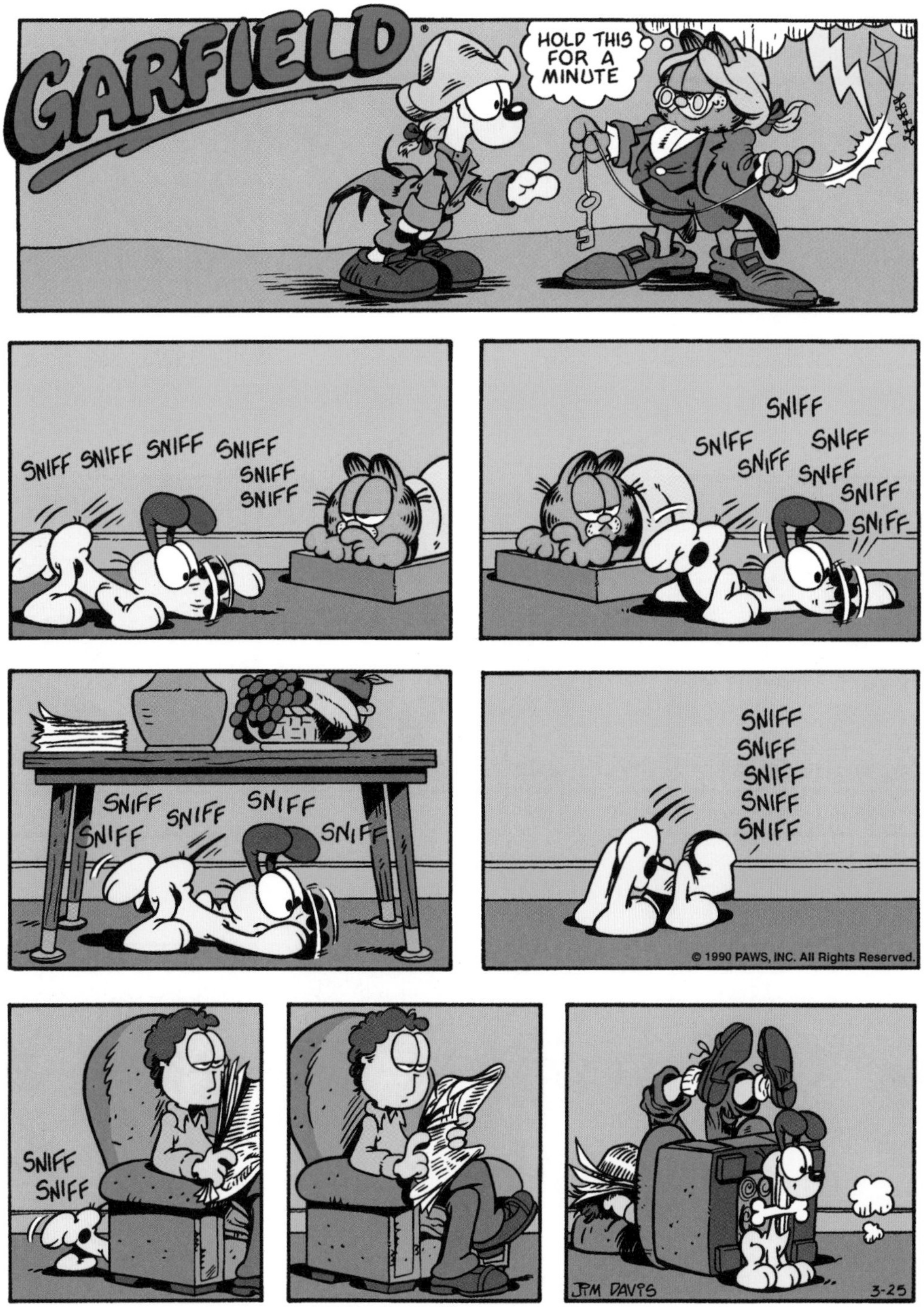
GARFIELD
HOLD THIS FOR A MINUTE
SNIFF SNIFF SNIFF SNIFF SNIFF SNIFF
SNIFF SNIFF SNIFF SNIFF SNIFF SNIFF SNIFF
SNIFF SNIFF SNIFF SNIFF SNIFF
SNIFF SNIFF SNIFF SNIFF SNIFF
SNIFF SNIFF
JIM DAVIS
3-25

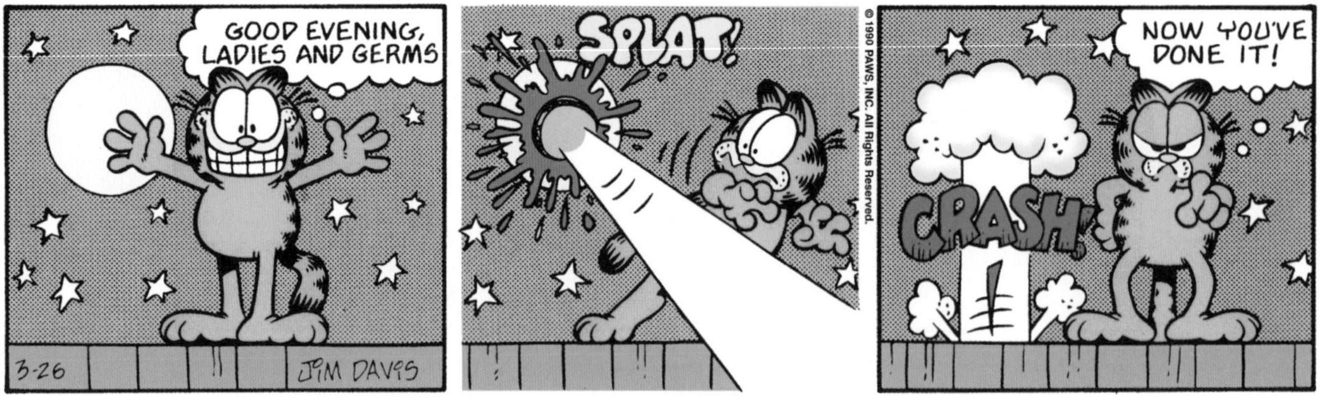
GOOD EVENING, LADIES AND GERMS
3-26
JIM DAVIS
SPLAT!
© 1990 PAWS, INC. All Rights Reserved.
NOW YOU'VE DONE IT!
CRASH!

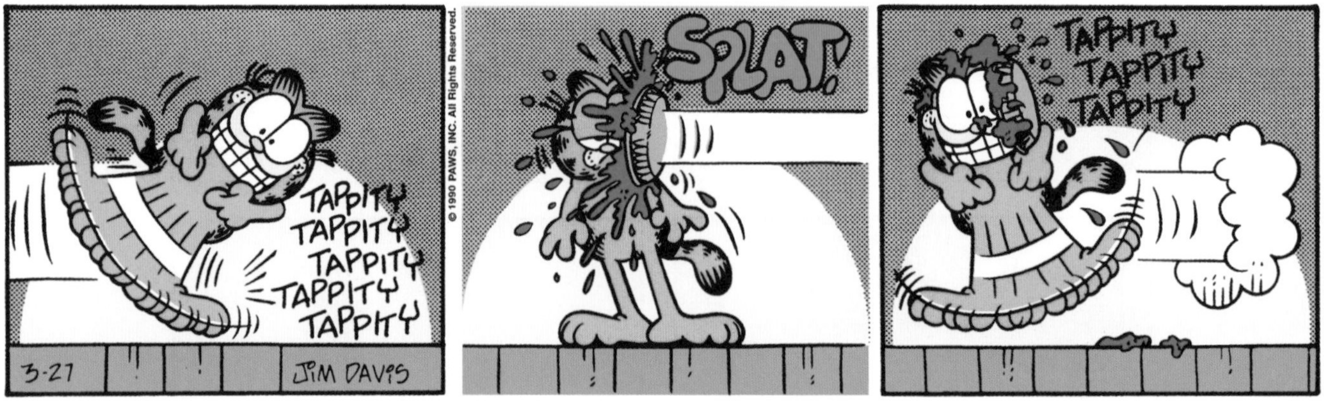
TAPPITY
TAPPITY
TAPPITY
TAPPITY
TAPPITY
3-27
JIM DAVIS
© 1990 PAWS, INC. All Rights Reserved.
SPLAT!
TAPPITY
TAPPITY
TAPPITY

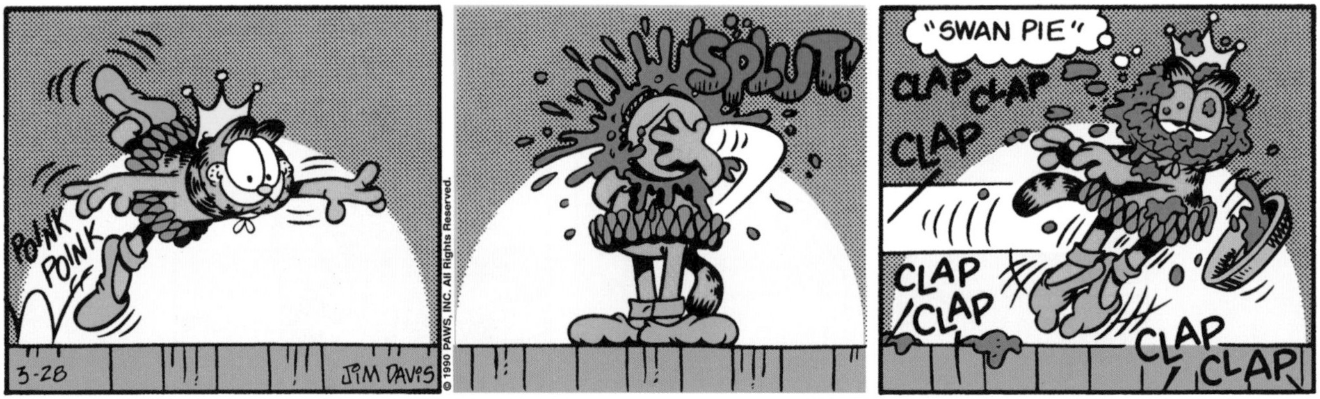
POINK
POINK
3-28
JIM DAVIS
© 1990 PAWS, INC. All Rights Reserved.
SPLUT!
"SWAN PIE"
CLAP CLAP
CLAP
CLAP
CLAP
CLAP
CLAP

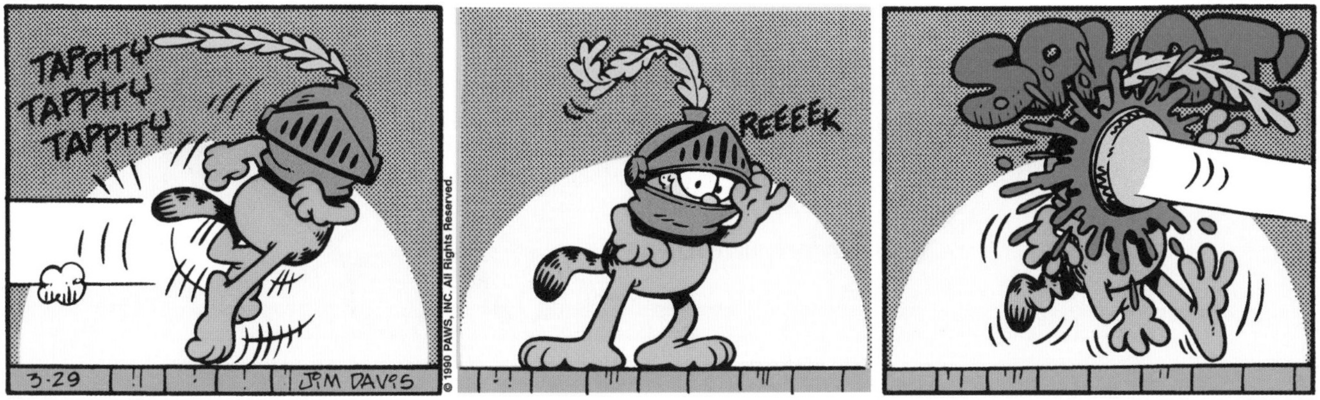
TAPPITY
TAPPITY
TAPPITY
3-29
JIM DAVIS
© 1990 PAWS, INC. All Rights Reserved.
REEEEK
SPLAT!

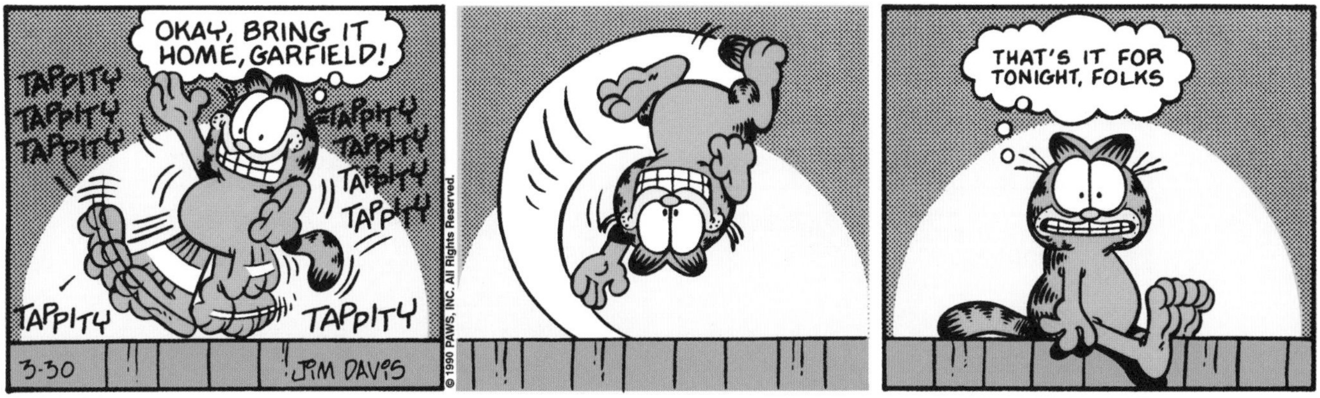
OKAY, BRING IT HOME, GARFIELD!
TAPPITY
TAPPITY
TAPPITY
TAPPITY
TAPPITY
TAPPITY
TAPPITY
TAPPITY
TAPPITY
3-30
JIM DAVIS
© 1990 PAWS, INC. All Rights Reserved.
THAT'S IT FOR TONIGHT, FOLKS

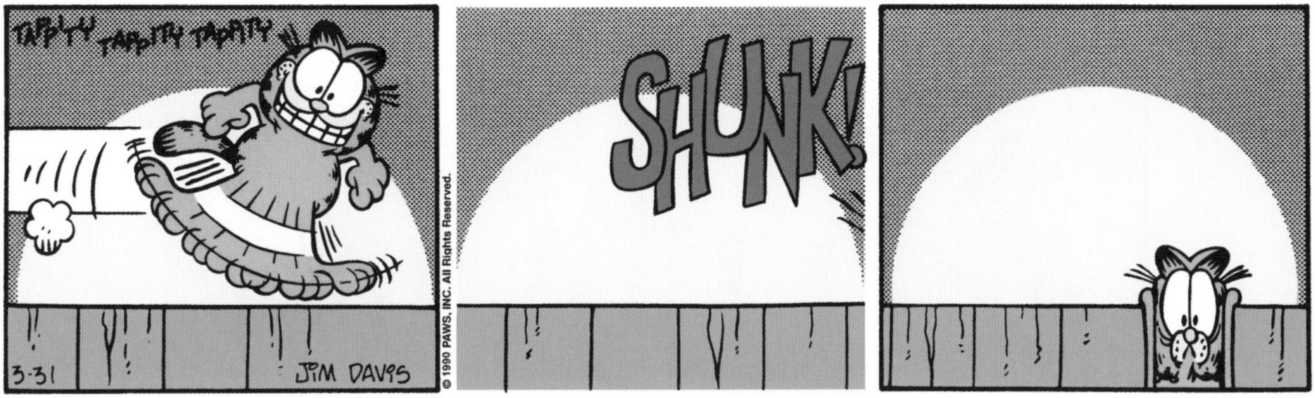
TAPPITY TAPPITY TAPPITY
3-31
JIM DAVIS
© 1990 PAWS, INC. All Rights Reserved.
SHUNK!

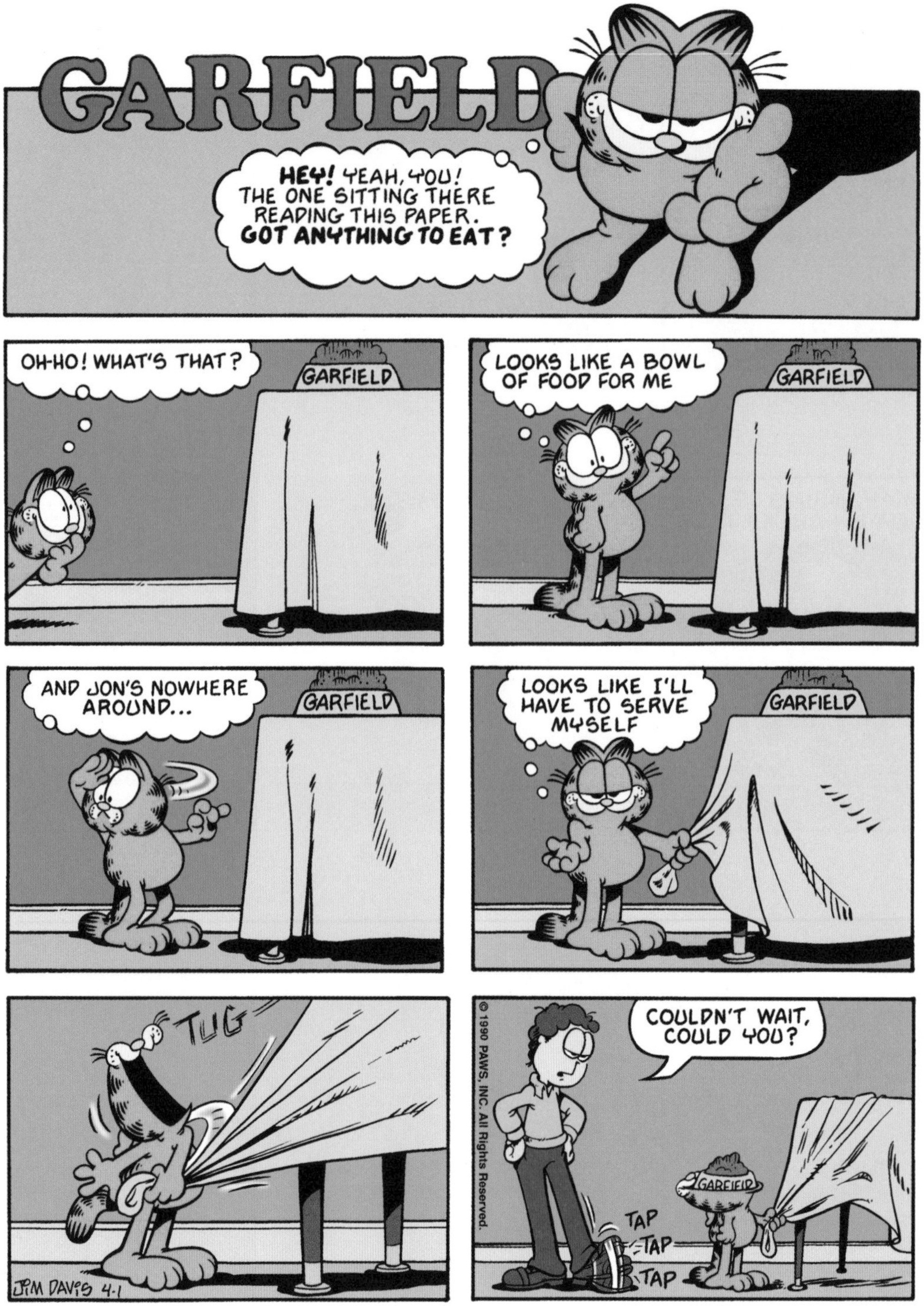
GARFIELD
HEY! YEAH, YOU! THE ONE SITTING THERE READING THIS PAPER. GOT ANYTHING TO EAT?
OH-HO! WHAT'S THAT?
GARFIELD
LOOKS LIKE A BOWL OF FOOD FOR ME
GARFIELD
AND JON'S NOWHERE AROUND...
GARFIELD
LOOKS LIKE I'LL HAVE TO SERVE MYSELF
GARFIELD
TUG
JIM DAVIS 4-1
© 1990 PAWS, INC. All Rights Reserved.
COULDN'T WAIT, COULD YOU?
GARFIELD
TAP
TAP
TAP

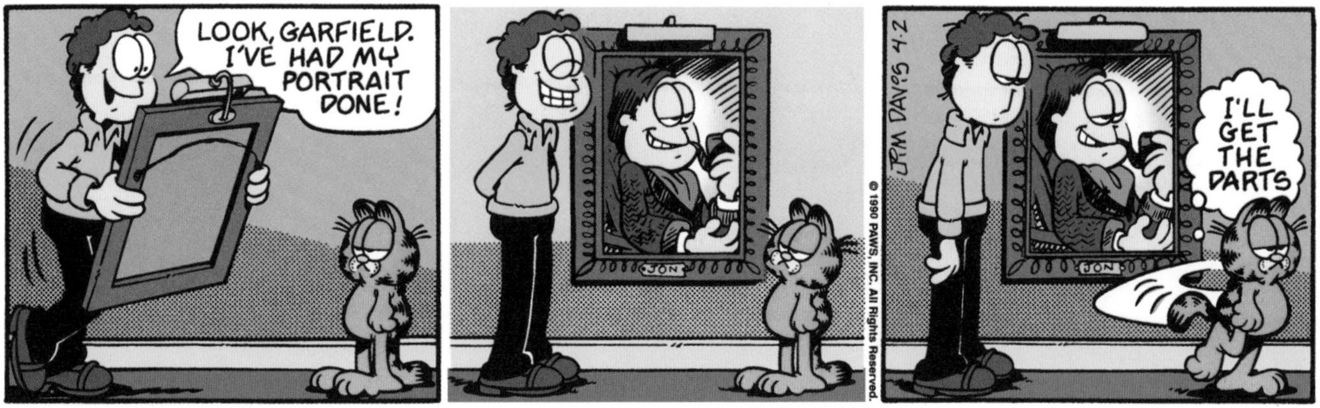
LOOK, GARFIELD. I'VE HAD MY PORTRAIT DONE!
JON
JIM DAVIS 4·2
© 1990 PAWS, INC. All Rights Reserved.
JON
I'LL GET THE DARTS

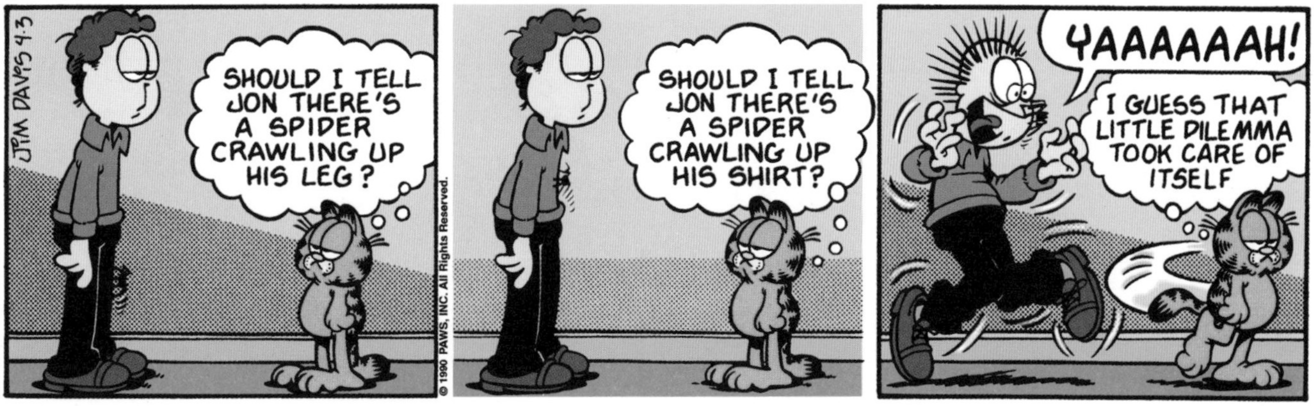
JIM DAVIS 4·3
SHOULD I TELL JON THERE'S A SPIDER CRAWLING UP HIS LEG?
© 1990 PAWS, INC. All Rights Reserved.
SHOULD I TELL JON THERE'S A SPIDER CRAWLING UP HIS SHIRT?
YAAAAAAH!
I GUESS THAT LITTLE DILEMMA TOOK CARE OF ITSELF

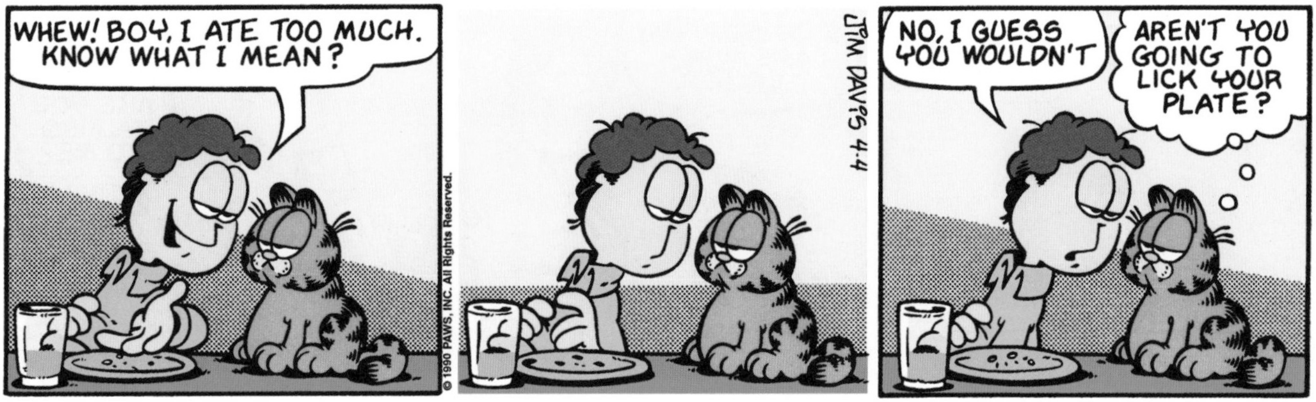
WHEW! BOY, I ATE TOO MUCH. KNOW WHAT I MEAN?
© 1990 PAWS, INC. All Rights Reserved.
JIM DAVIS 4·4
NO, I GUESS YOU WOULDN'T
AREN'T YOU GOING TO LICK YOUR PLATE?

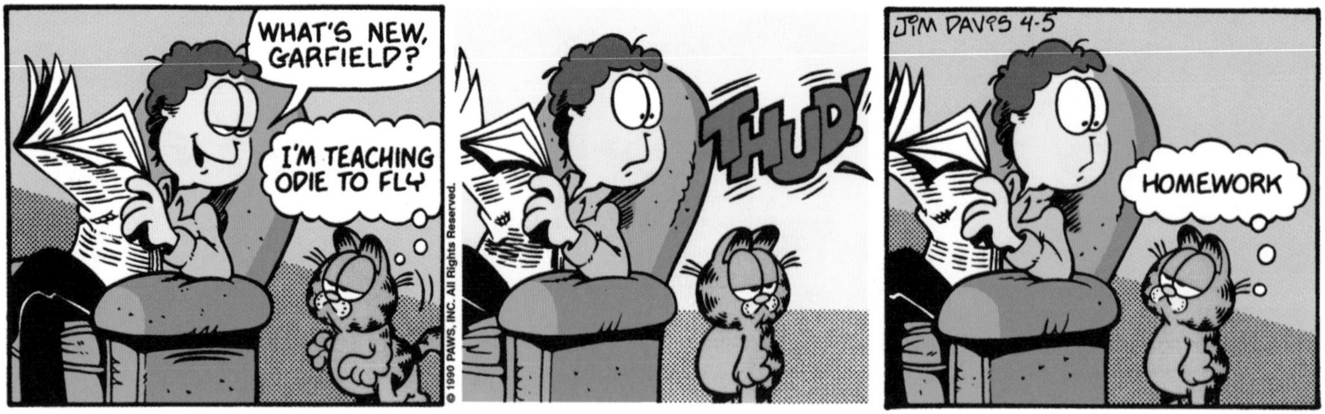
WHAT'S NEW, GARFIELD?
I'M TEACHING ODIE TO FLY
© 1990 PAWS, INC. All Rights Reserved.
THUD!
JIM DAVIS 4-5
HOMEWORK

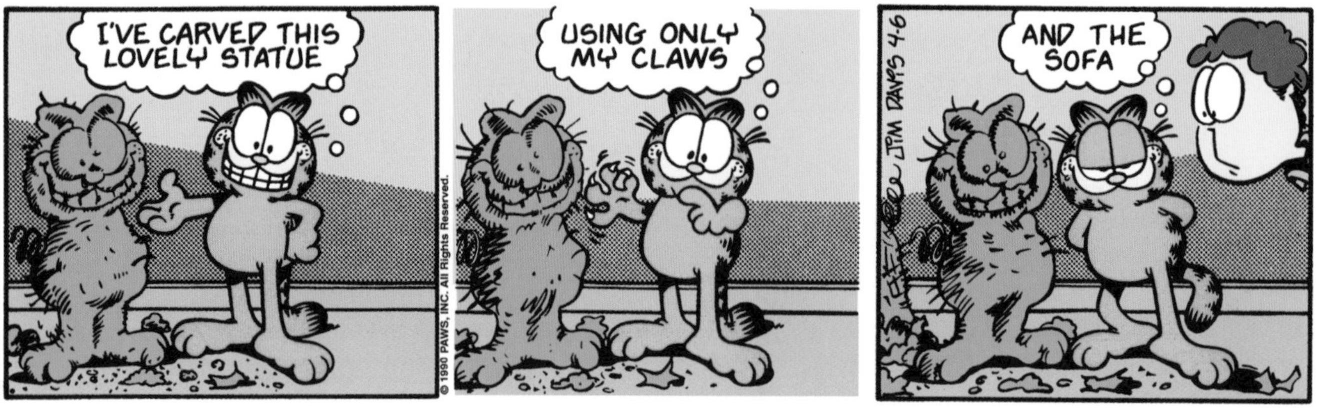
I'VE CARVED THIS LOVELY STATUE
© 1990 PAWS, INC. All Rights Reserved.
USING ONLY MY CLAWS
JIM DAVIS 4-6
AND THE SOFA

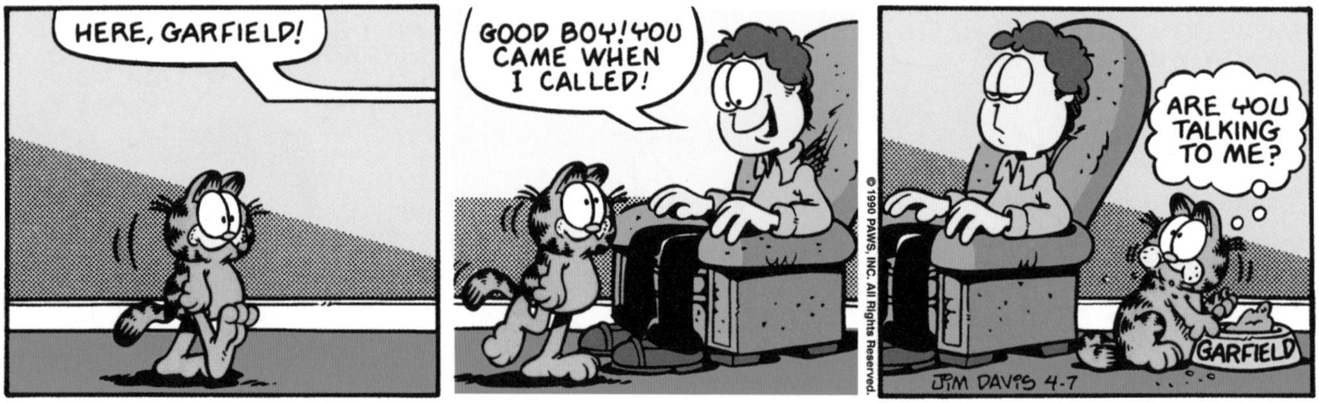
HERE, GARFIELD!
GOOD BOY! YOU CAME WHEN I CALLED!
© 1990 PAWS, INC. All Rights Reserved.
ARE YOU TALKING TO ME?
GARFIELD
JIM DAVIS 4-7

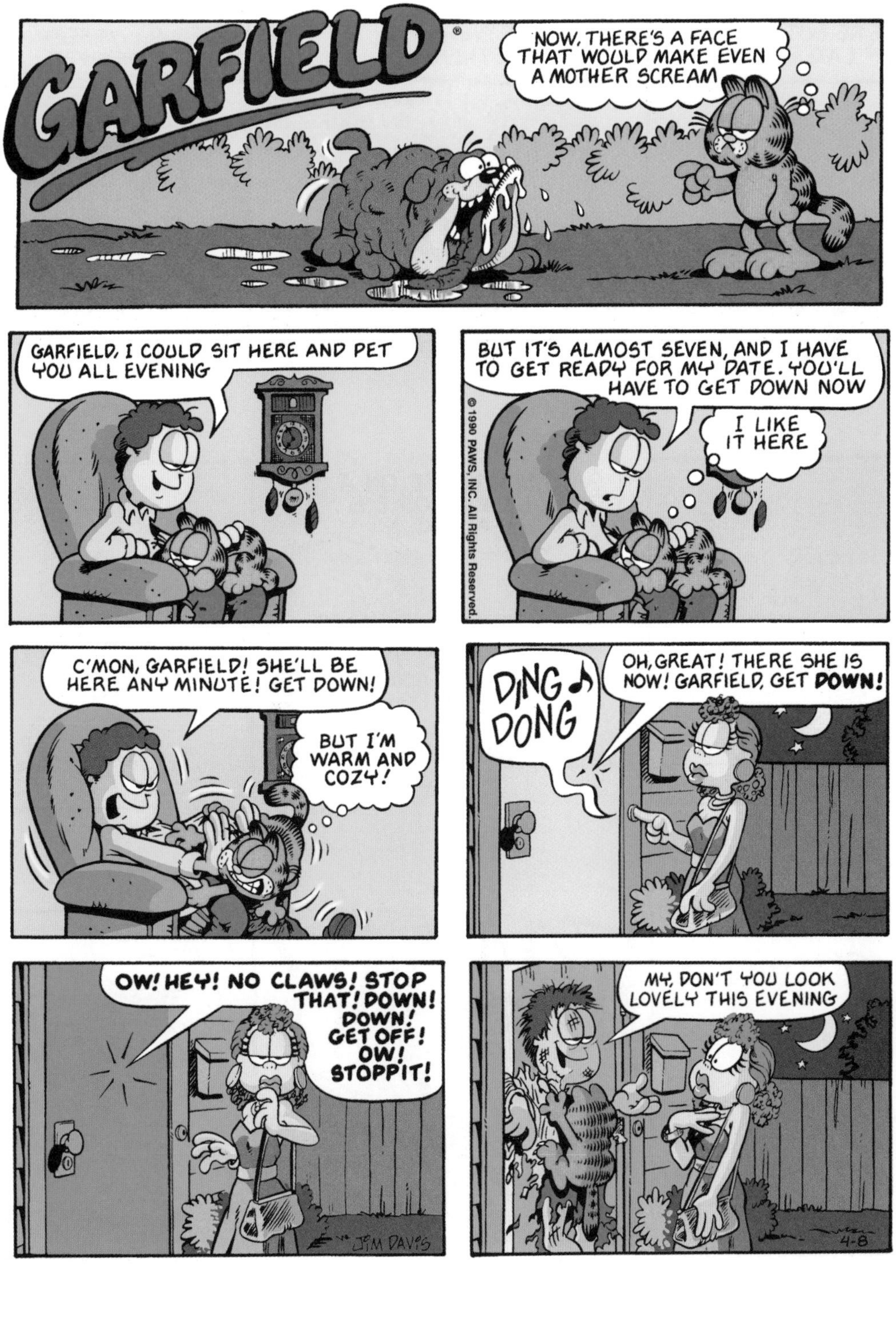
GARFIELD®
NOW, THERE'S A FACE THAT WOULD MAKE EVEN A MOTHER SCREAM
GARFIELD, I COULD SIT HERE AND PET YOU ALL EVENING
BUT IT'S ALMOST SEVEN, AND I HAVE TO GET READY FOR MY DATE. YOU'LL HAVE TO GET DOWN NOW
I LIKE IT HERE
C'MON, GARFIELD! SHE'LL BE HERE ANY MINUTE! GET DOWN!
BUT I'M WARM AND COZY!
DING DONG
OH, GREAT! THERE SHE IS NOW! GARFIELD, GET **DOWN**!
OW! HEY! NO CLAWS! STOP THAT! DOWN! DOWN! GET OFF! OW! STOPPIT!
MY, DON'T YOU LOOK LOVELY THIS EVENING
JIM DAVIS
4-8

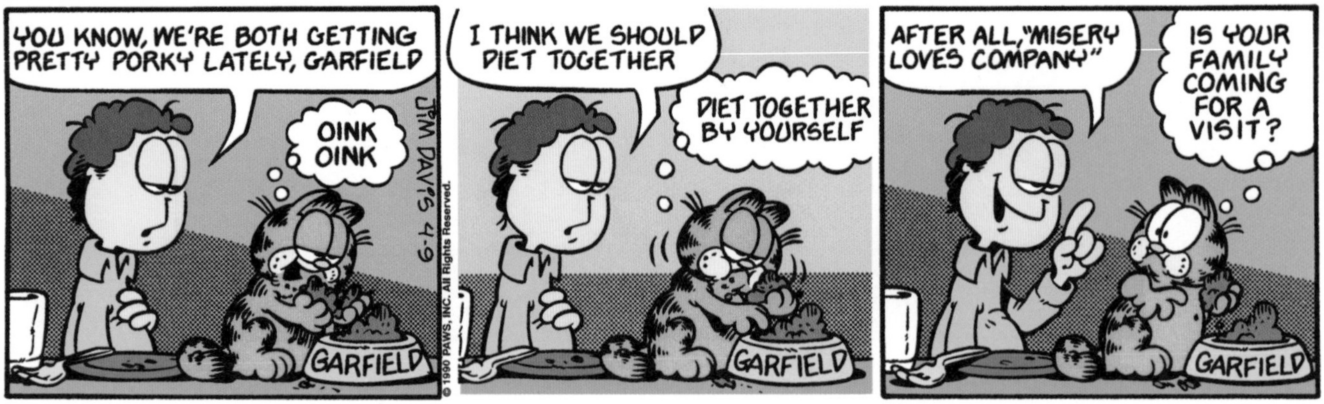
YOU KNOW, WE'RE BOTH GETTING PRETTY PORKY LATELY, GARFIELD
OINK OINK
JIM DAVIS 4-9
© 1990 PAWS, INC. All Rights Reserved.
GARFIELD
I THINK WE SHOULD DIET TOGETHER
DIET TOGETHER BY YOURSELF
GARFIELD
AFTER ALL, "MISERY LOVES COMPANY"
IS YOUR FAMILY COMING FOR A VISIT?
GARFIELD

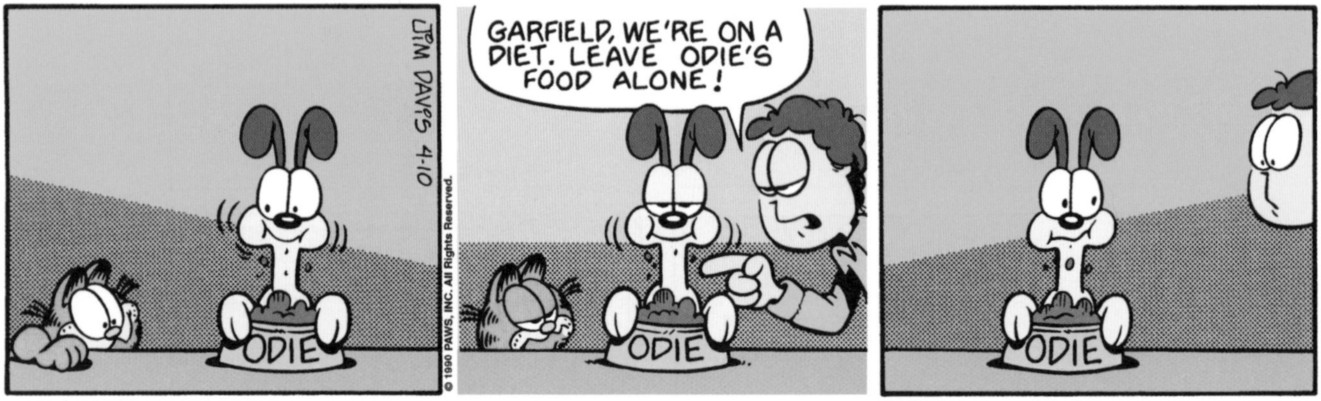
JIM DAVIS 4-10
© 1990 PAWS, INC. All Rights Reserved.
ODIE
GARFIELD, WE'RE ON A DIET. LEAVE ODIE'S FOOD ALONE!
ODIE
ODIE

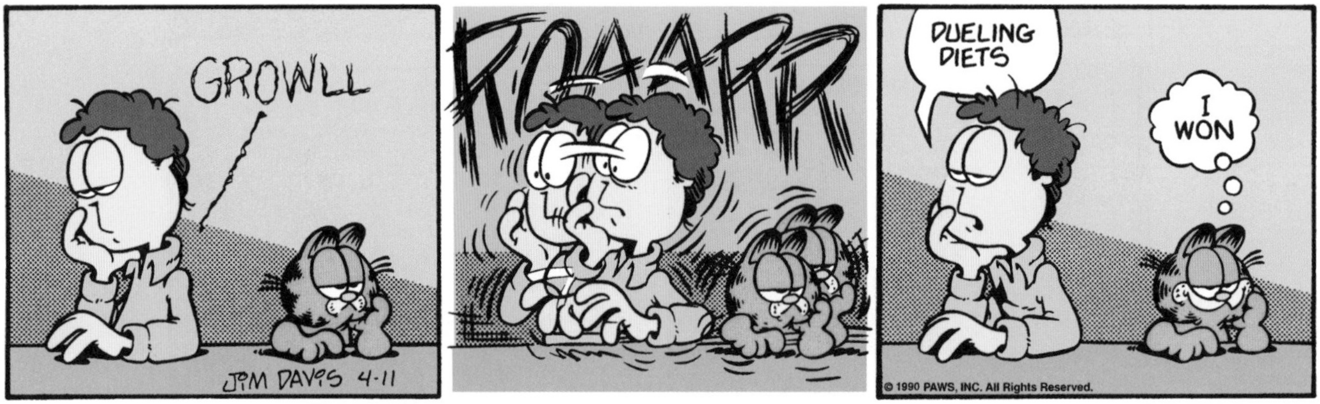
GROWLL
JIM DAVIS 4-11
ROAARR
DUELING DIETS
I WON
© 1990 PAWS, INC. All Rights Reserved.

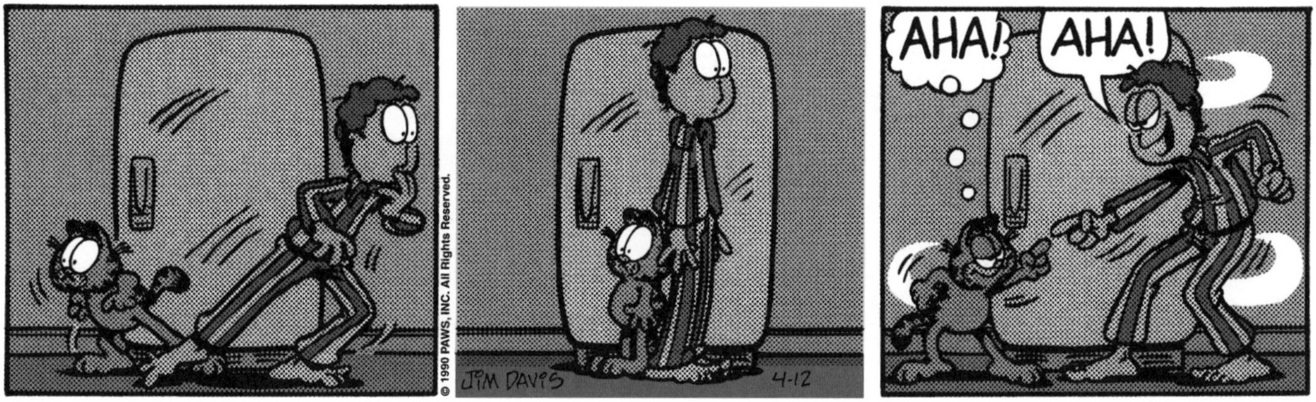
© 1990 PAWS, INC. All Rights Reserved.
JIM DAVIS 4-12
AHA!
AHA!

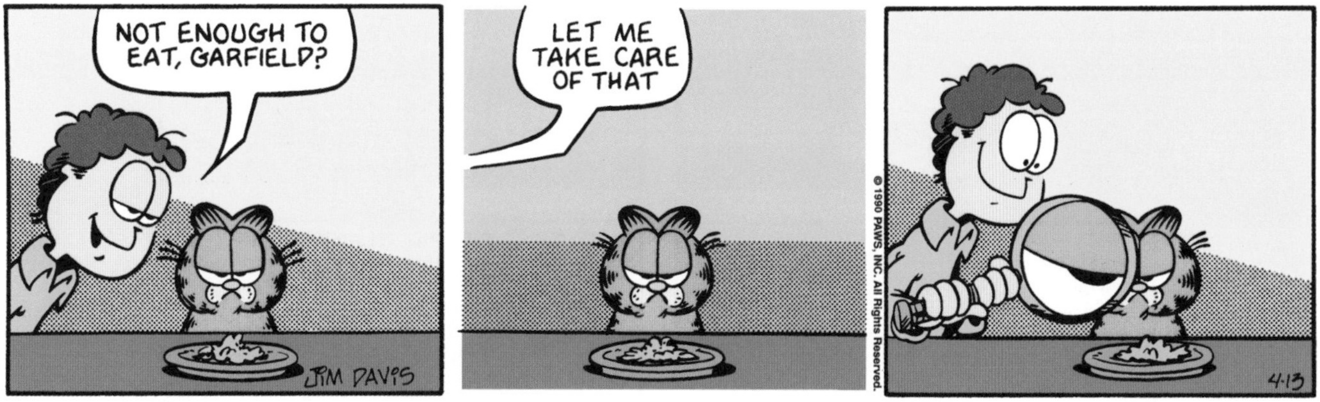
NOT ENOUGH TO EAT, GARFIELD?
JIM DAVIS
LET ME TAKE CARE OF THAT
© 1990 PAWS, INC. All Rights Reserved.
4-13

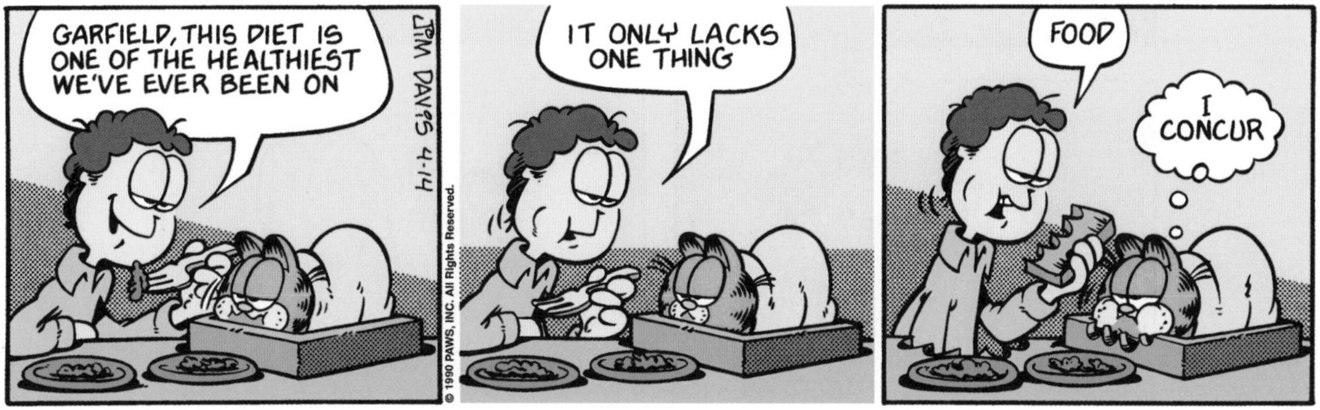
GARFIELD, THIS DIET IS ONE OF THE HEALTHIEST WE'VE EVER BEEN ON
JIM DAVIS 4-14
© 1990 PAWS, INC. All Rights Reserved.
IT ONLY LACKS ONE THING
FOOD
I CONCUR

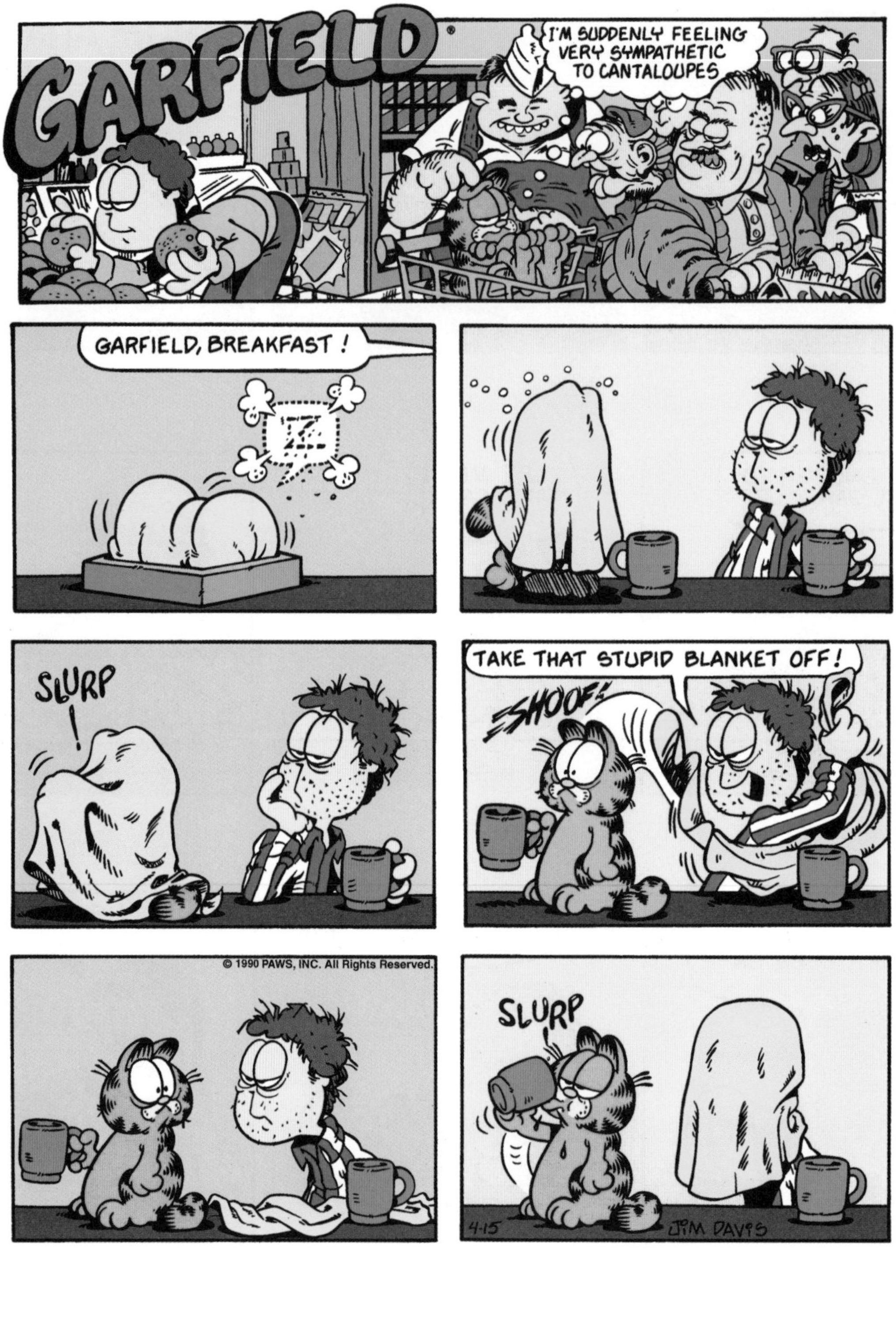
GARFIELD
I'M SUDDENLY FEELING VERY SYMPATHETIC TO CANTALOUPES
GARFIELD, BREAKFAST!
Z
SLURP
TAKE THAT STUPID BLANKET OFF!
SHOOF!
© 1990 PAWS, INC. All Rights Reserved.
SLURP
4-15
JIM DAVIS

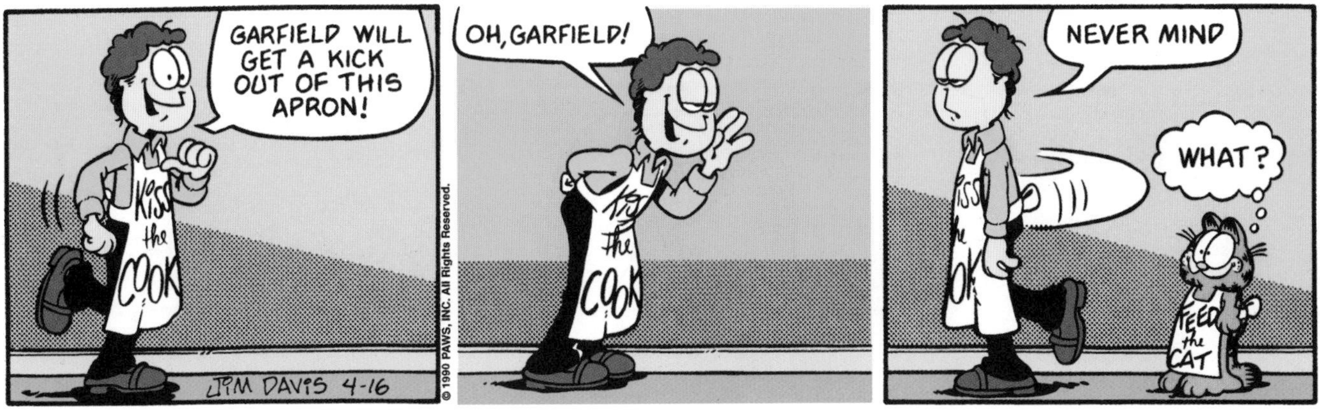
GARFIELD WILL GET A KICK OUT OF THIS APRON!
KISS the COOK
JIM DAVIS 4-16
© 1990 PAWS, INC. All Rights Reserved.
OH, GARFIELD!
NEVER MIND
WHAT?
FEED the CAT

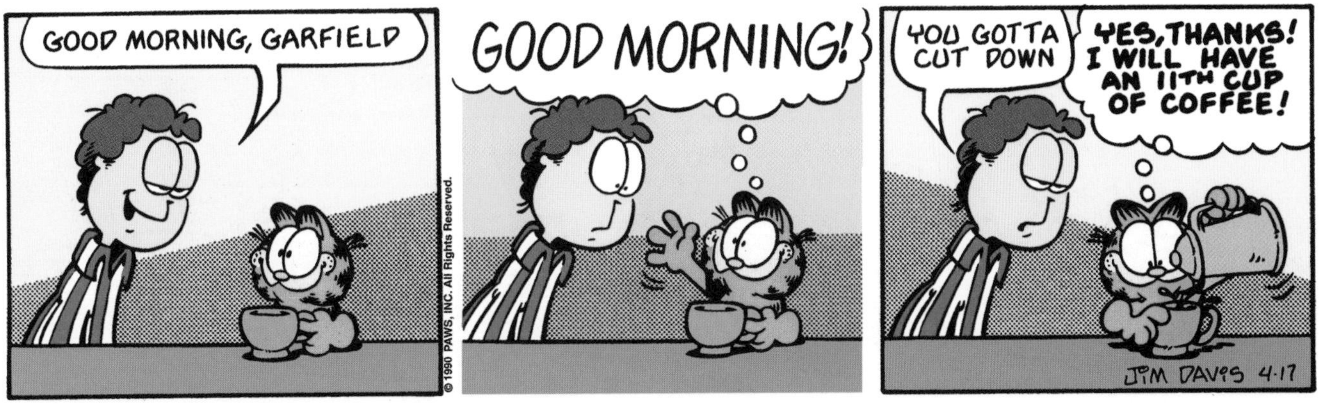
GOOD MORNING, GARFIELD
© 1990 PAWS, INC. All Rights Reserved.
GOOD MORNING!
YOU GOTTA CUT DOWN
YES, THANKS! I WILL HAVE AN 11TH CUP OF COFFEE!
JIM DAVIS 4-17

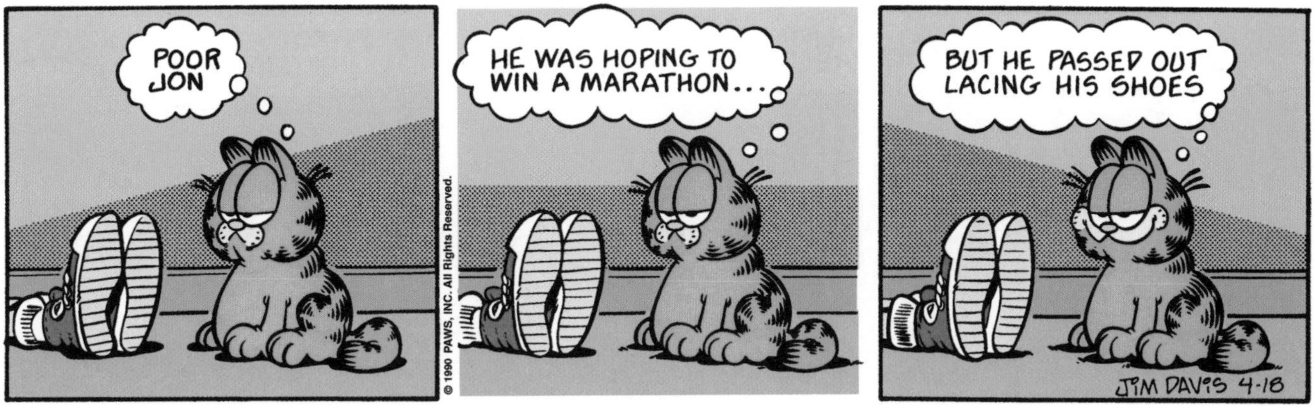
POOR JON
© 1990 PAWS, INC. All Rights Reserved.
HE WAS HOPING TO WIN A MARATHON...
BUT HE PASSED OUT LACING HIS SHOES
JIM DAVIS 4-18

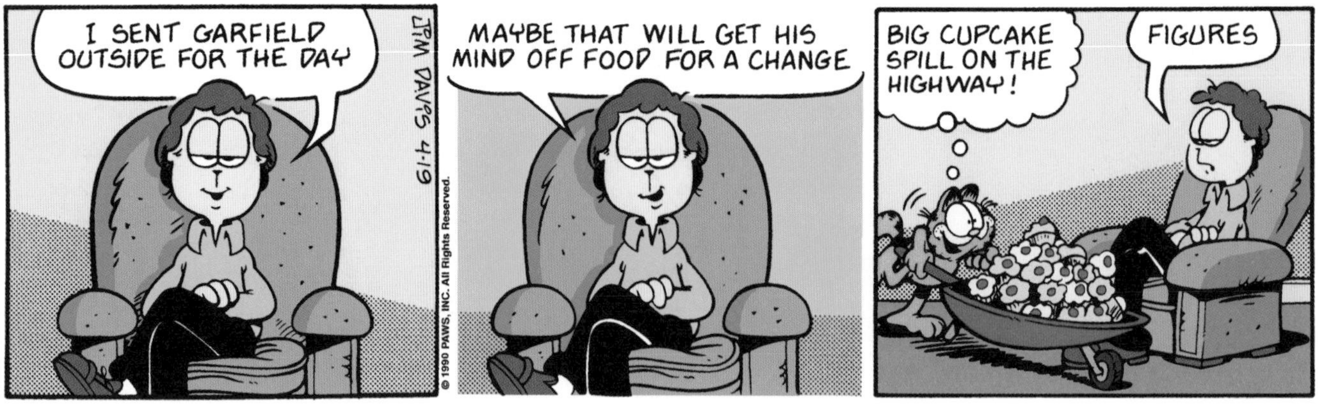
I SENT GARFIELD OUTSIDE FOR THE DAY
JIM DAVIS 4-19
MAYBE THAT WILL GET HIS MIND OFF FOOD FOR A CHANGE
© 1990 PAWS, INC. All Rights Reserved.
BIG CUPCAKE SPILL ON THE HIGHWAY!
FIGURES

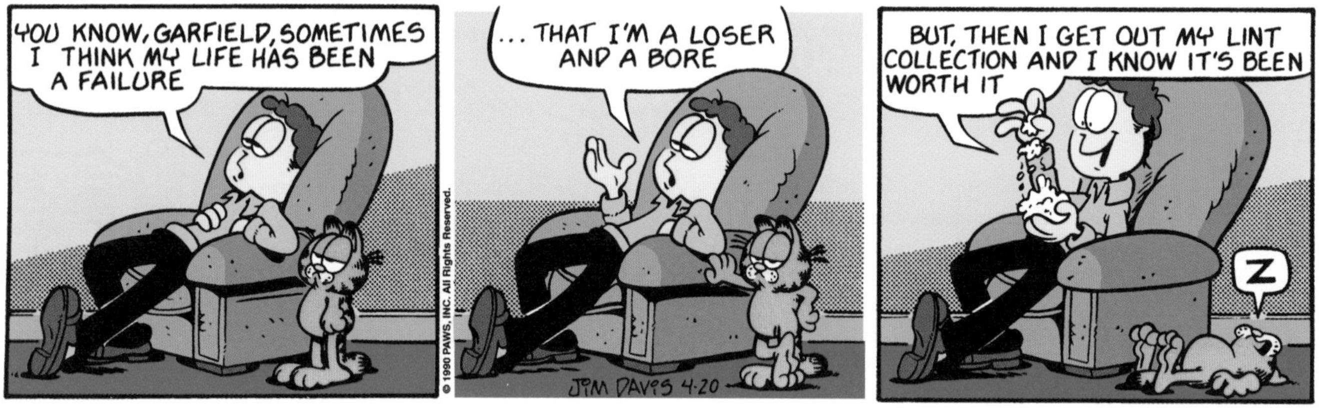
YOU KNOW, GARFIELD, SOMETIMES I THINK MY LIFE HAS BEEN A FAILURE
© 1990 PAWS, INC. All Rights Reserved.
... THAT I'M A LOSER AND A BORE
JIM DAVIS 4-20
BUT, THEN I GET OUT MY LINT COLLECTION AND I KNOW IT'S BEEN WORTH IT
Z

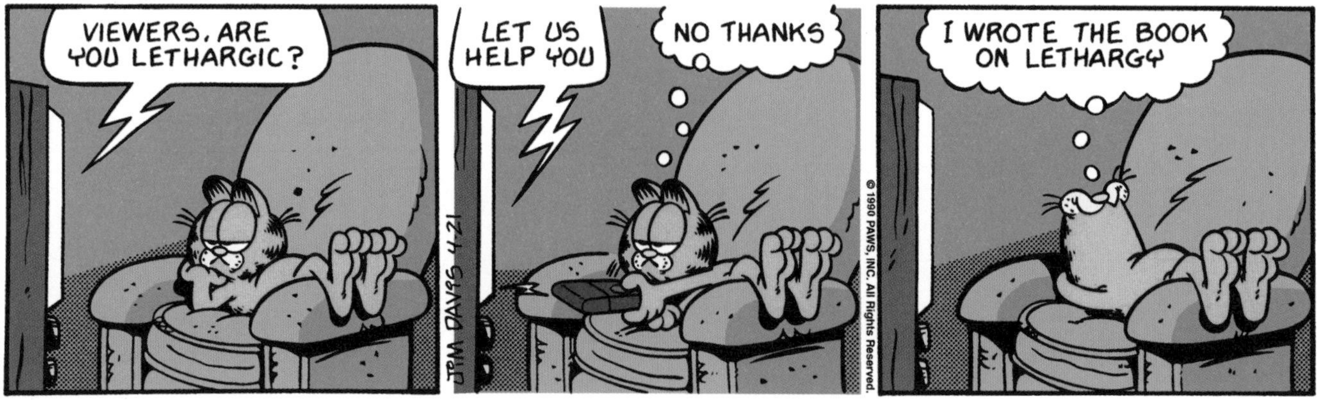
VIEWERS, ARE YOU LETHARGIC?
JIM DAVIS 4-21
LET US HELP YOU
NO THANKS
© 1990 PAWS, INC. All Rights Reserved.
I WROTE THE BOOK ON LETHARGY

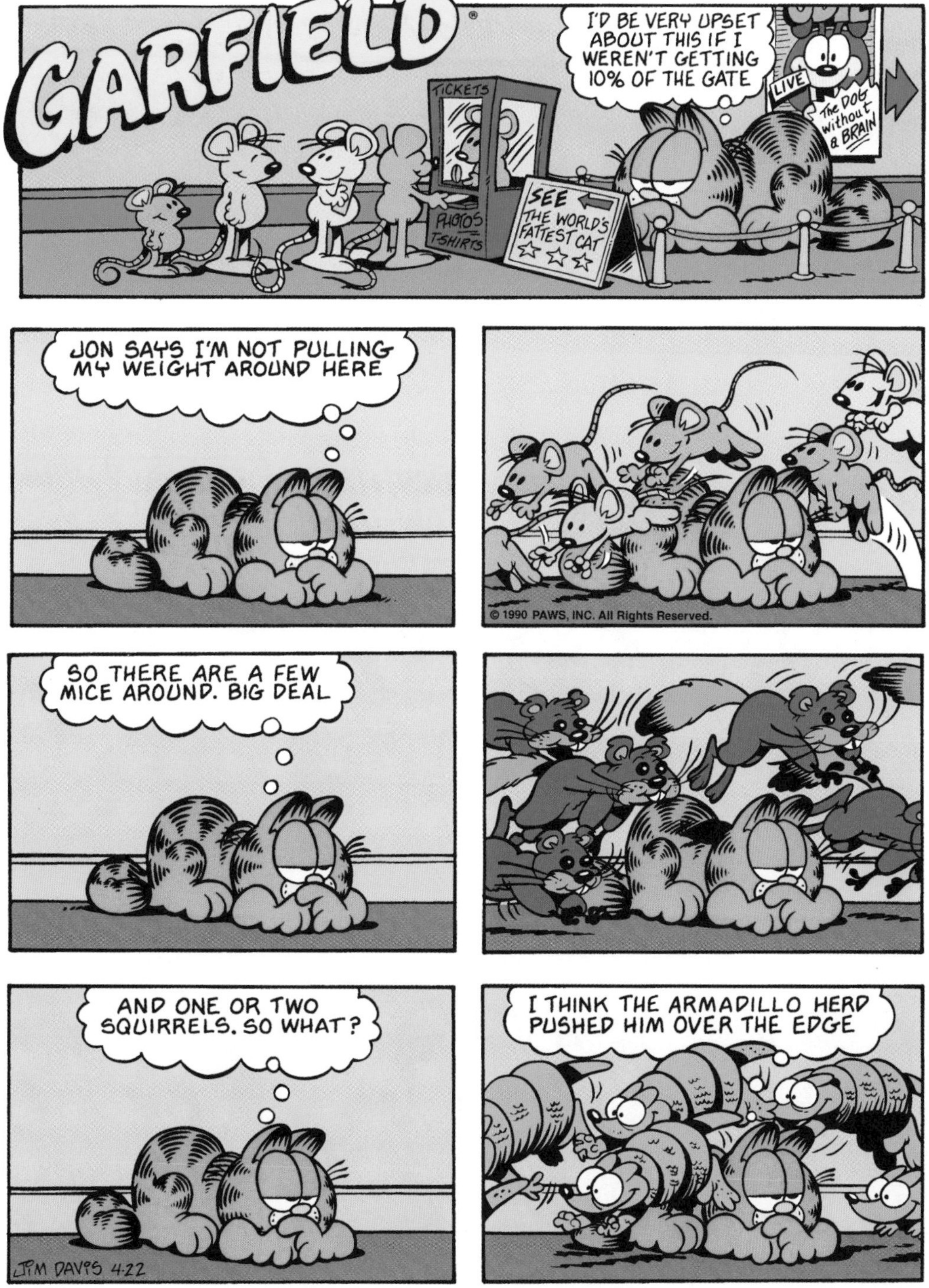
GARFIELD®
I'D BE VERY UPSET ABOUT THIS IF I WEREN'T GETTING 10% OF THE GATE
TICKETS
PHOTOS
T-SHIRTS
SEE THE WORLD'S FATTEST CAT
LIVE
The DOG without a BRAIN
JON SAYS I'M NOT PULLING MY WEIGHT AROUND HERE
© 1990 PAWS, INC. All Rights Reserved.
SO THERE ARE A FEW MICE AROUND. BIG DEAL
AND ONE OR TWO SQUIRRELS. SO WHAT?
JIM DAVIS 4-22
I THINK THE ARMADILLO HERD PUSHED HIM OVER THE EDGE

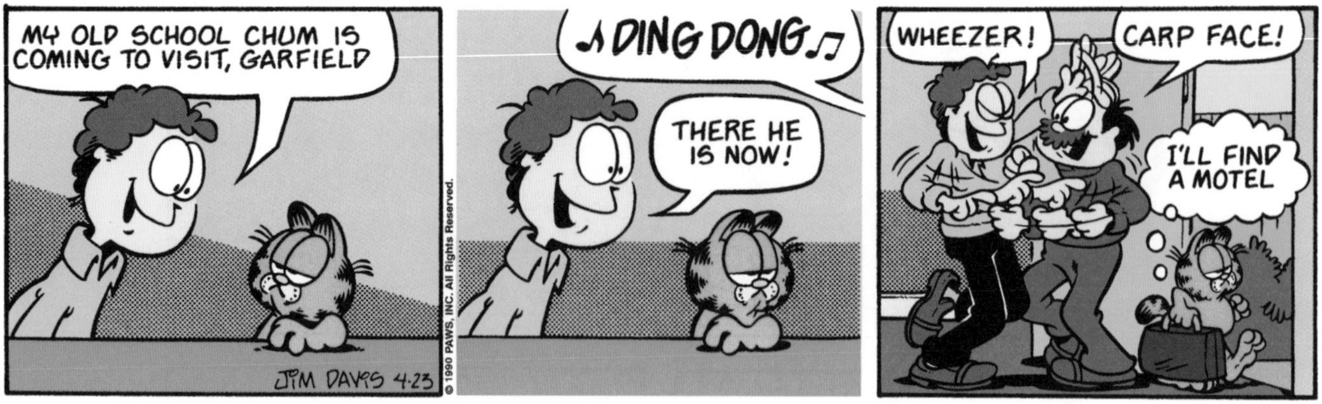
MY OLD SCHOOL CHUM IS COMING TO VISIT, GARFIELD
JIM DAVIS 4-23
© 1990 PAWS, INC. All Rights Reserved.
DING DONG
THERE HE IS NOW!
WHEEZER!
CARP FACE!
I'LL FIND A MOTEL

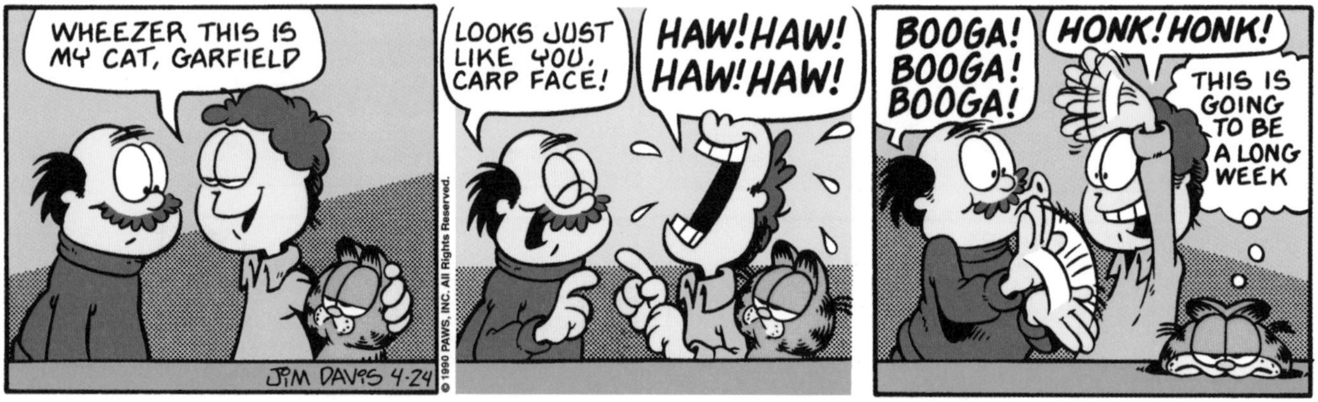
WHEEZER THIS IS MY CAT, GARFIELD
JIM DAVIS 4-24
© 1990 PAWS, INC. All Rights Reserved.
LOOKS JUST LIKE YOU, CARP FACE!
HAW! HAW! HAW! HAW!
BOOGA! BOOGA! BOOGA!
HONK! HONK!
THIS IS GOING TO BE A LONG WEEK

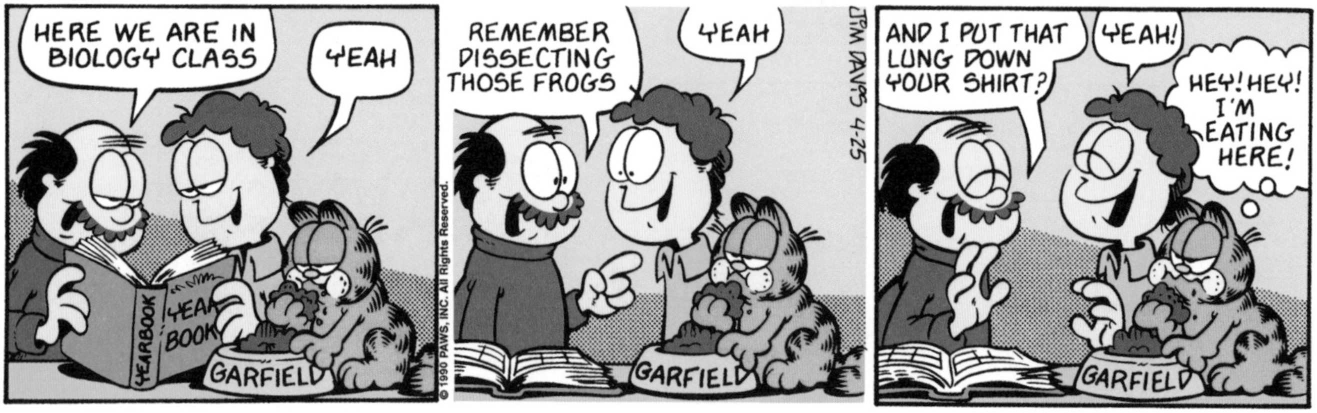
HERE WE ARE IN BIOLOGY CLASS
YEAH
YEARBOOK
YEARBOOK
GARFIELD
© 1990 PAWS, INC. All Rights Reserved.
REMEMBER DISSECTING THOSE FROGS
YEAH
GARFIELD
JIM DAVIS 4-25
AND I PUT THAT LUNG DOWN YOUR SHIRT?
YEAH!
HEY! HEY! I'M EATING HERE!
GARFIELD

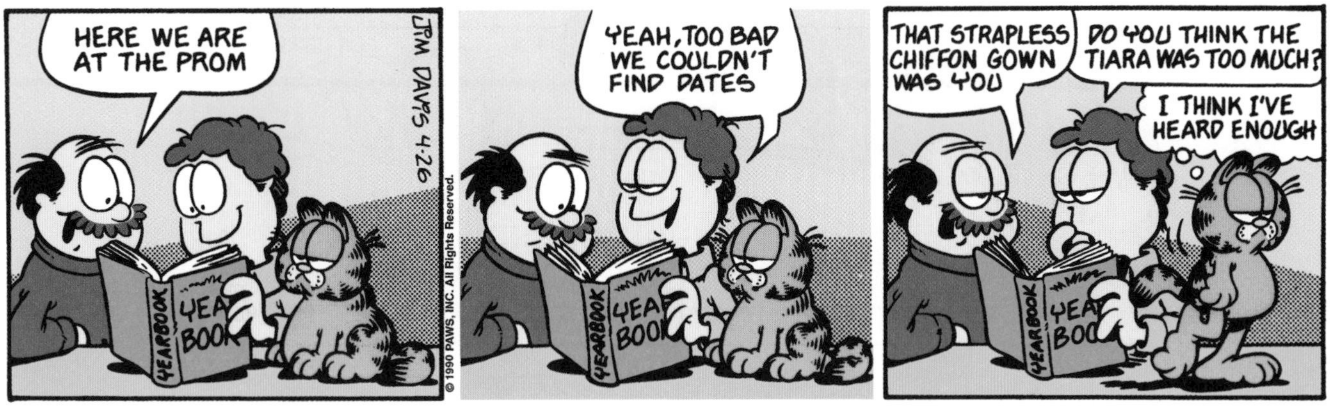
HERE WE ARE AT THE PROM
JIM DAVIS 4-26
© 1990 PAWS, INC. All Rights Reserved.
YEAH, TOO BAD WE COULDN'T FIND DATES
THAT STRAPLESS CHIFFON GOWN WAS YOU
DO YOU THINK THE TIARA WAS TOO MUCH?
I THINK I'VE HEARD ENOUGH

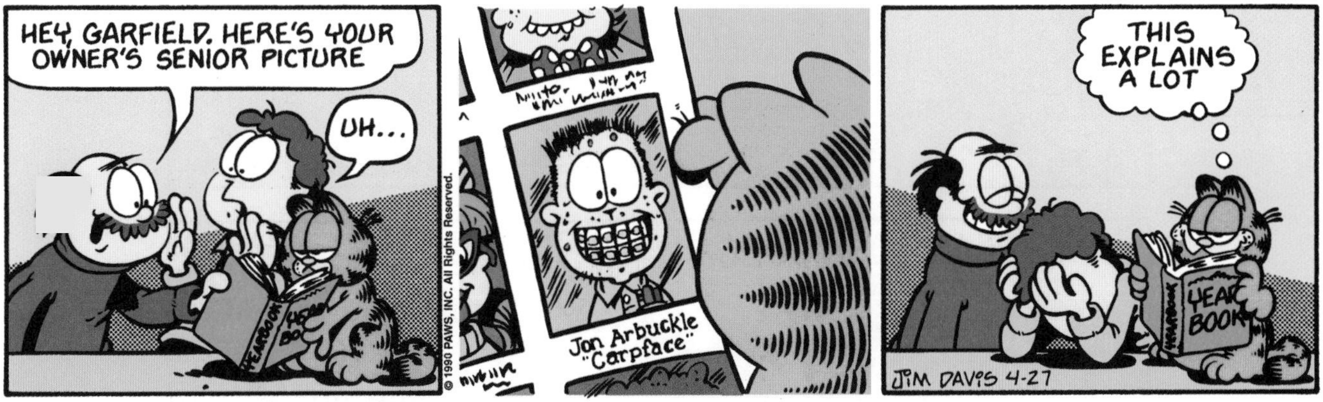
HEY, GARFIELD. HERE'S YOUR OWNER'S SENIOR PICTURE
UH...
© 1990 PAWS, INC. All Rights Reserved.
Jon Arbuckle "Carpface"
THIS EXPLAINS A LOT
JIM DAVIS 4-27

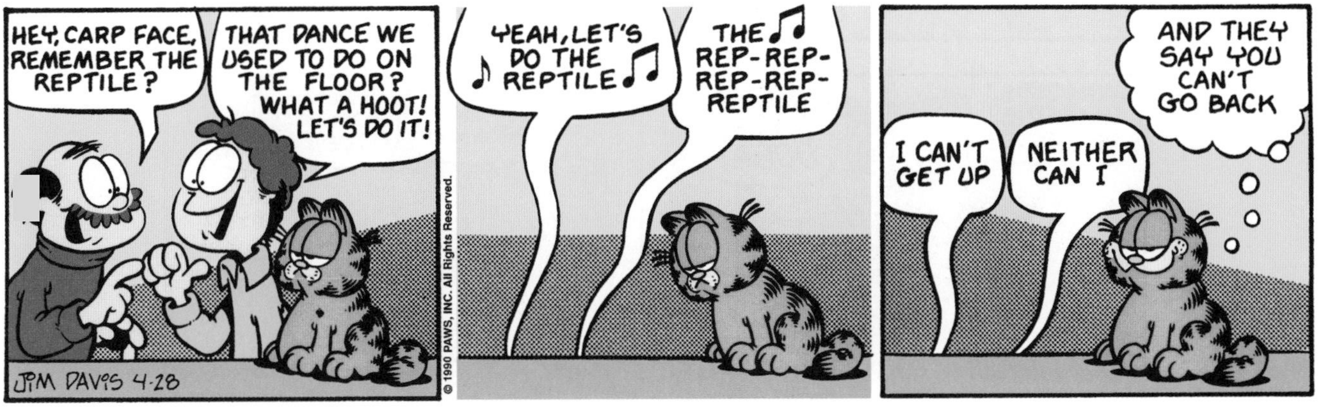
HEY, CARP FACE, REMEMBER THE REPTILE?
THAT DANCE WE USED TO DO ON THE FLOOR? WHAT A HOOT! LET'S DO IT!
JIM DAVIS 4-28
© 1990 PAWS, INC. All Rights Reserved.
YEAH, LET'S DO THE REPTILE
THE REP-REP-REP-REP-REPTILE
I CAN'T GET UP
NEITHER CAN I
AND THEY SAY YOU CAN'T GO BACK

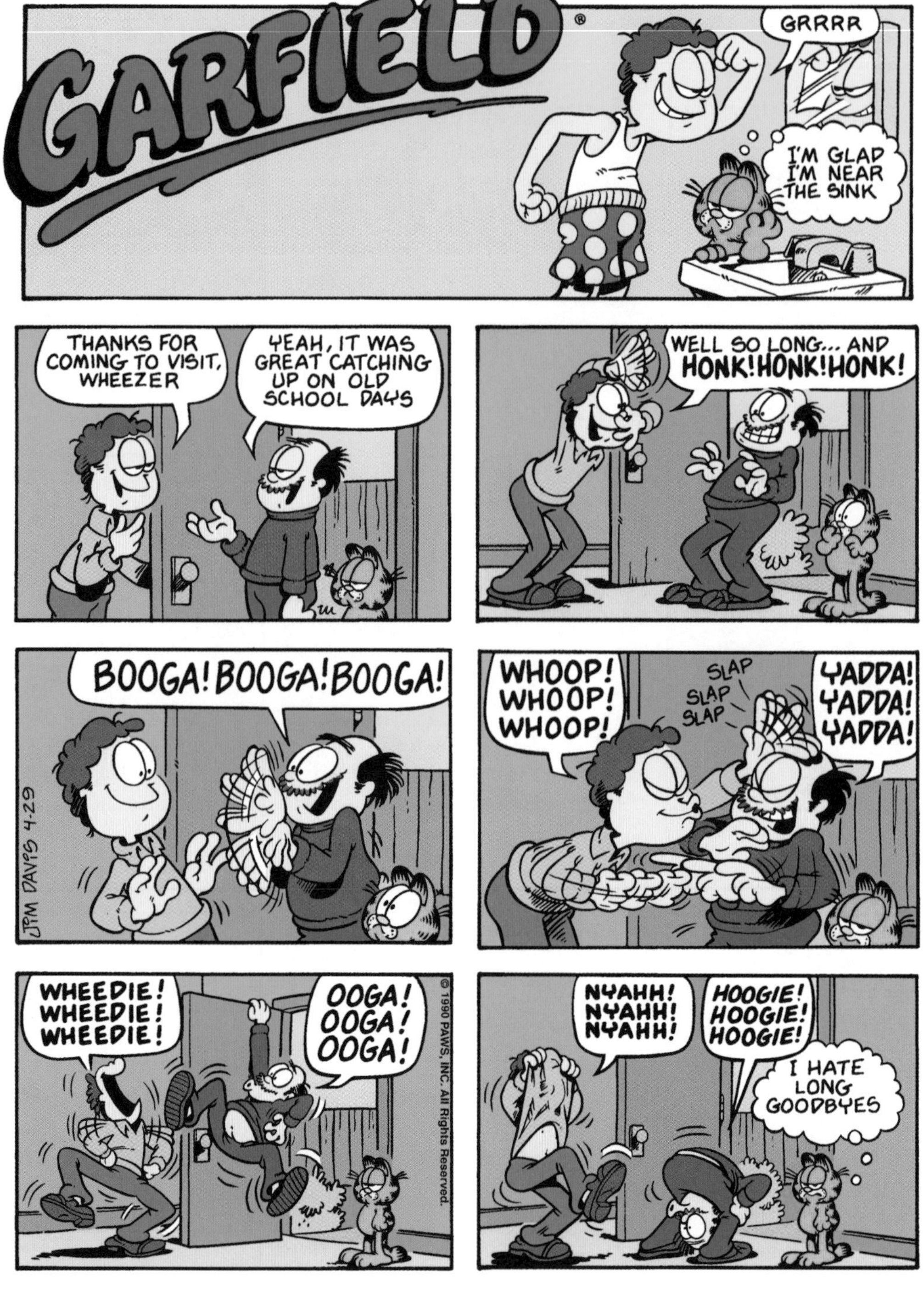
GARFIELD
GRRRR
I'M GLAD I'M NEAR THE SINK
THANKS FOR COMING TO VISIT, WHEEZER
YEAH, IT WAS GREAT CATCHING UP ON OLD SCHOOL DAYS
WELL SO LONG... AND HONK! HONK! HONK!
BOOGA! BOOGA! BOOGA!
JPM DAVIS 4-29
WHOOP! WHOOP! WHOOP!
SLAP SLAP SLAP
YADDA! YADDA! YADDA!
WHEEDIE! WHEEDIE! WHEEDIE!
OOGA! OOGA! OOGA!
© 1990 PAWS, INC. All Rights Reserved.
NYAHH! NYAHH! NYAHH!
HOOGIE! HOOGIE! HOOGIE!
I HATE LONG GOODBYES

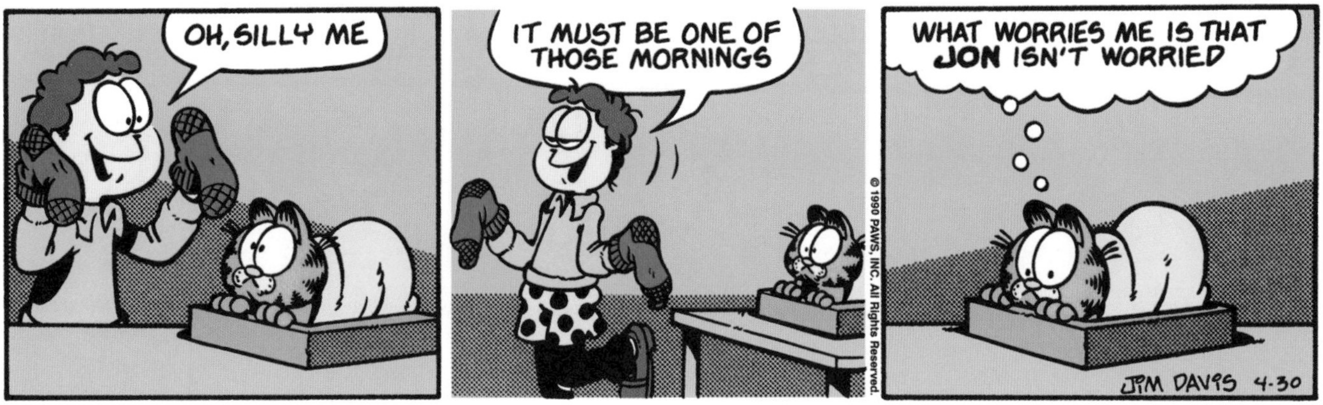
OH, SILLY ME
IT MUST BE ONE OF THOSE MORNINGS
WHAT WORRIES ME IS THAT **JON** ISN'T WORRIED
JIM DAVIS 4-30
© 1990 PAWS, INC. All Rights Reserved.

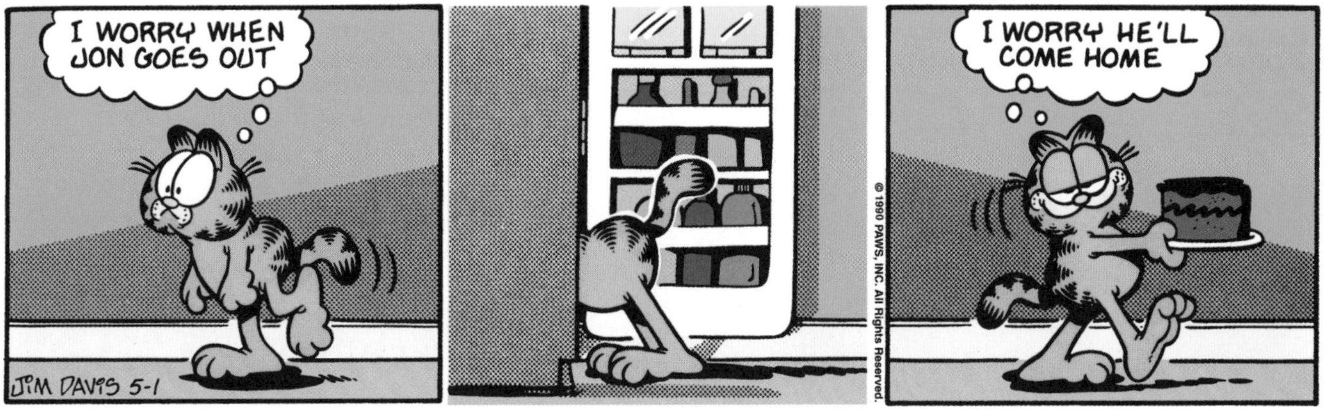
I WORRY WHEN JON GOES OUT
I WORRY HE'LL COME HOME
JIM DAVIS 5-1
© 1990 PAWS, INC. All Rights Reserved.

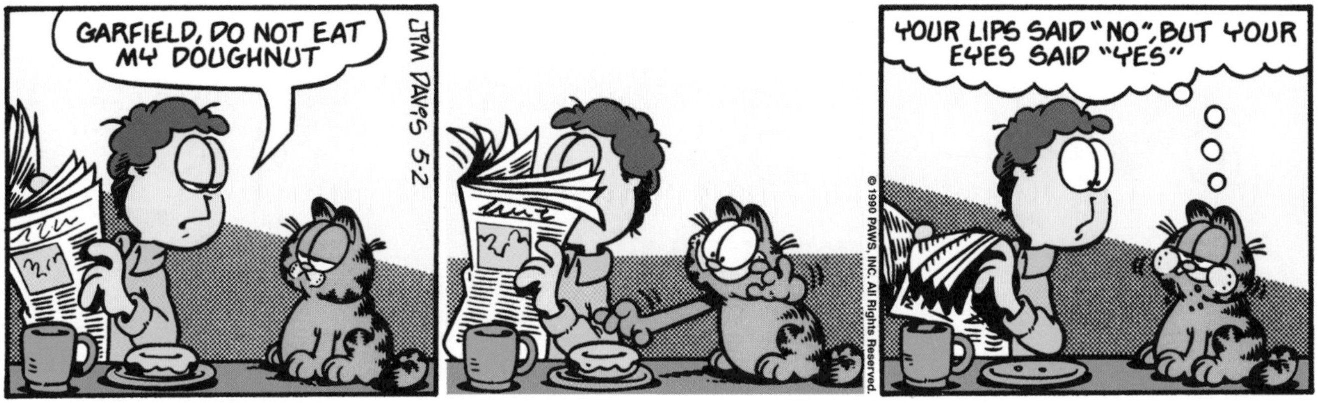
GARFIELD, DO NOT EAT MY DOUGHNUT
YOUR LIPS SAID "NO", BUT YOUR EYES SAID "YES"
JIM DAVIS 5-2
© 1990 PAWS, INC. All Rights Reserved.

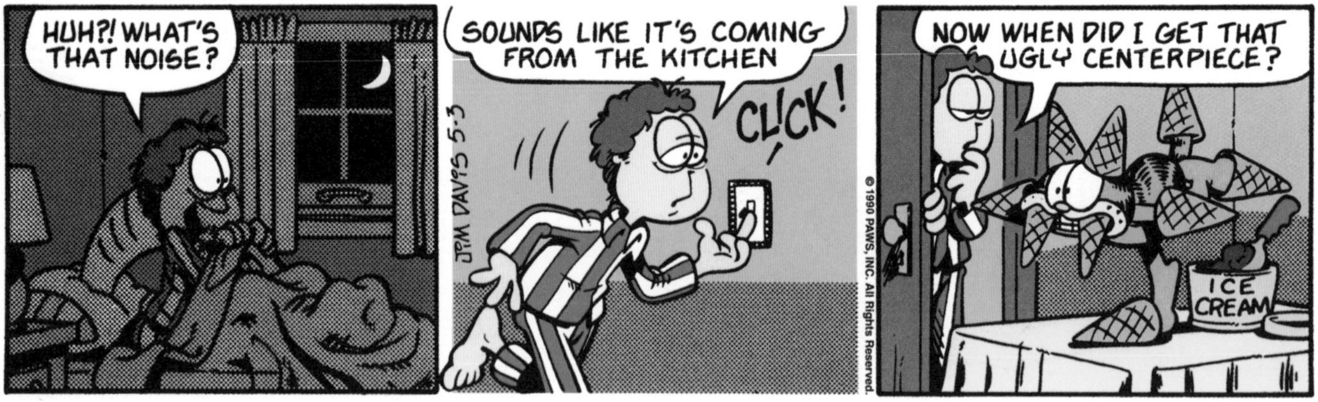
HUH?! WHAT'S THAT NOISE?
SOUNDS LIKE IT'S COMING FROM THE KITCHEN
CLICK!
JIM DAVIS 5-3
© 1990 PAWS, INC. All Rights Reserved.
NOW WHEN DID I GET THAT UGLY CENTERPIECE?
ICE CREAM

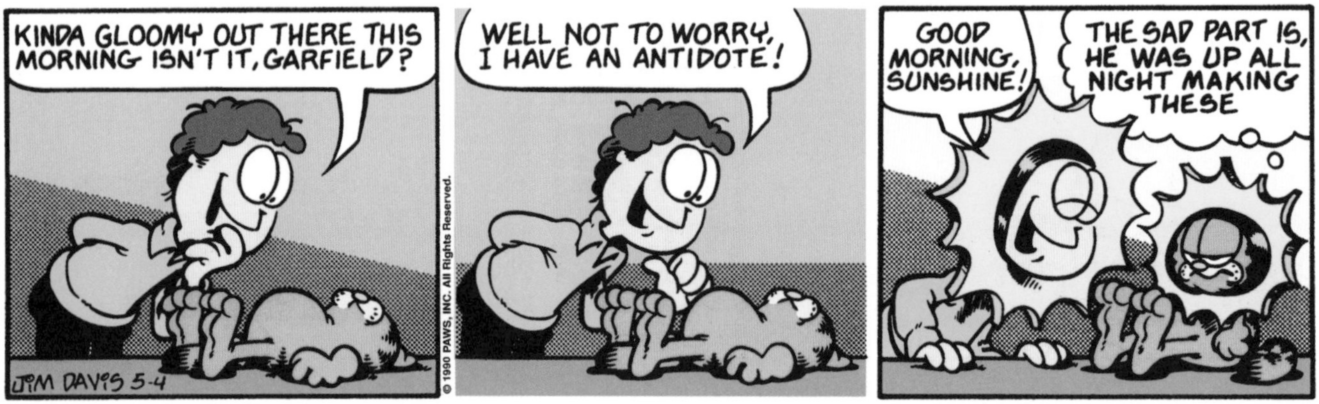
KINDA GLOOMY OUT THERE THIS MORNING ISN'T IT, GARFIELD?
JIM DAVIS 5-4
© 1990 PAWS, INC. All Rights Reserved.
WELL NOT TO WORRY, I HAVE AN ANTIDOTE!
GOOD MORNING, SUNSHINE!
THE SAD PART IS, HE WAS UP ALL NIGHT MAKING THESE

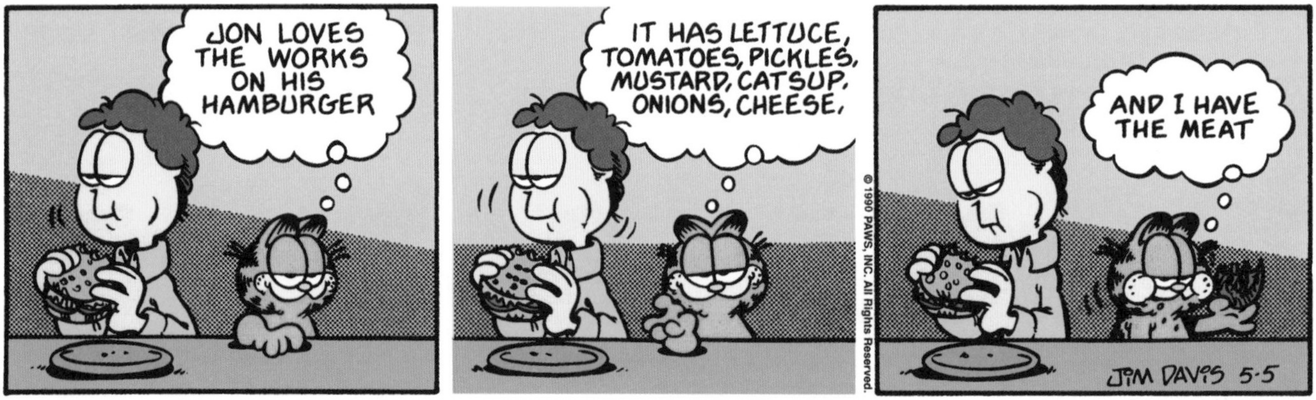
JON LOVES THE WORKS ON HIS HAMBURGER
IT HAS LETTUCE, TOMATOES, PICKLES, MUSTARD, CATSUP, ONIONS, CHEESE,
© 1990 PAWS, INC. All Rights Reserved.
AND I HAVE THE MEAT
JIM DAVIS 5-5

Garfield
says a
mouthful

BY JIM DAVIS

Ballantine Books • New York

Top Ten Signs That Your Cat Is a "Garfield"

10. Your food bill surpasses the national debt
9. He gets a court order requiring you to pamper him
8. He takes over everything in the house except the mortgage payment
7. Dogs in the neighborhood get anonymous hate mail
6. He has never strayed farther than three feet from the house
5. He treats you with no more respect than the drapes
4. Your plants die mysterious deaths
3. He's sometimes mistaken for Rhode Island
2. He tries to have **you** declawed
1. Can't tell if he's sleeping or dead

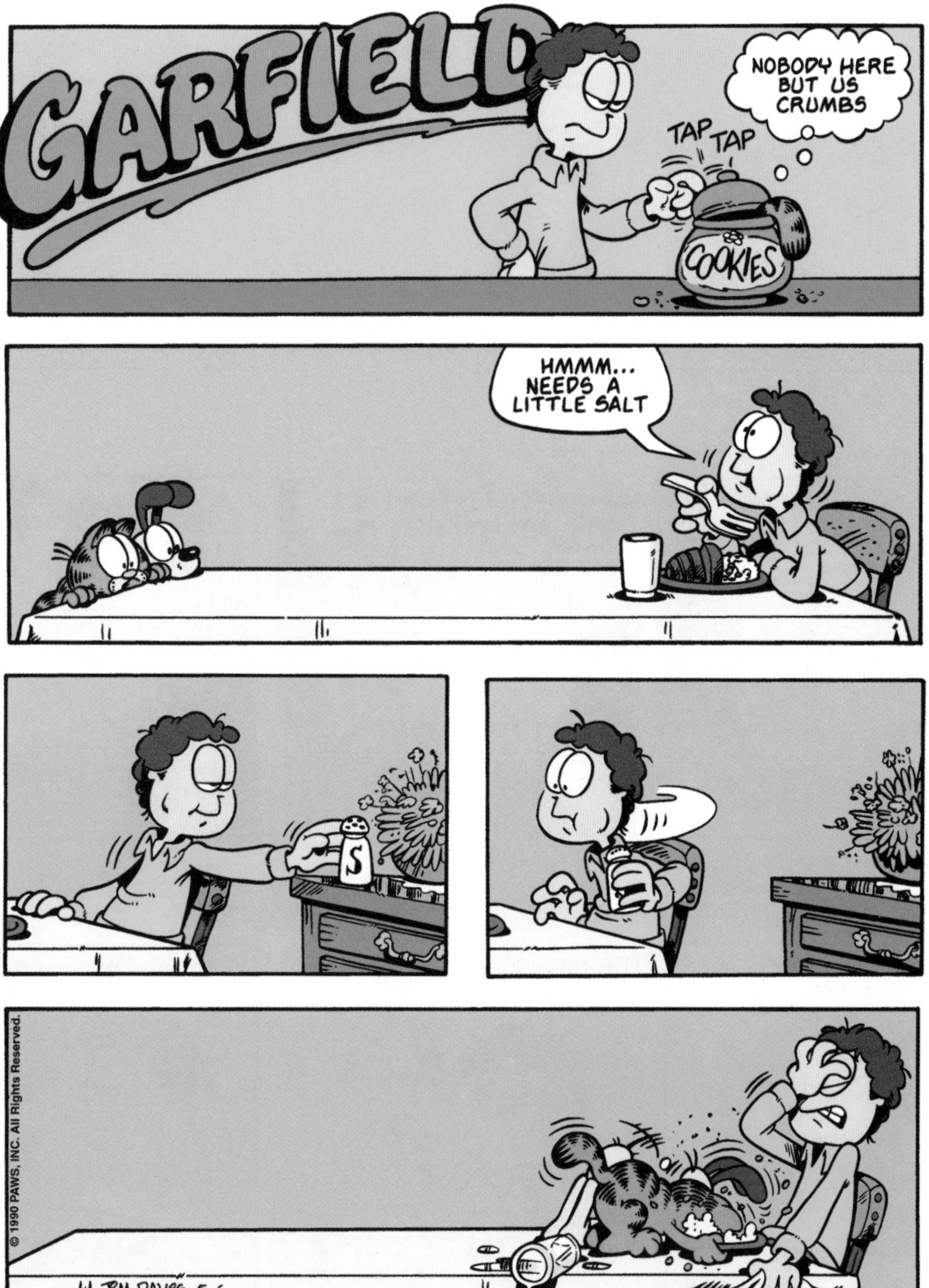
GARFIELD
NOBODY HERE BUT US CRUMBS
TAP TAP
COOKIES
HMMM... NEEDS A LITTLE SALT
S
© 1990 PAWS, INC. All Rights Reserved.
JIM DAVIS 5-6

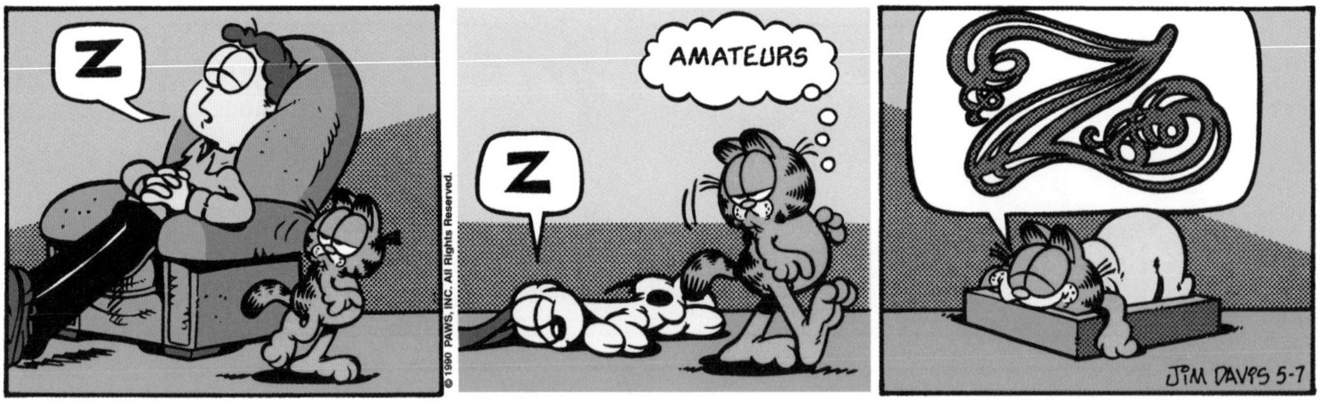
Z
Z
AMATEURS
JIM DAVIS 5-7
© 1990 PAWS, INC. All Rights Reserved.

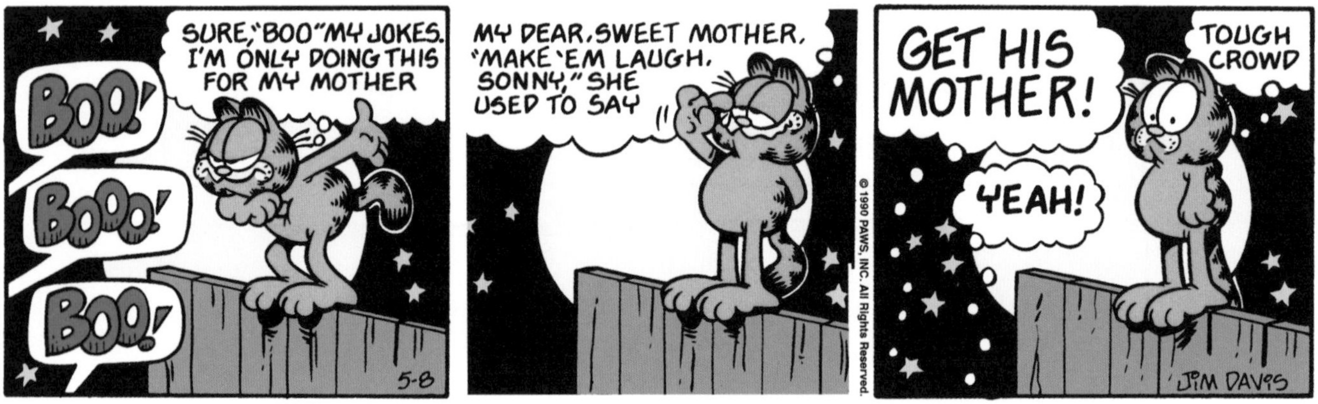
BOO!
BOOO!
BOO!
SURE, "BOO" MY JOKES. I'M ONLY DOING THIS FOR MY MOTHER
5-8
MY DEAR, SWEET MOTHER. "MAKE 'EM LAUGH, SONNY," SHE USED TO SAY
GET HIS MOTHER!
TOUGH CROWD
YEAH!
JIM DAVIS
© 1990 PAWS, INC. All Rights Reserved.

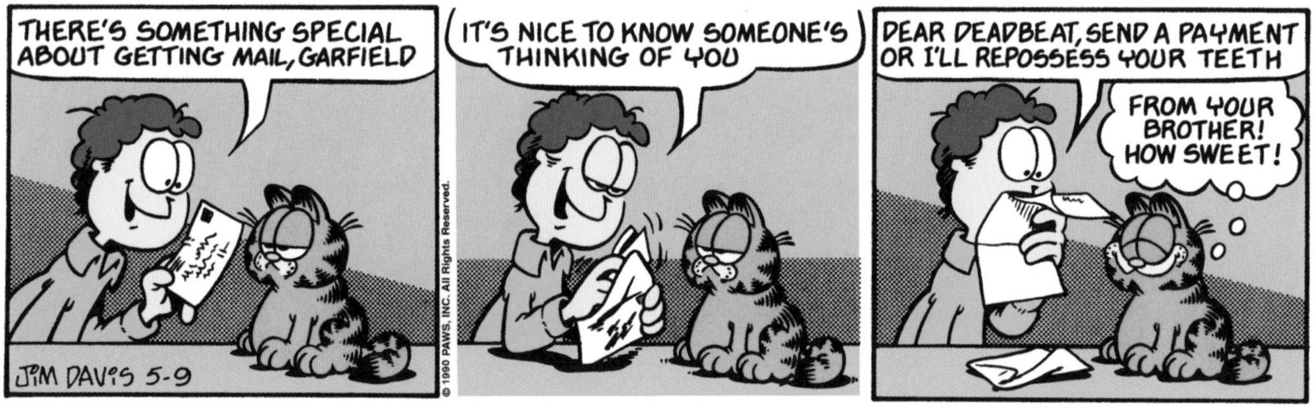
THERE'S SOMETHING SPECIAL ABOUT GETTING MAIL, GARFIELD
JIM DAVIS 5-9
IT'S NICE TO KNOW SOMEONE'S THINKING OF YOU
DEAR DEADBEAT, SEND A PAYMENT OR I'LL REPOSSESS YOUR TEETH
FROM YOUR BROTHER! HOW SWEET!
© 1990 PAWS, INC. All Rights Reserved.

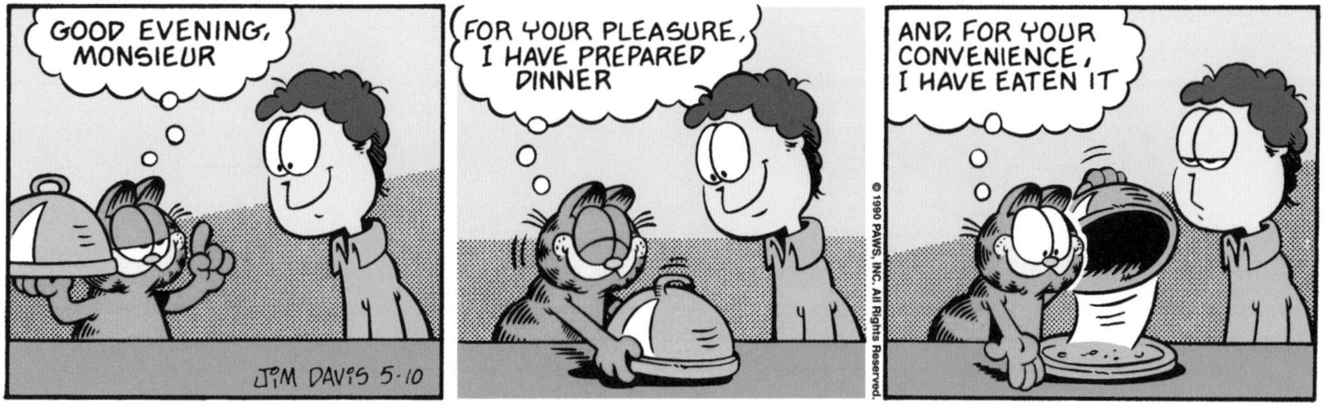
GOOD EVENING, MONSIEUR
JIM DAVIS 5-10
FOR YOUR PLEASURE, I HAVE PREPARED DINNER
© 1990 PAWS, INC. All Rights Reserved.
AND, FOR YOUR CONVENIENCE, I HAVE EATEN IT

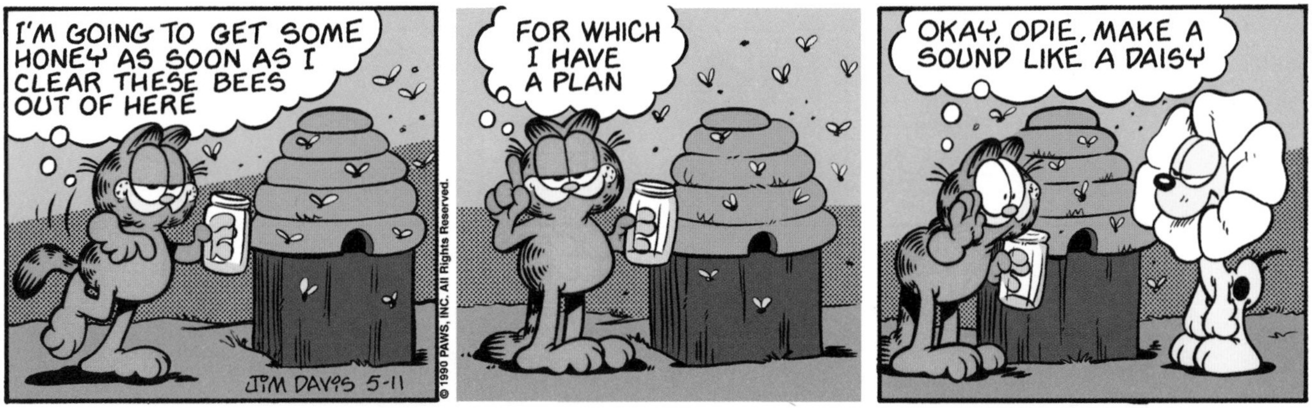
I'M GOING TO GET SOME HONEY AS SOON AS I CLEAR THESE BEES OUT OF HERE
JIM DAVIS 5-11
© 1990 PAWS, INC. All Rights Reserved.
FOR WHICH I HAVE A PLAN
OKAY, ODIE, MAKE A SOUND LIKE A DAISY

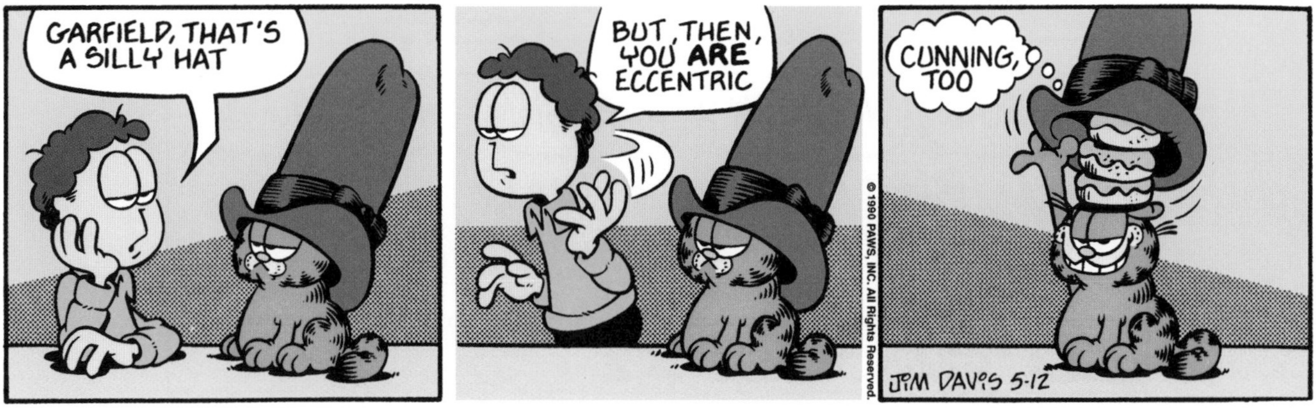
GARFIELD, THAT'S A SILLY HAT
BUT, THEN, YOU **ARE** ECCENTRIC
© 1990 PAWS, INC. All Rights Reserved.
CUNNING, TOO
JIM DAVIS 5-12

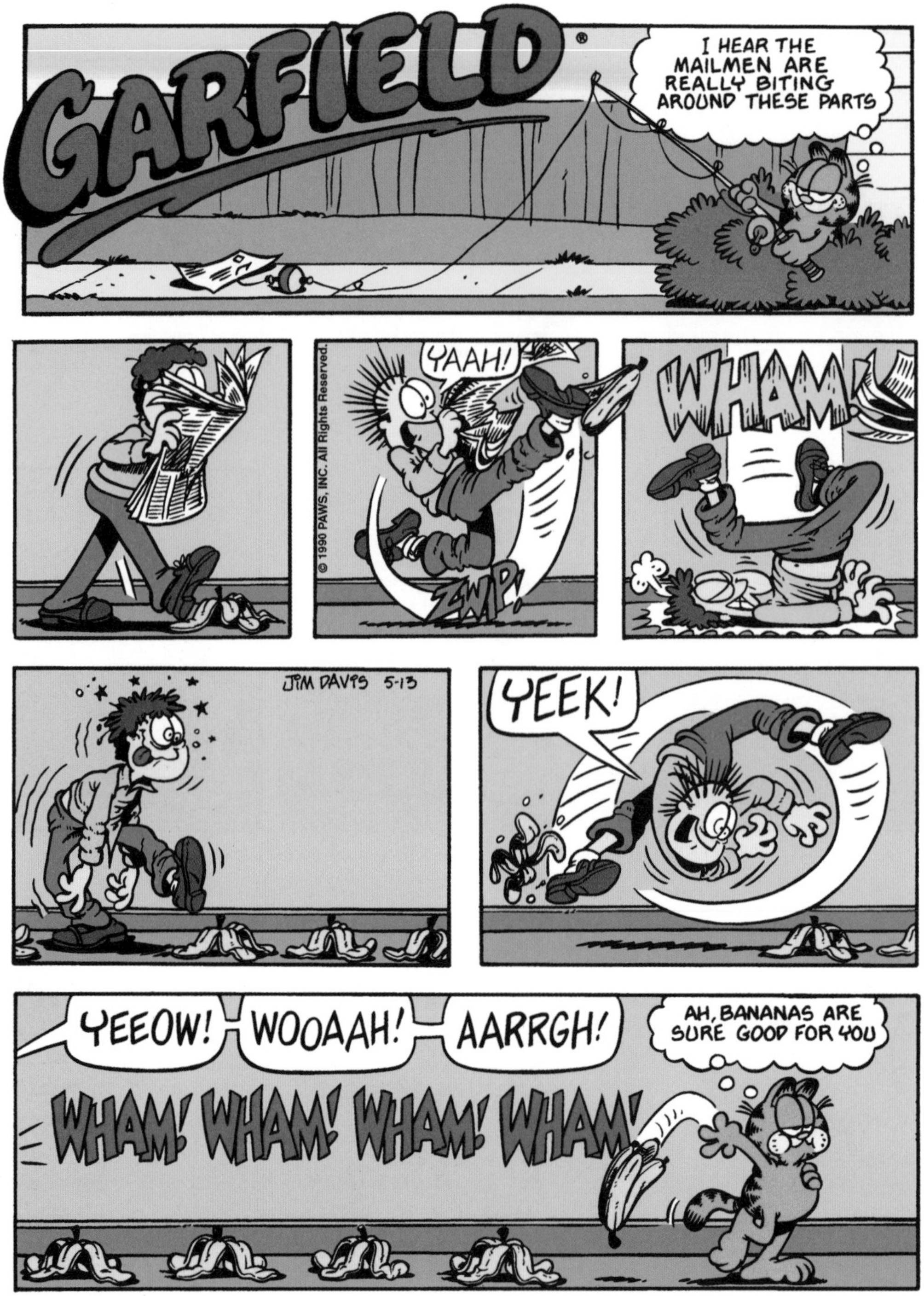
GARFIELD
I HEAR THE MAILMEN ARE REALLY BITING AROUND THESE PARTS
© 1990 PAWS, INC. All Rights Reserved.
YAAH!
ZWIP!
WHAM!
JIM DAVIS 5-13
YEEK!
YEEOW!
WOOAAH!
AARRGH!
AH, BANANAS ARE SURE GOOD FOR YOU
WHAM! WHAM! WHAM! WHAM!

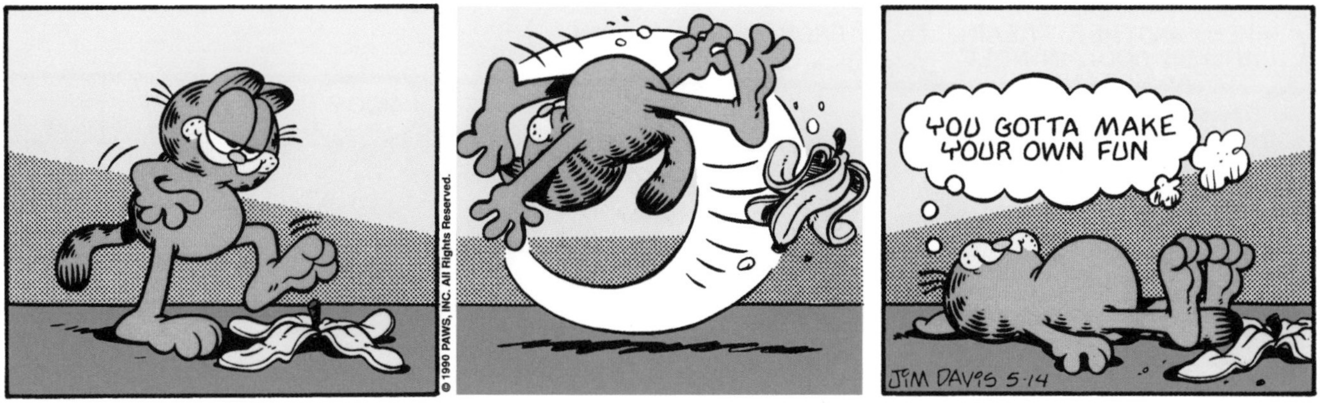
© 1990 PAWS, INC. All Rights Reserved.
YOU GOTTA MAKE YOUR OWN FUN
JIM DAVIS 5-14

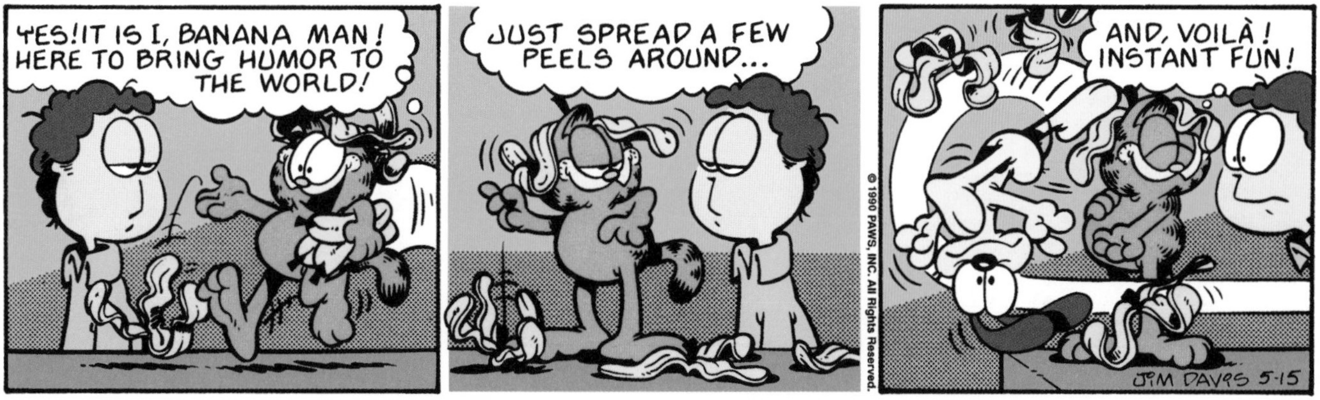
YES! IT IS I, BANANA MAN! HERE TO BRING HUMOR TO THE WORLD!
JUST SPREAD A FEW PEELS AROUND...
© 1990 PAWS, INC. All Rights Reserved.
AND, VOILÀ! INSTANT FUN!
JIM DAVIS 5-15

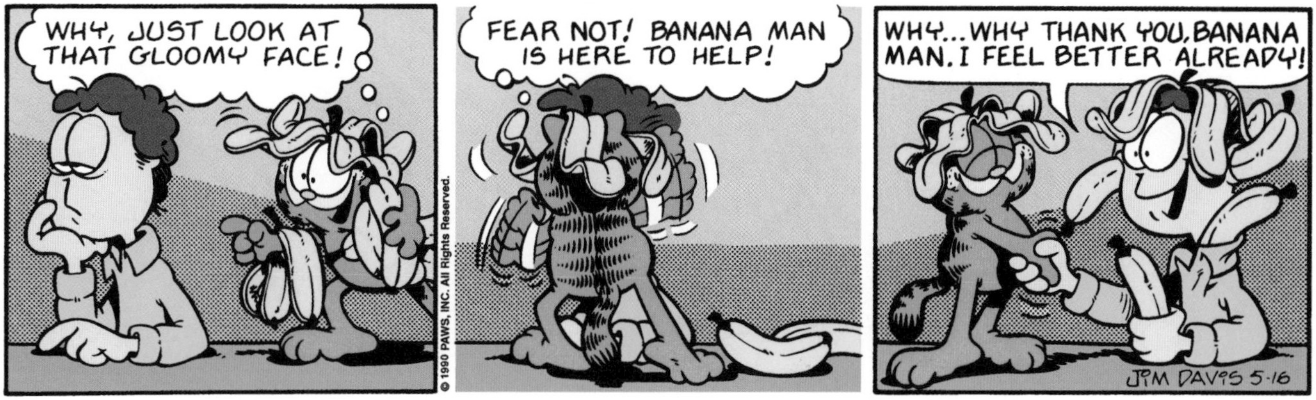
WHY, JUST LOOK AT THAT GLOOMY FACE!
© 1990 PAWS, INC. All Rights Reserved.
FEAR NOT! BANANA MAN IS HERE TO HELP!
WHY...WHY THANK YOU, BANANA MAN. I FEEL BETTER ALREADY!
JIM DAVIS 5-16

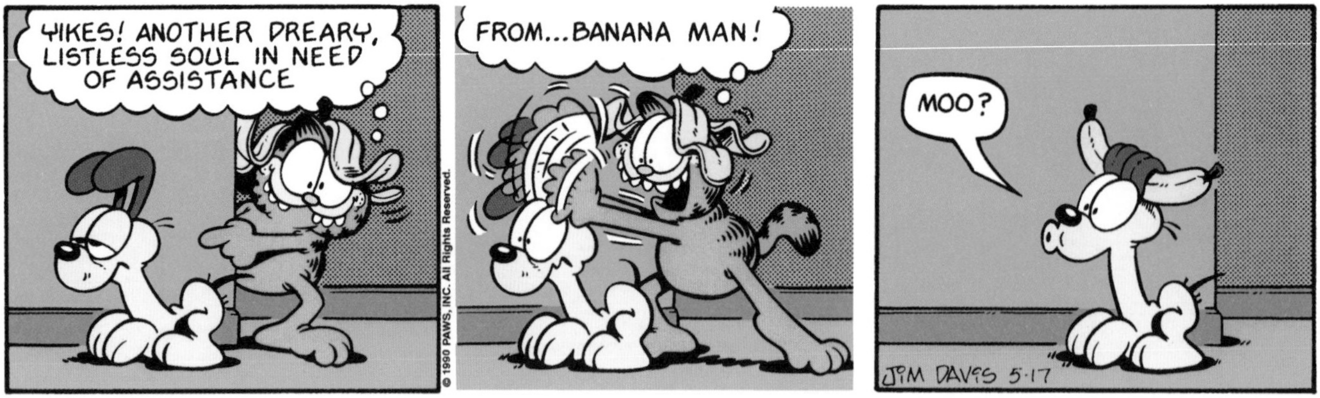
YIKES! ANOTHER DREARY, LISTLESS SOUL IN NEED OF ASSISTANCE
© 1990 PAWS, INC. All Rights Reserved.
FROM...BANANA MAN!
MOO?
JIM DAVIS 5-17

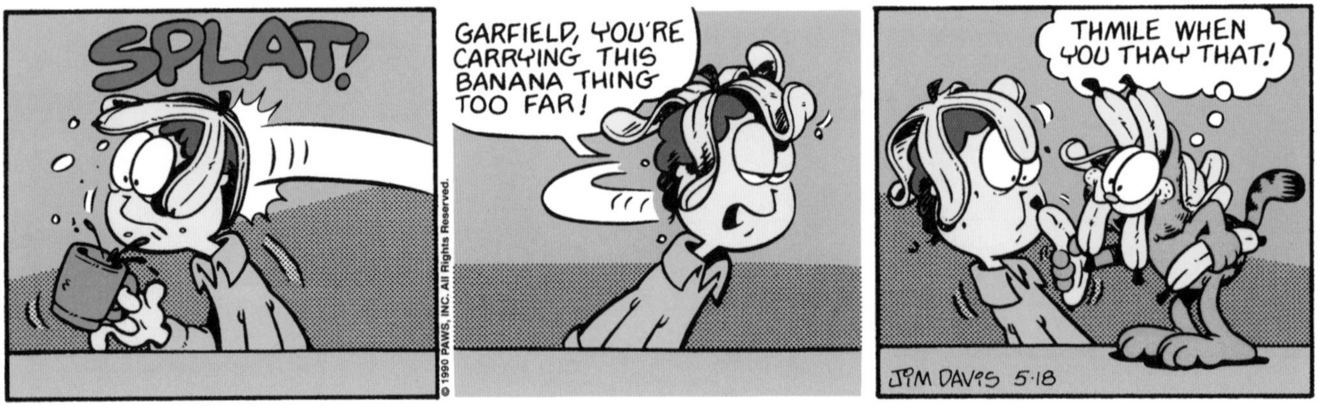
SPLAT!
© 1990 PAWS, INC. All Rights Reserved.
GARFIELD, YOU'RE CARRYING THIS BANANA THING TOO FAR!
THMILE WHEN YOU THAY THAT!
JIM DAVIS 5-18

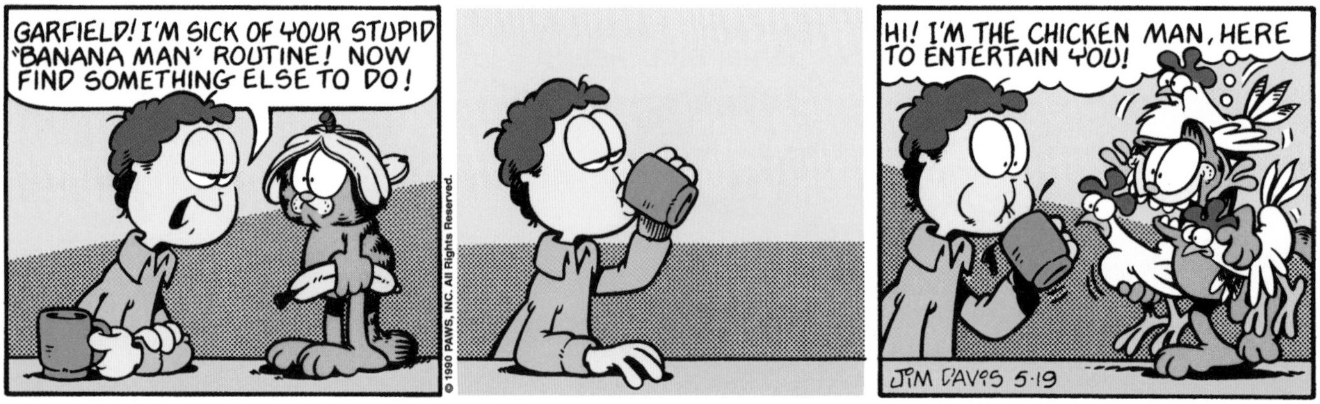
GARFIELD! I'M SICK OF YOUR STUPID "BANANA MAN" ROUTINE! NOW FIND SOMETHING ELSE TO DO!
© 1990 PAWS, INC. All Rights Reserved.
HI! I'M THE CHICKEN MAN, HERE TO ENTERTAIN YOU!
JIM DAVIS 5-19

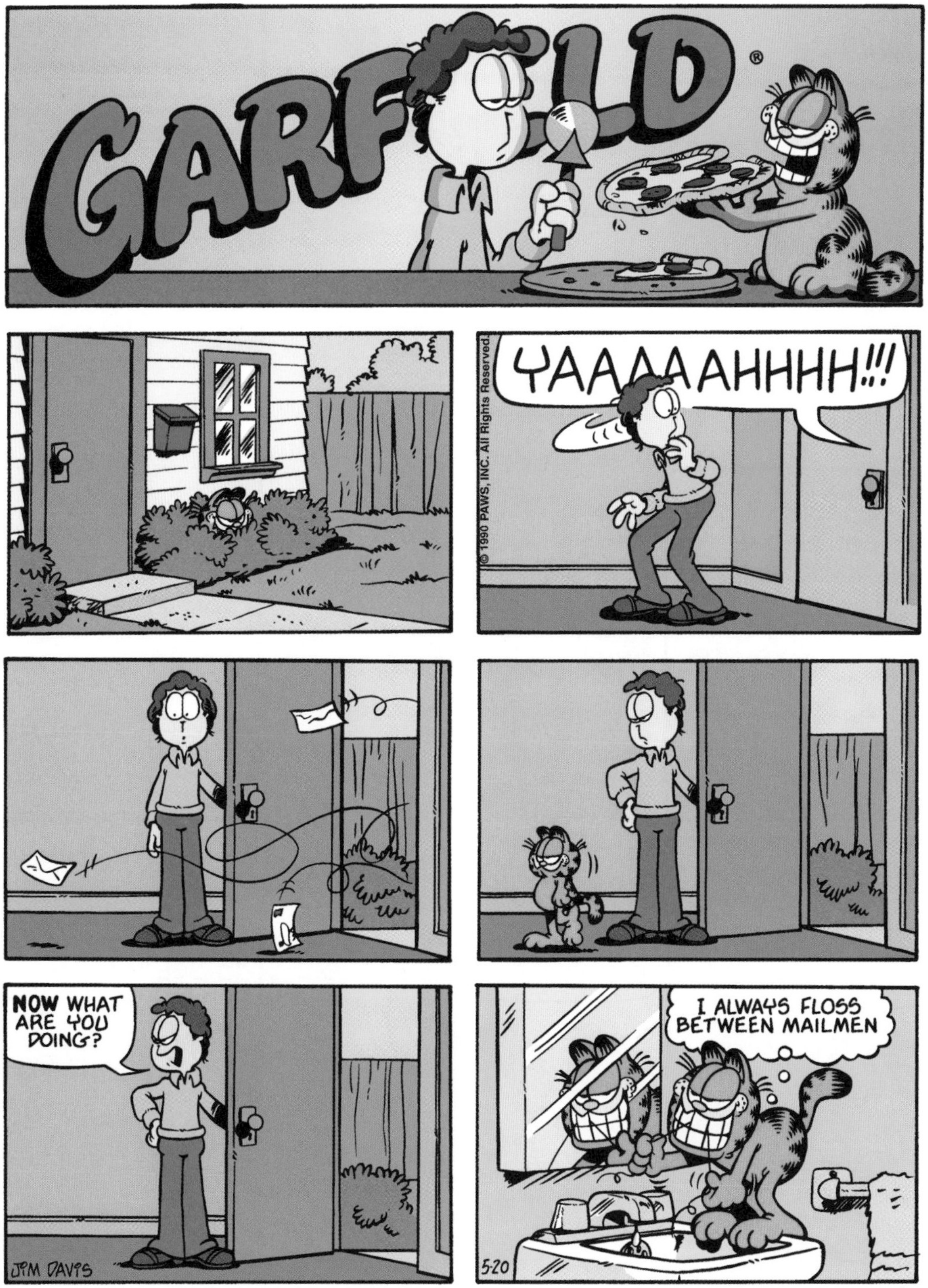
GARFIELD®
© 1990 PAWS, INC. All Rights Reserved.
YAAAAAHHHH!!!
NOW WHAT ARE YOU DOING?
I ALWAYS FLOSS BETWEEN MAILMEN
JIM DAVIS
5-20

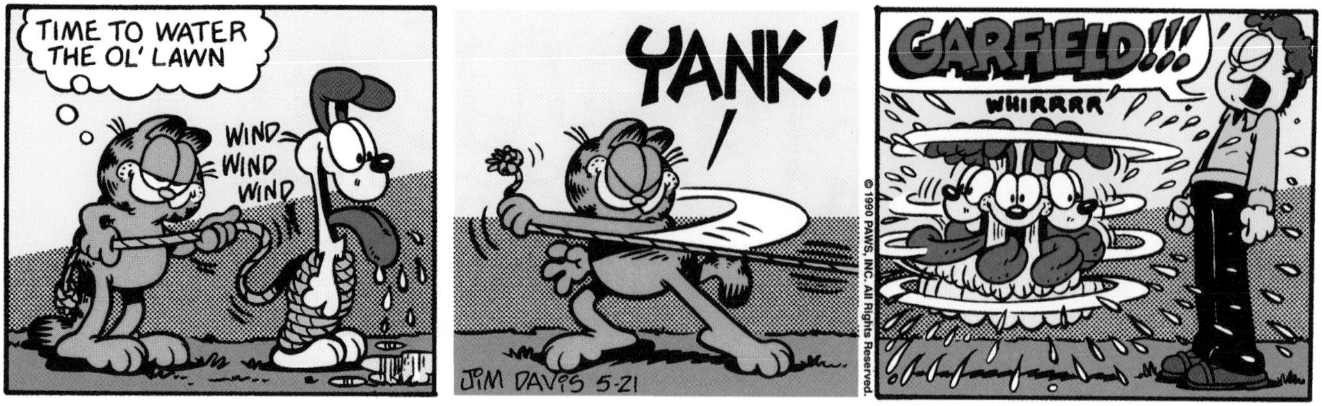
TIME TO WATER THE OL' LAWN
WIND WIND WIND
YANK!
JIM DAVIS 5-21
© 1990 PAWS, INC. All Rights Reserved.
GARFIELD!!!
WHIRRRR

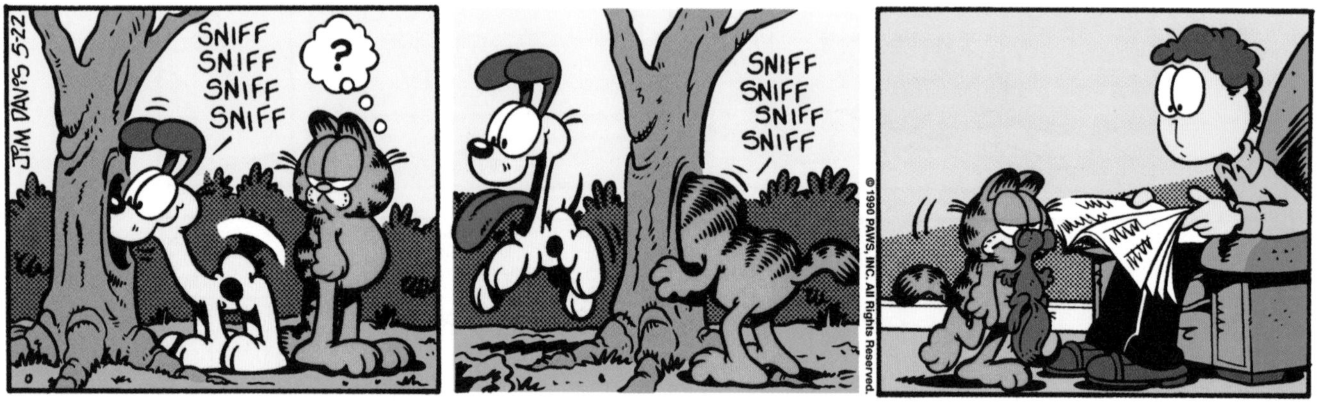
JIM DAVIS 5-22
SNIFF SNIFF SNIFF SNIFF
?
SNIFF SNIFF SNIFF SNIFF
© 1990 PAWS, INC. All Rights Reserved.

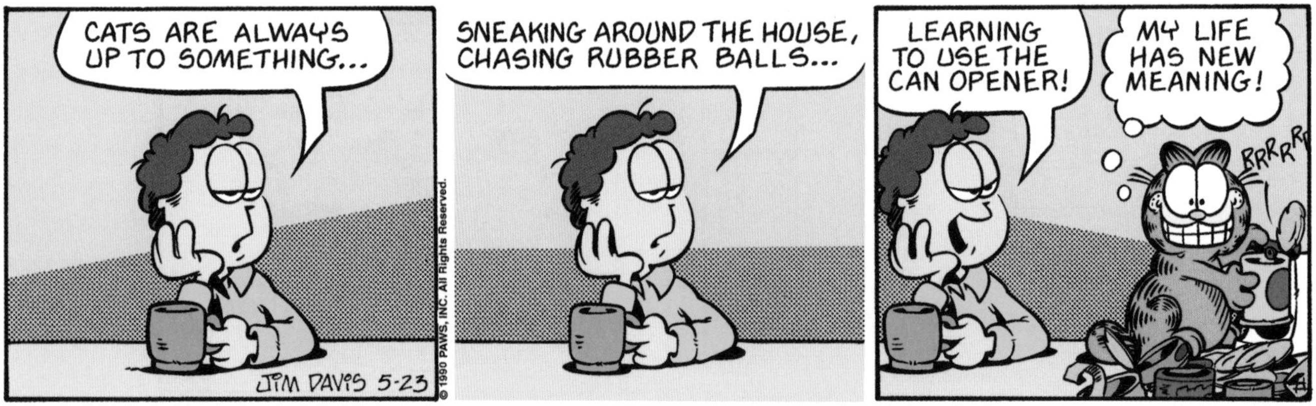
CATS ARE ALWAYS UP TO SOMETHING...
JIM DAVIS 5-23
© 1990 PAWS, INC. All Rights Reserved.
SNEAKING AROUND THE HOUSE, CHASING RUBBER BALLS...
LEARNING TO USE THE CAN OPENER!
MY LIFE HAS NEW MEANING!

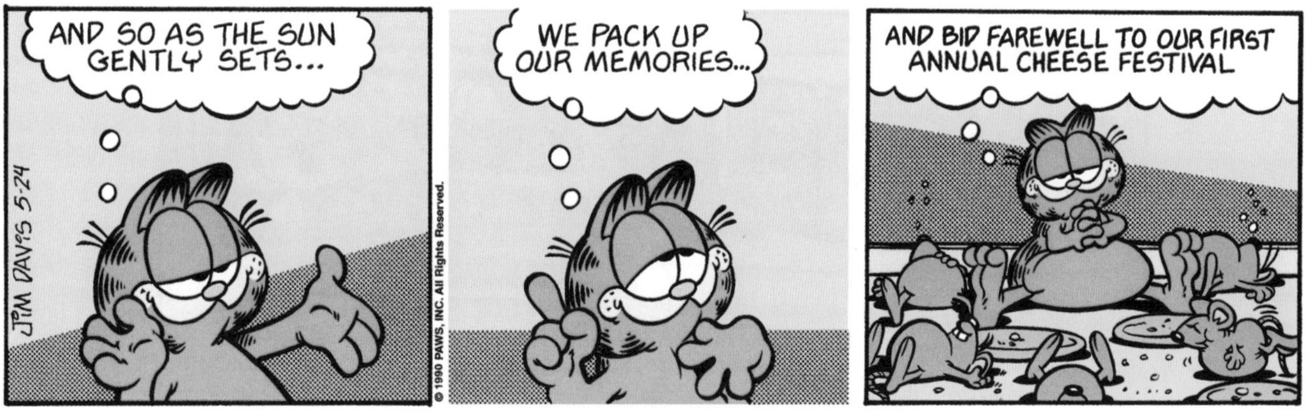
AND SO AS THE SUN GENTLY SETS...
JIM DAVIS 5-24
WE PACK UP OUR MEMORIES...
© 1990 PAWS, INC. All Rights Reserved.
AND BID FAREWELL TO OUR FIRST ANNUAL CHEESE FESTIVAL

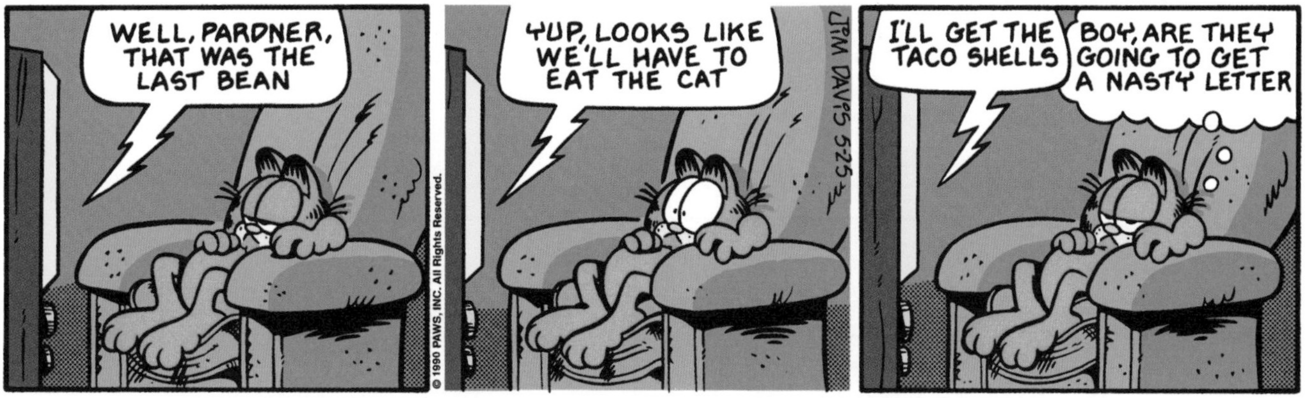
WELL, PARDNER, THAT WAS THE LAST BEAN
© 1990 PAWS, INC. All Rights Reserved.
YUP, LOOKS LIKE WE'LL HAVE TO EAT THE CAT
JIM DAVIS 5-25
I'LL GET THE TACO SHELLS
BOY, ARE THEY GOING TO GET A NASTY LETTER

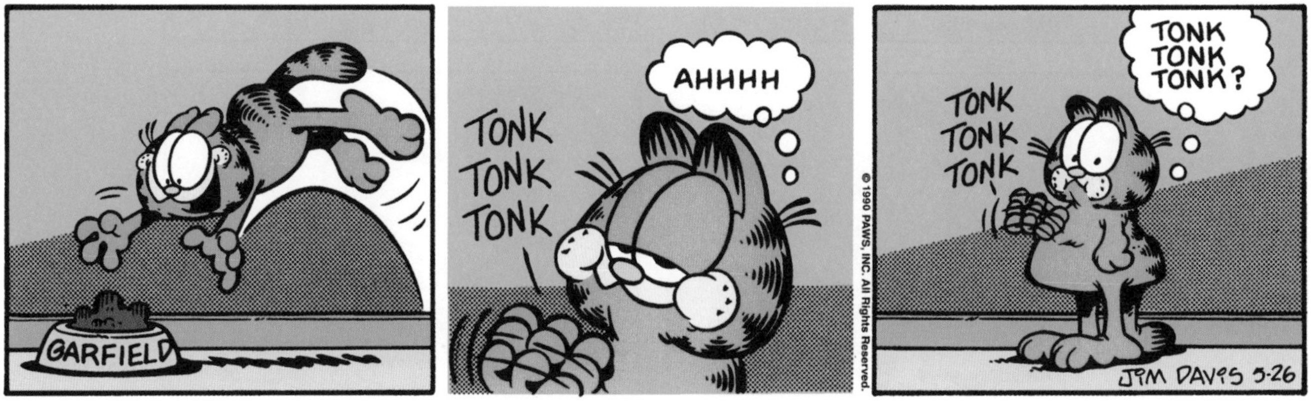
GARFIELD
AHHHH
TONK TONK TONK
© 1990 PAWS, INC. All Rights Reserved.
TONK TONK TONK
TONK TONK TONK?
JIM DAVIS 5-26

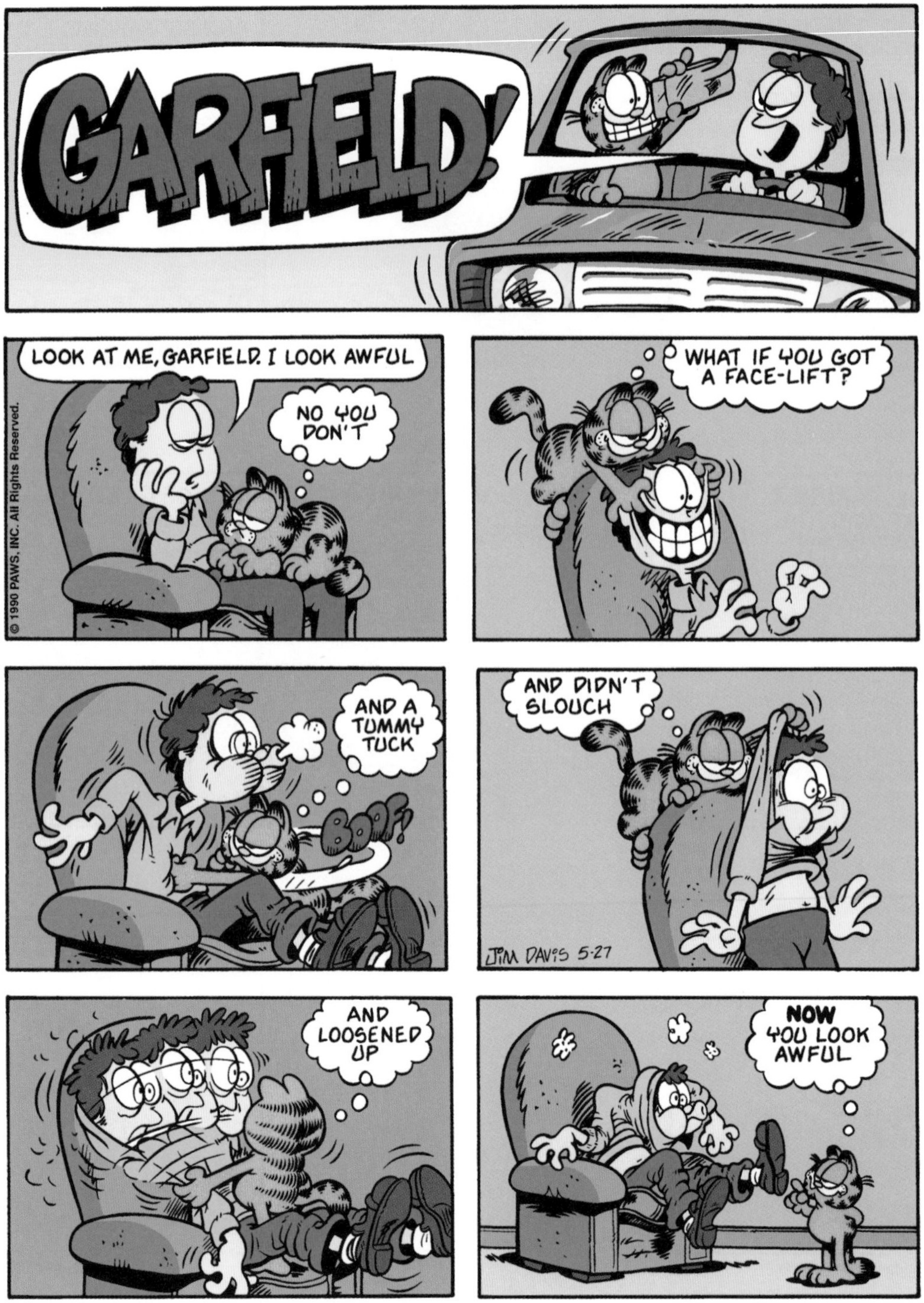
GARFIELD!
LOOK AT ME, GARFIELD. I LOOK AWFUL
NO YOU DON'T
WHAT IF YOU GOT A FACE-LIFT?
AND A TUMMY TUCK
BOOF!
AND DIDN'T SLOUCH
JIM DAVIS 5-27
AND LOOSENED UP
NOW YOU LOOK AWFUL

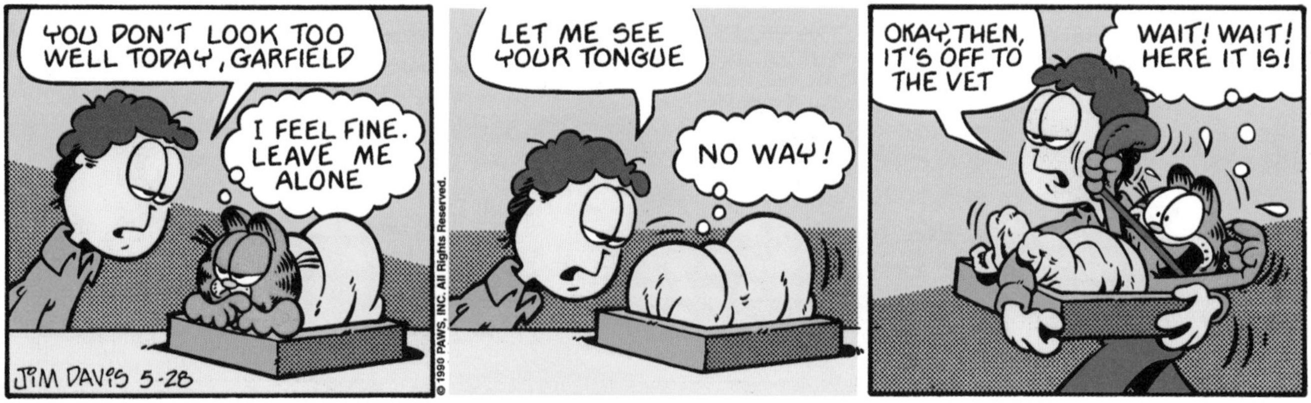
YOU DON'T LOOK TOO WELL TODAY, GARFIELD
I FEEL FINE. LEAVE ME ALONE
JIM DAVIS 5-28
© 1990 PAWS, INC. All Rights Reserved.
LET ME SEE YOUR TONGUE
NO WAY!
OKAY, THEN, IT'S OFF TO THE VET
WAIT! WAIT! HERE IT IS!

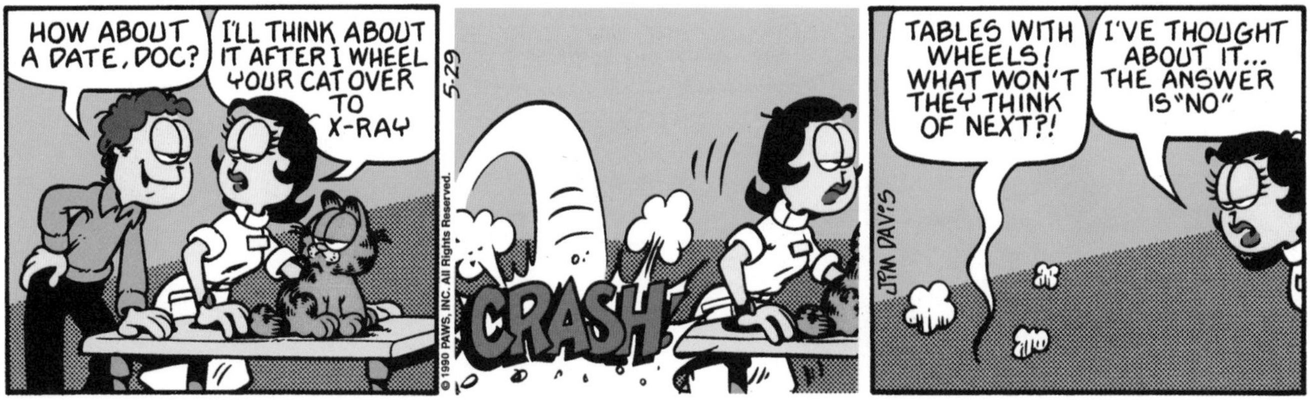
HOW ABOUT A DATE, DOC?
I'LL THINK ABOUT IT AFTER I WHEEL YOUR CAT OVER TO X-RAY
5-29
© 1990 PAWS, INC. All Rights Reserved.
CRASH
TABLES WITH WHEELS! WHAT WON'T THEY THINK OF NEXT?!
JIM DAVIS
I'VE THOUGHT ABOUT IT... THE ANSWER IS "NO"

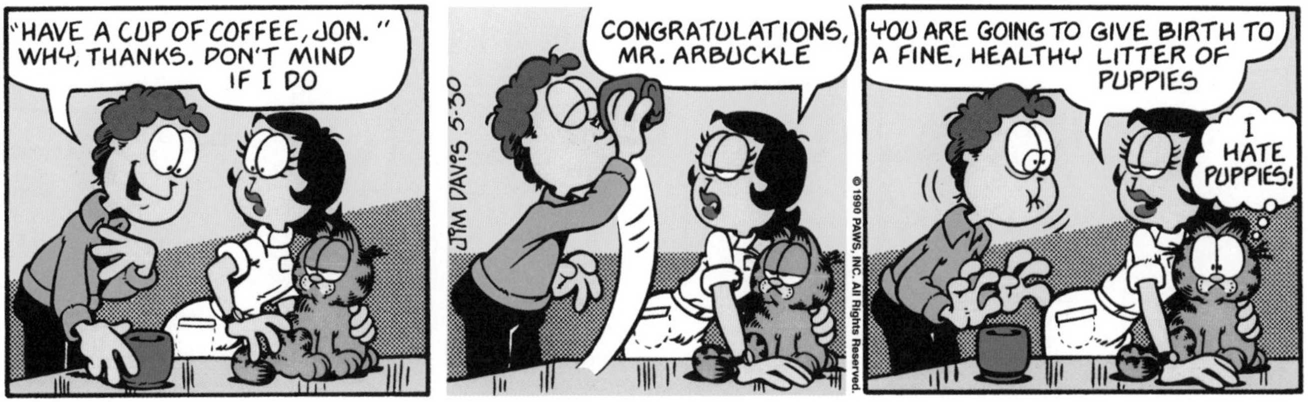
"HAVE A CUP OF COFFEE, JON." WHY, THANKS. DON'T MIND IF I DO
JIM DAVIS 5-30
CONGRATULATIONS, MR. ARBUCKLE
© 1990 PAWS, INC. All Rights Reserved.
YOU ARE GOING TO GIVE BIRTH TO A FINE, HEALTHY LITTER OF PUPPIES
I HATE PUPPIES!

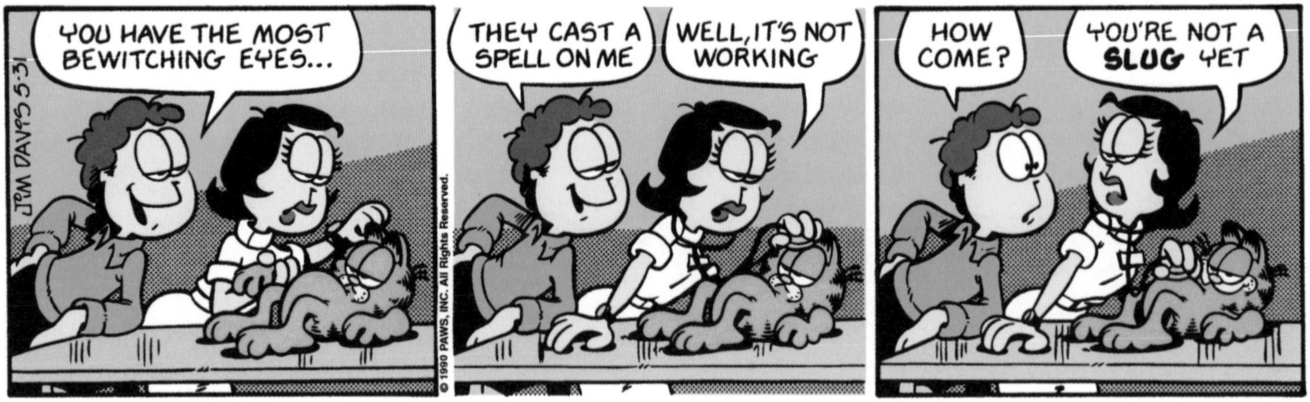
JIM DAVIS 5-31
YOU HAVE THE MOST BEWITCHING EYES...
THEY CAST A SPELL ON ME
WELL, IT'S NOT WORKING
HOW COME?
YOU'RE NOT A **SLUG** YET
© 1990 PAWS, INC. All Rights Reserved.

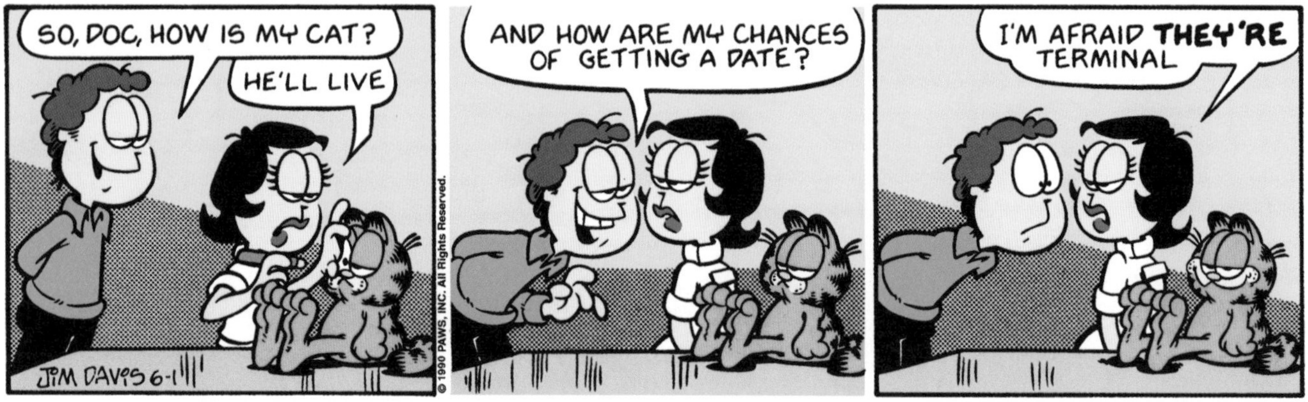
SO, DOC, HOW IS MY CAT?
HE'LL LIVE
JIM DAVIS 6-1
AND HOW ARE MY CHANCES OF GETTING A DATE?
I'M AFRAID **THEY'RE** TERMINAL
© 1990 PAWS, INC. All Rights Reserved.

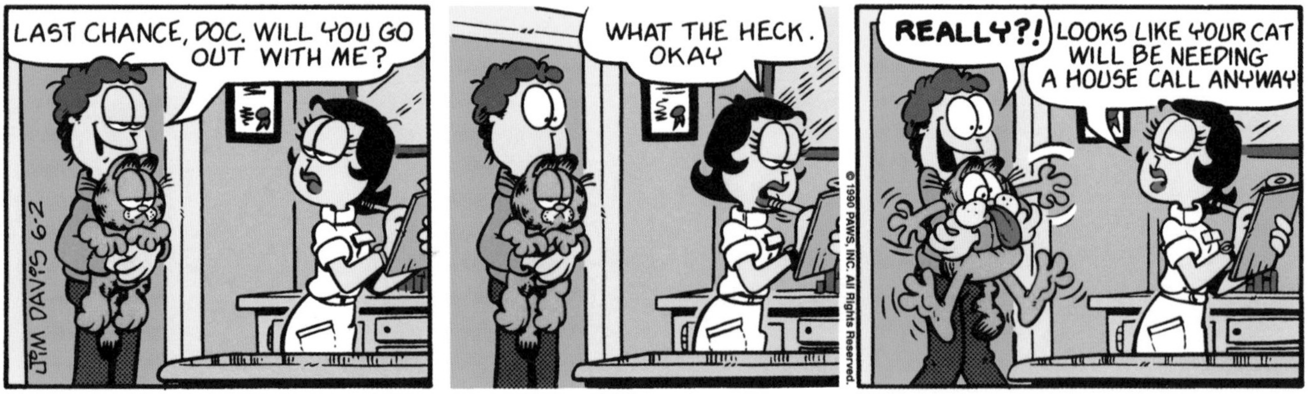
LAST CHANCE, DOC. WILL YOU GO OUT WITH ME?
JIM DAVIS 6-2
WHAT THE HECK. OKAY
REALLY?!
LOOKS LIKE YOUR CAT WILL BE NEEDING A HOUSE CALL ANYWAY
© 1990 PAWS, INC. All Rights Reserved.

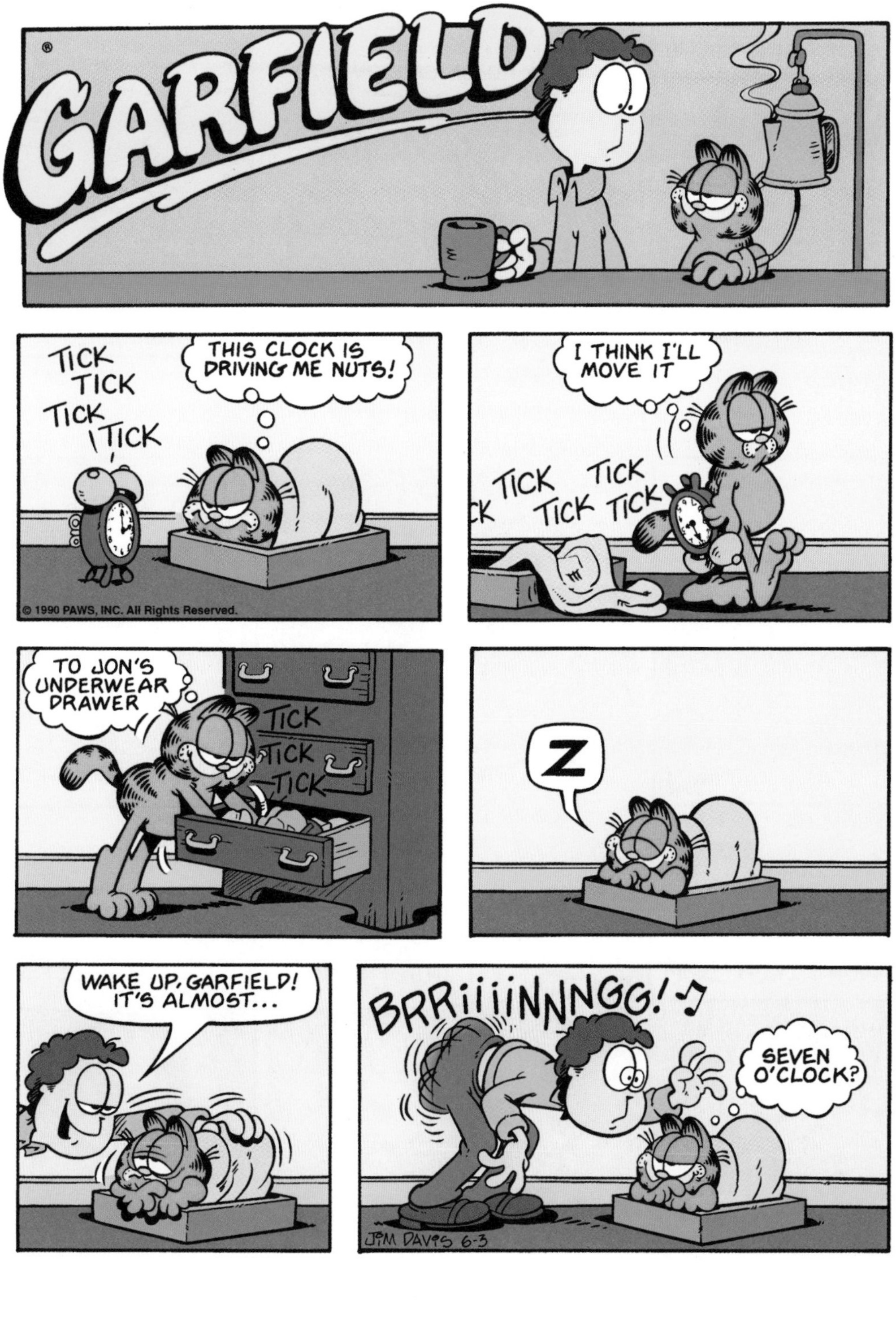
GARFIELD
TICK TICK TICK TICK
THIS CLOCK IS DRIVING ME NUTS!
I THINK I'LL MOVE IT
TICK TICK TICK TICK
TO JON'S UNDERWEAR DRAWER
TICK TICK TICK
Z
WAKE UP, GARFIELD! IT'S ALMOST...
BRRiiiiNNNGG!
SEVEN O'CLOCK?
JIM DAVIS 6-3

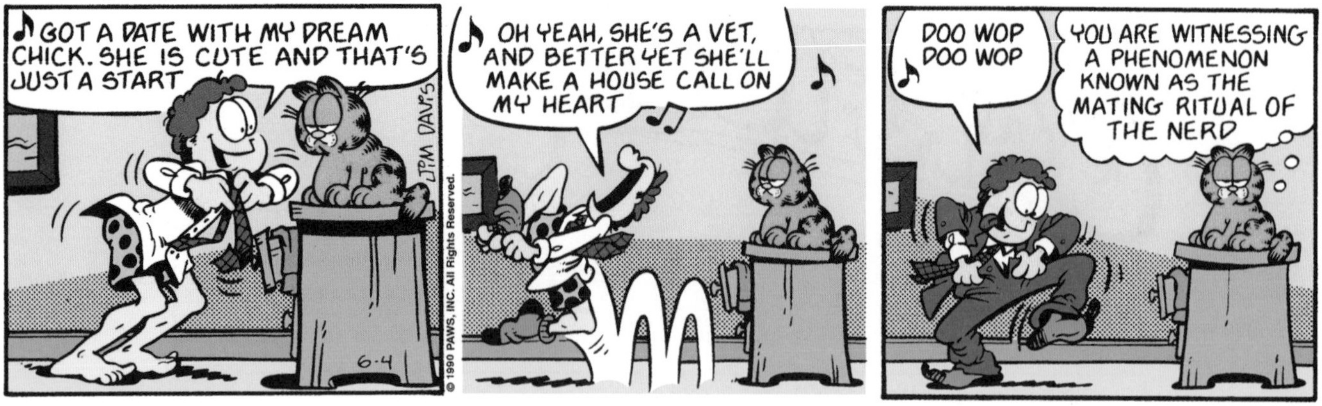
♪ GOT A DATE WITH MY DREAM CHICK. SHE IS CUTE AND THAT'S JUST A START
JIM DAVIS 6-4
© 1990 PAWS, INC. All Rights Reserved.
♪ OH YEAH, SHE'S A VET, AND BETTER YET SHE'LL MAKE A HOUSE CALL ON MY HEART
♪ DOO WOP DOO WOP
YOU ARE WITNESSING A PHENOMENON KNOWN AS THE MATING RITUAL OF THE NERD

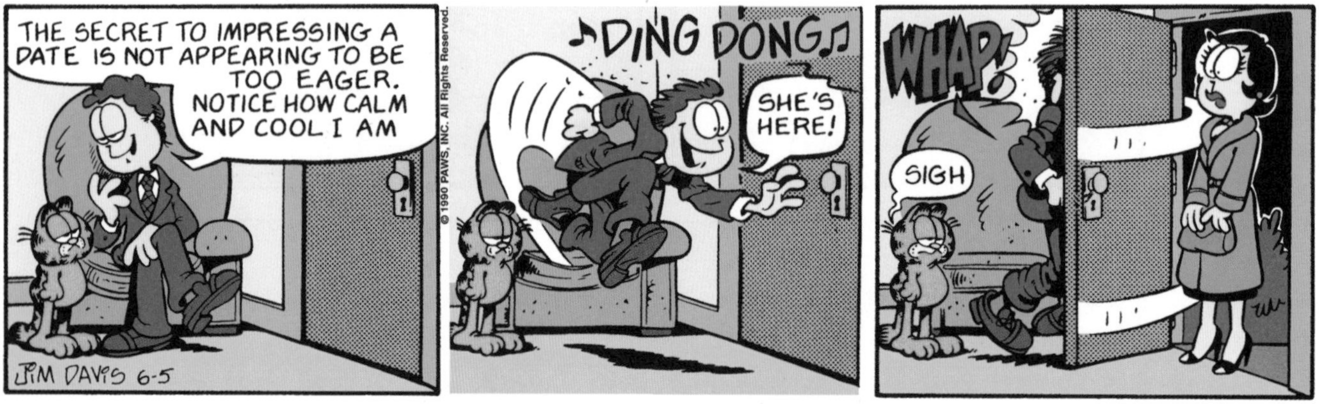
THE SECRET TO IMPRESSING A DATE IS NOT APPEARING TO BE TOO EAGER. NOTICE HOW CALM AND COOL I AM
JIM DAVIS 6-5
© 1990 PAWS, INC. All Rights Reserved.
♪DING DONG♫
SHE'S HERE!
WHAP!
SIGH

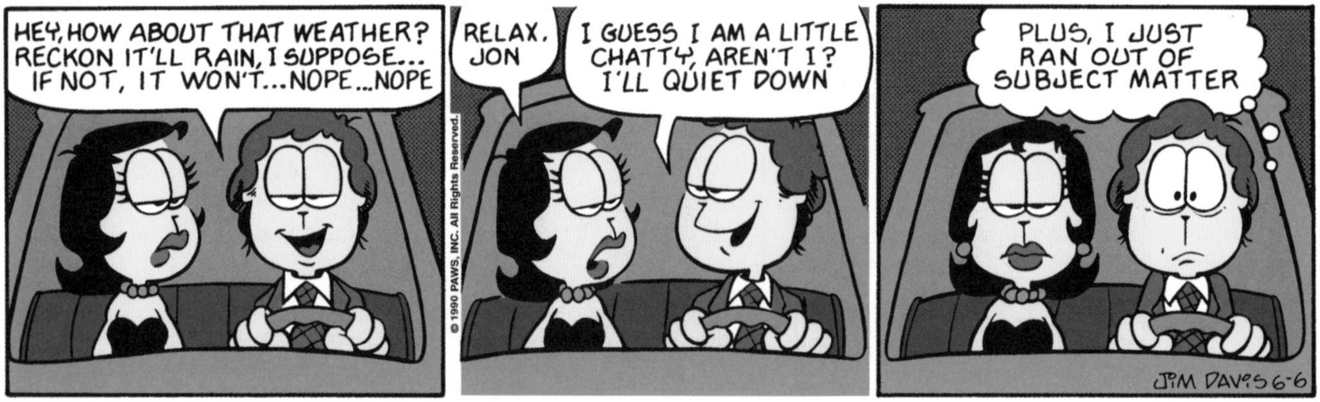
HEY, HOW ABOUT THAT WEATHER? RECKON IT'LL RAIN, I SUPPOSE... IF NOT, IT WON'T...NOPE...NOPE
© 1990 PAWS, INC. All Rights Reserved.
RELAX, JON
I GUESS I AM A LITTLE CHATTY, AREN'T I? I'LL QUIET DOWN
PLUS, I JUST RAN OUT OF SUBJECT MATTER
JIM DAVIS 6-6

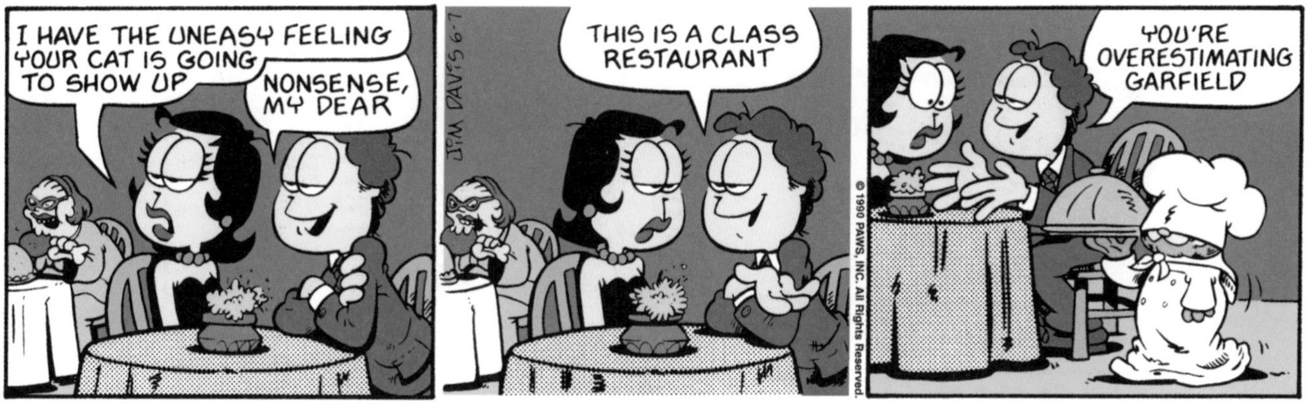
I HAVE THE UNEASY FEELING YOUR CAT IS GOING TO SHOW UP
NONSENSE, MY DEAR
JIM DAVIS 6-7
THIS IS A CLASS RESTAURANT
© 1990 PAWS, INC. All Rights Reserved.
YOU'RE OVERESTIMATING GARFIELD

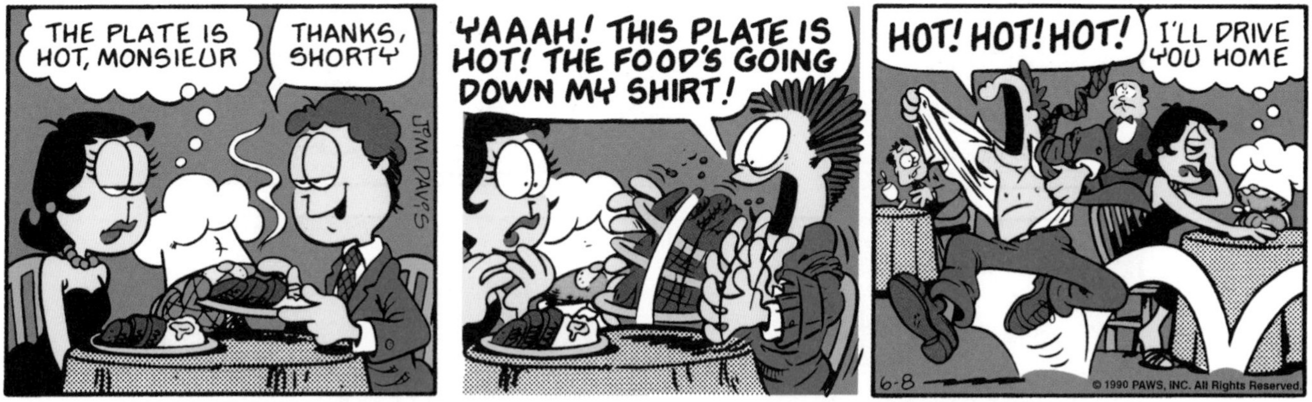
THE PLATE IS HOT, MONSIEUR
THANKS, SHORTY
JIM DAVIS
YAAAH! THIS PLATE IS HOT! THE FOOD'S GOING DOWN MY SHIRT!
HOT! HOT! HOT!
I'LL DRIVE YOU HOME
6-8
© 1990 PAWS, INC. All Rights Reserved.

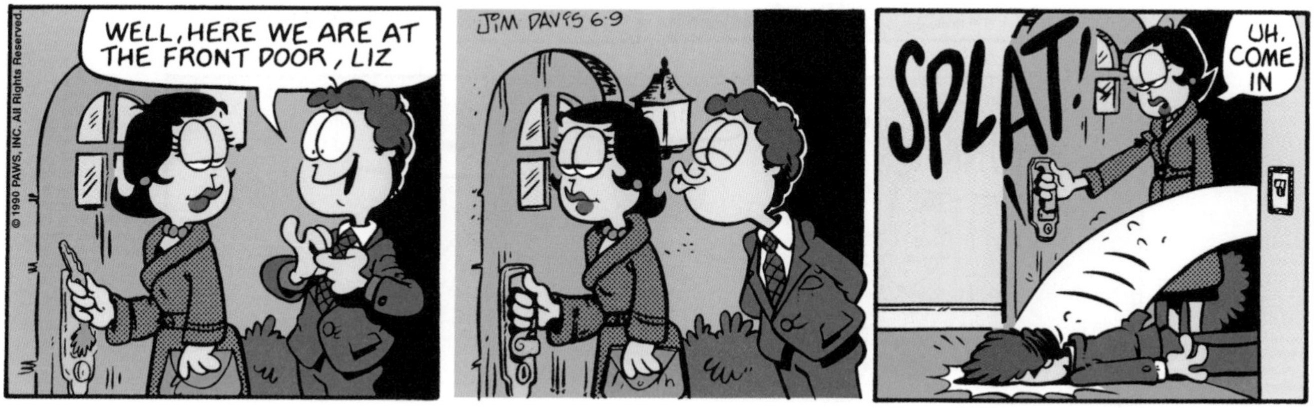
© 1990 PAWS, INC. All Rights Reserved.
WELL, HERE WE ARE AT THE FRONT DOOR, LIZ
JIM DAVIS 6-9
SPLAT!
UH. COME IN

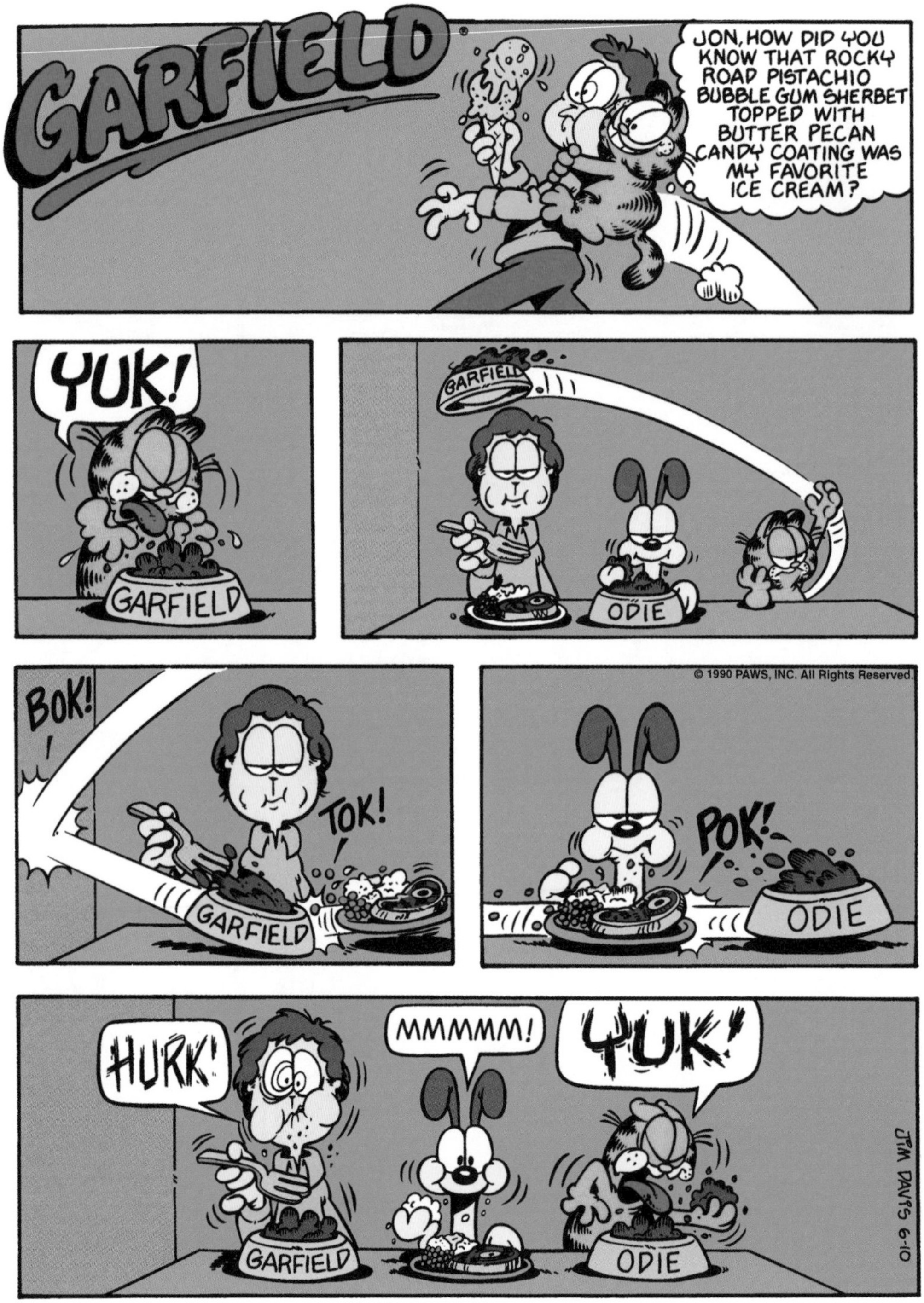
GARFIELD
JON, HOW DID YOU KNOW THAT ROCKY ROAD PISTACHIO BUBBLE GUM SHERBET TOPPED WITH BUTTER PECAN CANDY COATING WAS MY FAVORITE ICE CREAM?
YUK!
GARFIELD
GARFIELD
ODIE
BOK!
TOK!
GARFIELD
© 1990 PAWS, INC. All Rights Reserved.
POK!
ODIE
HURK!
MMMMM!
YUK!
GARFIELD
ODIE
JIM DAVIS 6-10

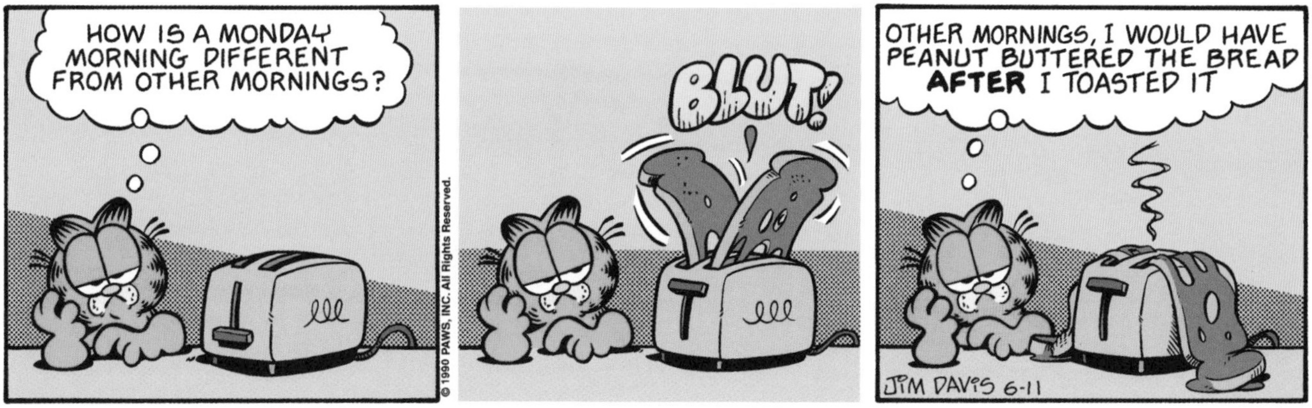
HOW IS A MONDAY MORNING DIFFERENT FROM OTHER MORNINGS?
© 1990 PAWS, INC. All Rights Reserved.
BLUT!
OTHER MORNINGS, I WOULD HAVE PEANUT BUTTERED THE BREAD **AFTER** I TOASTED IT
JIM DAVIS 6-11

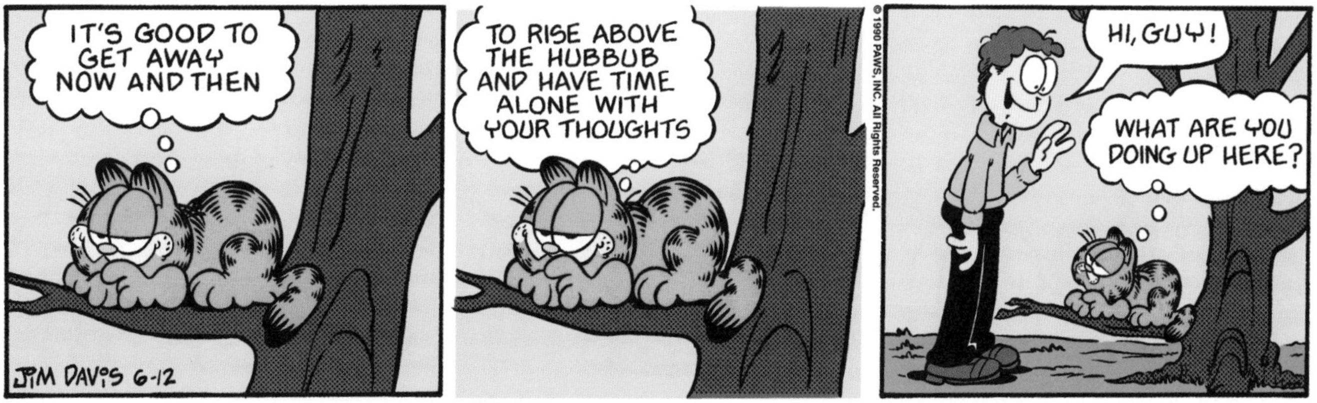
IT'S GOOD TO GET AWAY NOW AND THEN
JIM DAVIS 6-12
TO RISE ABOVE THE HUBBUB AND HAVE TIME ALONE WITH YOUR THOUGHTS
© 1990 PAWS, INC. All Rights Reserved.
HI, GUY!
WHAT ARE YOU DOING UP HERE?

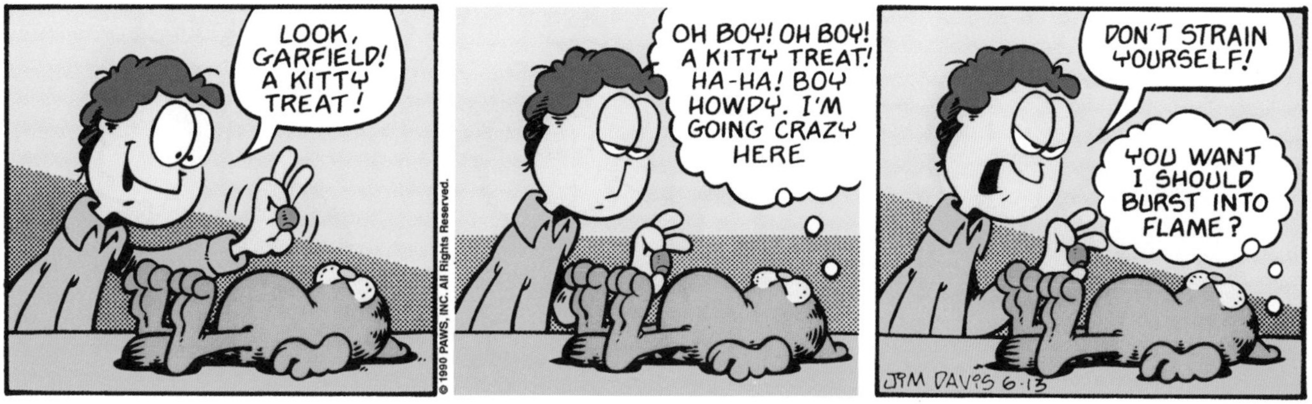
LOOK, GARFIELD! A KITTY TREAT!
© 1990 PAWS, INC. All Rights Reserved.
OH BOY! OH BOY! A KITTY TREAT! HA-HA! BOY HOWDY. I'M GOING CRAZY HERE
DON'T STRAIN YOURSELF!
YOU WANT I SHOULD BURST INTO FLAME?
JIM DAVIS 6-13

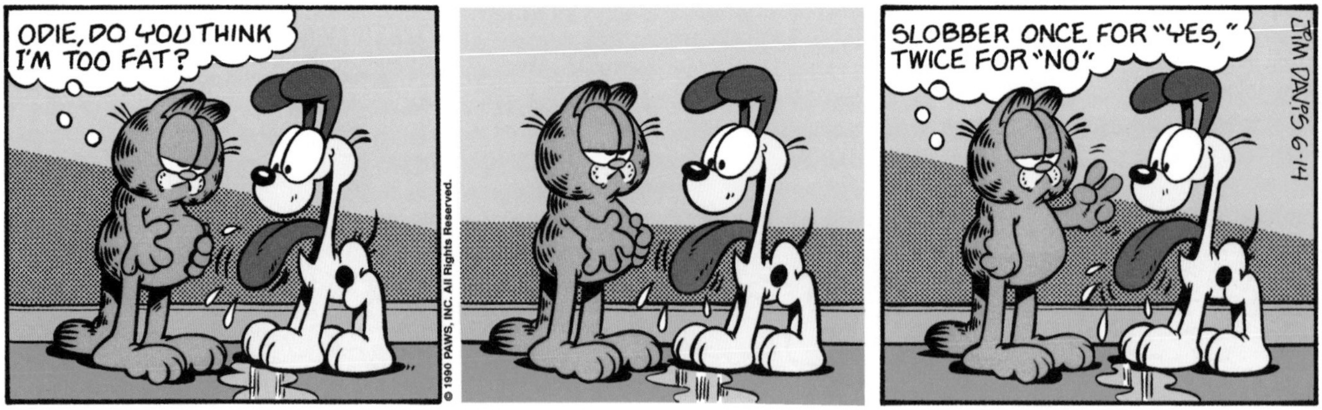
ODIE, DO YOU THINK I'M TOO FAT?
SLOBBER ONCE FOR "YES," TWICE FOR "NO"
JIM DAVIS 6-14
© 1990 PAWS, INC. All Rights Reserved.

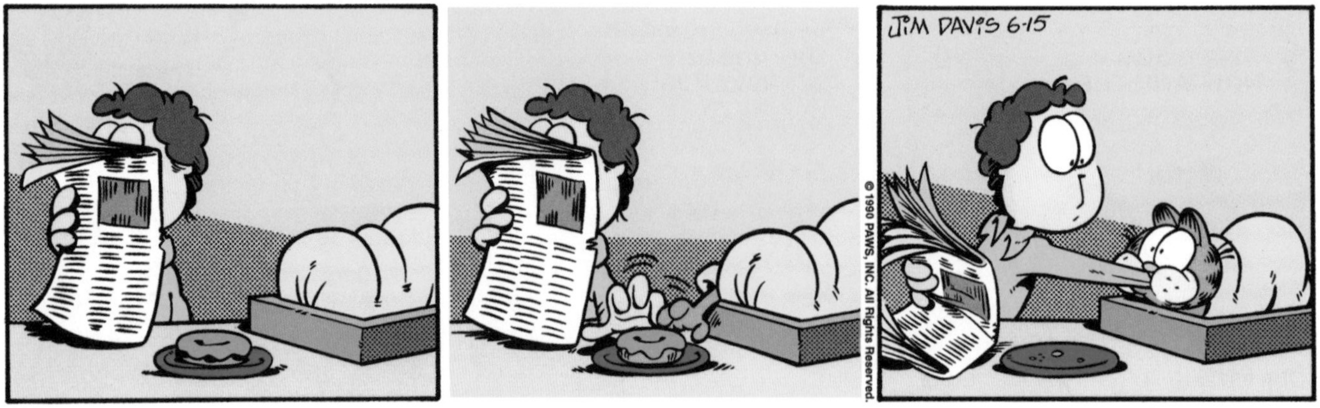
JIM DAVIS 6-15
© 1990 PAWS, INC. All Rights Reserved.

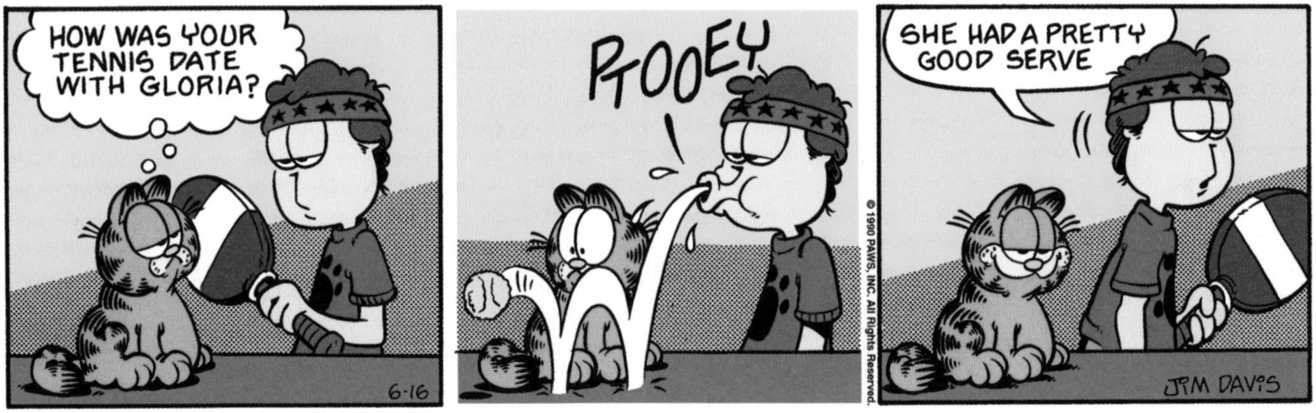
HOW WAS YOUR TENNIS DATE WITH GLORIA?
6-16
PTOOEY
© 1990 PAWS, INC. All Rights Reserved.
SHE HAD A PRETTY GOOD SERVE
JIM DAVIS

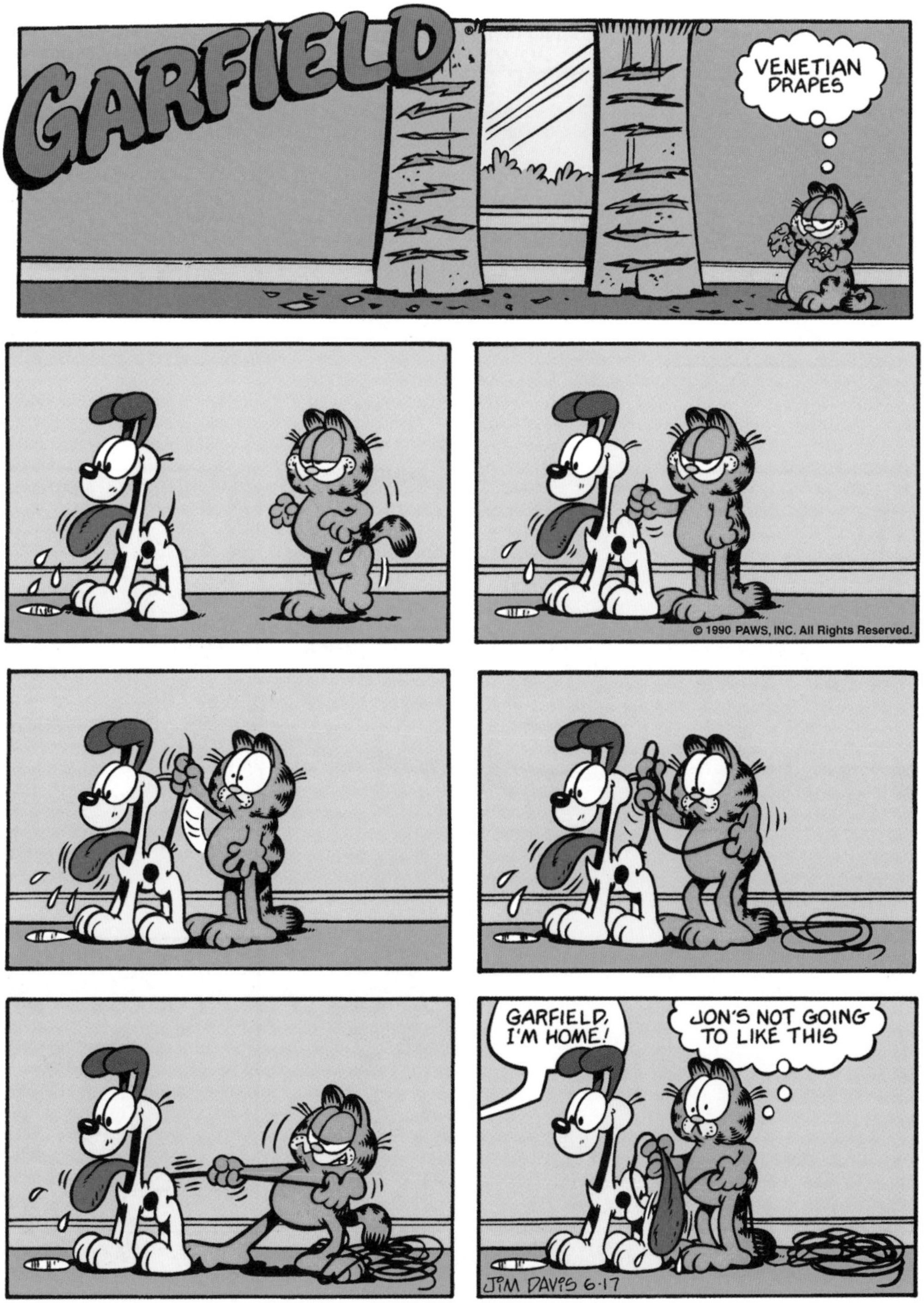
GARFIELD
VENETIAN DRAPES
© 1990 PAWS, INC. All Rights Reserved.
GARFIELD, I'M HOME!
JON'S NOT GOING TO LIKE THIS
JIM DAVIS 6-17

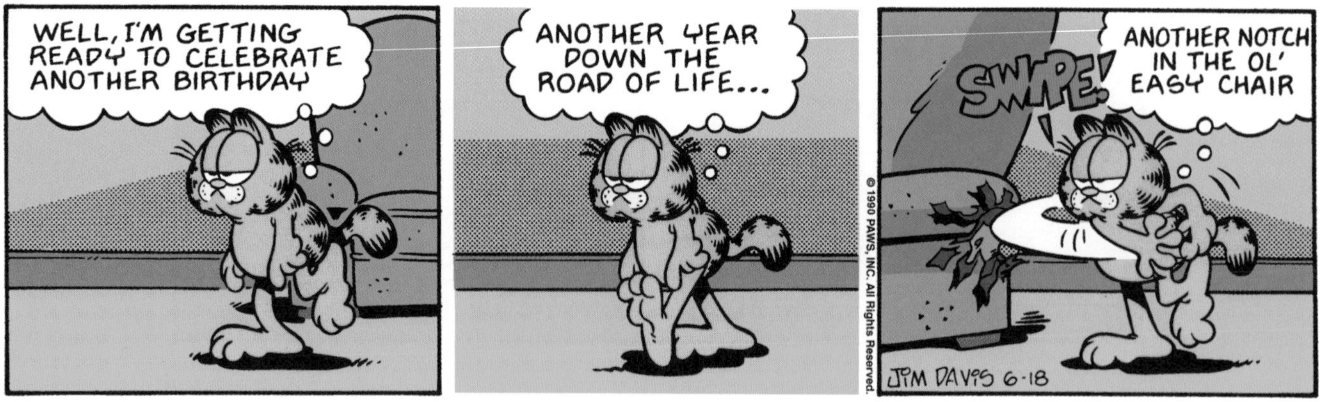
WELL, I'M GETTING READY TO CELEBRATE ANOTHER BIRTHDAY
ANOTHER YEAR DOWN THE ROAD OF LIFE...
SWIPE!
ANOTHER NOTCH IN THE OL' EASY CHAIR
© 1990 PAWS, INC. All Rights Reserved.
JIM DAVIS 6-18

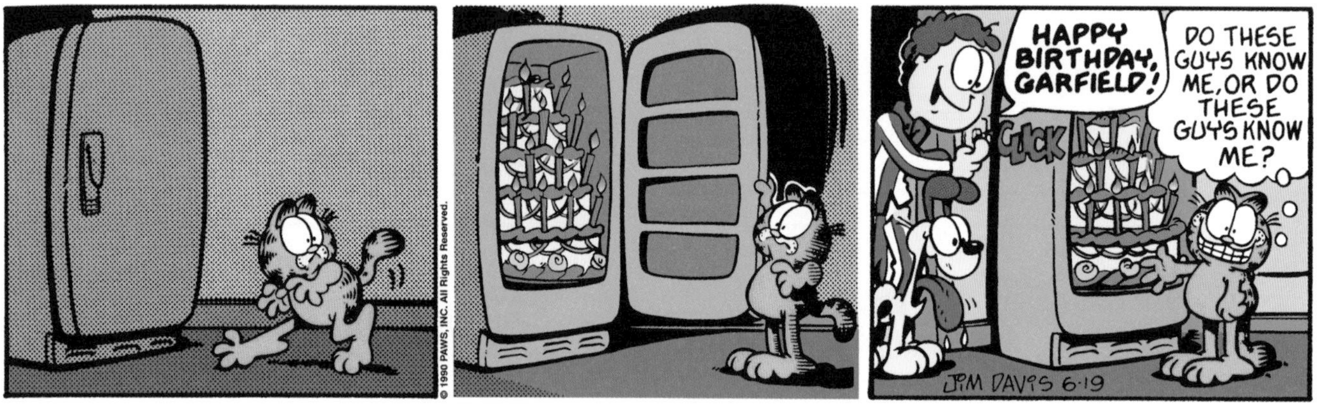
© 1990 PAWS, INC. All Rights Reserved.
HAPPY BIRTHDAY, GARFIELD!
GLICK
DO THESE GUYS KNOW ME, OR DO THESE GUYS KNOW ME?
JIM DAVIS 6-19

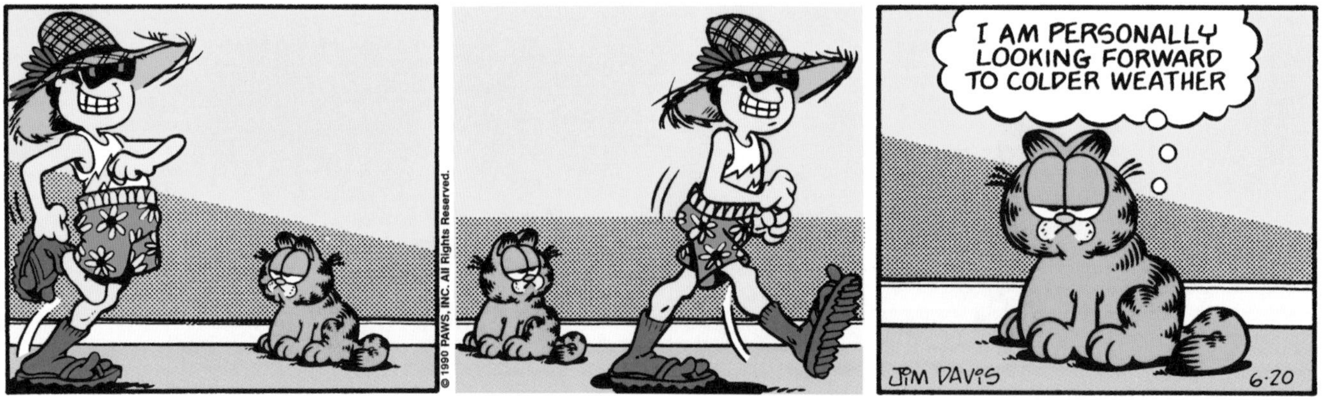
© 1990 PAWS, INC. All Rights Reserved.
I AM PERSONALLY LOOKING FORWARD TO COLDER WEATHER
JIM DAVIS
6-20

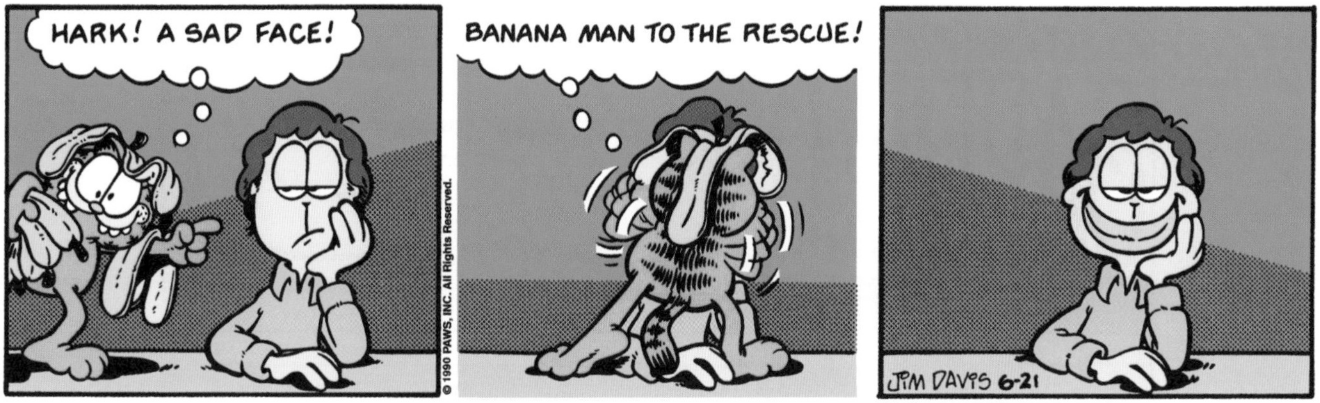
HARK! A SAD FACE!
© 1990 PAWS, INC. All Rights Reserved.
BANANA MAN TO THE RESCUE!
JIM DAVIS 6-21

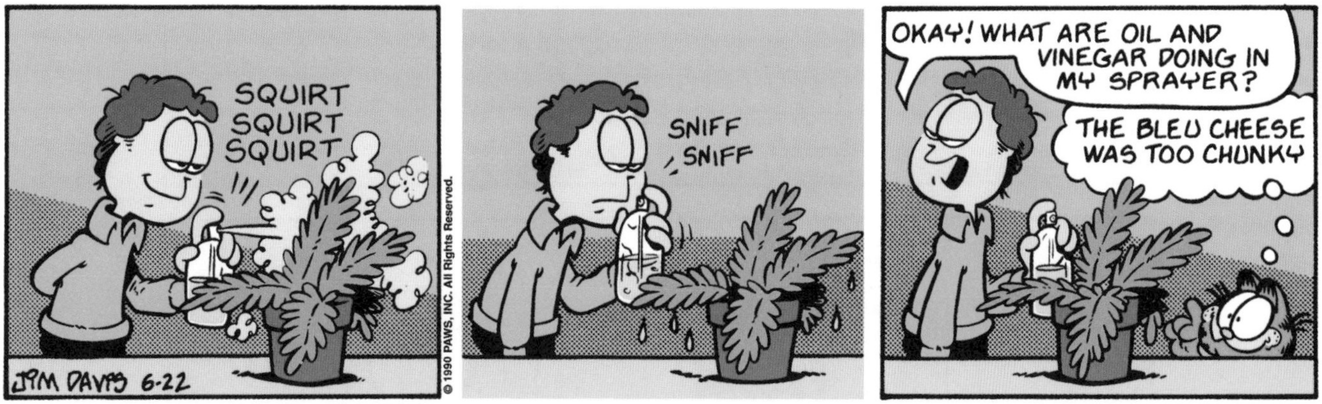
SQUIRT
SQUIRT
SQUIRT
JIM DAVIS 6-22
© 1990 PAWS, INC. All Rights Reserved.
SNIFF
SNIFF
OKAY! WHAT ARE OIL AND VINEGAR DOING IN MY SPRAYER?
THE BLEU CHEESE WAS TOO CHUNKY

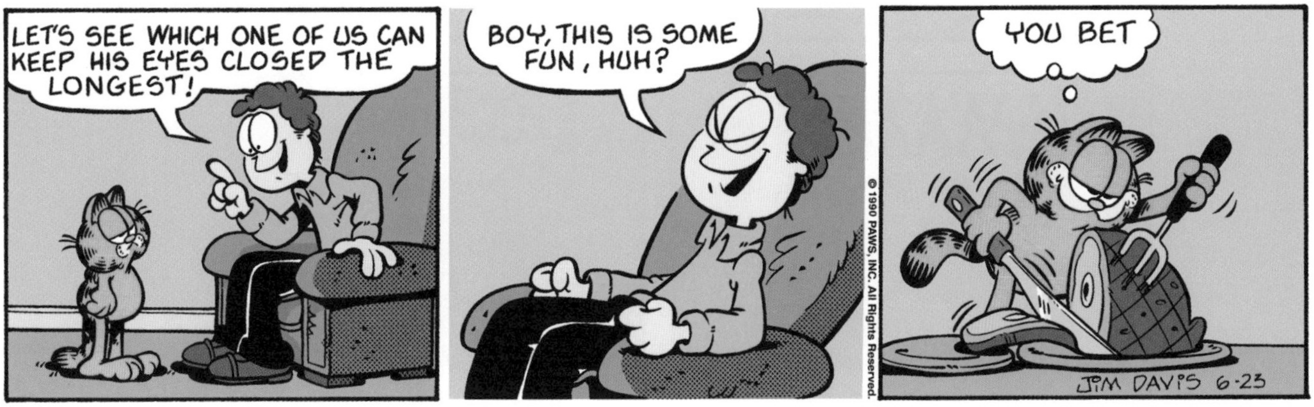
LET'S SEE WHICH ONE OF US CAN KEEP HIS EYES CLOSED THE LONGEST!
BOY, THIS IS SOME FUN, HUH?
© 1990 PAWS, INC. All Rights Reserved.
YOU BET
JIM DAVIS 6-23

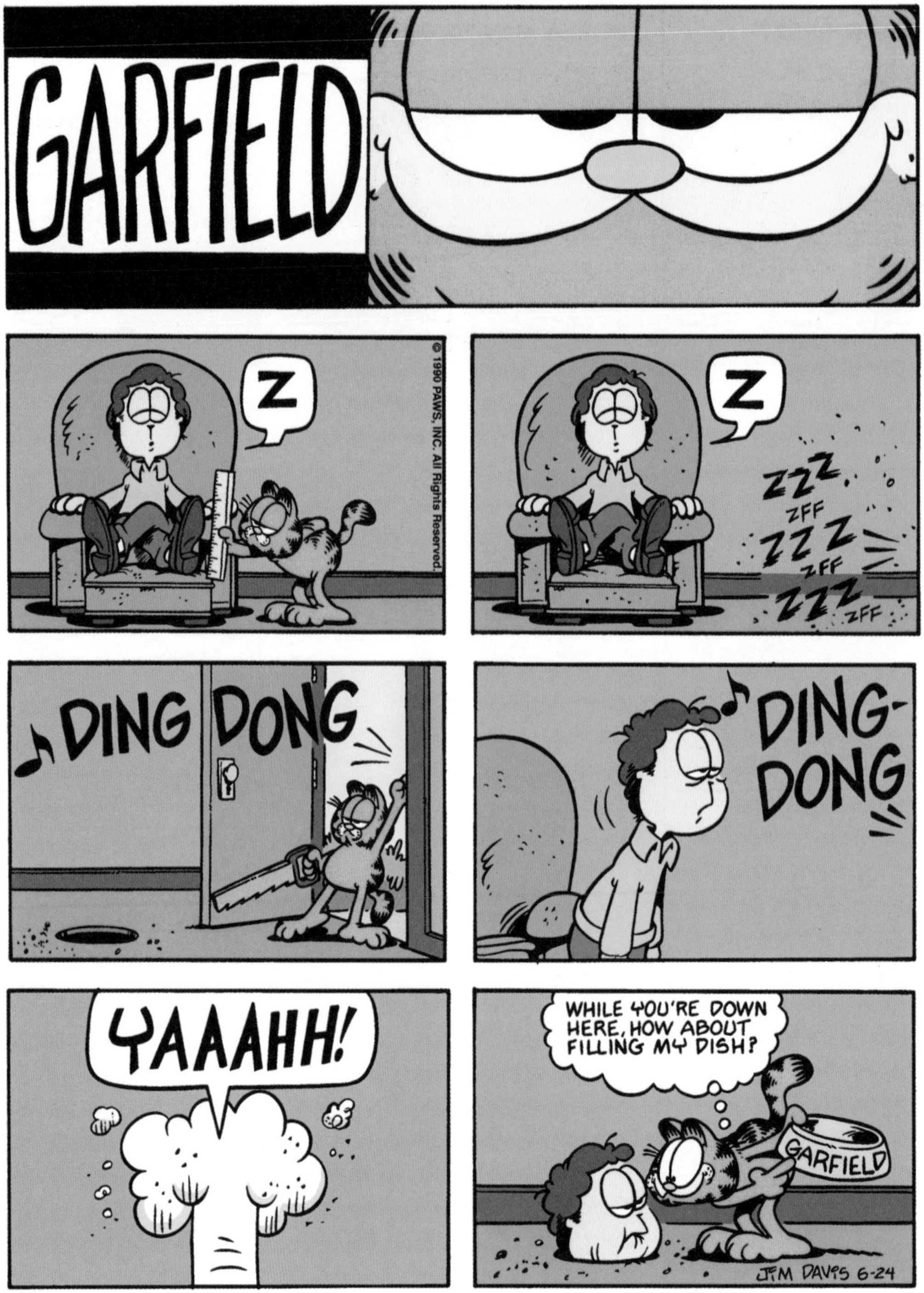
GARFIELD
© 1990 PAWS, INC. All Rights Reserved.
Z
Z
ZZZ ZFF ZZZ ZFF ZZZ ZFF
DING DONG
DING-DONG
YAAAHH!
WHILE YOU'RE DOWN HERE, HOW ABOUT FILLING MY DISH?
GARFIELD
JIM DAVIS 6-24

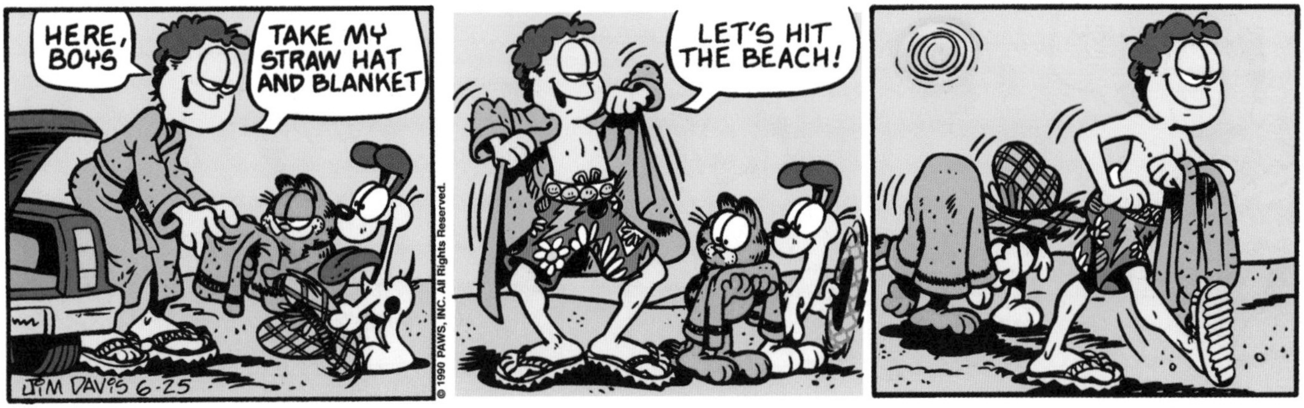
HERE, BOYS
TAKE MY STRAW HAT AND BLANKET
LET'S HIT THE BEACH!
JIM DAVIS 6-25
© 1990 PAWS, INC. All Rights Reserved.

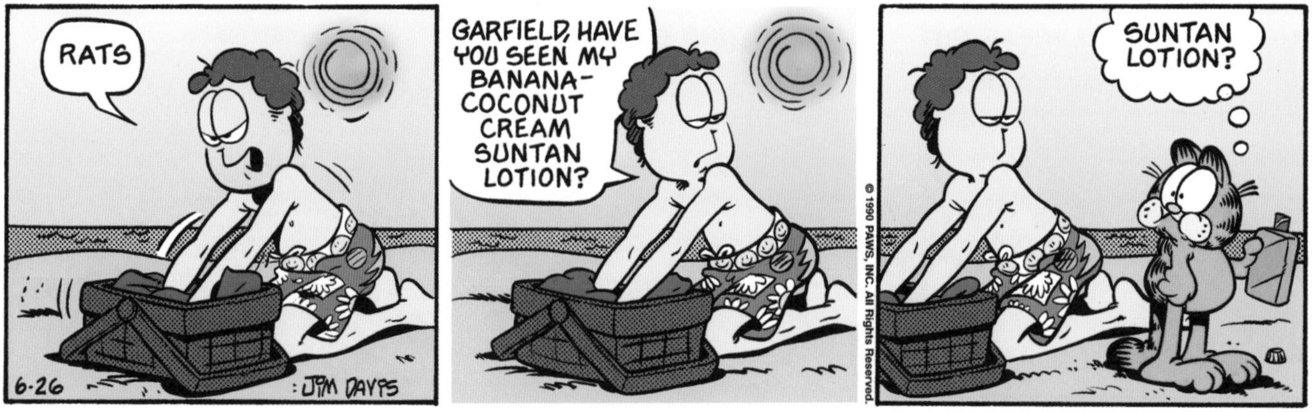
RATS
GARFIELD, HAVE YOU SEEN MY BANANA-COCONUT CREAM SUNTAN LOTION?
SUNTAN LOTION?
6-26
JIM DAVIS
© 1990 PAWS, INC. All Rights Reserved.

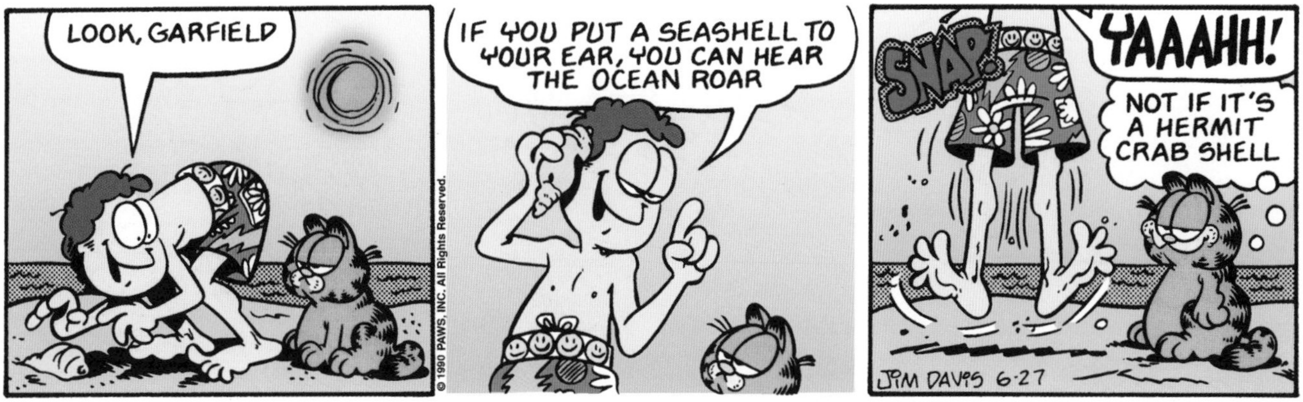
LOOK, GARFIELD
IF YOU PUT A SEASHELL TO YOUR EAR, YOU CAN HEAR THE OCEAN ROAR
SNAP!
YAAAHH!
NOT IF IT'S A HERMIT CRAB SHELL
JIM DAVIS 6-27
© 1990 PAWS, INC. All Rights Reserved.

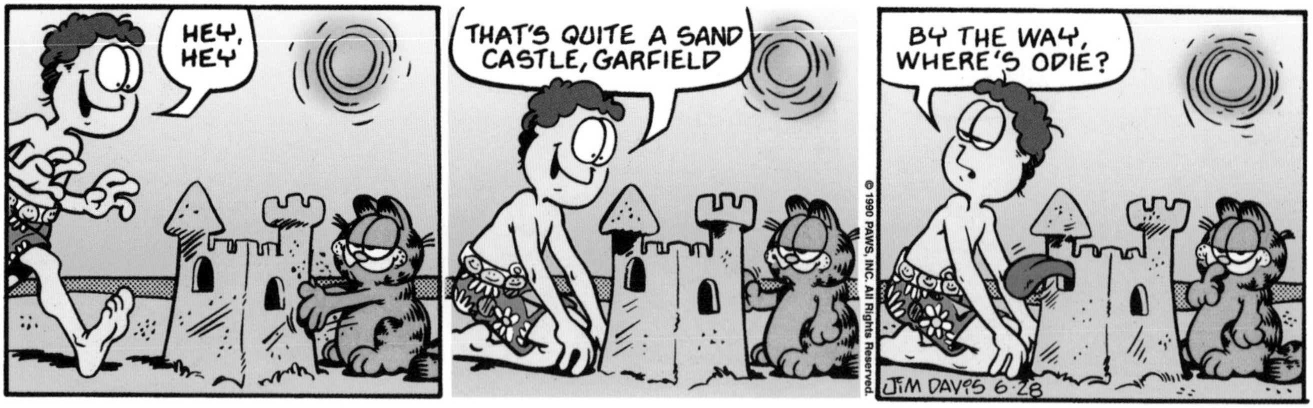
HEY, HEY
THAT'S QUITE A SAND CASTLE, GARFIELD
© 1990 PAWS, INC. All Rights Reserved.
BY THE WAY, WHERE'S ODIE?
JIM DAVIS 6-28

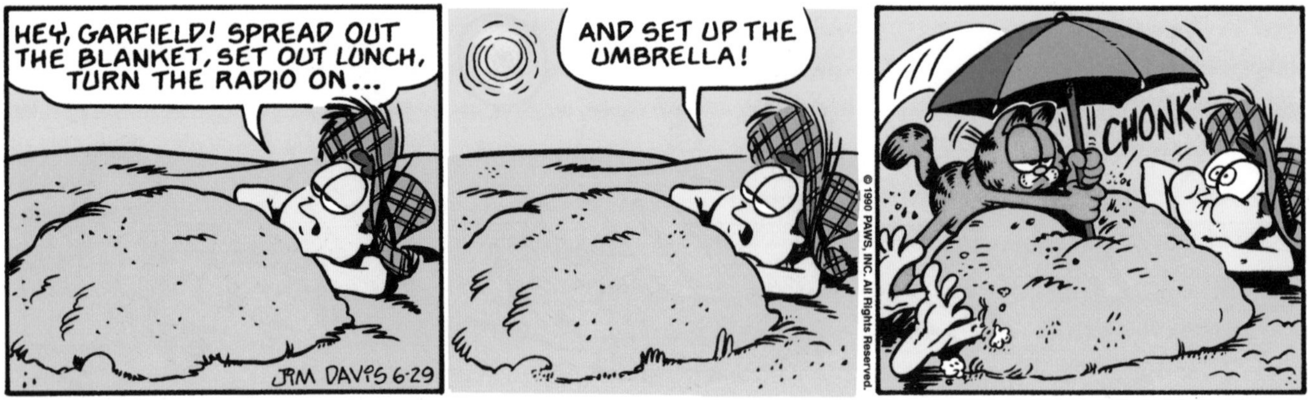
HEY, GARFIELD! SPREAD OUT THE BLANKET, SET OUT LUNCH, TURN THE RADIO ON...
JIM DAVIS 6-29
AND SET UP THE UMBRELLA!
© 1990 PAWS, INC. All Rights Reserved.
CHONK

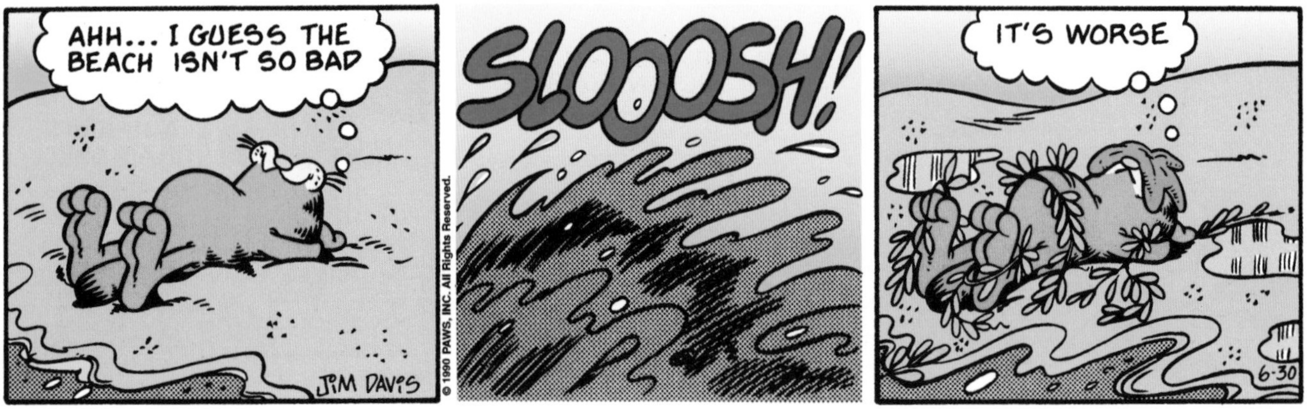
AHH... I GUESS THE BEACH ISN'T SO BAD
JIM DAVIS
© 1990 PAWS, INC. All Rights Reserved.
SLOOOSH!
IT'S WORSE
6-30

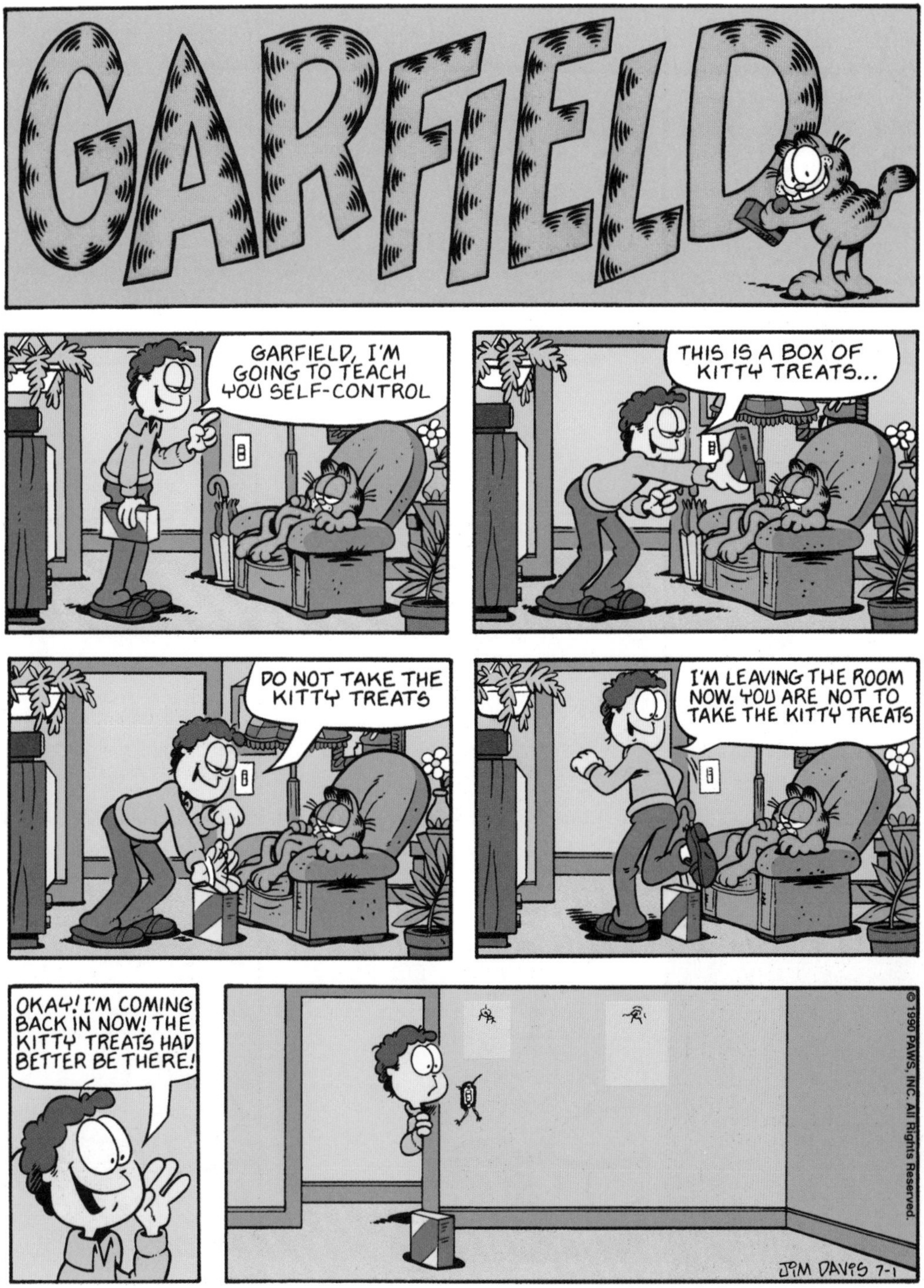
GARFIELD
GARFIELD, I'M GOING TO TEACH YOU SELF-CONTROL
THIS IS A BOX OF KITTY TREATS...
DO NOT TAKE THE KITTY TREATS
I'M LEAVING THE ROOM NOW. YOU ARE NOT TO TAKE THE KITTY TREATS
OKAY! I'M COMING BACK IN NOW! THE KITTY TREATS HAD BETTER BE THERE!
© 1990 PAWS, INC. All Rights Reserved.
JIM DAVIS 7-1

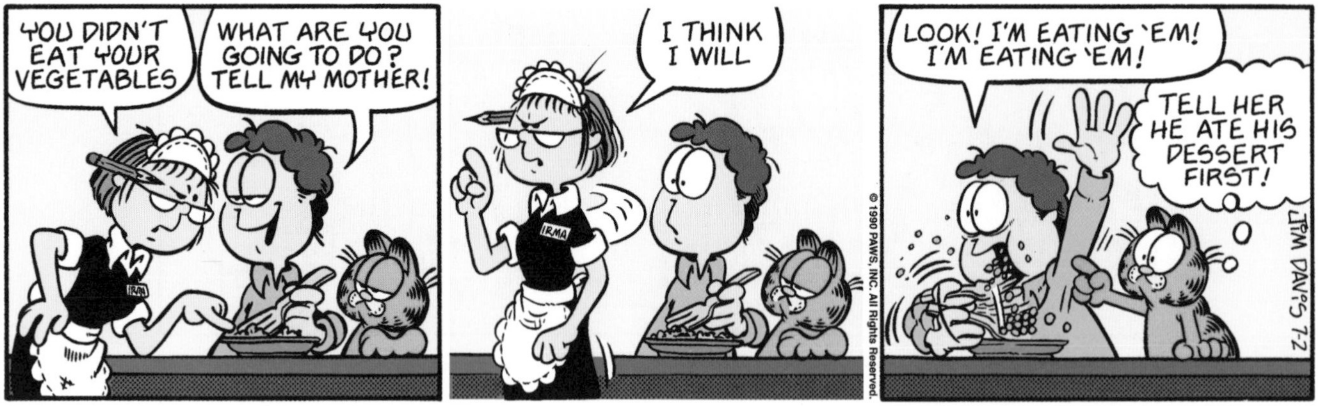
YOU DIDN'T EAT YOUR VEGETABLES
WHAT ARE YOU GOING TO DO? TELL MY MOTHER!
IRMA
I THINK I WILL
© 1990 PAWS, INC. All Rights Reserved.
LOOK! I'M EATING 'EM! I'M EATING 'EM!
TELL HER HE ATE HIS DESSERT FIRST!
JIM DAVIS 7-2

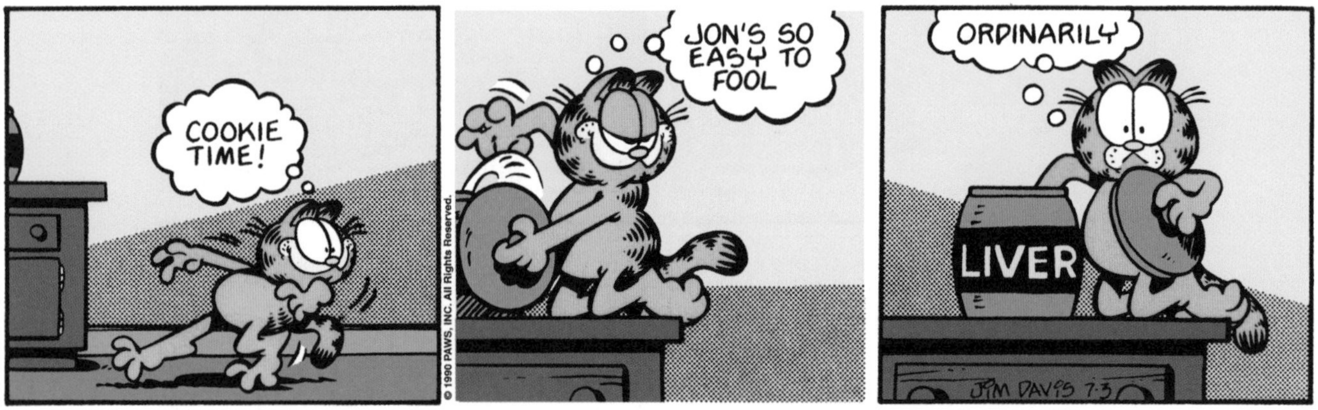
COOKIE TIME!
© 1990 PAWS, INC. All Rights Reserved.
JON'S SO EASY TO FOOL
ORDINARILY
LIVER
JIM DAVIS 7-3

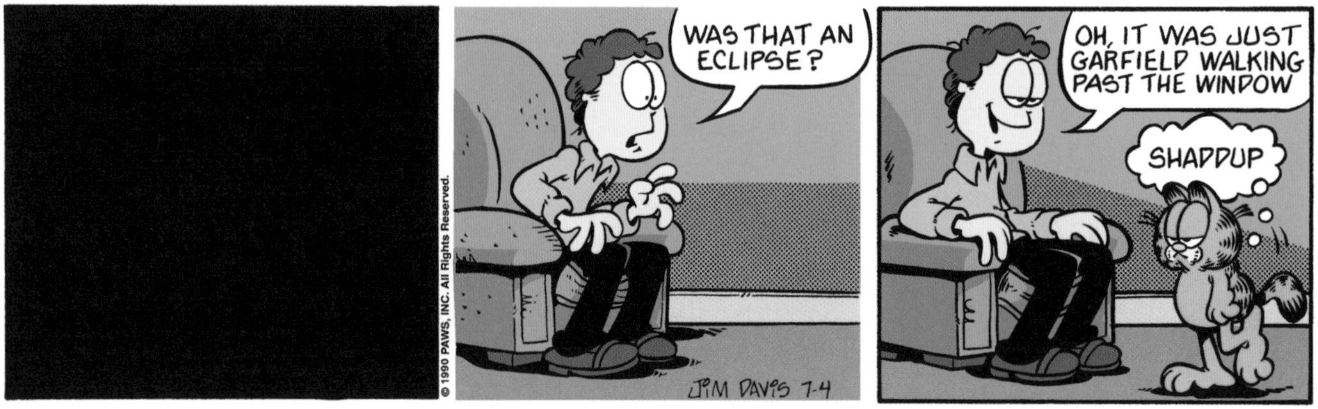
© 1990 PAWS, INC. All Rights Reserved.
WAS THAT AN ECLIPSE?
JIM DAVIS 7-4
OH, IT WAS JUST GARFIELD WALKING PAST THE WINDOW
SHADDUP

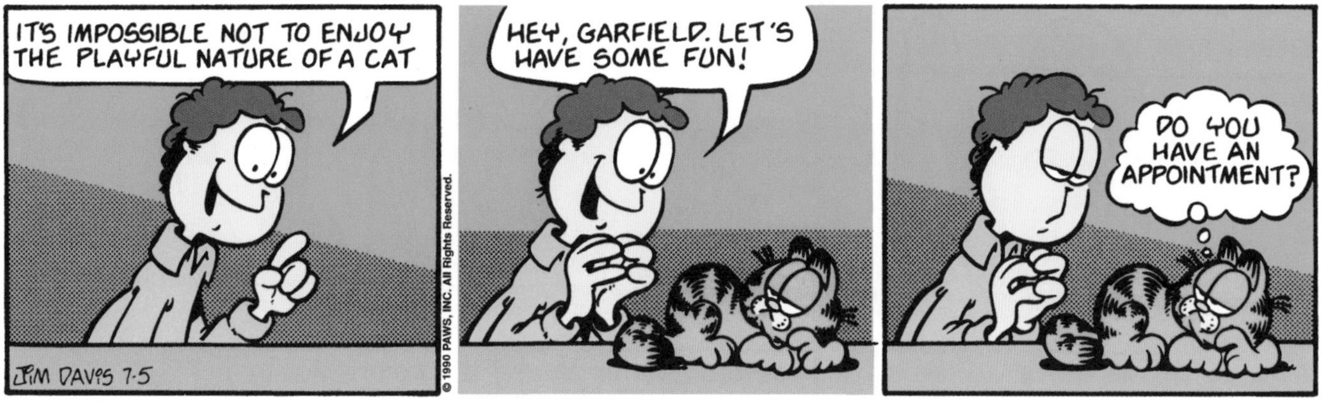
IT'S IMPOSSIBLE NOT TO ENJOY THE PLAYFUL NATURE OF A CAT
JIM DAVIS 7-5
© 1990 PAWS, INC. All Rights Reserved.
HEY, GARFIELD. LET'S HAVE SOME FUN!
DO YOU HAVE AN APPOINTMENT?

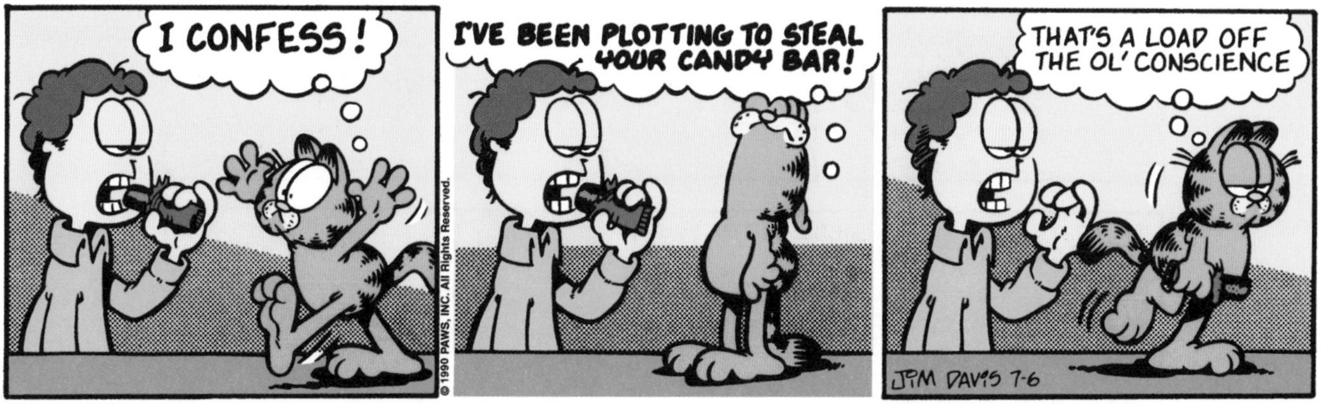
I CONFESS!
© 1990 PAWS, INC. All Rights Reserved.
I'VE BEEN PLOTTING TO STEAL YOUR CANDY BAR!
THAT'S A LOAD OFF THE OL' CONSCIENCE
JIM DAVIS 7-6

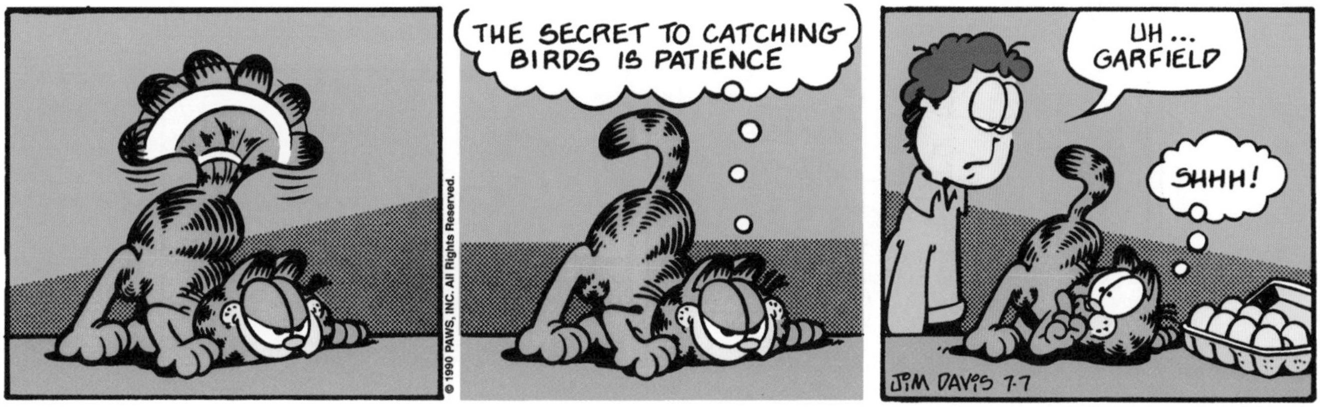
© 1990 PAWS, INC. All Rights Reserved.
THE SECRET TO CATCHING BIRDS IS PATIENCE
UH... GARFIELD
SHHH!
JIM DAVIS 7-7

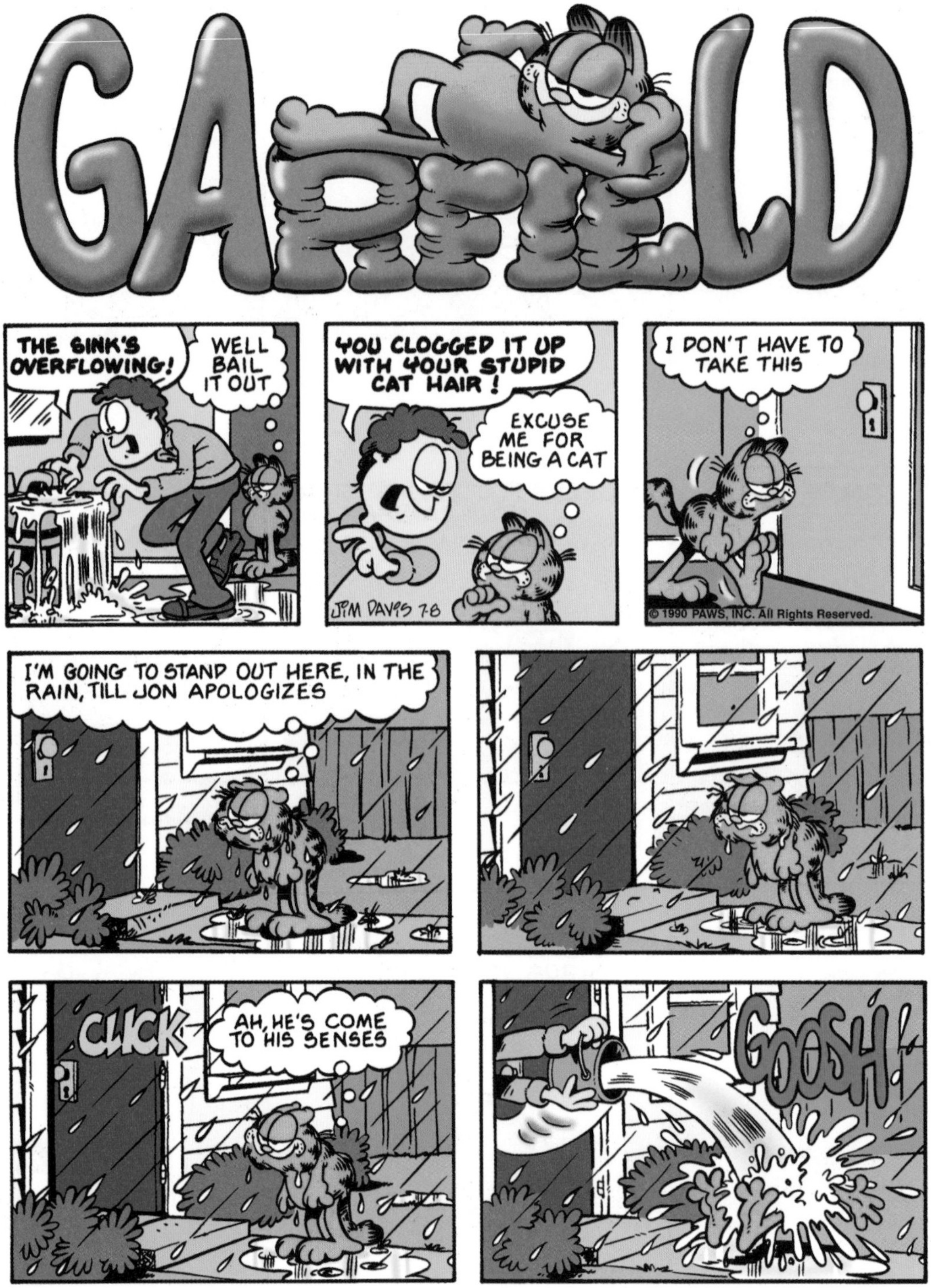
GARFIELD
THE SINK'S OVERFLOWING!
WELL BAIL IT OUT
YOU CLOGGED IT UP WITH YOUR STUPID CAT HAIR!
EXCUSE ME FOR BEING A CAT
JPM DAVPS 7-8
I DON'T HAVE TO TAKE THIS
© 1990 PAWS, INC. All Rights Reserved.
I'M GOING TO STAND OUT HERE, IN THE RAIN, TILL JON APOLOGIZES
CLICK
AH, HE'S COME TO HIS SENSES
GOOSH!

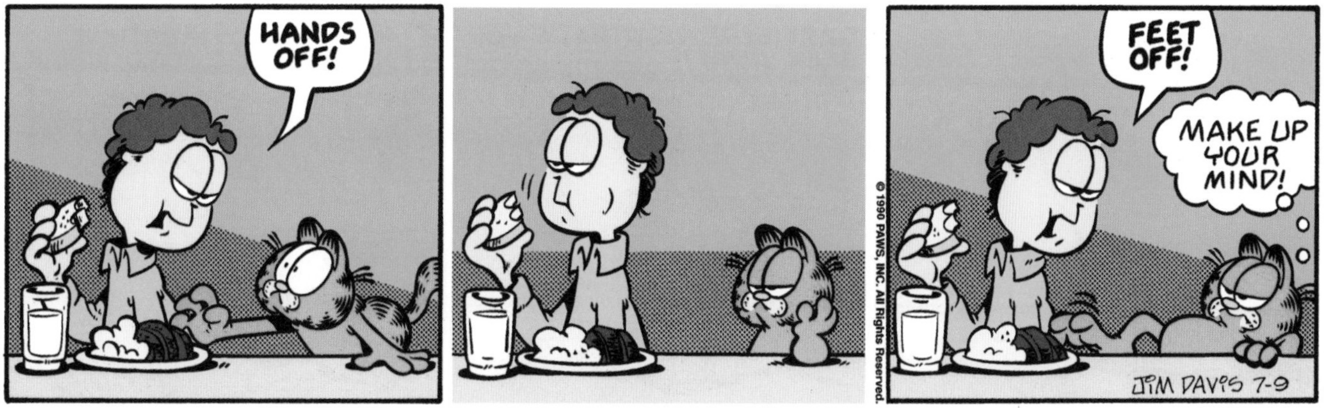
HANDS OFF!
FEET OFF!
MAKE UP YOUR MIND!
© 1990 PAWS, INC. All Rights Reserved.
JIM DAVIS 7-9

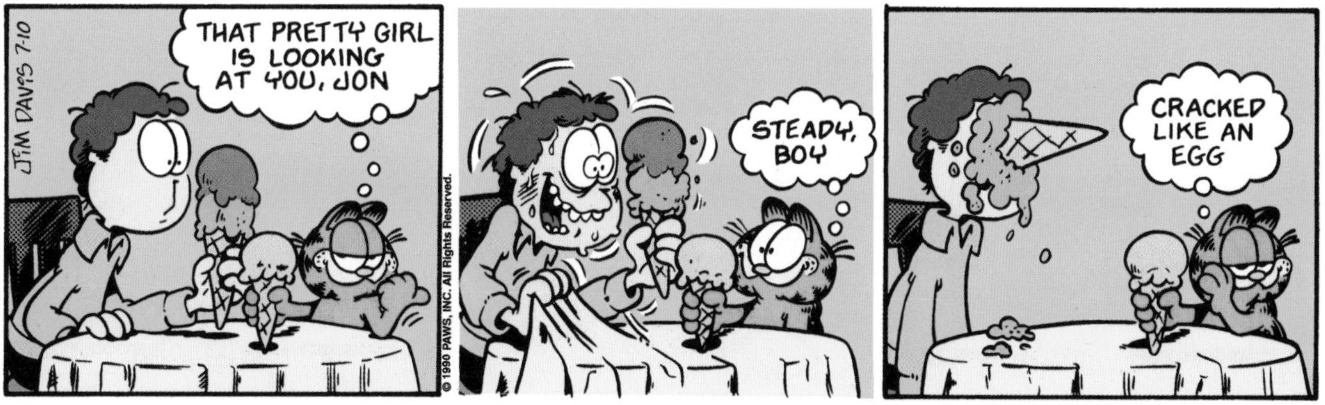
JIM DAVIS 7-10
THAT PRETTY GIRL IS LOOKING AT YOU, JON
© 1990 PAWS, INC. All Rights Reserved.
STEADY, BOY
CRACKED LIKE AN EGG

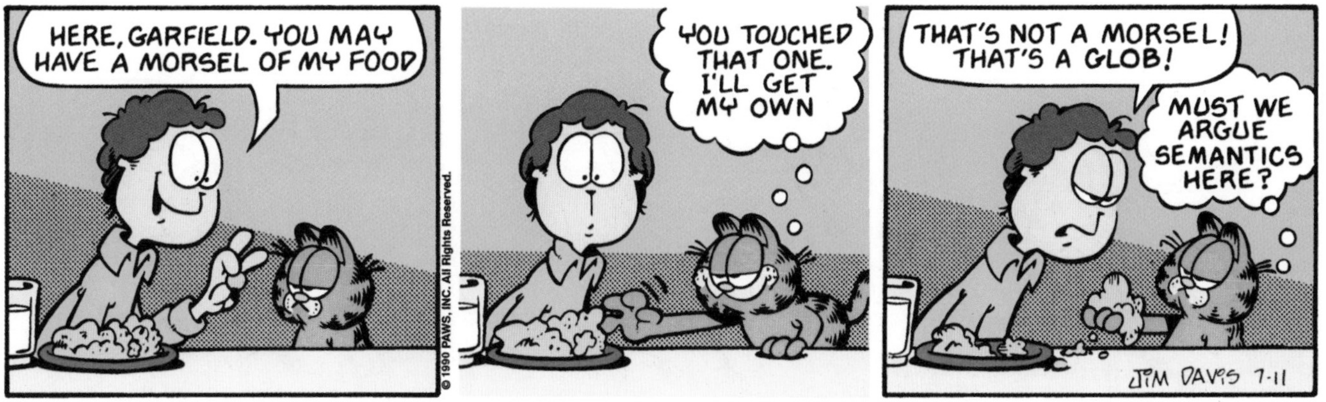
HERE, GARFIELD. YOU MAY HAVE A MORSEL OF MY FOOD
© 1990 PAWS, INC. All Rights Reserved.
YOU TOUCHED THAT ONE. I'LL GET MY OWN
THAT'S NOT A MORSEL! THAT'S A GLOB!
MUST WE ARGUE SEMANTICS HERE?
JIM DAVIS 7-11

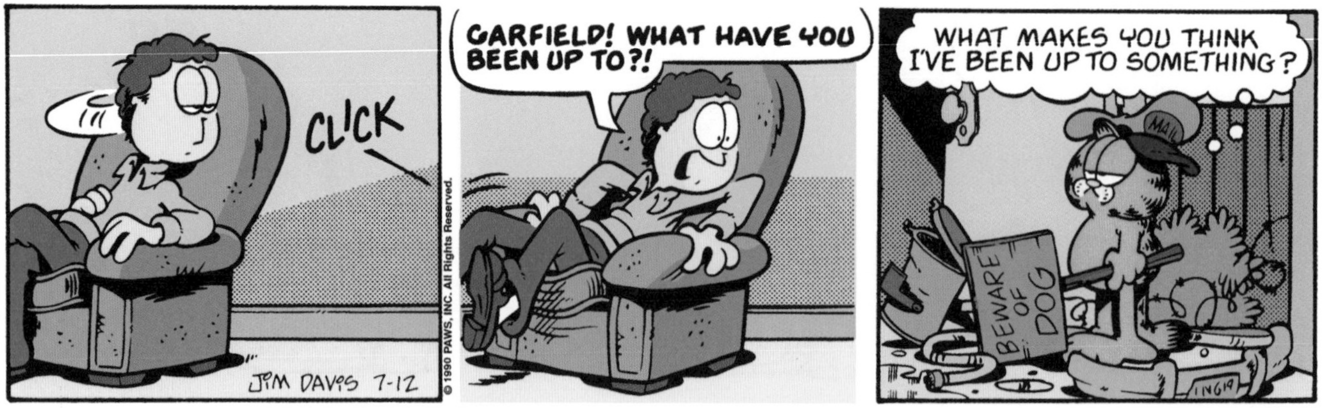
CLICK
JIM DAVIS 7-12
© 1990 PAWS, INC. All Rights Reserved.
GARFIELD! WHAT HAVE YOU BEEN UP TO?!
WHAT MAKES YOU THINK I'VE BEEN UP TO SOMETHING?
MAIL
BEWARE OF DOG

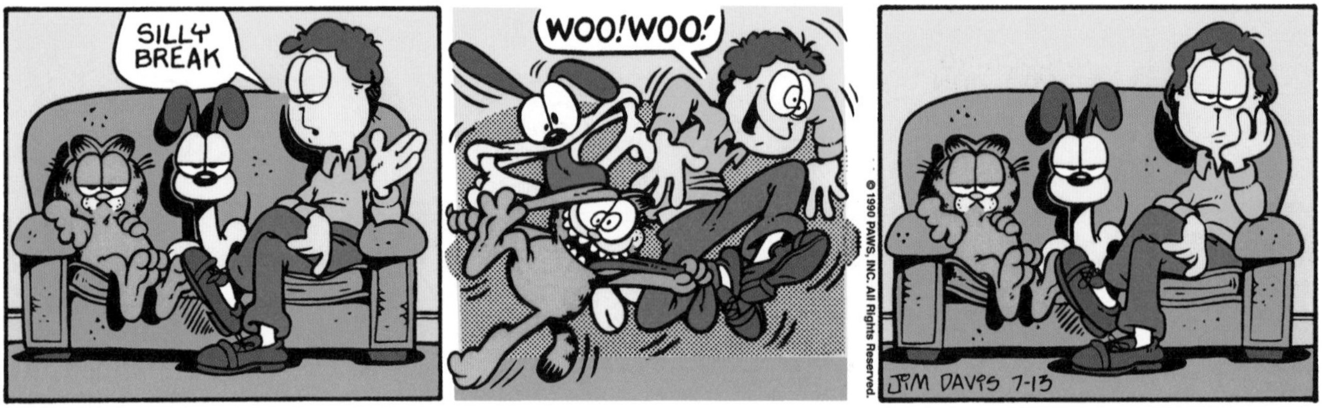
SILLY BREAK
WOO! WOO!
© 1990 PAWS, INC. All Rights Reserved.
JIM DAVIS 7-13

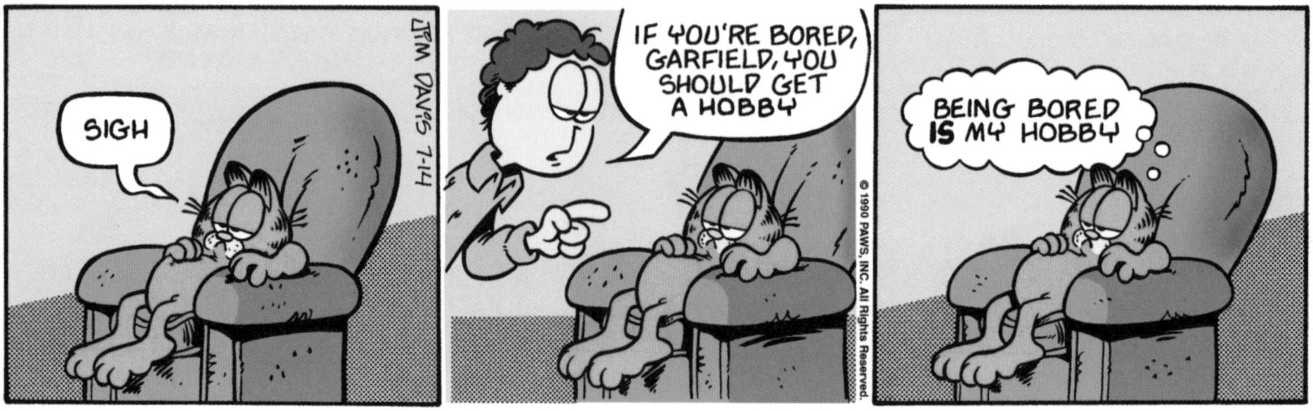
JIM DAVIS 7-14
SIGH
IF YOU'RE BORED, GARFIELD, YOU SHOULD GET A HOBBY
© 1990 PAWS, INC. All Rights Reserved.
BEING BORED **IS** MY HOBBY

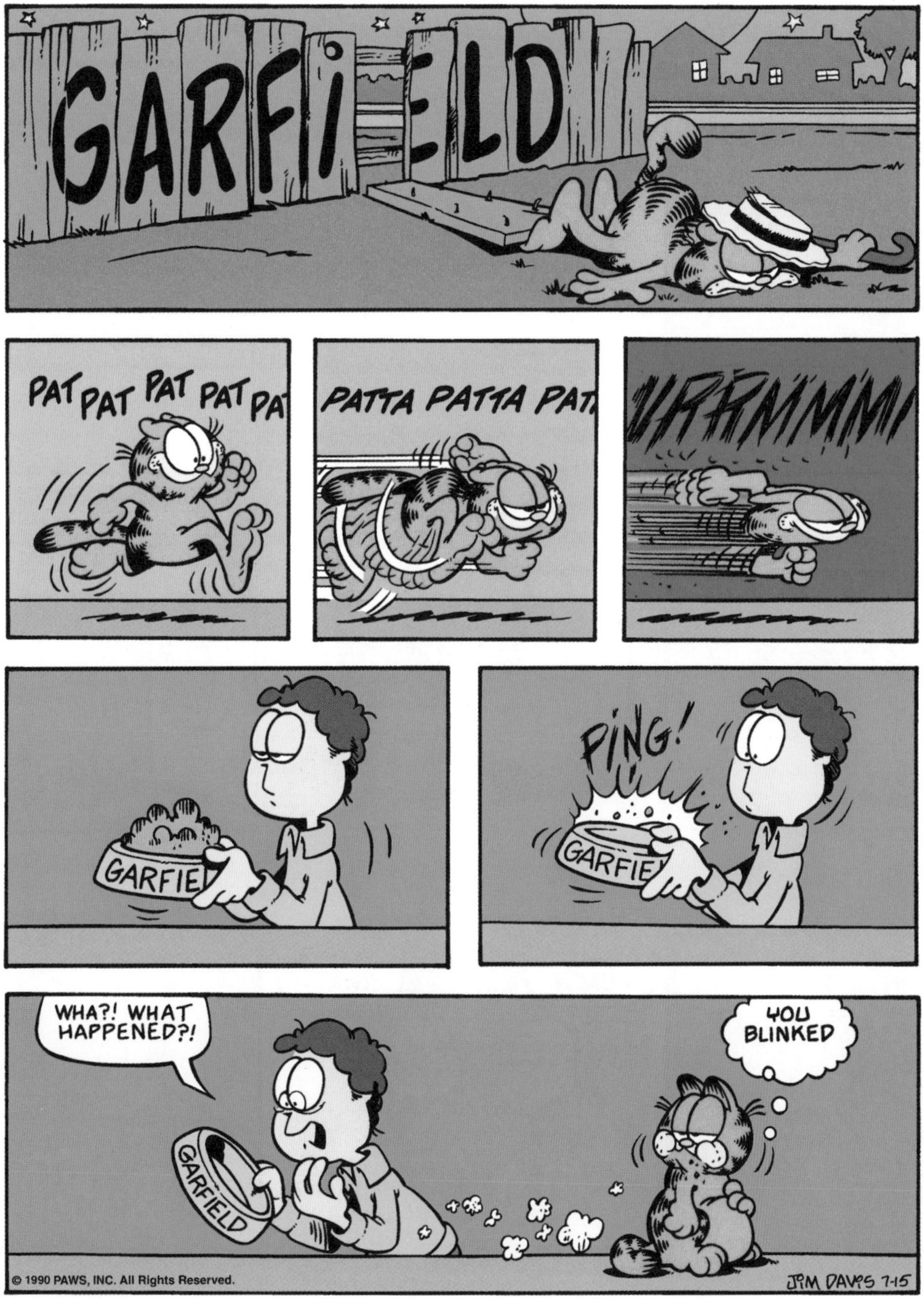
GARFIELD
PAT PAT PAT PAT PA
PATTA PATTA PAT
URRMMMM
GARFIE
PING!
GARFIE
WHA?! WHAT HAPPENED?!
YOU BLINKED
GARFIELD
© 1990 PAWS, INC. All Rights Reserved.
JIM DAVIS 7-15

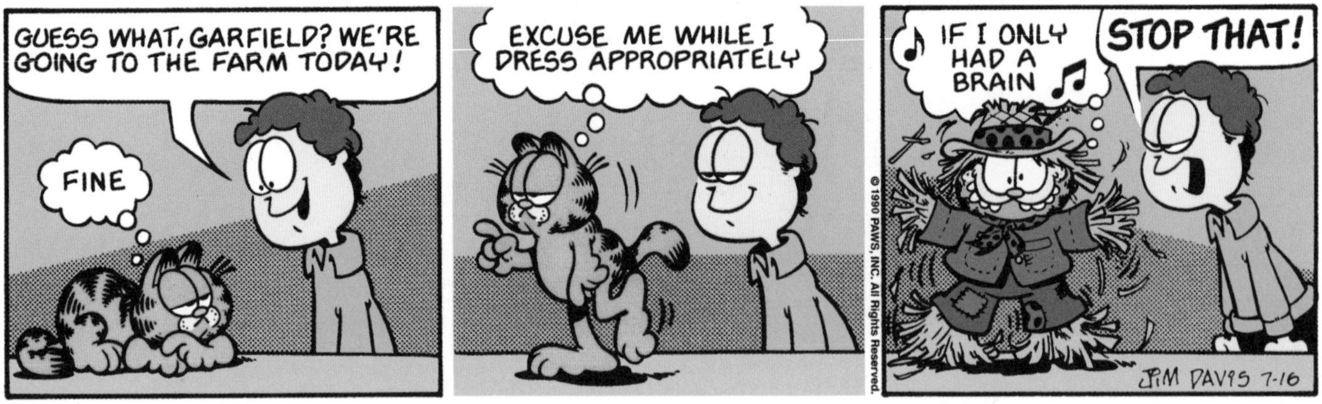
GUESS WHAT, GARFIELD? WE'RE GOING TO THE FARM TODAY!
FINE
EXCUSE ME WHILE I DRESS APPROPRIATELY
♪ IF I ONLY HAD A BRAIN ♫
STOP THAT!
© 1990 PAWS, INC. All Rights Reserved.
JIM DAVIS 7-16

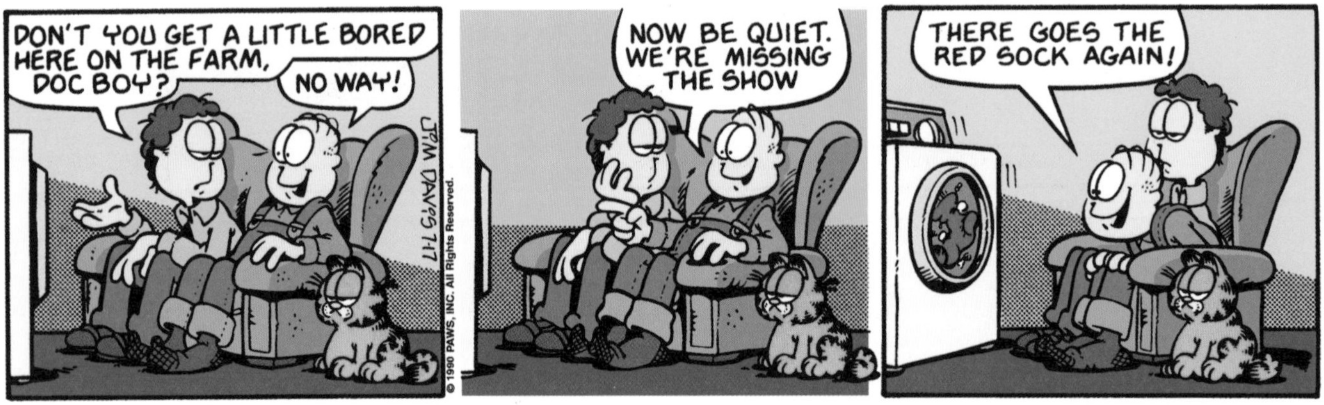
DON'T YOU GET A LITTLE BORED HERE ON THE FARM, DOC BOY?
NO WAY!
JIM DAVIS 7-17
© 1990 PAWS, INC. All Rights Reserved.
NOW BE QUIET. WE'RE MISSING THE SHOW
THERE GOES THE RED SOCK AGAIN!

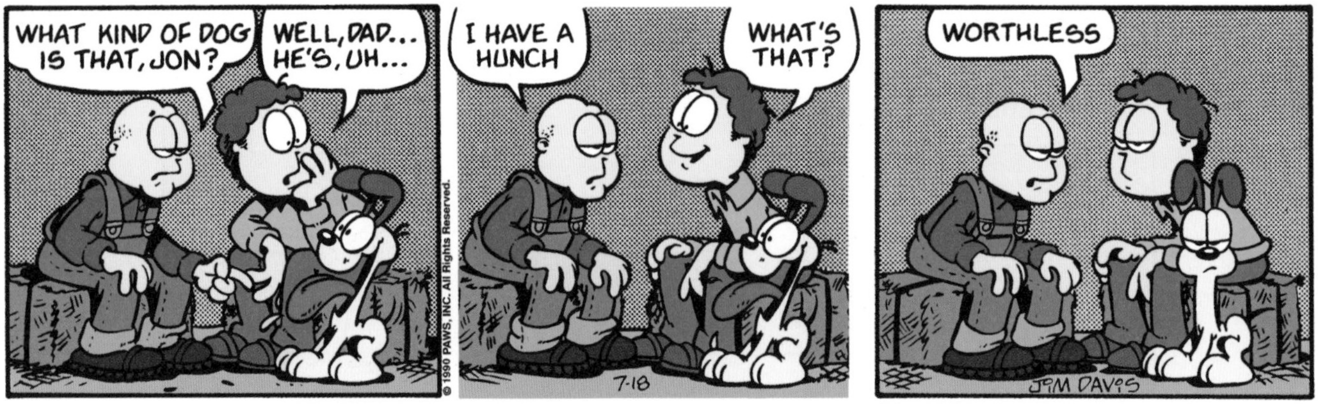
WHAT KIND OF DOG IS THAT, JON?
WELL, DAD... HE'S, UH...
© 1990 PAWS, INC. All Rights Reserved.
I HAVE A HUNCH
WHAT'S THAT?
7-18
WORTHLESS
JIM DAVIS

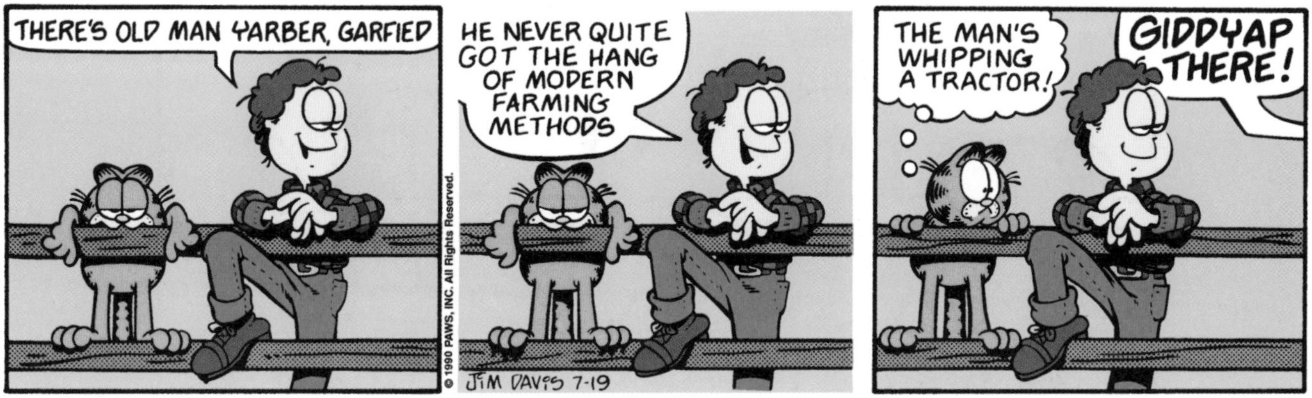
THERE'S OLD MAN YARBER, GARFIED
HE NEVER QUITE GOT THE HANG OF MODERN FARMING METHODS
© 1990 PAWS, INC. All Rights Reserved.
JIM DAVIS 7-19
THE MAN'S WHIPPING A TRACTOR!
GIDDYAP THERE!

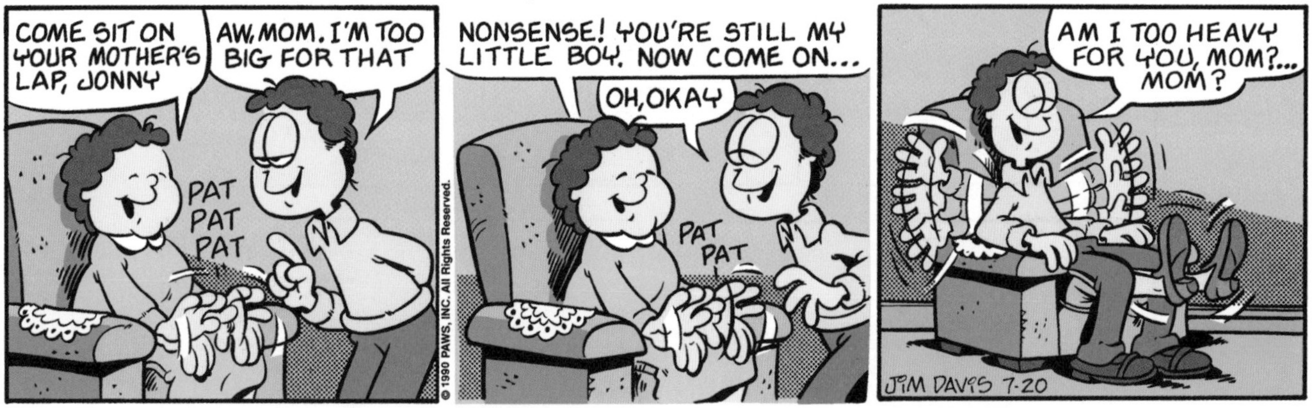
COME SIT ON YOUR MOTHER'S LAP, JONNY
AW, MOM. I'M TOO BIG FOR THAT
PAT PAT PAT
© 1990 PAWS, INC. All Rights Reserved.
NONSENSE! YOU'RE STILL MY LITTLE BOY. NOW COME ON...
OH, OKAY
PAT PAT
AM I TOO HEAVY FOR YOU, MOM?... MOM?
JIM DAVIS 7-20

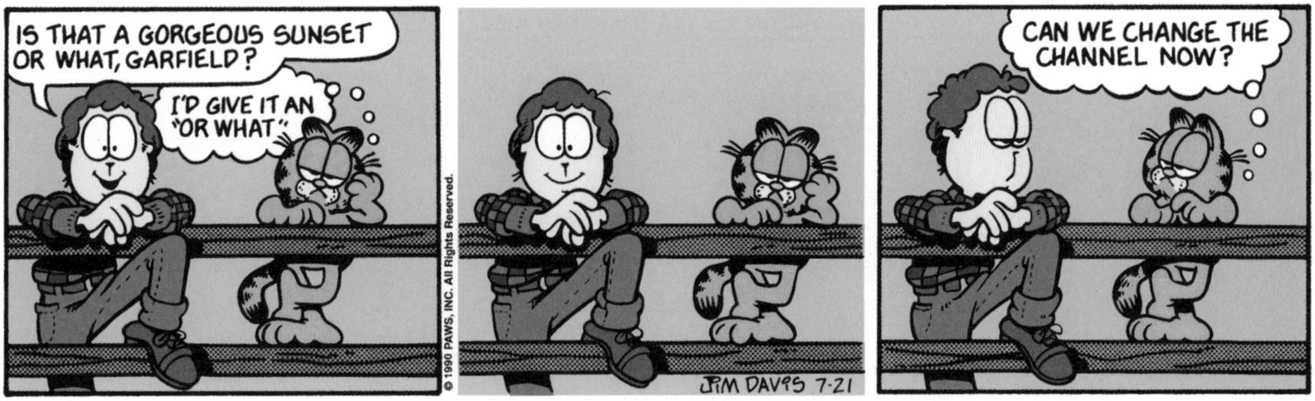
IS THAT A GORGEOUS SUNSET OR WHAT, GARFIELD?
I'D GIVE IT AN "OR WHAT"
© 1990 PAWS, INC. All Rights Reserved.
JIM DAVIS 7-21
CAN WE CHANGE THE CHANNEL NOW?

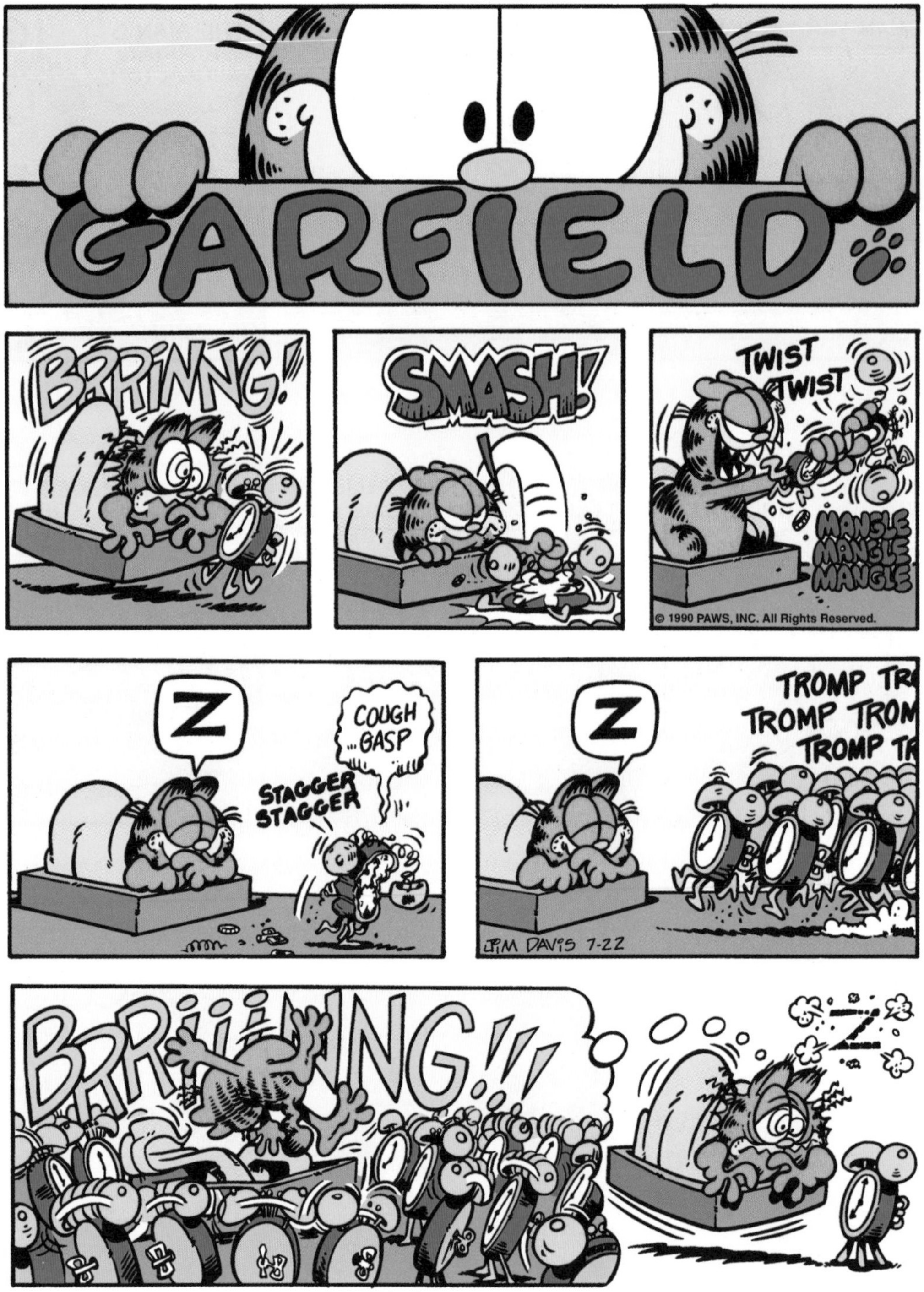
GARFIELD
BRRINNG!
SMASH!
TWIST TWIST
MANGLE MANGLE MANGLE
© 1990 PAWS, INC. All Rights Reserved.
Z
COUGH ...GASP
STAGGER STAGGER
Z
TROMP TR
TROMP TROM
TROMP TR
JIM DAVIS 7-22
BRRiiiiNNG!!!
Z

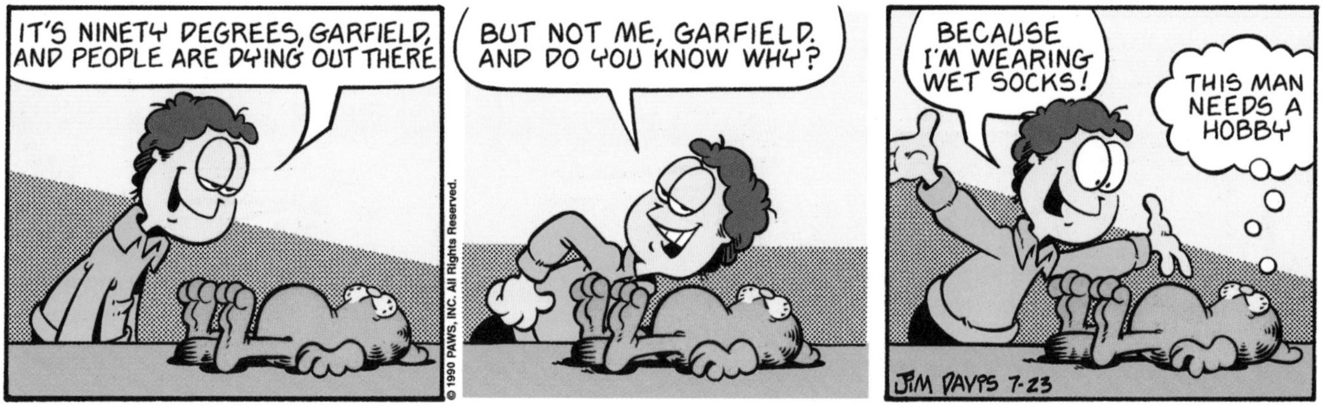
IT'S NINETY DEGREES, GARFIELD, AND PEOPLE ARE DYING OUT THERE
© 1990 PAWS, INC. All Rights Reserved.
BUT NOT ME, GARFIELD. AND DO YOU KNOW WHY?
BECAUSE I'M WEARING WET SOCKS!
THIS MAN NEEDS A HOBBY
JIM DAVIS 7-23

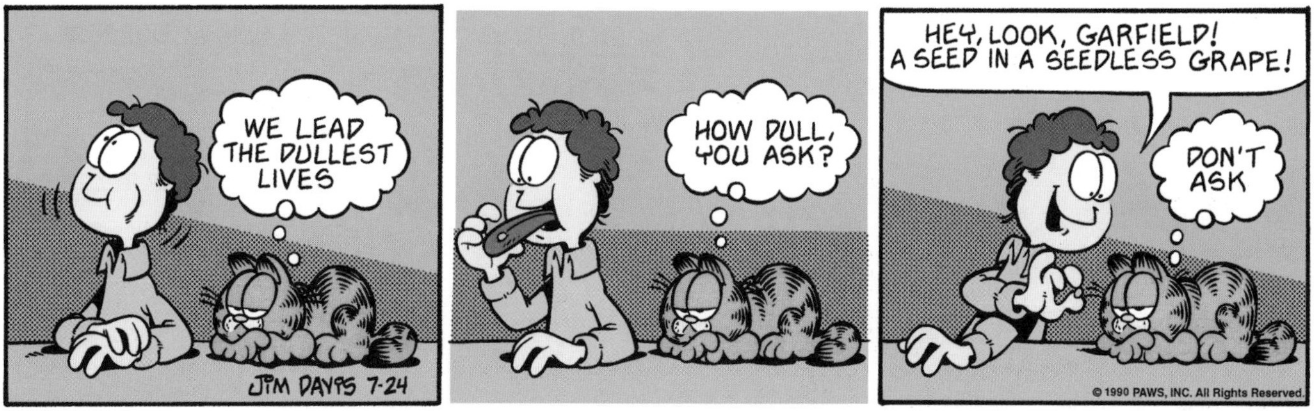
WE LEAD THE DULLEST LIVES
JIM DAVIS 7-24
HOW DULL, YOU ASK?
HEY, LOOK, GARFIELD! A SEED IN A SEEDLESS GRAPE!
DON'T ASK
© 1990 PAWS, INC. All Rights Reserved.

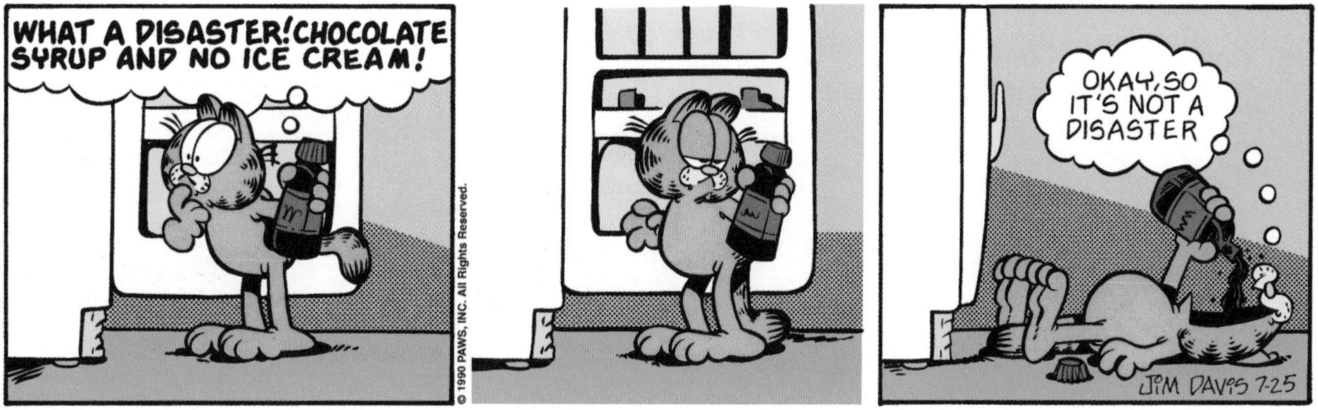
WHAT A DISASTER! CHOCOLATE SYRUP AND NO ICE CREAM!
© 1990 PAWS, INC. All Rights Reserved.
OKAY, SO IT'S NOT A DISASTER
JIM DAVIS 7-25

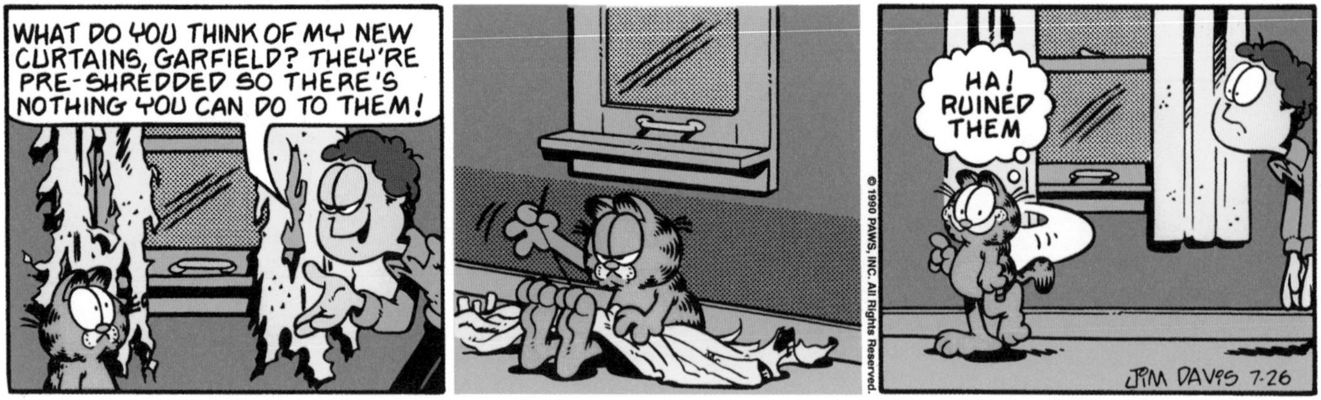
WHAT DO YOU THINK OF MY NEW CURTAINS, GARFIELD? THEY'RE PRE-SHREDDED SO THERE'S NOTHING YOU CAN DO TO THEM!
© 1990 PAWS, INC. All Rights Reserved.
HA! RUINED THEM
JIM DAVIS 7-26

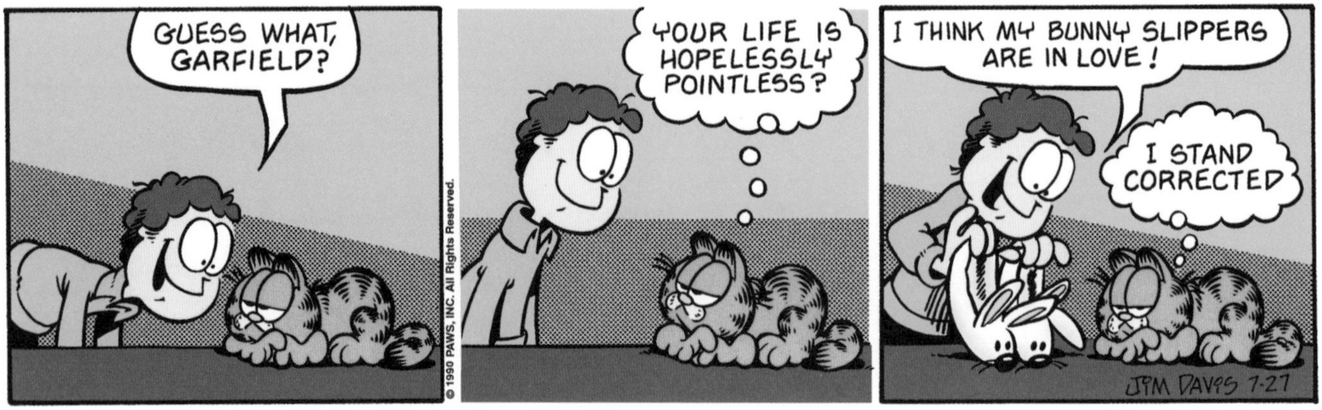
GUESS WHAT, GARFIELD?
© 1990 PAWS, INC. All Rights Reserved.
YOUR LIFE IS HOPELESSLY POINTLESS?
I THINK MY BUNNY SLIPPERS ARE IN LOVE!
I STAND CORRECTED
JIM DAVIS 7-27

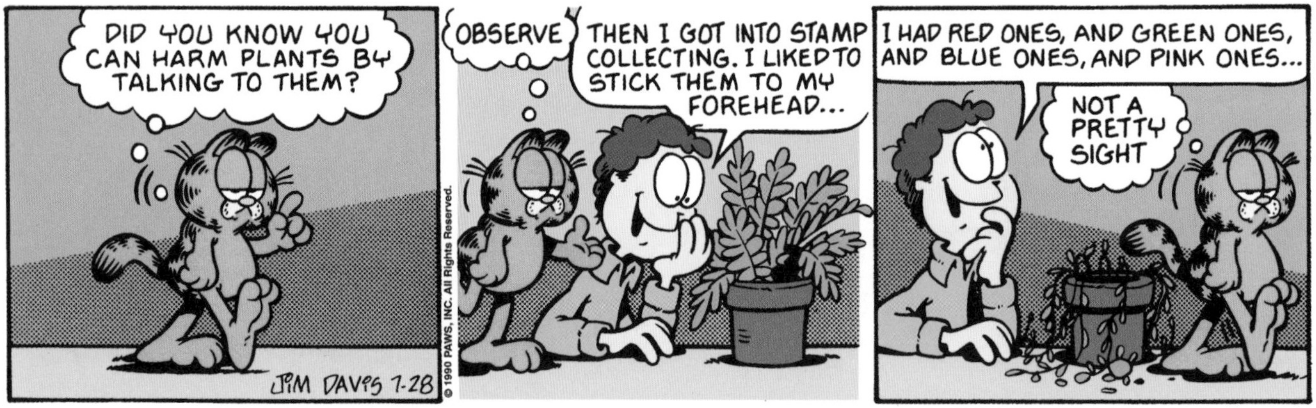
DID YOU KNOW YOU CAN HARM PLANTS BY TALKING TO THEM?
JIM DAVIS 7-28
© 1990 PAWS, INC. All Rights Reserved.
OBSERVE
THEN I GOT INTO STAMP COLLECTING. I LIKED TO STICK THEM TO MY FOREHEAD...
I HAD RED ONES, AND GREEN ONES, AND BLUE ONES, AND PINK ONES...
NOT A PRETTY SIGHT

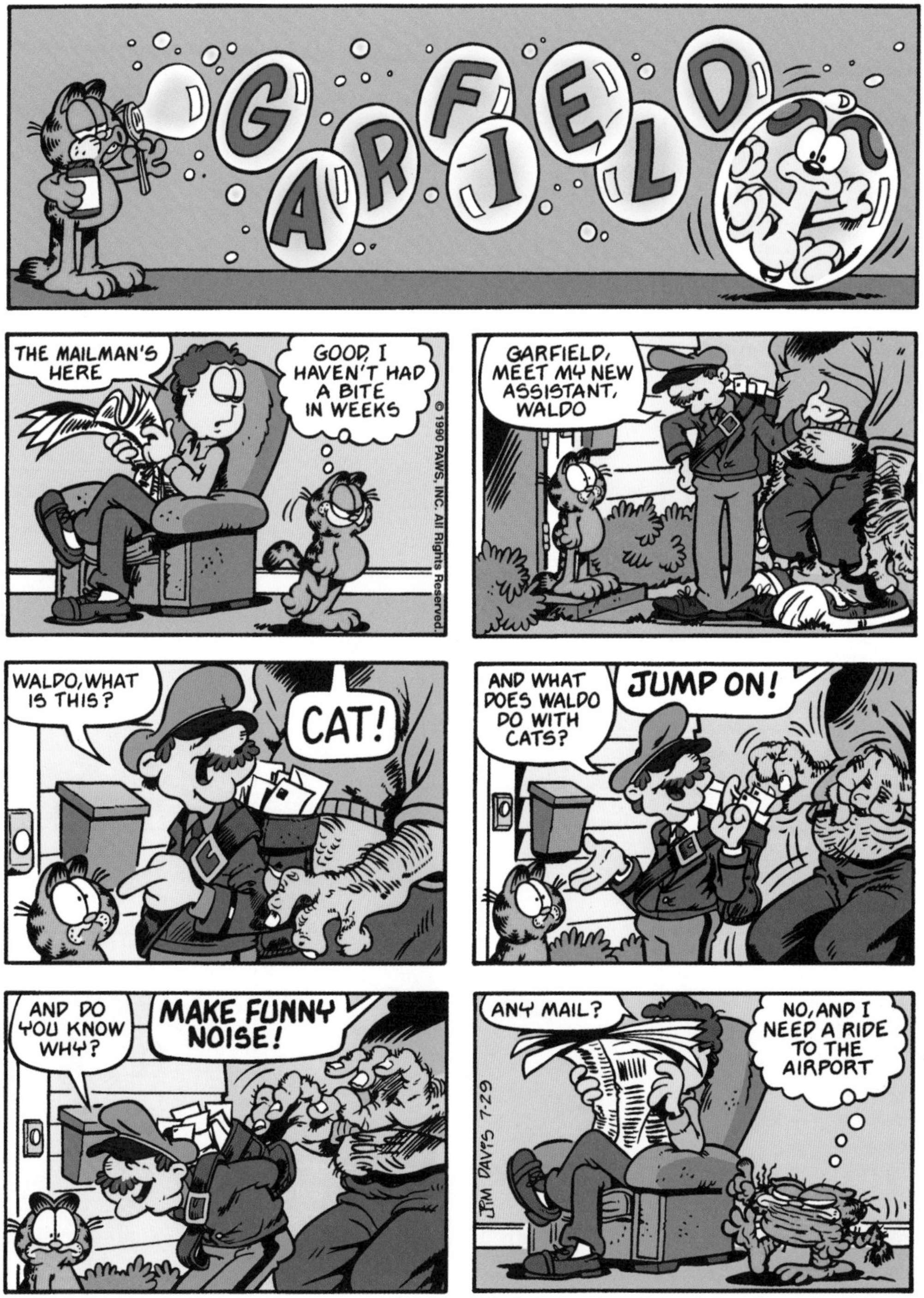
GARFIELD
THE MAILMAN'S HERE
GOOD, I HAVEN'T HAD A BITE IN WEEKS
© 1990 PAWS, INC. All Rights Reserved.
GARFIELD, MEET MY NEW ASSISTANT, WALDO
WALDO, WHAT IS THIS?
CAT!
AND WHAT DOES WALDO DO WITH CATS?
JUMP ON!
AND DO YOU KNOW WHY?
MAKE FUNNY NOISE!
JIM DAVIS 7-29
ANY MAIL?
NO, AND I NEED A RIDE TO THE AIRPORT

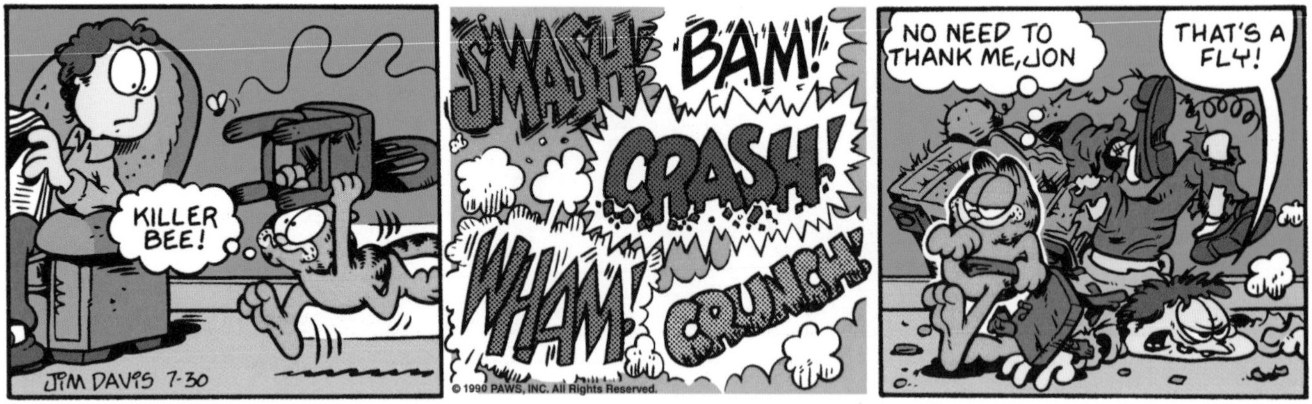
KILLER BEE!
JIM DAVIS 7-30
SMASH! BAM!
CRASH!
WHAM!
CRUNCH!
© 1990 PAWS, INC. All Rights Reserved.
NO NEED TO THANK ME, JON
THAT'S A FLY!

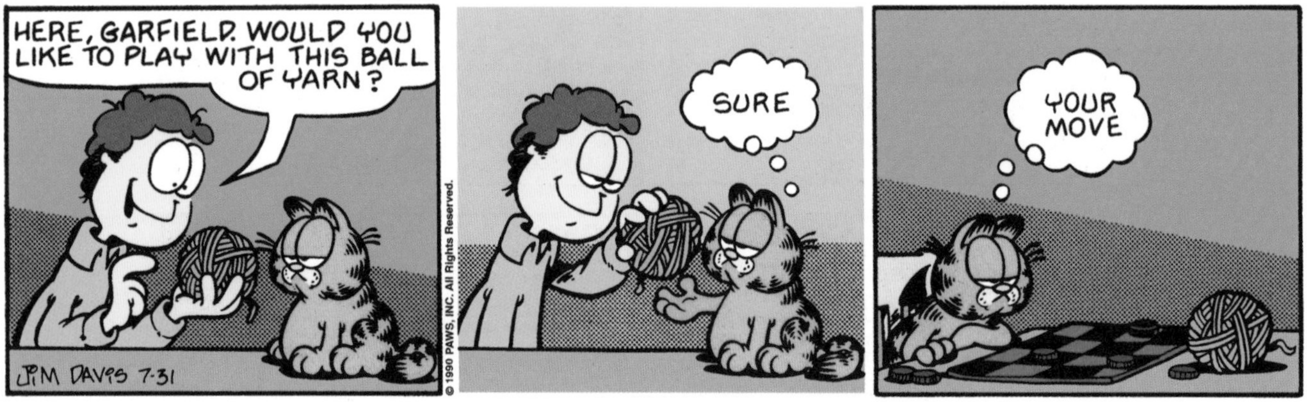
HERE, GARFIELD. WOULD YOU LIKE TO PLAY WITH THIS BALL OF YARN?
JIM DAVIS 7-31
© 1990 PAWS, INC. All Rights Reserved.
SURE
YOUR MOVE

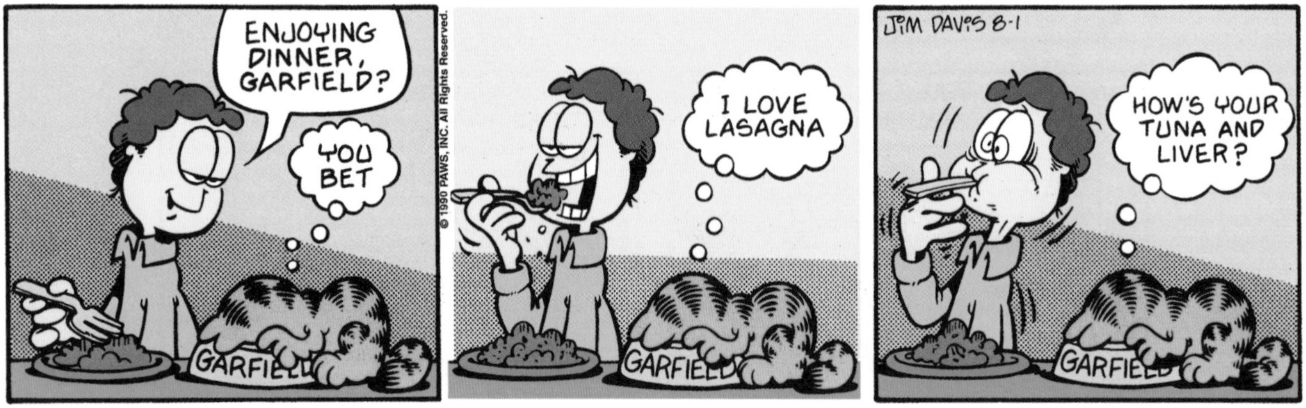
ENJOYING DINNER, GARFIELD?
YOU BET
GARFIELD
© 1990 PAWS, INC. All Rights Reserved.
I LOVE LASAGNA
GARFIELD
JIM DAVIS 8-1
HOW'S YOUR TUNA AND LIVER?
GARFIELD

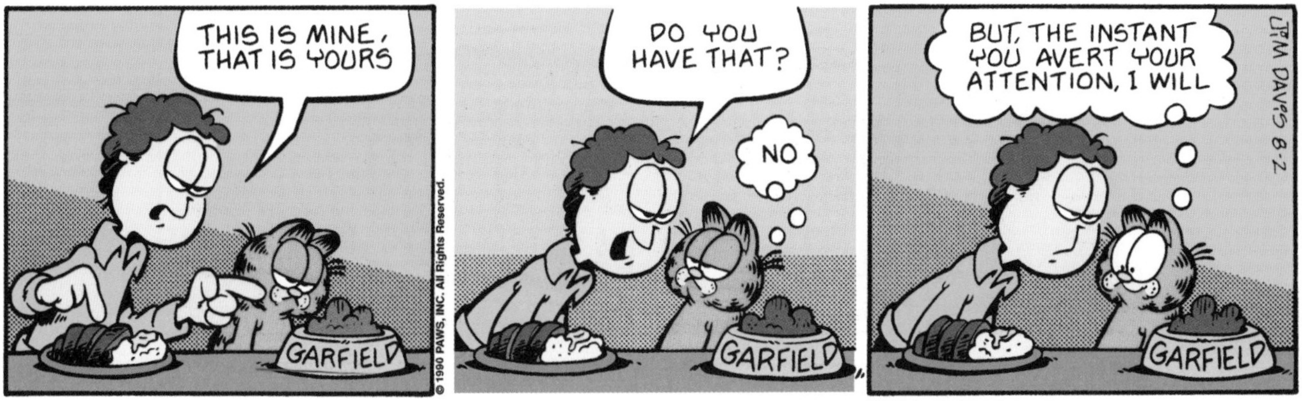
THIS IS MINE, THAT IS YOURS
GARFIELD
DO YOU HAVE THAT?
NO
GARFIELD
BUT, THE INSTANT YOU AVERT YOUR ATTENTION, I WILL
GARFIELD
JIM DAVIS 8-2
© 1990 PAWS, INC. All Rights Reserved.

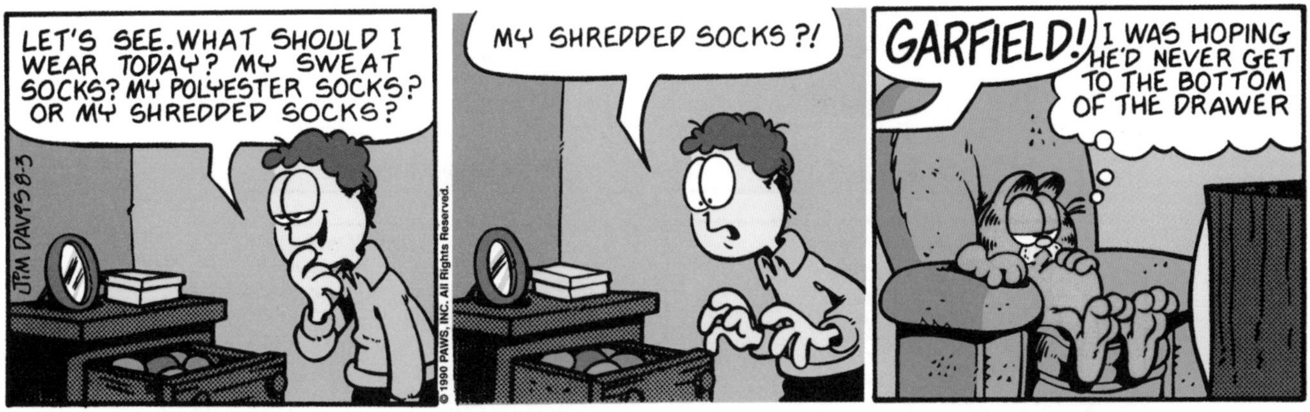
LET'S SEE. WHAT SHOULD I WEAR TODAY? MY SWEAT SOCKS? MY POLYESTER SOCKS? OR MY SHREDDED SOCKS?
JIM DAVIS 8-3
MY SHREDDED SOCKS?!
GARFIELD!
I WAS HOPING HE'D NEVER GET TO THE BOTTOM OF THE DRAWER
© 1990 PAWS, INC. All Rights Reserved.

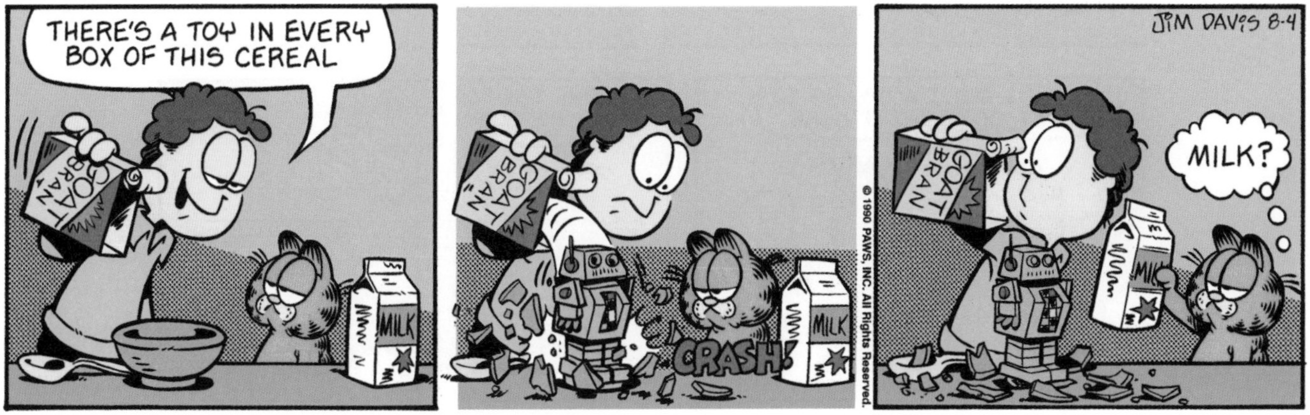
THERE'S A TOY IN EVERY BOX OF THIS CEREAL
GOAT BRAN
MILK
CRASH!
JIM DAVIS 8-4
MILK?
© 1990 PAWS, INC. All Rights Reserved.

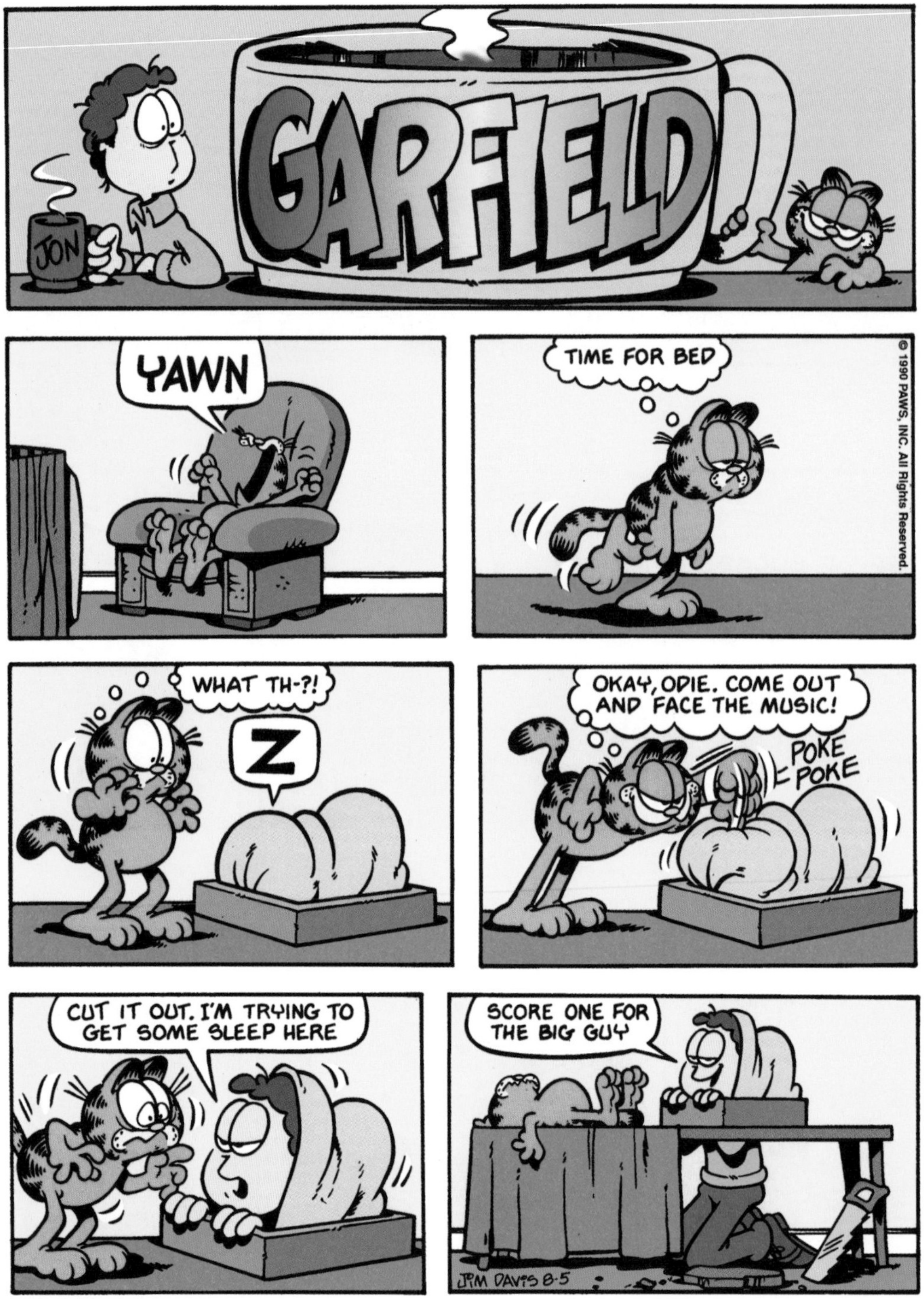
GARFIELD
JON
YAWN
TIME FOR BED
© 1990 PAWS, INC. All Rights Reserved.
WHAT TH-?!
Z
OKAY, ODIE. COME OUT AND FACE THE MUSIC!
POKE POKE
CUT IT OUT. I'M TRYING TO GET SOME SLEEP HERE
SCORE ONE FOR THE BIG GUY
JIM DAVIS 8-5

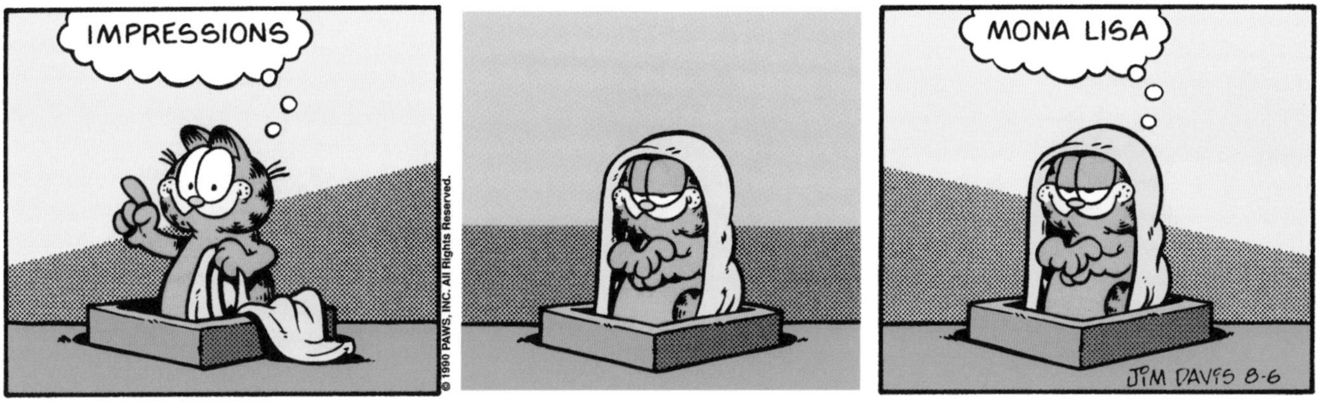
IMPRESSIONS
© 1990 PAWS, INC. All Rights Reserved.
MONA LISA
JIM DAVIS 8-6

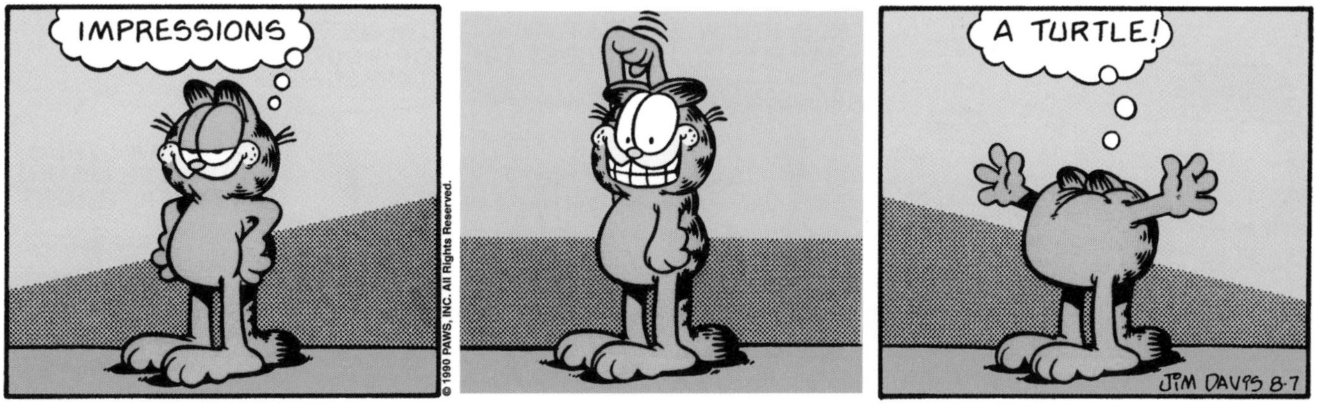
IMPRESSIONS
© 1990 PAWS, INC. All Rights Reserved.
A TURTLE!
JIM DAVIS 8-7

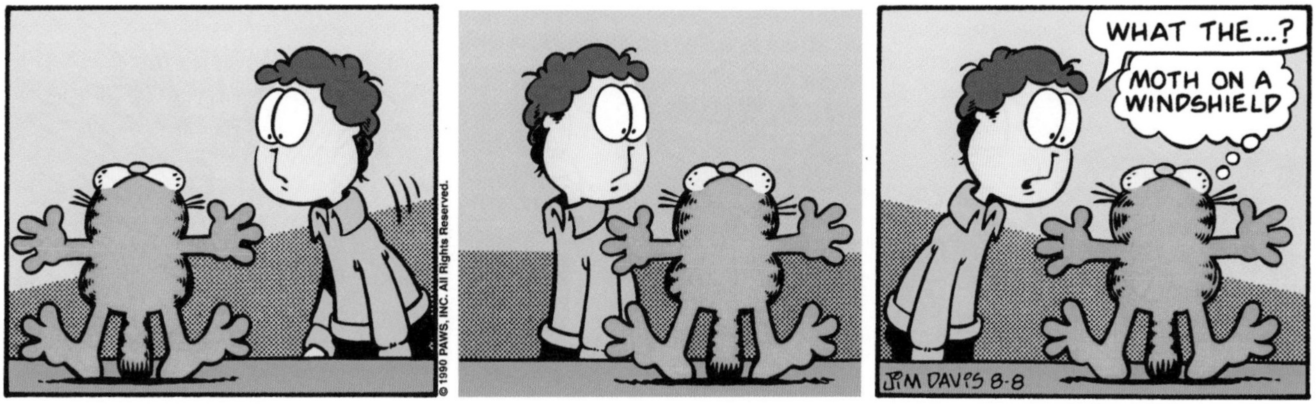
© 1990 PAWS, INC. All Rights Reserved.
WHAT THE...?
MOTH ON A WINDSHIELD
JIM DAVIS 8-8

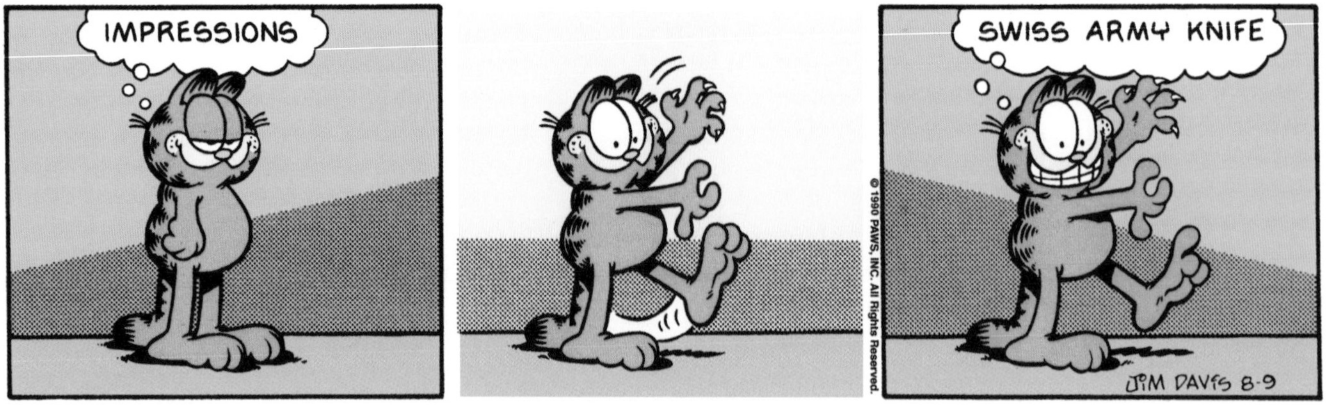
IMPRESSIONS
SWISS ARMY KNIFE
JIM DAVIS 8-9
© 1990 PAWS, INC. All Rights Reserved.

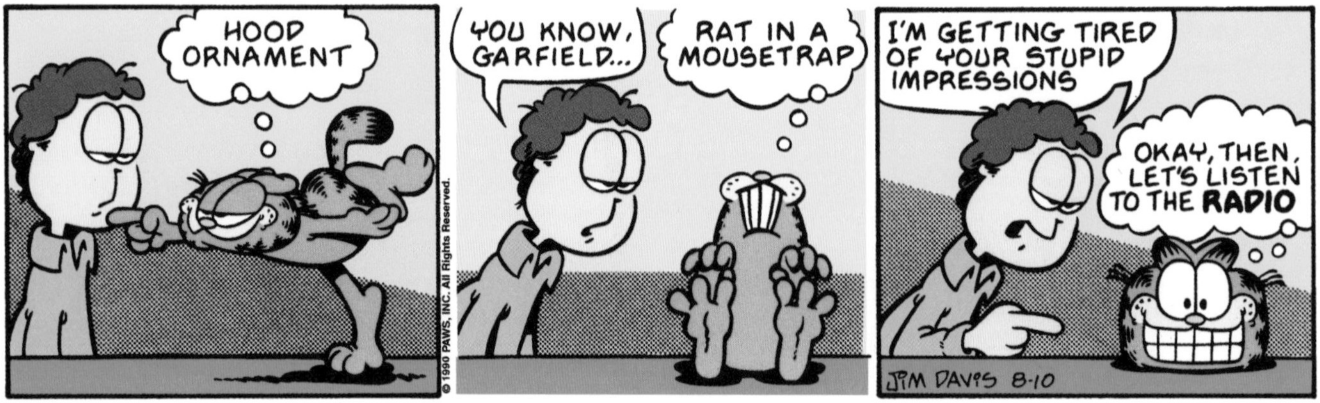
HOOD ORNAMENT
YOU KNOW, GARFIELD...
RAT IN A MOUSETRAP
I'M GETTING TIRED OF YOUR STUPID IMPRESSIONS
OKAY, THEN, LET'S LISTEN TO THE **RADIO**
JIM DAVIS 8-10
© 1990 PAWS, INC. All Rights Reserved.

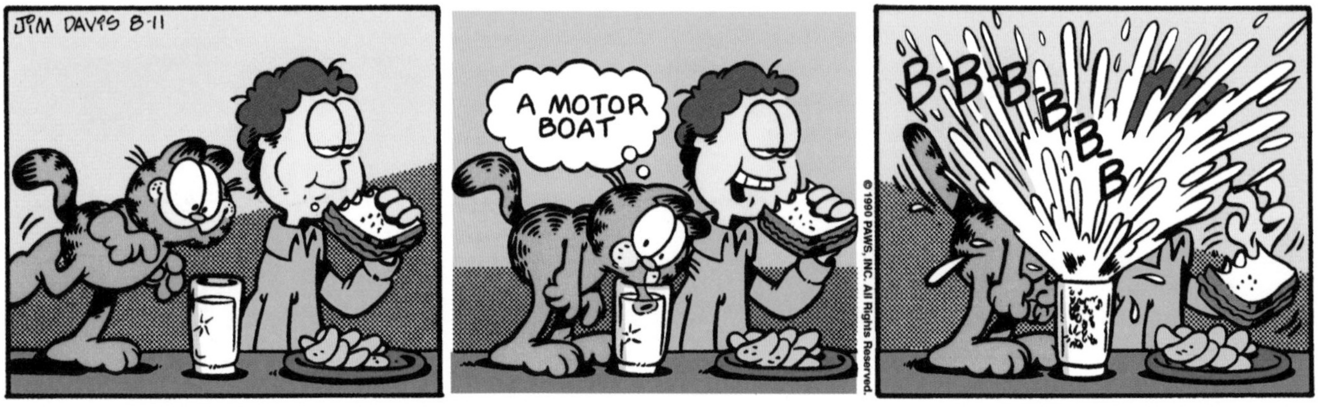
JIM DAVIS 8-11
A MOTOR BOAT
B-B-B-B-B-B
© 1990 PAWS, INC. All Rights Reserved.

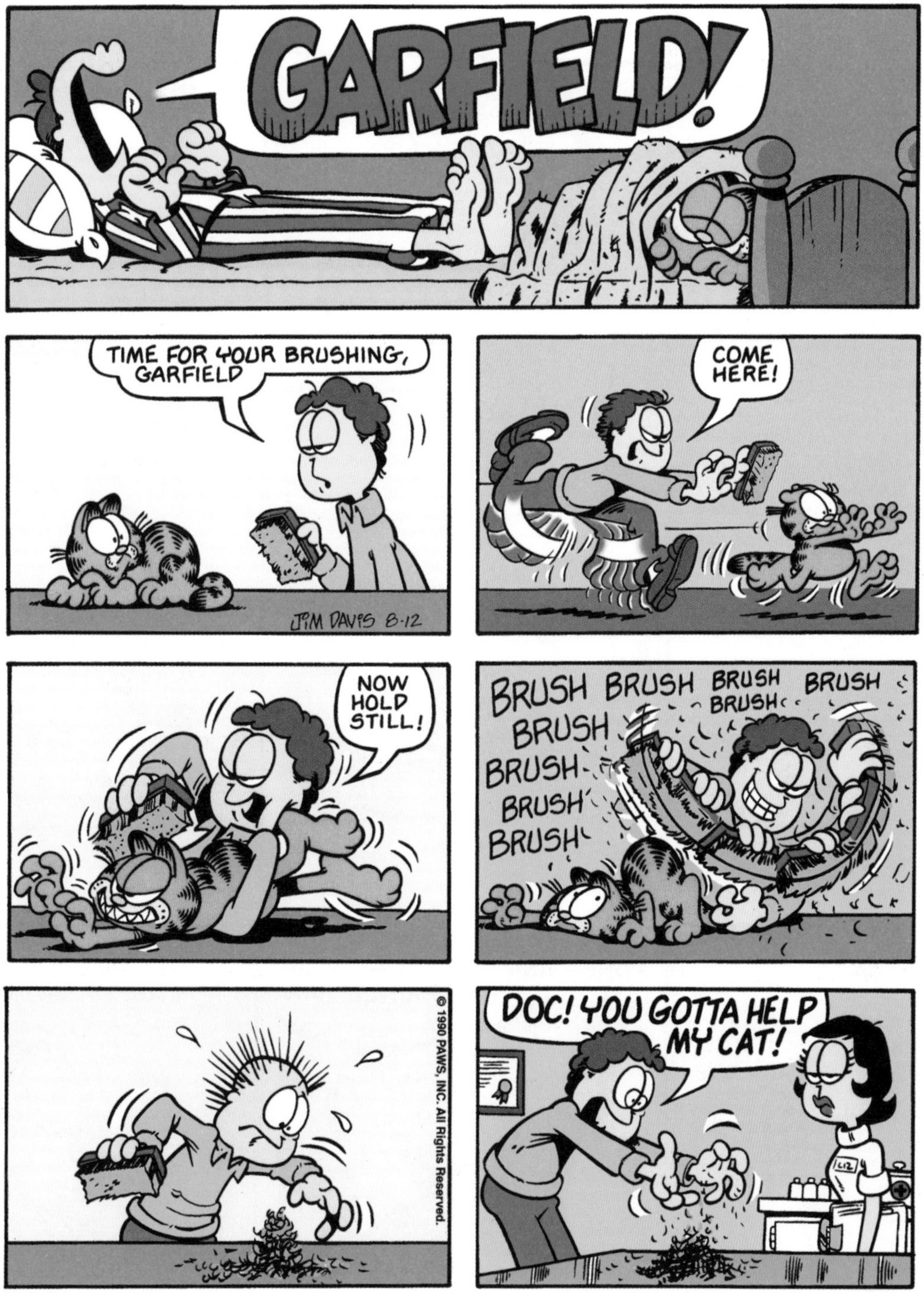
GARFIELD!
TIME FOR YOUR BRUSHING, GARFIELD
JIM DAVIS 8-12
COME HERE!
NOW HOLD STILL!
BRUSH BRUSH BRUSH BRUSH BRUSH BRUSH BRUSH BRUSH BRUSH BRUSH
© 1990 PAWS, INC. All Rights Reserved.
DOC! YOU GOTTA HELP MY CAT!
LIZ

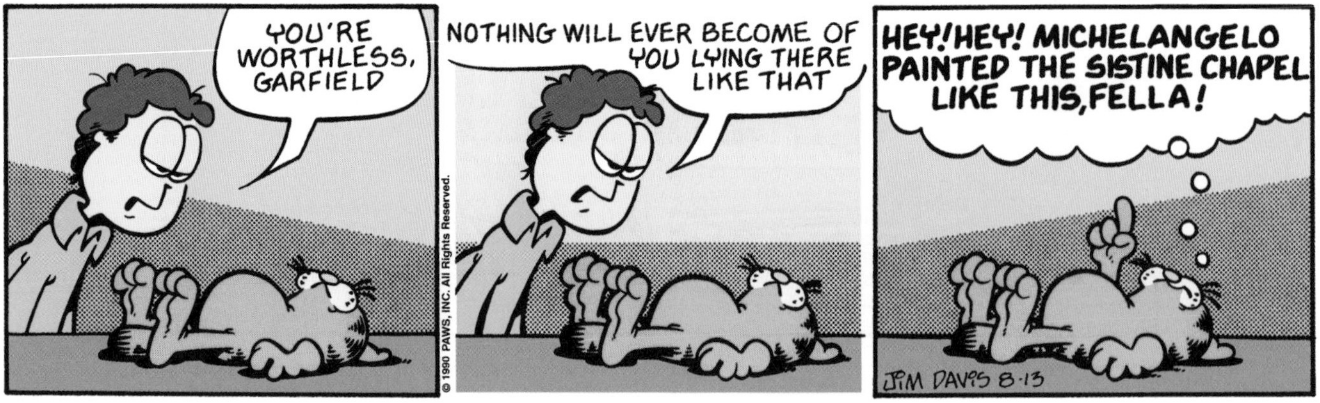
YOU'RE WORTHLESS, GARFIELD
© 1990 PAWS, INC. All Rights Reserved.
NOTHING WILL EVER BECOME OF YOU LYING THERE LIKE THAT
HEY! HEY! MICHELANGELO PAINTED THE SISTINE CHAPEL LIKE THIS, FELLA!
JIM DAVIS 8-13

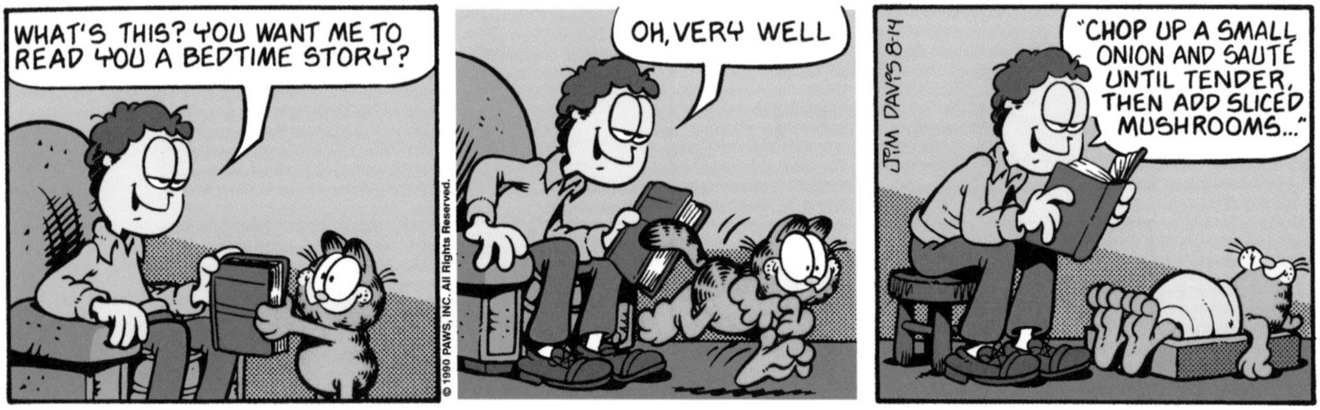
WHAT'S THIS? YOU WANT ME TO READ YOU A BEDTIME STORY?
© 1990 PAWS, INC. All Rights Reserved.
OH, VERY WELL
JIM DAVIS 8-14
"CHOP UP A SMALL ONION AND SAUTÉ UNTIL TENDER, THEN ADD SLICED MUSHROOMS..."

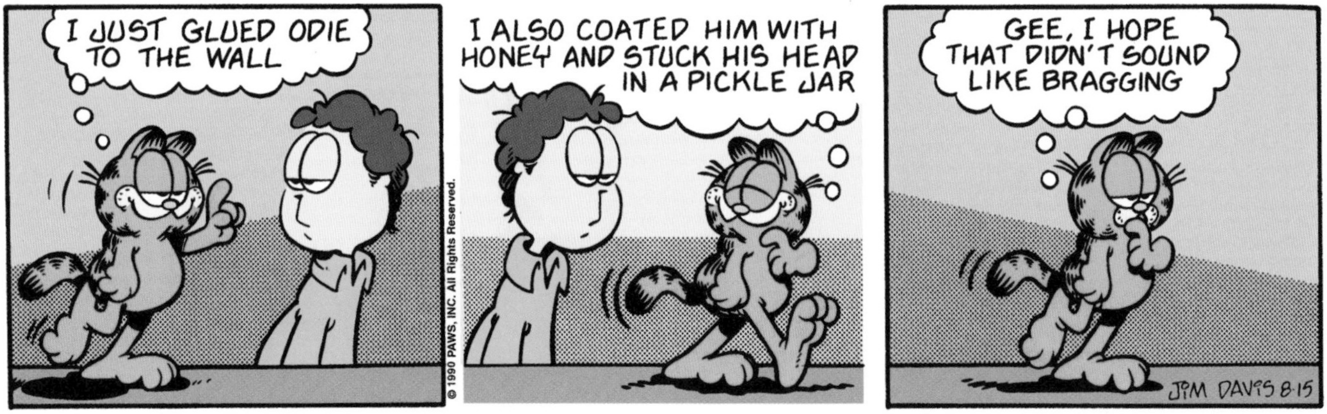
I JUST GLUED ODIE TO THE WALL
© 1990 PAWS, INC. All Rights Reserved.
I ALSO COATED HIM WITH HONEY AND STUCK HIS HEAD IN A PICKLE JAR
GEE, I HOPE THAT DIDN'T SOUND LIKE BRAGGING
JIM DAVIS 8-15

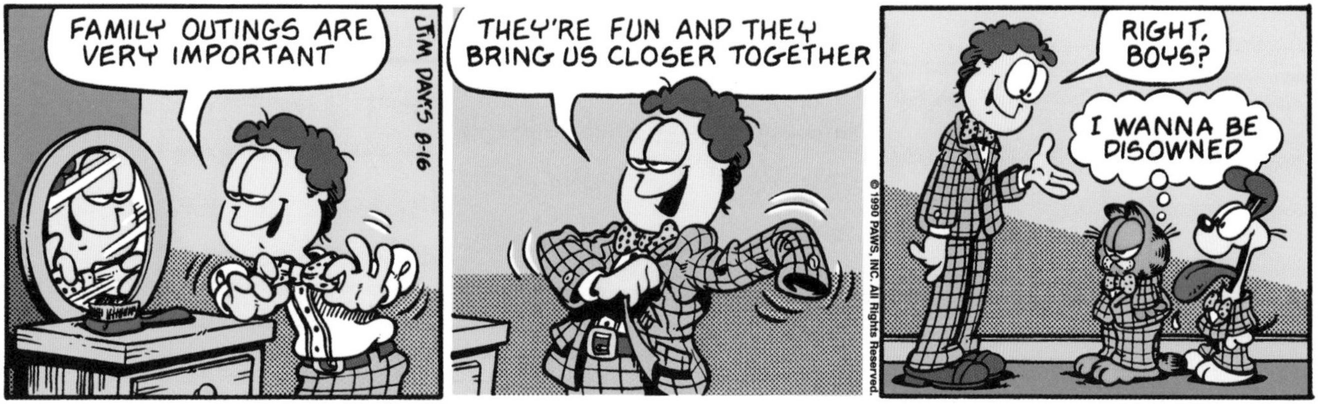
FAMILY OUTINGS ARE VERY IMPORTANT
JIM DAVIS 8-16
THEY'RE FUN AND THEY BRING US CLOSER TOGETHER
© 1990 PAWS, INC. All Rights Reserved.
RIGHT, BOYS?
I WANNA BE DISOWNED

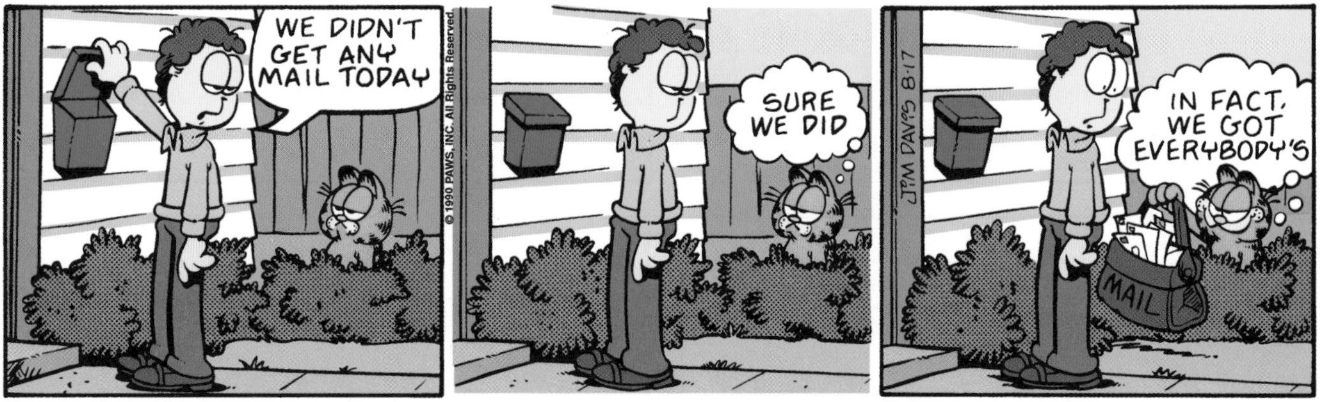
WE DIDN'T GET ANY MAIL TODAY
© 1990 PAWS, INC. All Rights Reserved.
SURE WE DID
JIM DAVIS 8-17
IN FACT, WE GOT EVERYBODY'S
MAIL

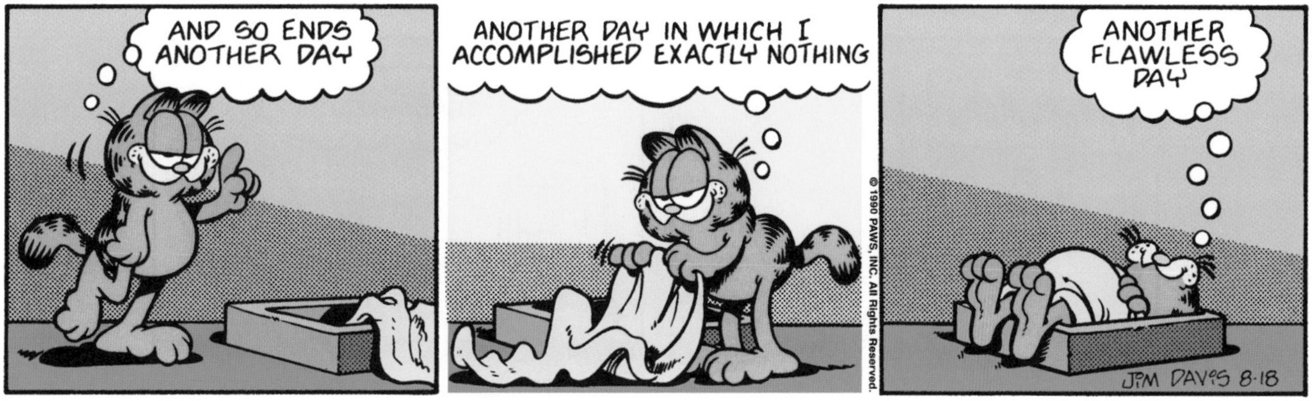
AND SO ENDS ANOTHER DAY
ANOTHER DAY IN WHICH I ACCOMPLISHED EXACTLY NOTHING
© 1990 PAWS, INC. All Rights Reserved.
ANOTHER FLAWLESS DAY
JIM DAVIS 8-18

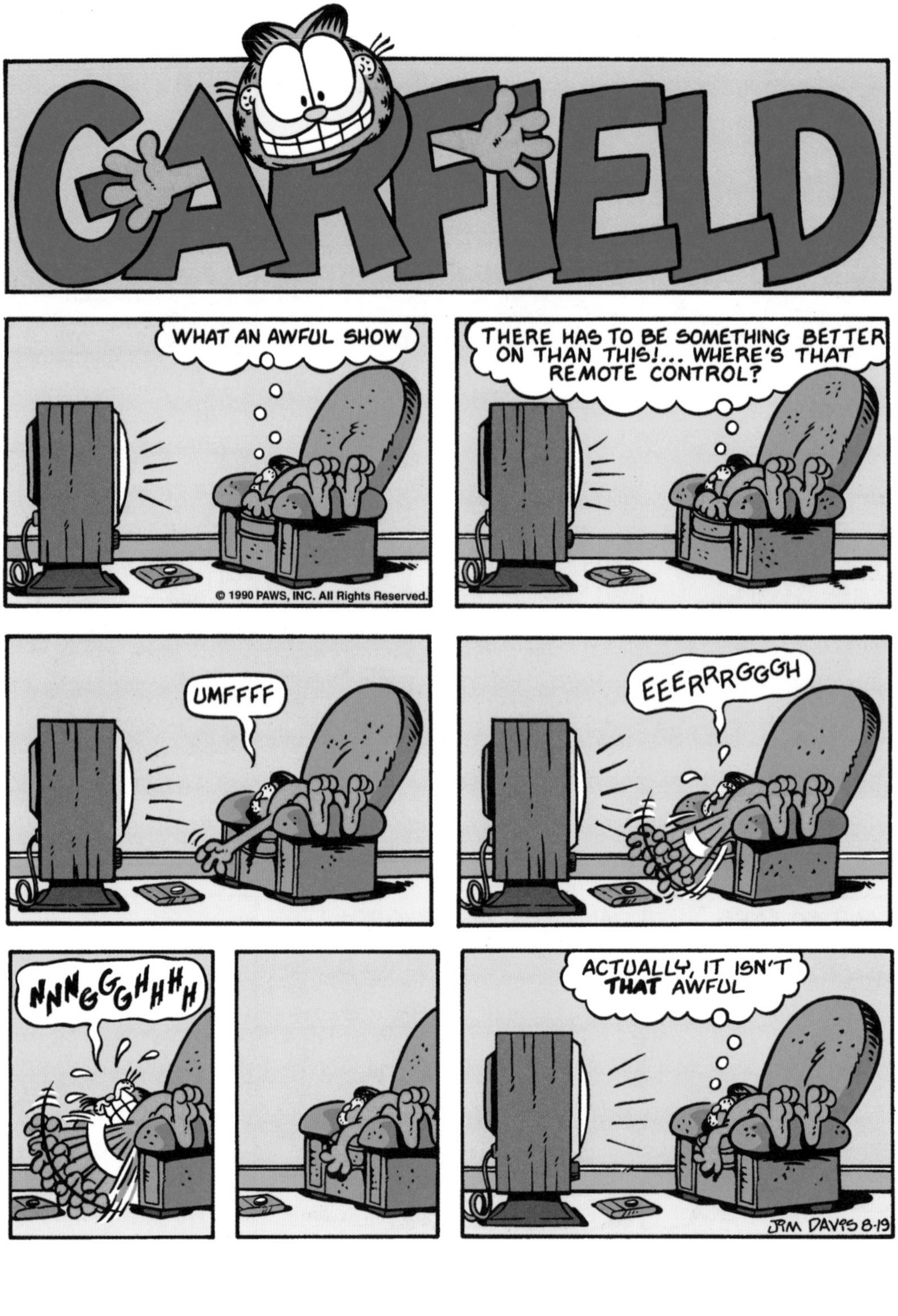
GARFIELD
WHAT AN AWFUL SHOW
THERE HAS TO BE SOMETHING BETTER ON THAN THIS!... WHERE'S THAT REMOTE CONTROL?
UMFFFF
EEERRRRGGGH
NNNGGGHHHH
ACTUALLY, IT ISN'T **THAT** AWFUL
JIM DAVIS 8-19

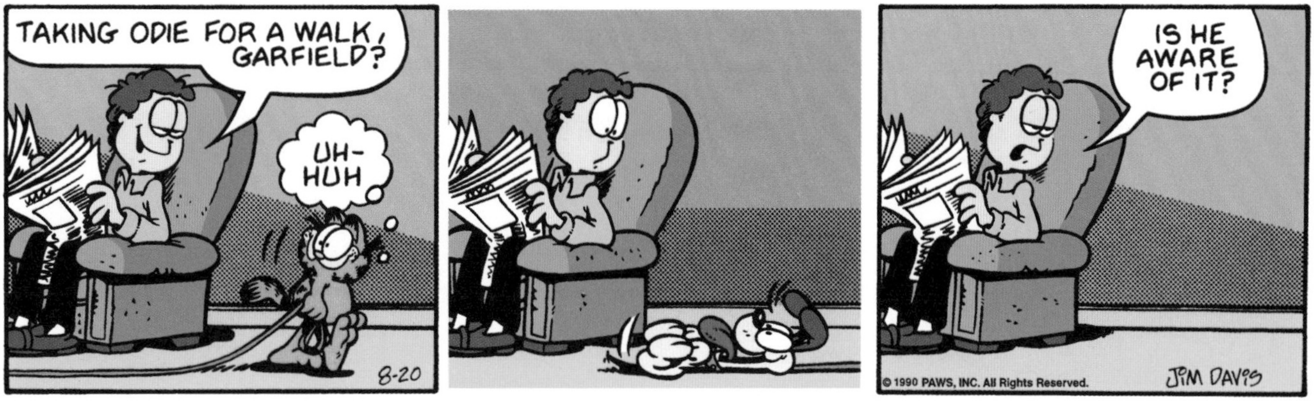
TAKING ODIE FOR A WALK, GARFIELD?
UH-HUH
8-20
IS HE AWARE OF IT?
© 1990 PAWS, INC. All Rights Reserved.
JIM DAVIS

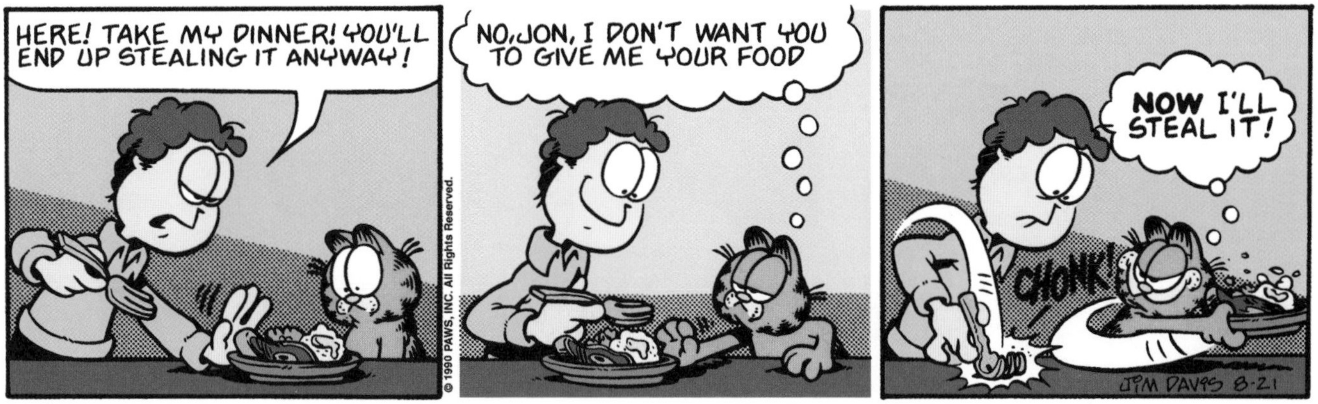
HERE! TAKE MY DINNER! YOU'LL END UP STEALING IT ANYWAY!
© 1990 PAWS, INC. All Rights Reserved.
NO, JON, I DON'T WANT YOU TO GIVE ME YOUR FOOD
NOW I'LL STEAL IT!
CHONK!
JIM DAVIS 8-21

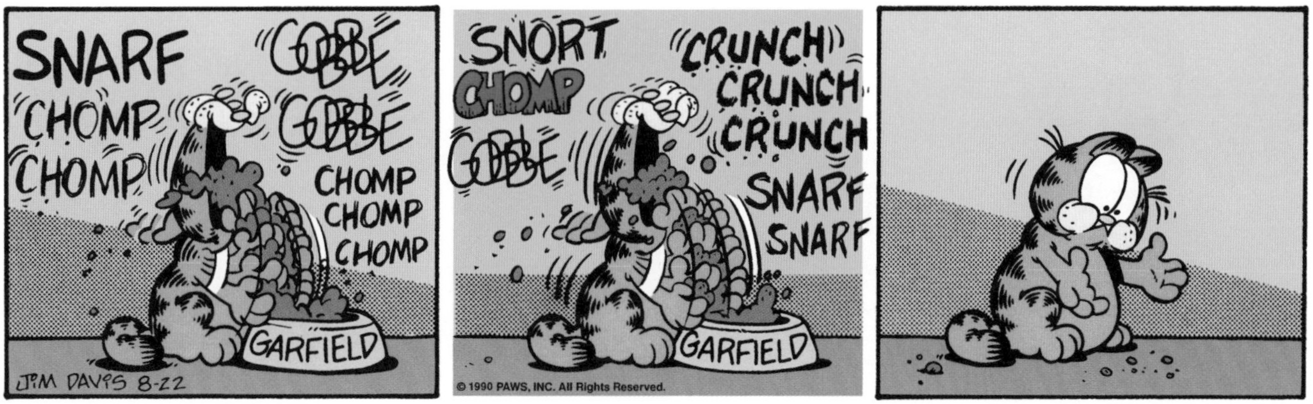
SNARF
GOBBLE
CHOMP
CHOMP
GOBBLE
CHOMP
CHOMP
CHOMP
GARFIELD
JIM DAVIS 8-22
SNORT
CHOMP
GOBBLE
CRUNCH
CRUNCH
CRUNCH
SNARF
SNARF
GARFIELD
© 1990 PAWS, INC. All Rights Reserved.

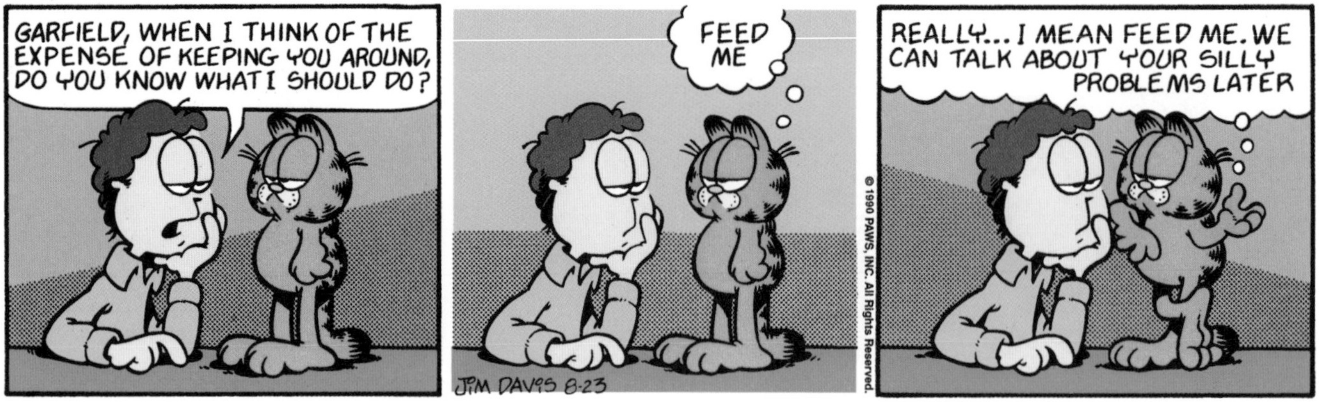
GARFIELD, WHEN I THINK OF THE EXPENSE OF KEEPING YOU AROUND, DO YOU KNOW WHAT I SHOULD DO?
FEED ME
JIM DAVIS 8-23
© 1990 PAWS, INC. All Rights Reserved.
REALLY... I MEAN FEED ME. WE CAN TALK ABOUT YOUR SILLY PROBLEMS LATER

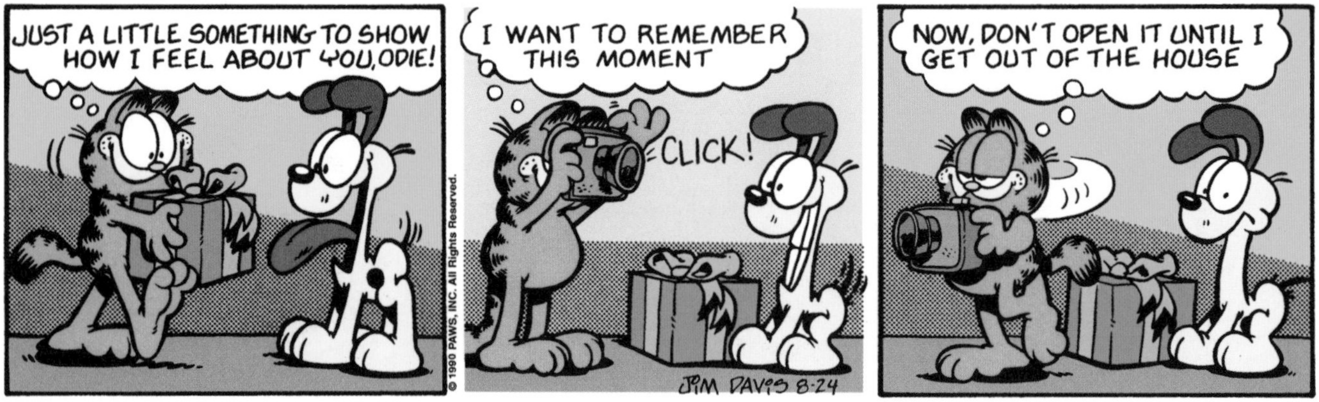
JUST A LITTLE SOMETHING TO SHOW HOW I FEEL ABOUT YOU, ODIE!
© 1990 PAWS, INC. All Rights Reserved.
I WANT TO REMEMBER THIS MOMENT
CLICK!
JIM DAVIS 8-24
NOW, DON'T OPEN IT UNTIL I GET OUT OF THE HOUSE

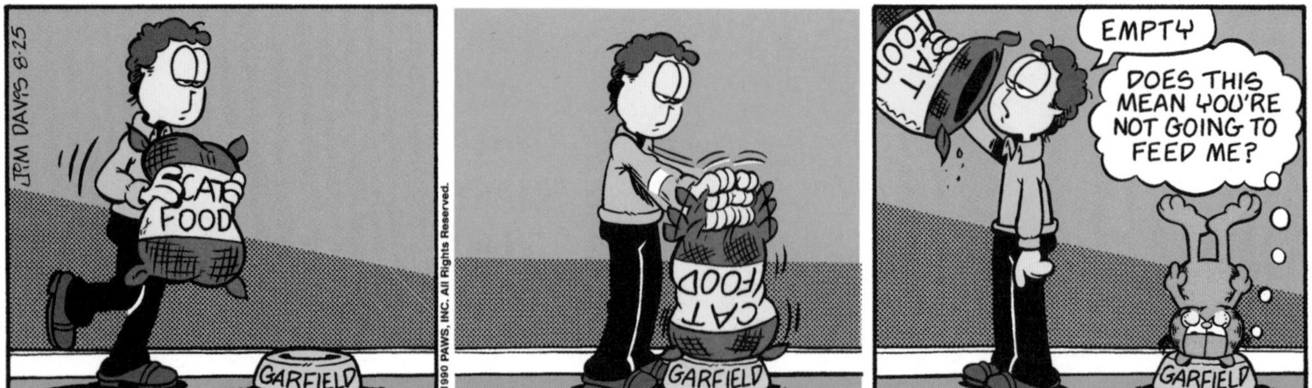
JIM DAVIS 8-25
CAT FOOD
GARFIELD
© 1990 PAWS, INC. All Rights Reserved.
CAT FOOD
GARFIELD
CAT FOOD
EMPTY
DOES THIS MEAN YOU'RE NOT GOING TO FEED ME?
GARFIELD

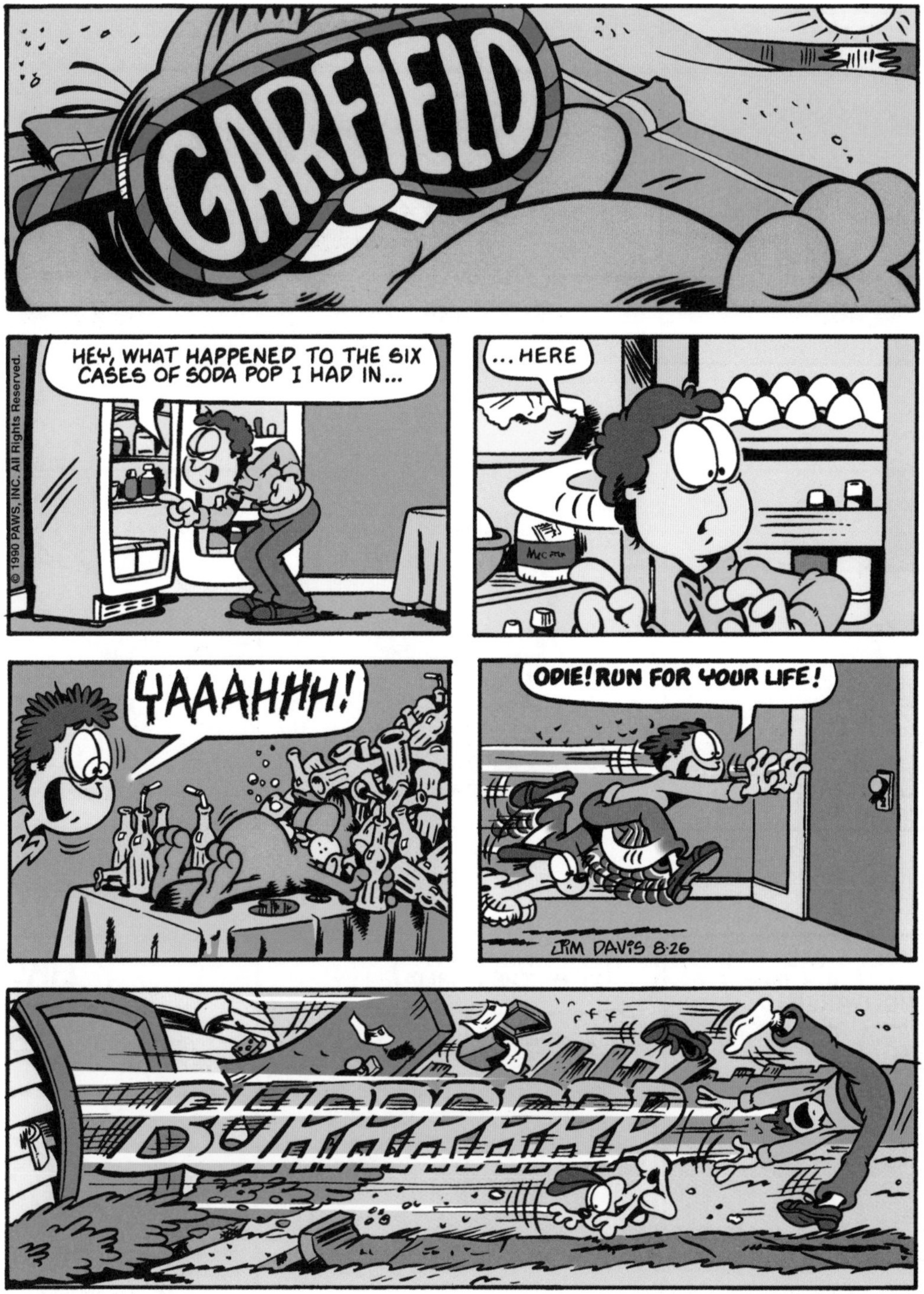
GARFIELD
© 1990 PAWS, INC. All Rights Reserved.
HEY, WHAT HAPPENED TO THE SIX CASES OF SODA POP I HAD IN...
... HERE
YAAAHHH!
ODIE! RUN FOR YOUR LIFE!
JIM DAVIS 8·26
BURRRRRRP

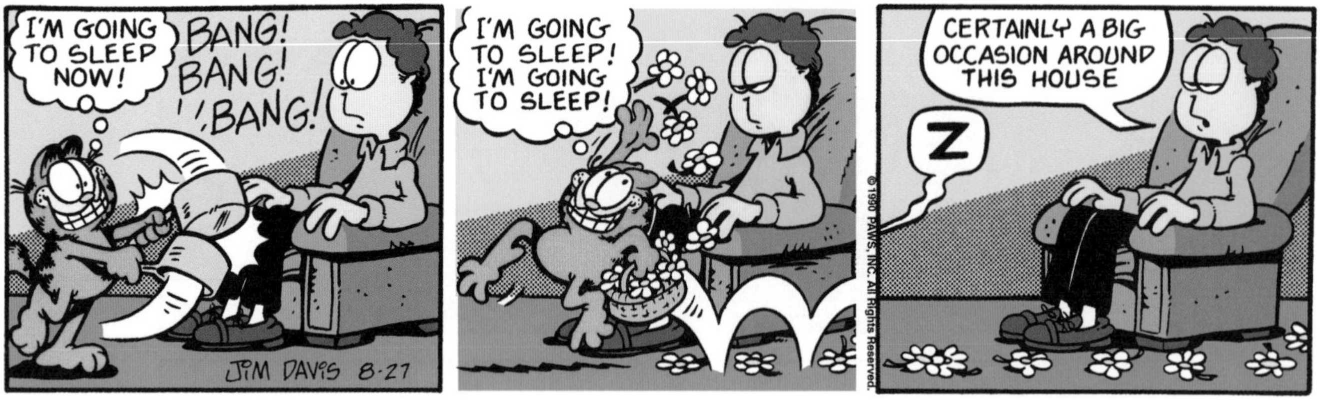

I'M GOING TO SLEEP NOW!
BANG! BANG! BANG!
JIM DAVIS 8-27
I'M GOING TO SLEEP! I'M GOING TO SLEEP!
© 1990 PAWS, INC. All Rights Reserved.
CERTAINLY A BIG OCCASION AROUND THIS HOUSE
Z

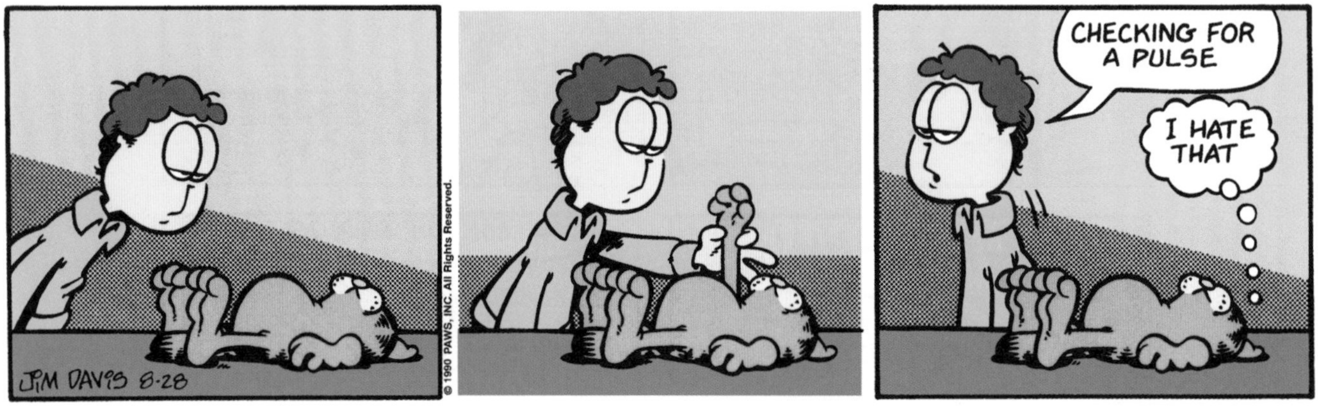

JIM DAVIS 8-28
© 1990 PAWS, INC. All Rights Reserved.
CHECKING FOR A PULSE
I HATE THAT

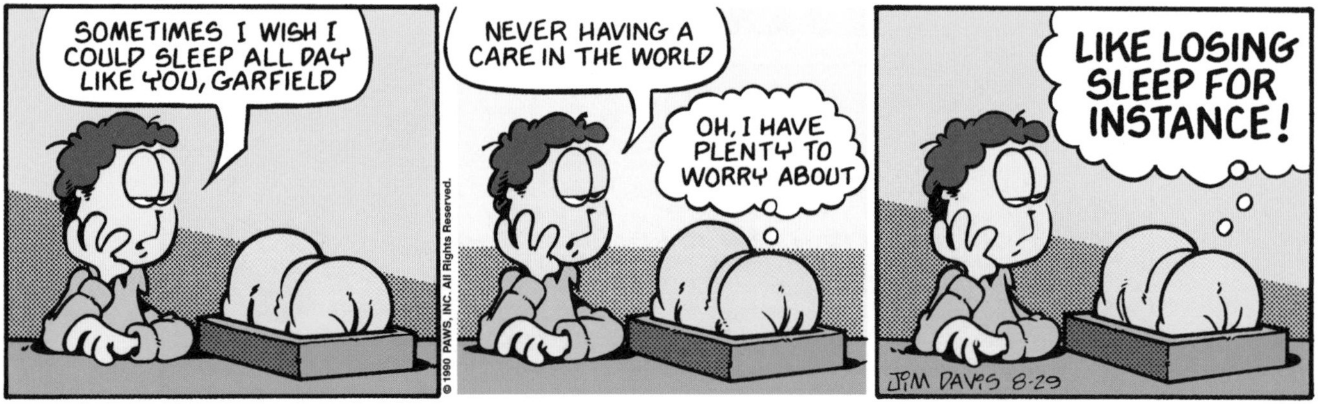

SOMETIMES I WISH I COULD SLEEP ALL DAY LIKE YOU, GARFIELD
© 1990 PAWS, INC. All Rights Reserved.
NEVER HAVING A CARE IN THE WORLD
OH, I HAVE PLENTY TO WORRY ABOUT
LIKE LOSING SLEEP FOR INSTANCE!
JIM DAVIS 8-29

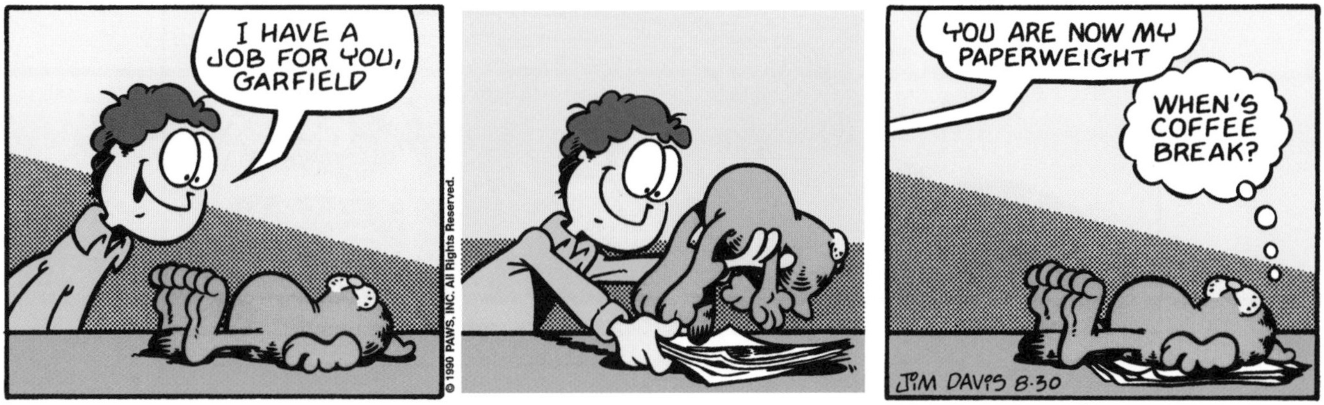
I HAVE A JOB FOR YOU, GARFIELD
© 1990 PAWS, INC. All Rights Reserved.
YOU ARE NOW MY PAPERWEIGHT
WHEN'S COFFEE BREAK?
JIM DAVIS 8-30

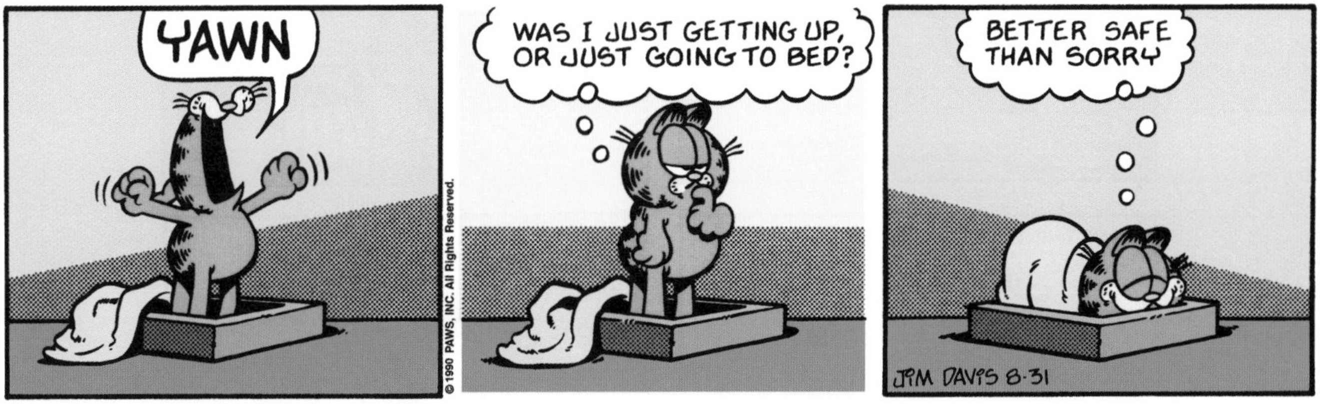
YAWN
© 1990 PAWS, INC. All Rights Reserved.
WAS I JUST GETTING UP, OR JUST GOING TO BED?
BETTER SAFE THAN SORRY
JIM DAVIS 8-31

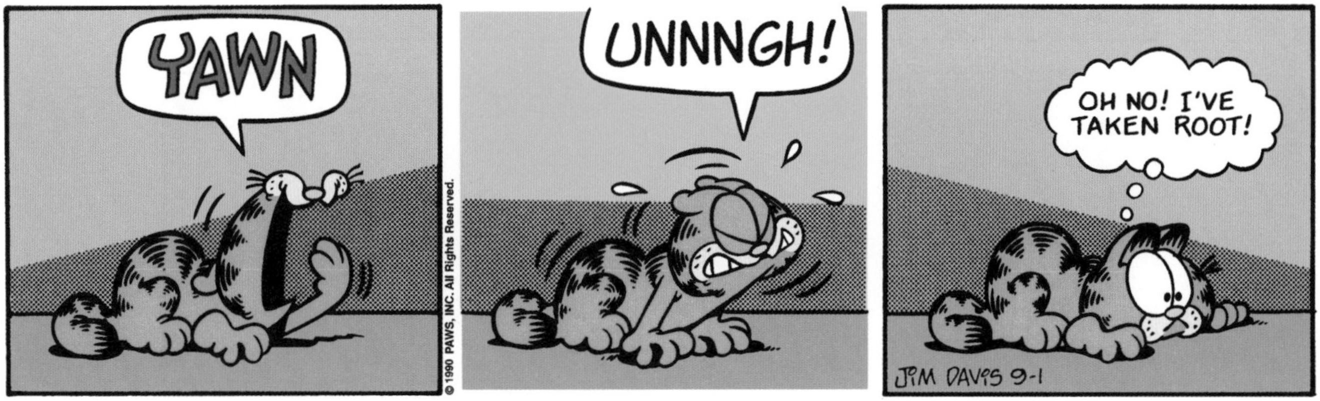
YAWN
© 1990 PAWS, INC. All Rights Reserved.
UNNNGH!
OH NO! I'VE TAKEN ROOT!
JIM DAVIS 9-1

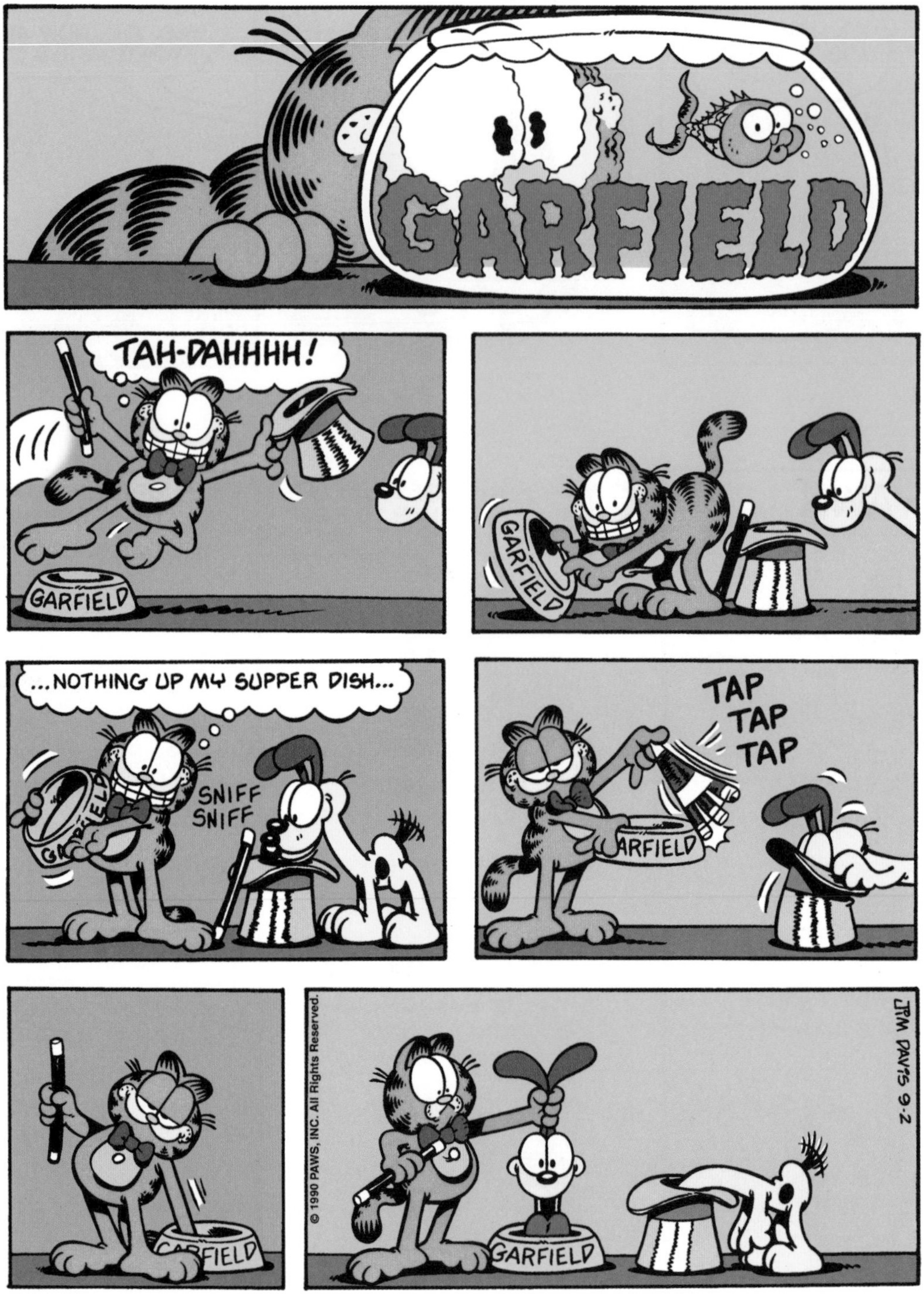
GARFIELD
TAH-DAHHHH!
GARFIELD
GARFIELD
...NOTHING UP MY SUPPER DISH...
SNIFF SNIFF
GARFIELD
TAP TAP TAP
ARFIELD
GARFIELD
© 1990 PAWS, INC. All Rights Reserved.
JIM DAVIS 9-2
GARFIELD

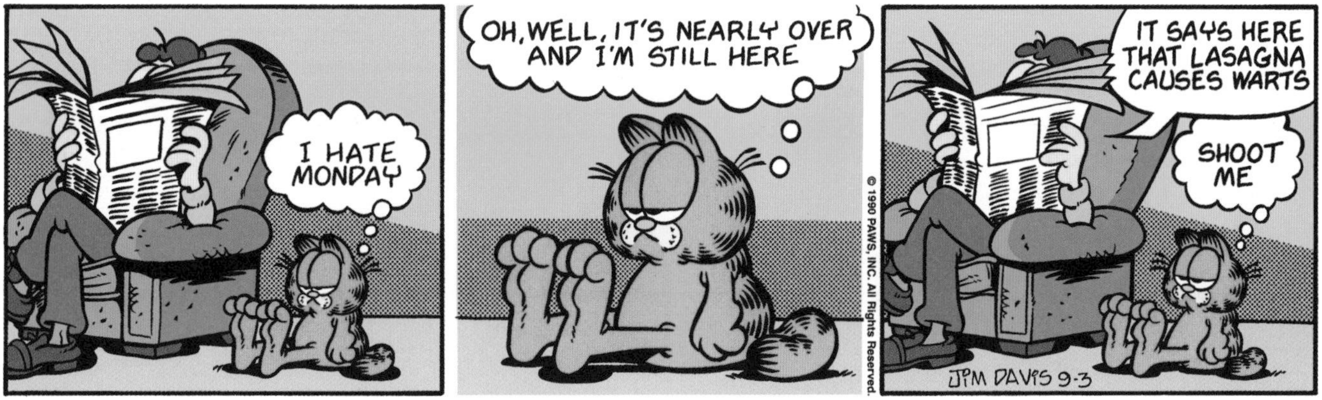
I HATE MONDAY
OH, WELL, IT'S NEARLY OVER AND I'M STILL HERE
© 1990 PAWS, INC. All Rights Reserved.
IT SAYS HERE THAT LASAGNA CAUSES WARTS
SHOOT ME
JIM DAVIS 9-3

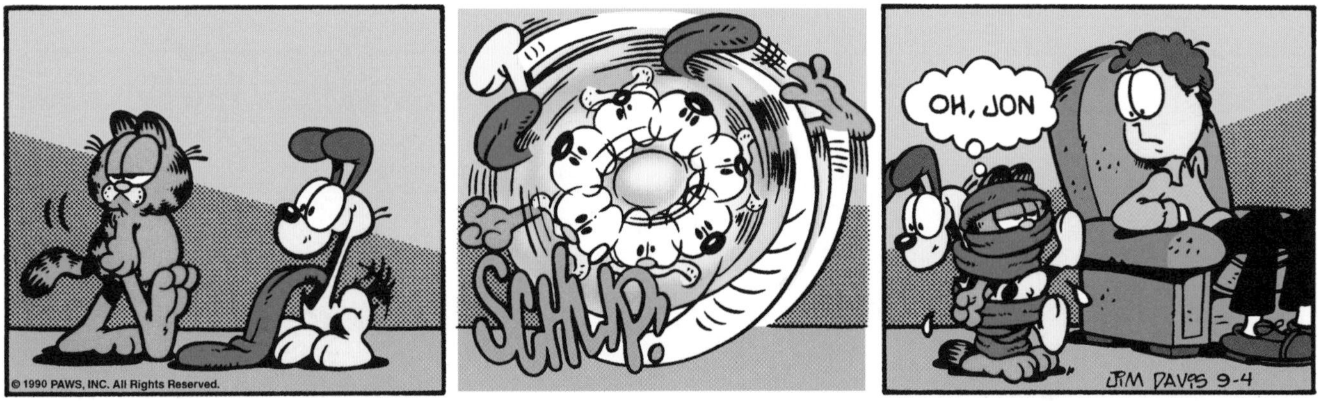
© 1990 PAWS, INC. All Rights Reserved.
SCHLUP
OH, JON
JIM DAVIS 9-4

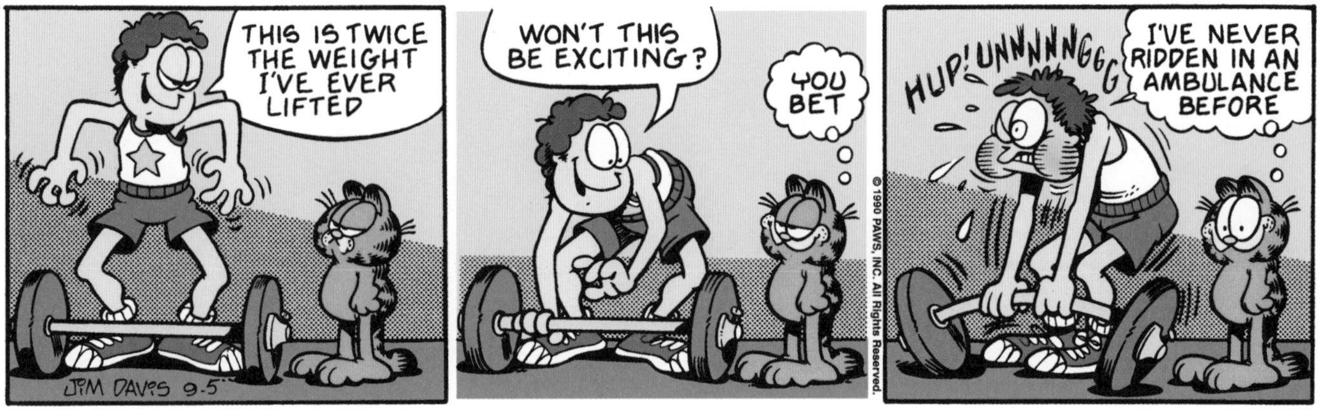
THIS IS TWICE THE WEIGHT I'VE EVER LIFTED
JIM DAVIS 9-5
WON'T THIS BE EXCITING?
YOU BET
© 1990 PAWS, INC. All Rights Reserved.
HUP! UNNNNNGGG
I'VE NEVER RIDDEN IN AN AMBULANCE BEFORE

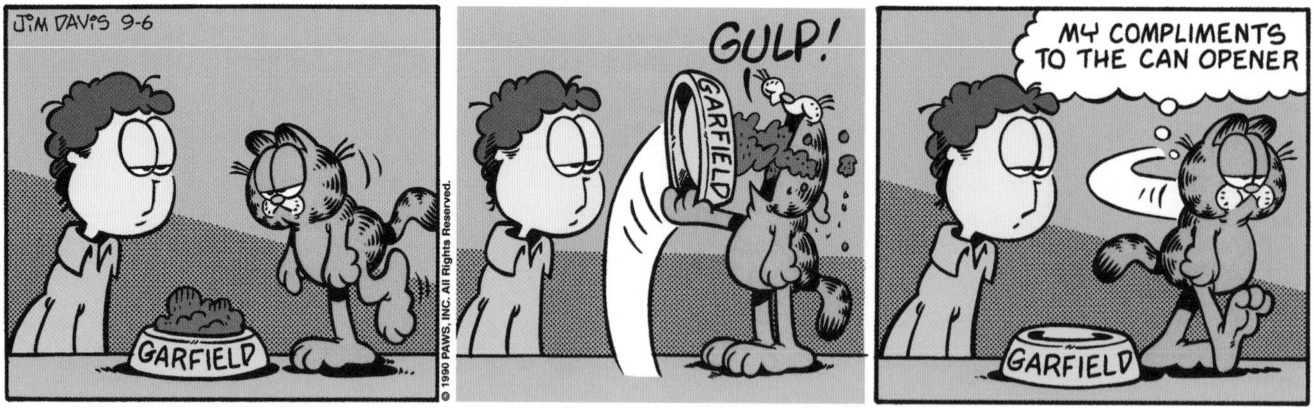
JIM DAVIS 9-6
GARFIELD
© 1990 PAWS, INC. All Rights Reserved.
GULP!
GARFIELD
MY COMPLIMENTS TO THE CAN OPENER
GARFIELD

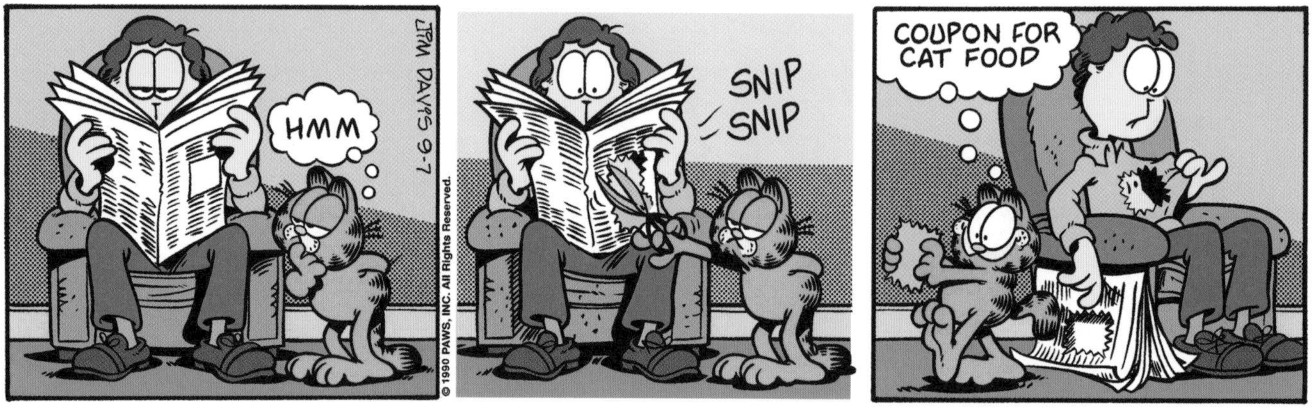
HMM
JIM DAVIS 9-7
© 1990 PAWS, INC. All Rights Reserved.
SNIP SNIP
COUPON FOR CAT FOOD

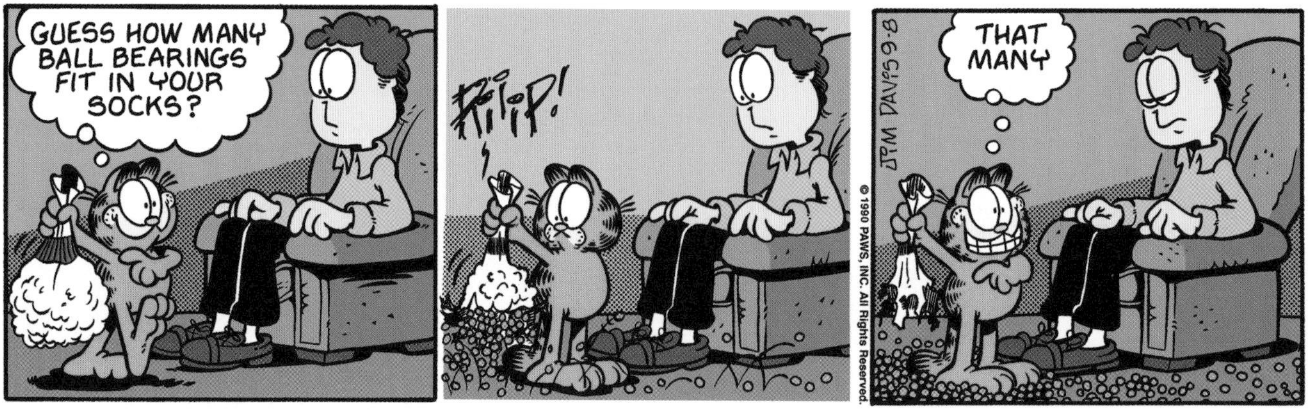
GUESS HOW MANY BALL BEARINGS FIT IN YOUR SOCKS?
RIIIP!
JIM DAVIS 9-8
© 1990 PAWS, INC. All Rights Reserved.
THAT MANY

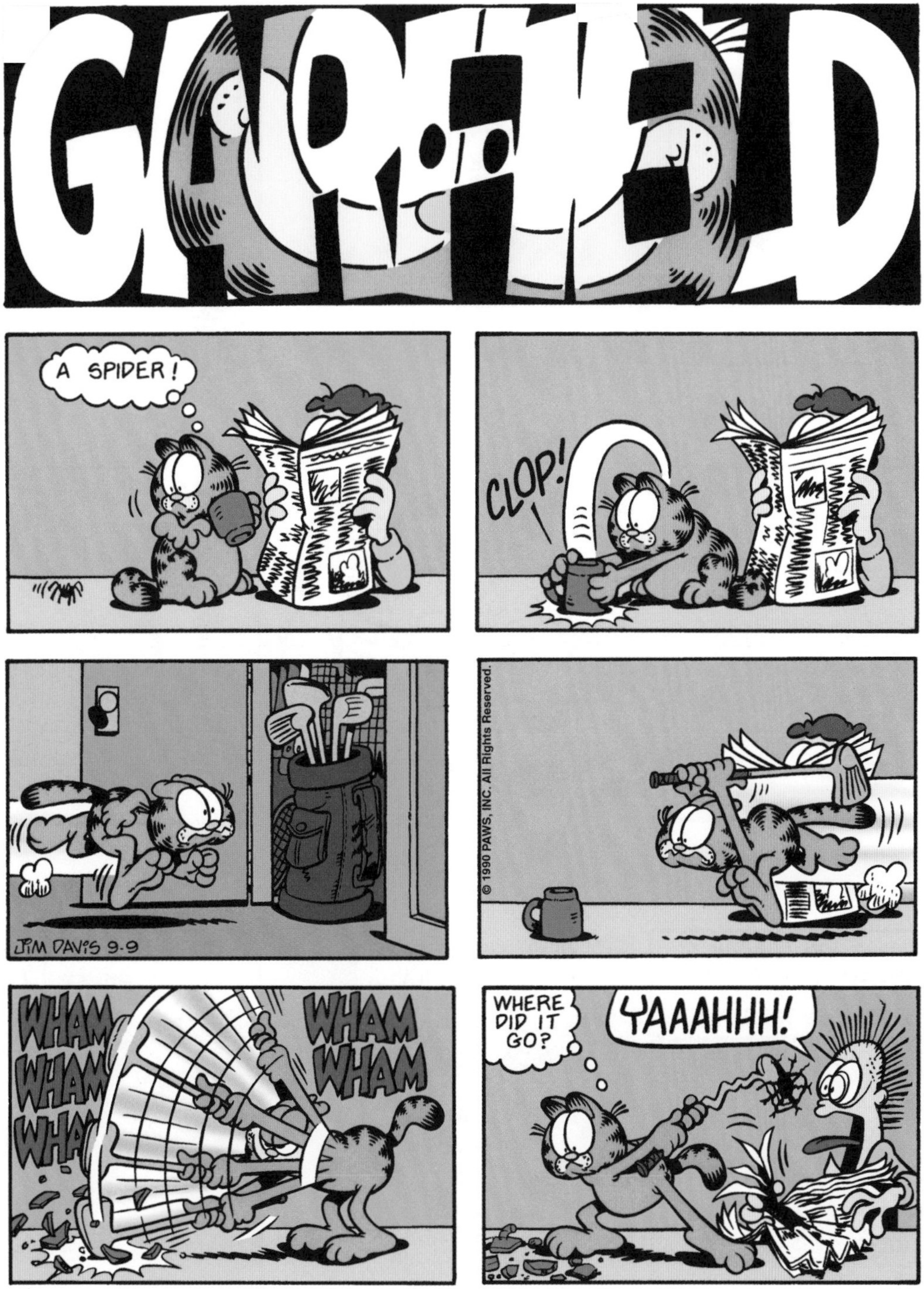
GARFIELD
A SPIDER!
CLOP!
JIM DAVIS 9-9
© 1990 PAWS, INC. All Rights Reserved.
WHAM
WHAM
WHAM
WHAM
WHAM
WHERE DID IT GO?
YAAAHHH!

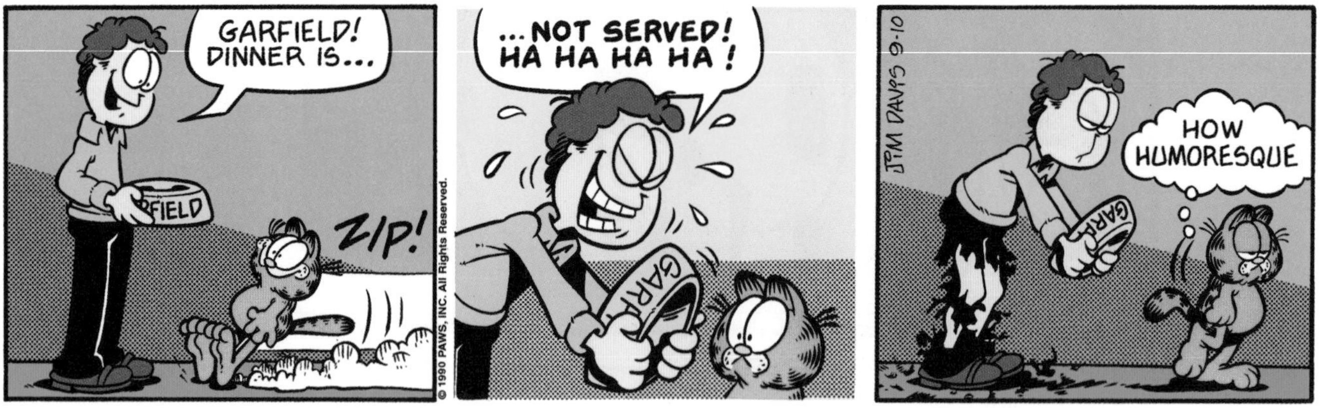
GARFIELD! DINNER IS...
FIELD
ZIP!
© 1990 PAWS, INC. All Rights Reserved.
...NOT SERVED! HA HA HA HA!
GARF
JIM DAVIS 9-10
HOW HUMORESQUE
GARF

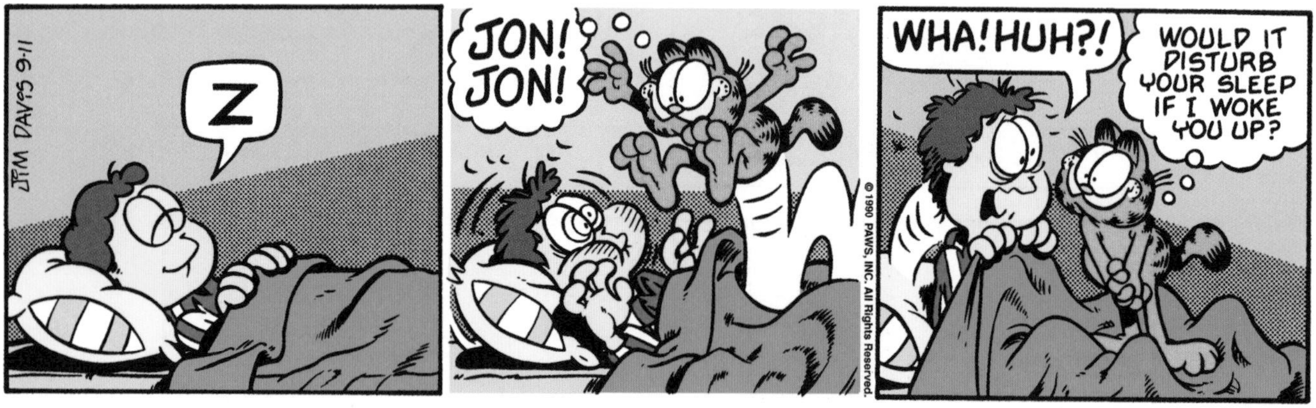
JIM DAVIS 9-11
Z
JON! JON!
© 1990 PAWS, INC. All Rights Reserved.
WHA! HUH?!
WOULD IT DISTURB YOUR SLEEP IF I WOKE YOU UP?

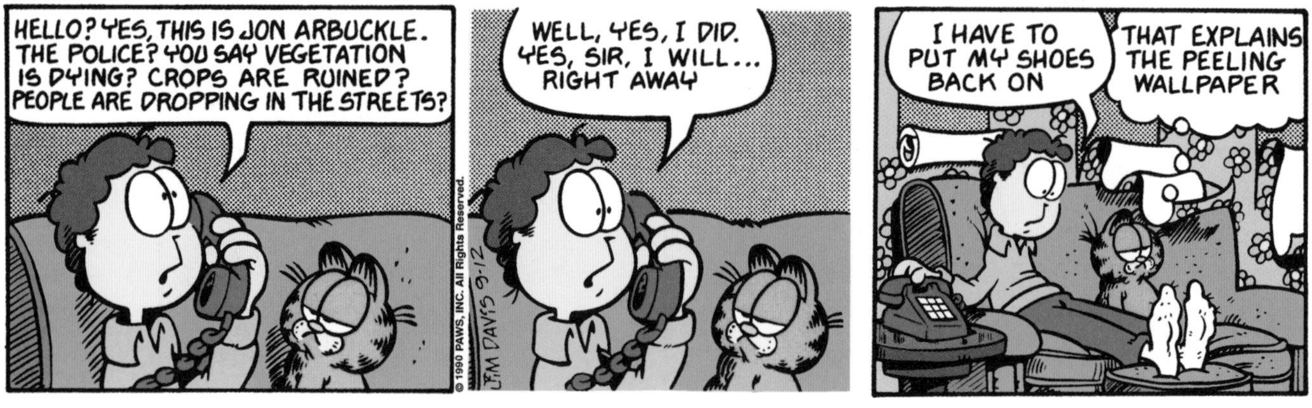
HELLO? YES, THIS IS JON ARBUCKLE. THE POLICE? YOU SAY VEGETATION IS DYING? CROPS ARE RUINED? PEOPLE ARE DROPPING IN THE STREETS?
© 1990 PAWS, INC. All Rights Reserved.
JIM DAVIS 9-12
WELL, YES, I DID. YES, SIR, I WILL... RIGHT AWAY
I HAVE TO PUT MY SHOES BACK ON
THAT EXPLAINS THE PEELING WALLPAPER

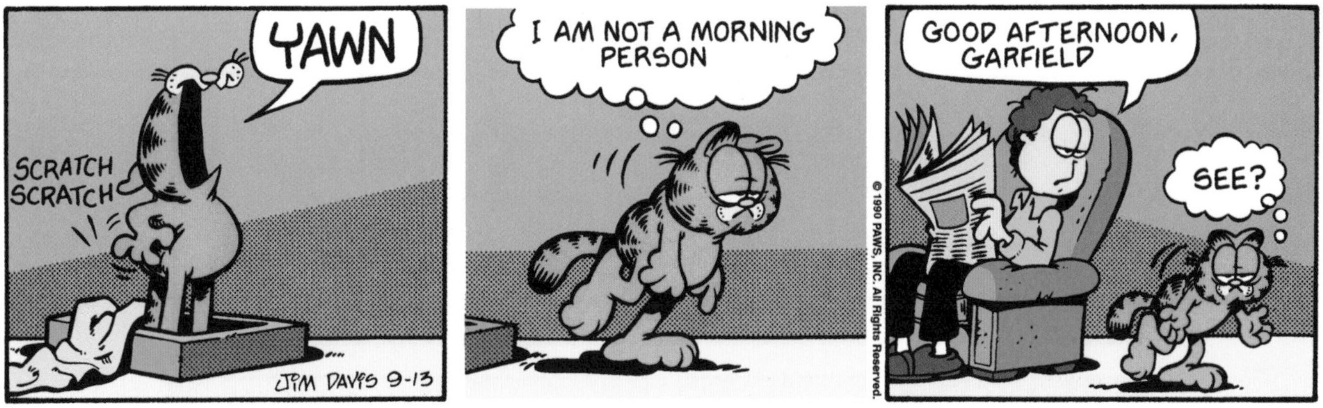
SCRATCH SCRATCH
YAWN
JIM DAVIS 9-13
I AM NOT A MORNING PERSON
© 1990 PAWS, INC. All Rights Reserved.
GOOD AFTERNOON, GARFIELD
SEE?

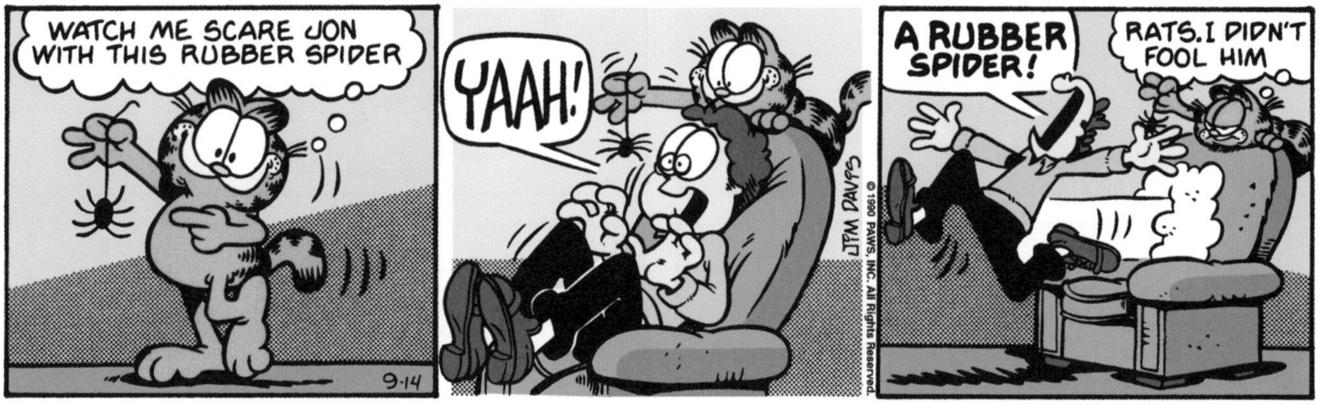
WATCH ME SCARE JON WITH THIS RUBBER SPIDER
9-14
YAAH!
JIM DAVIS
© 1990 PAWS, INC. All Rights Reserved.
A RUBBER SPIDER!
RATS. I DIDN'T FOOL HIM

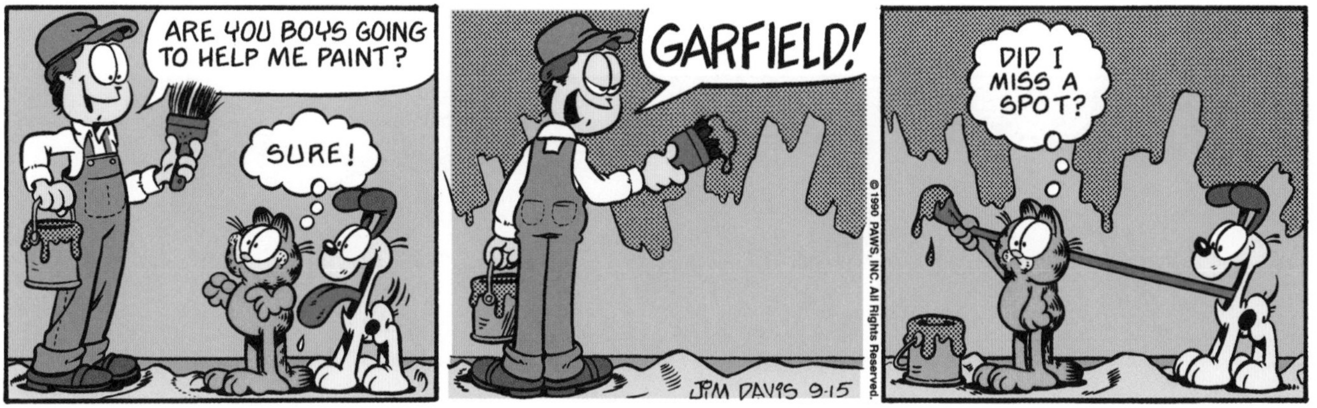
ARE YOU BOYS GOING TO HELP ME PAINT?
SURE!
GARFIELD!
JIM DAVIS 9-15
© 1990 PAWS, INC. All Rights Reserved.
DID I MISS A SPOT?

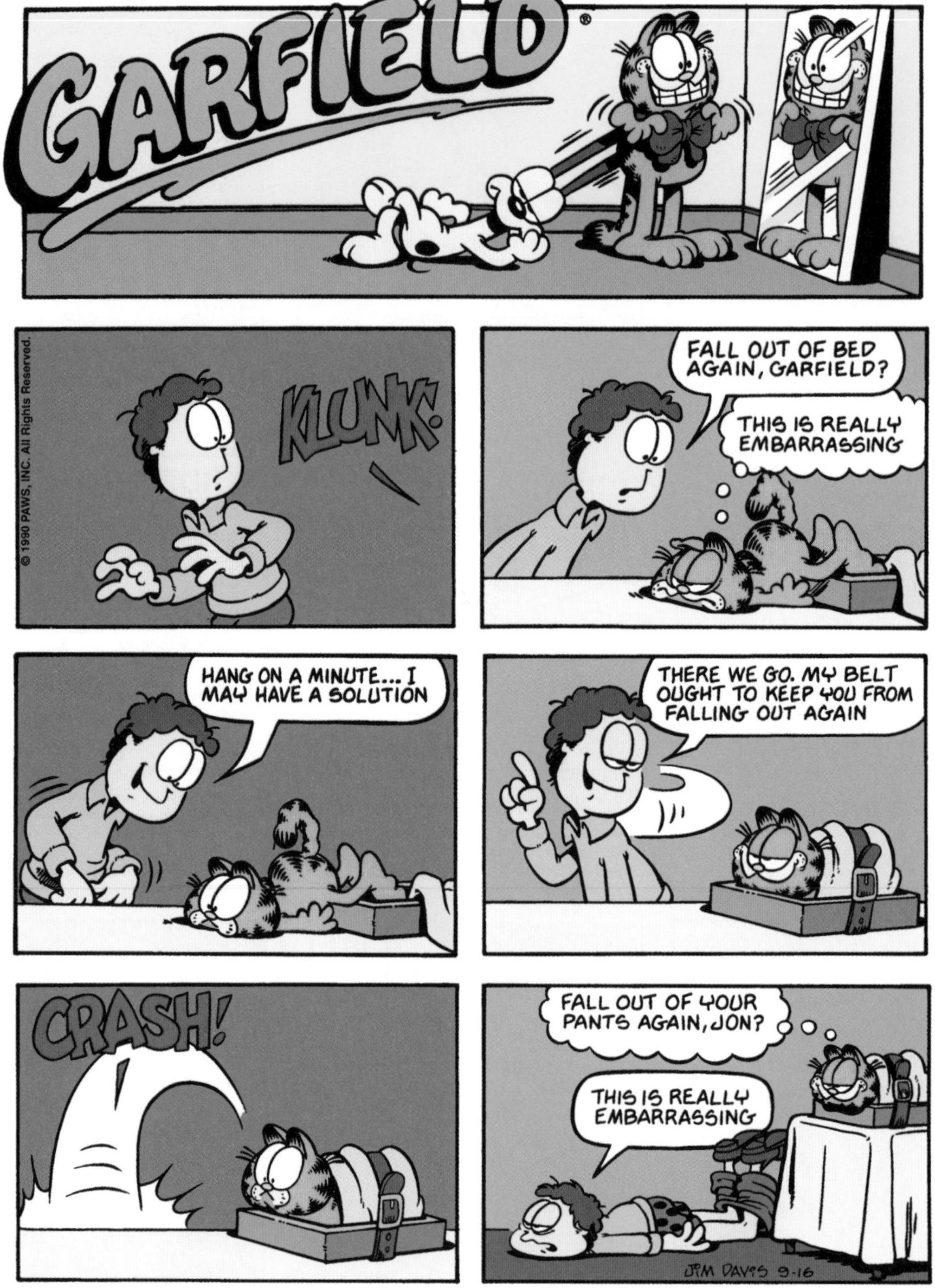
GARFIELD®
© 1990 PAWS, INC. All Rights Reserved.
KLUNK!
FALL OUT OF BED AGAIN, GARFIELD?
THIS IS REALLY EMBARRASSING
HANG ON A MINUTE... I MAY HAVE A SOLUTION
THERE WE GO. MY BELT OUGHT TO KEEP YOU FROM FALLING OUT AGAIN
CRASH!
FALL OUT OF YOUR PANTS AGAIN, JON?
THIS IS REALLY EMBARRASSING
JIM DAVIS 9-16

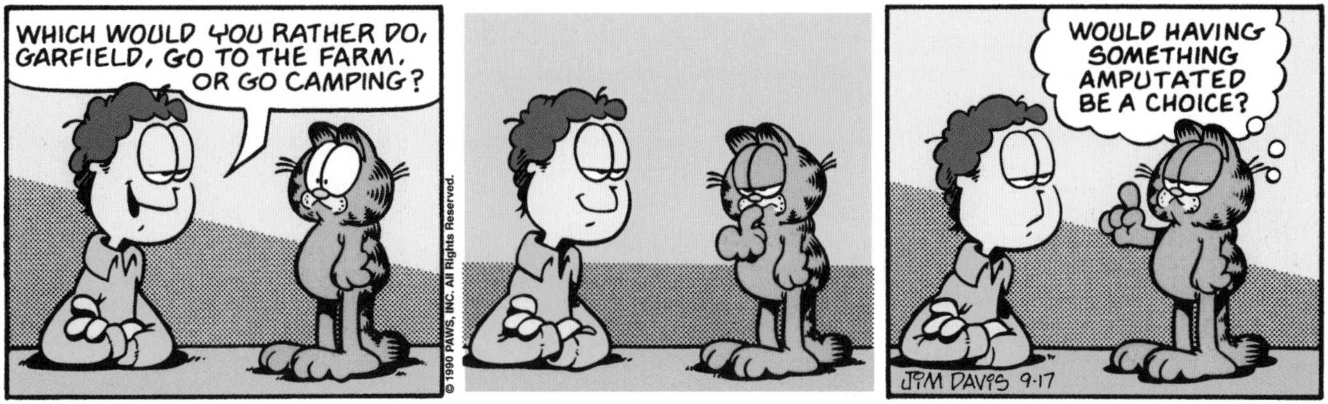
WHICH WOULD YOU RATHER DO, GARFIELD, GO TO THE FARM, OR GO CAMPING?
© 1990 PAWS, INC. All Rights Reserved.
WOULD HAVING SOMETHING AMPUTATED BE A CHOICE?
JIM DAVIS 9-17

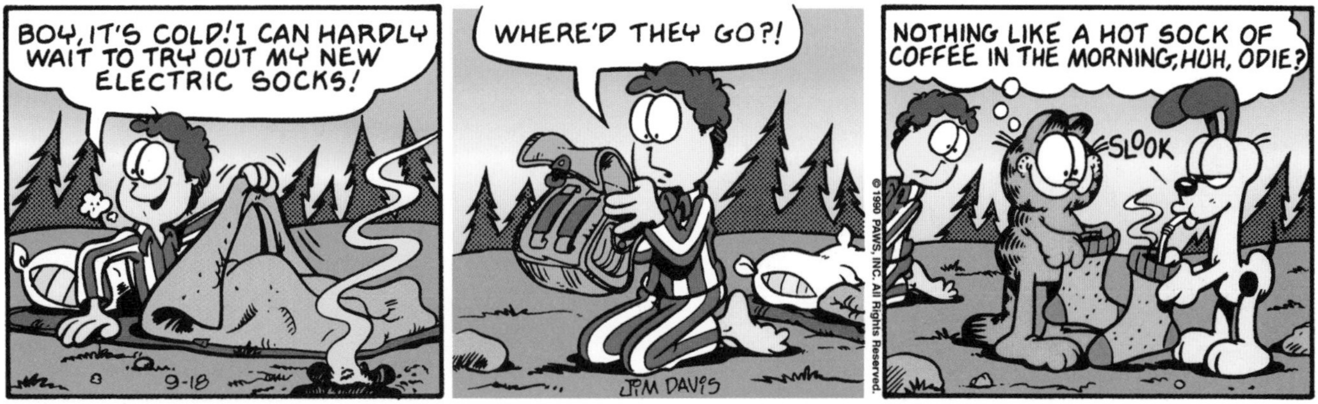
BOY, IT'S COLD! I CAN HARDLY WAIT TO TRY OUT MY NEW ELECTRIC SOCKS!
9-18
WHERE'D THEY GO?!
JIM DAVIS
© 1990 PAWS, INC. All Rights Reserved.
NOTHING LIKE A HOT SOCK OF COFFEE IN THE MORNING, HUH, ODIE?
SLOOK

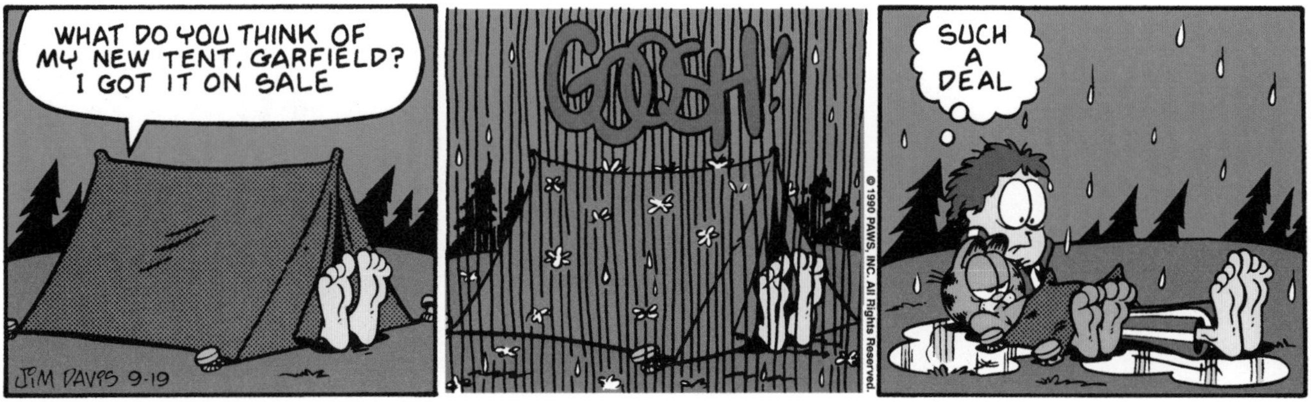
WHAT DO YOU THINK OF MY NEW TENT, GARFIELD? I GOT IT ON SALE
JIM DAVIS 9-19
GOOSH!
© 1990 PAWS, INC. All Rights Reserved.
SUCH A DEAL

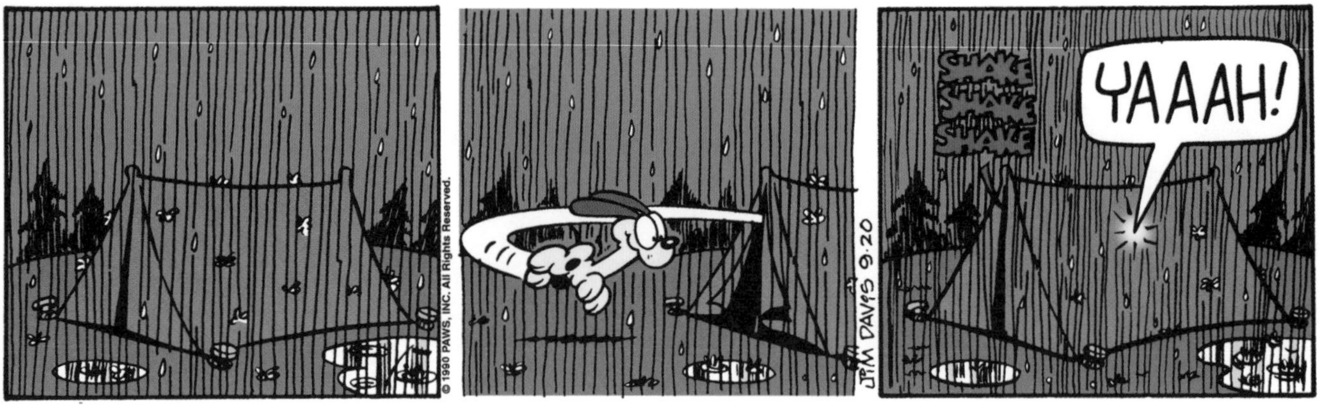
SHAKE
SHAKE
SHAKE
SHAKE
YAAAH!
© 1990 PAWS, INC. All Rights Reserved.
JIM DAVIS 9-20

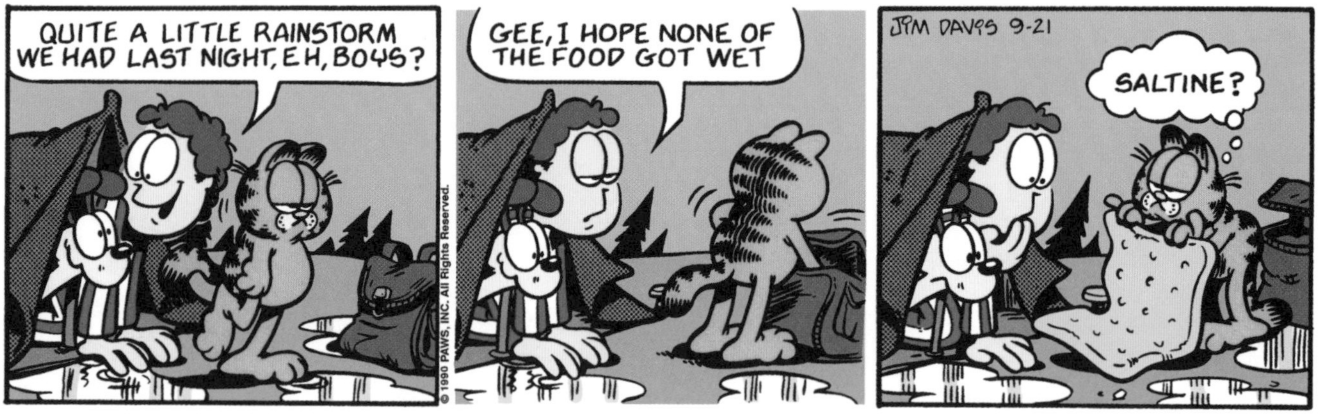
QUITE A LITTLE RAINSTORM WE HAD LAST NIGHT, EH, BOYS?
GEE, I HOPE NONE OF THE FOOD GOT WET
SALTINE?
© 1990 PAWS, INC. All Rights Reserved.
JIM DAVIS 9-21

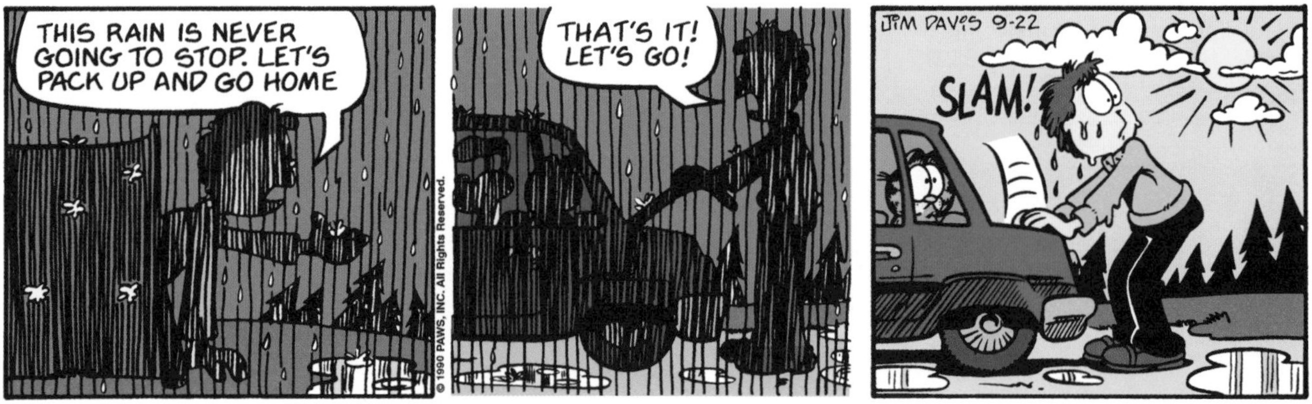
THIS RAIN IS NEVER GOING TO STOP. LET'S PACK UP AND GO HOME
THAT'S IT! LET'S GO!
SLAM!
© 1990 PAWS, INC. All Rights Reserved.
JIM DAVIS 9-22

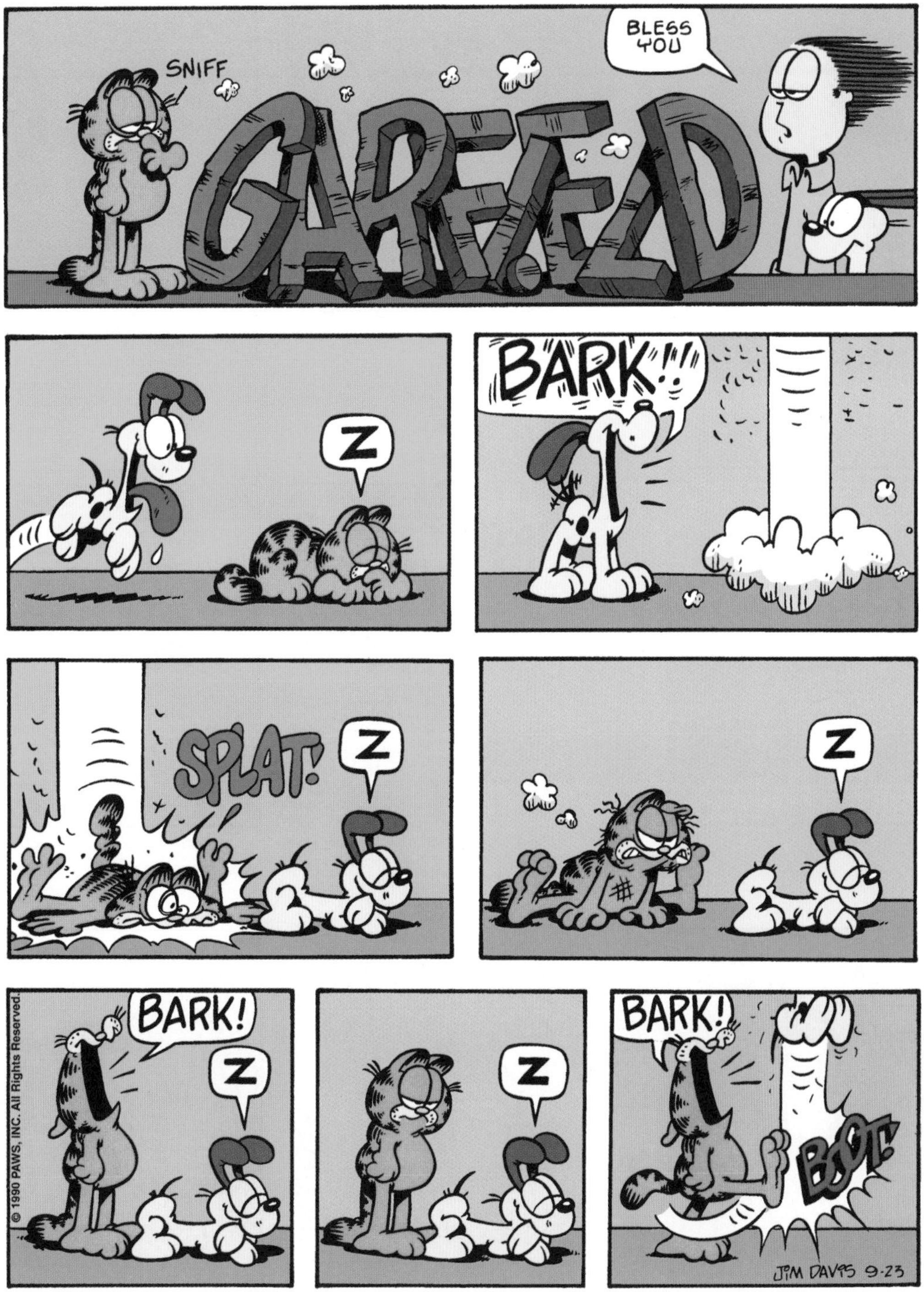

SNIFF
BLESS YOU
GARFIELD
Z
BARK!!
SPLAT!
Z
Z
© 1990 PAWS, INC. All Rights Reserved.
BARK!
Z
Z
BARK!
BOOT!
JIM DAVIS 9-23

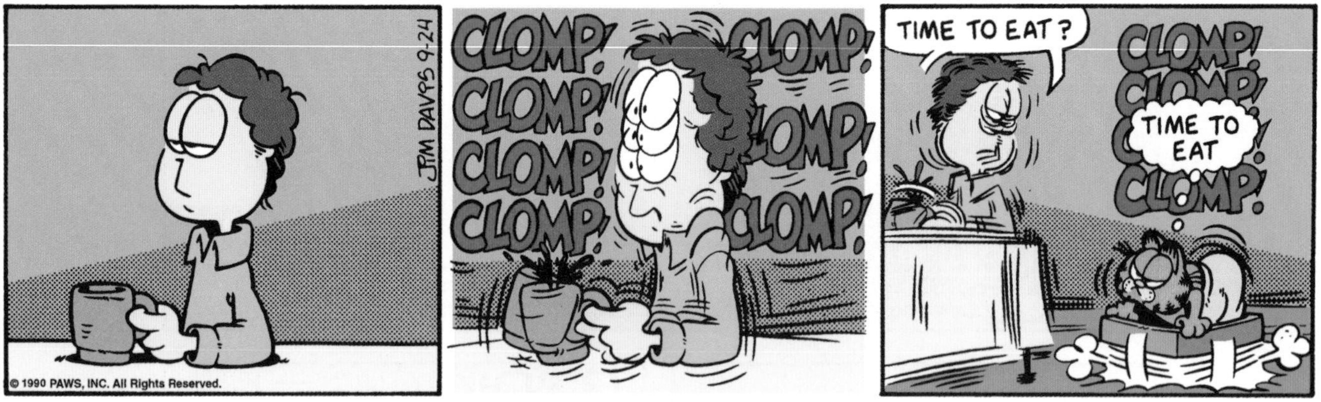
JIM DAVIS 9-24
© 1990 PAWS, INC. All Rights Reserved.
CLOMP! CLOMP! CLOMP! CLOMP!
CLOMP! CLOMP!
TIME TO EAT?
CLOMP! CLOMP!
TIME TO EAT
CLOMP!

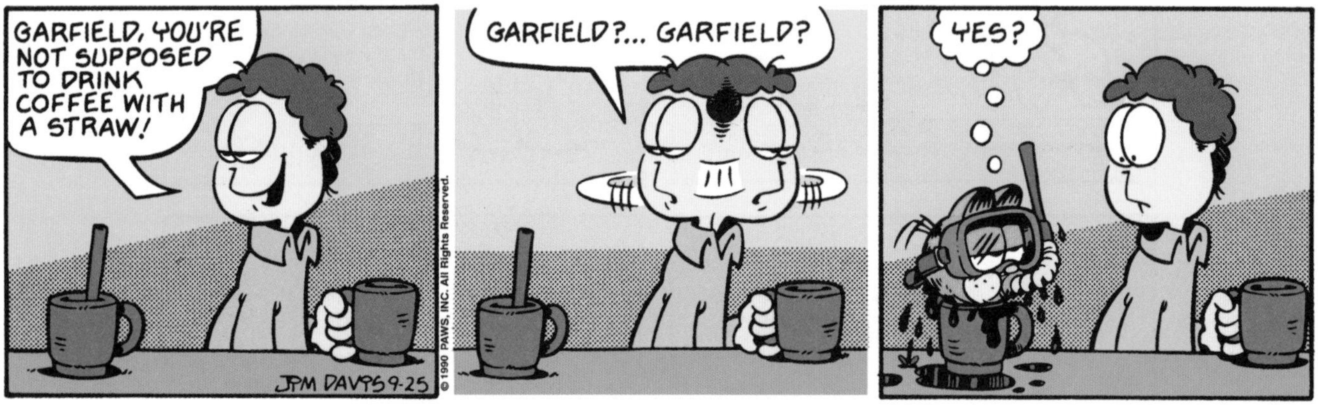
GARFIELD, YOU'RE NOT SUPPOSED TO DRINK COFFEE WITH A STRAW!
JIM DAVIS 9-25
© 1990 PAWS, INC. All Rights Reserved.
GARFIELD?... GARFIELD?
YES?

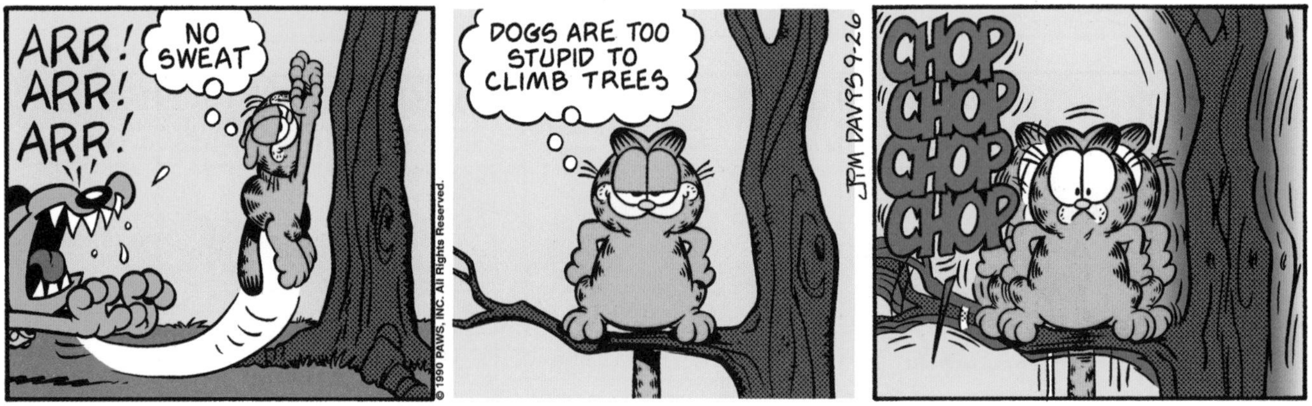
ARR! ARR! ARR!
NO SWEAT
© 1990 PAWS, INC. All Rights Reserved.
DOGS ARE TOO STUPID TO CLIMB TREES
JIM DAVIS 9-26
CHOP CHOP CHOP CHOP

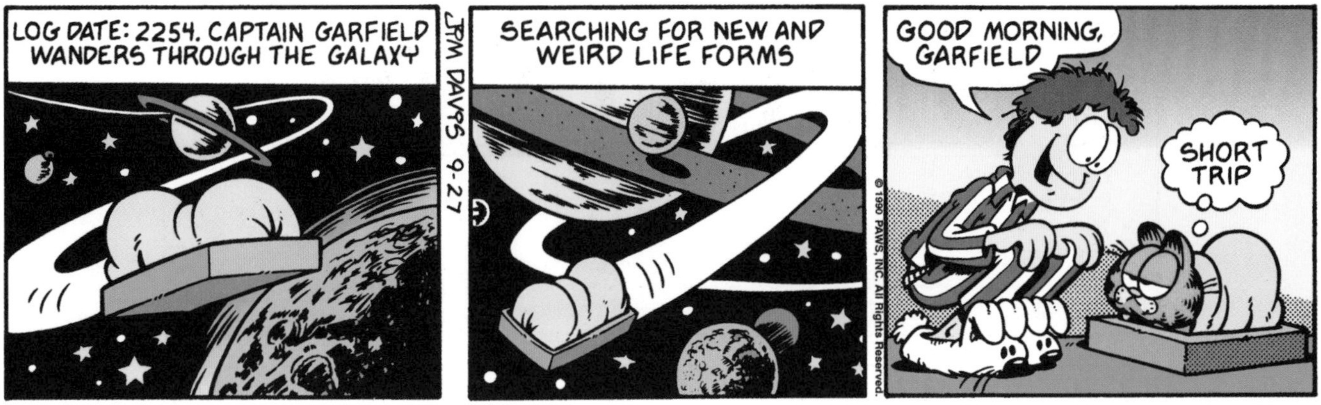
LOG DATE: 2254. CAPTAIN GARFIELD WANDERS THROUGH THE GALAXY
JIM DAVIS 9-27
SEARCHING FOR NEW AND WEIRD LIFE FORMS
GOOD MORNING, GARFIELD
SHORT TRIP
© 1990 PAWS, INC. All Rights Reserved.

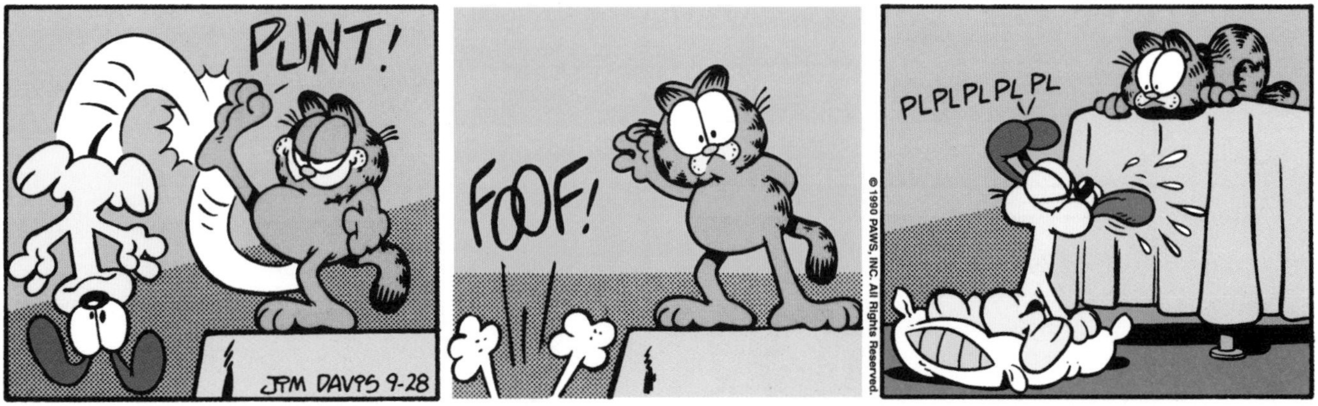
PUNT!
JIM DAVIS 9-28
FOOF!
PLPLPLPLPL
© 1990 PAWS, INC. All Rights Reserved.

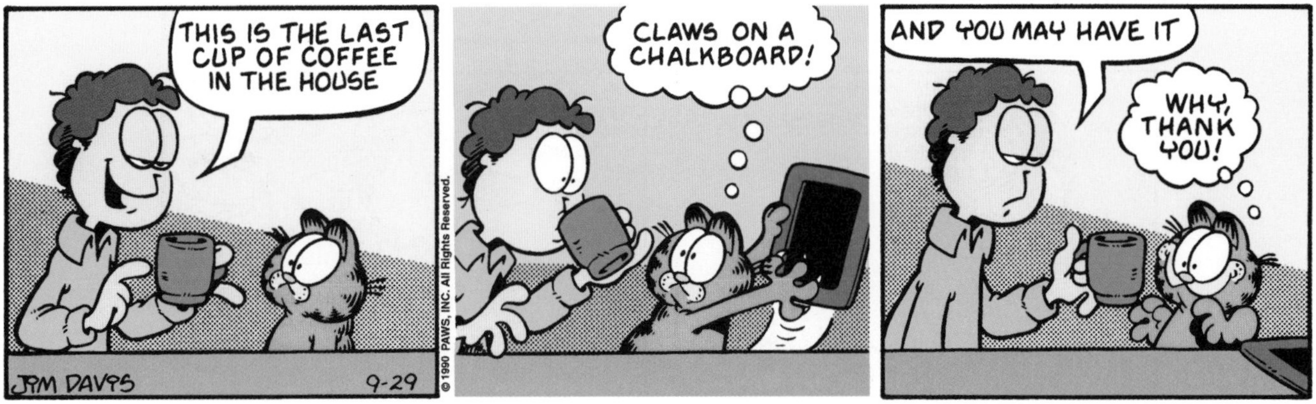
THIS IS THE LAST CUP OF COFFEE IN THE HOUSE
JIM DAVIS 9-29
CLAWS ON A CHALKBOARD!
© 1990 PAWS, INC. All Rights Reserved.
AND YOU MAY HAVE IT
WHY, THANK YOU!

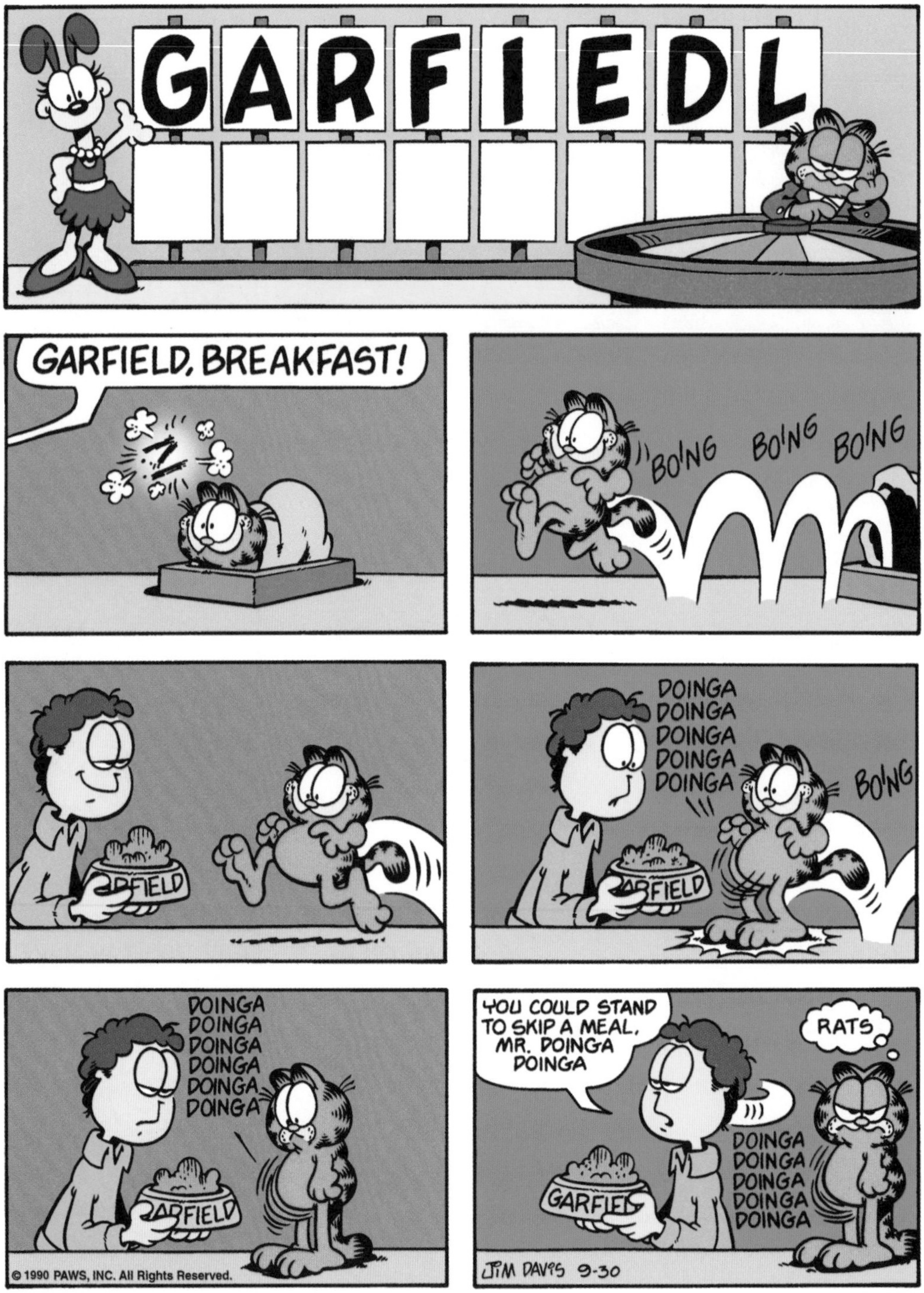
GARFIEDL
GARFIELD, BREAKFAST!
Z
BOING BOING BOING
ARFIELD
DOINGA
DOINGA
DOINGA
DOINGA
DOINGA
BOING
ARFIELD
DOINGA
DOINGA
DOINGA
DOINGA
DOINGA
DOINGA
ARFIELD
© 1990 PAWS, INC. All Rights Reserved.
YOU COULD STAND TO SKIP A MEAL, MR. DOINGA DOINGA
RATS
GARFIEL
DOINGA
DOINGA
DOINGA
DOINGA
DOINGA
JIM DAVIS 9-30

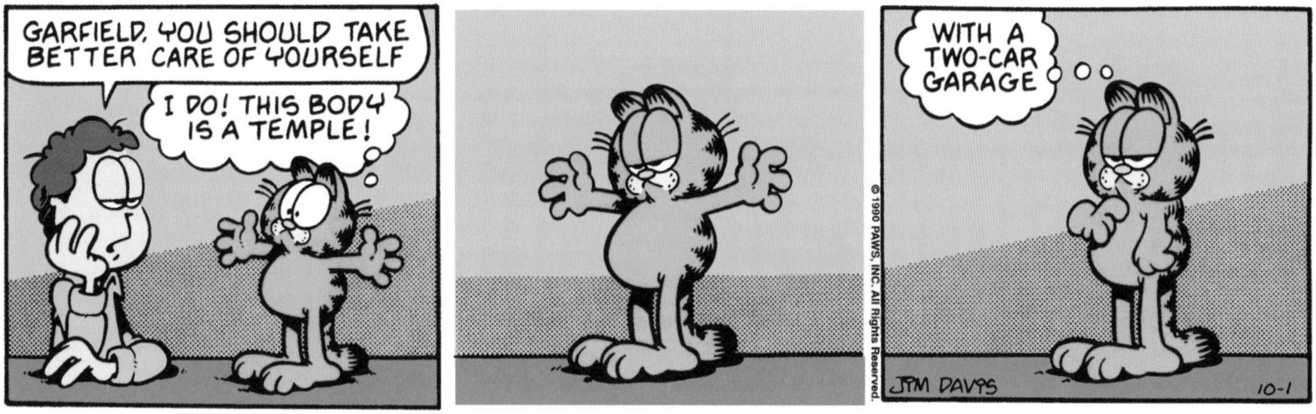
GARFIELD, YOU SHOULD TAKE BETTER CARE OF YOURSELF
I DO! THIS BODY IS A TEMPLE!
WITH A TWO-CAR GARAGE
JIM DAVIS
10-1

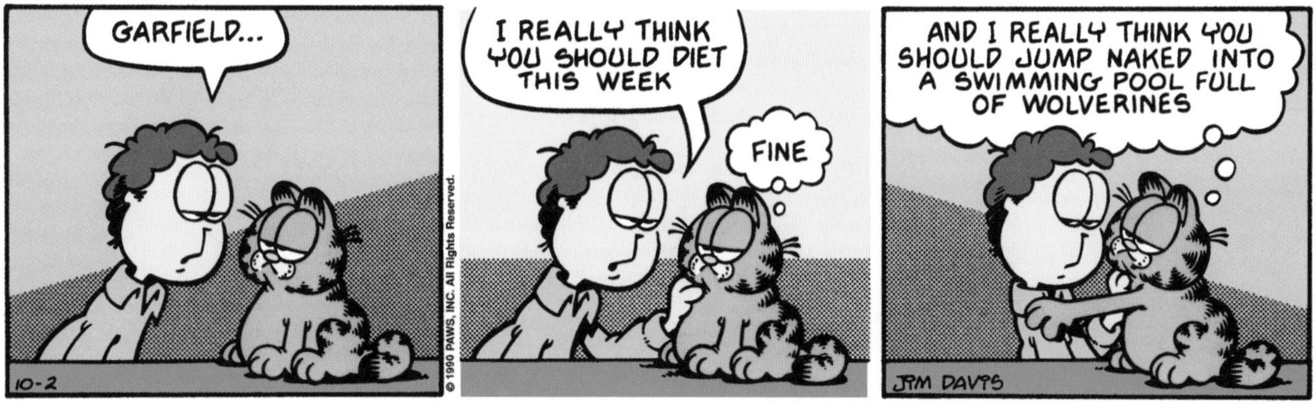
GARFIELD...
10-2
I REALLY THINK YOU SHOULD DIET THIS WEEK
FINE
AND I REALLY THINK YOU SHOULD JUMP NAKED INTO A SWIMMING POOL FULL OF WOLVERINES
JIM DAVIS

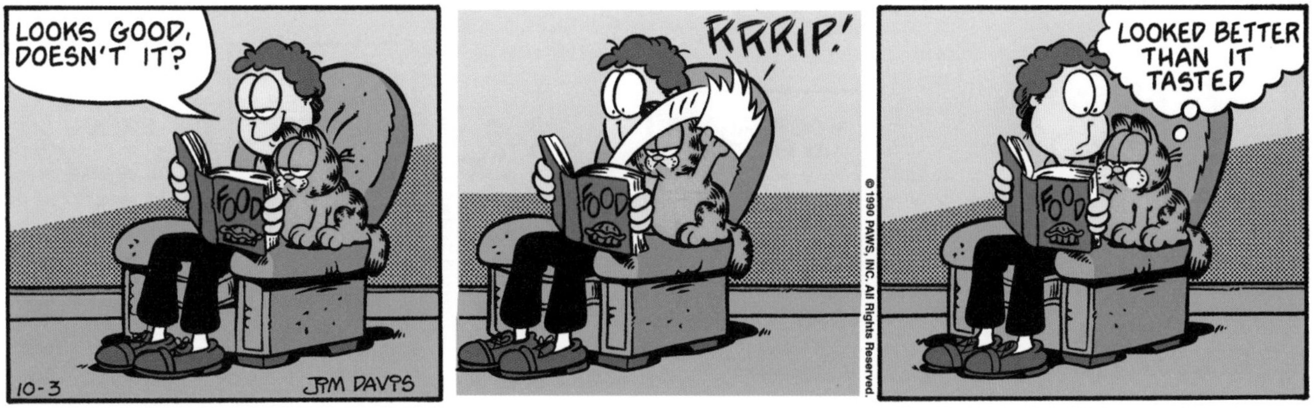
LOOKS GOOD, DOESN'T IT?
FOOD
10-3
JIM DAVIS
KRRIP!
LOOKED BETTER THAN IT TASTED

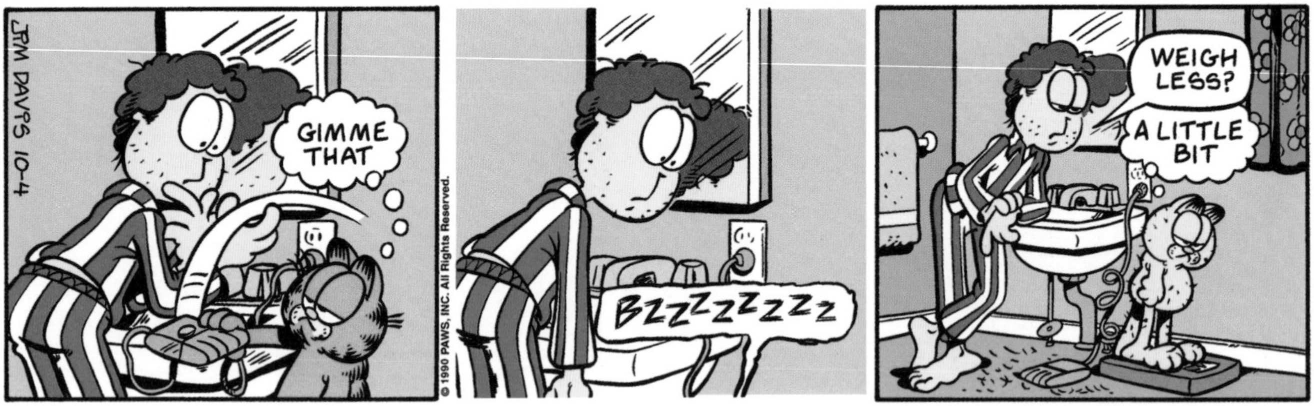
JIM DAVIS 10-4
GIMME THAT
© 1990 PAWS, INC. All Rights Reserved.
BZZZZZZZZZ
WEIGH LESS?
A LITTLE BIT

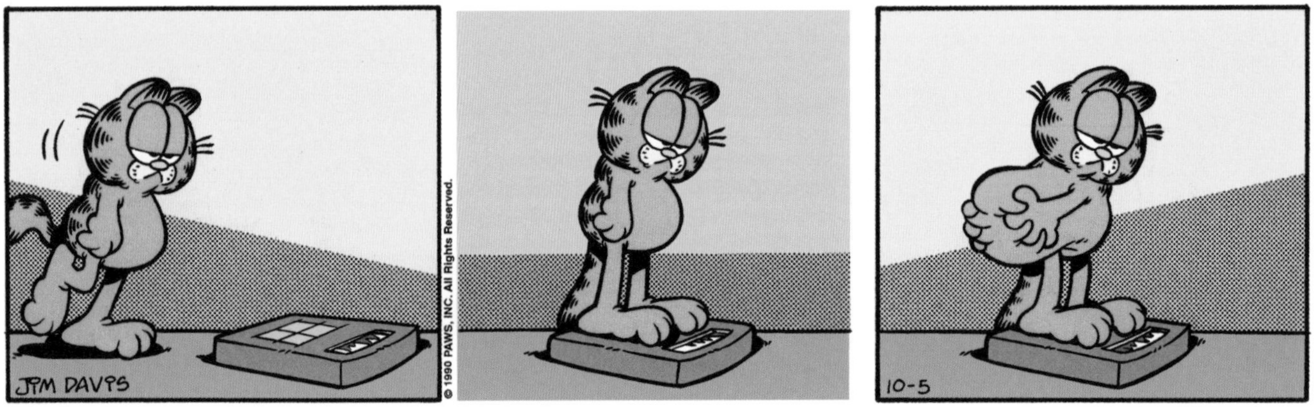
JIM DAVIS
© 1990 PAWS, INC. All Rights Reserved.
10-5

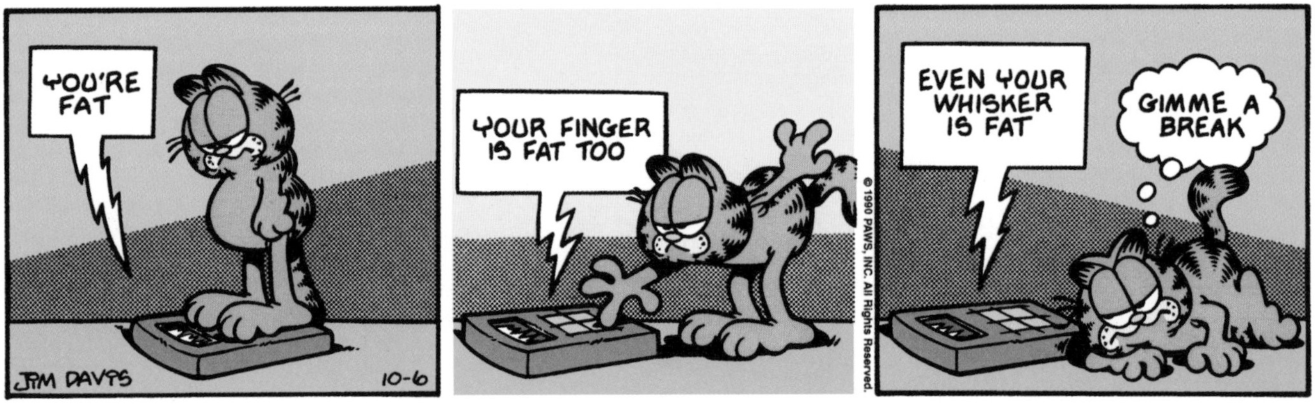
YOU'RE FAT
JIM DAVIS
10-6
YOUR FINGER IS FAT TOO
© 1990 PAWS, INC. All Rights Reserved.
EVEN YOUR WHISKER IS FAT
GIMME A BREAK

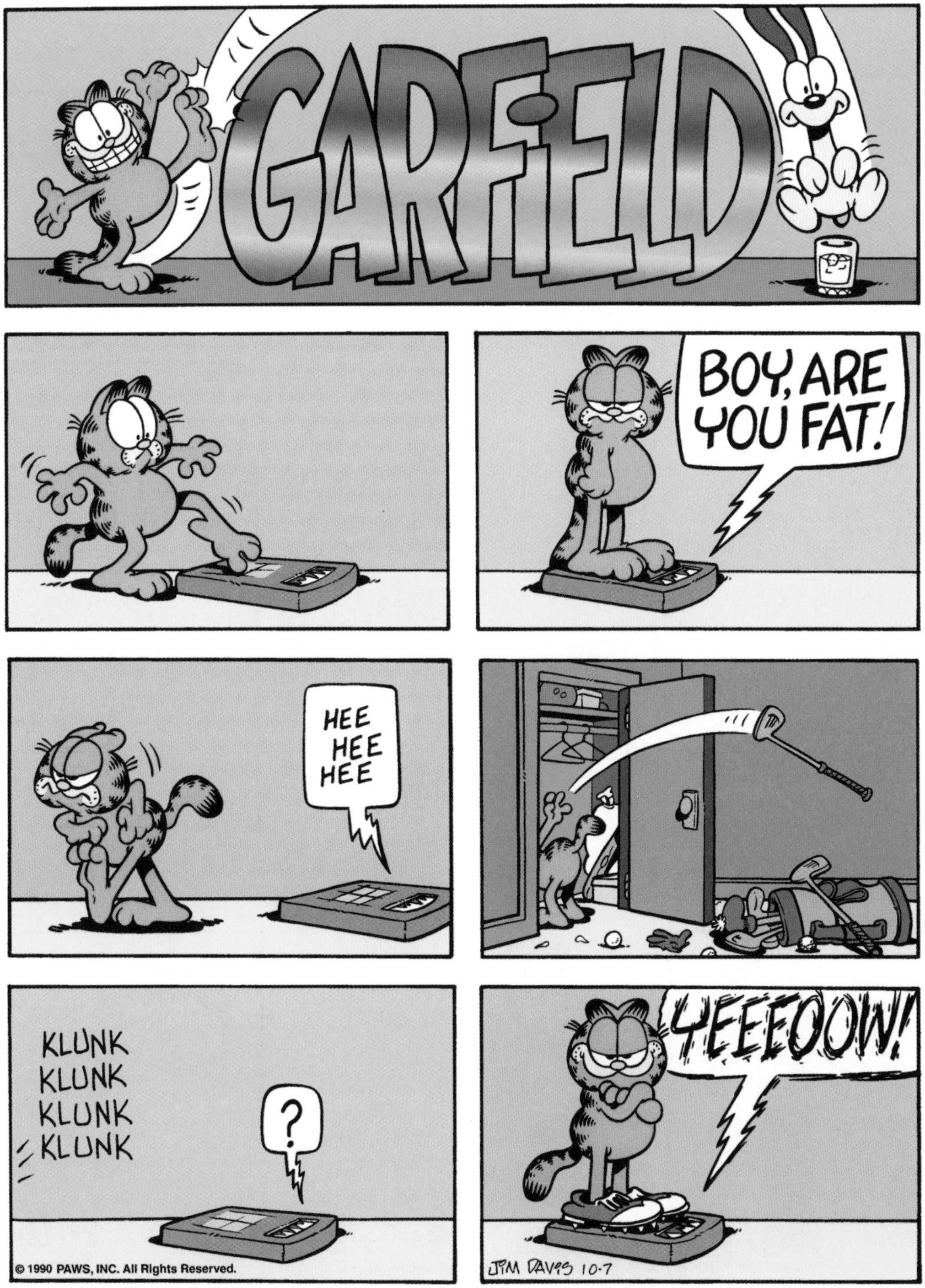
GARFIELD
BOY, ARE YOU FAT!
HEE HEE HEE
KLUNK KLUNK KLUNK KLUNK
?
YEEEOOW!
© 1990 PAWS, INC. All Rights Reserved.
JIM DAVIS 10-7

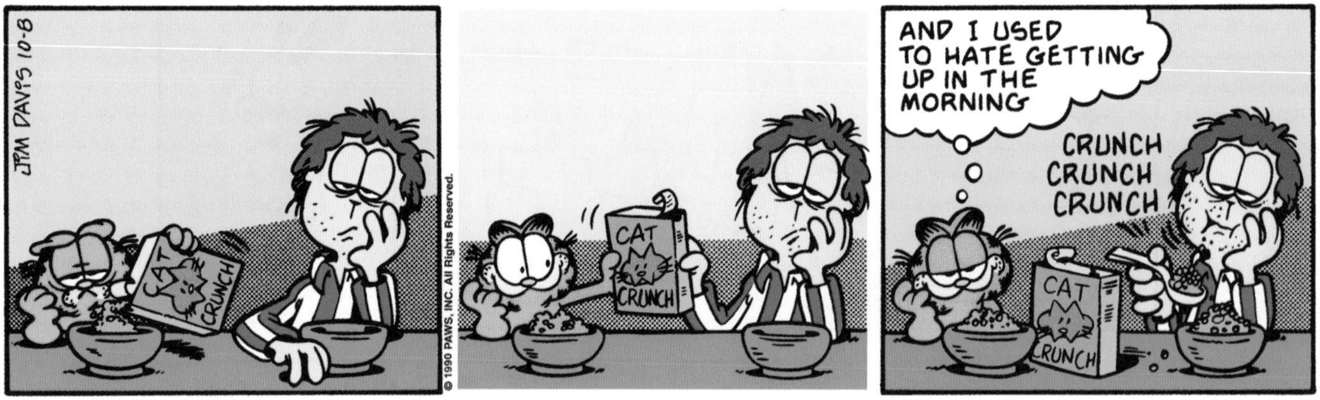
JIM DAVIS 10-8
CAT CRUNCH
© 1990 PAWS, INC. All Rights Reserved.
CAT CRUNCH
AND I USED TO HATE GETTING UP IN THE MORNING
CRUNCH CRUNCH CRUNCH
CAT CRUNCH

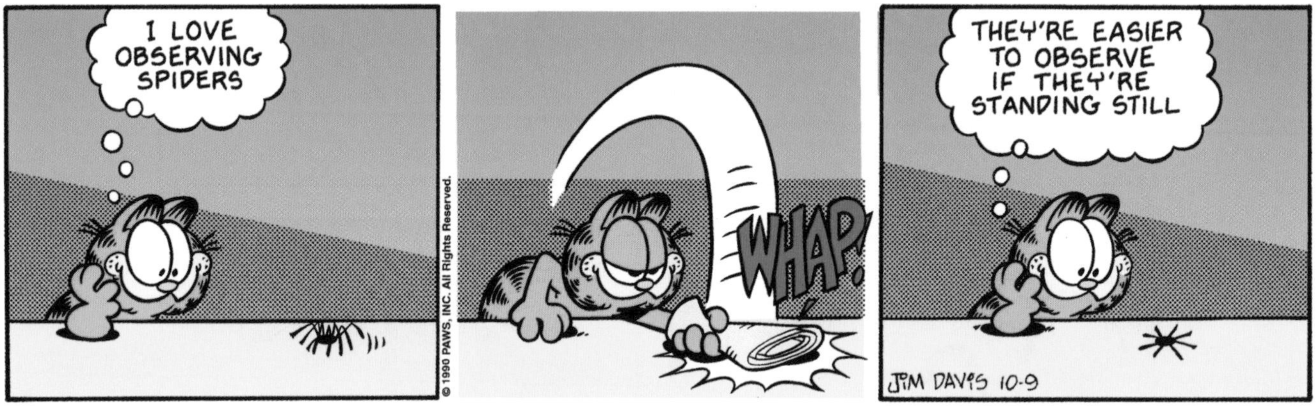
I LOVE OBSERVING SPIDERS
© 1990 PAWS, INC. All Rights Reserved.
WHAP!
THEY'RE EASIER TO OBSERVE IF THEY'RE STANDING STILL
JIM DAVIS 10-9

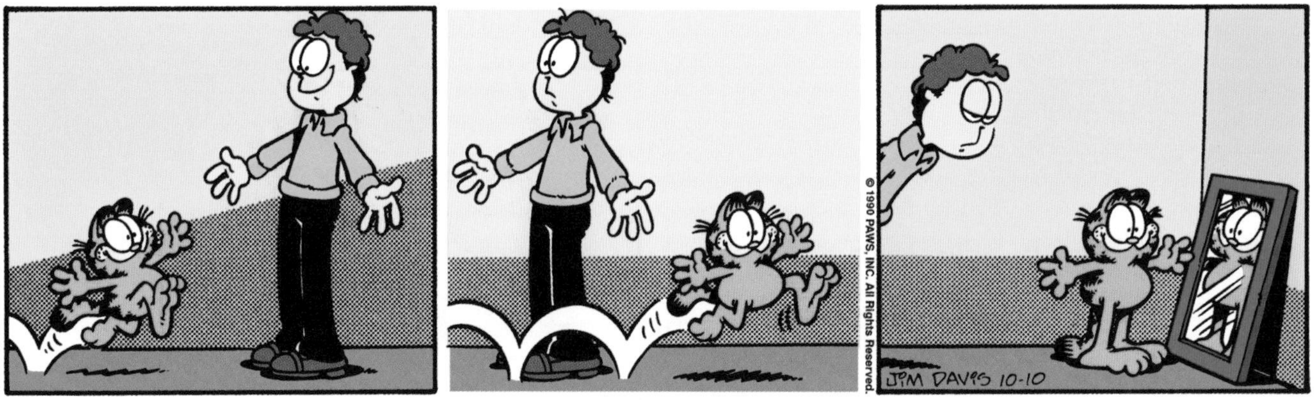
© 1990 PAWS, INC. All Rights Reserved.
JIM DAVIS 10-10

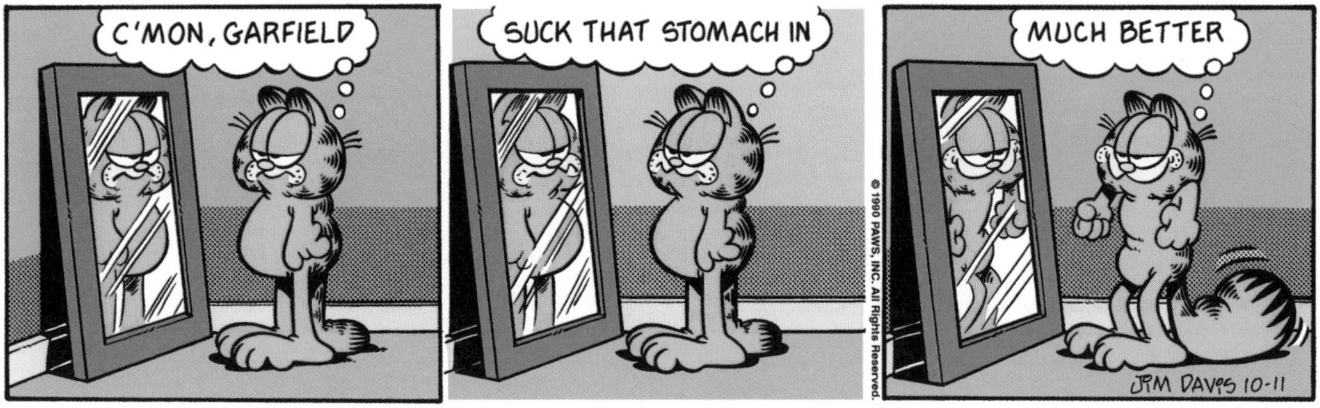
C'MON, GARFIELD
SUCK THAT STOMACH IN
© 1990 PAWS, INC. All Rights Reserved.
MUCH BETTER
JIM DAVIS 10-11

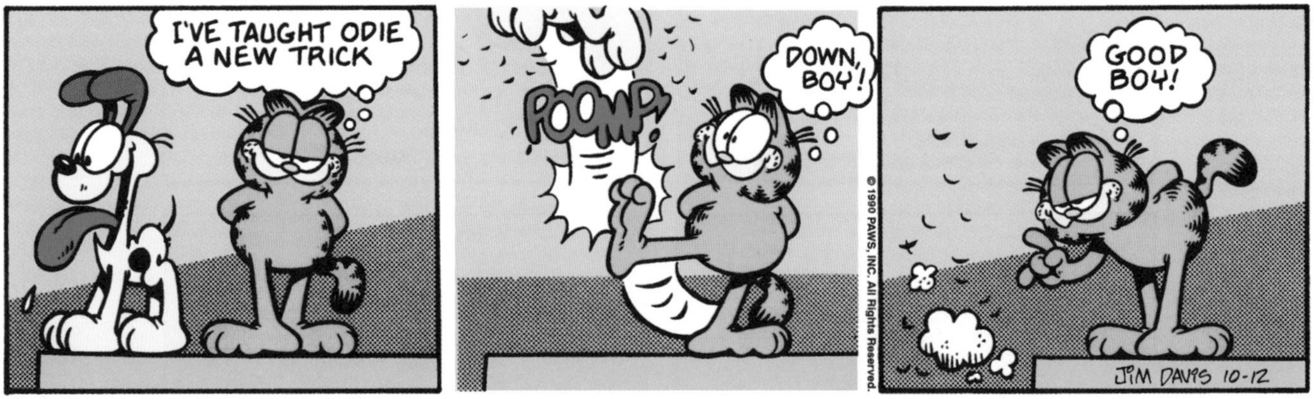
I'VE TAUGHT ODIE A NEW TRICK
POOMP!
DOWN, BOY!
© 1990 PAWS, INC. All Rights Reserved.
GOOD BOY!
JIM DAVIS 10-12

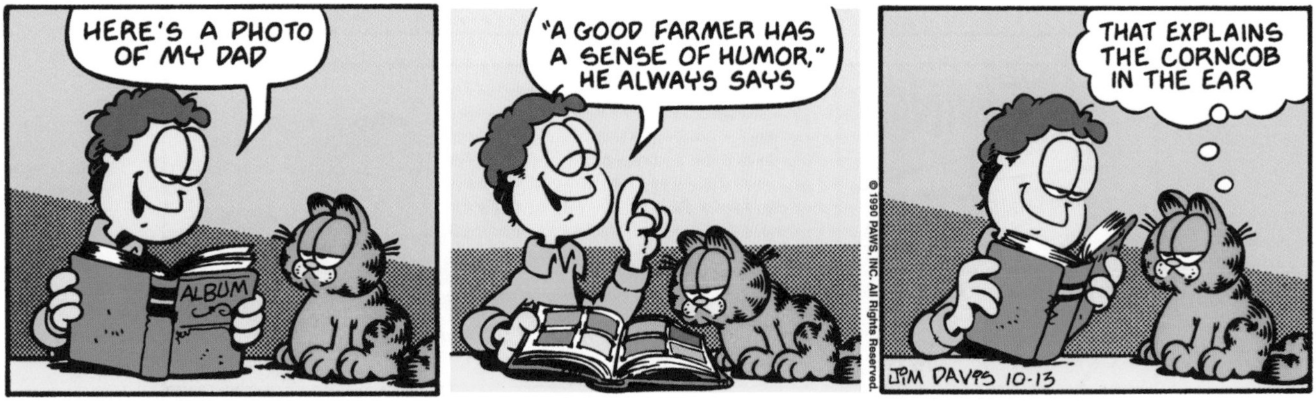
HERE'S A PHOTO OF MY DAD
ALBUM
"A GOOD FARMER HAS A SENSE OF HUMOR," HE ALWAYS SAYS
© 1990 PAWS, INC. All Rights Reserved.
THAT EXPLAINS THE CORNCOB IN THE EAR
JIM DAVIS 10-13

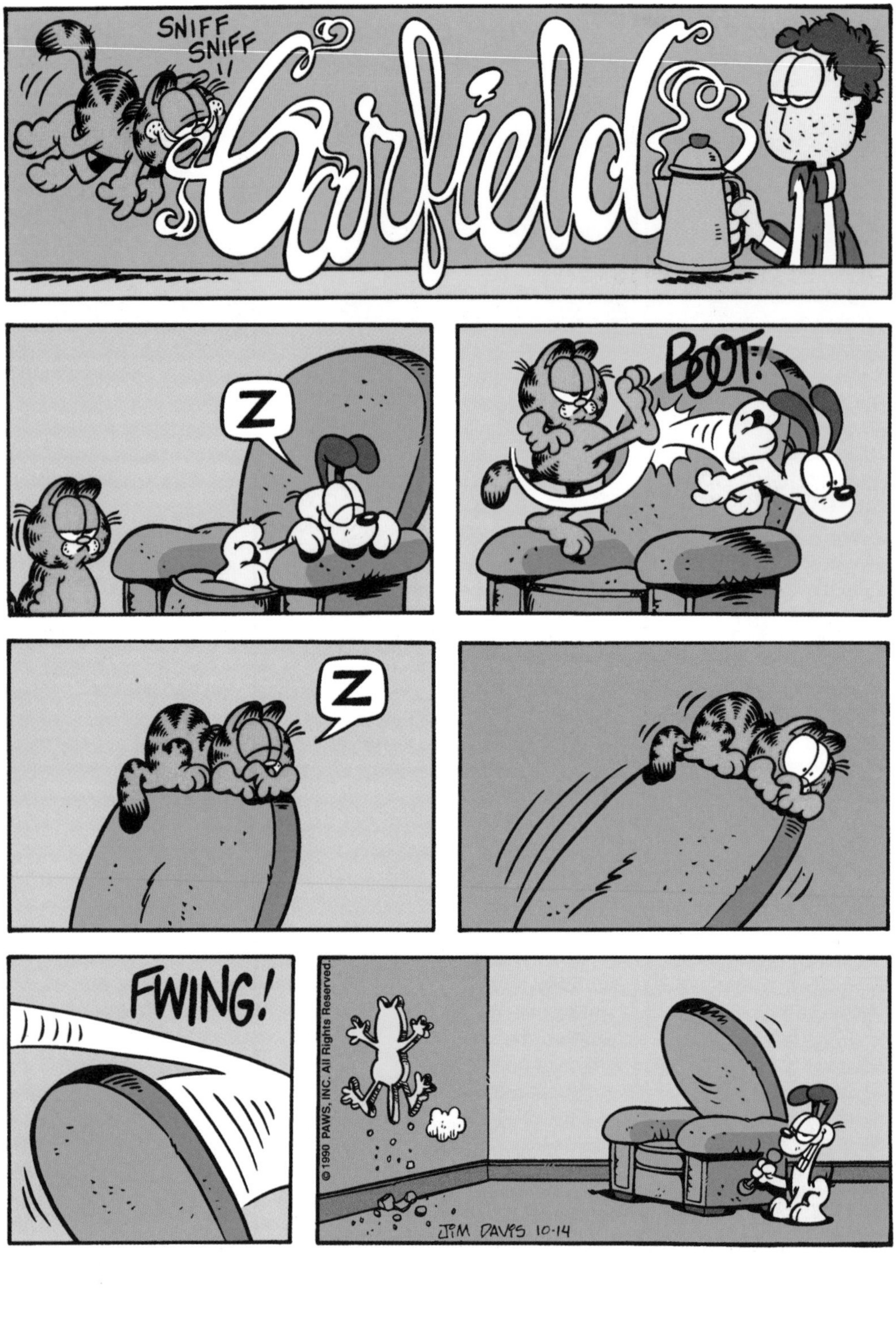
SNIFF SNIFF
Garfield
Z
BOOT!
Z
FWING!
© 1990 PAWS, INC. All Rights Reserved.
JIM DAVIS 10-14

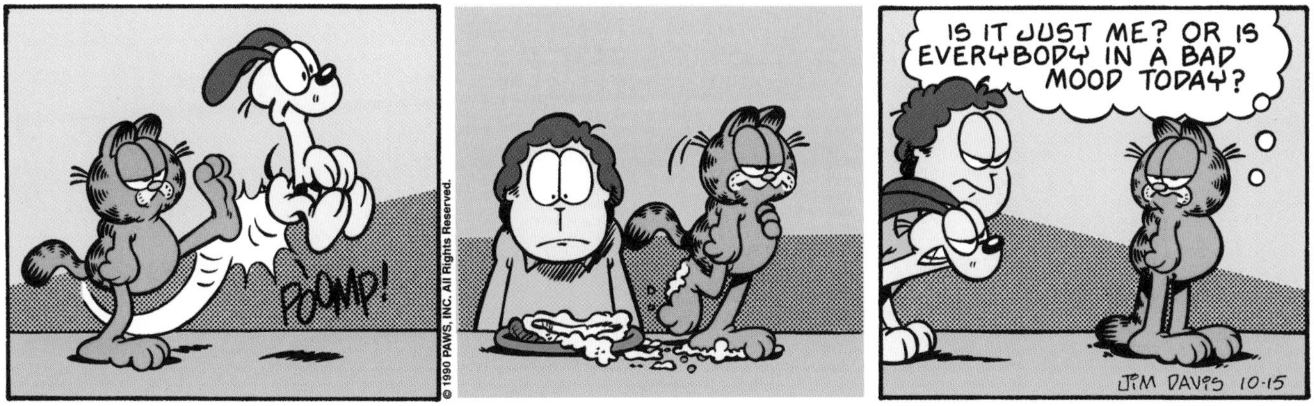
POOMP!
© 1990 PAWS, INC. All Rights Reserved.
IS IT JUST ME? OR IS EVERYBODY IN A BAD MOOD TODAY?
JIM DAVIS 10-15

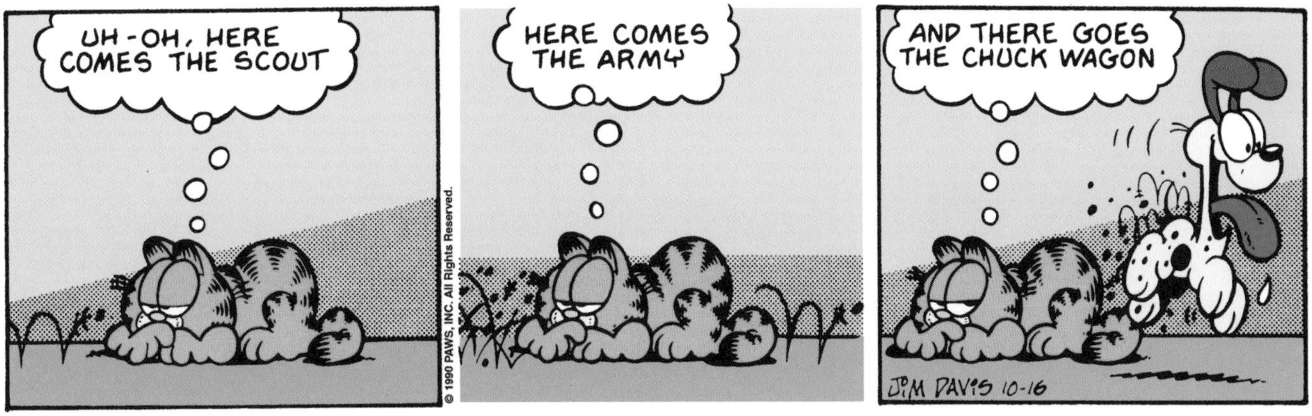
UH-OH, HERE COMES THE SCOUT
© 1990 PAWS, INC. All Rights Reserved.
HERE COMES THE ARMY
AND THERE GOES THE CHUCK WAGON
JIM DAVIS 10-16

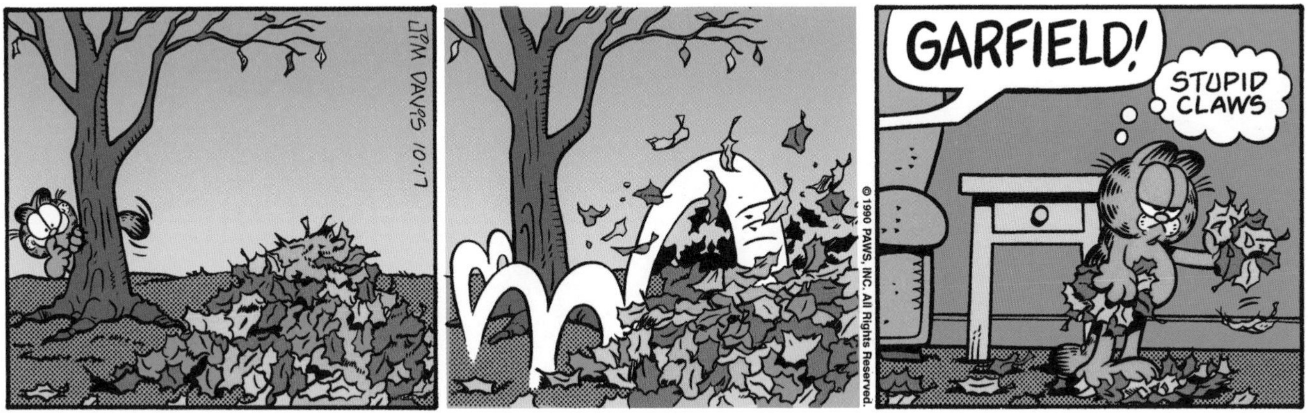
JIM DAVIS 10-17
© 1990 PAWS, INC. All Rights Reserved.
GARFIELD!
STUPID CLAWS

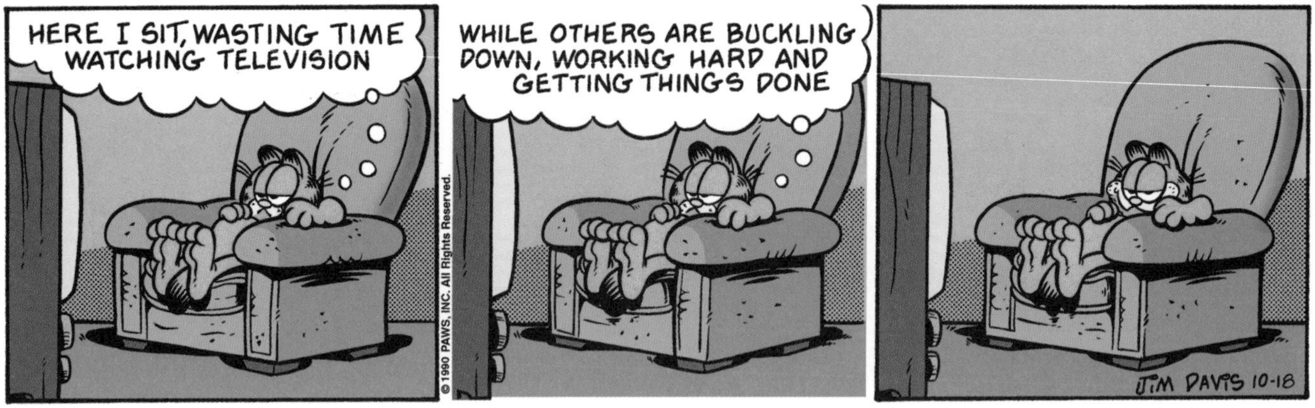
HERE I SIT, WASTING TIME WATCHING TELEVISION
WHILE OTHERS ARE BUCKLING DOWN, WORKING HARD AND GETTING THINGS DONE
© 1990 PAWS, INC. All Rights Reserved.
JIM DAVIS 10-18

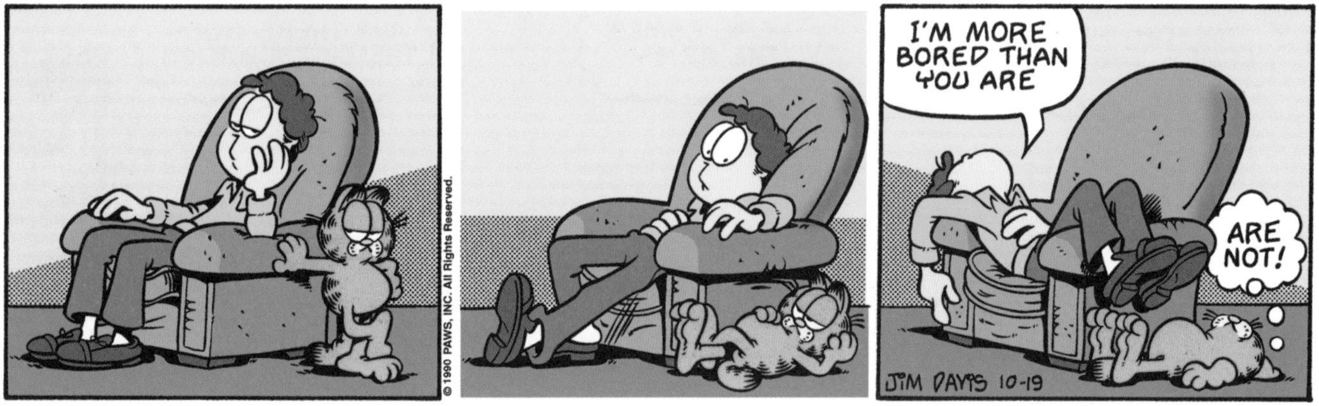
© 1990 PAWS, INC. All Rights Reserved.
I'M MORE BORED THAN YOU ARE
ARE NOT!
JIM DAVIS 10-19

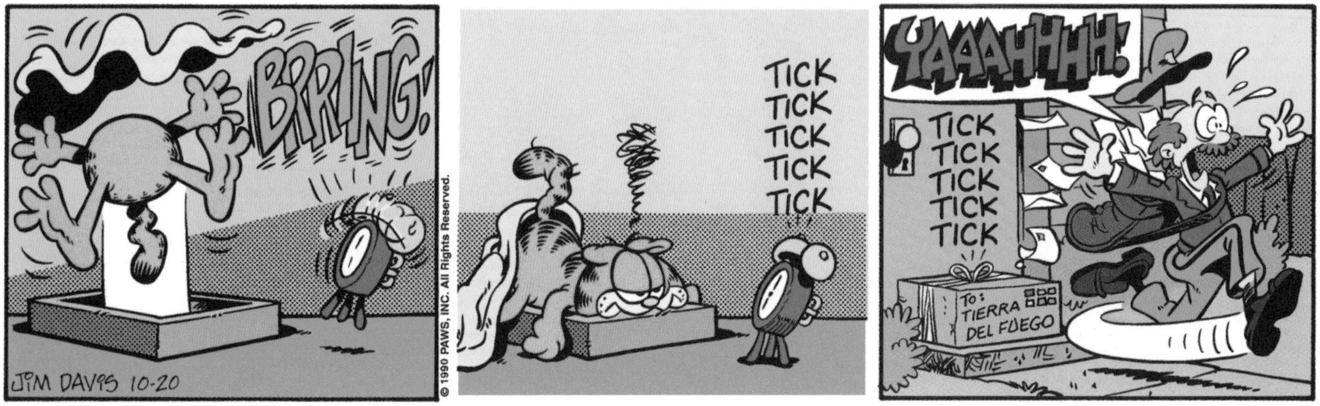
BRRING!
JIM DAVIS 10-20
© 1990 PAWS, INC. All Rights Reserved.
TICK TICK TICK TICK TICK
YAAAHHHH!
TICK TICK TICK TICK TICK
TO: TIERRA DEL FUEGO

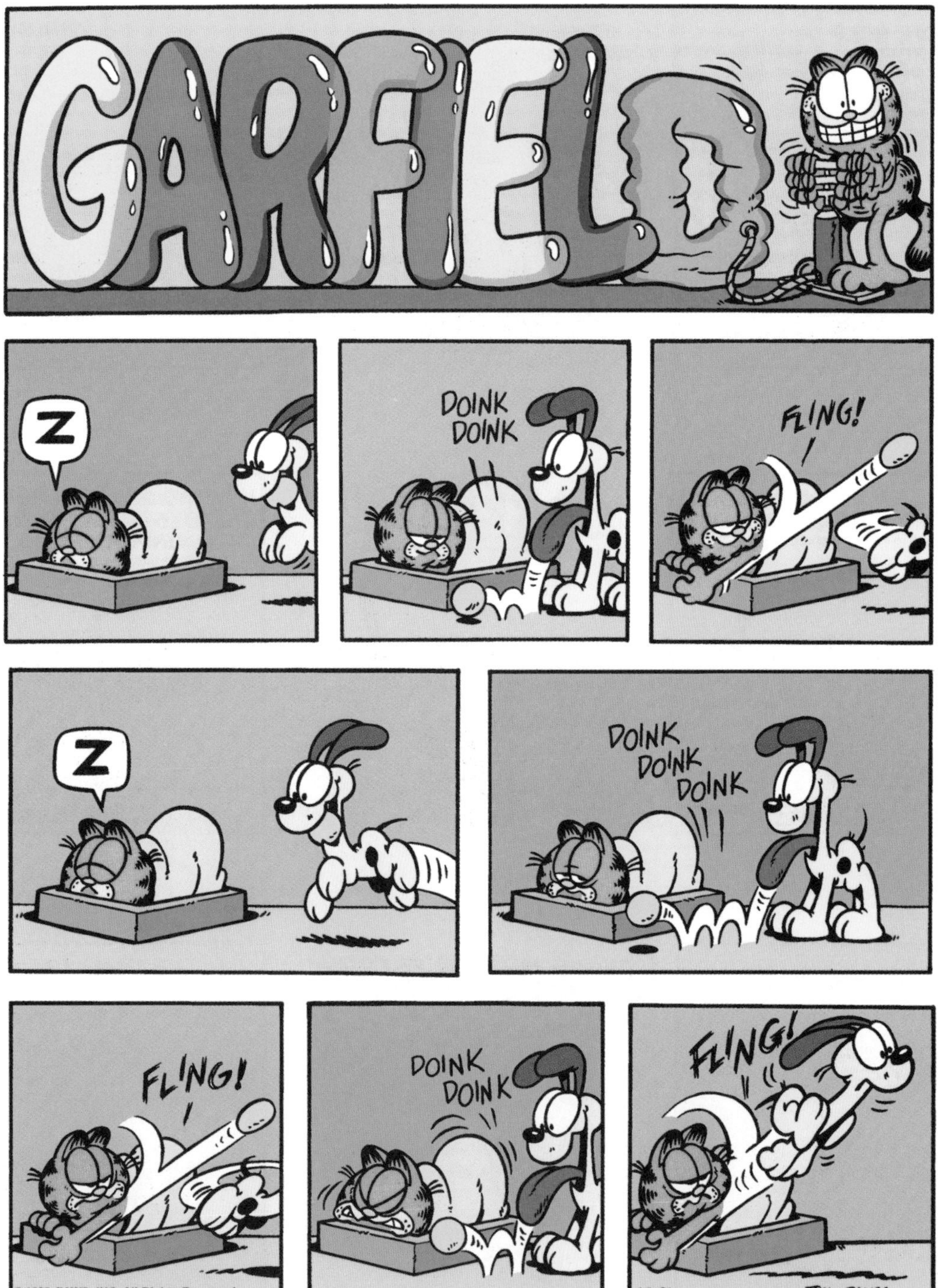
GARFIELD
Z
DOINK DOINK
FLING!
Z
DOINK DOINK DOINK
FLING!
DOINK DOINK
FLING!
© 1990 PAWS, INC. All Rights Reserved.
10-21
JIM DAVIS

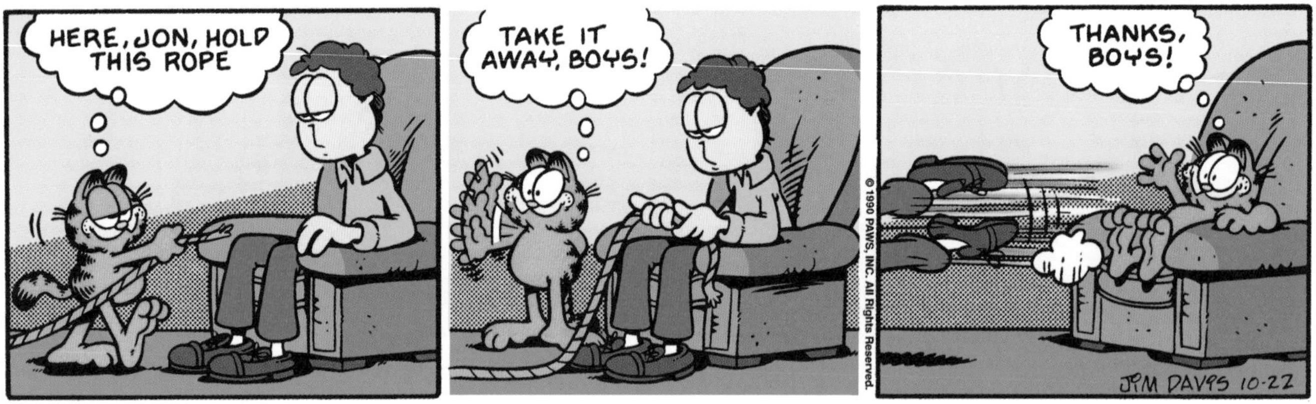
HERE, JON, HOLD THIS ROPE
TAKE IT AWAY, BOYS!
© 1990 PAWS, INC. All Rights Reserved.
THANKS, BOYS!
JIM DAVIS 10-22

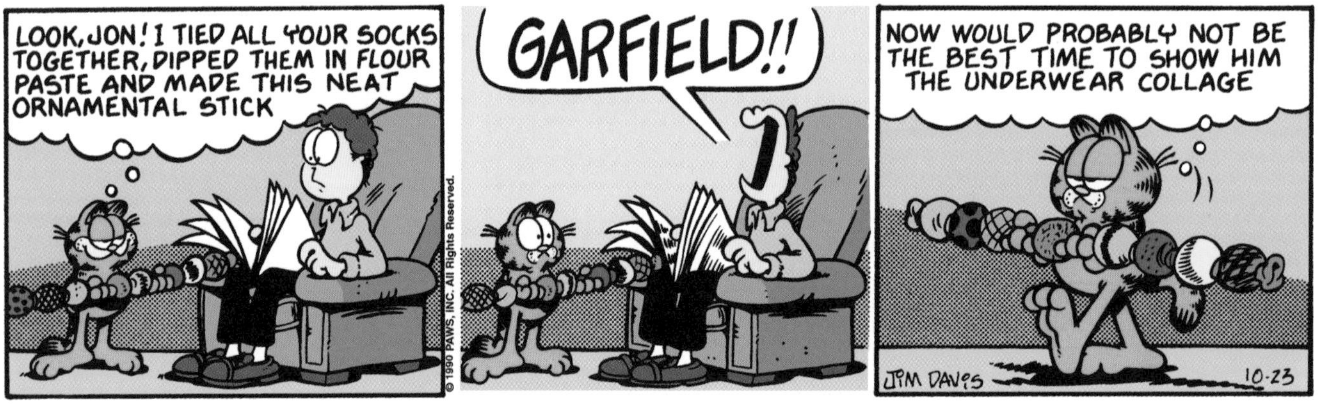
LOOK, JON! I TIED ALL YOUR SOCKS TOGETHER, DIPPED THEM IN FLOUR PASTE AND MADE THIS NEAT ORNAMENTAL STICK
© 1990 PAWS, INC. All Rights Reserved.
GARFIELD!!
NOW WOULD PROBABLY NOT BE THE BEST TIME TO SHOW HIM THE UNDERWEAR COLLAGE
JIM DAVIS 10-23

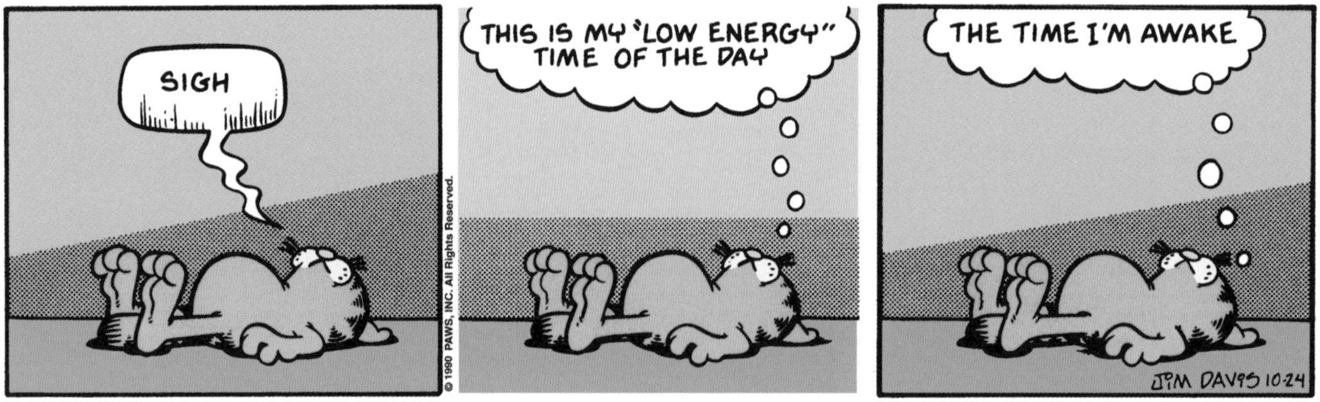
SIGH
© 1990 PAWS, INC. All Rights Reserved.
THIS IS MY "LOW ENERGY" TIME OF THE DAY
THE TIME I'M AWAKE
JIM DAVIS 10-24

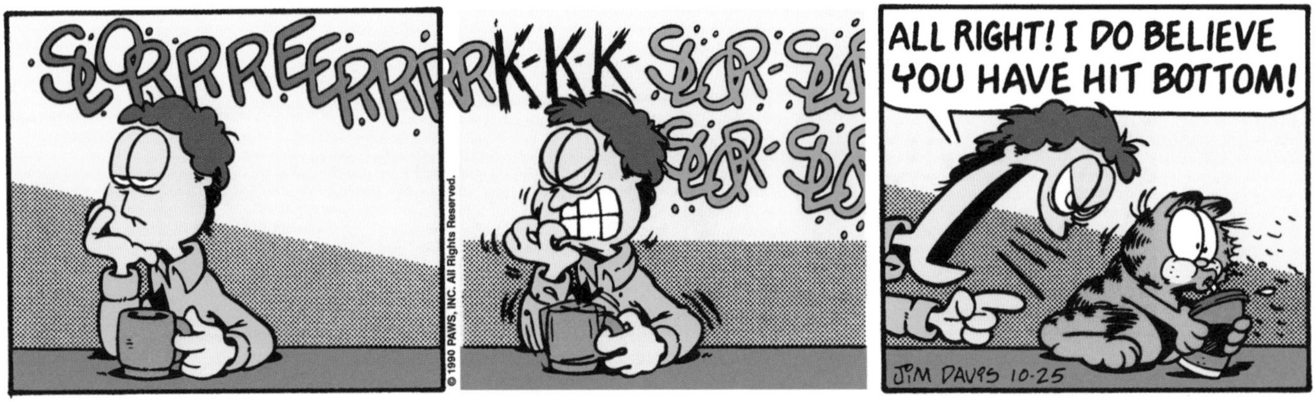
© 1990 PAWS, INC. All Rights Reserved.
ALL RIGHT! I DO BELIEVE YOU HAVE HIT BOTTOM!
JIM DAVIS 10-25

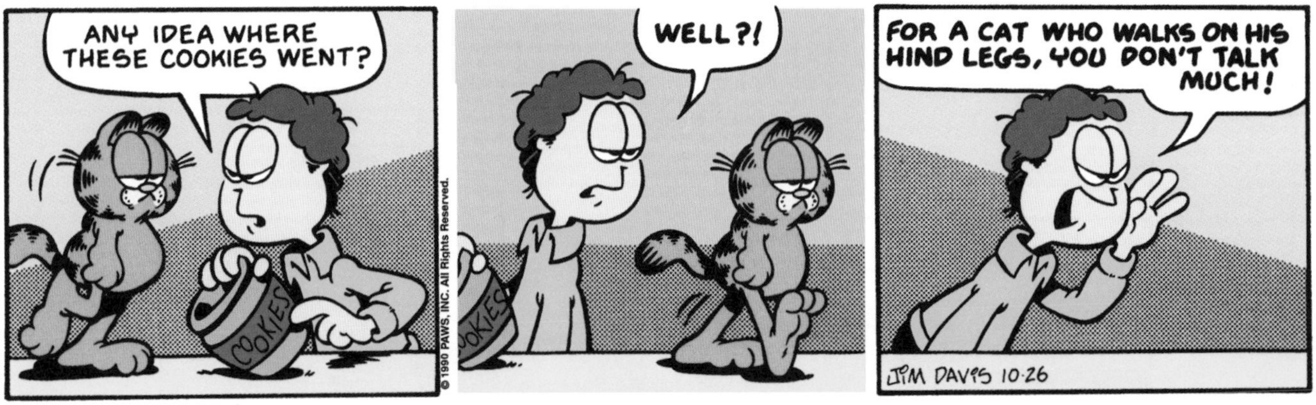
ANY IDEA WHERE THESE COOKIES WENT?
COOKIES
© 1990 PAWS, INC. All Rights Reserved.
WELL?!
FOR A CAT WHO WALKS ON HIS HIND LEGS, YOU DON'T TALK MUCH!
JIM DAVIS 10-26

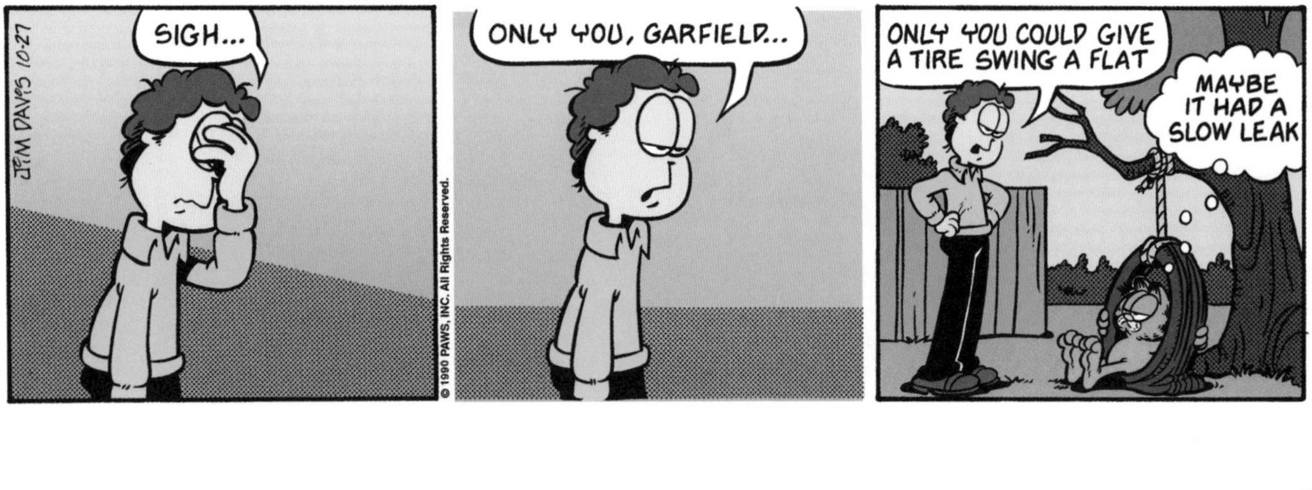
JIM DAVIS 10-27
SIGH...
© 1990 PAWS, INC. All Rights Reserved.
ONLY YOU, GARFIELD...
ONLY YOU COULD GIVE A TIRE SWING A FLAT
MAYBE IT HAD A SLOW LEAK

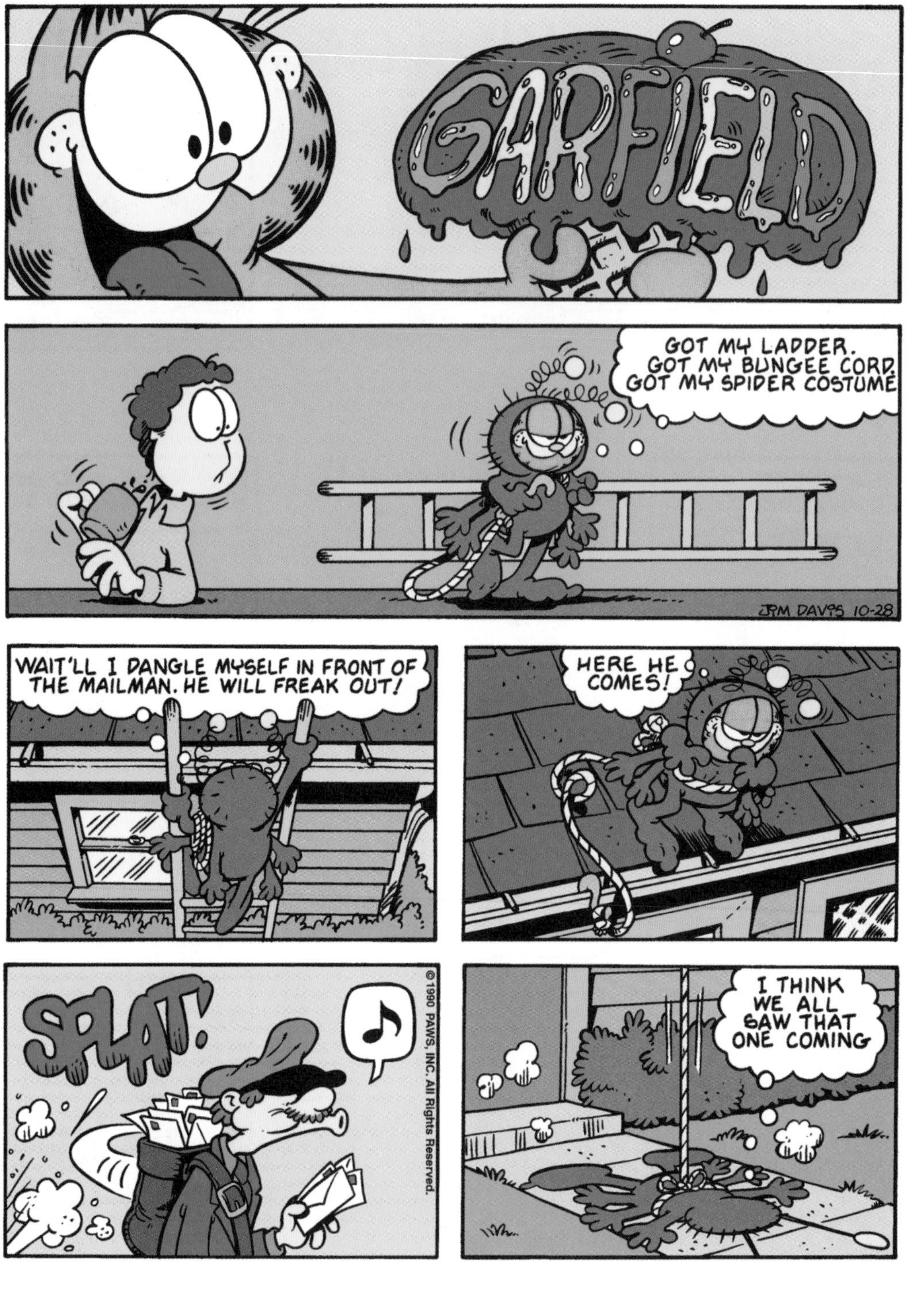
GARFIELD
GOT MY LADDER. GOT MY BUNGEE CORD. GOT MY SPIDER COSTUME
JPM DAVIS 10-28
WAIT'LL I DANGLE MYSELF IN FRONT OF THE MAILMAN. HE WILL FREAK OUT!
HERE HE COMES!
SPLAT!
♪
I THINK WE ALL SAW THAT ONE COMING

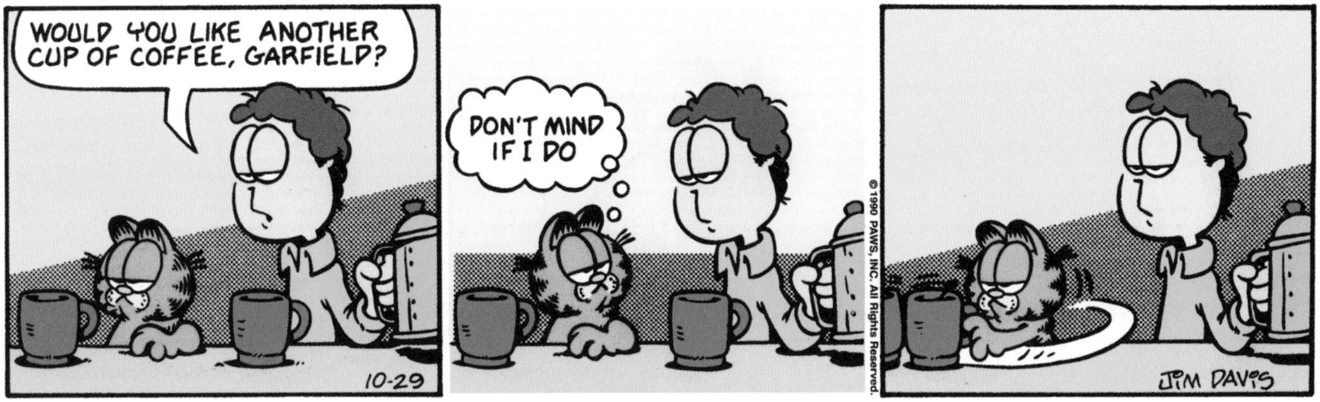
WOULD YOU LIKE ANOTHER CUP OF COFFEE, GARFIELD?
10-29
DON'T MIND IF I DO
© 1990 PAWS, INC. All Rights Reserved.
JIM DAVIS

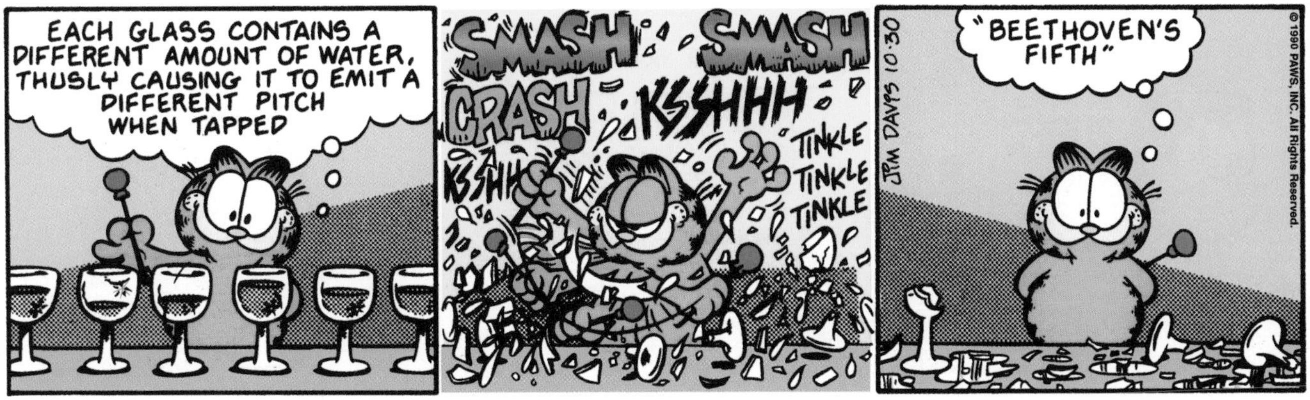
EACH GLASS CONTAINS A DIFFERENT AMOUNT OF WATER, THUSLY CAUSING IT TO EMIT A DIFFERENT PITCH WHEN TAPPED
SMASH SMASH
CRASH
KSSHHH
KSSHH
TINKLE TINKLE TINKLE
JIM DAVIS 10-30
"BEETHOVEN'S FIFTH"
© 1990 PAWS, INC. All Rights Reserved.

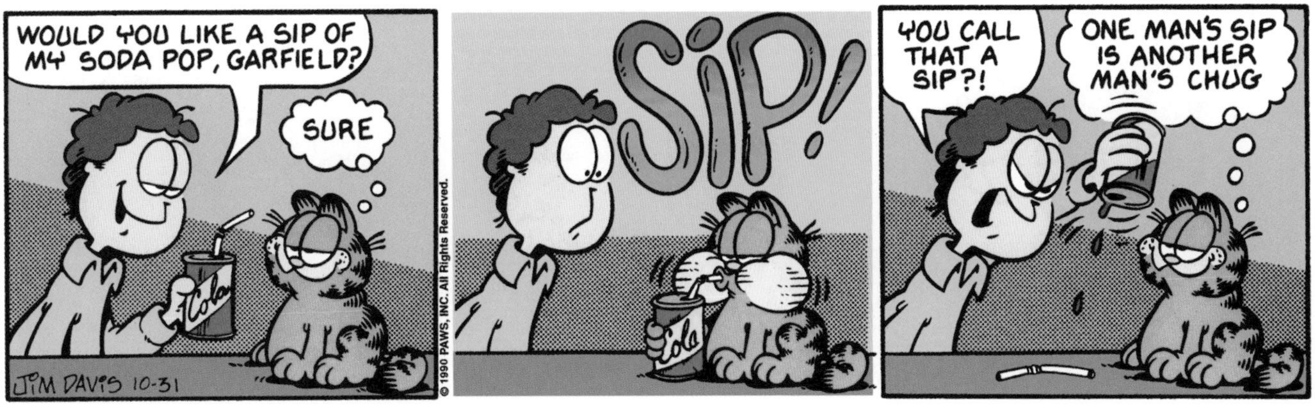
WOULD YOU LIKE A SIP OF MY SODA POP, GARFIELD?
SURE
JIM DAVIS 10-31
© 1990 PAWS, INC. All Rights Reserved.
SIP!
YOU CALL THAT A SIP?!
ONE MAN'S SIP IS ANOTHER MAN'S CHUG

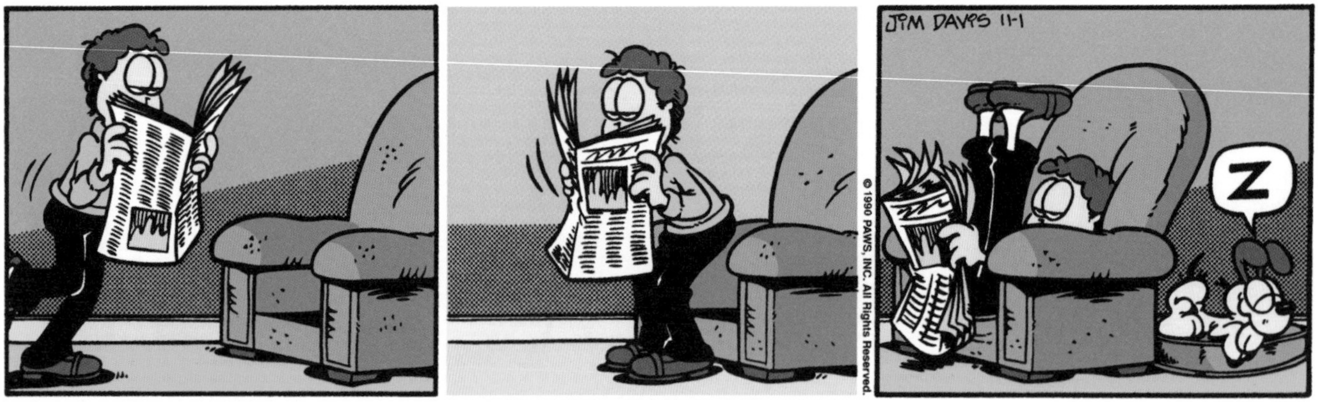
© 1990 PAWS, INC. All Rights Reserved.
JIM DAVIS 11-1
Z

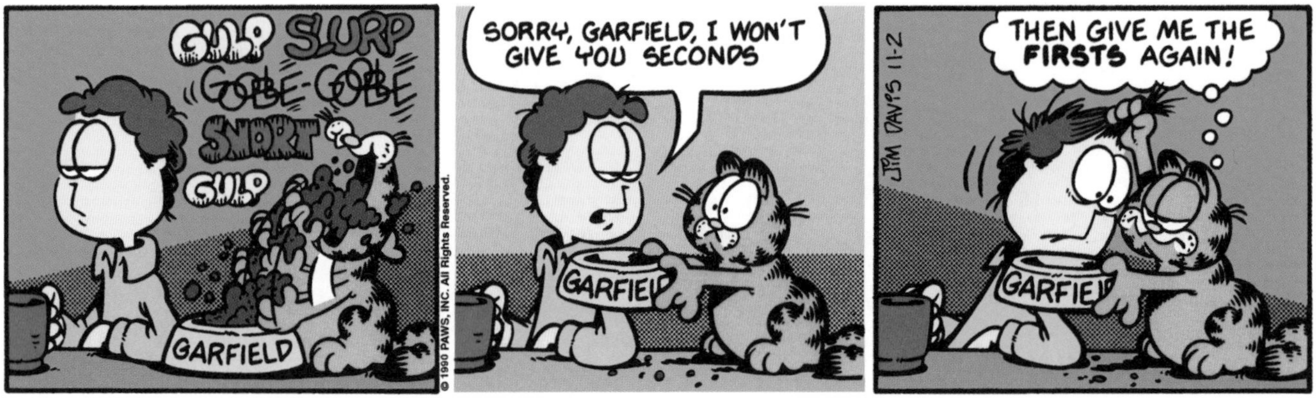
GULP SLURP
GOBLE-GOBLE
SNORT
GULP
GARFIELD
© 1990 PAWS, INC. All Rights Reserved.
SORRY, GARFIELD, I WON'T GIVE YOU SECONDS
GARFIELD
JIM DAVIS 11-2
THEN GIVE ME THE **FIRSTS** AGAIN!
GARFIELD

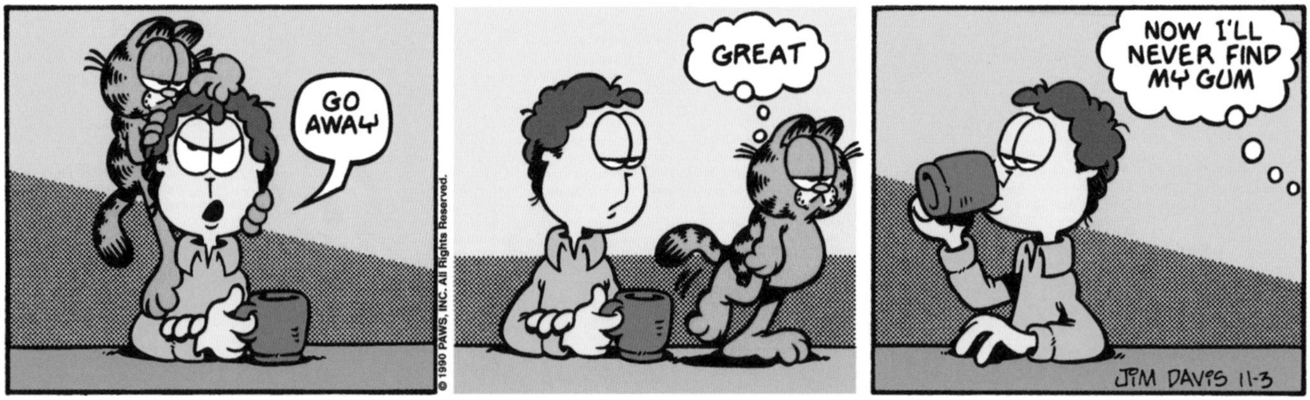
GO AWAY
© 1990 PAWS, INC. All Rights Reserved.
GREAT
NOW I'LL NEVER FIND MY GUM
JIM DAVIS 11-3

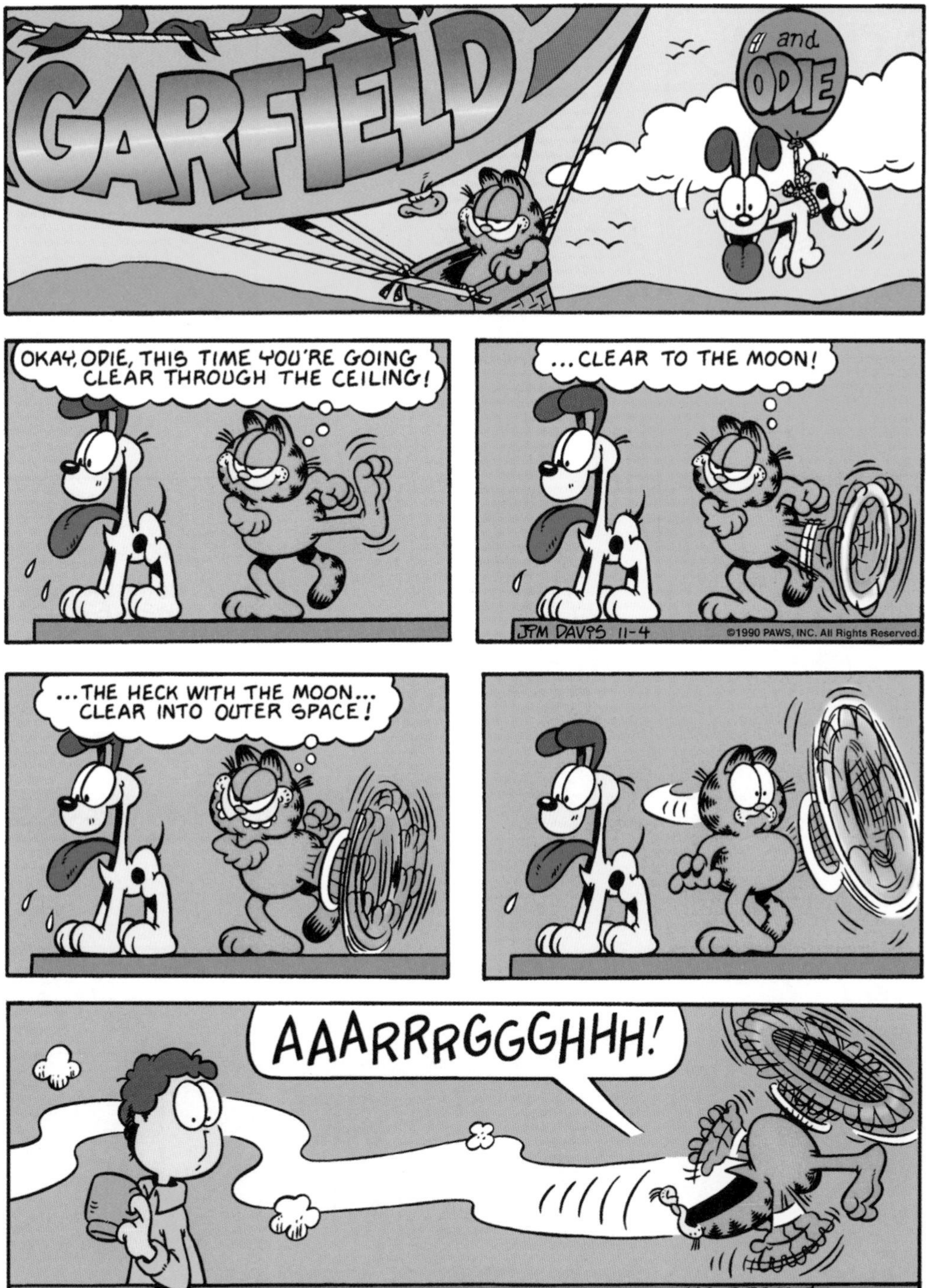
GARFIELD
and
ODIE
OKAY, ODIE, THIS TIME YOU'RE GOING CLEAR THROUGH THE CEILING!
...CLEAR TO THE MOON!
JIM DAVIS 11-4
©1990 PAWS, INC. All Rights Reserved.
...THE HECK WITH THE MOON... CLEAR INTO OUTER SPACE!
AAARRRGGGHHH!

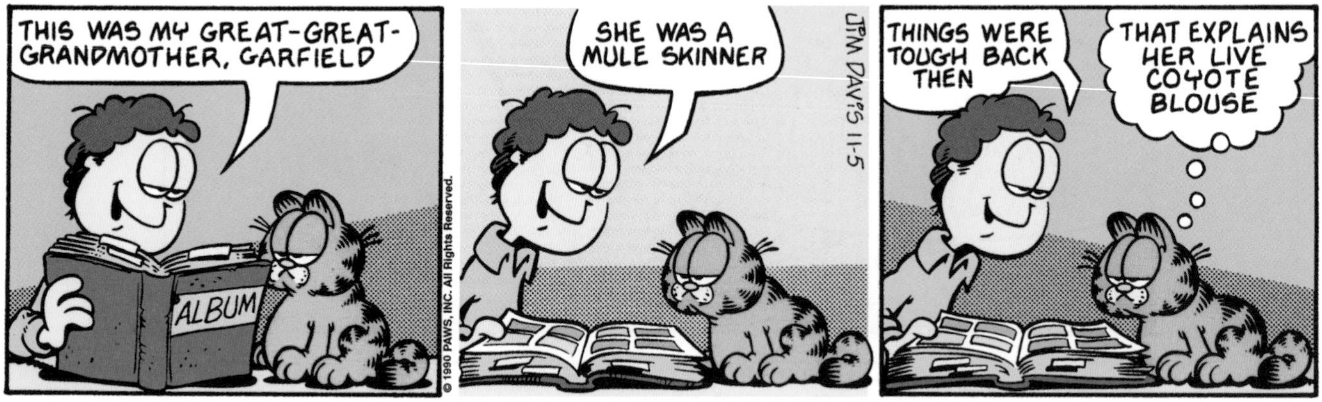
THIS WAS MY GREAT-GREAT-GRANDMOTHER, GARFIELD
ALBUM
SHE WAS A MULE SKINNER
JIM DAVIS 11-5
© 1990 PAWS, INC. All Rights Reserved.
THINGS WERE TOUGH BACK THEN
THAT EXPLAINS HER LIVE COYOTE BLOUSE

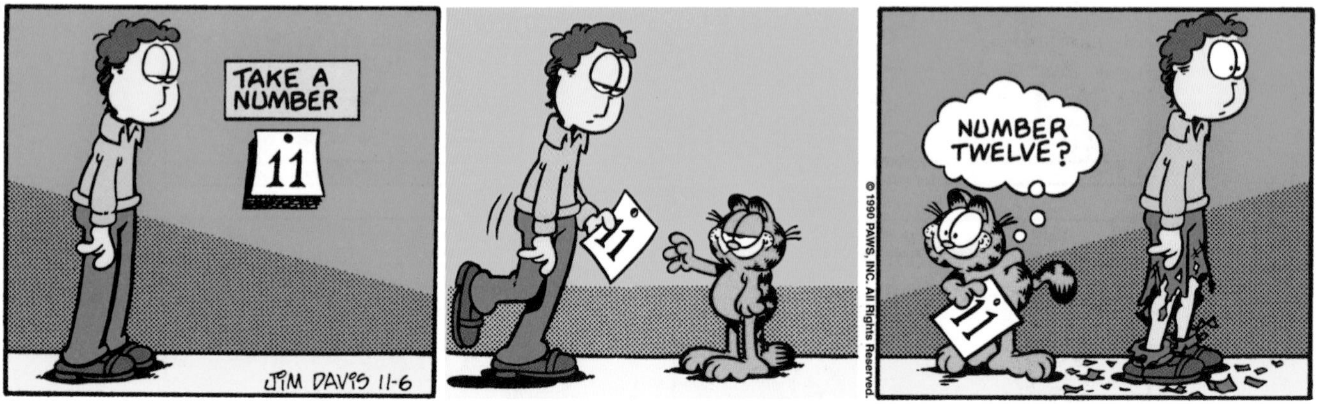
TAKE A NUMBER
11
JIM DAVIS 11-6
11
© 1990 PAWS, INC. All Rights Reserved.
NUMBER TWELVE?
11

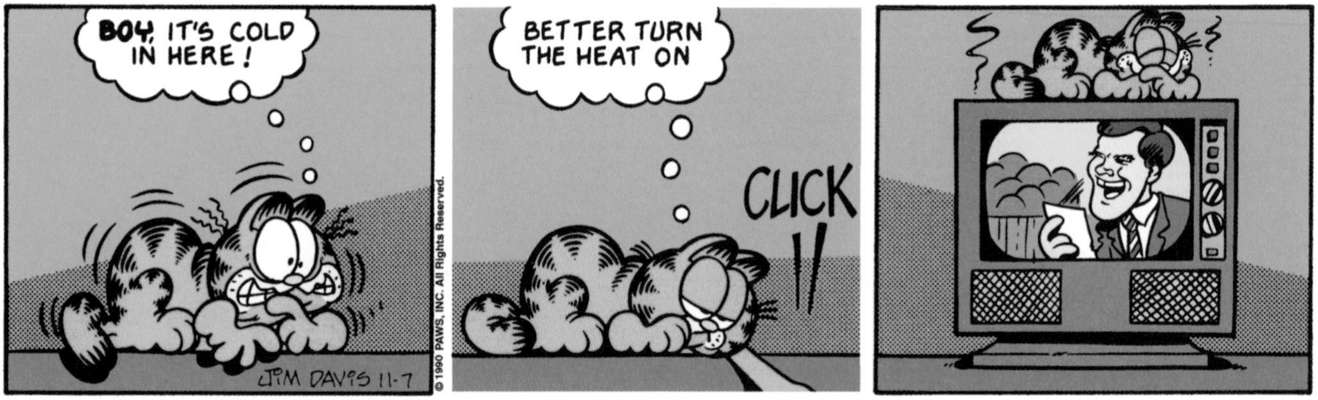
BOY, IT'S COLD IN HERE!
JIM DAVIS 11-7
© 1990 PAWS, INC. All Rights Reserved.
BETTER TURN THE HEAT ON
CLICK

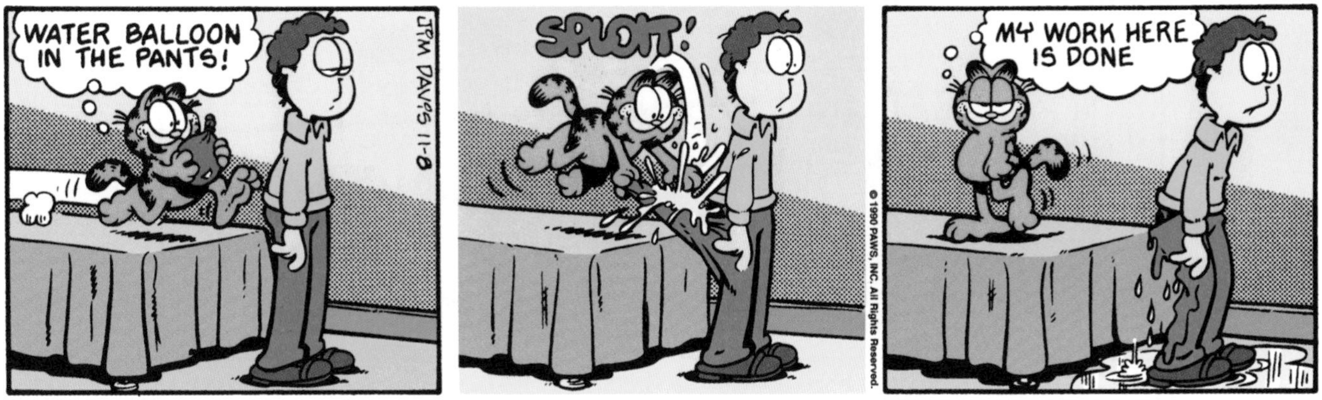
WATER BALLOON IN THE PANTS!
JIM DAVIS 11-8
SPLOIT!
MY WORK HERE IS DONE
© 1990 PAWS, INC. All Rights Reserved.

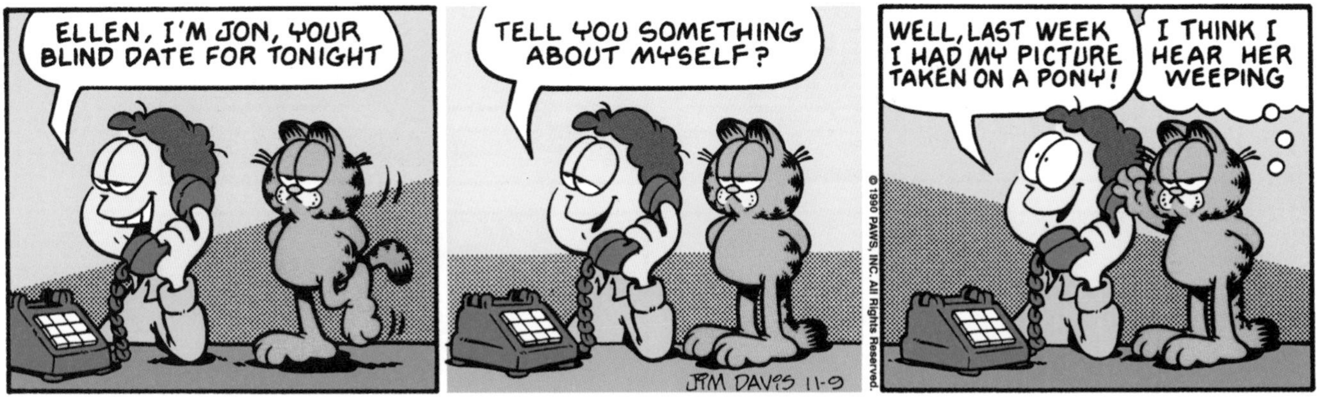
ELLEN, I'M JON, YOUR BLIND DATE FOR TONIGHT
TELL YOU SOMETHING ABOUT MYSELF?
JIM DAVIS 11-9
WELL, LAST WEEK I HAD MY PICTURE TAKEN ON A PONY!
I THINK I HEAR HER WEEPING
© 1990 PAWS, INC. All Rights Reserved.

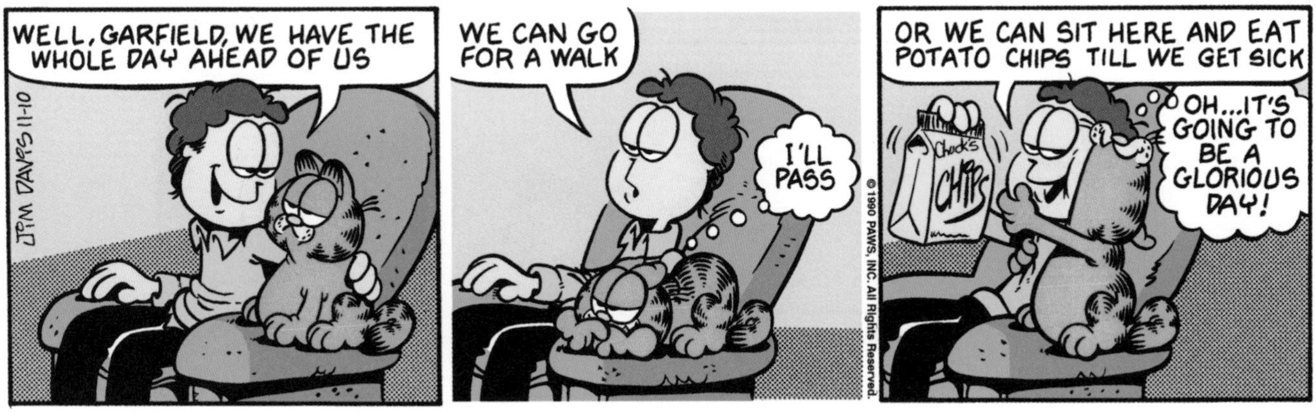
WELL, GARFIELD, WE HAVE THE WHOLE DAY AHEAD OF US
JIM DAVIS 11-10
WE CAN GO FOR A WALK
I'LL PASS
OR WE CAN SIT HERE AND EAT POTATO CHIPS TILL WE GET SICK
Chuck's CHIPS
OH...IT'S GOING TO BE A GLORIOUS DAY!
© 1990 PAWS, INC. All Rights Reserved.

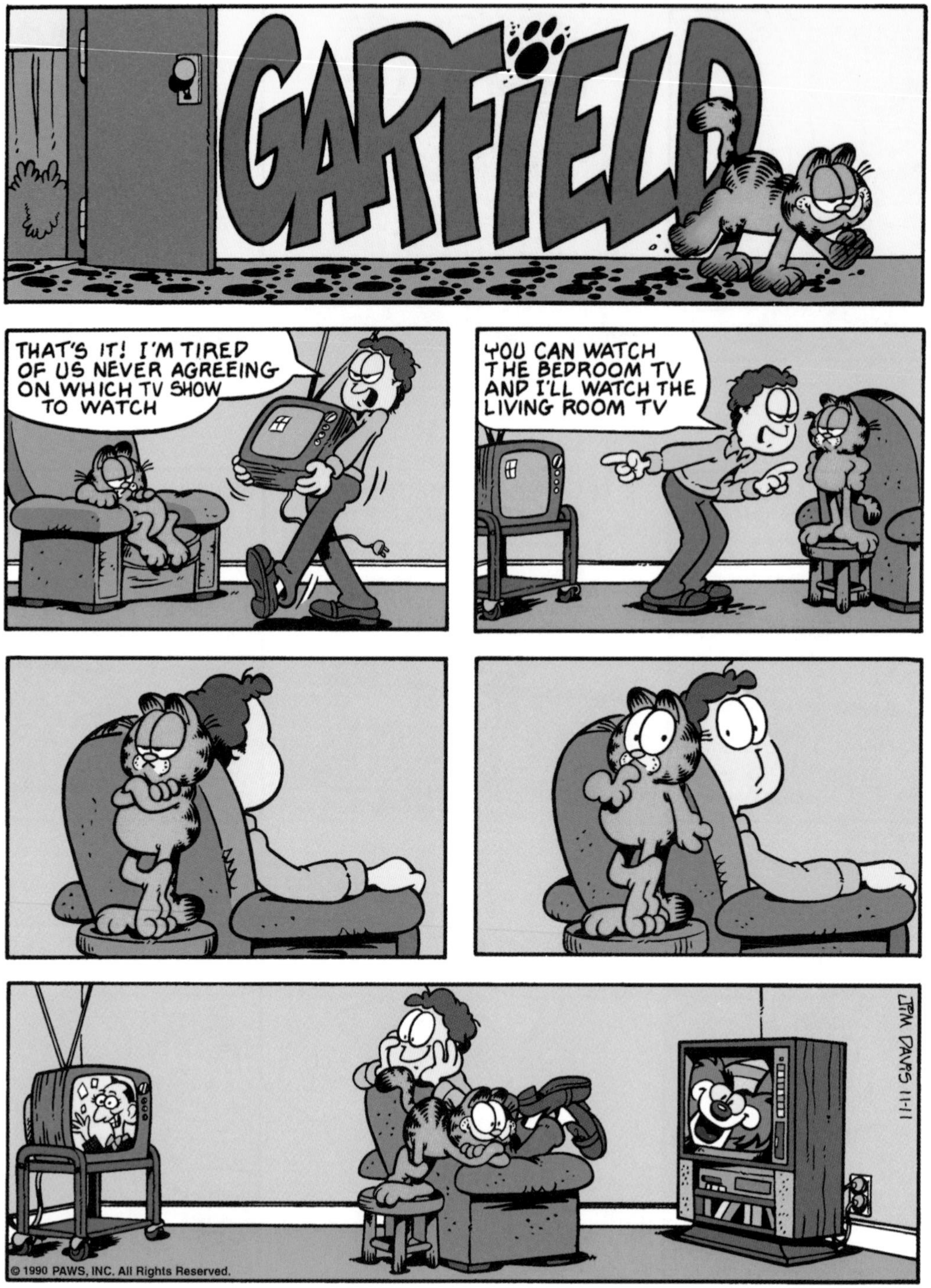
GARFIELD
THAT'S IT! I'M TIRED OF US NEVER AGREEING ON WHICH TV SHOW TO WATCH
YOU CAN WATCH THE BEDROOM TV AND I'LL WATCH THE LIVING ROOM TV
JIM DAVIS 11-11
© 1990 PAWS, INC. All Rights Reserved.

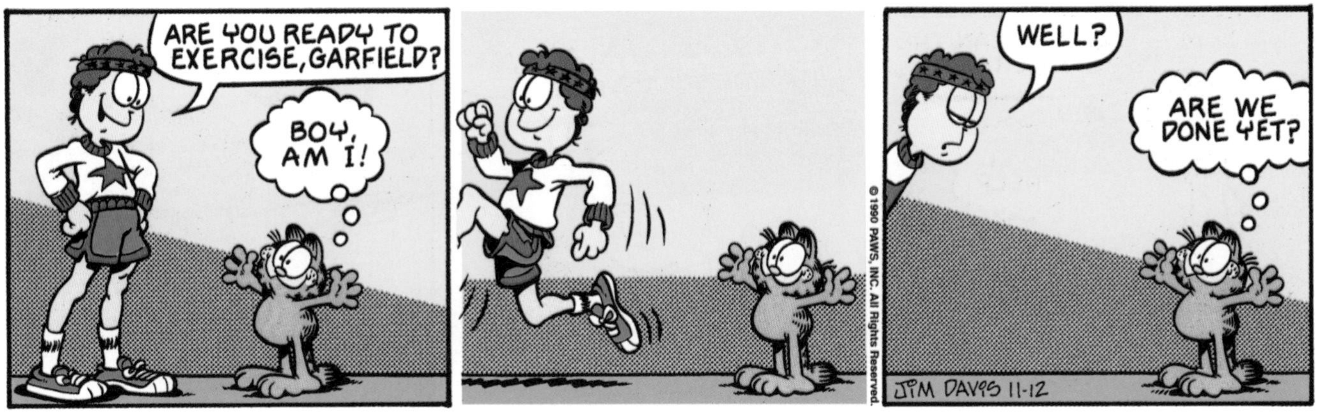
ARE YOU READY TO EXERCISE, GARFIELD?
BOY, AM I!
© 1990 PAWS, INC. All Rights Reserved.
JIM DAVIS 11-12
WELL?
ARE WE DONE YET?

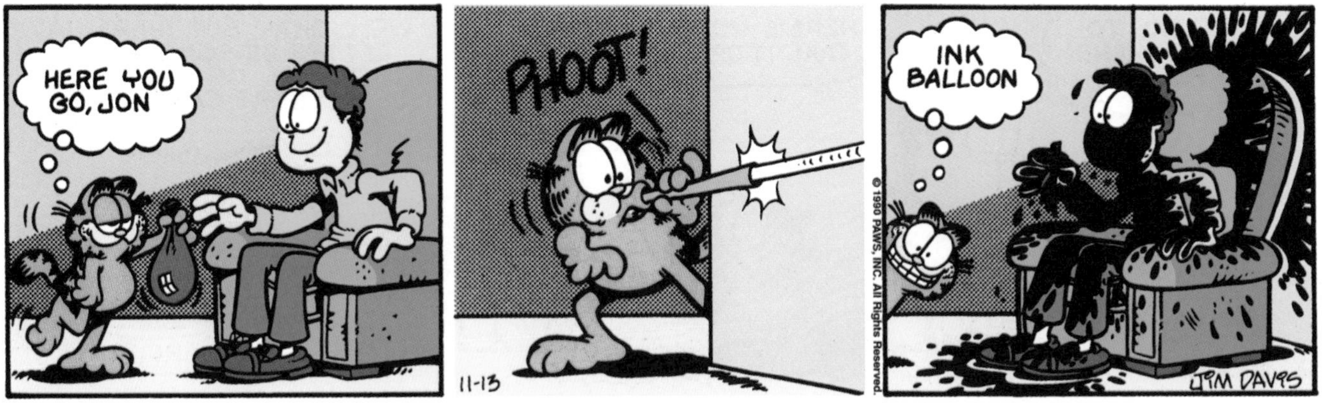
HERE YOU GO, JON
PHOOT!
11-13
© 1990 PAWS, INC. All Rights Reserved.
INK BALLOON
JIM DAVIS

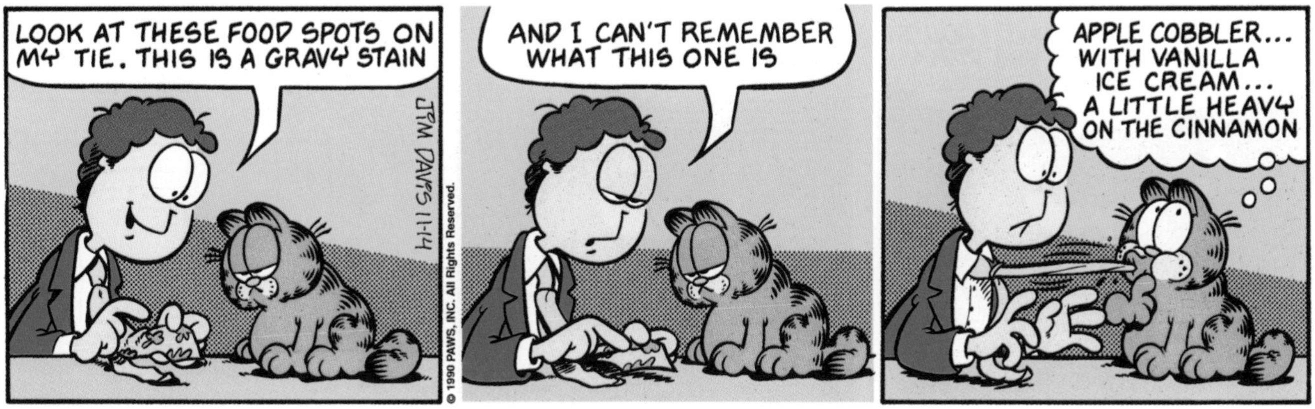
LOOK AT THESE FOOD SPOTS ON MY TIE. THIS IS A GRAVY STAIN
JIM DAVIS 11-14
© 1990 PAWS, INC. All Rights Reserved.
AND I CAN'T REMEMBER WHAT THIS ONE IS
APPLE COBBLER... WITH VANILLA ICE CREAM... A LITTLE HEAVY ON THE CINNAMON

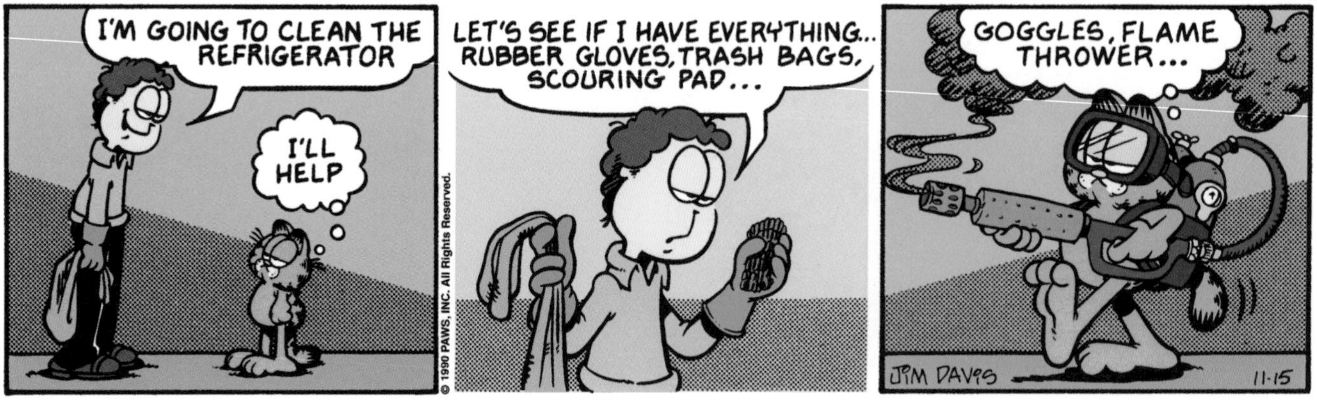
I'M GOING TO CLEAN THE REFRIGERATOR
I'LL HELP
© 1990 PAWS, INC. All Rights Reserved.
LET'S SEE IF I HAVE EVERYTHING... RUBBER GLOVES, TRASH BAGS, SCOURING PAD...
GOGGLES, FLAME THROWER...
JIM DAVIS 11-15

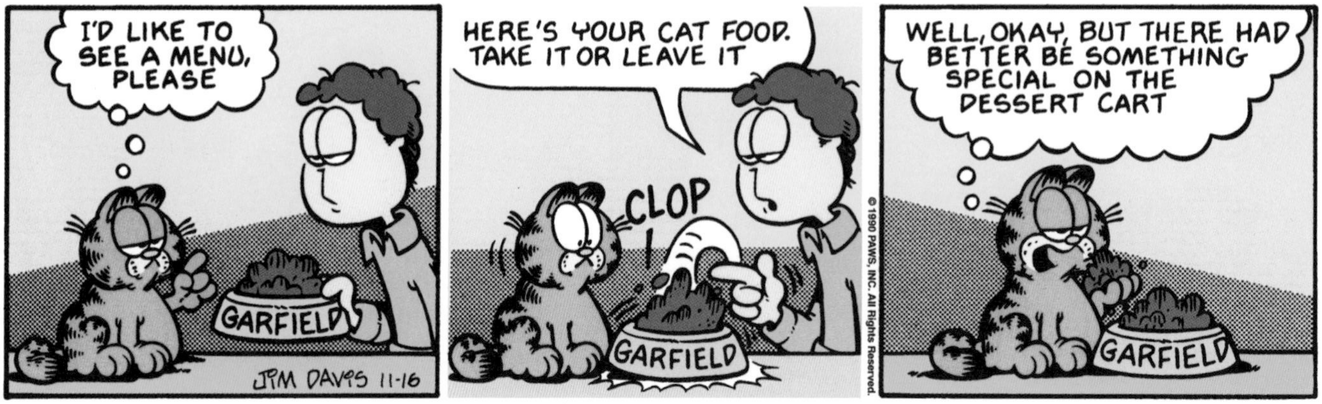
I'D LIKE TO SEE A MENU, PLEASE
GARFIELD
JIM DAVIS 11-16
HERE'S YOUR CAT FOOD. TAKE IT OR LEAVE IT
CLOP
GARFIELD
© 1990 PAWS, INC. All Rights Reserved.
WELL, OKAY, BUT THERE HAD BETTER BE SOMETHING SPECIAL ON THE DESSERT CART
GARFIELD

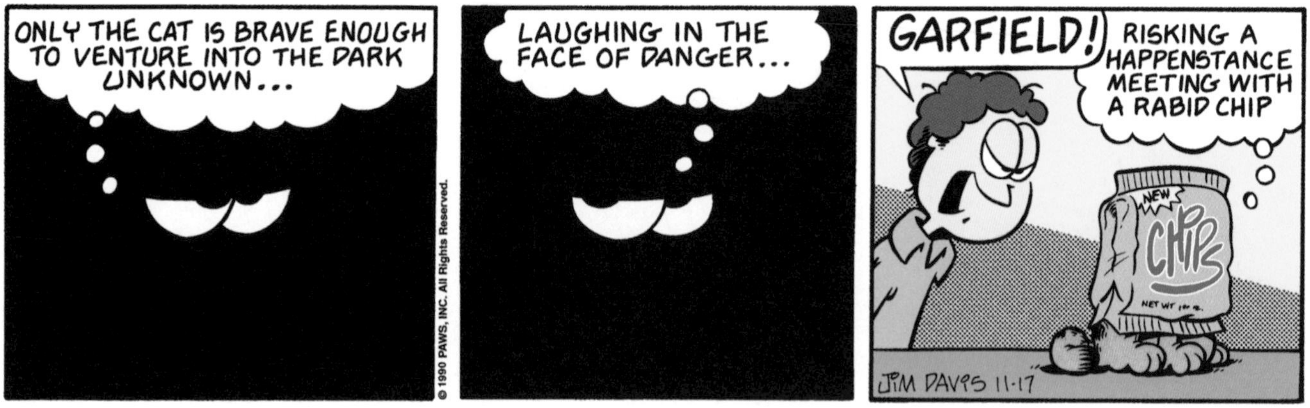
ONLY THE CAT IS BRAVE ENOUGH TO VENTURE INTO THE DARK UNKNOWN...
© 1990 PAWS, INC. All Rights Reserved.
LAUGHING IN THE FACE OF DANGER...
GARFIELD!
RISKING A HAPPENSTANCE MEETING WITH A RABID CHIP
NEW
CHIPS
JIM DAVIS 11-17

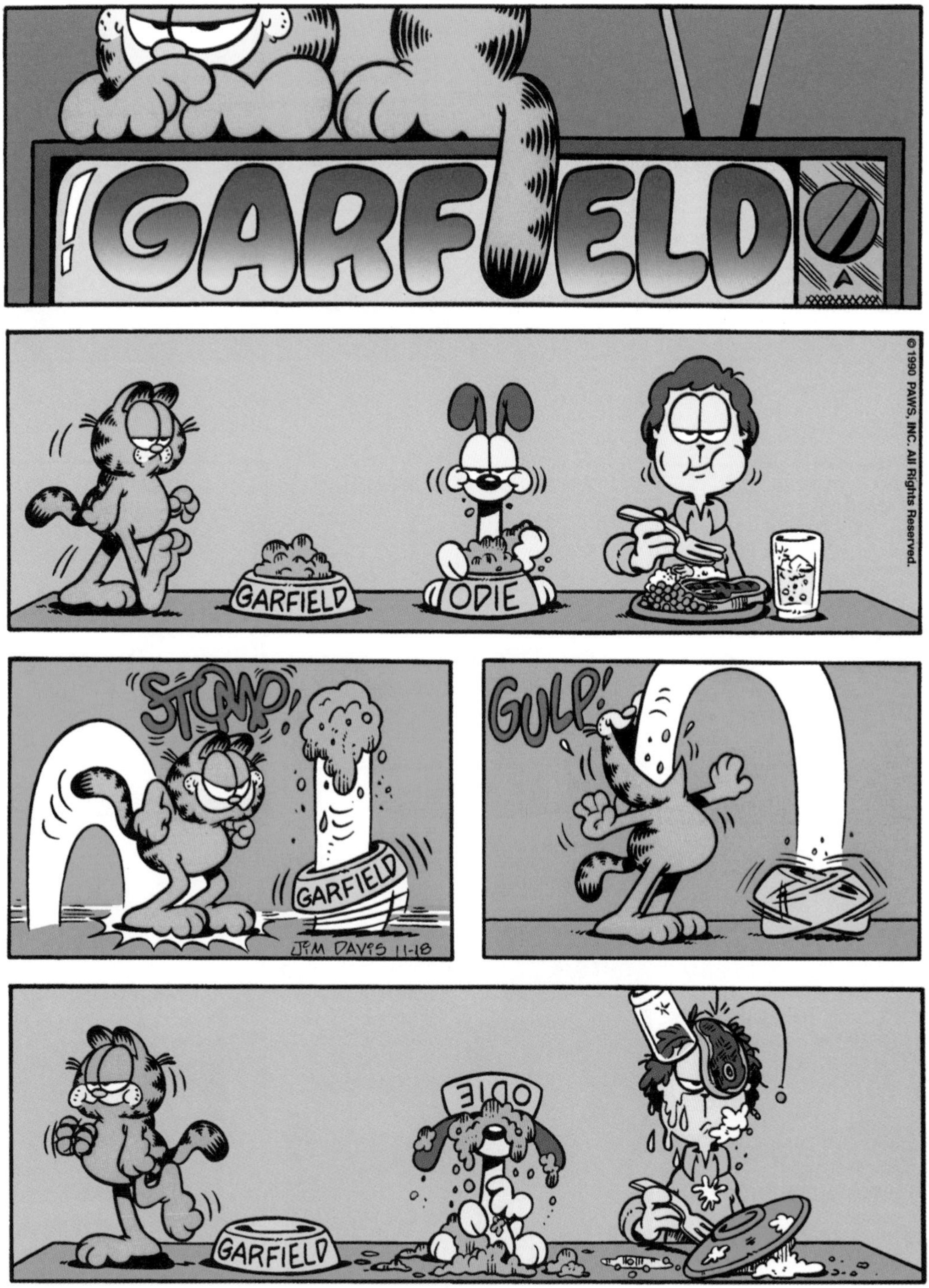
GARFIELD
© 1990 PAWS, INC. All Rights Reserved.
GARFIELD
ODIE
STOMP!
GARFIELD
JIM DAVIS 11-18
GULP!
ODIE
GARFIELD

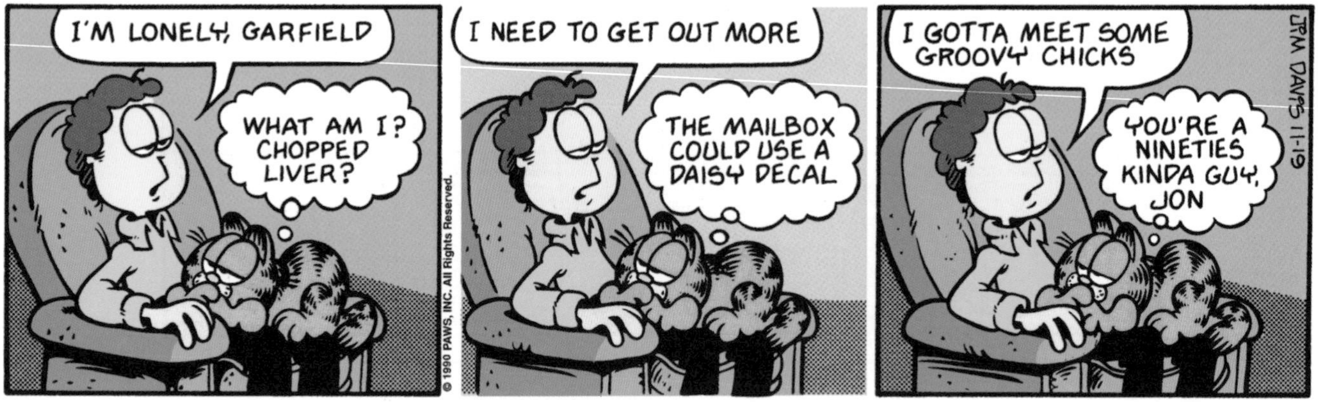
I'M LONELY, GARFIELD
WHAT AM I? CHOPPED LIVER?
© 1990 PAWS, INC. All Rights Reserved.
I NEED TO GET OUT MORE
THE MAILBOX COULD USE A DAISY DECAL
I GOTTA MEET SOME GROOVY CHICKS
YOU'RE A NINETIES KINDA GUY, JON
JIM DAVIS 11-19

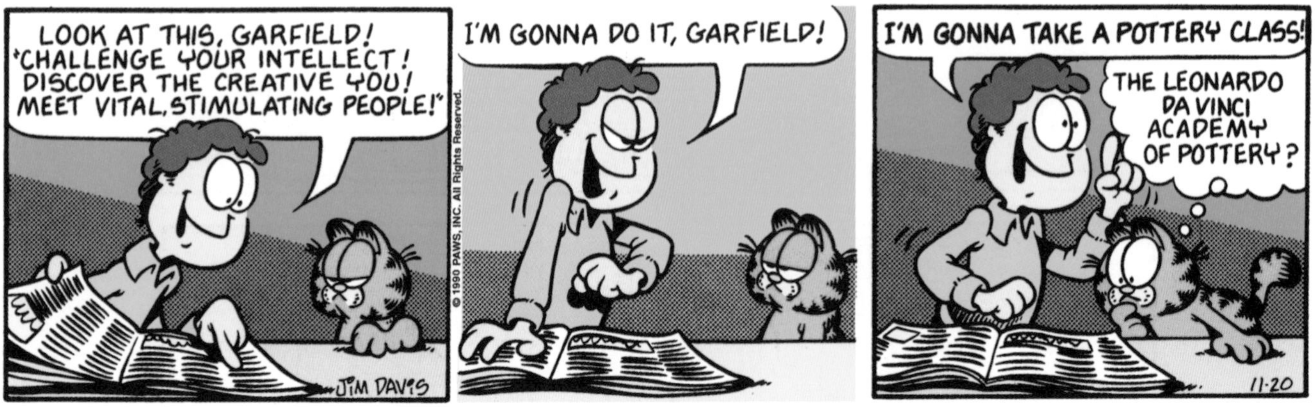
LOOK AT THIS, GARFIELD! "CHALLENGE YOUR INTELLECT! DISCOVER THE CREATIVE YOU! MEET VITAL, STIMULATING PEOPLE!"
JIM DAVIS
© 1990 PAWS, INC. All Rights Reserved.
I'M GONNA DO IT, GARFIELD!
I'M GONNA TAKE A POTTERY CLASS!
THE LEONARDO DA VINCI ACADEMY OF POTTERY?
11-20

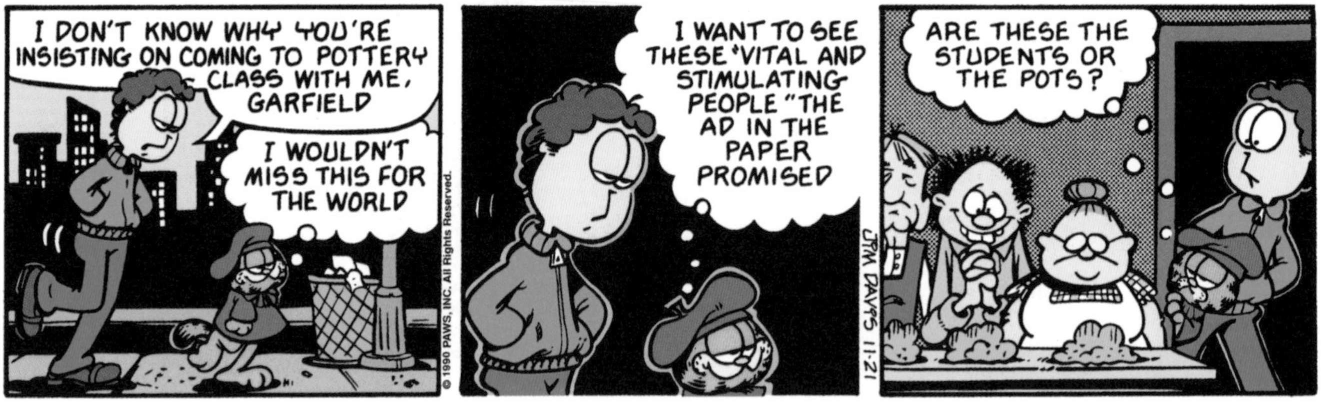
I DON'T KNOW WHY YOU'RE INSISTING ON COMING TO POTTERY CLASS WITH ME, GARFIELD
I WOULDN'T MISS THIS FOR THE WORLD
© 1990 PAWS, INC. All Rights Reserved.
I WANT TO SEE THESE "VITAL AND STIMULATING PEOPLE" THE AD IN THE PAPER PROMISED
JIM DAVIS 11-21
ARE THESE THE STUDENTS OR THE POTS?

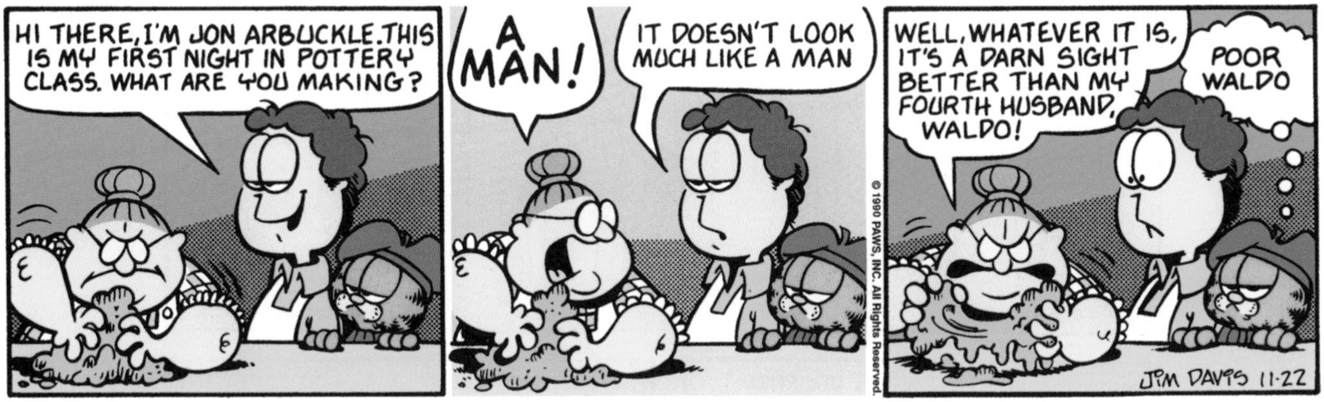
HI THERE, I'M JON ARBUCKLE. THIS IS MY FIRST NIGHT IN POTTERY CLASS. WHAT ARE YOU MAKING?
A MAN!
IT DOESN'T LOOK MUCH LIKE A MAN
WELL, WHATEVER IT IS, IT'S A DARN SIGHT BETTER THAN MY FOURTH HUSBAND, WALDO!
POOR WALDO
© 1990 PAWS, INC. All Rights Reserved.
JIM DAVIS 11-22

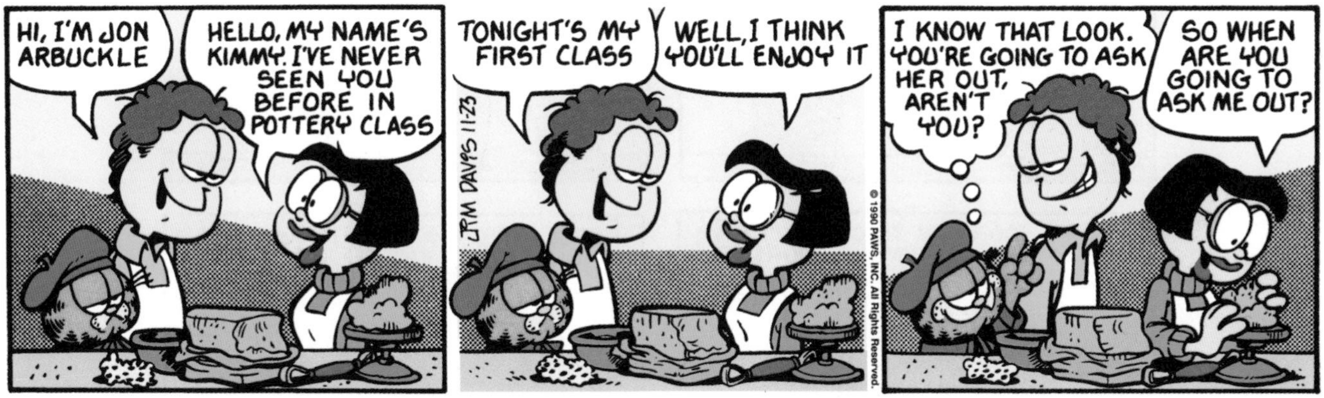
HI, I'M JON ARBUCKLE
HELLO, MY NAME'S KIMMY. I'VE NEVER SEEN YOU BEFORE IN POTTERY CLASS
TONIGHT'S MY FIRST CLASS
WELL, I THINK YOU'LL ENJOY IT
JIM DAVIS 11-23
© 1990 PAWS, INC. All Rights Reserved.
I KNOW THAT LOOK. YOU'RE GOING TO ASK HER OUT, AREN'T YOU?
SO WHEN ARE YOU GOING TO ASK ME OUT?

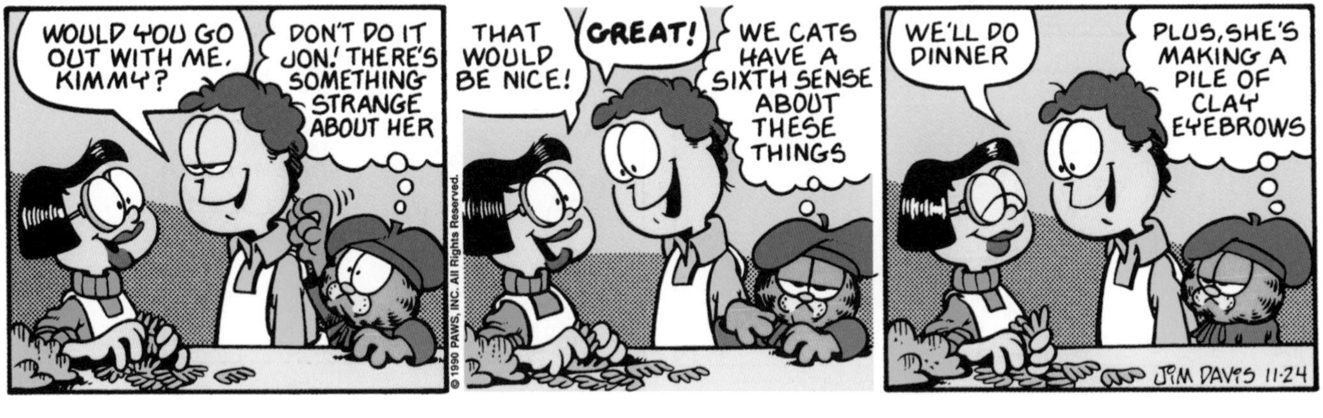
WOULD YOU GO OUT WITH ME, KIMMY?
DON'T DO IT JON! THERE'S SOMETHING STRANGE ABOUT HER
© 1990 PAWS, INC. All Rights Reserved.
THAT WOULD BE NICE!
GREAT!
WE CATS HAVE A SIXTH SENSE ABOUT THESE THINGS
WE'LL DO DINNER
PLUS, SHE'S MAKING A PILE OF CLAY EYEBROWS
JIM DAVIS 11-24

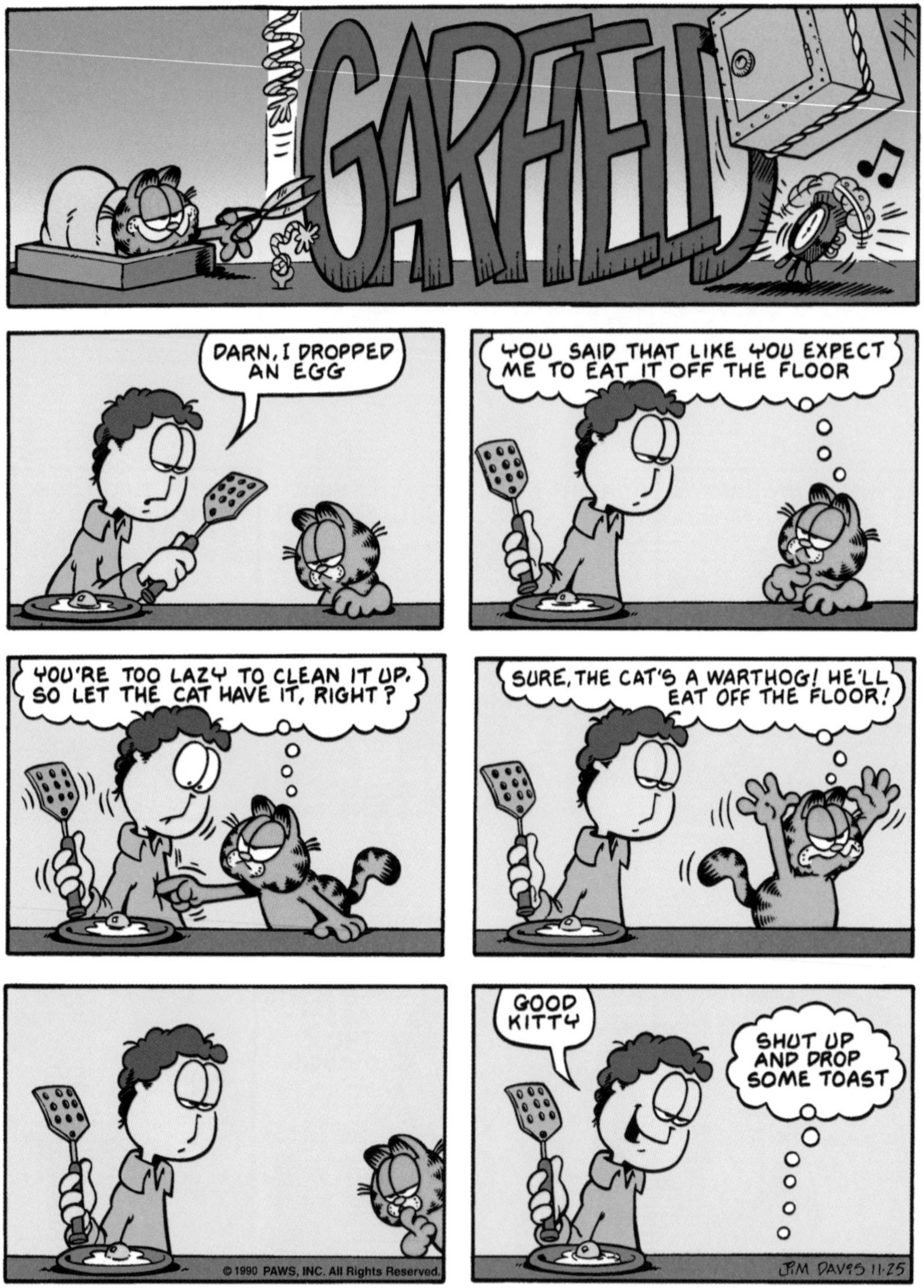
GARFIELD
DARN, I DROPPED AN EGG
YOU SAID THAT LIKE YOU EXPECT ME TO EAT IT OFF THE FLOOR
YOU'RE TOO LAZY TO CLEAN IT UP, SO LET THE CAT HAVE IT, RIGHT?
SURE, THE CAT'S A WARTHOG! HE'LL EAT OFF THE FLOOR!
© 1990 PAWS, INC. All Rights Reserved.
GOOD KITTY
SHUT UP AND DROP SOME TOAST
JIM DAVIS 11-25

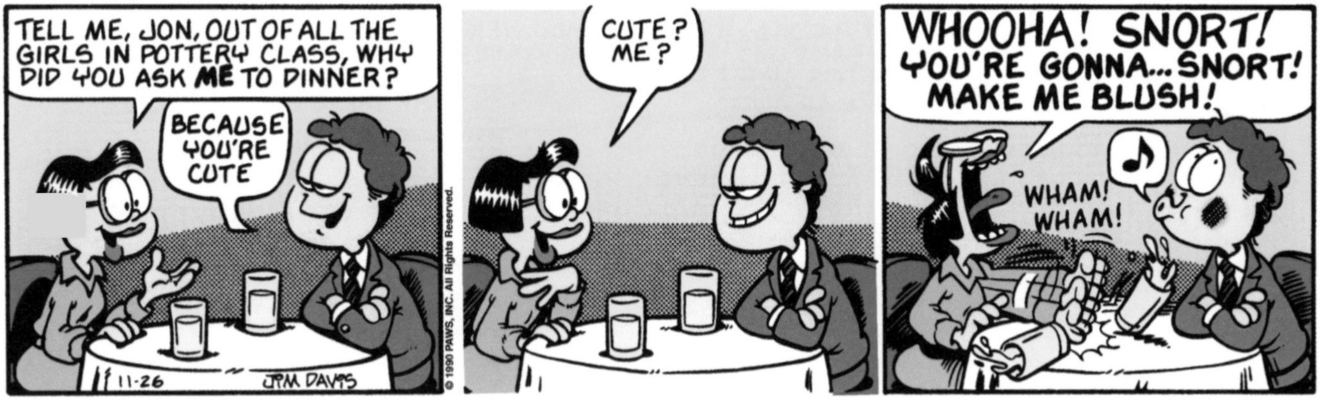
TELL ME, JON, OUT OF ALL THE GIRLS IN POTTERY CLASS, WHY DID YOU ASK ME TO DINNER?
BECAUSE YOU'RE CUTE
11-26
JIM DAVIS
© 1990 PAWS, INC. All Rights Reserved.
CUTE? ME?
WHOOHA! SNORT! YOU'RE GONNA... SNORT! MAKE ME BLUSH!
WHAM! WHAM!

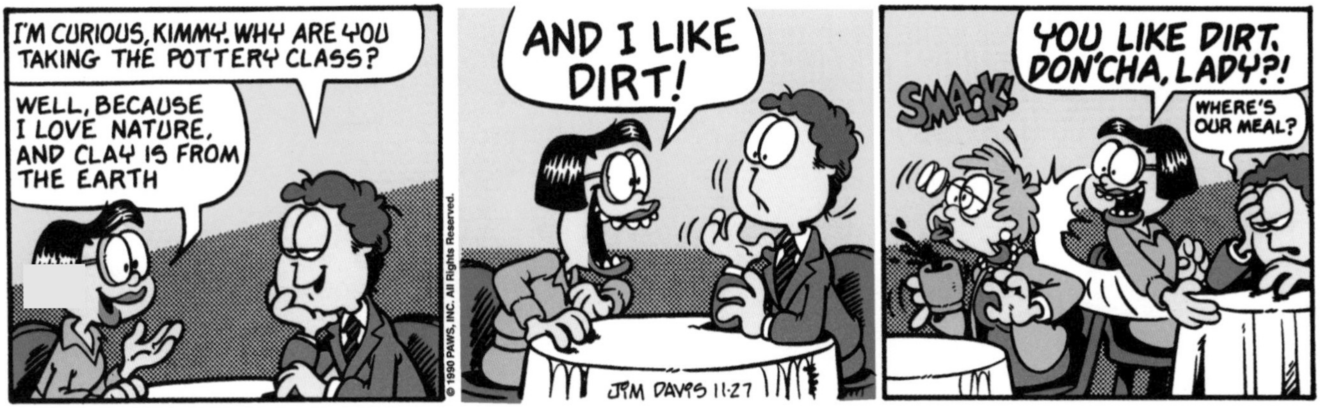
I'M CURIOUS, KIMMY. WHY ARE YOU TAKING THE POTTERY CLASS?
WELL, BECAUSE I LOVE NATURE, AND CLAY IS FROM THE EARTH
© 1990 PAWS, INC. All Rights Reserved.
AND I LIKE DIRT!
JIM DAVIS 11-27
SMACK!
YOU LIKE DIRT, DON'CHA, LADY?!
WHERE'S OUR MEAL?

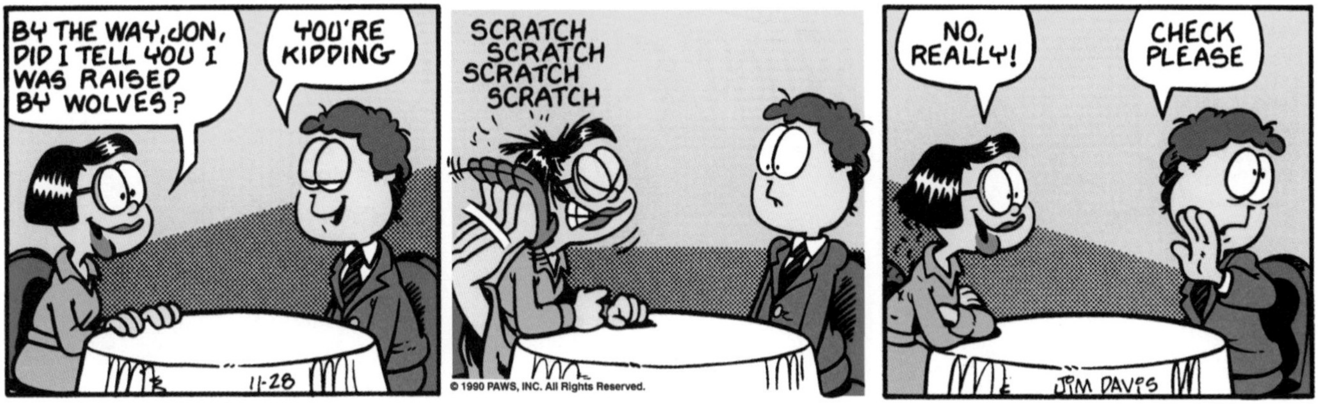
BY THE WAY, JON, DID I TELL YOU I WAS RAISED BY WOLVES?
YOU'RE KIDDING
11-28
SCRATCH SCRATCH SCRATCH SCRATCH
© 1990 PAWS, INC. All Rights Reserved.
NO, REALLY!
CHECK PLEASE
JIM DAVIS

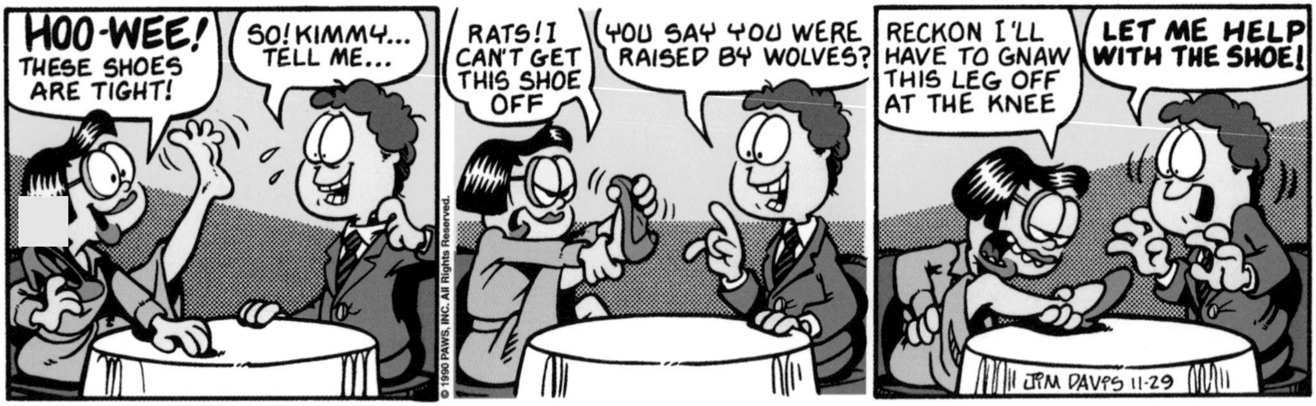
HOO-WEE! THESE SHOES ARE TIGHT!
SO! KIMMY... TELL ME...
© 1990 PAWS, INC. All Rights Reserved.
RATS! I CAN'T GET THIS SHOE OFF
YOU SAY YOU WERE RAISED BY WOLVES?
RECKON I'LL HAVE TO GNAW THIS LEG OFF AT THE KNEE
LET ME HELP WITH THE SHOE!
JIM DAVIS 11-29

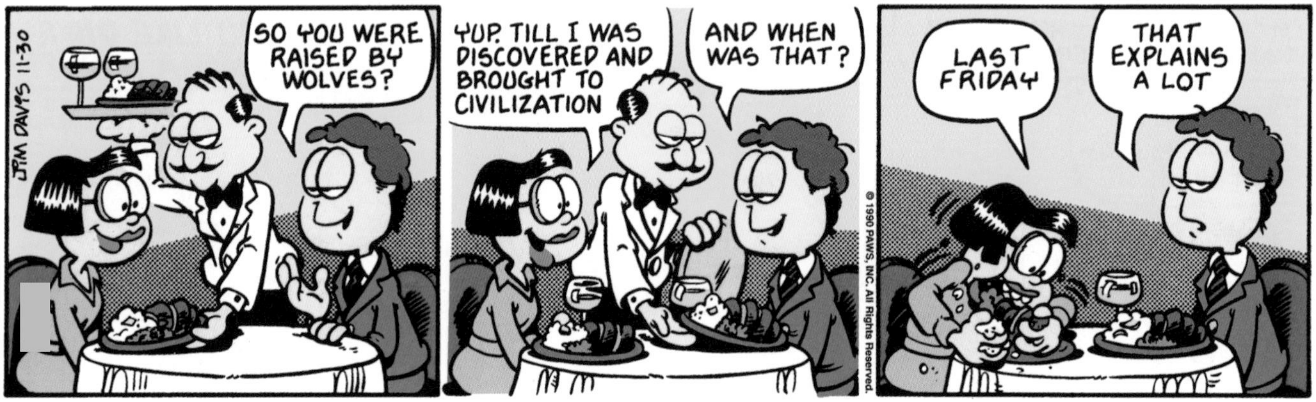
JIM DAVIS 11-30
SO YOU WERE RAISED BY WOLVES?
YUP. TILL I WAS DISCOVERED AND BROUGHT TO CIVILIZATION
AND WHEN WAS THAT?
© 1990 PAWS, INC. All Rights Reserved.
LAST FRIDAY
THAT EXPLAINS A LOT

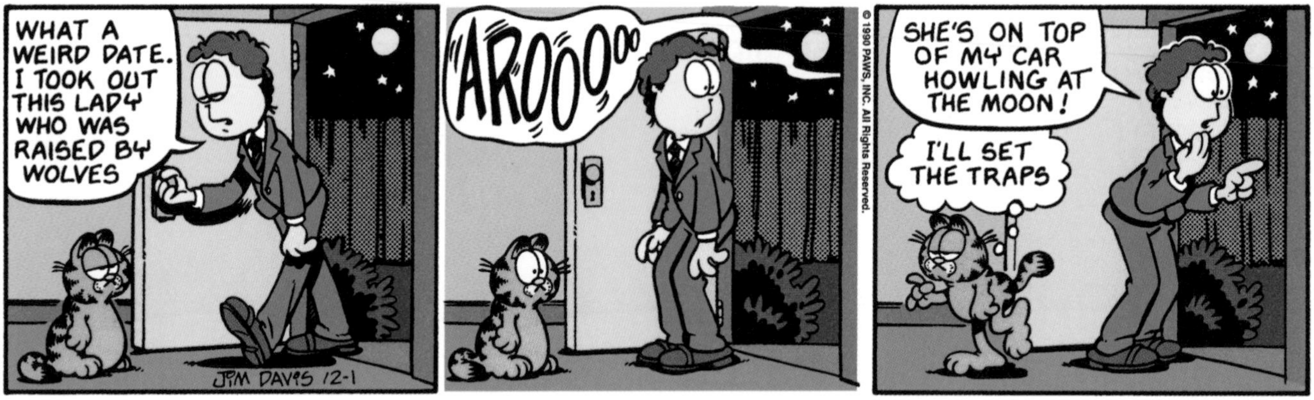
WHAT A WEIRD DATE. I TOOK OUT THIS LADY WHO WAS RAISED BY WOLVES
JIM DAVIS 12-1
AROOOOO
© 1990 PAWS, INC. All Rights Reserved.
SHE'S ON TOP OF MY CAR HOWLING AT THE MOON!
I'LL SET THE TRAPS

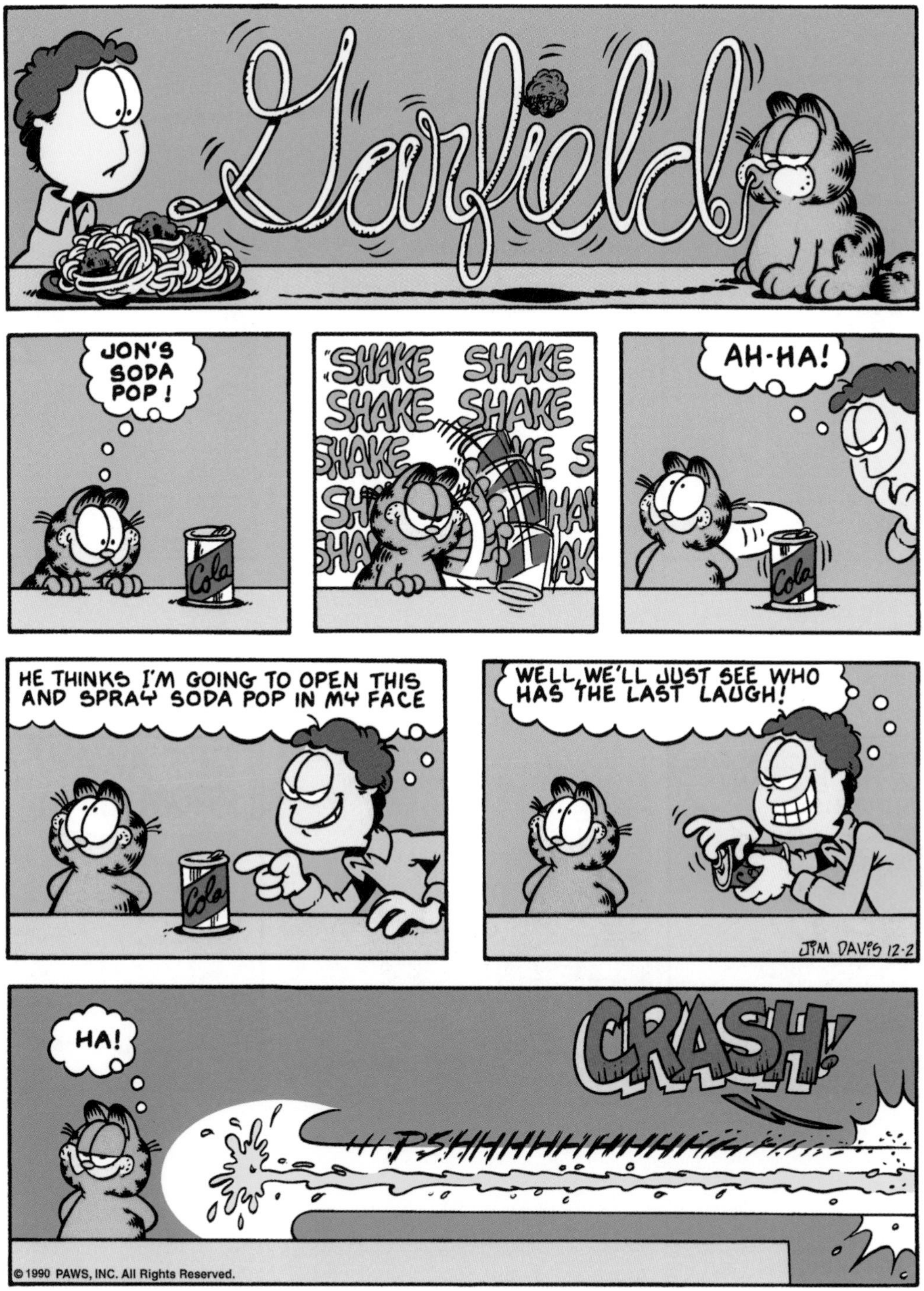
Garfield
JON'S SODA POP!
SHAKE SHAKE SHAKE SHAKE
AH-HA!
HE THINKS I'M GOING TO OPEN THIS AND SPRAY SODA POP IN MY FACE
WELL, WE'LL JUST SEE WHO HAS THE LAST LAUGH!
JIM DAVIS 12-2
HA!
CRASH!
PSHHHHHHHHHHH

OUT OF MY WAY! COMING THROUGH!
© 1990 PAWS, INC. All Rights Reserved.
STAND ASIDE! NO TIME TO CHAT! I'M A BUSY CAT!
Z
JIM DAVIS 12-3

THE SECRET TO A SUCCESSFUL HOTFOOT IS THE ELEMENT OF SURPRISE
© 1990 PAWS, INC. All Rights Reserved.
GET AWAY FROM ME!
MAYBE I WASN'T SUBTLE ENOUGH
JIM DAVIS 12-4

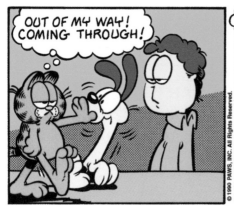

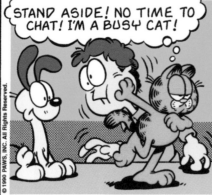

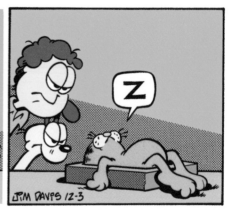

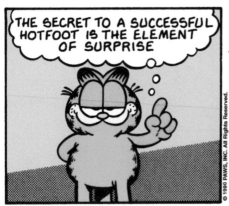

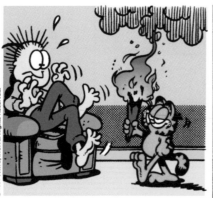

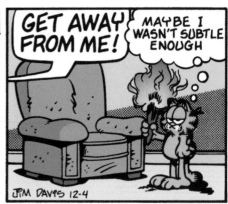

GARFIELD'S TOP TEN NIGHTMARES

10. **Nermal gets cloned**
9. **Vet prescribes "chain saw therapy"**
8. **Falls into vat of Odie drool**
7. **Fleas vote him "Most Bloodsuckable"**
6. **Inhales next to Jon's dirty socks**
5. **Forced to watch the "All Lassie" channel**
4. **Trapped for a week inside health food store**
3. **Cat fur the latest thing for women's coats**
2. **Meets huge spider with an attitude**
1. **Diet Monday!**